DRAMA
for Students

National Advisory Board

DRAMA
for Students

Presenting Analysis, Context, and Criticism on Commonly Studied Dramas

Volume 24

Jennifer Greve and Ira Mark Milne,
Project Editors

Foreword by Carole L. Hamilton

THOMSON

™

GALE

Detroit • New York • San Francisco • New Haven, Conn. • Waterville, Maine • London

Drama for Students, Volume 24

Project Editors
Jennifer Greve and Ira Mark Milne

Rights Acquisition and Management
Margaret Chamberlain-Gaston, Lisa Kincade,
Andrew Specht

Manufacturing
Drew Kalasky

Imaging
Lezlie Light, Mike Logusz, Kelly A. Quin

Product Design
Pamela A. E. Galbreath

Product Manager
Meggin Condino

ISBN-13: 978-0-7876-8120-3
ISBN-10: 0-7876-8120-2
e-ISBN-13: 978-1-4144-1037-1
e-ISBN-10: 1-4144-1037-9
ISSN 1094-9232

Printed in the United States of America
10 9 8 7 6 5 4 3 2 1

Table of Contents

The Study of Drama

We study drama in order to learn what meaning others have made of life, to comprehend what it takes to produce a work of art, and to glean some understanding of ourselves. Drama produces in a separate, aesthetic world, a moment of being for the audience to experience, while maintaining the detachment of a reflective observer.

Drama is a representational art, a visible and audible narrative presenting virtual, fictional characters within a virtual, fictional universe. Dramatic realizations may pretend to approximate reality or else stubbornly defy, distort, and deform reality into an artistic statement. From this separate universe that is obviously not "real life" we expect a valid reflection upon reality, yet drama never is mistaken for reality—the methods of theater are integral to its form and meaning. Theater is art, and art's appeal lies in its ability both to approximate life and to depart from it. For in intruding its distorted version of life into our consciousness, art gives us a new perspective and appreciation of life and reality. Although all aesthetic experiences perform this service, theater does it most effectively by creating a separate, cohesive universe that freely acknowledges its status as an art form.

And what is the purpose of the aesthetic universe of drama? The potential answers to such a question are nearly as many and varied as there are plays written, performed, and enjoyed. Dramatic texts can be problems posed, answers asserted, or moments portrayed. Dramas (tragedies as well as comedies) may serve strictly "to ease the anguish of a torturing hour" (as stated in William Shakespeare's *A Midsummer Night's Dream*)—to divert and entertain—or aspire to move the viewer to action with social issues. Whether to entertain or to instruct, affirm or influence, pacify or shock, dramatic art wraps us in the spell of its imaginary world for the length of the work and then dispenses us back to the real world, entertained, purged, as Aristotle said, of pity and fear, and edified—or at least weary enough to sleep peacefully.

It is commonly thought that theater, being an art of performance, must be experienced—seen—in order to be appreciated fully. However, to view a production of a dramatic text is to be limited to a single interpretation of that text—all other interpretations are for the moment closed off, inaccessible. In the process of producing a play, the director, stage designer, and performers interpret and transform the script into a work of art that always departs in some measure from the author's original conception. Novelist and critic Umberto Eco, in his *The Role of the Reader: Explorations in the Semiotics of Texts* (Indiana University Press, 1979), explained, "In short, we can say that every performance offers us a complete and satisfying version of the work, but at the same time makes it incomplete for us, because it cannot simultaneously give all the other artistic solutions which the work may admit."

Thus Laurence Olivier's coldly formal and neurotic film presentation of Shakespeare's *Hamlet* (in which he played the title character as well as directed) shows marked differences from subsequent adaptations. While Olivier's Hamlet is clearly entangled in a Freudian relationship with his mother Gertrude, he would be incapable of shushing her with the impassioned kiss that Mel Gibson's mercurial Hamlet (in director Franco Zeffirelli's 1990 film) does. Although each of the performances rings true to Shakespeare's text, each is also a mutually exclusive work of art. Also important to consider are the time periods in which each of these films were produced: Olivier made his film in 1948, a time in which overt references to sexuality (especially incest) were frowned upon. Gibson and Zeffirelli made their film in a culture more relaxed and comfortable with these issues. Just as actors and directors can influence the presentation of drama, so too can the time period of the production affect what the audience will see.

A play script is an open text from which an infinity of specific realizations may be derived. Dramatic scripts that are more open to interpretive creativity (such as those of Ntozake Shange and Tomson Highway) actually require the creative improvisation of the production troupe in order to complete the text. Even the most prescriptive scripts (those of Neil Simon, Lillian Hellman, and Robert Bolt, for example), can never fully control the actualization of live performance, and circumstantial events, including the attitude and receptivity of the audience, make every performance a unique event. Thus, while it is important to view a production of a dramatic piece, if one wants to understand a drama fully it is equally important to read the original dramatic text.

The reader of a dramatic text or script is not limited by either the specific interpretation of a given production or by the unstoppable action of a moving spectacle. The reader of a dramatic text may discover the nuances of the play's language, structure, and events at their own pace. Yet studied alone, the author's blueprint for artistic pro-

duction does not tell the whole story of a play's life and significance. One also needs to assess the play's critical reviews to discover how it resonated to cultural themes at the time of its debut and how the shifting tides of cultural interest have revised its interpretation and impact on audiences. And to do this, one needs to know a little about the culture of the times which produced the play as well as the author who penned it.

Drama for Students supplies this material in a useful compendium for the student of dramatic theater. Covering a range of dramatic works that span from 442 BC to the present, this book focuses on significant theatrical works whose themes and form transcend the uncertainty of dramatic fads. These are plays that have proven to be both memorable and teachable. *Drama for Students* seeks to enhance appreciation of these dramatic texts by providing scholarly materials written with the secondary and college/university student in mind. It provides for each play a concise summary of the plot and characters as well as a detailed explanation of its themes. In addition, background material on the historical context of the play, its critical reception, and the author's life help the student to understand the work's position in the chronicle of dramatic history. For each play entry a new work of scholarly criticism is also included, as well as segments of other significant critical works for handy reference. A thorough bibliography provides a starting point for further research.

This series offers comprehensive educational resources for students of drama. *Drama for Students* is a vital book for dramatic interpretation and a valuable addition to any reference library.

Source: Eco, Umberto, *The Role of the Reader: Explorations in the Semiotics of Texts,* Indiana University Press, 1979.

Carole L. Hamilton
Author and Instructor of English at
Cary Academy, Cary, North Carolina

Introduction

Purpose of the Book

The purpose of *Drama for Students* (*DfS*) is to provide readers with a guide to understanding, enjoying, and studying dramas by giving them easy access to information about the work. Part of Gale's "For Students" literature line, *DfS* is specifically designed to meet the curricular needs of high school and undergraduate college students and their teachers, as well as the interests of general readers and researchers considering specific plays. While each volume contains entries on "classic" dramas frequently studied in classrooms, there are also entries containing hard-to-find information on contemporary plays, including works by multicultural, international, and women playwrights.

The information covered in each entry includes an introduction to the play and the work's author; a plot summary, to help readers unravel and understand the events in a drama; descriptions of important characters, including explanation of a given character's role in the drama as well as discussion about that character's relationship to other characters in the play; analysis of important themes in the drama; and an explanation of important literary techniques and movements as they are demonstrated in the play.

In addition to this material, which helps the readers analyze the play itself, students are also provided with important information on the literary and historical background informing each work. This includes a historical context essay, a box comparing the time or place the drama was written to modern Western culture, a critical essay, and excerpts from critical essays on the play. A unique feature of *DfS* is a specially commissioned critical essay on each drama, targeted toward the student reader.

To further aid the student in studying and enjoying each play, information on media adaptations is provided (if available), as well as reading suggestions for works of fiction and nonfiction on similar themes and topics. Classroom aids include ideas for research papers and lists of critical sources that provide additional material on each drama.

Selection Criteria

The titles for each volume of *DfS* were selected by surveying numerous sources on teaching literature and analyzing course curricula for various school districts. Some of the sources surveyed included: literature anthologies; *Reading Lists for College-Bound Students: The Books Most Recommended by America's Top Colleges*; textbooks on teaching dramas; a College Board survey of plays commonly studied in high schools; a National Council of Teachers of English (NCTE) survey of plays commonly studied in high schools; St. James Press's *International Dictionary of Theatre*; and Arthur Applebee's 1993 study *Literature in the Secondary School: Studies of Curriculum and Instruction in the United States*.

Input was also solicited from our advisory board, as well as from educators from various areas. From these discussions, it was determined that each volume should have a mix of "classic" dramas (those works commonly taught in literature classes) and contemporary dramas for which information is often hard to find. Because of the interest in expanding the canon of literature, an emphasis was also placed on including works by international, multicultural, and women playwrights. Our advisory board members—educational professionals—helped pare down the list for each volume. If a work was not selected for the present volume, it was often noted as a possibility for a future volume. As always, the editor welcomes suggestions for titles to be included in future volumes.

How Each Entry Is Organized

Each entry, or chapter, in *DfS* focuses on one play. Each entry heading lists the full name of the play, the author's name, and the date of the play's publication. The following elements are contained in each entry:

- **Introduction:** a brief overview of the drama which provides information about its first appearance, its literary standing, any controversies surrounding the work, and major conflicts or themes within the work.

- **Author Biography:** this section includes basic facts about the author's life, and focuses on events and times in the author's life that inspired the drama in question.

- **Plot Summary:** a description of the major events in the play. Subheads demarcate the play's various acts or scenes.

- **Characters:** an alphabetical listing of major characters in the play. Each character name is followed by a brief to an extensive description of the character's role in the play, as well as discussion of the character's actions, relationships, and possible motivation.

    Characters are listed alphabetically by last name. If a character is unnamed—for instance, the Stage Manager in *Our Town*—the character is listed as "The Stage Manager" and alphabetized as "Stage Manager." If a character's first name is the only one given, it will appear alphabetically by that name. Variant names are also included for each character. Thus, the nickname "Babe" would head the listing for a character in *Crimes of the Heart,* but below that listing would be her less-mentioned married name "Rebecca Botrelle."

- **Themes:** a thorough overview of how the major topics, themes, and issues are addressed within the play. Each theme discussed appears in a separate subhead, and is easily accessed through the boldface entries in the Subject/Theme Index.

- **Style:** this section addresses important style elements of the drama, such as setting, point of view, and narration; important literary devices used, such as imagery, foreshadowing, symbolism; and, if applicable, genres to which the work might have belonged, such as Gothicism or Romanticism. Literary terms are explained within the entry, but can also be found in the Glossary.

- **Historical Context:** this section outlines the social, political, and cultural climate *in which the author lived and the play was created.* This section may include descriptions of related historical events, pertinent aspects of daily life in the culture, and the artistic and literary sensibilities of the time in which the work was written. If the play is a historical work, information regarding the time in which the play is set is also included. Each section is broken down with helpful subheads.

- **Critical Overview:** this section provides background on the critical reputation of the play, including bannings or any other public controversies surrounding the work. For older plays, this section includes a history of how the drama was first received and how perceptions of it may have changed over the years; for more recent plays, direct quotes from early reviews may also be included.

- **Criticism:** an essay commissioned by *DfS* which specifically deals with the play and is written specifically for the student audience, as well as excerpts from previously published criticism on the work (if available).

- **Sources:** an alphabetical list of critical material used in compiling the entry, with full bibliographical information.

- **Further Reading:** an alphabetical list of other critical sources which may prove useful for the student. It includes full bibliographical information and a brief annotation.

In addition, each entry contains the following highlighted sections, set apart from the main text as sidebars:

- **Media Adaptations:** if available, a list of important film and television adaptations of the play, including source information. The list may also include such variations on the work as audio recordings, musical adaptations, and other stage interpretations.

- **Topics for Further Study:** a list of potential study questions or research topics dealing with the play. This section includes questions related to other disciplines the student may be studying, such as American history, world history, science, math, government, business, geography, economics, psychology, etc.

- **Compare and Contrast:** an "at-a-glance" comparison of the cultural and historical differences between the author's time and culture and late twentieth century or early twenty-first century Western culture. This box includes pertinent parallels between the major scientific, political, and cultural movements of the time or place the drama was written, the time or place the play was set (if a historical work), and modern Western culture. Works written after 1990 may not have this box.

- **What Do I Read Next?:** a list of works that might complement the featured play or serve as a contrast to it. This includes works by the same author and others, works of fiction and nonfiction, and works from various genres, cultures, and eras.

Other Features

DfS includes "The Study of Drama," a foreword by Carole Hamilton, an educator and author who specializes in dramatic works. This essay examines the basis for drama in societies and what drives people to study such work. The essay also discusses how *Drama for Students* can help teachers show students how to enrich their own reading/viewing experiences.

A Cumulative Author/Title Index lists the authors and titles covered in each volume of the *DfS* series.

A Cumulative Nationality/Ethnicity Index breaks down the authors and titles covered in each volume of the *DfS* series by nationality and ethnicity.

A Subject/Theme Index, specific to each volume, provides easy reference for users who may be studying a particular subject or theme rather than a single work. Significant subjects from events to broad themes are included, and the entries pointing to the specific theme discussions in each entry are indicated in **boldface**.

Each entry may include illustrations, including a photo of the author, stills from stage productions, and stills from film adaptations, if available.

Citing Drama for Students

When writing papers, students who quote directly from any volume of *Drama for Students* may use the following general forms. These examples are based on MLA style; teachers may request that students adhere to a different style, so the following examples may be adapted as needed.

When citing text from *DfS* that is not attributed to a particular author (i.e., the Themes, Style, Historical Context sections, etc.), the following format should be used in the bibliography section:

> "*Our Town*." *Drama for Students*. Eds. David Galens and Lynn Spampinato. Vol. 1. Detroit: Gale, 1998. 227–30.

When quoting the specially commissioned essay from *DfS* (usually the first piece under the "Criticism" subhead), the following format should be used:

> Fiero, John. Critical Essay on *Twilight: Los Angeles, 1992*. *Drama for Students*. Eds. David Galens and Lynn Spampinato. Vol. 2. Detroit: Gale, 1998. 247–49.

When quoting a journal or newspaper essay that is reprinted in a volume of *DfS*, the following form may be used:

> Rich, Frank. "Theatre: A Mamet Play, *Glengarry Glen Ross*." *New York Theatre Critics' Review* Vol. 45, No. 4 (March 5, 1984), 5–7; excerpted and reprinted in *Drama for Students*, Vol. 2, eds. David Galens and Lynn Spampinato (Detroit: Gale, 1998), pp. 51–53.

When quoting material reprinted from a book that appears in a volume of *DfS*, the following form may be used:

> Kerr, Walter. "*The Miracle Worker*," in *The Theatre in Spite of Itself*. Simon & Schuster, 1963. 255–57; excerpted and reprinted in *Drama for Students*, Vol. 2, eds. David Galens and Lynn Spampinato (Detroit: Gale, 1998), pp. 123–24.

We Welcome Your Suggestions

The editor of *Drama for Students* welcomes your comments and ideas. Readers who wish to suggest dramas to appear in future volumes, or who have other suggestions, are cordially invited to contact the editor. You may contact the editor via E-mail at: **ForStudentsEditors@thomson.com.** Or write to the editor at:

Editor, *Drama for Students*
Thomson Gale
27500 Drake Rd.
Farmington Hills, MI 48331-3535

Literary Chronology

496 BC: Sophocles is born in 496 or 495 B.C. in Colonus, a rural community just northwest of Athens.

440 BC: Sophocles's *Women of Trachis: Trachiniae* is published between 440 and 430 B.C..

406 BC: Sophocles dies in 406 or 405 B.C.. The cause of his death is unknown, although the comic poet Phrynichus claims that he died without suffering, a happy man.

1592: *Arden of Faversham* is published.

1640: Many of the facts about the early life of the dramatist, poet, and novelist Aphra Behn are matters of conjecture. It is likely that she is born in the village of Harbledown, near Canterbury, Kent, England in 1640.

1670: Aphra Behn's *The Forc'd Marriage* is published.

1689: Aphra Behn dies on April 16 and is buried in Westminster Abbey.

1876: Susan Keating Glaspell is born July 1 in Davenport, Iowa.

1889: Jean Maurice Eugene Clement Cocteau is born to a wealthy family on July 5 in the small town of Maisons-Lafitte near Paris, France.

1926: John Keyes Byrne (aka Hugh Leonard) is born on November 9 in Dalkey, a small town near Dublin, Ireland, to an unmarried woman called Annie Byrne.

1927: Neil Simon is born on July 4 in the Bronx, New York.

1929: John James Osborne is born December 12 in London, England.

1930: Susan Glaspell's *Alison's House* is published.

1931: Susan Glaspell is awarded the Pulitzer Prize in Drama for *Alison's House*.

1932: Athol Harold Lannagan Fugard is born on June 11 in the Karoo village of Middleburg, South Africa.

1937: Arthur Lee Koenig is born May 10 in New York City, but his mother, Maxine, divorces his father when Arthur is very young, and she then marries George Kopit, a jewelry salesman.

1938: Jean Cocteau's *Indiscretions* is published.

1945: August Wilson is born on April 27 in Pittsburgh, Pennsylvania, the fourth of six children in a poor mixed-race family.

1948: Susan Glaspell dies of pneumonia on July 27.

1959: Richard Greenberg is born on February 22 in East Meadow, New York in 1958 or 1959 (official sources conflict).

1963: Though her exact birth date is not provided in online sources that give biographical information, it is believed that playwright and actress Claudia Shear is born about 1963.

1964: John Osborne's *Inadmissible Evidence* is published.

1968: Hugh Leonard's *The Au Pair Man* is published.

1969: Arthur Kopit's *Indians* is published.

1973: Neil Simon's *The Prisoner of Second Avenue* is published.

1975: Jessica Blank is born in 1975.

1981: Athol Fugard's *A Lesson from Aloes* is published.

1987: August Wilson is awarded the Pulitzer Prize in Drama for *Fences*.

1990: August Wilson's *Two Trains Running* is published.

1990: August Wilson is awarded the Pulitzer Prize in Drama for *The Piano Lesson*.

1991: Neil Simon is awarded the Pulitzer Prize in Drama for *Lost in Yonkers*.

2000: Claudia Shear's *Dirty Blonde* is published.

2002: Richard Greenberg's *Take Me Out* is published.

2002: Jessica Blank's and Eric Jensen's *The Exonerated* is published.

2005: August Wilson dies of liver cancer on October 2 in Seattle, Washington.

Acknowledgments

The editors wish to thank the copyright holders of the excerpted criticism included in this volume and the permissions managers of many book and magazine publishing companies for assisting us in securing reproduction rights. We are also grateful to the staffs of the Detroit Public Library, the Library of Congress, the University of Detroit Mercy Library, Wayne State University Purdy/Kresge Library Complex, and the University of Michigan Libraries for making their resources available to us. Following is a list of the copyright holders who have granted us permission to reproduce material in this volume of *DFS*. Every effort has been made to trace copyright, but if omissions have been made, please let us know.

COPYRIGHTED EXCERPTS IN *DFS*, VOLUME 24, WERE REPRODUCED FROM THE FOLLOWING PERIODICALS:

American Theatre, v. 12, July–August 1995 for "Sexual Relations," by Eileen Blumenthal. Copyright 1996 Theatre Communications Group. Reproduced by permission of the author./ October, 2002. Copyright © 2002, Theatre Communications Group. All rights reserved. Reproduced by permission.—*Ariel: A Review of International English Literature*, v. 20, January, 1989 for "Surviving in Xanadu: Athol Fugard's *Lesson from Aloes*," by Errol Durbach. Copyright 1989 The Board of Governors, The University of Calgary. Reproduced by permission of the publisher and the author.—*Educational Theatre Journal*, v. 18, March, 1966. Copyright © 1966 The Johns Hopkins University Press. Reproduced by permission.—*The Gay & Lesbian Review*, v. 10, May–June, 2003. Reproduced by permission.—*New York Post*, January 30, 2001. Copyright 2001 NYP Holdings, Inc. All rights reserved. Reproduced by permission.—*The New Yorker*, 2002 for "Play at the Plate: Losing It in the Locker Room," by John Lahr. Copyright © 2002 by John Lahr. Reprinted by permission of Georges Borchardt, Inc., on behalf of the author.—*Players: The Magazine of American Theatre*, v. 47, June–July, 1972. Copyright © 1972 by Byron Schaffer, Jr. Reproduced by permission.—*The Seattle Times*, June 10, 2002. Copyright © 2002 The Seattle Times Company. Reproduced by permission.—*Studies in American Drama, 1945–present*, v. 6, 1991 for "An Interview with Neil Simon," by Jackson R. Bryer. Copyright © 1991 by the Ohio State University Press. All rights reserved. Reproduced by permission of the author.—*Theatre Journal*, v. 55, May, 2003. Copyright © 2003, University and College Theatre Association of the American Theatre Association. Reproduced by permission of The Johns Hopkins University Press.—*Times Literary Supplement*, July 2, 1993. Copyright © 1993 by The Times Supplements Limited. Reproduced from *The Times Literary Supplement* by permission.—*Twentieth Century Literature*, v. 39, winter, 1993. Copyright 1993, Hofstra University Press. Reproduced by permission.—*Utne*, November–December, 2003. Copyright © 2003 by LENS Publishing Co. Reprinted by permission from *The Progressive*, 409

COPYRIGHTED EXCERPTS IN *DFS*, VOLUME 24, WERE REPRODUCED FROM THE FOLLOWING BOOKS:

From *Contemporary Authors Online*. "August Wilson," www.gale.com, Thomson Gale, 2006. Reproduced by permission of Thomson Gale.—From *Contemporary Authors Online*. "John (James) Osborne," www.gale.com, Gale, 2002. Reproduced by permission of Thomson Gale.—From *Contemporary Authors Online*. "John Keyes Byrne," www .gale.com, Thomson Gale, 2005. Reproduced by permission of Thomson Gale.—From *Contemporary Authors Online*. "(Harold) Athol Fugard," www.gale.com, Thomson Gale, 2004. Reproduced by permission of Thomson Gale.—Cohen, Stanley. From *The Wrong Men: America's Epidemic of Wrongful Death Row Convictions*. Carroll & Graf Publishers, 2003. Copyright © 2003. All rights reserved. Reproduced by permission of the publisher, Carroll & Graf, a division of Avalon Publishing Group, Inc.—Crowson, Lydia. From *The Esthetic of Jean Cocteau*. The University Press of New England, 1978. Copyright © 1978 by Trustees of University of New Hampshire. Reprinted by permission of University Press of New England, NH.—Gallagher, S. F. From an Introduction to *Selected Plays of Hugh Leonard: Irish Drama Selections 9*. Edited by S. F. Gallagher. Colin Smythe, 1992. Introduction copyright © 1992 by S. F. Gallagher. Reproduced by permission.—Guicharnaud, Jacques, and June Guicharnaud. From *Modern French Theatre: From Giraudoux to Genet*. Yale University Press, 1967. Copyright © 1967 by Yale University. All rights reserved. Reproduced by permission.—Hughes, Derek. From "First Impact: *The Forc'd Marriage*, in *The Theatre of Aphra Behn*. Palgrave, 2001. © Derek Hughes, 2001. All rights reserved. Reproduced with permission of Palgrave Macmillan—Knowles, Dorothy. From *French Drama of the Inter-War Years, 1918–39*. Barnes & Noble, 1968. Copyright © 1967 by Dorothy Knowles. All rights reserved. Reproduced by permission.—Kosok, Heinz. From "Hugh Leonard," in *Dictionary of Literary Biography, Vol. 13, British Dramatists Since World War II*. Edited by Stanley Weintraub. The Gale Group, 1982. Reproduced by permission of Thomson Gale.—Laughlin, Karen. From "Conflict of Interest: The Ideology of Authorship in *Alison's House*," in *Susan Glaspell: Essays on Her Theater and Fiction*. Edited by Linda Ben-Zvi. The University of Michigan Press, 1995. Copyright © 1995 by the University of Michigan. All rights reserved. Reproduced by permission.—Little, Jonathan. From "August Wilson," in *Dictionary of Literary Biography, Vol. 228, Twentieth-Century American Dramatists, Second Series*. Edited by Christopher J. Wheatley. The Gale Group, 2000. Reproduced by permission of Thomson Gale.—Walder, Dennis. From "Athol Fugard," in *Dictionary of Literary Biography, Vol. 225, South African Writers*. Edited by Paul A. Scanlon. The Gale Group, 2000. Reproduced by permission of Thomson Gale.—White, Martin. From an Introduction to *The Tragedy of Master Arden of Faversham*. Edited by Martin White. Ernest Benn, 1982. © Ernest Benn Limited 1982. Reproduced by permission of A & C Black Publishers, Ltd.—Wolfe, Peter. From *August Wilson*. Twayne Publishers, 1999. Copyright © 1999 Twayne Publishers. All rights reserved. Reproduced by permission of Thomson Gale.

Contributors

Bryan Aubrey: Aubrey holds a Ph.D. in English and has published many essays on drama. Entries on *Arden of Faversham*, *Dirty Blonde*, *The Exonerated*, and *The Forc'd Marriage*. Critical essays on *Arden of Faversham*, *Dirty Blonde*, *The Exonerated*, and *The Forc'd Marriage*.

Klay Dyer: Dyer holds a Ph.D. in English literature and has published extensively on literature, film, and television. He is also a freelance university teacher, writer, and educational consultant. Critical essays on *The Exonerated* and *Inadmissible Evidence*.

Joyce Hart: Hart is a freelance writer and published author. Critical essays on *The Au Pair Man* and *Dirty Blonde*.

David Kelly: Kelly is an instructor of English literature and composition. Entry on *Take Me Out*. Critical essay on *Take Me Out*.

Wendy Perkins: Perkins is a professor of twentieth-century American and British litera-ture and film. Entries on *Inadmissible Evidence*, *A Lesson from Aloes*, and *The Prisoner of Second Avenue*. Critical essays on *Inadmissible Evidence*, *A Lesson from Aloes*, and *The Prisoner of Second Avenue*.

Claire Robinson: Robinson has a Master of Arts in English. She is a writer and editor and a former teacher of English literature and creative writing. Entries on *The Au Pair Man* and *Indiscretions*. Critical essays on *Arden of Faversham*, *The Au Pair Man*, and *Indiscretions*.

Scott Trudell: Trudell is a doctoral student of English literature at Rutgers University. Entries on *Two Trains Running* and *Women of Trachis: Trachiniae*. Critical essays on *Two Trains Running* and *Women of Trachis: Trachiniae*.

Carol Ullmann: Ullmann is a freelance writer and editor. Entries on *Alison's House* and *Indians*. Critical essays on *Alison's House* and *Indians*.

pretends not to know where Knowles has gone. Irritated, Louise calls for her father-in-law, Mr. Stanhope, to question Ann. She admits to him that Knowles is here because of Alison. Mr. Stanhope is not perturbed, but Louise is distraught at the talk that will be stirred up. She brings up Mr. Stanhope's daughter, Elsa, comparing her to Alison, which angers him. Louise and Mr. Stanhope find out from Ann that Knowles is with Ted and has gone to see Alison's room. Louise continues to complain about the gossip she is sure will come, and Mr. Stanhope tells her to go into the dining room and pack china. Louise pleads with him to take these matters seriously then leaves. Mr. Stanhope tells Ann he wishes he did not have family to worry about.

Ted and Knowles return to the library, and Knowles is formally introduced to Mr. Stanhope. Mr. Stanhope tries to be stern with Knowles, but Knowles's sincerity touches him. Agatha, Mr. Stanhope's sister, enters, suspicious of Knowles. Mr. Stanhope diverts her and tells Knowles to leave. Knowles asks one last question: "Have all the poems of Alison Stanhope been published?" Mr. Stanhope says yes, but Agatha is distressed that Knowles may have found or taken something. Knowles gives his copy of his published poem to Ann and leaves, followed by Ted.

Agatha is upset that people will not leave Alison alone. Their packing is not going quickly, and Mr. Stanhope is stressed. Ann helps Agatha pack her mother's tea set. Agatha feels she and Alison are being turned out of their home. Mr. Stanhope replies, "Alison was at home in the universe." When Ted returns, his father rebukes him, but Ted thinks they are all foolish for keeping Alison to themselves. "She belongs to the world," he says. Agatha declares that she will continue to protect Alison, even if it kills her. Ted sits down to write a letter about Alison to his Harvard English professor. Mr. Stanhope yells at him, but Ted continues his task. Mr. Stanhope and Ann work on cataloging books, while Agatha quietly unpacks the tea set and leaves the room with just a basket full of straw.

Louise enters to collect a table that is to be sent to Cousin Marion. Ted tells his father that he needs information about Alison so that he can get a good grade with his professor, who is very interested in Alison Stanhope. The abandoned tea set is discovered under the table, and the family thinks Agatha is going crazy. Ted persists in asking questions about Alison, which irritates Mr. Stanhope and Louise.

Eben arrives and greets his family. They talk about selling the house to Cousin Marion, but Mr. Stanhope says she does not have the money so the sale is going to Mr. Hodges. Mr. Stanhope tells Eben that Agatha is overly excited and not dealing well with the move. None of them really wants to give the house up, although they all live in town, and only Agatha and Jennie live in the house now. Eben fondly remembers his childhood with Elsa at this house, when Alison was alive. Ted asks if Alison was a virgin, which scandalizes Louise. Mr. Stanhope tells Ted to leave the room, and Eben grabs Ted and shakes him, cursing him. Eben is deeply stirred by his memories of Alison, "how can we help but think of her—and feel her—and wonder what's the matter with us—that something from her didn't—oh Lord, *make* us something!"

Elsa arrives in time to hear her brother's passionate outburst, and she agrees with him. The family is astonished to see her. She asks her father's permission to enter. Louise is hostile toward Elsa, and Mr. Stanhope is speechless. Elsa wants to stay the night in the house, for old time's sake. Jennie cries out from upstairs that a fire has been set. Eben, Ted, Louise, Ann, and Mr. Stanhope go to see what is happening. Elsa is shaken that the house is on fire just after she arrives. Agatha returns to the room, in a daze. The fire is put out, and Mr. Stanhope comes in looking for Agatha to reassure her that the fire was stopped. Agatha is distressed. Eben enters and tells his father that the fire was set—straw and kerosene. Stunned, Mr. Stanhope calls Jennie into the room and interrogates her. Louise blames the reporter, so Mr. Stanhope calls Ann and Ted in and asks them about Knowles. Eventually, Mr. Stanhope notices the tea set and realizes it was Agatha who set the fire. Distraught that her fire was put out, Agatha starts talking nonsense and nearly swoons.

Act 2

In the library again, in the afternoon of the same day, Mr. Stanhope is sorting papers and dictating notes to Ann. They talk about Ann's mother, whom Mr. Stanhope was fond of. She has been dead for nine years. Eben brings in a box of old newspapers, and they reminisce. Eben and Mr. Stanhope talk about Agatha, and Eben says he thinks Agatha has something she wants to burn but could not do it so she tried to burn the whole house instead. They think it has something to do with Alison. Mr. Stanhope decides to save the old newspapers for their nostalgic value. They talk about the New Year's Eve dance this night, but Eben and Ann do not want to go because they would rather spend their time packing up the house. Ted returns to the library and his letter to his professor. Mr. Stanhope is irritated with Ted and tells him to stop telling other people the family business.

Jennie tells Mr. Stanhope that Mr. and Mrs. Hodges have arrived. Mr. Stanhope is aggravated because they were to wait until the move was finished. He is worried about Agatha. The Hodges enter cheerfully, declaring that they are trying to decide between this house and another. Mrs. Hodges wants to turn it into a boarding house with significant upgrades, all of which breaks Mr. Stanhope's heart. Eben implies that they do not want to sell after all, but Mr. Stanhope assures them that he will stand by his original price. The Hodges want a price break, but Mr. Stanhope is firm. Mr. Hodges will not commit to buying but wants to look at the upstairs rooms. Mr. Stanhope says no because Agatha is abed, but they convince him, and Ann takes the Hodges to look upstairs. Eben despairs of what they are going to do to his family's old house. Mr. Stanhope says he is glad it will be radically changed, so that it will not be the same house with other people living in it.

Eben and Mr. Stanhope talk about Elsa. Mr. Stanhope is angry with her for what she did because he and Alison were able to stop themselves from running off with the people they fell in love with. Mr. Stanhope says Louise is the only one with sense even though she goes about things wrong. Ted tells his father he wants to go into the rubber wheel business. Mr. Stanhope tells him he is going to practice law like he and Eben do. Eben wants to take time off—he is a bit dreamy, especially in regards to old times with Alison. Mr. Stanhope reminds him of Louise and his children. Eben knows he is being foolish but feels a pull to do something else. Ted offers to run away with Louise if Eben will write a new essay about Alison for him. Eben used to write when he was young but gave it up when he and Louise married.

Louise returns to the library and tells Mr. Stanhope she refuses to stay the night in the same house as Elsa. She is outraged when Mr. Stanhope tells her to stay with friends for the evening, and Eben, her husband, sides with his sister instead of her, his wife. Ted propositions Louise to take a trip with him back to Cambridge. Mr. Stanhope cuts them off, and they talk about the Hodges and Ann. The Hodges return to the library and Louise chats with them about their boarding house plans, going along with Mrs. Hodges's ideas. Mr. Hodges finally says that they will buy the house and immediately writes out a check. Mr. Stanhope is stunned.

Knowles returns to talk to Ann. Mr. Stanhope interrogates Knowles as to his purpose, but the reporter is embarrassed to say. Ted understands that he likes her, but Mr. Stanhope is suspicious of the young man. Mr. Stanhope finally sends for Ann, and meanwhile Knowles wonders aloud that something of Alison remains in all her family members. When Ann arrives in the library, Knowles implores her to walk with him, so that they might get to know each other better. Mr. Stanhope finally encourages her, and she agrees to go. While Ann is off getting ready, Mr. Stanhope gives Knowles a book of Ralph Waldo Emerson's poetry—Alison's favorite book, marked with her notes. Knowles and Mr. Stanhope take turns reading each other poems from the book.

After Ann and Knowles leave, Mr. Stanhope remarks that Ann is in love. Elsa comes into the room and tells Mr. Stanhope that Aunt Agatha is up and about. He leaves to see to her health. Elsa and Eben talk about how she ran away with a married man, and Eben points out that Alison, when she was in love with a married man, did not run off with him. Elsa admits that her boyfriend misses his family and that they are not happy all the time. Agatha enters the library carrying a bag and arguing that she has a right to be in her library. She is fixated on the fire Eben is tossing old papers into. Agatha believes she is being made to live with her brother because Elsa left him when she ran off with her married boyfriend. Agatha and Elsa sit close together, and Eben leaves them alone together. Agatha takes a leather portfolio out of her bag. Elsa senses her aunt's distress and offers to help her in any way she can. Agatha is conflicted but she cries out: "For—Elsa!" just before she collapses. Elsa cries out and her brother and father return to the library. Agatha is dead.

Act 3

Elsa is in Alison's room, preparing to look through the portfolio that Aunt Agatha gave her. Ann comes in to see Alison's room one last time. Elsa reminisces about Alison and Ann talks about falling in love. They look at the picture of the man, whom Alison loved. Elsa recounts how she fell in love with her boyfriend Bill all at once even though they knew each other since they were children. Ann asks Elsa for a picture of Aunt Agatha, for Knowles's story. They talk about Agatha, who was possessive of her sister Alison. Elsa is reluctant to give Ann her picture of Agatha or speak about her to Knowles because her father or Eben should approve first.

Eben joins Elsa and Ann in Alison's room. Ann admits she is going to marry Knowles. Eben is hesitant at first but gives Ann the picture of Agatha in her youth for Knowles to put in his story. Ann thanks them both profusely and leaves. Eben feels terrible for his father, who will be losing Ann, and so soon after losing his sister Agatha. Eben recalls beloved Aunt Alison aloud, what she looked like, and how she would sit and compose her now famous poetry. Elsa shows Eben the mysterious portfolio just as Mr. Stanhope joins his two grown children. Mr. Stanhope recognizes the portfolio as belonging to Alison, and Elsa recounts how Agatha bequeathed it to her with her dying breath.

Jennie enters, determined to carry out a wish of Agatha's. Mr. Stanhope figures out that Agatha made Jennie promise to burn the portfolio. Jennie does not know what it is, but she wants to do right by her employer and is distressed. Mr. Stanhope, Elsa, and Eben convince Jennie that she absolved of her promise because Agatha gave the case to Elsa at the last minute. Jennie is distraught that since Alison and Agatha are dead she has no one to look after. Mr. Stanhope says he needs her to look after him, and he sends her off to bed.

Elsa finally opens the contents of the portfolio and discovers packets of Alison's poetry—poems that no one has ever seen before. The three of them are absorbed with reading these poems, poems that are so revealing of the person they knew and loved, which is why she never published them. Ted arrives, apologizing for his tardiness. He was summonsed home after Aunt Agatha's death. Ted is astonished to see these new poems, but Eben sends him away so that Mr. Stanhope can have peace while he reads.

After they read for a while, Mr. Stanhope tells Elsa and Eben that he was instrumental in keeping Alison from running away with her beloved. She was in love with a professor at Harvard who was married with children. Ted returns, demanding to read the poems also. Mr. Stanhope becomes protective of Alison and says he will do what Agatha could not and burn Alison's poems. His children disagree, decrying that the poems belong to them as well. Ted is very passionate and even stuffs some of the poems in his pocket. Mr. Stanhope threatens to kill him and then is shocked by his own outcry. Elsa convinces Ted to leave, and Eben also goes out to get sherry. Elsa speaks a little with her father about the world of shame and happiness she lives in and how Alison would not disapprove of her. Eben returns, and they drink to Alison's memory.

The poems are gathered, and Eben says of them, "They were too big for just us. They are for the world." Ann, Ted, and Knowles come to the bedroom to add their voices to Eben and Elsa. Ann implores Mr. Stanhope to let Alison's poems go out in the world, invoking his forbidden love of her mother. Mr. Stanhope is stricken. Ann, Ted, Knowles, and Eben leave once Mr. Stanhope has been convinced to leave the poems to Elsa, as Agatha bequeathed. Alone, Elsa and her father talk about his unhappy marriage to her mother. He is angry with her for running off with a married man after he lived the lie all of his life, denying himself his true love, Ann's mother. They feel Alison's poems were written for each of them and take this as a sign of their universal appeal. Mr. Stanhope builds up the fire, takes the portfolio, and appeals to Elsa one last time to join him in protecting Alison's good name. As the hour strikes the new year and new century, Mr. Stanhope finally turns over the poems to Elsa and father and daughter embrace and are reunited.

CHARACTERS

Aunt Agatha

Aunt Agatha is the sister of Alison and of Mr. Stanhope. She lives alone in the historic family home in the Iowa countryside, near the Mississippi River, cared for by her maid, Jennie. Agatha is upset about being moved out of her home and repeatedly blames her brother for turning her out. She does not seem to regard his strained finances as any kind of justification for selling the house. All the talk about Alison that comes up from the move and from Knowles's arrival drives Agatha to worry about the unpublished poetry of Alison's, which she is hiding. Because of its scandalous content, Agatha knows she must destroy the poems, but she cannot bring herself to do it. Although Agatha never specifies, one might conclude from the other characters that Agatha is unable to destroy these poems because of their beauty. Agatha tries to burn the house down and later dies just after failing a second time to burn the portfolio. She leaves the poems to Elsa.

Father

See Mr. Stanhope

Mr. Hodges

Mr. Hodges buys the Stanhope family manor. He and his wife plan to drastically alter the building, making it into a summer boarding house. Mr. Stanhope and Eben are unhappy when they learn of these plans, but Hodges is either oblivious to their emotions or does not care. Hodges tries to negotiate a lower price because he says the house is in poor repair, but Mr. Stanhope stands firm, half-hoping Hodges will back out of the deal.

Mrs. Hodges

Mrs. Hodges, wife to Mr. Hodges, looks forward to modernizing the Stanhope house. She wants to rent its rooms to summer boarders. Like her husband, Mrs. Hodges seems completely insensitive to the Stanhopes' grief about losing their family house and about the prospect that it will be completely changed in renovation.

Jennie

Jennie, Aunt Agatha's servant, has been with the family for a long time; she once worked for Alison Stanhope as well. After Agatha dies, Jennie tries to carry out Agatha's wish to burn Alison's portfolio of poetry, but she is prevented by Mr. Stanhope, Eben, and Elsa. She is distressed at not being able to fulfill her promise to Agatha, but Mr. Stanhope reassures her that her earnest intent is fulfillment enough.

Richard Knowles

Richard Knowles, a young reporter from Chicago, comes to the Stanhope family house hoping to learn more about Alison before the house she lived in is sold and her century is past. A poet himself, Knowles loves Alison's poetry. He convinces Ted to show him Alison's room, something no outsider has ever seen. Later, he walks the banks of the Mississippi River, thinking about how Alison once did the same thing. When Mr. Stanhope realizes how much feeling Knowles has for Alison as a poet, he gives the young man Alison's marked copy of Emerson's *Poems*. Knowles and Ann fall in love soon after they meet, and they are engaged by the end of the play.

Ann Leslie

Ann Leslie, Mr. Stanhope's secretary, is no mere employee. She is very close to the family, having grown up with them. She is treated more like an extended family member. Ann falls in love with Knowles and his poetic soul, but she restrains herself from acting on her feelings until Mr. Stanhope, her surrogate father, gives his consent. In the third act, Ann speaks passionately to Mr. Stanhope in favor of publishing Alison's poetry because her

words were meant to live on beyond them all and their mortal concerns. Knowing the power of what she asks, she pleads with Mr. Stanhope to do it for her mother.

Miss Agatha Stanhope
See Aunt Agatha

Alison Stanhope

Alison Stanhope is the central character of *Alison's House*, although she is never seen on stage or heard from directly. She has been dead eighteen years at the time the play's action takes place. Through the dialogue of the other characters, it is revealed that Alison loved a married man and may have had an affair with him, but her brother, Mr. Stanhope, stopped her from leaving with him, behavior that would have been scandalous to the family in the mid-nineteenth century. Alison wrote beautiful, unique poetry. A few of her poems were published in her lifetime and just after, but those few earned her a fierce following. People such as Knowles are eager to discover and publish more of her writing. When Alison's secret stash of poems, which tell the story of her forbidden love, are discovered, Mr. Stanhope wants them destroyed so that Alison's honor and memory will not be tarnished.

Alison is modeled after American poet Emily Dickinson. Dickinson was a reclusive but witty woman, and the genius of her unique poetry was not discovered until after her death. Like the Stanhope family, the Dickinsons favored their privacy in the face of Emily Dickinson's fame and refused to let Glaspell use Dickinson's name or poetry in this play.

Eben Stanhope

Eben Stanhope, Mr. Stanhope's son and husband to Louise, works as a lawyer in the family business. He and Louise are cold toward each other and clearly do not have a happy marriage, although it is mentioned that they have children. Eben is overall unhappy with his life, but he does not have a forbidden, secret love like several of the other characters do. He feels an urge to do *something* different with his life, and that something may be writing, the love of which he seems to have inherited from his aunt Alison. Eben confesses to Ted that he gave up writing when he got married. Eben, like Elsa and the others, argues with Mr. Stanhope for the preservation of Alison's private poems.

Edward Stanhope

See Ted Stanhope

Elsa Stanhope

Elsa Stanhope, Mr. Stanhope's daughter, ran away with Bill who was married to Louise's best friend Margaret. Elsa and Bill live in exile from their families because of the scandal their relationship created. Elsa shyly returns home for a visit when she hears that her father is selling the family house. Louise is irate at Elsa's presence and will not stay in the house with her, but Mr. Stanhope permits Elsa to stay, despite the dishonor she has brought to the family. Elsa is given Alison's portfolio of unpublished poems by Aunt Agatha and fights with her father for their preservation. Elsa convinces him that they cannot destroy Alison's story and that it should be shared with the world. In his agreement, Mr. Stanhope also accepts Elsa. Elsa anticipates a new age when love is a more honorable foundation for a relationship than status or expectation. She completes the story of love and loneliness told through Alison's poetry. Elsa has her own, different loneliness, but now, with the acceptance of her family, it need not be as severe as it was for Alison.

Louise Stanhope

Louise Stanhope, Eben's wife, is an example of a typical, upstanding late-nineteenth-century woman, but her rigid character clashes with the Stanhope family. Louise worries more than anyone else about what other people are saying about their family. She and Eben have children, but they are not happily married. Although Eben has not fallen in love with another woman, Eben may eventually find a reason to leave her. Louise seems unconcerned that this could actually happen, probably because breaking up a marriage is still a very serious social transgression.

Mr. Stanhope

Mr. Stanhope, the patriarch of the family and Alison Stanhope's brother, lives in the city and is being forced to sell the historic family home where his sister, Agatha, and her maid, Jennie, now live. Mr. Stanhope is saddened to see the home in which he was born and grew up go to the soulless Hodges but strained finances and concern for Agatha are forcing him to sell. Like Alison, Mr. Stanhope has suffered his own share of heartache, pining after Ann's mother even as he remained in an unhappy marriage to the mother of his children. Nonetheless, he is a good father and close to his children. Rigid Louise is a foil for Mr. Stanhope, showing him to be reserved and private but not uptight or overly concerned with gossip. When Elsa arrives at the house unexpectedly, Mr. Stanhope will not turn her away even though he is upset with her for bringing shame to the family name. He is reluctant to give up Ann, who is like a daughter to him and his only remaining connection to the woman he once loved, but he see that Knowles is a kind man. Mr. Stanhope does not want to reveal what may be seen as a scandal regarding Alison, but for the first time in his life, he chooses love. Thus, he is able to reconcile with Elsa and release Alison's poems.

Ted Stanhope

Ted Stanhope, Mr. Stanhope's youngest son, is a student at Harvard University. Ted is too young to remember Alison and seems to lack the sensitivity toward life that Eben and Elsa exhibit, although he does not lack for passion and argues vehemently with his father for the preservation of Alison's lost poems. Throughout the play, Ted seeks new information about mysterious Aunt Alison in order to get better grades with his English professor, but his family refuses to cooperate with him. He does not understand what the big deal is—Ted is the only family member not touched by forbidden love. Ted also does not want to go into the family business and is more attracted to speculating in rubber.

THEMES

Forbidden Love

Forbidden love is a theme that runs throughout the lives of the characters in *Alison's House*. The title character, Alison Stanhope, is known to have loved a married man. She would have run away with him except that her brother stopped her. Her loneliness and love inform much of her unpublished poetry, which her sister and brother try to suppress. Alison's brother, Mr. Stanhope, has also experienced forbidden love. He was in love with Ann's mother even though he was married with three children. He denied himself this love although Mr. Stanhope kept Ann and her mother in his household so that he could enjoy Ann's mother's company.

Elsa is the only character who has acted on her forbidden love. Although it was scandalous to her family, Elsa ran away with the man she fell in love with, and he left his wife and children to be with her. It is perceived as improper for her to come back home, but she is moved to see her childhood home before it is sold, and her father and brothers

TOPICS FOR FURTHER STUDY

- Select your favorite Dickinson poem. Read it aloud to your class and explain what you think it is about and why you like it best.

- Individually or in small groups, select an author whose work you admire. Script a fifteen-minute dramatization of an important event in that person's life and perform your short play for the class. For added effect, work some of the author's writing into the script.

- Glaspell liked to write about her home state of Iowa where *Alison's House* is set. Research the history of Iowa and write a brief report about a significant event that took place in Iowa or an important person who lived there.

- In the early 2000s, divorce is much more commonplace and socially accepted in the United States than it was a century earlier. What are the divorce rates then as compared to now? Do you agree with Elsa's position to live only for love no matter what other people say or with Mr. Stanhope's position to deny love and stay in an unhappy marriage because that is what is proper, especially when one has children? Write a short essay defending your point of view, using evidence from Glaspell's play.

- Write a poem that reflects on one of the themes in *Alison's House*. Have a poetry slam party where participants read their poems using visuals, sound, lighting, performance, or audience interaction, as desired.

- *Alison's House* takes place on December 31, 1899, at the turn of the nineteenth century. How are people recognizing the turn of the century in this play? How does it compare to the recent millennial celebration at the turn of the twentieth century? How do you like to celebrate New Year's Eve? Write a short story about a fictional New Year's Eve celebration—set on December 31, 2099.

- Alison Stanhope is modeled after New England poet Emily Dickinson. Read a biography of this poet. Write an essay describing the similarities and differences between the poet's life and Glaspell's portrayal. What do we know about Dickinson and her family that Glaspell and Dickinson's biographers did not know in the 1930s? Do you feel *Alison's House* is an accurate portrayal of the Dickinson family?

- Emily Dickinson admired the work of Ralph Waldo Emerson, an American poet and philosopher who first expressed the philosophical ideas of American transcendentalism in his long essay *Nature* (1836). Research American transcendentalism, including reading *Nature*, and prepare a poster or other visual aid that summarizes this philosophy, gives examples of works that are considered transcendental, and describes some well-known adherents from the nineteenth century to today. Display your poster in the classroom or school public space.

- Dickinson and Walt Whitman were two influential American poets from the nineteenth century. They were very different in their personalities and writing styles. Read a selection of poems from each poet. Which do you prefer and why? Be specific in your answers: point to specific lines, images, or emotions, and use literary device terminology. Share your responses with your classmates in a roundtable discussion of the lives and works of these two prominent American poets.

- Theater-going has declined since the 1930s, when *Alison's House* was produced. Select a show to attend at a nearby theater, whether civic or professional. You can go individually to different shows or as a class to the same show. Write a review of the play you see, focusing on the performances, sound, lights, setting, directing, writing, and anything else that catches your attention. Include compliments as well as criticisms to make your review balanced. For extra credit, submit your review to a local newspaper for publication consideration.

do not really want to disown her even if society expects it of them. Elsa's brother Eben suffers from a nebulous need to do something other than be married with children and work in the family business. He is not sure what he wants to do instead, but it might be writing, the only conversation topic in the play that excites Eben.

Alison's House takes place at the end of the nineteenth century. Mores concerning marriage and family were strict and clearly defined. Although men and women could legally get divorced, doing so carried a much greater stigma then than it does in the early 2000s. People who left their families to run off with a lover were even more disgraceful than those who got divorced. Their behavior was considered to be immoral and selfish and reflected badly upon family members, who often disowned the person in an effort to distance themselves from the shame. What readers see in the context of Glaspell's play is that people who deny their love (Mr. Stanhope and Alison) are no worse or better off than the people who indulge their feelings at the expense of their family (Elsa). The playwright offers no simple answer.

Ownership

Ownership of the Stanhope family house, of its furnishings, and, ultimately, Alison's unpublished poetry is the problem that the characters of this play struggle to solve. Mr. Stanhope must sell the house he and his children were born in because they have all moved away to the city except for his elderly sister, Agatha, and Mr. Stanhope cannot afford both homes any longer. Interestingly, none of the Stanhopes ever considers moving back to the country, although they are all deeply saddened to see the house sold. While they can have no control over what becomes of the house, Mr. Stanhope and Eben are upset to learn that the Hodges plan to dramatically overhaul the house: modernize it, partition the rooms, cut down very old trees, and, in general, transform the place into something that little resembles the old Stanhope home.

As part of the moving process, the family belongings are being divided up. Agatha is to take her mother's china tea set. Mr. Stanhope is sharing the library of books with Eben and Elsa. He even gives a volume of poetry to Knowles after the young reporter impresses Mr. Stanhope with the sincerity of his feelings for Alison's poetic works. Very few of her poems have been published. Her published work is small but dearly loved by her family and immensely popular with readers. Although she has been dead eighteen years, reporters and scholars still periodically probe the family for more information about the reclusive Alison and to learn if any more unpublished poems have been found. But the Stanhope family has been close-mouthed about their beloved Alison. When Alison's secret stash of poems is found in the third act, held by Agatha all these years, the question of ownership arises again. Mr. Stanhope, like Agatha, wants to destroy the poems because they reveal Alison's love for a married man, which threatens to bring scandal to her name and to the Stanhope family all over again. Elsa, to whom Agatha gave the poems before she died, sees her own experiences in forbidden love reflected in Alison's writing and determines that the poems must not be destroyed. Elsa, Eben, Ted, Ann, and Knowles argue for the universal truth and beauty in Alison's writing, which belongs to the whole world and not just one small family. Mr. Stanhope, seeing something of his own life's suffering in Alison's words, finally consents that the poems can be published and returns them to Elsa's care.

The play explores, then, the rights of ownership and privacy in a case in which relatives of a famous artist face the dilemma of either saving their privacy at the expense of the artwork or running the risk of having assumptions made about their relative and themselves if the artwork is published. The family members know readers ought to distinguish the writing from the life experience that generated it, but this distinction is often overlooked by those who seek sensational inferences regarding an artist's life in the work that artist produces. In the end, however, the Stanhopes affirm that the poetry is more important than any potential comfort they would gain by suppressing it.

Loneliness

Loneliness is a significant theme in Emily Dickinson's poetry, and Glaspell evokes this theme in her play. Although the major characters are related in some fashion, each is isolated from the others because of private miseries. Elsa has run off with a married man, effectively cutting herself off from her family and friends. Although she and Bill are happy with each other, they are also unhappy because they are estranged from others. Eben is in a loveless marriage and working in a job he dislikes, which happens to be the family business. He is cold toward his wife and only comes to life when he thinks about the past, especially the good times he had as a child around his aunt Alison. Although surrounded by family, he is close to no one and unable to express true emotion. Ann, although embraced by the Stanhopes as one of their own, seems to have no immediate family of her own now that her mother is dead. Agatha lives alone in the Stanhope ancestral home. Her isolation is physical as well as emotional. With her sister Alison dead, Agatha has little companionship, refusing to move into the city with her brother until he forces her to by selling the house. Mr. Stanhope, as family patriarch, brings his loneliness upon himself by taking on the mantel of family leader. He denied himself true love with Ann's mother because he was already married and had children. He has carried the pain of this unfulfilled love with him much of his life, keeping Ann near as a reminder of her mother. Alison wrote her loneliness into her poetry, which becomes a balm to her family and seems to show them each a way to cope.

STYLE

Foreshadowing

In *Alison's House*, Knowles arrives in act 1, asking about Alison and gently inquiring if there might be some of her poetry yet unpublished. His questions, on top of the move itself, stir up memories of Alison for all of the family, and the subject of a possible body of unpublished work lingers and repeats. This foreshadows the eventual discovery of the poems in act 3. Aunt Agatha appears in act 2 with a leather portfolio of unnamed contents, drawing heightened interest to this possibility. The Stanhopes' certainty that all of Alison's poetry has been found and published lends dramatic tension to the final discovery.

Setting

This play is set in Iowa, where Glaspell herself grew up. She chose Iowa as her setting in part because she knew and loved the area and in part because Emily Dickinson's family refused to allow her to directly use their name or likenesses in her dramatization of the discovery of Dickinson's body of work. The action of the play takes place in the library and in Alison's room of the Stanhope family house, a large country manor near the Mississippi River. The house is old-fashioned and a little run down and in this way reflects the family who loves it. *Alison's House* takes place at the turn of the century, on December 31, 1899. Even as the family members are ensconced in their familiar territory, they are preparing to enter the unknown: a new century and a life without their ancestral home.

Historical Parallels

Glaspell's play is a creative work that parallels in characters and events actual historical people and their experiences. While purporting to be about the Iowan family called Stanhope, *Alison's House* is actually about Emily Dickinson's family, who discovered her writings after she died. In Dickinson's lifetime, only a few of her poems were published. Her family found more than eight hundred poems in hand-bound volumes after she died. Dickinson's style is unique and compelling, but she and her family were very private people. Over forty years after Dickinson's death, her family would not permit Glaspell to use the Dickinson name or any of Emily Dickinson's poetry in her play. By fictionalizing the characters and the setting, Glaspell was able to explore the dilemma that faced Dickinson's family. The play shows characters grappling with whether creative work is a private thing, for one's family, or part of the culture in which it occurs and thus something that really belongs to everyone.

Climax and Denouement

The climax is the turning point of a story and is often the most exciting part. The denouement, which is a French word that means untying, follows the climax and resolves the plot. In *Alison's House*, the climax occurs at the end of act 2, when Agatha fails to destroy Alison's poetry and bequeaths it all to Elsa. This event is considered the turning point in the story partly because of its placement two-thirds of the way into the play and partly because Agatha's gift and subsequent death irrefutably change the outcome that was expected up to that point, which was the destruction of Alison's portfolio.

The denouement occurs in act 3 when Elsa and her family discover Alison's lost poetry. The question posed throughout the play of whether Alison wrote more poetry is finally answered. The family struggles over whether to share these revealing poems with the rest of the world, but sympathies expressed throughout the play suggest the eventual outcome that Mr. Stanhope relinquishes his grip on Alison's privacy and permits the poems to be known to the world.

HISTORICAL CONTEXT

Roaring Twenties

The Roaring Twenties is a name for the decade of the 1920s. In the United States, it was a time of prosperity and social advances, especially for women

COMPARE
&
CONTRAST

- **1890s:** Popular poets of this decade include Emily Dickinson, Paul Laurence Dunbar, A. E. Housman, Rudyard Kipling, and Henry Wadsworth Longfellow.

  1920s: Robert Frost is a popular poet in this decade, as well as Edna St. Vincent Millay, William Carlos Williams, E. E. Cummings, and T. S. Eliot.

  Today: Popular poets include Mary Oliver, Maya Angelou, Donald Hall, Billy Collins, and Louise Glück.

- **1890s:** Realism dominates the theater of the nineteenth century. Realist playwrights of this decade include Henrik Ibsen, George Bernard Shaw, and Anton Chekhov.

  1920s: Harlem Renaissance literary movement flourishes during this decade and includes the playwrights Langston Hughes, Angelina Weld Grimke, and Thelma Myrtle Duncan.

  Today: Absurdism, which takes hold in U.S. theater in the 1960s, continues to be a fashionable movement in playwriting. Popular absurdist playwrights are Edward Albee, Sam Shepard, and Maria Irene Fornes.

- **1890s:** In the United States, a new dye makes mauve a more accessible color in fashion, and it is extremely popular for about a decade.

  1920s: The flapper style is popular during this decade. It is characterized by short dresses with a straight, androgynous silhouette.

  Today: Fashion is widely varied in the United States but tends heavily toward retro styles, sometimes combining a mix of styles from former decades. Looser fits, which have not been seen since the grunge period of the early 1990s, are more prevalent.

who were granted the right to vote in 1920 with the passing of the Nineteenth Amendment. World War I was over, and growing communication and transportation technologies made the world a smaller place. Mass production made automobiles less expensive and more readily available. Radio broadcasting production also became less costly, and thus radio was the main form of mass communication in this decade. Coal was being replaced by electricity and telephones were in more and more households. Jazz was the popular music, as was the flapper fashions, which emphasized an androgynous figure for women at a time when they sought equality of treatment with men. The Harlem Renaissance artistic movement was at its height in the 1920s and produced a wealth of literary, artistic, musical, and critical works. The Roaring Twenties were also marked by Prohibition: the Eighteenth Amendment to the U.S. Constitution, passed in 1920, forbade the sale or manufacture of alcohol. Instead of alleviating social ills, Prohibition increased criminal activity as people sought illegal ways to make or buy alcohol. A repeal of Prohibition was not

passed until 1933. Despite Prohibition, the Roaring Twenties was an exciting time when people looked forward optimistically. This joyful prosperity came to a halt in 1929 with the Black Tuesday crash of the New York Stock Exchange. The stock market crash was devastating to the U.S. economy and signaled the Great Depression of the 1930s. In all, the 1920s was a permissive decade, one particularly recognized for a more liberal view of women's roles and social options. Audiences for Glaspell's play would have tended to view the Stanhopes' concern for propriety as outdated and approve of those emotional choices the Stanhopes view as posing a threat to social conventions and family reputation.

Theater in the Early Twentieth Century

The realism movement of the nineteenth century continued without pause in the early twentieth century although experimental forms of theater became more and more prevalent. These experimental forms include absurdism and epic or Brechtian theater. Eugene O'Neill was a popular playwright associated with twentieth century realism although he also experimented with his style during the 1920s. O'Neill was introduced professionally by the Provincetown Players, a small theater group dedicated to preserving the creative process, which its members saw disappearing from the very conventional shows that appeared on Broadway. Experimental forms continued to gain critical attention until the breakthrough text, *Theater of the Absurd*, was published in 1962 by British scholar and critic Martin Esslin. Esslin named Samuel Beckett as one of the first playwrights to address absurdism in his work. Bertolt Brecht was a creative German playwright whose fame was unfortunately overshadowed in his lifetime by World War II and the Nazis. His style is sometimes called epic theater and is shaped around argument and ideas. Brecht preferred to call it dialectic theater, but many have opted simply for the term Brechtian. Postmodern approaches from the end of the twentieth century drew significantly from experimental roots in the early part of the century. Postmodernism is anti-ideological, which means that it eschews exclusive bodies of belief in favor of a broader view.

Poster for a Federal Theatre Project staging of Alison's House   Library of Congress

CRITICAL OVERVIEW

Glaspell was an esteemed author and playwright in her own time and also well-known for cofounding the Provincetown Players and launching the career of Eugene O'Neill. In 1918, the *New York Times* hailed her as "one of the two or three foremost and most promising contemporaneous writers of the one-act play." Despite her popularity, however, *Alison's House* was never a resounding success. J. Brooks Atkinson, reporting for the *New York Times* on the off-Broadway production of *Alison's House* in December 1930, writes that it is "haunted by genius" but that it is "a disappointingly elusive play." John Chamberlain, as an aside while reviewing Glaspell's novel *Ambrose Holt*, comments that *Alison's House* "does its best before a badly sentimental close."

When it was announced in May 1931 that Glaspell had won the Pulitzer Prize for Drama with *Alison's House*, critics became more heated in their remarks. Atkinson devoted an entire column to belittling the judges' choice for the drama award. He acknowledges that Glaspell is "one of our most gifted writers," but her efforts in *Alison's House* are not her best. He argues that it is "a play of flat statement—of assertions, of sentimentally literary flourishes and of perfunctory characterizations." The anonymous review, "Prize Play on Broadway," of the revived Broadway performance states that the audience "clapped its hands in a gentle approval which, however, never threatened to become an ovation." Interestingly, in response to Atkinson's commentary that *Alison's House* was a poor choice for the Pulitzer, two people wrote letters proclaiming their admiration and enjoyment of the play and their disagreement with Atkinson. Despite these proclamations, Glaspell's play closed on Broadway after two weeks and was not revived for more than sixty years. When it was restaged in 1999 at the Mint Theater in New York City, reviews were nostalgic but still lukewarm. Elyse Sommer for the online magazine *CurtainUp* writes that *Alison's House* is "old-fashioned and slow-paced" but still enjoyable. Victor Gluck, reviewing for *Back Stage*, summarizes the conflicting opinions with his simple description of Glaspell's play as "talky, old-fashioned, and dated" but also "dramatic, engrossing, and moving." *Alison's House* was and continued to be in the early 2000s viewed as a lesser, more conventional work in the oeuvre of a woman who did not shy away from radical social statement elsewhere in her work.

CRITICISM

Carol Ullmann

Ullmann is a freelance writer and editor. In the following essay, she explores the function and characterization of the unseen, unheard Alison Stanhope, who is the focus of Glaspell's Alison's House.

Alison's House, by Susan Glaspell, is a play in which the central character never appears on stage. Alison Stanhope has been dead for eighteen years when the play begins. Her sister, her brother, and his children are breaking up the house they all grew up in, and in this process, they stir up memories that have laid in waiting, unfaded and powerful. The house itself belongs to Alison's brother, Mr. Stanhope, who is the patriarch of the family, but many of the house's contents give references to Alison, famous for her poetry and particularly dear to each of her family members who remember her with fierce affection. Alison lived as a near-recluse, but despite her hermitic life, she was larger-than-life to the people close to her and full of whimsy and wisdom. Eben and Elsa's memories of Alison from their childhood are charged with wonder. They all feel that she was the greatest of them and in some way more alive, stronger, more authentic.

The play's title refers to Alison's metaphorical house: the world she built with words. Alison's poetry, although never recited during the course of the play, is understood to be a thing of great beauty, wisdom, and love. It is fitting, therefore, that the first two acts of the play take place in the library, a common area where everyone can come together and be surrounded by words—both hers and others—which may express secondhand thoughts and feelings readers do not know to say themselves.

The first person to bring up Alison in Glaspell's play is the young reporter from Chicago, Richard Knowles. Unlike other reporters the Stanhope family has encountered, Knowles is sensitive, a poet himself, and passionate about Alison's writings. Knowles is representative of Alison's earnest fans. The family is suspicious of him as they are of any outsider, but as romance blossoms between Knowles and Ann, they slowly accept him. Mr. Stanhope, warming to Knowles as he feels he must, seems to finally accept that Alison's spirit also lives on in those who truly love her poetry. He gives Knowles one of Alison's favorite books, marked by her own hand, Ralph Waldo Emerson's *Poems*. From this volume, Mr. Stanhope reads the poem, "The House," for Knowles, which evokes Alison's presence: "She

"ALISON'S UNSEEN PERSON ACTS AS A LENS TO FOCUS THE EMOTIONS OF THE OTHER CHARACTERS AS THEY CIRCLE AROUND HER AND HER STORY."

lays her beams in music / In music every one." The end of the poem seems to describe Alison's family: "That so they shall not be displaced / By lapses or by wars / But for the love of happy souls / Outlive the newest stars." Knowles immediately understands what Mr. Stanhope is describing: "Alison's house," he says.

The poem Knowles reads to Mr. Stanhope from the Emerson volume is titled "Forbearance," which is a commentary by the playwright on how the Stanhope family has practiced self-control, even to its detriment: "And loved so well a high behavior / In man or maid, that thou from speech refrained." Alison, in her lifetime, was unable to cleave to the man she loved, and her brother stayed in an unhappy marriage while loving another woman. But Alison's niece, Elsa, born into a different time, had the bravery to do what they could not. She followed her love.

Act 3 takes the audience into the innermost chamber of the house, Alison's bedroom. It has been left untouched—partly because the room was not needed in the mostly empty house and partly in tribute to the beloved poet, aunt, and sister. Alison's room is the last one to be packed. The family seems reluctant to disturb this shrine. When Alison's secret stash of poems is discovered in act 3, the question quickly rises about whether it should be published because doing so would generate a scandal. Alison, although a recluse, was a passionate woman. She once fell in love with a married man and may have carried on an affair with him. Mr. Stanhope reveals near the end of the play to Eben and Elsa that he was instrumental in keeping Alison from running off with her lover. She stayed only because he requested it. Elsa, reading the new poems, says, "It's here—the story she never told. She has written it, as it was never written before. The love that never died—loneliness that never

WHAT DO I READ NEXT?

- *The Visioning* (1911), Glaspell's second novel, tells the story of young Katie Jones who questions the conventions of her day. *The Visioning* addresses social issues such as gender roles, divorce, and labor unions. This novel is in the public domain in the United States, and Project Gutenberg has made it available free for download at http://www.gutenberg.org/etext/11217.

- Eugene O'Neill's first play, *Bound East for Cardiff* (1916), was among the first plays produced by Glaspell's theater company, Provincetown Players. It was also O'Neill's first produced play and launched his professional playwriting career. *Bound East for Cardiff* is a one-act play that takes place at sea on a steamship where a sick sailor who is dying talks about his life and the life he wished he had lived.

- "A Jury of Her Peers" (1917), from the short story collection by the same name, is a widely anthologized story by Glaspell, based on her popular play *Trifles* (1916). The short story and play are about an investigation into the death of an abused woman's husband. Glaspell was inspired to write *Trifles* after covering a similar court case as a reporter. "A Jury of Her Peers" is available in *The Best American Short Stories of the Century* (1999), edited by John Updike. *Trifles* is in the public domain and is available as a free download from Project Gutenberg at http://www.gutenberg.org/etext/10623.

- *Inheritors* (1921) is a popular play by Glaspell about a young college woman who stands up against her college and her government when two Hindu students are discriminated against for protesting. The themes and questions raised by this play remain relevant. *Inheritors* is in the public domain and is available as a free download from Project Gutenberg at http://www.gutenberg.org/etext/10623.

- *A Room of One's Own* (1929), an extended essay by Virginia Woolf, argues that women writers are capable of producing work as great as that produced by men. Woolf, a contemporary of Glaspell, did not shy away from writing about controversial social issues.

- *Renascence and Other Poems* (1917) is the first published volume of poetry by Edna St. Vincent Millay, an American poet known for her bohemian lifestyle. Millay's poetry is lyrical and technically precise. She won the Pulitzer Prize for Poetry in 1923. This collection is in the public domain and available as a free download from Project Gutenberg at http://www.gutenberg.org/etext/109.

- *Cambridge Companion to American Women Playwrights* (1999), edited by Brenda Murphy, is a collection of fifteen essays, which examine the role of female playwrights in the history of U.S. theater. Glaspell, Lillian Hellman, and Wendy Wasserstein are among the more than dozen playwrights discussed.

- *The Awakening* (1899), by Kate Chopin, is a slim novel about a woman who is married to a wealthy man but is in turmoil about the conflicts she feels between the role of wife and the role of artist. Chopin's novel was so controversial at the time that it was published that the author was blacklisted.

- *Nature* (1836), by Ralph Waldo Emerson, is an important essay, which explains the philosophy of transcendentalism; it explores the metaphysical aspects of the natural world.

- *Leaves of Grass* (1891) is a collection of poetry by Walt Whitman, who was a contemporary of Dickinson. Whitman's style contrasts sharply to that of Emily Dickinson.

died—anguish and beauty of her love!" Alison embraced her loneliness as none of the other characters are able to, which imbues her with strength. Agatha fails repeatedly to burn Alison's poetry, crying out that it was too lonely to do such a thing. Mr. Stanhope also cannot do away with Alison's private poems because to do so would be too lonely. With Alison's poetry, they need never feel alone because she is watching over them, guiding them with her words.

The character of Alison is modeled after Emily Dickinson (1830–1886) who has long been a figure of mystery because of her reclusive nature and her family's earnest wish for privacy. Glaspell's play is based on incomplete information about Dickinson's life but also draws from the stories her poems seem to tell. The playwright holds forth that the Dickinson family reticence may have had more to do with their tangled hearts than a quirk of personality. It was a time in history very different than one hundred years later. Cheating on a spouse was a kind of social death; people like the Dickinsons and the Stanhopes would sooner give up their own happiness than bring that kind of shame onto themselves and their families. Forty years after Dickinson's death, her poetry and something of the story of her life was well-known to Glaspell's theater-going audience. Although Glaspell was unable to use the Dickinson name or Emily's poetry, her audience knew who this play was about. This knowledge brings full circle the characterization of a woman who is central to the story but is never seen or heard.

Alison materializes in the play in other ways. She is the focus of conversation throughout the drama, from Ted's inquiries for his letter to his Harvard professor to Elsa and Eben's reminisces of their childhood. Knowles himself, a great fan of her work and hoping to write an article about her, seeks out her spirit and keeps her poetry alive and in the minds of people by writing about her. The book of Emerson's poetry speaks for Alison indirectly. The love that quickly springs up between Knowles and Ann is also a product of Alison's passion as is Elsa's less sanctioned romance with Bill. Agatha and Mr. Stanhope's pain over Alison's scandalous relationship being publicly revealed is a facet of their love for her. They want to protect her, but Alison, in writing and keeping these poems, does not seek protection. She did the right thing when she was alive, but the time has come when her love, her story, and her strength should be shared.

Alison's ephemeral presence is strongest in act 3, when her family gathers in her bedroom and reads her story through for the first time. Despite her isolation, Alison was a woman of high emotion and creative expression. Her story of love and loneliness has universal appeal—both Mr. Stanhope and Elsa say they feel as if her poems were written just for them. Elsa then points out that other people are sure to feel the same way, and thus Mr. Stanhope should release his hold on his dead sister and share her, her wisdom, and the beauty of her poetry with the world. It is a difficult decision for Mr. Stanhope, who has protected Alison's story for so many decades and even lived through the anguish of frustrated longing himself. But he made it clear earlier in the play that he did not care as much as he should about what outsiders will say or think. Ultimately, Mr. Stanhopes chooses life for Alison: "She loved to make her little gifts. If she can make one more, from her century to yours, then she isn't gone."

Glaspell's decision to focus on an historical figure that does not actually appear in the action of the play is unusual. Alison's unseen person acts as a lens to focus the emotions of the other characters as they circle around her and her story. She has been dead eighteen years, but her influence is strong. In modeling Alison after Dickinson, Glaspell lends plausibility to her tale as well as the drama of exploring the life of a mysterious woman. *Alison's House* has been criticized for being overly conventional compared to Glaspell's other works, but in fact the playwright is making a bold statement to the effect that no one needs to go through the anguish and loneliness that shaped Alison's or Dickinson's life because the new century heralds different times. Elsa has demonstrated this herself and tells her father that while some things are difficult, she does not regret choosing love above all else.

Source: Carol Ullmann, Critical Essay on *Alison's House*, in *Drama for Students*, Thomson Gale, 2007.

Karen Laughlin

In the following essay, Laughlin explores the shaping of the female poet protagonist in Alison's House, *"the ideological tensions at work in this construction" and the parallels in character to the poet Emily Dickinson.*

One of the acknowledged hallmarks of Susan Glaspell's dramatic writing is the device of the "absent center," the structuring of the play around a female character who never appears but whose impact on the present characters and action is powerfully felt. In *Alison's House*, Glaspell's last play and the one that brought her the 1931 Pulitzer Prize,

GLASPELL BRINGS
ALISON'S AUTHORIAL PERSONA
INTO FOCUS BY RELYING, AT
LEAST PARTLY, ON ALLUSIONS
TO THE DICKINSON BIOGRAPHY
AND LEGEND."

the absent character is Alison Stanhope, a thinly veiled likeness of Emily Dickinson, whose house is being prepared for sale eighteen years after her death. While her presence is evoked in the play's earliest scenes, Alison's influence becomes pervasive upon the discovery of an unpublished packet of poems expressing her unfulfilled love for a married man.

As if anticipating recent critical theory's pronouncements of the "death of the author," this final absent heroine in Glaspell's theater is a *writer*, and one about whom, even by 1930, a considerable legend had been built up. *Alison's House* opened at Eva Le Gallienne's Civic Repertory Theatre on December 1, 1930, just nine days before the centenary of Emily Dickinson's birth, and it appears that Le Gallienne carefully promoted the play on the basis of the Alison-Dickinson link.

Contemporary reviews of the play were, at best, mixed, and the subsequent awarding of the Pulitzer Prize was generally seen as either an outright error or a misguided attempt to reward Glaspell and Le Gallienne for their "artistic integrity and high purpose" (Toohey 92). In 1944 one of the Pulitzer jurors justified the award in terms that hint at the play's conventional outlook:

> The choice, really, was between a play [*Elizabeth the Queen*] acted with great acclaim . . . in the older fashion of romantic verse drama, and a play acted down on 14th Street by Miss Le Gallienne's struggling Civic Repertory Company which *plumbed the deep American love of home and family* still existing outside the confines of New York cubby hole apartments, and which also brought the strange story of Emily Dickinson to dramatic life. (Toohey 93; my emphasis)

More recently, critics have also been somewhat dismissive of the play, noting its "capitulation to commercialism and conventionality" (Adler 134). Even

C. W. E. Bigsby, whose recent edition of four of Glaspell's earlier plays has done much to enhance the current revival of interest in Glaspell's drama, describes *Alison's House* as "perhaps, a rather slight affair." While noting the connection with Dickinson, Bigsby's critique emphasizes a different biographical connection, that between Alison's story and that of Glaspell herself, describing the play as "a piece of self-justification by a woman who had, in effect, run off with a married man and who in this play offers a justification of her violation of social taboo" (*Drama* 33).

Certainly *Alison's House* is not Glaspell's most experimental play. Its style is realistic, and its family-oriented three-act structure concludes with the expected reconciliation of Alison's brother, the current Stanhope patriarch, and his wayward daughter, Elsa. But whatever its literary or theatrical merits, Glaspell's dramatization of the absent poet offers a fascinating look at the construction of the female author and the ideological tensions at work in this construction. Far from being a straightforward "piece of self-justification," the shaping of Alison by both Glaspell and the play's characters reveals a number of ideological contradictions. As Bigsby's remarks suggest, a basic tension in the play exists between what women, in Glaspell's view and experience, *are*—that is to say, sexual beings, desiring subjects, as well as creative artists— and what they *ought to be*, as implied in Bigsby's reference to "social taboo." In Alison and her more modern counterpart, Elsa, Glaspell adds to her dramatic repertoire two assertive and expressive female characters who challenge patriarchal constraints on female behavior through their frank acknowledgment and expression of their own desire. Yet Glaspell's supposed defense of this rebellion not only acknowledges the power of the social ideals and institutions that limit and mediate their self-expression but also reinforces this power even as it purports to challenge it. "The women have their way with this drama," as one early reviewer puts it (Hutchens 100), but "their way" is itself contradictory, as the play explores the competing interests of propriety and property, or class and gender, as well as of different models of female sexuality.

In *The Proper Lady and the Woman Writer* Mary Poovey offers a broad definition of ideology as both "virtually inescapable"—since it governs not just political and economic relations but also social relations and even psychological stresses— and as "always developing. As ideology evolves, its internal dynamics may change, its implications for a particular group may alter, or its inherent tensions may be exposed in what is generally perceived as a crisis of values" (xiv). Glaspell seems to be invoking just such a "crisis of values" when she sets her play on the last day of the nineteenth century, in the "old Stanhope homestead in Iowa." Setting the play eighteen years after Alison Stanhope's death (twenty years after that of Dickinson) enables Glaspell to establish the conflicting values at work in the Alison-Dickinson story in terms of a conflict of generations, essentially opposing the traditional, Victorian values of Alison's brother and her sister, Agatha, to the modern outlook of Father Stanhope's children, Eben, Ted, and Elsa, as well as his young secretary, Ann. Poised uncertainly between these two positions stands the figure of Alison, the poet.

The play's opening immediately gives prominence to the act of writing as the curtain rises on Ann sitting at a typewriter in the library, sorting papers she retrieves from a horsehair trunk. Glaspell quickly dispels the possibility that Ann might be the anticipated Dickinson figure with the entrance of an outsider, a reporter named Knowles, who shares the audience's curiosity about the papers on which Ann is at work and asks to see "the room that was used by Miss Alison Stanhope." Knowles's interest in Alison's house—he has been assigned to write a newspaper story about its closing—immediately foreground's Alison's position as *author*, about whom he wishes to collect relevant data. It appears, however, that at this point in the story there is a significant gap between Alison's person (or persona) and her poetry. The family, notes Ann, has "published her poems," but, according to Knowles, Alison herself "isn't dead. Anything about her is alive. She belongs to the world. But the family doesn't seem to know that." In a striking parallel to the workings of Foucault's author-function, we see that Knowles isn't satisfied with the mere existence of Alison's published work, though this provides him with a starting point. A published poet himself, he has come to retrieve the author he admires: "where—how—[the poems] were written. The desk she sat at. The window she looked from." For Knowles, at least, glimpsing the traces of Alison's life provides a way of "explaining events" or images in her work and of pinning down their meaning (see Foucault 984, 988).

Glaspell brings Alison's authorial persona into focus by relying, at least partly, on allusions to the Dickinson biography and legend. Knowles's sensitive search for information about Alison finds a crude parallel in the questions posed by Ted, a crass and rather dull-witted college student, who was

only two when his Aunt Alison died. In a sharp jab at academia's involvement in authorial construction, Glaspell portrays Ted gathering information for his Harvard English professor, who is eager to hear about everything from Alison's eating habits to that central facet of the Dickinson legend, her unfulfilled (?) "love affair." What he can't supply by copying down his family's reminiscences, Ted makes up, in a desperate attempt to salvage a failing grade.

The fond reminiscences of Alison's nephew, Eben, capture Dickinson's legendary love for nature and kindness to children, linking them explicitly to Alison's poetry:

> The fun we used to have down here as kids—Elsa and I. Especially when Alison was here. Remember how she was always making us presents? . . . An apple—pebbles from the river—little cakes she'd baked. And always her jolly little verses with them.

Eben's wife, Louise, on the other hand, is made uncomfortable by Knowles's probing, afraid that it will "revive the stories about Alison," stories that "she was different—a rebel." And while Stanhope accepts the fact that "you can't have a distinguished person in the family without running into a little public interest," he is visibly upset by Louise's suggestion that Alison's oddness might be somehow related to Elsa's more recent, and ongoing, affair with a married man. As the play progresses, both Stanhope and, more pointedly, Alison's sister, Agatha, increasingly take on the role of protectors of Alison's privacy, seeking to shield her personal life from the probing of either Knowles or Ted. "Why can't they let her rest in peace?" Agatha asks in exasperation when she first hears of the reporter's presence, and her desire to protect Alison from public scrutiny climaxes in her unsuccessful attempt to burn the mysterious envelope later revealed to contain Alison's unknown love poems. Act 2 ends with the rather melodramatic death of Agatha, who, unable to burn the envelope, entrusts it to Elsa. The play's final act, then, develops the consequences of this gesture, with the family arguing over whether these, Alison's most personal poems, should be burned as she, or at least Agatha, apparently wished, or else released to Elsa and, eventually, to Alison's reading public.

The play's developing construction of the figure of Alison thus comes to revolve around the issue of privacy, as it relates to Alison's personal life and that of the Stanhope family in general. The legend of Emily Dickinson's reclusiveness, of course, makes this an apparently natural focal point for Glaspell. Dickinson scholars have long discussed privacy as a factor in both Dickinson's personal life and her poetic language. Christopher Benfey's *Emily Dickinson and the Problem of Others* takes the privacy question a step further than most, however, when he links it with an increasingly acute concern for privacy in late-nineteenth-century society in general. Benfey cites three major sources to explain this renewed interest in privacy: (1) Hannah Arendt's contention that during this period "the older distinction between public and private, a distinction heavily dependent upon notions of private property, yields to the modern opposition of the social and the intimate" ; (2) Roland Barthes's tracing of the role of photography in creating "a new social value, which is the publicity of the private"; and (3) an 1890 *Harvard Law Review* article by Louis Brandeis and Samuel Warren that responded to the invasion of private life threatened by both photography and newspaper reporting by establishing the first legal definition of privacy in the United States (Benfey 56).

As Benfey notes, Brandeis and Warren are "at pains to indicate the extent to which privacy is constitutive of the person." Linking privacy explicitly with the issue of publication, they write, "The principle which protects personal writings and all other personal productions, not against theft and physical appropriation, but against publication in any form, is in reality not the principle of private property, but that of an inviolate personality" (qtd. in Benfey 57). Now legally defined as the "[license] to be still," privacy, according to this argument, separates from the question of private property and becomes linked, instead, with a concern for "the social and the intimate" (in Arendt's formulation) or with a notion of personal integrity and the right to refrain from sharing the secrets of one's inner life.

In Glaspell's exploration of privacy in *Alison's House* we see this restructuring at work. Knowles's characterization as a reporter indicates journalism's role in breaking down the barriers between private and public life. And the very fact that act 3 centers on the *debate* over whether the family should make the newly discovered (and highly revealing) love poems available for publication, on the one hand, demonstrates Glaspell's acceptance of the family's right to privacy. On the other hand, in the passionate arguments of Eben, Elsa, Ann, and Knowles in favor of publication, Glaspell suggests that it is the family's social responsibility to relinquish that right. Echoing Knowles's initial insistence that Alison "belongs to the world," Eben applies this argument to the newly discovered poems late in the third act: "No question about it," he concludes.

"They were too big for just us. They are for the world."

In his critique of the play Thomas Adler describes the resolution of this debate as a foregone conclusion. Identifying the outsider/journalist Knowles as the play's *raisonneur*, Adler argues that Glaspell answers the question of whether Alison and her poems "belong to the family or to the world . . . at the onset [of the play], so even though the exact content of the poems remains hidden, the dramatist's stance is immediately clear, diluting audience interest." I do not think Glaspell's answer to this question is quite so simple. And I would argue that it is the fact of asking this question, or, more precisely, the *process* of answering it, that gives this play its interest. As the play's third act unfolds, the debate about privacy or publication suggests that the transition from a concern for private property to a link between privacy and identity (or between "the social and the intimate") may not be a smooth one, especially when that which is to be kept private involves a woman's sexuality and creative expression.

To begin with, Adler's formulation of the play's central question immediately invokes the question of property. To whom does Alison, and especially her poetry, *belong*? The answer to this question apparently was not difficult so long as Alison was seen as the author of "jolly little poems" about bees, flowers, and cookies (Adler 125). But now the poems also reveal Alison's explicitly sexual desire, which is all the more threatening to the social order Stanhope represents because the apparent object of her affection was a married man. Eben, Elsa, their father, and, eventually, Ted read the poems in the privacy of Alison's room, which, significantly, serves as the setting for the play's final act. Even before knowing the contents of the portfolio, Stanhope lays claim to it as family (i.e., *his*) property, suggesting that "Agatha didn't know what she was doing" when she gave it to Elsa. Once aware of its contents Stanhope again invokes his patriarchal privilege, announcing his plan to "burn them in [Alison's] own fireplace—before her century goes."

In explaining his motives, Glaspell's patriarch also makes clear the link between the poems, as family property, and the nineteenth-century ideal of feminine propriety. Chivalrously, he plans to "protect" his sister, arguing that she *chose* privacy by not publishing her poems, since "she was of an age when people did not tell their love." In planning, in effect, to censor the love poems, Stanhope seemingly frames his actions in terms of Arendt's distinction between the social and the intimate. The poems, since they tell of a forbidden love Alison voluntarily renounced, are too personal for public circulation and should be destroyed, as Alison apparently wished. Already implicit in this argument, of course, is the role of chastity as a key ingredient in the nineteenth-century view of correct feminine behavior. Alison's dual renunciation (of her married lover and of making her love for him public by publishing her poetry) indicates the extent to which she apparently internalized this ideal, even at the cost of self-denial. In appealing to the principle of intimacy (as well as that of individual autonomy), Stanhope seeks to replicate Alison's renunciation, thereby maintaining the public image of Alison as the sexless, nineteenth-century "Angel of the House."

In contrast with Stanhope's chivalry, the opportunistic Ted apparently could care less about his aunt's intimate feelings or "inviolate personality." Also appealing to his family privilege and his desire to "protect" Alison, he argues in favor of the poems' publication because he sees them as a marketable commodity. While Glaspell leads us to sympathize with Ted's desire to see the poems published, she also appears to dismiss Ted's modern form of chivalry as simply masking another attempt to salvage his failing grade, or as another of his get-rich quick schemes. The contrast between Stanhope's appeal to the apparently modern conception of privacy and Ted's proprietary concerns is summed up in Stanhope's line, "I promise you my sister's intimate papers are not going into your vulgar world."

Between Stanhope's attempt to maintain Alison's "inviolate personality" and Ted's crass view of the author as producer of marketable goods stands the romantic or expressive view of authorship advanced by both Elsa and Ann. Breaking up the fight between Ted and his father and brother, Elsa claims to know the value of Alison's poetry "as no one else knows." Like Stanhope himself, Elsa recognizes the poems as expressive of Alison's passion, of a "love that never died—the loneliness that never died." But whereas Stanhope wants to keep that expression private and personal, Ann urges Stanhope to leave the matter of the poems' fate to Elsa:

STANHOPE: Elsa! Why should I leave it to Elsa?
ANN: To a woman. Because Alison said it—for women.
STANHOPE: Alison was not like Elsa. Alison stayed.

ANN: Then let her speak for Elsa, and Mother, and me. Let her have *that* from it. [For her own sake—let her have that from it!]

For Ann, at least, Alison's self-expression is explicitly gendered, an overt acknowledgment of female sexuality and the desires that the nineteenth-century code or propriety either controlled or denied. Though she may have written without personally seeking notice, as a *writer* Alison broke the code of female modesty to take on the position of speaking (or authorial) subject. In love themselves, Ann and Elsa insist that Alison's writing should not remain a self-enclosed act of personal expression. Rather, they argue, the poems are inherently "social" (to return to Arendt's formulation). Alison spoke "for women," and it is through publication of her poems that Alison's love will, albeit indirectly, be fulfilled.

For Stanhope, Ann's argument is compelling, especially when she evokes the now virtually complete convergence of Alison and her poetry by referring to Stanhope's plan to burn the manuscripts as tantamount to taking life. But Glaspell does not resolve the debate until there is one final exchange between Stanhope and Elsa, now left alone in Alison's room. Resorting to his final, most telling argument, Stanhope himself lays claim to direct affinity with Alison's self-expression, by affirming that he, too, renounced an illicit love, staying in an unhappy marriage with Elsa's mother for the sake of the children, and especially for Elsa. What comes into focus here is what Bigsby calls the "reiterated pattern of would-be and adulterous affairs," which Stanhope invokes as he attempts to lay the blame for the poems' destruction on Elsa. While, for the moment, only Elsa's ongoing affair with a married man is a matter of public record, publishing the passionate love poems would allow people to see *all* of the Stanhopes as potential adulterers.

With this argument we glimpse, with Glaspell, a further function of the ideal of feminine propriety and a basic conflict of interest at work in the play. What Stanhope seeks to protect is not Alison's personal privacy or even her choice to avoid public recognition of her poetic gift but, rather, the family name—in other words, the family's social standing and, by implication, the property to which that social standing is attached. Though much of Glaspell's dialogue (as spoken by characters on all sides of the debate) invokes the "modern" reformulation of privacy as intimacy and personal identity, these closing arguments suggest that even this reworked definition ultimately functions to protect "men's property and their peace of mind."

On the surface of things Glaspell appears to reject this view in the play's conclusion. As the village bells ring in the new century, Stanhope hands the poems over to Elsa, recalling Alison's love for making "little gifts," and embraces his wayward daughter, apparently convinced that he no longer needs to repudiate her for her violation of the social code. In a scene eerily reminiscent of the closing of Strindberg's *The Father*, Elsa and Stanhope mutually acknowledge each other: "Father! My Father?" Elsa cries, and Stanhope replies lovingly, "Little Elsa."

Within the context of the play there is something very satisfying both in Stanhope's act of handing over poems to their "rightful owner," Elsa, and in the reconciliation of father and daughter as the curtain falls. The powerful love poems are, we assume, to be published, as a "gift" from Alison's century to Elsa's, and Elsa's sins against the old social code are forgiven. But in this link between the poem's potential publication and the renewed bond between Stanhope and his daughter we can see further complexities of Glaspell's construction of authorship and of Glaspell's own position within ideology.

First, the presentation of the poems themselves as another of Alison's "little gifts" recalls Hélàne Cixous's discussion, in "The Laugh of the Medusa," of "the whole deceptive problematic of the gift." Responding to Derrida's discussion of Nietzsche, Cixous writes: "Woman is obviously not that woman Nietzsche dreamed of who gives only in order to. Who could ever think of the gift as gift-that-takes? Who else but man, precisely the one who would like to take everything?" Alison's poems, in the play, are in some senses a gift from one woman to another: in Alison's experience of love they speak to Elsa's, and, at the close of act 2, they were explicitly handed to Elsa by Alison's sister, Agatha. But now, as the play closes, they are given to Elsa by Stanhope, and his very act of giving them in Alison's name can be construed not as a "woman's gift" but, rather, as a "gift-that-takes." In effect, Alison's poems, like her house (which Stanhope sells to another couple in the play's second act), are still Stanhope's to dispose of. And this gesture also suggests the extent to which the publication of Alison's writing, and hence the expression of her desire, is mediated by her socially powerful brother, much as its subsequent interpretation may be mediated by the likes of Ted and his Harvard professor.

Glaspell herself further mediates Alison's sexuality by accepting the heterosexual myth that based Emily Dickinson's withdrawal from the world on her renunciation of a male lover. In contrast with Adrienne Rich's call for a lesbian feminist reading of Dickinson and her work, Glaspell's focus on the love poems in constructing her Dickinson figure does appear to assume "heterosexual romance as the key to a woman artist's life and work" (Rich 158). This is hardly surprising given the biographies available to Glaspell at the time she wrote the play and the critical fashion for tracing the masculine references in Dickinson's poems to a mysterious male lover. But in working out Alison's influence on her other female characters, Glaspell maintains a connection between the persistent myth of heterosexual romance and the Victorian code of propriety these women supposedly reject. Alison's love, we are repeatedly told, was both heterosexual and chaste, sublimated in her writing. While female sexual desire occasionally bubbles up (like the disruptions of language from Kristeva's semiotic) in the play's dialogue, as in Elsa's admission to Ann that "when you love you want to give your man— everything in the world," in general it is "love," not desire, that drives and wounds the characters in the play. Though Elsa has broken with propriety in her choice of a lover, she repeatedly idealizes her passion, internalizing her father's emphasis on propriety and redefining it in terms of romantic love, which, for Glaspell, has now become the "proper" way to contain female desire.

The reconciliation of Stanhope and Elsa, in all of its conventionality, is equally complex. While we can infer that, in forgiving Elsa, Stanhope may jeopardize his standing in his narrow-minded community, the father-daughter embrace visibly acknowledges Stanhope's standing within the family. This gesture suggests that Elsa, like Strindberg's little Bertha, has now acknowledged Stanhope as her true parent. While Elsa, now infantilized as "Little Elsa," may still be involved with her married lover, the image with which Glaspell leaves us is that of Elsa now assuming her "proper place" as her father's daughter. Like that of other women whose lives were ruled by the Victorian social code, Elsa's power, though not entirely negligible, is largely restricted to the power to influence her father. And while the balance of power does seem to be tipping in favor of the younger generation as the play closes, Glaspell cannot envision "a revision of the family unit so complete that patriarchy would be unacceptable." Nor can she completely dismantle the class privilege that Stanhope's patriarchal control continues to uphold.

This is hardly surprising given Glaspell's own position as a woman author whose literary career began at about the time she portrays Elsa as receiving the poems from her father. Perhaps we see in these ideological conflicts the struggles of Glaspell herself to reconcile a middle-class family background and her own efforts to maintain a semblance of family life with the social and aesthetic rebellions in which she also played an active part. But rather than resorting to biographical detail to justify Glaspell's conventionality, by way of conclusion I want to return to Bigsby's criticism of *Alison's House* to consider how the ideology of authorship I have been exploring in the play functions in Bigsby's construction of Glaspell as author of *Alison's House*. After dismissing the play as exposing "the extent to which Glaspell still felt it necessary to engage in a debate with her own past and with a morality which, if scarcely irrelevant, had lost a great deal of its immediacy," Bigsby goes on in the introduction to his edition of Glaspell's plays to praise Glaspell for "having written some of the most original plays ever to have come out of America." These highly original plays, we assume, are the ones Bigsby has chosen to anthologize, and, not surprisingly, *Alison's House* is omitted. The latter play, Bigsby implies, is not forward looking enough, since its concerns about "morality" were not especially pressing in the 1930s and, by implication, are even less so today.

In this argument Bigsby is assuming a progress in social attitudes, presumably toward adultery and the "New Woman," which Glaspell questions in her play (and which we in turn might question given the decline suffered by feminism after women won the vote in 1920). In playing off against each other changing definitions of privacy and feminine propriety, *Alison's House* seems to suggest that the myth of progress may be a way of mystifying the relations, particularly relations of ownership, that are still being used to keep women from controlling their own property—be it personal or literary. Even if Glaspell has, to some extent, "sold out" to commercialism and convention in *Alison's House* (as critics like Bigsby contend), Glaspell and her own work may be subject to an expropriation similar to that experienced by Alison and Elsa, as they and their work end up, literally, in patriarchal hands. This expropriation occurs not only in the initial lack of recognition of Glaspell's contributions to American theater but also in a "recovery" of her work by critics whose appreciation of her contribution seems grudging at best and whose readings tend to overlook the ideological conflicts of interest that give a

play like *Alison's House* its resonance and relevance even today.

Source: Karen Laughlin, "Conflict of Interest: The Ideology of Authorship in *Alison's House*," in *Susan Glaspell: Essays on Her Theater and Fiction*, edited by Linda Ben-Zvi, University of Michigan Press, 1995, pp. 219–32.

SOURCES

Atkinson, J. Brooks, "The Play," in *New York Times*, December 2, 1930, p. 35.

———, "Pulitzer Laurels," in *New York Times*, May 10, 1931, p. X1.

Chamberlain, John, "A Tragi-Comedy of Idealism in Miss Glaspell's Novel," in *New York Times Book Review*, April 12, 1931, p. BR3.

Glaspell, Susan, *Alison's House*, Samuel French, 1930.

Gluck, Victor, Review of *Alison's House*, in *Back Stage*, Vol. 40, No. 40, October 8, 1999, p. 80.

"Prize Play on Broadway," in *New York Times*, May 12, 1931, p. 33.

Sommer, Elyse, Review of *Alison's House*, in *CurtainUp*, 1999, http://www.curtainup.com/alisonshouse.html (accessed September 22, 2006).

"Who Is Susan Glaspell?" in *New York Times*, May 26, 1918, p. X7.

FURTHER READING

Ben-Zvi, Linda, *Susan Glaspell: A Life*, Oxford University Press, 2005.
    Ben-Zvi presents a scholarly analysis of the life and work of Glaspell in this biography. She also gives a critical analysis of each of Glaspell's major works.

Dickinson, Emily, *The Complete Poems of Emily Dickinson*, edited by Thomas H. Johnson, Little, Brown, 1960.
    This collection of Dickinson's poetry contains all 1,775 poems in chronological order, a layout that is unusual for Dickinson collections but presents a refreshing view of her development as a writer.

Emerson, Ralph Waldo, *Poems*, J. Munroe, 1847.
    Emerson's poetry was beloved by Dickinson even though he was more popular as an essayist and philosopher. His poetry is in the public domain and easy to find in various editions, including online.

Sewall, Richard Benson, *The Life of Emily Dickinson*, 2 vols., Farrar, Straus, Giroux, 1974.
    Sewall's extensive biography of Dickinson brings new information to light about the life and work of this reclusive poet. This book won the National Book Award in 1975.

Arden of Faversham

ANONYMOUS

1592

The Tragedy of Master Arden of Faversham was first published in London in 1592, although it may have been written and performed several years earlier than that. The play appeared during the golden age of English drama that occurred toward the end of the Elizabethan Age, which refers to the reign of Elizabeth I, from 1558 to 1603.

Arden of Faversham was published anonymously, and as of the early 2000s, the author remains unknown. It is possible that it was written by one of the three leading dramatists of the day: Thomas Kyd, Christopher Marlowe, or William Shakespeare. The play appears to have been popular during its time, being reprinted in 1599 and again in 1633, and it has been revived on many occasions in modern times.

The play, which is classified as a domestic tragedy, is based on a sensational crime that took place in the small town of Faversham in the county of Kent, England, in 1551. The most prominent Faversham citizen, the wealthy landowner Thomas Arden, was murdered by two men hired by Arden's wife, Alice, who wanted to get rid of her husband because she was having an affair with a man named Mosby.

In this chapter, all quotations are from the edition of *Arden of Faversham* edited by M. L. Wine, in the Revels Plays series published by Methuen. In some sources, the name Faversham is spelled Feversham.

AUTHOR BIOGRAPHY

The author of *Arden of Faversham* is unknown. The play was first published in London in 1592, although it may have been both written and performed several years earlier. Various theories have been advanced over the years regarding its author's identity. Minor Elizabethan dramatists, such as Robert Greene and George Peele, have been mentioned, but because of the high quality of the play, scholars have often investigated the possibility that it was written by one of the three most accomplished dramatists of the era: Thomas Kyd, Christopher Marlowe, or William Shakespeare.

Thomas Kyd (1558–1594) is known in the early 2000s for his play, *The Spanish Tragedy*. But few other plays can be confidently ascribed to him. The case for his authorship of *Arden of Faversham* once rested on a belief that Kyd wrote the play *Soliman and Perseda* and a pamphlet, *The Murder of John Brewen*. There are, it is alleged, parallels between the two works and *Arden of Faversham*. However, modern scholarship in general regards Kyd's authorship of *Soliman and Perseda* as doubtful and has discredited the notion that Kyd wrote *The Murder of John Brewen*. There is no other evidence, either internal (the themes and language of the play) or external (contemporary documents), that would link Kyd to *Arden of Faversham*.

Christopher Marlowe (1564–1593) was the author of six plays, including *Tamburlaine the Great* (1587), *The Jew of Malta* (first performed in 1592), and *Dr. Faustus* (first published 1604). Marlowe is usually proposed as a collaborator on *Arden of Faversham* rather than as its sole author. Some scholars have noted similarities in the imagery used in *Arden of Faversham* and in Marlowe's plays. It is also pointed out that Marlowe came from Kent, and there are many references to places in Kent in the play. However, as with Kyd, there is no external evidence linking Marlowe to *Arden of Faversham*, and few if any scholars in the early 2000s would be prepared to argue the case for his authorship of this play.

Claims have been made that William Shakespeare (1564–1616) was the author in whole or part of *Arden of Faversham*. However, as with the other candidates, there is no external evidence to support such a claim. None of the early editions of Shakespeare's work included *Arden of Faversham*, which until 1770 was never linked to any particular author, either in published editions or play catalogues (with the one exception of a list of plays published in 1656, since discredited, which attributed it to Shakespeare).

Some critics argue that *Arden of Faversham* bears no relation to Shakespeare's plays in style or theme. Others have found similarities between *Arden of Faversham* and Shakespeare's *Henry VI* trilogy (1590–1592) and *Richard III* (1592–1593). In *Marlowe's Imagery and the Marlowe Canon*, Marion Bodwell Smith found close parallels between Shakespeare's imagery in the early plays and the histories and the imagery in *Arden of Faversham*. She also found parallels with Marlowe's imagery and raised the possibility of collaboration between Marlowe and Shakespeare on *Arden of Faversham*. M. L. Wine, an editor of *Arden of Faversham* (1973), argues that although nothing could be known for certain about the authorship of the play, Shakespeare was the strongest candidate: "characterization, structure, underlying theme, and appropriateness of language figure more prominently and more suggestively with him than they do with any other writer proposed." However, the conclusion of Martin White, who has also edited an edition of the play, was that "the undoubted strengths of the play . . . demonstrate that the author was a master playwright, but one whose identity must remain (at least on present evidence), tantalizingly unknown."

PLOT SUMMARY

Scene 1

As *Arden of Faversham* begins, Thomas Arden is talking with his friend, Franklin. Franklin tells him that the Lord of Somerset has given Arden all the lands that were formerly owned by the Abbey of Faversham. But this does not lift Arden's melancholy mood. He is grief-stricken because his wife is having an affair with Mosby, whom he contemptuously refers to as a "botcher," a tailor who does repairs. Arden is jealous and vows that Mosby must die. Franklin advises him to treat his wife gently and suggests that Arden and he spend some time in London.

When Arden's wife enters, Arden tells her he heard her speak Mosby's name in her sleep. Alice makes light of it, saying that was probably because they had been talking about Mosby the previous evening. When Arden says he is going to London for a month, Alice pretends to be distressed, saying she cannot live unless he returns within a day or two. After Arden and Franklin exit, Alice soliloquizes that she is glad her husband is going to London, because she is in love with Mosby.

MEDIA ADAPTATIONS

- In 1799, the Sadler's Wells Company in London transformed *Arden of Faversham* into a ballet.

- In 1967, Alexander Goehr's opera, *Arden Must Die*, commissioned by the Hamburg State Opera, received its first performance. The play was not available as of 2006 on either VHS tape or DVD.

Adam from the Flower-de-Luce inn enters and tells Alice that Mosby is in town, but she may not visit him. Alice wants to know if Mosby is angry with her. She gives Adam a pair of silver dice to give to Mosby with the message that he should come to her door that morning and greet her as a stranger, so as to avoid suspicion. After Adam exits, Alice says she knows Mosby loves her, but he is afraid of her husband. She says she hates her husband and vows that he must die.

Arden's servant, Michael, enters. At Alice's request, he has sworn to kill Arden within a week. In exchange, Alice has promised him the hand of Susan, Mosby's sister. Michael says he has heard that Susan has been promised to a painter, Clarke, but Alice tells him this is not so.

Mosby enters and Michael exits. He speaks roughly to Alice, and she tells him to go away. He complains about the fickleness of women, but they are soon reconciled. Mosby tells her he knows a painter who can paint a picture with poisoned oils that will kill anyone who looks at it.

The painter, Clarke, enters, and says he will paint such a picture in exchange for Susan's hand in marriage. Mosby agrees. After Mosby tells Clarke that he and Alice do not like the idea of the poisoned picture, Clarke gives them a poison to put in Arden's drink.

Arden and Franklin enter, and Arden asks Mosby why he is in his wife's company. He insults him and plucks Mosby's sword away from him, saying that only gentlemen are allowed to wear one. Mosby asks to be judged by what he is now rather than what he formerly was. Mosby admits he once loved Alice but no longer does. He comes to the house only because his sister is Alice's maid. Arden accepts this explanation and offers his friendship. Franklin suggests that Mosby should stay away from Arden's house, but Arden says that he should come more often so that everyone may see that he trusts his wife.

Alice enters with breakfast, but Arden thinks there is something wrong with the broth. Alice throws the broth to the ground and laments that nothing she does pleases him. Arden tries to appease her; she protests that she loves him. They appear to be reconciled. Alice demands that he write to her every day from London or she will die of sorrow.

After Arden exits, Alice and Mosby complain about the ineffective poison. Mosby says he cannot continue to love her, since he made an oath to Arden that he would not. Alice protests, but Mosby insists that as long as Arden lives, he will not break his oath. Alice says they will have her husband murdered in the streets of London.

Greene enters and Mosby leaves. Greene is angry that his land has been transferred to Arden. He claims Arden has wronged him and vows revenge. Alice pretends to him that Arden is a bad husband, and she lives in fear of him. Greene takes the bait and is even angrier at Arden. Alice gives him ten pounds to hire someone to kill her husband, promising twenty more when Arden is dead. Greene says he will go immediately to London to arrange for Arden's murder.

After Greene exits, Mosby and Clarke enter. Alice encourages Clarke to woo Susan, telling him that she no longer thinks about Michael. Alice then tells Mosby about what happened in her encounter with Greene. Mosby is concerned that Alice is telling too many people about their plans. Clarke returns, and Mosby asks one favor before he will consent to allowing his sister to marry Clarke. He asks the painter to produce a poisoned crucifix. Clarke agrees to do so within ten days.

Scene 2

On the way to London, Bradshaw, a goldsmith, meets Black Will, with whom he served in the army at Boulogne, on the English Channel. Bradshaw tells Will he is facing trial for handling at his pawnshop a stolen plate belonging to a nobleman, Lord Cheyne. Bradshaw is going to London to find the thief. He describes a man, and Black Will recognizes him as Jack Fitten, who is in prison awaiting trial on other charges. Bradshaw is relieved and resolves to inform Lord Cheyne. Greene gives

Bradshaw a letter from Alice and hires Will and his companion Shakebag to murder Arden.

Scene 3

Michael reads a letter he has written to Susan, urging her to return his affection. Arden and Franklin overhear him. Arden is angry that Michael wants to marry Mosby's sister and says he will dismiss her from his service when he returns home.

Greene points out Arden to the hired murderers but tells them to spare Michael. An apprentice at a bookstall shuts the stall and accidentally hits Black Will on the head with the window. In the confusion that follows, Arden escapes, unaware of the plot on his life.

Greene returns and wants to know why Arden has not been killed. Will and Shakebag explain what happened and vow to find another opportunity to carry out the murder.

Michael enters and admits to Black Will he has vowed to kill his master to please Mosby and win Susan's hand in marriage. But Will says that he, Will, is the man who will do the deed. Michael promises to leave the doors of Arden's house in Aldersgate unlocked, but after the others leave, he reveals how troubled he is about betraying his master. But he knows that if he should default on his promise, Will and Shakebag will kill him.

Scene 4

Arden pours out his grief about his unfaithful wife to Franklin, and Franklin tries to comfort him. After Arden and Franklin go to bed, Michael gives expression to his conflicting emotions. He cries out, and Franklin and Arden, roused by the noise, come to see what is wrong. Michael explains he was having a nightmare. Arden discovers the unlocked doors and rebukes Michael for his negligence.

Scene 5

Black Will and Shakebag arrive at Arden's house, only to find the doors locked. They presume Michael has betrayed them and vow to punish him for it. They will watch for him in the morning and carry out their revenge.

Scene 6

Arden tells Franklin that he had a dream in which he was hunted like a deer. He woke up trembling. Franklin tries to reassure him that he was picking up on Michael's fear, but Arden replies that often his dreams come true. They agree to dine together then return to Faversham that evening.

Scene 7

Shakebag and Black Will confront Michael, who swears he left the doors unlocked and it was Franklin who locked them. He tells the assassins they may find Arden at Rainham Down, a village in Kent. They agree to meet later at the Salutation inn, where they will concoct a murder plan.

Scene 8

Mosby soliloquizes about his distressed state of mind. He was happy when he was poor, but now that he is wealthy, he fears he may lose what he has. He looks forward to Arden's death so that he may enjoy Alice, and he also vows to kill Greene and engineer a quarrel between Michael and Clarke so they will kill each other. However, he does not trust Alice, thinking she will be unfaithful to him, so he plans to get rid of her, too.

Alice enters. She is troubled by the planned murder of her husband and tells Mosby she regrets becoming involved with him. She wants to return to being an honest wife and blames Mosby for bewitching her. Mosby curses Alice, saying he passed up the chance of marrying a woman far more beautiful than she, with a large dowry. He claims that he is the one who was bewitched, but the spell is over now. He wonders how he ever thought she was beautiful and tells her to go away. Alice replies that what her friends told her turns out to be true, that he loved her only for her wealth. However, she offers to do penance for offending him and tries to win back his favor. Eventually, Mosby relents and says he will forget their quarrel.

Bradshaw enters with a letter for Alice from Greene, informing her that they have not yet killed Arden but plan to do so soon. Alice and Mosby wish Arden were already dead.

Scene 9

Greene, Will, and Shakebag enter. They are at Rainham Down. The two ruffians quarrel and begin to fight; Greene has to separate them, saying that if they turn on each other, Arden may get away. Greene then leaves, hoping they will accomplish the deed while he is gone.

Arden, Franklin, and Michael enter. Michael pretends his horse is lame and that he must go to Rochester to get a shoe removed. After Michael exits, Franklin continues telling Arden a story about an adulterous woman, but before he can finish, Lord Cheyne enters with his men. He invites Arden and Franklin to his home for supper. Arden politely declines but accepts the invitation Cheyne extends for the following day. Lord Cheyne then spots Black Will, whom he knows as a robber, and rebukes him. Lord Cheyne gets one of his men to give Will a crown and tells him to reform his life.

After Lord Cheyne, Arden, Franklin, and Michael exit, Will and Shakebag grumble about Cheyne's untimely appearance, which came just as they were about to kill Arden. Greene enters, and Will and Shakebag explain what happened. Will promises he will follow Arden back to Faversham and shoot him the next day.

Scene 10

In the early morning at his home in Faversham, Arden tells Alice that he is leaving for the Isle of Sheppey to dine with Lord Cheyne. Alice protests at his departure, and at Franklin's suggestion, Arden invites her to come with them. Alice refuses.

Arden and Franklin depart, while Michael is delayed because, he says, he must look for his lost purse. The real reason is that he knows Arden is going to his death.

Clarke enters, and he and Michael quarrel over Susan. Clarke strikes Michael in the head. Alice, Mosby, and Greene enter, and Alice rebukes Michael. She asks Clarke if he has the poisoned crucifix. Clark replies that he has. Alice and Mosby affirm their love for each other, but Greene is eager to find out whether Shakebag and Will have done their business yet.

Scene 11

Arden and Franklin greet the ferryman, and they go down to the boat. Arden remarks on how misty it is, and the ferryman makes cryptic allusions to the fickleness of women.

Scene 12

Shakebag and Will enter. They have lost their way in the mist but still hope for a chance encounter with Arden. Shakebag falls into a ditch, and the ferryman comes to his assistance. He tells the villains that Arden and Franklin have already departed.

The mist clears as the sun rises, and Greene, Mosby, and Alice enter. Shakebag admits that yet again, Arden has escaped. He says that he and Will will wait there until Arden and Franklin come back. Alice gives them some money so they can go to the Flower-de-Luce and rest. Mosby is discouraged and thinks they should abandon the plot, but Alice proposes that she and Mosby should walk arm-in-arm to meet Arden and thus provoke a quarrel. She can

then call out for Shakebag and Will, and Arden will be murdered.

Scene 13

Dick Reede approaches Arden, claiming that Arden has wrongfully taken a plot of land from him, and his wife and children are suffering as a result. Arden threatens to have Reede locked up. Reede curses him and says he will pray for Arden's destruction. After Reede exits, Arden insists that he did him no wrong. As they near home, Arden thinks his wife may perhaps come to meet him.

Alice and Mosby enter, arm-in-arm. To inflame Arden more, they kiss. Enraged, Arden and Franklin draw their swords, as does Mosby. Alice screams for help, and Will and Shakebag appear. Franklin wounds Shakebag, and Arden wounds Mosby. Mosby, Will, and Shakebag exit, and Alice reproaches Arden for his jealousy, claiming that she and Mosby were coming to meet him in friendship, joining arms only as a way to try his patience. In other words, it was just a joke. Then she complains that he is always misunderstanding her. Arden accepts her explanation and asks to do penance. She asks him to go after Mosby, ensure that his wound is cared for, and apologize to him. Arden asks Alice to come with him as a mediator. Franklin protests, saying it would be dangerous to go to Mosby, but Arden will not listen.

Scene 14

Will, Shakebag, and Greene enter. An exasperated Greene says it is time to give up their plot, since they will never succeed. Shakebag insists they will try again, and Will boasts of his violent exploits in the past and seems amazed that he cannot accomplish the murder of Arden.

Alice and Michael enter. Michael tells Alice that Arden and Mosby are reconciled and that Arden has invited Mosby, Franklin, Bradshaw, Adam Fowle, and others to dinner at his house that night. Alice tells Michael to ask Mosby to come to her and promises him that Susan will be his. Alice also invites Will and Greene to the dinner, and Will tries to explain why their attempt on Arden's life failed; he promises they will stab him in a crowd.

Alice speaks about how she almost murdered her husband in their bedroom. They then discuss the plan hatched by Mosby. Greene is to keep Franklin away from the scene while Mosby and Arden play backgammon. At a given signal, Will and Shakebag will emerge from the countinghouse and commit the murder. Alice gives Will twenty pounds and promises forty more when Arden is dead.

After Will and Shakebag exit, Michael enters. Alice informs him of what is to happen and gives him permission to tell Susan. Michael brings the backgammon tables in as Arden and Mosby enter. Alice pretends that she is not happy to see Mosby and refuses to welcome him. Mosby sits down, and Michael brings wine while Alice continues her pretense of disliking Mosby. Arden and Mosby play backgammon. At the given signal, Will emerges, covers Arden with a towel and pulls him down. Mosby, Shakebag, and Alice all stab him to death. They lay the body in the countinghouse, and Will and Shakebag depart. Susan is summoned to wash the floor of blood, but she cannot get it clean. Nor can Alice, who expresses remorse for her actions.

The guests enter. Alice pretends to be worried because her husband is still out. Susan is concerned that they will all be found out, and Michael seeks poison to kill Alice so she will not betray them. Franklin is suspicious, but all the guests leave. Susan and Alice carry Arden's body in from the countinghouse. Michael announces that the mayor and the watch are on their way to the house. Mosby, Greene, Susan, and Michael carry the body to the fields, and Mosby and Greene go to the Flower-de-luce for the night. The mayor enters with a warrant for the arrest of Black Will; they go to search the house for him. Franklin brings the news that Arden has been murdered and produces the bloody towel and the knife that Michael failed to dispose of. Alice claims that the blood stains are pig's blood, but Franklin points to other evidence that Arden was murdered in the house. The mayor notices the blood-stained floor. Alice protests, but Franklin orders that Michael and Susan be detained and that someone go to the Flower-de-luce to arrest Mosby.

Scene 15

Shakebag says he sought refuge with an old lover, but she would not admit him. He threw her down the stairs, cut her throat, and robbed her. Now he seeks sanctuary somewhere else.

Scene 16

The mayor urges Alice to confess to the murder, and she does so. Mosby admits he hired Will and Shakebag to murder Arden. Franklin vows they will not escape.

Scene 17

Will can find nowhere to hide in England, so he plans to hide in a boat that is going to Flushing, in Holland.

Scene 18

The mayor enters with the prisoners. Bradshaw has been condemned to death even though he claims, and Alice confirms, that he was unaware of the plot. Mosby and Alice indulge in mutual recriminations. Susan protests that she knew nothing until after the murder. Michael wishes he had never consented to the crime. The mayor condemns Mosby and Susan to be executed at Smithfield in London. Alice will be burnt at the stake in Canterbury. Michael and Bradshaw will be executed in Faversham.

Epilogue

Franklin announces that Shakebag was murdered in Southwark; Black Will was burnt on a scaffold in Flushing; Greene was hanged at Osbridge in Kent. Clarke fled, and the details of his death are unknown. At the spot in the field where Arden's body was laid, the grass did not grow for over two years after the murder.

CHARACTERS

Alice Arden

Alice Arden is the ruthless, immoral wife of Thomas Arden. She does not love her husband and is carrying on an affair with Mosby. She is so much in the grip of this passion that she plans and carries out the murder of her husband. She commits this murder even though she recognizes from time to time that Mosby is not a very admirable character. In scene 1, she taunts him as a "Base peasant" and says she was bewitched by him. Before she fell in love with him, she says, she was deeply in love with her husband. She acknowledges that Arden is a "gentleman" and that Mosby comes from a lower class. Yet she cannot free herself from her infatuation, which leads her to lie, deceive, and ultimately to murder. After Arden is murdered, Alice is at first filled with remorse, but then she pulls herself together and tries to deceive her guests, saying she is worried about Arden's safety because it is late and her husband has not returned. Then she becomes fearful about what she has done, but her fear quickly turns to a new resolve, and she seems almost gleeful, telling Mosby that they will spend the night "in dalliance and in sport." After that, she takes charge of the situation, directing the moving of the body and telling Mosby and Greene how to escape. After Alice is arrested, she repents of her actions. She is sent to Canterbury to be put to death by burning.

Thomas Arden

Thomas Arden, the husband of Alice, has recently become the owner of much land around the Abbey of Faversham, the property having being redistributed by order of the Duke of Somerset. Arden is therefore newly wealthy, but he makes enemies of former small landowners such as Greene and Reede, whose land he has taken. When they complain, he treats them in a high-handed manner, and this contributes to his violent death, since Greene vows to murder him and Reede curses the land that Arden took from him. Arden behaves in a heartless and arrogant way towards those he can control and whom he deems his inferiors. For example, when he finds out that Susan is the subject of the amorous attentions of both Michael and Clarke, he says he will dismiss her from his service. However, Arden is gracious, even obsequious, to his social superior, Lord Cheyne.

Arden is well aware of his wife's infidelity with Mosby, and it causes him great grief. He does not appear to be a bad husband, and it seems he still loves his wife. He is contemptuous of Mosby because of the latter's low social origins. When Mosby and Alice try to manipulate him into believing in their innocence, Arden on the surface goes along with this charade, even offering Mosby his friendship. But he later reveals that he is fully aware of the truth about his wife's conduct: "But she is rooted in her wickedness, / Perverse and stubborn, not to be reclaimed." This will cause grief in his heart until the day he dies, he says. Since Arden suspects nothing of the murder plot (even though he has a dream about a hunt in which he himself becomes the hunted) he is an easy target, the incompetence of the villains notwithstanding.

Black Will

Black Will is one of the low-life criminals hired by Greene to kill Arden. He was once a soldier at Boulogne, but since then has lived a life of crime in London. He likes to boast about his violent ways, telling Greene that "For a cross word of a tapster I have pierced one barrel after another with my dagger and held him by the ears till all his beer hath run out." He has run a protection racket in which prostitutes had to pay him a fee before he would allow them to set up a whorehouse. Even Lord Cheyne knows about Black Will's lawless ways and predicts that he will hang one day. Black Will is eager to kill Arden and talks a lot about how it is his destiny to do the deed and how efficiently he is going to do it. When he sees Arden, Franklin, and Michael together, he says he will kill all three of them. When

it comes to action, however, Black Will is not so efficient. When a shopfront falls on him, bloodying his head, the whole murder plan is ruined. Still he vows, "From hence ne'er will I wash this bloody stain / Till Arden's heart be panting in my hand." His role in the slaughter is to pull Arden down with a towel, allowing the others to stab him. After the murder, Black Will is brought to justice and burnt on a scaffold in Flushing, Holland.

Bradshaw

Bradshaw, a goldsmith, knows Black Will from their time together as soldiers at Boulogne and seems proud of the fact that he now owns his own shop. But Bradshaw is in trouble; he appears unwittingly to have handled a stolen plate belonging to Lord Cheyne and is facing a trial. Will supplies him with information about the thief, that Bradshaw plans to use to get himself acquitted. At the end of the play, Bradshaw is condemned to death for being an accomplice to the murder, even though both he and Alice swear that he knew nothing of it.

Lord Cheyne

Lord Cheyne, a nobleman, appears only in scene 9, when he enters with his men just as Black Will and Shakebag are about to murder Arden. Lord Cheyne is on good terms with Arden and invites him and Franklin to his home for supper. Lord Cheyne also knows Black Will, and when he sees him he rebukes him, saying that he will likely end up hanged. Behaving with the easy assurance of the born aristocrat, Lord Cheyne gives Will a crown and tells him that he must reform his disreputable life.

Clarke

Clarke is a painter who desperately wants to win the hand of Susan, Mosby's sister. He is so unscrupulous that he agrees to Mosby's request to create a painting that will poison anyone who looks at it. Mosby promises him Susan's hand in return. When Mosby and Alice decide they do not like the idea of a poisoned picture, he agrees to produce a poisoned drink that can be used to kill Arden. After that does not work, Clarke agrees to produce a poisoned crucifix. After the murder, which is actually carried out without any of his materials, Clarke flees, and no details of his fate are known.

Adam Fowle

Adam Fowle, the landlord of the Flower-de-Luce inn, appears in scene 1, bringing a message for Alice from Mosby. Alice gives him a pair of silver dice to take to Mosby.

Franklin

A loyal friend of Thomas Arden, Franklin is the only man to whom Arden can confide his inner thoughts and feelings. Franklin always tries to cheer Arden up. He gives his friend sound advice about how to handle the difficult situation with Alice, suggesting that he treat her gently. He suggests in scene 4, as a way of comforting Arden, that others have to bear greater woes. When Arden says he cannot bear to be in his own house, Franklin invites him to stay with him in London. Just after this, Franklin's soliloquy shows that he has genuine compassion for Arden. After Arden talks about his nightmare, Franklin tries to reassure Arden that it does not mean that anything bad is about to happen to him. Franklin always has Arden's interests at heart, as when he suggests that Mosby stay away from Arden's house. Arden appreciates Franklin and the friendship he offers: "Franklin, thy love prolongs my weary life; / And, but for thee, how odious were this life."

Greene

Greene is a tenant on land that has recently been passed by higher authority to Arden. Formerly, Greene owned the land on which he lived. He is indignant about the situation because he believes that Arden is being greedy and has cheated him of what is rightfully his. He vows to have his revenge, and Alice pays him money to arrange for Arden's murder in London. It is Greene who hires Shakebag and Black Will to carry out the plan. He gets increasingly exasperated by the incompetence of the two villains and at one point wants to give up the whole enterprise. He has a direct hand in the murder by keeping Franklin away from the scene and then dragging the body out to the fields. He is hanged.

Michael

Michael, Arden's servant, wants to marry Susan, Mosby's sister and for that reason agrees to take part in the plot against Arden. He is also a greedy, immoral man who tells Alice that to win Susan he will even get rid of his elder brother so that ownership of his brother's farm will pass to him and he will be wealthy. Michael agrees to betray his master to the killers, but he is troubled by his conscience, and in his confusion, he manages unwittingly to foil the plot to kill Arden in his own house. However, he plays a significant role in the actual murder, for which he is condemned to execution in Faversham.

Mosby

Mosby, the lover of Alice Arden, was formerly a low-born tailor, but he has managed to climb the social scale and is now steward in the house of the nobleman, Lord Clifford. He is conscious of his humble origins, and when Arden insultingly reminds him of them, he asks that he should be judged by what he is now, not what he was formerly. Mosby is a determined and ruthless man who is also conscious of the price he has paid for his successful social climbing. He admits that when he was poor he was happy, but now that he has more wealth and prestige, he worries about losing them. He is fully aware of the dangers of the course he is pursuing with Alice in their joint effort to get rid of Arden, but he knows that he cannot pull back from it. He is too much in love with Alice. Mosby is the active planner of the two; it is he who solicits Clarke to produce the poisoned painting, and he is unscrupulous enough to bribe the painter with the promise of marriage to Susan if he does what he is asked. Mosby lies to Arden directly, swearing he has no interest in Alice, but then he has a fit of conscience and tells Alice he cannot court her because he has promised Arden he would not. Although he appears to be sincere in this promise, he soon abandons it.

Mosby reveals the full extent of his cunning and his ruthlessness in his soliloquy in scene 8, when he says he will not be safe even when Arden is dead. Greene and Michael must be killed, too, lest they cause trouble for him. He even decides that he will also have to kill Alice because he does not trust her. He states his ambition clearly with the words, "I sole ruler of mine own." He wants to rid himself of anyone who could possibly be a threat to him.

After the murder, Mosby is arrested, and his love of Alice turns to hatred. He is taken to Smithfield, London, to be executed.

Dick Reede

Dick Reede, a sailor and inhabitant of Faversham, appears only in scene 13, when he confronts Arden with a complaint similar to that of Greene. He claims that Arden has taken a plot of land that was his. Although he is going off to sea, he needs the land for his wife and children. Arden tries to brush him off, and Reede responds by cursing the land that Arden took. He says he hopes Arden will be murdered there or meet some other bad end.

Shakebag

Shakebag is one of the two ruffians whom Greene hires to kill Arden. He prides himself on being a vicious cutthroat and boasts that he has stolen more money as a pick-pocket than his partner in crime, Black Will. At one point, he and Will get into a fight with each other. After the murder, in which Shakebag is the second man to stab Arden, Shakebag manages to find sanctuary in some unspecified place, and it appears that he evades capture by the authorities. However, Shakebag meets a bad end, murdered in Southwark.

Susan

Susan is Mosby's sister and Alice Arden's maid. Both Michael and Clarke want to marry her; Michael is even prepared to kill in order to win her hand. After the murder, Susan tries to wash the blood off the floor, and she also helps to move the body. Although she claims that she knew nothing about the plot against Arden until after he had been killed, she is condemned to death and executed at Smithfield in London.

THEMES

Awareness of Class Differences

Although only one character in the play is of noble birth (Lord Cheyne), the issue of social class is an important theme. Characters are very conscious of their positions in the social hierarchy. One of the reasons Arden despises Mosby is that the latter was not content to remain in the class in which he was born. He made a living as a humble tailor but then rose through the patronage of a nobleman to become steward in the nobleman's house, a position that gives him considerably more wealth and prestige than he had as a mere repairer of other people's clothes. Mosby also aspires to marrying Alice Arden, who was, as she herself says, "descended of a noble house," so that he can rise to an even higher social status.

Arden prides himself on his high social status. "I am by birth a gentleman of blood," he tells Franklin, and when he speaks venomously about Mosby, it is Mosby's low social origins that annoy him the most. "She's no companion for so base a groom," he says directly to Mosby about Alice. He further taunts Mosby, saying that his rival has no right to wear a sword, because of a statute that bans anyone under the rank of gentleman from doing so. Arden continues to insult Mosby by harping on his former occupation: "Now use your bodkin, / Your Spanish needle, and your pressing iron," he says and then calls Mosby a "goodman botcher." "Goodman" was a form of address used to those whose rank was lower than that of a nobleman. Once he

has started it, Arden simply cannot stop this line of attack. He insults Mosby as "a velvet drudge" and "base-minded peasant." Curiously, it seems as if Arden's anger is due to Mosby's perceived impertinence in trying to rise above his social origins than to the fact that the former tailor is committing adultery with Arden's wife.

Interestingly, when Mosby tries to defend himself from Arden's verbal attack ("Measure me what I am, not what I was"), the language he uses unconsciously reveals his origins at the very time he is trying to show that he has transcended them, since "measuring" is what a tailor does. Notably also, when Mosby finally gets to stab Arden, he says, "There's for the pressing iron you told me of," as if the insult about his being a former tailor is the reason for the murder, not the fact that Mosby wants the victim's wife for himself.

Alice is also aware of the gap in social status between herself and Mosby and between Mosby and Arden. Like her husband, when she quarrels with her lover, she cannot resist having a dig at his social status: "A mean artificer, that low-born name," she says, referring to him.

This awareness of social class extends even to the lower characters. Black Will and Bradshaw served in the military together, but when Will hails him as a fellow and recalls their army days together, Bradshaw says, "O Will, times are changed. No fellows now," to which Will replies, "'No fellows now' because you are a goldsmith and have a little plate in your shop?" In other words, even though Bradshaw has climbed only a few rungs on the social ladder, he is keenly aware that he has bettered himself and makes sure his old friend knows it.

Greed and Immorality

Consciousness of class differences feeds into another main theme of the play, which is simple greed. People want more than they have and are prepared to do anything to get it. The servant Michael contemplates the murder of his elder brother, who owns a farm, because he thinks this will help him be a worthy husband of Susan. Greene accepts money from Alice in order to hire someone to murder Arden. Bradshaw says of Black Will, "I warrant you he bears so bad a mind / That for a crown he'll murder any man."

The ruthless, manipulative Alice is acutely aware of how greed for money makes the immoral, pitiless world depicted in the play go round. She knows very well that ruffians may be hired to kill if the price is right: "They shall be soundly fee'd

TOPICS FOR FURTHER STUDY

- Research the dissolution of the monasteries in England that took place between 1538 and 1541. Write an essay in which you explain why Henry VIII closed the monasteries. What were the consequences for English society and culture, and how is that shown in *Arden of Faversham*?

- Reread the play and pick out your three favorite passages of two to ten lines or more. Explain to the class why you like these quotations. What appeals to you about the use of language in them? Then select from your favorite Shakespeare play three of the most memorable short passages. Read them to the class also, explaining the dramatic context in which they occur. Whose lines are more memorable—Shakespeare's or those of the anonymous author of *Arden of Faversham*? Explain your answer.

- After the sensational murder in Faversham in 1551, Alice's story was told in a popular ballad. Team up with one other student and write a ballad or other type of song in which you tell Alice's story. Perform your song for the class.

- Read Holinshed's account of Arden's murder in his *Chronicles of England, Scotland, and Ireland*. You can find this account in the appendices to both editions of the play mentioned in this chapter. Write an essay in which you show how the dramatist handled his source material. Did he stay close to Holinshed's account in every way? In what ways did he shape the material to make powerful drama? Make sure you mention the character Dick Reede in your essay. How does the dramatist seize on this small detail in Holinshed and make it dramatic?

---

to pay him home," meaning that the assassins will be well paid to send Arden to his death. To this end, she offers Greene money and promises more when the deed is done. In scene 14, just before the murder, she promises Will "golden harmony" (that is, money), in addition to what she has already paid through Greene. Alice seems very much at home in this world where greed overrides morality at every turn. Earlier in the play, she appeals to Mosby's greed when she points out that her husband has saved much money and has gone to London "to unload the goods that shall be thine."

Arden also contributes to this world of greed. He has been granted a lot of land by the authorities, but he is blind to the social obligations that accompany his good fortune. He treats Greene and Dick Reede without any sympathy or understanding. All he cares about is the fact that his own wealth and power has increased, and the fact that others have been displaced and impoverished as a result is of no interest to him.

The world of the play is, therefore, one in which all sense of decency, of a man's obligations

to others and to the social fabric, has been obliterated. It is a dark play with few chinks of light. The only good character is Franklin, and he is completely ineffective in saving his friend Arden.

STYLE

Domestic Tragedy

Arden of Faversham is the first example of a new genre in the history of English drama, the domestic tragedy. Before this play, tragedies had always been about characters of high social rank—kings and nobility. In contrast, the domestic tragedy features characters lower in the social scale. The historical Thomas Arden, for example, although he was a wealthy landowner and the chief citizen of the small town of Faversham, was not a nobleman and appears to have gained his local importance from hard work, a successful career, and the good fortune that came from cultivating relationships with those who had more wealth and power than he did.

Domestic tragedies presented realistic scenes from ordinary life. The plot usually centered on a murder and was based on an actual crime in recent history that had been recorded in a chronicle, a ballad, or pamphlet. Domestic tragedy evolved from the traditional morality play. It offered moral lessons to the audience by presenting them with people whom they could recognize as members of their own societies. The emphasis is often on sin and punishment, as in *Arden of Faversham*, but domestic tragedies also explore matters of forgiveness and repentance.

Noting that domestic tragedy appealed to the large middle-class element in the audience, Madeleine Doran writes that the genre "has the characteristics of bourgeois literature in its heavy moral emphasis and in its combination of sensationalism and sentiment."

Other domestic tragedies include Thomas Heywood's *A Woman Killed with Kindness* (acted in 1603) and the anonymous *A Yorkshire Tragedy* (1608).

HISTORICAL CONTEXT

The Murder in Faversham

The historical Thomas Arden, like the dramatic version of him in the play, was a man who knew how to climb the social ladder. The year of Arden's birth is unknown, but it appears he came from a good family. He soon rose to prominence, serving Sir Edward North in the court appointed by Henry VIII to arrange for the dispersal of church lands after the dissolution of the monasteries in 1538. Arden married well, from a social point of view, since his bride, reported to be many years younger than he, was the stepdaughter of Sir Edward. After the marriage, Arden was placed in charge of customs at the thriving port of Faversham, in Kent. This was a lucrative position at the time. Arden also received, as the play makes clear, some lands that had formerly been the property of the abbey at Faversham. He was mayor of Faversham in 1548, and at the time of his murder in 1551, he was the most powerful citizen in the town.

The murder took place in Arden's parlor at about seven o'clock in the evening on Sunday, February 15. It was a cold night and snow lay on the ground. When the news of the murder spread, it caused quite a stir, both locally and nationally. Then as now, a crime with sensational elements— a wife and her lover conspiring with ruffians to murder the wife's wealthy husband—was food for gossip and moralizing for many years to come. The

crime even reached the attention of the historian Raphael Holinshed, who allowed himself a four-page digression in his *Chronicles of England, Scotland, and Ireland* (1587) in which to tell the story.

Holinshed's work was the source used by the author of *Arden of Faversham* to write the play. Although the anonymous dramatist was entirely dependent on Holinshed for his plot, he also shaped the historian's narrative for his own dramatic purposes. The character Franklin, for example, does not appear in Holinshed; it is likely that the dramatist created him in order to give Arden someone to whom he could confess his feelings. The dramatist also invented the ferryman, while eliminating Arden's daughters, who are mentioned by Holinshed. The dramatist also enlarged the role of Shakebag, who is mentioned in Holinshed only a few times, with no details. The dramatist also developed more fully the characters of Arden, Alice, and Mosby, carefully exploring their motives. In some other respects, however, Holinshed gave more details of the event than the dramatist. His description of the murder is particularly lurid. As Holinshed told it, Black Will covered Arden's neck with the towel in order to strangle him, and then Mosby hit him on the head with a fourteen-pound pressing iron. Arden fell down groaning. He was still alive when they carried him to the countinghouse, where he continued to groan until Black Will slashed him in the face, killing him. Black Will then took all the money from Arden's purse and removed the rings from the dead man's fingers. Then as he left the countinghouse, he demanded his money from Alice, and she duly handed over ten pounds.

Elizabethan Drama

Arden of Faversham was written and performed during the Elizabethan Age, the period when Queen Elizabeth I was on the throne of England (1558–1603). The last two decades of Elizabeth's reign produced the golden age of English drama, which is known principally for the plays of William Shakespeare. During this period, there were a number of large public theaters in London, some holding as many as three thousand spectators. The capacity of the Globe theater, for which Shakespeare wrote many of his plays, was just over two thousand.

The stage was a small platform surrounded on three sides by the audience. Conditions were cramped. At the Globe, no spectator was more than fifty feet from the actors, and those who stood at the front in the yard (the standees were known as groundlings) could rest their arms on the stage. The price of admission to the theater was cheap. The groundlings could get in for only one penny, which

COMPARE & CONTRAST

- **1590s:** In the Elizabethan theater, plays take place in the afternoon, in natural light. The audience is boisterous and unruly, surrounds the actors on three sides, and interacts with them. All classes of society attend the theater.

  Today: Plays take place in a darkened theater, and the largely middle-class audiences are generally more subdued than their Elizabethan counterparts. Talking during the performance is frowned upon. There is a convention of the fourth wall that describes the invisible barrier between stage and audience; the performers act as if the audience does not exist.

- **1590s:** Having defeated the Spanish Armada in 1588, England is a strong and united kingdom under the capable leadership of Queen Elizabeth 1. English sailors explore the world and begin to lay the basis for the nation's emergence as a powerful maritime and colonial power.

  Today: The United Kingdom of Great Britain and Northern Ireland is no longer a colonial power. Having given up its empire by the mid-twentieth century, it is now a member of the European Community. Britain has retained its monarchy, however, and Elizabeth II is a popular queen, although her power is merely symbolic. English people remain extremely proud of the Elizabethan era which they regard as a golden age in their history.

- **1590s:** The English language undergoes a period of rapid development and attains a new richness and flexibility in expression. Shakespeare in particular molds and expands the English tongue, introducing many new words into the language. However, English is spoken only by between five and seven million English people.

  Today: English is the dominant world language. It is used by at least 750 million people and possibly as many as one billion. It is more widely spoken and written than any language in history.

---

even the artisan class could afford. It is estimated that about one in ten Londoners attended a play every week, and the audience was a large cross-section of society. The theaters were open to the elements, but there is no record of any play being rained off. The performance simply continued, rain or shine.

Elizabethan drama evolved out of a number of earlier elements, including medieval morality plays and a kind of drama known as the interlude, which arose in the late fifteenth century and stimulated the secularization of the drama. Another influence was classical Roman drama, including Seneca (for tragedy) and Plautus and Terence (for comedy). Also, during the sixteenth century, a tradition developed in England of writing and performing plays at universities. Many of these playwrights, known as the University Wits, later went to London and wrote for the public stage. This was from the late 1580s, around the time *Arden of Faversham* was written, until the mid-1590s. The greatest of these university-educated men was Christopher Marlowe; others were Robert Greene, Thomas Nash, and Thomas Kyd. These playwrights had an innovative approach to tragedy and also developed the use of blank verse (a form used effectively by the author of *Arden of Faversham*), which was then taken to its highest form of expression by Shakespeare. However, by no means all the dramatists who wrote for the Elizabethan stage were university educated. Shakespeare himself, who was probably educated at Stratford Grammar School, is believed to have had no other formal education.

The principle genres in Elizabethan drama are the history play, such as Shakespeare's *Richard III* and *Henry V*; tragedy, such as Kyd's *The Spanish Tragedy* (which was part of a subgenre known as revenge tragedy); and comedy, including such plays as Shakespeare's *A Midsummer Night's Dream*.

The house where Thomas Arden was murdered by his wife and her lover in Faversham, England in 1551 Faversham Society

CRITICAL OVERVIEW

There are no records of any production of *Arden of Faversham* until the eighteenth century, but it is likely that the play was a popular one, performed frequently both before and after its publication in 1592. It was published again in 1599 and 1633. The first documented performance was in 1730, at Faversham, in Kent.

During the twentieth century, there were many productions of *Arden of Faversham*. In 1970, the play was directed by a Romanian, Andrei Sherban,

for the La Mama Experimental Theatre Club in New York. Clive Barnes comments in a review in the *New York Times* that the production expresses a worldview "so savage in its necessities that survival itself becomes the solitary virtue" (quoted in Wine's edition of the play).

A 1990 production in London's Old Red Lion Theatre, mounted by Classics on a Shoestring and directed by Katie Mitchell, was reviewed in the London *Times* by Jeremy Kingston. Kingston was not impressed by the play itself, which he refers to as a "foolishly earnest drama." Commenting on the many unsuccessful attempts by the villains to murder Arden, Kingston writes:

> So protracted is this business of trying to shuffle off his mortal coil that I am inclined to picture a Bankside mogul slamming the first draft down on a tavern table with the words, "I'll tell you something, Mr. Anon. You wanna write a good show; you gotta delay your climax."

Kingston also comments on the performance of Ian Reddington, who "characterises Arden with the realistic detail of a nervy businessman, rubbing his fingers and bravely smiling."

In 2004, the Metropolitan Playhouse in New York City staged a production of the play, directed by Alex Roe. Mary Bly, who reviewed the production favorably for the *Shakespeare Bulletin*, comments that the play was presented as more comedy than tragedy: "Once a performance whose moral resonance extended into every household, it is now limited to the local and silly." Bly makes the point that a modern audience, with quite different sexual and moral values than were common during the sixteenth century, can no longer take the play seriously as a stern warning against the sin of adultery.

One reason for the comic effect of this production was that the director, building on what Bly describes as the "homosocial nature of early modern culture" (male friends address each other in intimate terms of endearment) offered a production with homosexual overtones:

> Tod Mason, as Arden, swishes onto the stage in a little midnight blue velvet miniskirt dress with gold buttons. He dresses with the prim enthusiasm of a society matron. . . . If there was an early modern closet, he's not very far into it. . . . Franklin, played by Jason Alan Griffin, is a muscled sidekick in lavender stockings who acts a bewildered Watson to Arden's fluttering Judy Garland.

When the pair are awakened from sleep by Michael's shouting, "Arden trots onto the stage in a laced pale blue nightgown, clutching a teddy bear; Franklin is bare-chested and annoyed."

Comedy aside, Bly has high praise for Mason's "truly brilliant performance as Arden," which allowed the audience to both like and mistrust him. Bly comments further:

> Mason manages to bring out the uncaring side of the character's nature. Arden here is a sort of righteous evangelical: capable of great brutality, enacted with the solemn and cheerful resolution that he is in the right.

For over four centuries after its publication, *Arden of Faversham* has shown its staying power. It will likely be staged many times during the twenty-first century, in new and challenging interpretations.

CRITICISM

Bryan Aubrey

Aubrey holds a Ph.D. in English and has published many essays on drama. In the following essay, he discusses why some scholars argue that Arden of Faversham *was quite possibly written by William Shakespeare.*

Although lovers of Elizabethan drama might be able to locate and attend one of the infrequent productions of *Arden of Faversham*, it is more likely that they will be compelled to study this fascinating play at home or in a library. Perhaps with some help from reviews of past productions, readers will have to imagine for themselves how the callous landowner Arden, his adulterous wife Alice, the social climber Mosby, and the villains Shakebag and Black Will might be effectively presented on a modern stage. But given the structure of the plot, this may be no easy task. In *Themes and Conventions of Elizabethan Tragedy*, no less an authority than M. C. Bradbrook, a renowned scholar of Elizabethan drama, put on record her own reaction to the play. She notes that there are six unsuccessful attempts on the life of Arden "until the spectator feels positively irritated that she [Alice] should not succeed." Bradbrook also points out, however, that in repeatedly postponing the fatal moment, the author of *Arden of Faversham* was making use of a popular device in Elizabethan drama, the "cumulative plot," in which "the same type of incident was repeated again and again, in a crescendo and with quickening tempo, up to the catastrophe." Bradbrook notes that Marlowe, in *Tamburlaine the Great*, uses a similar device, although she makes no mention of any play by Shakespeare, the greatest Elizabethan dramatist of them all, that employs it.

Shakespeare's name has often been mentioned in connection with the anonymous *Arden of Faversham*, and indeed, for many readers, part of the interest the play holds lies in the possibility that it might just be a work by Shakespeare. It seems highly likely that Shakespeare would have known the story of the murder at Faversham, since it appears in Holinshed's *Chronicles of England, Scotland, and Ireland* (1587), which was Shakespeare's source for his history plays. Shakespeare knew Holinshed's work well.

In 1940, Marion Bodwell Smith, in *Marlowe's Imagery and the Marlowe Canon*, made the intriguing argument that the imagery in *Arden of Faversham* calls to mind the imagery used by

MOSBY HAS LOST CONTROL OF HIS OWN DESTINY, AND THE HARDER HE TRIES TO CONTROL IT THE MORE HELPLESS HE BECOMES. LIKE SHAKESPEARE'S MACBETH, HE KNOWS HE WILL BE LED ON FROM ONE EVIL DEED TO ANOTHER, COMPELLED BY THE DARK LOGIC OF HIS OWN INSECURITIES."

Shakespeare in his early plays, especially the histories. According to the classification made by Smith, over one-third of the images in *Arden of Faversham* are drawn from daily life, especially the "daily occupations and trades, from sports, and from war." The sports images are taken from archery, riding, and the hunting of birds. Smith notes that, similarly, many of Shakespeare's images from daily life are drawn from sport. She highlights several images of bird hunting. Greene's comment to Black Will, for example, "Lime your twigs to catch this weary bird" is an image that occurs frequently in Shakespeare's *Henry VI* trilogy. Smith also argues that the images of the unweeded or untended garden in *Arden of Faversham* recall the frequent use of similar images in Shakespeare's histories from the *Henry VI* trilogy to *Richard II*. Smith claims that not only single images but whole passages in *Arden of Faversham* are reminiscent of the early Shakespeare. As an example, she cites Arden's dream and compares it to Clarence's dream in act 1, scene 4 of Shakespeare's *Richard III*.

Some may find this evidence by itself to be less than convincing—the unweeded garden as an image of a misgoverned society was a commonplace during the period—and Smith herself did not claim to have proved that Shakespeare wrote *Arden of Faversham*, only that the imagery "point[s] in his direction."

However, the case for Shakespearean authorship has been argued from other aspects of the play. The characterization has been widely admired, and

some scholars believe that such an achievement would have been beyond the capabilities of any other dramatist of the period. The inner conflicts of the characters are laid bare, and they emerge as multi-dimensional figures rather than simple portraits of people in the grip of evil passions. Even the servant Michael, a comparatively minor character, is presented in scene 4 as being torn by his conscience over his betrayal of his master. He has sufficient self-awareness to know that his actions are contemptible, even if he does not have the courage or the moral strength to change them. Also, his comment, "My master's kindness pleads to me for life," suggests in passing another dimension to the character of Arden. Arden may be callous and avaricious, but it appears that at least he treats his servant well. Other aspects of the play also modify the negative impression Arden creates by his ill-treatment of Greene and Dick Reede. His friend Franklin is completely loyal to him; he undoubtedly loves his wife dearly (as she herself attests), and once, before she became entranced by Mosby, she loved him; and he is on good terms with Lord Cheyne, who insists on inviting him to dinner. These small hints all suggest that although Arden may not be a fully sympathetic character, he may not quite deserve the cruel end he meets either.

Scholars often refer to scene 8 when they discuss the dramatist's in-depth characterization. In this scene, Alice and Mosby quarrel and are reconciled. It begins with a forty-three line soliloquy by Mosby. (A soliloquy is a dramatic convention in which a character, alone on the stage, speaks his thoughts aloud.) Often in drama, when a character bares his soul in a soliloquy he immediately becomes more sympathetic to the audience, which gets a glimpse of his full humanness. A well-known example is King Claudius in Shakespeare's *Hamlet*, who appears little more than a stage villain until he reveals his own troubled soul in his soliloquy in act 3, scene 3. Like Claudius, Mosby begins his soliloquy by revealing his "troubled mind . . . stuffed with discontent." He has sufficient self-awareness to know that his newfound wealth and prestige has brought him neither happiness nor peace and that his "golden time" was in fact when he was poor. He is also aware of the dangerous course on which he is set with Alice, but he is so much in the grip of his passion and his hopes for social advancement that he knows he cannot turn back. But whatever sympathy he may generate in the audience by these honest self-revelations, it is soon dissipated. As he speaks not only of the murder of Arden but also of his desire to be rid of Greene, Michael, and even

WHAT DO I READ NEXT?

- *A Yorkshire Tragedy*, a play by Thomas Middleton, is available in a reprint edition published by Kessinger Publishing (2004). The play was first published in 1608 and is classified as a Jacobean domestic tragedy. Like *Arden of Faversham*, it is based on an actual incident. In the county of Yorkshire, England, in 1605, a cruel, violent husband, addicted to gambling, finally repents but, stricken by shame, kills his two children and wounds his wife.

- *The Witch of Edmonton*, a play by William Rowley, Thomas Dekker, and John Ford, was first performed in December 1621 or possibly earlier. It is a domestic tragedy, based on a story of betrayal and deceit. The witch of the title was based on Elizabeth Sawyer, who was hanged for witchcraft in 1621 after a frenzied witch hunt swept through her community. The dramatists were quick to see the dramatic potential in the sensational story, and the play was performed within a few months of the actual event. The play is available in a well-annotated edition, edited by Peter Corbin and Dekker Sedge and published by Manchester University Press (1999).

- *Plays on Women* (Manchester University Press, Student edition, 2000), edited by Kathleen McCluskie, includes four Elizabethan plays in which women play a variety of prominent roles, ranging from adulteresses to victims and faithful wives. The plays are *Arden of Faversham*; *The Roaring Girl*, by Thomas Middleton and Thomas Dekker; Middleton's *A Chaste Maid in Cheapside* (known as a city comedy); and Thomas Heywood's *A Woman Killed with Kindness* (a domestic tragedy).

- *The Death of a Salesman*, by Arthur Miller, is one of the best examples of a modern tragedy in which the protagonist is not a high-ranking hero but an ordinary man. First published in 1949, it is available in a Penguin edition (1998). The salesman of the title is the self-deluded Willy Loman. Some have seen him as a pathetic figure, but Miller himself believed that Willy attained tragic status. The Penguin edition contains, in addition to the text of the play, a chronology of its productions, photos from various stagings, and a new preface by the playwright.

Alice herself, he shows himself to be a frightened soul, terrified of losing what he has and without any moral compass to guide him. Mosby has lost control of his own destiny, and the harder he tries to control it the more helpless he becomes. Like Shakespeare's Macbeth, he knows he will be led on from one evil deed to another, compelled by the dark logic of his own insecurities. Isolated and desperate, Mosby is a very dangerous man.

When Alice enters, part of the dynamic that propels her relationship with Mosby is revealed. They seem to be engaged in a mutually manipulative dance. When he sees her holding a prayer book, Mosby guesses that something is wrong and says, at the end of his soliloquy, that he must flatter her. He thinks that Alice is putting on a show of sadness in order to hurt him emotionally, and he tells her so. But she surprises him by revealing her guilty feelings about their adulterous affair. If she is sincere, this adds a dimension to her character that the audience has not seen before. She knows that what she is doing with Mosby is wrong; she is ashamed of it and can hardly bear to speak about it. After she broaches the subject of how much her husband loves her, she continues:

> And then—conceal the rest, for 'tis too bad,
> Lest that my words be carried with the wind
> And published in the world to both our shames.

She tells Mosby that their affair must end—is she being genuine or manipulative, the audience wonders—and then blames him for bewitching her. He responds by blaming *her* for bewitching *him*; it appears that any self-understanding that might emerge from this encounter is about to be buried by mutual finger-pointing. As the scene continues, it does seem that it is Alice who emerges with the upper hand by making a show of submission. She may well be the stronger character of the two. She continues to manipulate Mosby emotionally, saying she will do penance for offending him, that she will kill herself unless he looks at her. Then quite shamelessly, knowing his weakness, she flatters him:

> Thou hast been sighted as the eagle is,
> And heard as quickly as the fearful hare,
> And spoke as smoothly as an orator,
> When I have bid thee hear or see or speak.

When that does not seem to work, she flatters him again ("Sweet Mosby is as gentle as a king"), finally managing to win him back by appeasing his insecurities about his low-born origins (which she had herself used against him only a few moments earlier). Having lost the initiative, Mosby is defenseless against her manipulation. Even as he knows what she is doing, he is powerless to resist this complex and strong-willed woman, whose emotions seem to change rapidly—a quality that is seen again in the murder scene when remorse, fear, defiance, and cunning all show themselves in her in the space of a few minutes.

It is characterization like this that has prompted comparisons between Alice Arden and some of the great Shakespearean female characters, such as Cleopatra and Lady Macbeth. Lovers of Shakespeare may be tempted to go even further. Who could not be tempted by the hope that in the comic roguery of Black Will and Shakebag, the audience is seeing the predecessors of those immortal denizens of the Boar's Head in Eastcheap, especially the braggart soldier Pistol, boisterous companion of Sir John Falstaff in *Henry IV, part 2*? Unfortunately, pending some sensational find of an old manuscript in the attic of a country house somewhere in England that would definitively identify the author of *Arden of Faversham*, readers will never know for sure.

Source: Bryan Aubrey, Critical Essay on *Arden of Faversham*, in *Drama for Students*, Thomson Gale, 2007.

Claire Robinson

Robinson has a Master of Arts in English. She is a writer and editor and a former teacher of English literature and creative writing. In the following essay, Robinson examines how Arden of Faversham *portrays a world in chaos, both on the individual and societal levels.*

The opening exchange of *Arden of Faversham* sets up the framework of values for the rest of the play. Franklin tells a melancholy Arden to cheer up because he has been granted the lands of the Abbey of Faversham. Franklin's remark implies that for men like Arden, happiness is contingent upon the acquisition of land. As becomes clear in the rest of the play, Arden's greed for land ruins the livelihoods and happiness of others, causing so much resentment as to provide one character, Greene, with a motive for murder.

The exchange comments on a process of change in land ownership that was occurring in England at the time the play was set (1551) and that was still a topic of contention at the time it was written (most commentators suggest a date between 1587 and 1591). This process of change caused immense social upheaval. As much as 90 percent of the population lived directly off the land, so the question of who owned it could mean the difference between life and death. Such questions were raised by the life of the historical figure Thomas Arden, whose story the play dramatizes. In many ways, he was a man typical of the Tudor period. He enjoyed success in his career working for Sir Edward North, who had obtained land and wealth from King Henry VIII's dissolution of the monasteries (1538–1541). The dissolution is the process by which the monasteries and their land holdings were broken up and confiscated by the crown, to be sold off or granted to the king's favorites. Prior to the dissolution, much of the monasteries' land had been leased to tenant farmers. The historical Thomas Arden made a good marriage to Alice, Sir Edward's stepdaughter, and obtained the land and revenues of the Abbey of Faversham from Sir Thomas Cheiny, who had received it from Henry VIII. Thomas Arden moved into a house on the land and, according to Lionel Cust, cited by Martin White in his Introduction to *The Tragedy of Master Arden of Faversham*, "continued to amass wealth and dispossess the other owners of Abbey lands, until he became the foremost citizen in Faversham."

Criticism of men like the historical Thomas Arden was widespread and bitter. A "Prayer for Landlords" was even included in the 1553 *Book of Private Prayer*. White, in his Introduction, cites the prayer as follows:

> We heartily pray thee, to send thy holy Spirit into the hearts of them that possess the grounds, pastures, and dwelling places of the earth, that they . . . may not rack and stretch out the rents of their houses and lands . . . after the manner of covetous worldlings.

The playwright of *Arden of Faversham* portrays the age as characterized by covetousness. Its most successful proponent is Arden, though the other characters follow suit. Arden's first conversation with Alice is preceded and followed by talk of commodities and trade. Just as Arden covets and acquires goods and land, Mosby covets and acquires

Alice. Alice covets Mosby. In an attempt to obtain him, she over-reaches herself, hiring no less than three potential assassins—Michael, Clarke, and Greene, whom she advises to subcontract the work to "some cutter"—to rid her of her husband.

People have become commodities, to be desired, bought, hired, stolen, or bartered. When Arden challenges Mosby over his relationship with Alice, he speaks of her as if she were as much a commodity as the land he owns: "But I must have a mandate for my wife; / They say you seek to rob me of her love." A "mandate" is a deed of ownership. Mosby seeks to rob Arden of Alice, just as Arden robs others of their land. Alice claims that Mosby has "rifled" her of her good reputation, using terminology that is usually applied to robberies. Human values are reduced to the level of material goods. Alice shows herself to be even more ruthless a businesswoman than Arden when she barters away Susan Mosby as payment for the promised assassination of her husband. Even in this deal, there is no honor, as Alice double-deals, selling Susan to two men, Michael and Clarke. She is willing to let her go to the one who does the job of killing Arden first. Mosby and Alice's courtship involves playing at dice for kisses in place of the usual money.

In the context of this grim and heartless trading of commodities, the holy sacrament of marriage, which belongs in a more spiritual realm, is dismissed by Alice as being "but words": "Oaths are words, and words is wind, / And wind is mutable." In *Arden of Faversham*, that which should be eternal is expendable, and that which is transient rules supreme. This development is portrayed as being against the natural order of things and as symptomatic of societal breakdown.

Arden's remarks to Franklin about Mosby reveal another aspect of the social upheaval of the time: increased social mobility of the classes. Though Arden has profited from the changes in land ownership, he resents the social mobility that has come with it. Arden contemptuously dismisses Mosby as a "botcher, and no better at the first," who has "Crept into service of a nobleman" by flattery. He looks down upon Mosby because he is in trade (a tailor) and of lowly birth, unlike Arden, who, as a member of the landowning classes and "a gentleman of blood," believes himself superior. Arden is as angry about Mosby's social climbing, his usurpation of the accoutrements of gentility and nobility, as he is about his stealing his wife. Arden repeatedly insults Mosby for his low birth and status as a tailor, calling him "a velvet drudge," a "base-minded peasant," and "so base a groom." He humiliates

IN *ARDEN OF FAVERSHAM*, THAT WHICH SHOULD BE ETERNAL IS EXPENDABLE, AND THAT WHICH IS TRANSIENT RULES SUPREME."

Mosby during their quarrel over Alice by pointing out that by law, Mosby, being below the rank of a gentleman, is not allowed to wear a sword. Arden's confiscation of Mosby's sword at a moment when Mosby is threatening Arden symbolizes unmanning or castration. Arden again taunts Mosby with his tradesman status, telling him to use his tailor's needle and clothes pressing iron instead of the sword.

This, as it turns out, is a fatal insult. In the murder scene (scene 14), Mosby uses his iron to deliver one of the blows that kills Arden, in revenge "for the pressing iron you told me of." This is Mosby's acknowledgement that the enmity between him and Arden is more about class warfare than overwhelming love or desire for Alice.

From his side, though Mosby claims to have loved Alice once, his soliloquy in scene 8 suggests that in his affair with her, a woman of higher social rank, he is primarily motivated by ambition "to build my nest among the clouds." His choice of monetary language when he tells her that he has "wrapped my credit in thy company" confirms this. Alice implicitly acknowledges his ulterior motives when she soothes him into making up their quarrel by calling him "as gentle as a king," with "gentle" meaning "of noble birth"; she is appealing to his desire for higher social status. Because their relationship is not founded on love, but on self-interest—from her side, sexual passion, and from his, ambition, covetousness, and greed—he does not trust her. He also reveals in his soliloquy that he believes she will dispose of him even as she disposed of Arden, and so he plans to get rid of her, though whether he means to abandon her or to kill her is not made clear. The point is that in a world that has elevated self-interest above humane considerations, even close relationships have changed their nature. No longer safe refuges from the perils of the world, they have become the very center of danger and betrayal. As Mosby comments, " 'Tis fearful sleeping in a serpent's bed."

Another inversion of the natural order in relationships is seen in the suborning of Michael. As Arden's servant, Michael should protect his master, particularly as Michael admits that Arden has always been kind and generous to him. But he allows himself to be bribed by Alice to kill Arden, with Susan as the prize. Later he is persuaded by Black Will and Shakebag to leave the doors of Arden's house unlocked so that they can enter and kill him.

The playwright frequently uses the imagery of hunting, or of predator and prey, to emphasize the dehumanizing effects of this society of greed and appetite. Several characters in the play hunt Arden in order to kill him. The symbolism is heavily emphasized in Arden's dream of being hunted in scene 6. An Elizabethan audience would assume that it is part of the natural order for people to hunt animals, but not for people to hunt people, particularly for a servant such as Michael to hunt his master. Michael's soliloquy in scene 3 speaks of Arden as a "lamb," an image of innocence that connotes Christ, the Lamb of God. Michael has become a predator, "The hunger-bitten wolf" who "takes advantage to eat him up." However, there is an ambiguity even in this image that is typical of this play. The wolf that stalks Arden is "hunger-bitten," a reference, perhaps, to those people, embodied in the character of Reede (scene 13), whom Arden has caused to go hungry by taking their land. That this reference is deliberate is reinforced by Shakebag's similar description of himself as Arden's potential assassin as "the starven lioness." These images suggest that while predators such as Shakebag and Michael are brutal in their desire for Arden's death and bestial in their ruthless appetite for material reward, their brutality and bestiality is a grosser manifestation of the more civilized greed of men such as Arden. Michael's characterization of Arden as "harmless" as a lamb is ironically undermined by Arden's seeming willingness to let Reede's family starve. The irony is driven home by the fact that when Arden brutally dismisses Reede, he and Franklin have just returned from enjoying sumptuous hospitality at Lord Cheiny's and are looking forward to a supper cooked by Alice. This expectation in turn is ironically subverted by the audience's knowledge that on his return home he is likely to be served not with a delicious meal, but with death.

In spite of the ambiguous light in which Arden is presented, there is no question of his deserving his grisly fate. Yet a beneficent power seems to be trying to prevent it. Time and again, when he is being stalked by Black Will and Shakebag, fate appears to intervene to save his life. For

example, Michael's attempt to leave the doors of Arden's house open to allow the assassins to enter fails when Michael's drowsy cry of fear rouses his master and Franklin, who then lock the doors. This is not mere chance at work: Michael's troubled conscience gives him bad dreams of robbers. On another occasion, Black Will is prevented from killing Arden by a shopkeeper's window dropping onto his head; on yet another occasion, a fog prevents Black Will and Shakebag from seeing Arden until he has safely passed. A bemused Black Will can only conclude that "doubtless he is preserved by miracle." Fate in this play is not neutral but a manifestation of divinely ordered justice, in which the innocent enjoy a degree of divine protection and the wicked are punished. This is in line with the unabashedly moralistic title page of the play, which describes the play as showing "the great malice and discimulation of a wicked woman, the unsatiable desire of filthie lust and the shamefull end of all murderers."

In this context, Alice and Mosby subvert the divine order with their unnatural and unsanctified love. This is expressed by various inversions of Christian belief connected with these characters. They commission a poisoned crucifix from Clarke the painter. The crucifix is designed to kill whoever looks at it, and Alice and Mosby intend that this will be Arden. The irony lies in the inversion of the Christian belief that Christ died on the cross for the sins of mankind in order to give man eternal life. In this instance, Alice and Mosby are using the symbol of the giver of life to bring about Arden's death. The religious symbolism continues in scene 8, when Alice meets Mosby with a prayer book in her hands. Here, she has moments of repentance. In an ugly episode of mutual recrimination, each accuses the other of bewitchment, a serious charge in an era when witchcraft was punishable by death. Mosby calls Alice "unhallowed." His reference to her as a "serpent" connects her with the devil, who tempted Eve in the Biblical Garden of Eden in the form of a serpent. Alice quickly makes up her quarrel with Mosby, but in a way that an Elizabethan audience would have viewed as irreligious. First, she threatens to kill herself, though suicide was widely believed to be a cardinal sin against God. Then, she offers to do penance for offending Mosby and to worship him and threatens to burn her prayer book. Alice thereby places her lover in a position rightly occupied by God and Christ, an act of blasphemy.

In this disordered universe, there is no final restoration to order, no triumph of love and forgiveness. Arden's dead body is first dragged onto the Abbey lands that caused so much contention and is then laid in his counting house, a striking image weighty with symbolism that sums up the life of one whose preoccupation was the acquisition of land and wealth. After Arden's murder, Alice's repentance in scene 16 is unconvincing. It comes only after all her attempts to cover up her guilt have failed and consists mostly of attempting to insinuate her way into her dead husband's favor in much the same manner that she employed during his life. Mosby expresses only disgust for Alice, wanting only to get away from "that strumpet," and curses all women. Susan feels that she is a victim of injustice, and Michael proclaims that he does not care about heaven as long as he dies with Susan. Nothing of value has been gained or learned by any of the characters. For all its moral lessons and apparent justice, *Arden of Faversham* is a pessimistic play, its end showing a world that remains in the grip of the inverted values that governed the characters throughout.

Source: Claire Robinson, Critical Essay on *Arden of Faversham*, in *Drama for Students*, Thomson Gale, 2007.

Martin White

In the following excerpt, White covers the involvement that the avarice of landlords, like Arden, had in eroding the bond between landlord and tenant during the 1500s, which helped solidify the social hierarchy.

. . . Thomas Arden was murdered in 1551, the fourth year of Edward VI's brief reign. The date is important, for it coincides with a time of great social unrest. The debasement of the coinage; marked increases in the already spiralling trend of rising prices; bad harvests; and widespread enclosure of common land, were all factors that contributed to the discontent that at times during Edward's reign erupted into open rebellion. Although, today, we may be able to distinguish the various causes of the hardship suffered by the agrarian population, it was inevitable that, at the time, directly observable causes should be blamed. Among those singled out as being particularly responsible for the widespread distress were the landlords, and especially those 'new men' who had benefitted from the distribution of land that followed the dissolution of the monasteries, and who looked on that land as the passport to wealth and social status, to gain which they were prepared to break the traditional bonds between landlord and tenant: in other words men like Thomas Arden.

Arden was, in many ways, a typical man of his time, made and raised by the Tudors. Born in Wye

> IN FACT, *ARDEN* PRESENTS WHAT AMOUNTS TO A MICROCOSM OF RURAL TUDOR SOCIETY. FROM LORD CHEINY AT THE APEX DOWN TO REEDE AT THE BOTTOM, ALL THE CHARACTERS ARE CLEARLY PLACED IN THE SOCIAL HIERARCHY."

(about 12 miles south of Faversham), apparently of a good family, he first made his mark working for Sir Edward North (who had done as well as any out of the Dissolution), in the Court of Augmentations, which had been set up to deal with the revenue and litigation arising from the Crown's disposal of the monastic land. Arden's career progressed well, and marriage to Sir Edward's stepdaughter, Alice Mirfyn, was followed by his appointment to the lucrative post of Controller of the Customs for the port of Faversham. Settled in Kent, Arden soon obtained the land and revenues of the Abbey of Faversham from Sir Thomas Cheiny, who had received the land from Henry VIII in 1540. Once possessed of the property, Arden and his family took up residence in a house by the Abbey wall and he 'continued to amass wealth and to dispossess the other owners of Abbey lands, until he became the foremost citizen in Faversham.'

Inevitably, with nine-tenths of the population living and working directly on the land, criticism of the behaviour of men like Arden was extensive. It was frequently the topic of pamphlets and sermons, and a special 'Prayer for Landlords' was even included in the 1553 *Book of Private Prayer*:

> We heartily pray thee, to send thy holy Spirit into the hearts of them that possess the grounds, pastures, and dwelling places of the earth, that they . . . may not rack and stretch out the rents of their houses and lands . . . after the manner of covetous worldlings.

There is a striking similarity between certain speeches in the play attacking Arden's public actions, and pamphlets attacking the landlords. In one such pamphlet, *An Informacion and Peticion* (1548), the author, Robert Crowley, condemns the landlords' lack of compassion to those dependent on them with the same vehemence as Reede uses in cursing Arden in the play:

> And if any of them perish through your default, know then for certain that the blood of them shall be required at your hands. If the impotent creatures perish for lack of necessaries, you are the murderers, for you have their inheritance and do not minister unto them.

In *The Way to Wealth* (a pamphlet which appeared in the same year as Arden died) the same author indicted men like Arden in terms very similar to Greene's in Scene I, accusing them of being:

> Men without conscience. Men utterly void of God's fear. Yea, men that live as though there were no God at all! Men that would have all in their own hands; . . .

What has not previously been noted, however, is the *significance* of this particular parallel, for *The Way to Wealth* is not simply an attack on the avariciousness of landlords, but a discussion of the causes and dangers of civil unrest, a constant fear throughout the sixteenth century, and a burning issue in the wake of the uprisings of the late 1540s. Although Crowley naturally condemns sedition, he isolates as one of its main causes the provocation to the poor of the landlords' rack-renting, engrossing, and enclosing for their own profit, the effect of which, he argues, was to drive normally peaceful, God-fearing men to extremes of action, just as, in the play, Arden's actions drive Greene and Reede to take desperate measures.

Although, as E. P. Cheyney writes, the 'greatest distress among the people . . . falls in the short reign of Edward VI', the problems caused by those who put their 'private profit before common gain' were not confined to the middle years of the sixteenth century, and neither was the criticism of their actions.

The closing years of Elizabeth's reign witness the beginning of the retreat of the 'moral economy.' By the middle of the seventeenth century the split had become clearly defined between those who continued to apply traditional moral censure to economic practice and those who argued that such strictures were irrelevant since economic behaviour was determined by necessity rather than human weakness. But even then, when the 'critical link between action and responsibility had been cut', specific areas of economic activity 'remained vulnerable to the scrutiny of moralists': the grain trade (in times of famine); usury; and the enclosure of land. For although by the time of the play's composition enclosing was past the peak levels of the mid-century, its effects were well remembered. The whole question of land ownership and use 'still in-

spired outspoken sermons from the pulpit, and stirred passions and community loyalties in the field', and *moral* condemnation of 'men that would have all in their own hands' was as sharp as when Crowley wrote his pamphlet . . .

The audiences who saw *Arden* performed from the late 1580s through to the 1630s would, therefore, have perceived the social issues and implications of the play as being directly relevant to their own time, and not as just the historical background to a murder story. They would have recognized in the character of Arden a contemporary type—a social criminal whose 'creed . . . was a doctrineless individualism', and whose actions were a threat to the stability of society.

So while it is true that the play is not merely a 'dramatized sociological tract', to see Arden as a 'good man touched somewhat by avarice', or to suggest that his behaviour as a 'grasping and unscrupulous' landholder is 'not given any emphasis in the play until the strange appearance of Reede', is to fail to grasp that the playwright could expect a knowledge of, and attitude towards, Arden and his actions, without the need to elaborate more than he does.

The points made so far also indicate that the playwright's efforts to establish the sense of a physical environment and of a community where men have 'occupations as well as passions' are the result of his desire to create—within the theatrical means at his disposal—as realistic and tangible a setting as possible for a play in which public actions figure so prominently.

Even more significant is the care with which the social structure within the play is defined. In fact, *Arden* presents what amounts to a microcosm of rural Tudor society. From Lord Cheiny at the apex down to Reede at the bottom, all the characters are clearly placed in the social hierarchy. Even Black Will and Shakebag, far from being merely stock dramatic types, are representative of 'that dread of sixteenth-century society—the masterless man', who haunted the streets of London and the road to the coast.

Perhaps Franklin provides the best example of the dramatist's concern to locate each character's social status as precisely as possible. The playwright's own invention, Franklin's main function in the play is to provide someone to whom Arden can confess his inmost thoughts without the constant need for soliloquy, and to act as a spokesman on the otherwise isolated Arden's behalf. Beyond this, the character remains largely undeveloped as an individual personality. His social status is made quite clear, however, not only by implication as Arden's friend, but also by the obvious significance of his name and by the reference to his 'house in Aldersgate Street', which at the time of the play's composition was one of the most fashionable addresses in London—a fact that would certainly not go unnoticed by the original audience.

With certain characters—Lord Cheiny and Dick Reede, for example—the playwright deliberately indicates no more than their position in the social hierarchy, since in each case it is this rather than any individual qualities that is of greatest importance. It should be realized, however, that if the world these characters inhabit is clearly defined in terms of its social structure—through, for example, close attention to costume, speech and social behaviour, class attitudes—this method of presentation will make them no less effective dramatically than those characters who are more fully drawn.

The 'private' world of the play is centred around the personalities and relationships of the three main characters, the struggle between them and—more strikingly—within themselves, as the playwright explores with remarkable psychological depth their 'disturbed thoughts' and inner conflicts.

Arden alone of the three main protagonists inhabits both the 'public' and 'private' worlds of the play. His is the central, pivotal role, and to sustain it the playwright has created possibly his most complex character. He is torn between his avowedly deep love for Alice, and his loathing for her adultery, a reaction made the more acute by the fact that her lover is of such inferior social status in his eyes ('A botcher, and no better at the first'), and because the affair has become the 'common table-talk' of 'all the knights and gentlemen of Kent.' It is this mixture of conflicting attitudes in Arden that accounts for the contradictory nature of much of his behaviour. Although, for example, an audience might find his sudden capitulation to Alice in Scene XIII bewildering or foolish, even derisory, if the contradictions within him are established from the beginning, and if each attitude is played with equal conviction, the audience will come to recognize that the 'devil' that drives Arden is his own confused mind, and that the contradictions in his behaviour are a result of this, not of the dramatist's failure to present a consistent characterization.

The changes made by the playwright in his source material indicate (as with other main characters) his desire to avoid a one-sided, one-dimensional portrayal of Arden, but despite these changes, and the other points that might be advanced

in Arden's favour (eg. Franklin's friendship, Cheiny's respect, Michael's acknowledgement of his kindness), his public actions weigh heavily against him. The playwright highlights them by, for example, the telling juxtaposition of Arden's apparent willingness to see Reede's family starve, with his and Franklin's smugly satisfied appraisal of the 'most bounteous and liberal' hospitality they themselves have just enjoyed, and it is hard to find in this fascinatingly complex—but still unattractive—character the 'best instincts for affection, generosity and trust' of which Wine writes, especially in his dealings with those who need the benefit of such instincts most . . .

As I have tried to show, the social comment constitutes the 'public' world of the play (with the central motif of *land*), and the exploration of the personalities and relationships of Arden, Alice, and Mosby constitutes the 'private', although in practice, of course, the play is less schematized, the issues less separable, than my analysis may suggest. The playwright is concerned to show that in both public and private life—though their objectives may be different—men and women are driven to commit immoral acts by similar covetous urges, and the structure of the play is designed to establish the affinity between *all* these actions . . .

Source: Martin White, "Introduction," in *The Tragedy of Master Arden of Faversham*, edited by Martin White, Ernest Benn, 1982, pp. xi–xxvii.

SOURCES

Bly, Mary, Review of *Arden of Faversham*, in *Shakespeare Bulletin*, Vol. 22, No. 3, Fall 2004, pp. 84–86.

Bradbrook, M. C., *Themes and Conventions in Elizabethan Tragedy*, Cambridge University Press, 1969, p. 41.

Doran, Madeleine, *Endeavors of Art: A Study of Form in Elizabethan Drama*, University of Wisconsin Press, 1964, p. 145.

Kingston, Jeremy, Review of *Arden of Faversham*, in *Times* (London), August 10, 1990.

Smith, Marion Bodwell, *Marlowe's Imagery and the Marlowe Canon*, University of Pennsylvania, 1940, pp. 126, 128.

The Tragedy of Master Arden of Faversham, A & C Black, 1990.

The Tragedy of Master Arden of Faversham, Norton, 1982.

White, Martin, "Introduction," in *The Tragedy of Master Arden of Faversham*, A & C Black, 1990, p. xix.

———, "Introduction," in *The Tragedy of Master Arden of Faversham*, Norton, 1982, p. xvii.

Wine, M. L., "Introduction," in *The Tragedy of Master Arden of Faversham*, Methuen, 1973, pp. lvi, lxxxviii.

FURTHER READING

Reynolds, George Fullmer, *The Staging of Elizabethan Plays at the Red Bull Theater, 1605–1625*, Modern Language Association of America, 1940, reprint Kraus Reprint Corporation, 1966, pp. 115–21.

    Reynolds analyzes how the play was staged in the Elizabethan Age, emphasizing the use of the stage doors, which are significant in every scene.

Schutzman, Julie R., "Alice Arden's Freedom and the Suspended Moment of *Arden of Faversham*," in *Studies in English Literature, 1500–1900*, Vol. 36, No. 2, Spring 1996, pp. 289–314.

    Schutzman argues that although Alice Arden ends up suffering the death penalty, she was able to exercise her will by subverting and manipulating the patriarchal social order that curtailed women's freedom to act as autonomous agents.

Sullivan, Garrett A., Jr., "'Arden Lay Murdered in that Plot of Ground': Surveying, Land and *Arden of Faversham*," in *ELH*, Vol. 61, No. 2, Summer 1994, pp. 231–52.

    Sullivan examines the concept of land in the play. In the Elizabethan era, technological innovations in the science of estate surveying threatened to reduce land to a commodity to be sold and manipulated. The play offered a near-metaphysical view of land as a force that can be offended and which also has the power to punish covetousness and social irresponsibility.

Youngblood, Sarah, "Theme and Imagery in *Arden of Feversham*," in *Studies in English Literature*, Vol. 3, 1963, pp. 207–18.

    Youngblood shows how distorted or perverted images from religion and nature reinforce the theme of moral degeneration and lack of spiritual growth.

The Au Pair Man

HUGH LEONARD
1968

The Au Pair Man, by the Irish author Hugh Leonard (John Keyes Byrne), was first produced and published in 1968. It is the first play in the collection *Selected Plays of Hugh Leonard*, which was published in 1992. The play is a reversed-gender *Pygmalion*, a 1912 play by George Bernard Shaw in which a professor makes a bet that he can turn a working-class flower girl into a lady. In *The Au Pair Man*, Eugene, a rough Irish bill collector, becomes a sexual slave to Mrs. Elizabeth Rogers, a wealthy English lady, who tries to turn him into a gentleman. The play is a satirical allegory regarding the battle between Britain and Ireland. It is also a witty comedy of Anglo-Irish manners, full of amusing observations reminiscent of the styles of George Bernard Shaw and Oscar Wilde.

AUTHOR BIOGRAPHY

Hugh Leonard (the pseudonym of John Keyes Byrne) was born on November 9, 1926, in Dalkey, a small town near Dublin, Ireland, to an unmarried woman called Annie Byrne. His name was originally John Byrne, but he was adopted soon after birth by Nicholas Keyes, a gardener, and his wife Margaret, and later called himself John Keyes Byrne. In 1941, he won a scholarship to Presentation College, Glasthule, Co. Dublin. In 1945, he joined the Irish civil service, where he worked until 1959.

Hugh Leonard © Geray Sweeney/Corbis. Reproduced by permission

During his time as a civil servant in the Land Commission, Leonard became involved in amateur dramatics and began to write plays. The second play he submitted to the Abbey Theatre, Dublin, *The Big Birthday Suit*, was accepted for production in 1956. He submitted this play under the pseudonym Hugh Leonard, the name of a character in *The Italian Road* (1954), the play that the Abbey had earlier rejected. When the second play was accepted, he felt he had to keep the successful pseudonym.

Leonard moved to London in the 1960s but returned to Ireland to live in 1970, after a change in the tax laws. He was a prolific writer for the stage, films, and television in England and Ireland, and became known for his darkly humorous stories focusing on the less admirable aspects of human nature. His witty style has been compared with that of his fellow Irish authors, George Bernard Shaw and Oscar Wilde.

Leonard became known in the United States after the 1973 production of *The Au Pair Man* (first produced in 1968) in New York. However, his best-known play was *Da*, which was first produced at the Olney Theater, Olney, Maryland, in 1973. In 1977, that production was presented off-Broadway at the Hudson Guild Theater and then moved to Broadway and the Morosco Theater. In 1978, it was awarded the Drama Critics Circle Award for Best Play, the Drama Desk Award for Outstanding New Play, a Tony for Best Play of the 1977–1978 theater season, and the Outer Critics Circle Award as Best Play of that season.

Other plays by Leonard are *Stephen D* (1962), *The Patrick Pearse Motel* (1971), *A Life* (1979), and *Love in the Title* (1999). His best-known screenplays are for the film adaptation of *Da* (1988) and *Widow's Peak* (1986).

As of 2006, Leonard was the literary manager of the Abbey Theatre in Dublin and a reviewer for *Plays and Players* magazine, published in London. He lived in Dalkey, where he grew up. In 1999, Paule, his wife of forty-five years, died from an asthma attack. In an attempt to come to terms with his grief, Leonard wrote a series of letters to her and published them in a book, *Dear Paule* (2001).

Leonard has described his early life in a working-class Catholic family and his emergence as a writer in two volumes of autobiography, *Home before Night* (1979) and *Out after Dark* (1989). These books were reprinted in the Methuen Biography Series in 2002.

Leonard's work has attracted a host of awards. He received the Italia Prize, International Concourse for Radio and Television, and the Writers Guild of Great Britain Award of Merit, both in 1967, both for the television play *Silent Song* (1966); a Tony Award nomination, in 1974, for *The Au Pair Man*; and a Harvey Award for *A Life*.

PLOT SUMMARY

Act 1

The Au Pair Man opens in the London home of Mrs. Rogers. The doorbell rings, chiming the English national anthem. Mrs. Rogers answers the door. Her visitor is Eugene, an Irishman employed by the furniture company Weatherby and Fitch. He has come to collect payment on a wall unit that she bought some time before but never paid for. She is using it as a room divider, though it should be put against a wall. Mrs. Rogers explains that there was once a wall behind the unit, but it fell down. The wall unit is holding up what is left of the ceiling. Mrs. Rogers denies that she bought the unit, claiming it was a gift. Eugene says that Weatherby and Fitch have sent him, the newest employee, to collect Mrs. Rogers's debt as an initiative test.

Mrs. Rogers plies Eugene with whiskey. She admires his fountain pen and asks to borrow it. She says that she has no intention of paying for the wall unit but acknowledges that if he fails to collect on the bill, he will be fired. She reassures him that there are other jobs. In fact, she is advertising for an au pair man. Her husband is often away selling his collection of stamps from the British colonies and needs someone to keep his collection in order, write letters, and pay bills. She emphasizes that she needs an au pair, not a secretary, as a secretary is paid but an au pair is not. She adds that Eugene would not be suitable. Eugene at first says he does not want the post as he wants a job with prospects, but then he demands to know why he is not good enough. She lists his failings, including dirty fingernails, ungrammatical speech, and body odor. Eugene is irritated that she is discriminating against him on the grounds of class.

Eugene tells her that some time ago, a previous employee of Weatherby's called Wilson took all her records and went to her house to collect the money that she owes. He did not return for a long time. When he finally reappeared, he looked emaciated and worn out. He offered to return Mrs. Rogers's address to the firm in return for being reinstated in his job. Mrs. Rogers reveals that Wilson was her previous au pair man. Wilson had begged her to give him the job, but she had found him lazy, and his fountain pen defective. Two days earlier, he had left without saying goodbye. Though Wilson had told her that he had torn up her records, he was evidently lying.

Eugene says that he would never tell her that he had torn up the papers but would do so in front of her. He does so. Each time he makes a tear, Mrs. Rogers lets out a little groan. He asks her to make him her au pair man. Mrs. Rogers is evasive and vanishes into her bedroom. Eugene, thinking he will have to go back to Weatherby's, tries to piece together the torn papers. Mrs. Rogers's head appears through a hatch. She warns him that she is watching him. She asks him who he is. Eugene tells her a story of how he went to the cinema and was groped sexually by an unknown girl. He had reciprocated, but when the lights came on at the end of the film, the girl had looked at him and shouted, "You're not Charlie." Mrs. Rogers enters, wearing a negligee. Eugene tells her with some shame that he is not Charlie. She picks up the torn papers and puts them in the waste bin. She says that Charlie was probably tiresome and fondles his hair. As he gazes at her legs, he wonders how Wilson became so emaciated.

Eugene reflects that he feels more cheerful than when he came in. Mrs. Rogers says that this is because she has cultivated the art of being feminine, and she always aims to please men. She promises that she is never jealous or possessive. She offers him the job of au pair man on a trial basis. Eugene agrees. Together, they set fire to the papers in the waste bin. He eagerly follows Mrs. Rogers into her bedroom.

Act 2

Some time has passed. Eugene is reading aloud from a book. He is dressed in expensive new clothes and his diction is improved. The book consists of points, written by Benjamin Franklin, explaining why older women are better sexual partners than young ones. Mrs. Rogers enters from the bedroom. She is educating Eugene in English history and tells him a story about Queen Elizabeth I. Eugene wonders how practical such knowledge will be; he would rather be instructed in the art of witty conversation. Mrs. Rogers reminds him how well he is being looked after and how comfortable his room is (the area behind the wall unit), with its canopy over the bed to catch the falling plaster. She cannot understand how he could be interested in the world outside her home, which has become a frightening place full of foreigners. Eugene is disturbed to discover that it is not part of Mrs. Rogers's plan to make him better equipped for the outside world, and that he is her prisoner. He wants a wealthy lifestyle, with fast cars and beautiful women. He also wants to go home dressed in a smart suit to impress his mother. Mrs. Rogers reminds him that she is not possessive and that he can go home one day. But when he mentions that he has been traveling on a bus, she interrogates him about where he went. Then she asks to borrow his fountain pen. He tells her to get her own, as she is wearing his out. She steals it, locks it in a box, and puts the key down her décolletage, challenging him to retrieve it. He refuses and breaks open her box. To his horror, many fountain pens fall out.

One night, Eugene comes in drunk. He has to go through Mrs. Rogers's bedroom to reach his own. He tries to creep into his room without waking her. She is heard calling him by the names of Queen Elizabeth I's favorites; she is, perhaps, asleep and dreaming that she is the queen. Eugene takes a shelf out of the wall unit and tries to dive headfirst through the hole, but gets stuck midway, his trousers round his ankles. Mrs. Rogers comes in and switches on the lights. She is angry, telling him that he could have broken the wall unit, and that walls are vital because they provide segregation. She quizzes Eugene about where he has been and with whom, and he admits that he went to a nightclub. He reminds her that she claimed never to be jealous or possessive. Mrs. Rogers says that if she seems possessive, it is because he is untrustworthy. She could not be jealous, as there is no emotional involvement between them. How could there be, she asks, as he is so "sadly underdeveloped"?

Mrs. Rogers adopts a conciliatory approach, saying that friends should have no secrets from one another. She asks him why he drank so much. He replies that when he is drunk, he can remember his homeland. He says that after getting drunk in the club, he picked up a woman and pinned her against a tree. Unfortunately, she turned out to be a policewoman. He stole her police whistle and walked away. He shows Mrs. Rogers the whistle. Jealous of his giving attention to another woman, she taunts and insults him. Furious, he goes to pack his things. She tells him he cannot leave, as "the streets are filled with Australians." She tries to charm him into staying by promising him his own coat of arms but cannot resist another insult. Eugene kicks the wall unit, and one of the legs flies off. She takes the whistle and blows it to summon the police.

Act 3

Time has passed. The wall unit is buckling from the pressure of the walls and ceiling. Eugene appears outside, dressed in a suit and bowler hat, and rings the doorbell. Mrs. Rogers, who has invited him, asks him in. She compliments him on his smart appearance. It becomes clear that Eugene has learned the English manners that she was trying to teach him.

Eugene warns her that her house is badly dilapidated and compares it to the *Titanic*, the British ship that sank in 1912. He reveals that he has a girlfriend called Rose, whose family owns several large houses. They do not work, as they have a rich relative who supports them. Rose does not approve of their idle lives. Mrs. Rogers suggests that marriage to Eugene might correct her attitude. Eugene says he is now working for the estate agent Loman and Selway, as Rose insisted that he have a job. Mrs. Rogers says he must get ahead quickly in his career and then throw it aside, as a gentleman only works as a hobby.

Eugene tells her that he is on another initiative test. He has been sent to evict Mrs. Rogers from her home. She protests that she owns it, but he replies that the land on which it is built belongs to a landlord for whom Loman and Selway acts as

agent. He shows her a glossy brochure: the landlord is offering to move Mrs. Rogers to a new development called Runnymede. Mrs. Rogers reacts hysterically. Acting like Queen Elizabeth I under threat, she shouts for imaginary guards, seizes an old sword, attacks Eugene and threatens to behead him, and runs the brochure through. Finally, she plunges the sword into the wall, where it sticks. Eugene points out that the house is a wreck and even the electricity has been cut off because Mrs. Rogers refuses to spend any of her huge wealth on it. Mrs. Rogers tells him to leave. Eugene persists, saying that she has broken the lease by not doing repairs and the house is dragging down the neighborhood. He produces an ancient lease, which states that if she, the tenant, fails to keep the house in order, it will revert to the landlord. In any case, the local authority has slated the house for demolition on public health grounds. Mrs. Rogers reluctantly signs a document agreeing to go to Runnymede. Then she reveals that she is Rose's rich relative. Eugene, speechless, drops his papers.

Mrs. Rogers tells him that after he left her employ, she arranged for Rose to look after him. She predicts that in ten years' time, Rose will have lost her rebelliousness and be exactly like her. She has Eugene within her power: if she refuses to go to Runnymede, he will lose his job with Loman and Selway and his marriage prospects with Rose; if she goes to Runnymede, Rose will be angry that she has been dispossessed, and he will also lose her. She suggests that Eugene catch up with the work that needs to be done in her house. As she briefly steps out of the room, Eugene seizes the sword and seems ready to kill her. She comes in carrying the waste bin and orders him to tidy up his papers. He drops to his knees, picks them up, and puts them in the bin. The clock chimes, but the chimes sound like a record that is running down.

CHARACTERS

Eugene Hartigan

Eugene Hartigan is a rough Irish bill collector who calls on Mrs. Rogers to obtain her payment of a debt for the wall unit she keeps in her house. In the allegory of the play, he stands for Ireland, and, more specifically, for those Irish rebels who sought to drive the British out of their country. Far from extracting payment from Mrs. Rogers, he ends up being exploited by her as her unpaid au pair man and sexual slave. In part, he finds himself in this position because his sensitivity about being working-class and discriminated against makes him so eager for acceptance that he pushes his way into a job that can offer him nothing. Though Eugene is not unintelligent, he is naïve and always one step behind Mrs. Rogers. He is ambitious, but while at first he believes that working for her could be a route to advancement, he soon finds out that there is no reward in the job apart from acquiring some of the manners and diction of an Englishman. Though at the beginning of act 3 he believes he is forging a life for himself independently of Mrs. Rogers, her power over his fiancée, Rose, means that he cannot escape her clutches.

Mrs. Elizabeth Rogers

Mrs. Rogers is a wealthy English lady who lives in a crumbling house in London. In the allegory of the play, she stands for Britain, and her house is the declining British Empire. She is a lascivious middle-aged woman whose husband (if he really exists) is generally abroad selling his colonial stamp collection. She co-opts Eugene into her service as an unpaid au pair man, or, as it turns out, a sexual slave and general drudge. Alternately charming, cruel, insulting, and terrifying, she seduces, threatens, and coerces Eugene into doing her will. When crossed, she flies into a rage, calling in the police or attacking Eugene physically. Mrs. Rogers is a staunch monarchist whose doorbell chimes the English national anthem and who expects Eugene to toast the royal family when he drinks. Seemingly without scruples, she never has any intention of paying for the wall unit that holds up her house. Throughout, she pursues only her own interests, though she hypocritically claims that she is helping Eugene by teaching him refined English manners. To her, it is the veneer of civilization that matters; she is oblivious to the deeper humanitarian values.

Rose

Rose does not appear in the play in person. She is a young person whom Eugene meets and hopes to marry. Eugene is aware that she is a member of a wealthy family that owns several large houses and travels between them shooting game. What he does not know, until Mrs. Rogers informs him, is that Rose is her relative and that the family receives its vast allowance from her. In the allegory of the play, Rose stands for Northern Ireland.

Matthew Wilson

Matthew Wilson does not appear in the play in person. He is a former employee of Weatherby and Fitch who disappears after being sent on an initiative test to collect on Mrs. Rogers's debt. He reappears some time later, looking emaciated and worn out, after having been co-opted as Mrs. Rogers's sexual slave. His successor in the post is Eugene.

THEMES

The Battle between Britain and Ireland

The Au Pair Man is an allegory. An allegory is a work in which the characters, actions, and sometimes the setting, are contrived to make sense on the literal level and also to communicate a second level of meaning. On the literal level, the play is about an English lady hiring an Irish man as her au pair man. On the second level of meaning, the play comments satirically on the battle between Britain (or more specifically, England) and Ireland.

Britain has occupied Ireland for many centuries. Irish nationalists, who are mostly Catholic, have opposed the occupation, wanting a unified Ireland independent of Britain. This conflict is embodied in the only two characters in the play, the wealthy English lady, Mrs. Elizabeth Rogers, who represents Britain, and the rough Irish bill collector, Eugene Hartigan, who represents Ireland. Mrs. Rogers's dilapidated house is the crumbling British Empire, while Rose, whom Eugene hopes to marry, represents Northern Ireland, the area of Ireland that is unified with Britain (Irish people who support union with Britain, called unionists, are mostly Protestant and concentrated in Northern Ireland).

Eugene becomes Mrs. Rogers's sexual slave, underlining Leonard's view that the relationship between Britain and Ireland is an exploitative one. As well as being a relationship between occupier and occupied, it is also a relationship between the upper- and middle-class British people and the working-class Irish. It should be noted, however, that Leonard has stated that in his play, the exploitation runs both ways. S. F. Gallagher, in his introduction to *Selected Plays of Hugh Leonard*, writes:

> Leonard . . . who has confessed his fascination with the class structure in Britain—"Class is about the only facet of English life which excites me or about which I care intensely"—says *The Au Pair Man* is about an outsider despising this structure while using it for his own material good."

Eugene is not paid for being Mrs. Rogers's au pair man, but he is provided with expensive clothes and

TOPICS FOR FURTHER STUDY

- Research and write a report on the history of the Troubles in Northern Ireland. Bring your report up to date with a summary of the current situation in Northern Ireland.

- Write an essay comparing one or more plays by Hugh Leonard with one or more plays by one of the following Irish writers: George Bernard Shaw, W. B. Yeats, Oscar Wilde, or John Millington Synge. In your opinion, what, if anything, distinguishes both writers as identifiably Irish?

- Read about the military occupation of one country by another at any time between 1960 and the present and about any country that formed part of the British Empire from the nineteenth century to the first half of the twentieth century. Write a report comparing the more recent occupation with the older British occupation. Consider such factors as the reasons given for the occupation by the occupying nation; the reasons given for the occupation by independent analysts; tactics used by the occupier to maintain or extend power; responses by the occupied nation; and reasons why the occupier left. In your answer, include sources from among the occupiers and the occupied.

- Write a poem, play, or short story either from the point of view of the British occupiers of Ireland or from the point of view of the occupied Irish. You may use any period in history when occupation was current.

- Study a literary or artistic work that was created by a writer or artist at a time when his or her country was at war with, or occupied by, a foreign power. Give a presentation on what the work says about the war or occupation and associated issues. Include in your presentation your view of what is lost or gained by saying these things through art or literature instead of through factual means as in a documentary report.

- At some periods in history in some places, certain languages or dialects have been banned by the ruling or occupying government. The Irish language, suppressed by the British, is one example. Research one such ban and write a report on your findings. Include in your answer reasons given for the ban by the perpetrators; reasons given for the ban by its victims; effects of the ban; resistance to the ban; and the fate of the banned language.

---

food and an education in what she considers to be superior English manners. This is a satirical reference to the arguments often used by Irish unionists who want to maintain the union of Northern Ireland with Britain: Northern Ireland benefits economically and developmentally from alliance with the historically more prosperous Britain. Nevertheless, Leonard portrays the more powerful half of this relationship, Mrs. Rogers, with little sympathy. While remaining an amusing comic character, she comes across as dishonest, manipulative, cruel, contemptuous, vengeful, and possessive, leaving the audience in no doubt that she is not excused for her actions and has no claim to the moral high ground. Britain is to be viewed similarly.

The Arrogance of the Occupier

The Au Pair Man draws attention to the habit of Britain and other imperial powers of justifying their occupation of other nations by claiming that they are civilizing those countries. By the latter half of the twentieth century, the civilization claim was mostly based on material examples, such as the introduction of technological advancements and institutions for education and health care. In the nineteenth century, of which Mrs. Rogers is a relic, British justifications were more likely to focus on the alleged positive influence of British manners, learning, and customs. After World War II, awareness grew of various atrocities committed in the name of civilizing nations, and there was a corresponding change in the language of imperial powers. Talk of civilization (which carries an unacceptable implication of superiority of the occupying nation over the occupied) gave way to talk of bringing democracy. However, it could be argued that while the rhetoric changed, the underlying assumption—that the occupier is of superior intelligence and development to the occupied, who should therefore see the occupation of their nation as a boon—remains the same.

British Xenophobia

Leonard uses the character of Mrs. Rogers to highlight what he sees as British xenophobia (fear of foreigners) and ignorance of other cultures. The irony lies in the discrepancy between the fact that the British have a history of occupying foreign countries by force and the fact that the British are terrified of foreigners. Mrs. Rogers likes to stay in her house and responds with terror to the idea of leaving it because "foreign persons" and "dusky gentlemen" "infest" the streets. When Eugene threatens to leave, she tells him he cannot as "the streets are filled with Australians." At the same time, she retains the delusion that the Indians whom her father "was obliged to crucify" because they "behaved rather badly," "all adored him." (This is a reference to the British occupation of India. Indian resistance peaked in Mahatma Gandhi's Quit India movement of civil disobedience and ended with India's independence in 1947.) Mrs. Rogers assumes that the occupied nation can only be grateful to men like her father for their gift of civilization. Similarly, she expects gratitude from Eugene for her teaching him English manners, at the same time that she abuses and insults him.

In 1968, when the play was written, the type of xenophobia embodied by Mrs. Rogers was already seen as old-fashioned and redundant by much of an increasingly multicultural society. This is shown by Mrs. Rogers's increasing sense of alienation in a world where people who were once her friends now "pretend" that "everyone is as good as everyone else." However, such xenophobia was perceived to persist in British policy in Ireland, which at that time retained laws discriminating against Catholics.

STYLE

Allegory of Character, Action, and Setting

Political allegory in *The Au Pair Man* extends beyond the two main characters to a character that does not physically appear. This is Wilson, Eugene's predecessor as Mrs. Rogers's au pair man. When Wilson emerges from his time with Mrs. Rogers, he is emaciated and worn out. On the literal level, this is a comic comment on Mrs. Rogers's sexual appetite. On the level of political satire, this probably refers to the Irish potato famine between 1845 and 1850. Britain is widely considered to have been partly responsible for the famine, because of British-imposed land ownership laws and changes in the rural economy brought in by British and Anglo-Irish landlords.

The play's setting also carries a great deal of allegorical significance. Mrs. Rogers's dilapidated house stands for the declining British Empire. The fact that Mrs. Rogers believes she owns it and later finds out that the land on which it is built belongs to someone else refers to the conviction of the British-occupying government that it has a right to be in Ireland. Eugene's attempt to evict her from the house symbolizes Irish resistance to British occupation; the fact that he is unsuccessful implies that Leonard does not believe that Ireland will achieve independence from Britain.

The allegory is carried into the internal layout of the house. The wall unit, which Mrs. Rogers uses as a partition and to brace the walls and ceiling, represents the partition of Ireland into the British-owned Northern Ireland and the independent Republic of Ireland. Mrs. Rogers sleeps on one side of the partition, and Eugene on the other. The atrocious state of the house behind the wall unit refers to the economic deprivation of the mainly Catholic Republic of Ireland at the time of writing. The collapse of the wall unit over time refers to the vulnerability and instability of the British system of partition.

Symbolism

Throughout the play, the fountain pen is a comic phallic symbol. Mrs. Rogers repeatedly borrows Eugene's fountain pen and becomes angry when he withholds it. She is delighted with its quality, though she is contemptuous of the fountain pen of his predecessor Wilson, which, in line with his lethargic and lazy character, always proved defective. Act 1 ends with the desperate Mrs. Rogers stealing Eugene's pen and locking it in her box. When he forces the box open, many fountain pens fall out. Eugene gives her a significant look, as he knows what this means: he is one in a long line of au pair men whose pens she has stolen.

The pen may also have a secondary symbolic meaning. Ireland has produced a disproportionately large number of great writers, who are revered in Britain. Mrs. Rogers's obsessive desire for Eugene's fountain pen may comment on the gap between British attitudes toward Irish literature and toward the nation of Ireland as a whole. In addition, British policies in Ireland and a stigma attached to the Irish language have suppressed its use, meaning that most Irish writers before the 1990s wrote in English. In a sense, then, the Irish lost their writers to the British, just as the series of au pair men lose their pens to Mrs. Rogers.

Mrs. Rogers's taunting of Eugene as "Stripey" is an insult that works on the literal and symbolic levels. On the literal level, it mocks the poverty of Eugene's family, as the term refers to the striped material used by his family to lengthen an ancient shirt that he had long since out grown. In Ireland, striped wool or cotton calico fabric was commonly used for shirts by poorer rural people. On the symbolic level, "Stripey" is a reference to the tricolor, the triple-striped flag of the Irish Republic and the nationalists.

Speech Styles

The Au Pair Man's debt to Irish author George Bernard Shaw's play *Pygmalion* has often been noted. In Shaw's play, a large part of the professor's success in passing the London flower girl off as a lady springs from the changes he teaches her to make in her speech. Shaw knew that in the England of his time, perhaps more than any other place in the world, accent and speech patterns defined class. He commented in the preface to *Pygmalion* (cited in *The Oxford Dictionary of Quotations*), "It is impossible for an Englishman to open his mouth, without making some other Englishman despise him." This point is illustrated in *The Au Pair Man*, as Mrs. Rogers constantly sneers at Eugene's Irish accent and dialect and tries to teach him to speak like an upper-class Englishman. When Eugene rebels against Mrs. Rogers's authority, he provokes her by returning to his Irish vernacular, such as saying "voilence" instead of "violence." The historical British suppression of the Irish language (though suppression also came from Irish sources) is reflected in Mrs. Rogers's arrogant statement, "Your mind was a blank page and I wrote my name on it." To Mrs. Rogers, the Irish language is merely a blank.

HISTORICAL CONTEXT

The Troubles

During the twentieth century, there have been two periods of unrest in Ireland, which have become known as the Troubles. The first was the Irish War of Independence, a guerrilla campaign conducted by the Irish Republican Army (often called the Old IRA to distinguish it from the later IRA) against the British government in Ireland from 1919 until the truce in 1921. The peace talks led to the Anglo-Irish Treaty (1921), which allowed the mostly Protestant Northern Ireland to opt out of the mostly Catholic Irish Free State. Northern Ireland did so and became part of the United Kingdom of Great Britain and Ireland. The Irish Free State, that part of Ireland that declared itself independent from Britain, was named the Republic of Ireland, or simply Ireland.

The second period of Troubles centered on the violence involving paramilitary organizations such as the IRA, the Royal Ulster Constabulary (RUC, the Northern Irish police), the British Army, and other groups in Northern Ireland from the late 1960s until the 1998 peace settlement known as the Good Friday Agreement. The conflict began when the Northern Ireland Civil Rights Association (NICRA), formed in 1967, campaigned for civil rights for Northern Ireland's Catholic minority. NICRA drew its inspiration from the civil rights movement in the United States. NICRA's demands included an end to the manipulation of voting regions, which gave unionists control over local government even in towns with nationalist majorities; an end to discrimination against Catholics in government employment and local authority housing; disbandment of the B Specials section of the RUC, which was viewed by many Catholics as a Protestant vigilante force; and repeal of the Special Powers Acts of 1922, 1933, and 1943. The Special Powers Acts allowed arrest without charge or warrant, internment without trial, flogging or execution of suspects, use of witness testimony as evidence without requiring the witnesses to be present for cross-examination or rebuttal, destruction of buildings, requisition of land or property, and banning of any organization, meeting, or publication. These measures were seen as being aimed against the nationalists.

In practice, the power to intern without trial under the Acts of 1922, 1933, and 1943 was only used immediately after the partition of Ireland (1921) and during World War II (1939–1945). The 1971 law reactivating internment without trial, passed in Northern Ireland, was a different matter. Though the British government claimed that the law was for the purpose of fighting terrorism from either side, Irish Catholics saw it in practice as another tool to repress them. Between 1971 and 1975,

COMPARE & CONTRAST

- **1960s:** The Northern Ireland Civil Rights Association (NICRA) is formed in 1967 to campaign for civil rights for Northern Ireland's Catholic minority. NICRA activities culminate in an anti-internment march in 1972, which ends with the British Army's shooting of unarmed demonstrators, an event which comes to be known as Bloody Sunday.

  Today: The Northern Ireland Assembly, a home rule legislature established in Northern Ireland under the Good Friday Agreement of 1998, is under suspension as of 2002. The assembly is designed to ensure that both unionist and nationalist communities in Northern Ireland participate in governing the region. The suspension occurs because of unionist impatience at perceived remaining links between nationalist party Sinn Féin and the IRA. The Police Service of Northern Ireland, successor to the RUC, alleges that Sinn Féin employed spies at the assembly.

- **1960s:** The Republic of Ireland is predominantly an agricultural economy and continues to struggle with poverty, high unemployment, and emigration. The situation is exacerbated by the Troubles in Northern Ireland.

  Today: Economic growth in the Republic of Ireland averages an exceptional 10 percent from 1995–2000, and 7 percent from 2001–2004. The phenomenon leads to the country being called the Celtic Tiger. Industry replaces agriculture as the country's leading sector, and Ireland is a leading exporter of computer hardware, software, and pharmaceuticals. One of the factors cited in the Republic of Ireland's success is the peace process in Northern Ireland.

- **1960s:** The geographical, political, and economic isolation of both the Republic of Ireland and Northern Ireland make them largely dependent on past and present British policies in Ireland.

  Today: After Britain (including Northern Ireland) and the Republic of Ireland join the European Union in 1973, the political and economic center of power increasingly shifts from London towards the wider trading bloc. Both Irish economies improve thereafter.

---

of 1,981 people who were detained, 1,874 were Catholic/nationalist, and only 107 were Protestant/unionist. The NICRA took up the issue in their campaigns. At a NICRA anti-internment march in the Northern Irish city of Derry on January 30, 1972, twenty-six unarmed demonstrators were shot by the British Army, of whom thirteen died immediately and a fourteenth died a few months later as a result of his injuries. The incident became known as Bloody Sunday. Following this, the NICRA lost support as many nationalists lost faith in peaceful protest and turned to the Provisional IRA. The backlash against internment led to the 1972 decision of the British government under Prime Minister Edward Heath to suspend the Northern Ireland government and replace it with direct rule from London.

Potato Famine

Another historical event that may be reflected in the play in the sad tale of Wilson, the Weatherby and Fitch employee who becomes emaciated and worn out in Mrs. Rogers's service, is the Irish potato famine (1845–1850). The famine was caused by a blight that destroyed the potato crop, the staple food of Irish rural people. British policy in Ireland is widely considered to have been partly responsible for the devastation caused by the famine. First, British penal laws dating from the late 1500s meant that Catholics could face confiscation of their property. As a result, by the time of the potato famine, most Catholics held small amounts of land. Second, British penal laws forbade Irish Catholics to pass on family land to a single son.

This prohibition led to subdivision of plots with every generation, meaning that by the time of the famine, most family plots were extremely small. Potatoes were the only crop that could be grown in sufficient quantity to feed a family on such plots, leading to a dangerous dependence on a single crop. Third, much of the best land was packaged into large estates owned by absentee British landlords, who, even while the famine was in progress, continued to use it to grow cash crops for export. This arrangement meant that Irish Catholics could not be self-sufficient in food, except for the potato crops grown on small plots of poor soil.

It should be noted that many landlords of large estates did try to help their starving tenant farmers. They organized soup kitchens and relief works such as building (mostly superfluous) roads and walls, for which they paid the farmers. Some estates bankrupted themselves in the process. As a result of the potato famine, around two million Irish people emigrated to Britain, the United States, Canada, and Australia.

Speech Characteristics as a Sign of Class

Mrs. Rogers's constant attempts to correct Eugene's Irish pronunciation and dialect to a more English style may refer to the historical suppression of the Irish language by the British. The language has traditionally been viewed as a tool of Irish nationalists, and in the twentieth century, it was perceived as indicating links to the IRA. Before 1871, the Irish language was banned in Ireland's primary schools, and only English was taught, by order of the British government. Not all suppression of the Irish language came from Britain, however. Many Irish-speaking parents discouraged their children from speaking Irish, as a strong stigma attached to the language. The Irish Catholic Church also discouraged the use of Irish in its schools until 1890, as economic opportunities were seen as being within English-speaking countries.

CRITICAL OVERVIEW

The Au Pair Man was first produced to popular acclaim in Dublin, Ireland, at the Dublin Theatre Festival in 1968, before a mainly Irish audience. The following year, it was produced in London but received a less enthusiastic reception. The theater critic of the *Times*, Michael Billington, comments that while in the context of the Dublin Festival the play might seem "a joyously irreverent attack on Britain's fading Imperial grandeur," in Britain, "its analysis of the British malaise looks oddly insubstantial, and its satire infinitely less wounding than one had hoped." Billington finds the story contrived:

> what makes the comic allegory unconvincing is that it never seems to grow out of a plausible realistic situation: instead one feels Mr. Leonard has decided on a thesis and then looked around for a way of illustrating it.

The play fared better with critics in the United States, when it was produced at the Lincoln Center's Vivian Beaumont Theater in New York in 1973. The performances of the two leads, Julie Harris and Charles Durning, were widely praised. One *Time* magazine critic found the audience "captivated, fascinated and pleasurably teased" by the characters. This critic notes that while the narrative line occasionally meandered, "much of the evening consists of a fiendishly clever talkfest," reminiscent of the plays of George Bernard Shaw. *Los Angeles Times* critic William Glover remarks that "Leonard is out to uphold the Irish playwriting tradition for ironic mockery," drawing a comparison with the works of the Irish writer Oscar Wilde. Glover sums up the production as a "generally beguiling, brilliantly performed parable."

The 1994 production of the play at the Irish Repertory Theater in New York drew a lukewarm review from David Richards, writing in the *New York Times*. Richards states, "Unfortunately, the characters are saddled with so much symbolic weight they aren't particularly believable as people." Richards notes that this production suffered in comparison with the Vivian Beaumont Theater's from the absence of Harris and Durning, who "lent their considerable personal charisma to the roles."

As of 2006, the play seems less likely than previously to be taken up by theater producers because the political situation it portrays is specific to a certain time. Ireland is a different place, more engaged in looking to the future and to Europe than to its past relationship with Britain. Britain, too, has changed: the British Empire as portrayed in the play is all but gone, although Britain still occupies other countries by military force. This latter trend, however, has given rise to new forms of political satire more specific to the age.

The Au Pair Man *is an allegory of the battle between Ireland and England that is depicted here in a* *1968 march for Northern Ireland's civil rights* © Hulton-Deutsch Collection/Corbis. Reproduced by permission

CRITICISM

Claire Robinson

Robinson has a Master of Arts in English. She is a writer and editor and a former teacher of English literature and creative writing. In the following essay, Robinson examines the relationship between Britain and Ireland as it is enacted in Hugh Leonard's The Au Pair Man.

The Au Pair Man is a satirical allegory on the fraught relationship between Britain and Ireland, a country that Britain has occupied for centuries. Britain is represented by the ardent royalist, Mrs. Rogers. Her crumbling home, along with her stamp-collecting husband, who is abroad "selling his colonials," represents the declining British Empire. Ireland is represented by the rough Irish bill collector, Eugene. The evolving relationship between the two reflects Leonard's view as an Irishman on the dynamics of the Britain-Ireland conflict.

It is significant that both Eugene and his predecessor, Wilson, initially go to Mrs. Rogers's house in order to claim payment on a debt that she owes to their firm. Allegorically, they represent the Irish rebels who demand justice and freedom from British rule. In a rapid reversal, however, the men who want change end up shoring up the status quo. The British theater critic Irving Wardle, quoted by S. F. Gallagher in his introduction to *Selected Plays of Hugh Leonard*, calls *The Au Pair Man* "an object lesson (very pertinent to the 1960s) in how the establishment disarms plebian rebels." Both Eugene and Wilson fall victim to Mrs. Rogers's charm, threats, and domineering behavior. Both find themselves being exploited as her sexual slaves and unpaid laborers. At the beginning of act 3, Eugene turns up at Mrs. Rogers's house dressed in the uniform of the 1960s English businessman: suit, bowler hat, and umbrella. He drinks sherry now, the favored drink of the English upper- and middle-class, having abandoned the traditional Irish drink, whiskey. This metamorphosis reflects Leonard's view of the time-honored tactics of the occupying power, which, when faced with rebels, either terrorizes them into submission or co-opts them into its service. Eugene has become almost English. Historically, such assimilation was the pragmatic response to British rule of the majority of Northern Irish.

The character of Mrs. Rogers reflects Leonard's view of the class warfare between the

"

LEONARD NEVER LETS
THE AUDIENCE LOSE SIGHT OF
THE VIOLENCE UNDERLYING MRS.
ROGERS'S VENEER OF CHARM,
SUGGESTED IN HER COMMENT TO
EUGENE, 'I THOUGHT OF SENDING
A GUNBOAT, BUT AN INVITATION
PROVED JUST AS EFFECTIVE.'"

British occupiers and the Irish. While exploiting
Eugene as her sexual slave and for unpaid labor,
she repeatedly tells him that he is of inferior intelligence, learning, and manners. She says:

> We are separate islands. I am lush and crammed with
> amenities, a green and pleasant land; you have good
> fishing but are sadly underdeveloped. We aren't even
> in the same archipelago.

The reference to good fishing is to the fondness of
upper-class British people for visiting their country estates in Ireland to fish or hunt. There is also
a humorous allusion to the traditional symbolism
of fish to mean the sexual organs, in the light of
Eugene's role as sexual slave.

Mrs. Rogers is zealously pro-monarchy. The
monarch of Britain is commonly viewed as a symbol of the British Empire and British rule. In Northern Ireland, the mostly unionist population tends to
be pro-monarchy, whereas in the Republic of Ireland, the mostly nationalist population tends to be
anti-monarchy or indifferent. Mrs. Rogers expects
Eugene to toast the royal family and her doorbell
plays the national anthem of the United Kingdom,
"God Save the Queen." She has a bust of Queen
Victoria (ruled 1837–1901) and in moments of
stress, falls into the utterance of Queen Elizabeth I
(ruled 1558–1603). Both these queens reigned during periods when England massively increased its
power and influence abroad. Mrs. Rogers shares her
initials, E. R., with Queen Elizabeth I and Queen
Elizabeth II, who became queen in 1953. When applied to queens, E. R. is short for Elizabeth Regina,
Latin for Elizabeth the Queen. In act 2, when Eugene enters the house drunk, she is heard calling,
perhaps in her sleep, for "my lord Essex." The Earl

of Essex was a favorite of Elizabeth I, and the queen
sent him to Ireland to put down a rebellion against
English rule. Mrs. Rogers's sporadic belief that she
is Elizabeth I underlines her unshakeable assumption that she has an inborn right to supreme power
over Eugene and her other au pair men.

One of the major themes of *The Au Pair Man*
is the arrogance of the occupier, as typically an occupying nation justifies its occupation with the belief that it is doing a favor to the occupied nation
by bringing it the gift of civilization. Not only is
Mrs. Rogers convinced of her right to rule, but she
believes that Eugene should be grateful to be her
subject. This delusion underpins her account of her
father in British India, twirling his moustache and
making an "austere little speech" to a group of Indians who had "behaved rather badly," and whom
he had been "obliged to crucify." Literally, as the
nails were "hammered in," he lectured them. She
claims: "They all adored him. That kind of gentleness isn't to be found any more." In this account,
Leonard juxtaposes Mrs. Rogers's tone of genteel
nostalgia with a horrific incident to make his satirical point about the brutality underlying the arrogance of empire.

The delusion that the occupier is doing a favor for the occupied nation is also at work in Mrs.
Rogers's comparison of the crimes of rape and
theft. While she considers theft, even of an object
as trivial as a police whistle, to be a serious crime,
rape is another matter: "even at its worst it is no
more than pressing an unwanted gift upon another
person." Leonard's satirical message is that Britain
(Mrs. Rogers) is raping Ireland (Eugene) but persuades itself that it is doing nothing worse than be-
stowing an unwanted gift on the country. This is
confirmed by Mrs. Rogers's repeated insistences
that Eugene should be grateful to her for all that
she does for him. Mrs. Rogers's lenient attitude toward rape also draws attention to Leonard's view
of the difference in values between the two nations.
The materialistic British, he implies, care more
about crime against property (theft) than crime
against people (rape).

There is an additional point that the whistle
that Eugene steals is the property of the police,
who, in the form of the Royal Ulster Constabulary
(RUC), have traditionally been viewed by Irish nationalists as agents of the illegitimate British occupiers. This viewpoint is allegorically suggested
at the end of act 2, when Eugene, maddened by
Mrs. Rogers's possessiveness and insults, decides
to leave. Mrs. Rogers's response is to blow the

WHAT DO I READ NEXT?

- Six of Hugh Leonard's plays are collected in *Selected Plays of Hugh Leonard* (1992). The collection includes *The Au Pair Man* (1968), *The Patrick Pearse Motel* (1971), and Leonard's most famous play, *Da* (1973).

- Hugh Leonard's first novel, *Parnell and the Englishwoman* (1991), is based on the life of Charles Stewart Parnell, who led the struggle for Irish home rule in the nineteenth century, and his romance with an English married woman, Kitty O'Shea.

- George Bernard Shaw's play *Pygmalion* (1912) is one of his most popular. Its story of how a professor tries to pass off a flower girl as a lady is mirrored in *The Au Pair Man*. Leonard's style is also frequently likened to Shaw's, with both writers favoring brilliantly witty aphorisms that subvert the reader's expectations. The play is available in a 1994 Dover publication.

- William Butler Yeats is widely considered to be Ireland's greatest poet. Many of his most memorable poems and four plays are collected in *Selected Poems and Four Plays* (1996), edited by M. I. Rosenthal. Subjects are the big ones, ranging from love, wisdom, and death to Ireland's landscape and the passions ignited by Irish nationalism. Yeats's use of language is often musical and incantatory and sometimes classically spare, but always powerful.

whistle in order to summon the police, just as the British, in the opinion of many Irish people, called upon the RUC to enforce British government policy.

The tactics used by Mrs. Rogers to keep Eugene at her side comment on Leonard's view of the tactics used by Britain to keep Ireland in submission. The fact that Mrs. Rogers keeps Eugene a virtual prisoner reflects the hated British policy of internment without trial, which, in practice, was used far more often against Catholic nationalists (who opposed British rule) than unionist Protestants (who supported British rule). Her interrogation of Eugene whenever he goes out mirrors the deeply unpopular mass surveillance of Northern Ireland's population instituted by the British government. Ultimately, Leonard suggests, Britain's power over Ireland rested in its superior military force and its willingness to use it. Leonard never lets the audience lose sight of the violence underlying Mrs. Rogers's veneer of charm, suggested in her comment to Eugene, "I thought of sending a gunboat, but an invitation proved just as effective." Finally, the veneer cracks when Eugene tries to persuade her to vacate her house and move to Runnymede. In a scene in which she believes herself to be, first, Jesus Christ (she repeats the words he spoke on the cross) and then Queen Elizabeth I, her fury erupts in a full-blown physical attack on Eugene. Runnymede is the place where Magna Carta, a bill of rights limiting the power of the monarch, was signed in 1215, so Eugene's attempt to make her move to a development with that name represents Irish attempts to make Britain respect their civil rights.

Eugene is not, however, an entirely innocent victim. He wants to better himself. He has dreams of a luxurious lifestyle, with fast cars and beautiful women, and at first hopes that working for Mrs. Rogers will provide the means to advancement. He is disturbed to discover that it is no part of her plan to teach him skills that will be useful in the wider world. Instead, she tells him stories about Queen Elizabeth I, corrects his pronunciation, and advises him not to work except as a hobby, making him into her idea of an English gentleman. He finds that working for Mrs. Rogers leads to one destination only, and that is working for Mrs. Rogers. Finally, Eugene stays with her because he has nowhere else to go. This is a situation which Mrs. Rogers herself engineers by refusing to pay for her wall unit, thus ruining his chances of continued employment.

At the beginning of act 3, Eugene believes he has slipped out of Mrs. Rogers's clutches and has found an independent route to success and happiness by marrying Rose. (Rose stands for Northern Ireland, with a reference to the rose as a traditional symbol of England.) What is more, he looks likely to achieve justice for his firm of estate agents and evict Mrs. Rogers from her house. But there is no escape for Eugene, or for Ireland. In a cruel twist, Mrs. Rogers reveals that Rose is her relative and financially dependent upon her. If he evicts Mrs. Rogers, Rose will be angry and refuse to marry him, and if he does not, he will lose his job and Rose will reject him. This means that Eugene remains in Mrs. Rogers's power as surely as Northern Ireland remains in Britain's power. Eugene and Mrs. Rogers are inextricably bound together, suggesting that the conflict between Britain and Ireland will endure forever.

Source: Claire Robinson, Critical Essay on *The Au Pair Man*, in *Drama for Students*, Thomson Gale, 2007.

Joyce Hart

Hart is a freelance writer and published author. In the following essay, she studies the personality flaws of the characters of this play and the characters' symbiotic relationship.

Hugh Leonard's play *The Au Pair Man* is about two weak people, Mrs. Rodgers and Eugene Hartigan, who find one another through a series of coincidences and discover that two vulnerable people can better protect themselves if they band together. Theirs is not a healthy relationship, but it is in their coming together that they find they are better equipped to deal with life. Like the piece of furniture—the wall unit that Mrs. Rodgers bought but forgot to pay for—that holds up the ceiling and walls of Mrs. Rodgers's dilapidated house, the two characters lean upon one another in order to keep their lives from collapsing in on them. Although the play begins with the characters exploring their differences, as the play continues, it becomes obvious, if not to the characters at least to the audience, that Mrs. Rodgers and Eugene are very much alike and that they need each other.

Though Mrs. Rodgers and Eugene would much rather see only how they are different from one another, it is easy to see their similarities and their disparities as soon as the play begins. Mrs. Rodgers loves to look down on Eugene, subtly (and not so subtly) claiming higher social status and appreciation of the finer things in life than Eugene knows. However, it is obvious from the way Mrs. Rodgers speaks to Eugene that both of them are afraid, insecure, and very much on edge when dealing with everyday occurrences as simple as a conversation between strangers. For example, Eugene stands outside Mrs. Rodgers's door, nervous about confronting the woman about her overdue bill for the oak wall unit that sits inside her living room. On her part, Mrs. Rodgers opens the door and, without any attempt at offering even the simplest salutation to the stranger who stands on the other side, goes on the attack. "What do you want of me?" she asks in the first line of the play. This assault is not provoked from anything that Eugene has done other than his ringing her door bell. From this, one can surmise that the irritation that Mrs. Rodgers feels comes not from anything Eugene has done but rather it comes from inside herself. She is as nervous as Eugene is in confronting a stranger. On the surface, Mrs. Rodgers may convince herself that she is aggravated because Eugene has invaded her privacy, but deep down, as the audience soon finds out, Mrs. Rodgers is really irritated with herself. She is lonesome, which makes her defensive when someone reminds her of her isolation. Eugene, once he becomes more comfortable in his encounter with Mrs. Rodgers, also exposes his own loneliness, another of the many traits that the two characters share.

Because of her insecurities, Mrs. Rodgers continually attempts to keep Eugene on unstable ground. She needs to have the upper hand in her relationship with the world. If she expresses any vulnerability, she is afraid she will fall to pieces. Her false bravado is the prop she uses to present the fragile image she has built up around herself, an image that has little to do with reality. So whenever Eugene makes even the simplest and most obvious statement, Mrs. Rogers questions it. First, Eugene asks that she confirm her name. "Mrs. Rogers?" Eugene asks. Mrs. Rogers responds: "Well, that depends." A little later, when Eugene steps into the house and notices the wall unit, he says: "I see you still have it." Mrs. Rogers's response is: "Have I?" Then when Eugene points out that she is using the wall unit as a room divider, Mrs. Rogers asks: "Am I?" All of these exchanges seem absurd. What does Mrs. Rogers believe she is hiding? Everything is out there in front of her staring her in the face. But the fact that she questions it makes Eugene stand a little off kilter, makes him second-guess his own assumptions. Maybe he has stated something that is not true. So he has to explain himself further. When he tries to offer a statement that might clarify what he sees, Mrs. Rogers tells Eugene that he is being rude. What a great game Mrs. Rogers is playing. Of course, if Eugene were stronger in himself, he would have nothing to do with this game. He would see that Mrs. Rogers is strange and mentally frail. Instead, Eugene goes on the defensive. He apologizes to her. He turns his statements around so he can agree with her. This play can be easily likened to a boxing match, a competition that will first go one way and then another as the two anxious characters try, not to find strength in themselves, but to zap any strength that they might happen upon in their opponent. Eugene should definitely have the upper hand, as he is there to shame Mrs. Rogers into paying her debt. Eugene has the law on his side if nothing else, and yet Mrs. Rogers makes Eugene feel ill at ease. Mrs. Rogers has won, at least, the first round.

The playwright Leonard offers a deeper reflection on Mrs. Rogers's character when he has her explain why she is using the wall unit as a room divider. When Eugene suggests that the piece of furniture looks odd, sticking out into the room as it does, "it must look odd from the other side," Mrs. Rogers replies, "I don't look at it from the other side." The room on the other side of the wall unit has totally collapsed, and Mrs. Rogers does not want to see it. Here, the playwright is offering two insights. First, Mrs. Rogers does not want to look at reality. She does not want to see the damage and ruin that is corrupting her life. She does not want to deal with facts, such as the one about not having paid her debts or the one that confirms that her life is falling apart. The other insight that Leonard proposes is that Mrs. Rogers is rigid in her views. She believes what she sees is truth. Anyone who sees otherwise is wrong in their assumptions. In her statement that she does not look at things from the other side she implies that she does not consider other people's perceptions; she will not accept another person's point of view. She wants to control her life at all costs, which, the audience soon learns, includes her never stepping outside her home. Eugene wants control, too. He has not yet stated this and may not even be aware of it yet, but he craves status. He wants people to notice him because of his clothes or the way he carries himself. He is excited when someone refers to him respectfully, calling him, sir. He wants to control other people's perceptions of him, those people who do not dismiss him or make him invisible by ignoring him. Although Eugene wants recognition from the outside world and Mrs. Rogers wants parameters set around her inner world, they both need that sense of control of their surroundings.

Although these two people eventually find a relationship by which each of them becomes a little stronger, it is at the expense of the other that

> IN THE END, THERE ARE NO REAL WINNERS IN THIS PLAY. THERE ARE JUST TWO LOSERS WHO KEEP TELLING THEMSELVES THE SAME STORY IN HOPES THAT THEY WILL EVENTUALLY CONVINCE EACH OTHER THAT THERE IS A WAY TO WIN EVEN IF IT EXISTS ONLY IN THEIR IMAGINATIONS."

they make the relationship work. Mrs. Rogers must convince Eugene that he is inferior to her and that he needs her in order to advance. She proves this by bringing up French and German phrases, for instance, that Eugene often does not understand. When he asks her to explain, she makes statements such as "I don't mean to be patronizing, but if you have to ask, you can't possibly afford to know." Of course, she means to be patronizing. She has to belittle him to maintain her own superiority.

In addition to her demeaning comments, Mrs. Rogers also dangles things in front of Eugene, teasing him. Sometimes the teasing is sexual in nature. She makes tantalizing insinuations, for example, concerning his fountain pen, which she describes as large, burly, and serviceable. She wants to hold the pen at first. Then when Eugene asks for it back, Mrs. Rogers tells him that he should not wear it on the outside but rather should hide it so that not everyone knows he has such a great instrument. This exchange, like many others in the play, is Mrs. Rogers' way of testing Eugene's sexual interest in her. The pen is a phallic symbol. It represents something private, something that only Eugene uses. It is also something that Mrs. Rogers does not want anyone else, but her, to share. It is not clear if the two of them ever have an intimate relationship, but the sexual overtones are often present in their conversations. Sex is used as a form of control by both of them, either by tantalizing one another or by rousing jealousy.

In addition to the sexual insinuations, Mrs. Rogers also dangles the au pair job in front of Eugene, first telling him about it then stating that he is not worthy of the position. The dialogue that occurs over this topic is indicative of the push and pull of their relationship. When the subject of the au pair job is first broached, Mrs. Rogers refers to it as "Mother's help." Then she quickly adds: "No, I'm being naughty. Father's help, really." This statement is very telling. Why would she consider her statement naughty? It is not an obviously mischievous comment. A mother's helper might insinuate helping around the house with food or cleaning or children. However, with Mrs. Rogers's bent of mind, her thoughts might have once again slipped to the bedroom, exposing her desires for sex. She attempts to cover this up, telling Eugene that the job would really be taking care of her husband's business affairs. What is interesting to note is that Mrs. Rogers only mentions her husband in order to provide Eugene with missing information, namely that her husband (if there really is a husband) is seldom home. Mrs. Rogers is setting the scene in this part of the dialogue. She is adding color to the offer of the au pair position that she is going to describe and then take away, removing it from Eugene's grasp but hoping that in doing so, Eugene will just want it more. She describes herself as helpless and housebound, needing someone to help her fill in the gaps in her life. Then she turns back, emphasizing yet another time that her husband is "incurably and inescapably absent from home." When Eugene takes the bait, asking for a deeper explanation of the position of au pair, Mrs. Rogers defines it as a position that gives "a mutual service, without payment." At this, Eugene prepares to leave. He puts the papers back into his briefcase and sets down his glass. Of course, Mrs. Rogers notices this and immediately tries to manipulate him another way. "But I'm afraid you wouldn't be in the least bit suitable," she says, challenging Eugene to react again.

Eugene does not take the bait, to Mrs. Rogers's dismay; at least he does not bite right away. He looks like he is going to make a run for it. He wants a job with a future, and an au pair does not sound like it will lead to anything. But before he walks out the door, a thought strikes him. He becomes curious. At first he might have thought that the job was beneath him. But then he wonders if Mrs. Rogers might have insulted him in some way. "*Why wouldn't I be suitable?*" he needs to know. When he questions her further, he realizes that Mrs. Rogers has been critical of him, and his feelings are hurt.

Eugene now becomes defensive. He explains how he has been victimized because of his heritage and lack of education. By the time he is finished defending himself, he has not bettered the situation but rather has made it worse. He has also made a sexual suggestion. His is more vulgar or at least less subtle than Mrs. Rogers's, and he believes this is his downfall. He tries to make a joke by referring to "pubic" school rather than to "public" school, but the joke falls flat. Mrs. Rogers pretends to be offended and begins to suggest that it is time for Eugene to leave. At this point in the play the playwright exposes Eugene's biggest flaw. Eugene is very class conscious and believes that he is low class. It is while "in the presence of a gold-embossed accent," or "in a room with a bit of décor in it" that Eugene says that he falls apart. Mrs. Rogers makes him nervous, in other words. Mrs. Rogers also appears to have won another round. She has made herself seem to be of higher stature than Eugene by pointing out all of Eugene's faults and opening the wounds of his childhood insecurities. She has set him up nicely, and all he wants to do is submit. He will take her nonpaying au pair job no matter what she says. By the time Mrs. Rogers offers Eugene the job, he believes he has won something. After all, he has proven he is worthy of this go-nowhere position.

The next round also appears to be won by Eugene, when he makes Mrs. Rogers feel insecure about her sexuality and her age. After Eugene has worked for her for awhile, he goes out at night looking for younger women. He is unfaithful to Mrs. Rogers, in other words, in that he is looking beyond what she has to offer. Mrs. Rogers can no longer hold Eugene back. She has taught him enough for him to go out in society with confidence. Even though Eugene successfully leaves, there is still one more round to go.

In the final act, Eugene returns after a long absence. From all appearances, he is thriving. By contrast, Mrs. Rogers's house is in an even worse state of disrepair. Her dwelling is only one step from the wrecker ball. The wall unit is barely keeping the house standing. Eugene comes back this time, not with an unpaid bill but rather with money in hand. He offers her a brand new house in exchange for her leaving this one. The suggestion is unthinkable for Mrs. Rogers. She has not stepped outside her house in a long time, and she is against doing so now. Just as she refuses to look at the room on the other side of the wall unit, she will not step outside to look at her house from the outside. If she does so, her whole make-believe reality might collapse. Mrs. Rogers believes that she is one of the last few dignified people on Earth. She believes she has a traveling husband. She also believes that she is sexually attractive to younger men. All of these beliefs are based on the flimsy fabric of her imagination. Should she admit any one of these is a delusion, it would be like removing the wall unit from her living room. Everything would come down on her head. So Eugene's offer is unacceptable. Mrs. Rogers cannot leave her imaginary existence and face being the old, lonely woman that she is. So she allows Eugene to talk. While she listens, she conceives another story, one that will turn to her advantage.

Eugene is defeated when he discovers that his new love, Rose, is Mrs. Rogers's niece, that Mrs. Rogers is behind his new relationship with Rose, and that if he does not do as Mrs. Rogers tells him (or maybe even if he does), he will probably lose Rose. Mrs. Rogers regains the upper hand. Eugene, in the meantime, is on the floor picking up the trash of his grand scheme to get Mrs. Rogers out of his life.

In the end, there are no real winners in this play. There are just two losers who keep telling themselves the same story in hopes that they will eventually convince each other that there is a way to win even if it exists only in their imaginations.

Source: Joyce Hart, Critical Essay on *The Au Pair Man*, in *Drama for Students*, Thomson Gale, 2007.

Thomson Gale

In the following essay, the critic gives an overview of John Keyes Byrne's work.

Irish playwright, screenwriter, and novelist John Keyes Byrne, who writes under the name Hugh Leonard, is known for his wickedly humorous story lines that focus on humanity's dark nature. At his birth in Dublin, he was named John Byrne; following his adoption by a working-class family, he began using his adoptive father's name, "Keyes," as his middle name. Byrne began his writing career as a civil servant in the Department of Lands. While with the department, he became involved with amateur theater and began writing for and about the stage. Byrne's pseudonym, Hugh Leonard, is the name of a character in his first play, *The Italian Road*, which was originally rejected by the Abbey Theatre. After three of his plays were staged in Dublin, he became a professional writer, drafting serious dramas as well as scripts for television and films.

Since 1960 Byrne's plays have been staged nearly every year at the Dublin Theatre Festival. Among Byrne's numerous plays are *The Au Pair Man*, *The Patrick Pearce Motel*, *Da*, *A Life*, and

> A *VARIETY* CRITIC NOTED THAT THE PLAY 'SHOWS THE BRITISH EMPIRE CRUMBLING BUT DEFIANTLY CLINGING TO ITS OUTWORN PAST, ARROGANT, BROKE, BUT STILL LOFTILY TRYING TO IGNORE THE NEW WORLD AND CONTROL "THE PEASANTS."'"

Love in the Title. Jeremy Kingston called Byrne's play, *The Au Pair Man*, a "witty social parable" in which the author pokes fun at the British. The comedy revolves around Mrs. Elizabeth Rogers, whose initials indicate she is a parody of Queen Elizabeth (Elizabeth Regina). Her poverty-stricken but royal residence is soon invaded by a gauche young Irish debt collector endeavoring to reclaim a wall-unit. Considering how valuable this unit is to her, Mrs. Rogers seduces the young man and gradually transforms him into a personage possessing social grace. A *Variety* critic noted that the play "shows the British Empire crumbling but defiantly clinging to its outworn past, arrogant, broke, but still loftily trying to ignore the new world and control 'the peasants.'" He added: "Some of [Byrne's] dialog has the air of secondhand Oscar Wilde, but he provides . . . . many splendid flights of fancy and airy persiflage."

A more recent play, *The Patrick Pearce Motel*, met with an enthusiastic reception. Critics praised the work for its artful combination of farce and satire. A *Plays and Players* critic observed that the play "is both an act of conscious homage to Feydeau and a pungent, witty, acerbic attack on the Irish *nouveau riche*—in particular on their exploitation of their country's political and folk heritage as a tourist attraction." The two principal characters are prosperous Irish business partners whose new venture, a motel, has recently been constructed. In an effort to attract customers, the entrepreneurs name each room after a famed Irish hero. The story begins at the celebration of the motel's opening and rapidly becomes a farcical comedy of misunderstanding and sexual innuendo involving the businessmen, their discontented wives, a rambunctious television personality, the nymphomaniac motel manager, and the night watchman. *Stage*'s R. B. Marriott hailed Byrne's efforts, asserting that while he "creates vivid personalities among his bizarre characters, he also creates strong, smoothly progressive farcical situations with rich trimmings." Marriott continued that Byrne's "wit can be sharp, his humour splendidly" rowdy.

The author's next play received rave reviews and won several drama awards. *Da* is an autobiographical comedy-drama about a bereaved son, Charlie, on his return to Ireland and the scene of his boyhood. Charlie's father, Da, has recently died and the son tries to exorcise himself of the painful memory of his parent while sitting in his father's vacant cottage discarding old papers. Da returns, however, in the form of a ghost, and the father and son remember the past together. "*Da* is a beguiling play about a son's need to come to terms with his father—and with himself," disclosed Mel Gussow of the *New York Times*. "Warmly but unsentimentally, it concerns itself with paternity, adolescence, the varieties of familial love and the tricks and distortions of memory." He concluded that "*Da* is a humane and honest memory play in which, with great affection and humor, we are invited to share the life of a family." Similarly complimentary, John Simon of *New York* remarked: "A charming, mellow, saucy, and bittersweet boulevard comedy, but from a boulevard whose dreams are not entirely housebroken and have a bit of untamable Hiberian wilderness left fluttering in them." Byrne later wrote the screenplay for a film version of *Da*, starring Martin Sheen as Charlie.

Love in the Title is the story of Katie, a thirty-seven-year-old Irish novelist, who, while enjoying a picnic in a meadow, is joined by her mother and grandmother in earlier stages of their lives. Cat, Katie's grandmother, is a twenty-year-old, free-spirited girl in 1932. Triona, Katie's mother, is an uptight, conservative woman from the 1960s. Together, the three women compare the Ireland of the present to the Ireland of the past. Steve Winn of the *San Francisco Chronicle* observed: Byrne's "fanciful meeting of mother, daughter, and granddaughter in an Irish meadow takes a beguiling look at how both past and future exert a powerful hold." In the *Guardian*, Mic Moroney noted that while the play is "uneven," it is "by far the most probing and perhaps honest of Leonard's plays in many years."

In addition to his plays and screenplays, Byrne has written several books. In *Home before Night*, Byrne rehashes some of the incidents he already

covered in *Da*. Richard Eder stated in the *New York Times Book Review:* "The book's sketches, touching or comical though many of them are, lack the vitality that they had when dramatized onstage." Susan von Hoffmann of the *New Republic* also spotted annoying similarities between the play and book; however, she asserted that "a three-character play by nature lacks the richer texture of the memoir and these rough spots melt away in the larger view of Ireland and of a boy's slow and often painful discovery that his life is in the end a journey home." A *New Yorker* reviewer called *Home before Night* an "eloquent little book of merry and bitter reminisce," noting that Byrne "has led a life of classic Irish disarray."

Out after Dark, the sequel to *Home before Night*, continues Byrne's autobiographical account of his boyhood in Ireland. This second volume tells the story of his adolescence in the 1940s and 1950s and his first experiences as a writer.

A Wild People, Byrne's first novel, is the story of TJ Quill, a film critic chosen as the archivist for his favorite Western filmmaker, Sean O'Fearna. Karen Traynor wrote in the *Library Journal*, "The authenticity of [Byrne's] characters captures the essence of Irish culture." A reviewer in *Publishers Weekly* said the plot was "haphazard" at first, but it "gradually grows into a complex social comedy."

Byrne's book *Dear Paule* is a collection of letters that appeared in his weekly column in the London *Sunday Independent*. The letters, addressed to his wife, Paule, helped Byrne work through his grief over her sudden death. A compilation of memories of their life together, the column expresses how the smallest things in life remind him of her. Pauline Ferrie, a reviewer for *Bookview Ireland*, wrote that Byrne's letters are a "realization that he cannot fulfill his promise to remember his wife without first facing up to her absence."

Byrne once told *CA:* "I am not an Irish writer, but a writer who happens to be Irish. This is not hair-splitting: I find that the former is usually categorized as someone who writes quaint, charming, witty, idiomatic dialogue, but whose work has no real validity outside of Ireland. The people I write about are those in the small seaside town I was born in and in which I now live, ten miles from Dublin. I use them as a means of exploring myself, which is what I believe writing is about. I usually pick an emotional or biological crossroads: the realization of middle age (*Summer*), the death of a parent (*Da*), or the onset of death (*A Life*). The themes are weighty, but I treat them in terms of comedy—serious comedy, that is. I write without knowing where I am going; it is a journey for me as well as the audience, and I write about recognizable human beings. If a play of mine does not evoke recognition in Buffalo, Liverpool, Lille, or Melbourne, then it is an utter failure. I try not to repeat myself; life is too short to chew the same cabbage twice. I think that basically I am that unfashionable thing: an optimist. My work says that life may be bad, but we can change it by changing ourselves, and of course my best play is always the next one."

Source: Thomson Gale, "John Keyes Byrne," in *Contemporary Authors Online*, Thomson Gale, 2005.

S. F. Gallagher

In the following excerpt, Gallagher discusses the "lightness" of Leonard's plays, the political and social implications, and Leonard's conscious effort not to be an "Irish writer." Leonard states that The Au Pair Man *is about an outsider who, though he detests the English class structure, uses it for his own material gain.*

Christopher Fitz-Simon has described Hugh Leonard as 'the most prolific and the most technically assured of modern Irish playwrights' (*The Irish Theatre*, 1983, p. 191). He may also be the least pretentious. During the 1985 rehearsals of *The Mask of Moriarty*, based on characters culled from stories by A. Conan Doyle, Leonard, asked by a journalist why he had not written 'a Festival play that Says Something', replied:

> I *am* saying something, if with a small 's', and it is this. If you care to come in out of the rain for a couple of hours, I shall attempt to entertain you and send you out again feeling as if you have had a good meal. Mind, I may not be successful in this intention, for I am not using the crutches of either the missionary or the Artist (capital 'A'), which, if they do not keep the play upright, at least excite our pity and indulgence.
>
> (Introduction, *The Mask of Moriarity*, 1987, p. 16)

As the journalist leaves, Leonard overhears him wail to a companion, 'Oh God, why couldn't Jack at least have written an Irish play?' (*ibid.*).

The episode encapsulates two—perhaps they are really one?—fairly common charges against Leonard as dramatist: that his plays are lightweight or insubstantial, and that they fail to address current Irish problems. Christopher Murray, in the *Irish University Review* (Spring, 1988), readily recognizes Leonard as 'a craftsman of the highest order, inventive, witty and humorous', but avers, 'The problem is that these qualities, divorced from a social or political impulse, seem to be no longer

entirely in favour. A writer such as Tom Stoppard, for example, who shares with Leonard the qualities just mentioned, has had to take account in his work of the increasing interest in dilemmas that have a political as well as a moral implication . . .' (p. 136). Leonard is hardly impervious to such comments; he seems, indeed, to have anticipated something of the sort. As early as 1973, he had observed: 'I am conscious that my main faults are the cleverness (in the structural sense) . . . and at times an irresponsible sense of comedy which is not so much out of place as inclined to give my work an unintended lightness' (*Contemporary Dramatists*, 4th edn., 1988, p. 321). A less modest writer might have cited, as corroboration, O'Casey's lively defence of Shaw against similar misconceptions:

> By many, too, Shaw was thought to be 'an irresponsible joker'; but his kind of joking is a characteristic of the Irish; and Shaw in his temperament is Irish of the Irish. We Irish, when we think, and we often do this, are just as serious and sober as the Englishman; but we never hesitate to give a serious thought the benefit and halo of a laugh. That is why we are so often thought to be irresponsible, whereas, in point of fact, we are critical realists, while Englishmen often mistake sentimental mutterings for everlasting truths.
>
> (*The Green Crow*, New York, 1956, p. 204)

The unidentified journalist's Parthian shot—'Oh God, why couldn't Jack at least have written an Irish play?'—not only seems incredibly oblivious of the predominantly Irish content in Leonard's plays but may also symptomize an insularity that Leonard perceives as bedevilling too much of Irish drama in recent decades, an insularity that in his own work he strives to avoid: 'Being an Irish writer both hampers and helps me: hampers, because one is fighting the preconceptions of audiences who have been conditioned to expect feyness and parochial subject matter . . . Ireland is my subject matter, but only to the degree in which I can use it as a microcosm . . .' (*Contemporary Dramatists*, p. 321). When in 1986 he was lured to a conference in Monaco on 'Irishness in a Changing Society', the provocative title of his address was 'The Unimportance of Being Irish' and he told the select assembly of scholars, writers, journalists, librarians, publishers and policymakers:

> My belief is that our attitude towards Irish writing is as parochial as the communal water-tap and the horse-trough at the end of the village street. Poets, novelists, and playwrights—unless the names happen to be Yeats or Joyce or Beckett—write about Irishmen first, as a separate species that is, and mankind a very distant and unimportant second. And, yes, I have read Blake on the virtue of seeing the world in

a grain of sand and heaven in the wild flower. Indeed, why else, one might say, does the commonplace exist in art if not to contain the universal? Pardon me if I say that I find little that is universal in the contemplation of the navel that passes for our literature.

(*Irishness in a Changing Society*, 1988, pp. 19–20)

The Au Pair Man (1968) has a Pygmalion-like plot. An older woman, Mrs. Elizabeth Rogers, who lives in a cluttered London town-house that resembles a museum for a British Empire on which the sun has long set—the doorbell plays the National Anthem and the clock chimes out 'Land of Hope and Glory'—induces an uncouth but ambitious young Irishman, Eugene Hartigan, to abandon his 'initiative test' as a bill-collector and become her live-in 'secretary', ultimately to the point of sexual exhaustion, in return for which she undertakes to teach him how to be a gentleman.

Mrs. Rogers' husband, a philatelist, is 'out there somewhere, selling his colonials'. At one time he had an enormous collection and was forever adding to it, but 'after all those years of blood, toil, tears and perspiration', decided that in an 'age of specialization' it would be better 'to concentrate on one's British collection and ignore the rest'. She, herself, is 'hopelessly housebound', not daring to venture on streets that now 'teem with incivility, infested with foreign persons' pretending 'that everyone is as good as everyone else'. It is all quite unlike the old days when people knew how to behave themselves; when even some natives of India that Daddy was 'obliged to crucify'—they had 'behaved rather badly'—were touched by the 'austere little speech' he made while the nails were being hammered in, 'all the time with a twinkle in his eye and the occasional chuckle'. 'That kind of gentleness', she sighs, 'isn't to be found any more'.

Eugene's eyes, however, are fixed on the future. He endures his indentures only in order to realize what he frankly calls his 'ignoble ambitions' of materialistic success. He does suffer the odd bout of nostalgia: 'When I'm jarred, I go back home . . . that's all. It's like standing on a hill and seeing the two bays . . . next to one another like a pair of spectacles cut across the middle . . . I miss them', Whatever the sexual commerce between Eugene and Mrs. Rogers, neither expects any emotional involvement. As she puts it, 'We are separate islands. I am lush and crammed with amenities, a green and pleasant land; you have good fishing . . . but are sadly underdeveloped. We aren't even in the same archipelago.'

There are enough of such exchanges to prompt some commentators—the kind of critic, Leonard chides, 'whose byword is serendipity'—to read the play as an allegory of the age-old conflict between England and Ireland. Irving Wardle, who acknowledges that the cleverness of *The Au Pair Man* may tempt one to read too much into it, still praises 'its precision as a comedy of Anglo-Irish manners, and an object lesson (very pertinent to the 1960s) in how the establishment disarms plebeian rebels'. He notes Mrs. Rogers' initials (E. R.) and that when her territory is threatened she reverts to 'the full-blooded utterance of Elizabeth I'. The debt Eugene was assigned to collect is for a wall-unit now being used as a room-divider. And Rose, whom Eugene is surreptitiously courting but apparently doomed to lose—he discovers that Mrs. Rogers is Rose's favourite rich relative; 'We're having such trouble getting that girl settled', Mrs. Rogers admits—might well stand for Northern Ireland. Leonard, however, who has confessed his fascination with the class structure in Britain—'Class is about the only facet of English life which excites me or about which I care intensely'—says '*The Au Pair Man* is about an outsider despising this structure whilst using it for his own material good'

(*A Paler Shade of Green*, p. 198).

Leonard doubts that he could have written *The Au Pair Man* had he remained in Ireland, but even before he returned to Dalkey in 1970 he had developed an acute interest in what he saw emerging in Ireland as a new aristocracy—more a plutocracy, perhaps—situated primarily in the affluent south-Dublin suburb, Foxrock: 'It has sprung up full of new business executives, all of whom seem to be called Brendan. It's a classless aristocracy' (*ibid.*). 'The folks', he has elsewhere dubbed them, 'that live on the Pill'.

Source: S. F. Gallagher, "Introduction," in *Selected Plays of Hugh Leonard: Irish Drama Selections 9*, edited by S. F. Gallagher, Colin Smythe, 1992, pp. 3–7.

Heinz Kosok

In the following essay, Kosok gives a critical analysis of Hugh Leonard's work.

Hugh Leonard was born in Dublin. As he records in his autobiographical volume, *Home Before Night* (1979), his name was originally John Byrne, but he was adopted soon after his birth and later on called himself John Keyes Byrne, using the name of his adoptive father as his middle name. He grew up in the vicinity of Dublin, won a scholarship in 1941 to Presentation College Glasthule, and in 1945 joined the Irish civil service. *Home Before Night* is a moving account of his early life in a working-class family that, despite his adoptive parents' conflicting characters, provided an atmosphere of warmth and shelter. During his time as a civil servant in the land commission, he became involved in amateur theatricals and began to write for as well as about the stage. The second play he submitted to the Abbey Theatre, *The Big Birthday* (originally called "Nightingale in the Branches"), was accepted for production in 1956. When he sent in this play he used the pseudonym Hugh Leonard, ironically choosing the name of a character in *The Italian Road* (1954), his play that the Abbey had rejected earlier.

After two more of his plays, *A Leap in the Dark* (1957) and *Madigan's Lock* (1958) had been performed in Dublin, Leonard saw a chance to realize his lifelong ambition to become a professional writer. In 1959, four years after he had married Paule Jacquet, a Belgian by birth, he left the civil service, at first supporting himself by writing serials for sponsored radio. Ever since, Leonard has been successful at combining the career of a serious dramatist with the breadwinning activities of a commercial writer. In 1961 he joined Granada Television in Manchester as a script editor, and from 1963 to 1970 he worked as a free-lance writer in London, adapting novels for television, writing film scripts and television serials. In 1967 he received the Italia Award for one of his television plays.

In the meantime, Leonard had had a number of successes on the Dublin stage. Almost from the start he was associated with the Dublin Theatre Festival. Nearly every year since 1960 a play of his has been produced during the festival. Some of these plays are adaptations of well-known literary works, such as *The Passion of Peter Ginty* (1961), a modernized and Dublinized version of Henrik Ibsen's *Peer Gynt*. *Stephen D.*, which became Leonard's first great international success, premiered at the 1962 festival. The play went on from Dublin to London, Hamburg, New York, and many other cities and eventually was even produced at the Abbey Theatre. *Stephen D.* is a curious work to have made Leonard famous, because, as he himself emphasized repeatedly, it was written in a few weeks and hardly contains a word of his. It is based on James Joyce's *A Portrait of the Artist as a Young Man* (1916), with additional material taken from *Stephen Hero*, Joyce's first draft for *A Portrait of the Artist as a Young Man*, wherever the former did not yield sufficient plot or dialogue. Leonard decided to use Joyce's words, and made only an occasional change of tense or pronoun. However, the praise *Stephen D.* elicited everywhere may be

" ON THIS LEVEL, THE PLAY IS AS PINTERESQUE AS ANYTHING LEONARD HAS WRITTEN: A THEATER-OF-THE-ABSURD SITUATION COMPOSED OF MINUTE FRAGMENTS OF CLOSELY OBSERVED REALITY THAT BECOMES GROTESQUE— SIMULTANEOUSLY COMIC AND FRIGHTENING—THROUGH AN UNUSUAL ARRANGEMENT OF THE FRAGMENTS."

attributed in large part to Leonard's craftsmanship, his wealth of experience as an adaptor, and his excellent sense of stage effectiveness.

After *Stephen D.*, roughly one third of Leonard's output for the stage consisted of adaptations. He took up Joyce again when in 1963 he dramatized *Dubliners* (1914) as *Dublin One*. It was followed by *The Family Way* (1964), adapted from a play by Eugene Marin Labiche. The 1965 festival saw *When the Saints Go Cycling In* from Flann O'Brien's novel *The Dalkey Archive* (1964). Later, he wrote *Some of My Best Friends Are Husbands* (1976) from another Labiche play, and *Liam Liar* (1976) from *Billy Liar* (1960), a play by Keith Waterhouse and Willis Hall. However, to state that Leonard is a successful adaptor is not to say that he is not an original playwright. In addition to his adaptations, he has written almost twenty original plays, at least five of which—*The Poker Session* (1963), *The Au Pair Man* (1968), *The Patrick Pearse Motel* (1971), *Da* (1973), and *Summer* (1974)—merit detailed attention.

Typical of Leonard's plays, *The Poker Session* is witty, clever, brittle, and skillfully constructed, with an ingenious twist that will surprise even the wariest theatergoer. First staged at the 1963 Dublin Theatre Festival, *The Poker Session* is representative of the kind of plays that became fashionable in the early 1960s. Assembled around a table are a group of people whose seeming respectability is stripped off layer by layer. This type of play requires little stage action because it merely displays a situation, the result of past events that are being rediscovered in analytical technique. In *The Poker Session*, the Beavis family meet for a game of poker to celebrate Billy Beavis's discharge from a mental asylum. Billy appears to be cured; he has learned to face his own situation with ruthless frankness and applies the same attitude to his relations as well. With the help of Teddy, his roommate from the institution, Billy succeeds in stripping their characters to the bare bones of egotism and self-interest. There remains only one mystery nearly to the end: why did his brother-in-law Des fail to turn up for the poker session? It is solved with the final curtain when one suddenly realizes that Billy has killed Des just before the play began, thus confirming his own madness and perhaps involving in it his relations, whom he seems now to resemble in sanity. The play is witty in a cruel sense, reflecting on the near-identity of madness and sanity. It is also critical, in a fairly conventional way, of bourgeois respectability. And it has some of the makings of a tragedy of character, the tragic aspect consisting of Billy's insight into his own situation without the power to change it. Leonard himself, in his production note, sees in *The Poker Session* elements of a detective play, a comedy, a thriller, a tragedy, an allegory, and a black farce. In other words, the play is rich in meanings to the point of meaninglessness; where any interpretation is possible, taken together they tend to cancel each other out. Its effect on an audience is therefore paradoxical, its very fullness of conflicting meanings resulting in a sensation of emptiness.

The Poker Session is Irish only in the sense that it happens to take place in the suburbs of Dublin. In some of his subsequent plays, Leonard was much more clearly concerned with Ireland and her specific social and historical conditions. *The Au Pair Man*, it is true, is set in London, but the Irishness of one of its two characters is essential to its deeper meaning. Superficially, the play shows the confrontation between Mrs. Rogers, a grass widow of nebulous aristocratic origin who never leaves her dilapidated house, and Eugene, a raw young man, insecure and undereducated, whom Mrs. Rogers takes in as an au pair man, that is, an unpaid companion-cum-servant. Eugene receives an education in fashionable behavior and finally breaks away to take a job with a firm of estate agents. He comes back to turn Mrs. Rogers out of a derelict house, which is about to be demolished, but to his

dismay discovers that the girl whom he intends to marry is Mrs. Rogers's niece, which makes him as dependent on the grass widow as ever. On this level, the play is as Pinteresque as anything Leonard has written: a theater-of-the-absurd situation composed of minute fragments of closely observed reality that becomes grotesque—simultaneously comic and frightening—through an unusual arrangement of the fragments. Yet the play contains (as Pinter's works do not) certain fairly obvious hints at an allegorical meaning. Mrs. Rogers, whose doorbell plays the British national anthem and whose clock chimes "Land of Hope and Glory," becomes the personification of a decaying empire, while Eugene is obviously Irish in more than an individual sense. Once such a context of political allegory has been established, even small details take on an added significance: when Mrs. Rogers repeatedly borrows Eugene's fountain pen, this can be seen as a reference to the role of Irish writers in English literature, and the wall unit that separates Eugene's room from the rest of the flat becomes reminiscent of another border in the North of Ireland. The play is funny and effective even without these allegorical associations, but it reveals a wealth of additional ideas once the subterranean meaning has been grasped.

The Au Pair Man had been preceded by *The Late Arrival of the Incoming Aircraft*, televised in Britain in 1964, *Mick and Mick* (originally called *All the Nice People* and produced under this title in 1976), a Dublin Theatre Festival production in 1966, and *The Quick, and The Dead* (1967), a double bill of two short plays. *The Barracks* (1969) and *The Patrick Pearse Motel* (1971) followed *The Au Pair Man*. *The Barracks* was the last of Leonard's plays to be written in London, because early in 1970 he decided to terminate his semi-exile and return to Dublin. Although Leonard rejects the idea that he ever was self-exiled, his subsequent plays show an increased awareness of specific problems of Ireland and contemporary Irish society.

The Patrick Pearse Motel is a particularly interesting example because it deals with a dominant theme of modern Irish literature: Ireland's relationship to her immediate past and the discrepancy between the Irish people's professed hero worship and their actual materialism. The Patrick Pearse Motel is a commercial venture about to be opened on the edge of the Wicklow Mountains. Each of the rooms, complete with full-length portrait, is named after one of the heroes of Irish history, and the restaurant ("best steaks in Ireland") is in the Famine Room. The owners have even succeeded in engaging as caretaker a participant in the 1916

Easter Rising against the British. This patriotic setting becomes the scene of a farcical action in the best tradition of English stage farce, with characters playing hide-and-seek in the bedrooms, always missing each other or meeting the wrong person. The accretion of improbabilities is such that it precludes any semblance of reality. The characters—two married couples, who own the motel, the future manageress, and a television personality—are exaggerated in the tradition of farce, with one dominant characteristic that monopolizes the personality of each. They all become mere counters in a turbulent charade, all the more hilarious because they bear the names of figures from Irish mythology, such as Dermod, Grainne, Niamh, and Usheen (Ossean). It is Leonard's specific achievement that the farcical situations of his play add up to a bitter satire on present-day Irish society, its superficiality, materialism, hypocrisy, lack of values, neglect of the past, and cynical attitude toward religion. As one character remarks, "After all, it's the same God we all disbelieve in."

Up to the early 1970s, Leonard's writings had been remarkably impersonal and objective. However personal some of his plays may appear to Leonard himself, such relations are hidden behind a glazing of irony, sarcasm, and detachment. In his choice of plot and characters, too, he had seemed determined to keep out any reference to his own life. This approach was changed completely with *Da*, and perhaps this play's resonant international success was due to the fact that Leonard here touched upon very personal matters and showed himself emotionally more vulnerable than one would have thought possible. *Da*, the story of Leonard's relationship with his adoptive father, is one of the most decidedly autobiographical plays of the modern stage. The term *story* is not misapplied, because in its technique the play owes a great deal to the epic tradition of the international theater. Essentially a play of memories, *Da* utilizes material that Leonard was to use again for his autobiography *Home Before Night*. A successful middle-aged writer has come back from London to the small Dublin corporation house of his youth for the funeral of his adoptive father. When he sits in the house alone at night, burning the last papers and trying to break with the past, Da steps out of the shadows, and the two reenact those scenes from the past, significant and insignificant, that the writer will never be able to forget. He realizes that Da's infuriating foibles, worn-out jokes, his stubbornness, ignorance, and naiveté are all part of his life, and when finally the son sets out for London, Da is ready to go with him because, as Da says, "you can't get rid of a bad thing." The

play, for all its gruff abruptness and understatement, is a deeply moving account of a man's attempt to come to terms with his past, to reappraise, in the moment of ultimate loss, what he has always taken for granted, and to understand a love that has never been put into words. Technically, *Da* is a remarkable achievement. It is reminiscent in part of Arthur Miller's *Death of a Salesman* (1949), but Leonard succeeds, even better than Miller, in completely fusing the past and the present. When *Da* eventually reached Broadway in 1978, on being transferred from the Hudson Guild Theatre to the Morosco Theatre, it received both the New York Drama Critics Circle Award and the Antoinette Perry Award for the best play of the 1977-1978 season.

The first American production of *Da*, in 1973, marked the beginning of Leonard's close relationship with the theater group at Olney, Maryland, where several of his subsequent plays were produced for the first time and others had their American premiere. *Summer*, his next play, like *Da* had its world premiere at Olney. The play is an analysis of the problems of bourgeois middle age, a theme that Edward Albee had made fashionable with *Who's Afraid of Virginia Woolf?* (1962). Three well-to-do married couples meet for a picnic on the hills above Dublin city. Leonard brilliantly copies the small talk of conventionalized conversation: witty, ironical, daring up to a point where it will shock nobody, and carefully avoiding the pitfalls of genuine emotion and those facts that one does not talk about. But Leonard just as clearly reveals the underlying frustrations, the failure to keep up financially with the rest, the emptiness of a pro-forma marriage, the secret desires, the heartbreak occasioned by a desperate attempt to find a more meaningful relationship, the inconveniences caused by the necessity to hush up an affair, the fear of disease and death. When, in act 2, the couples meet again after a six-year interval, the impression one has formed of them in act 1 is confirmed, but the resignation, the frustration, the fear are deepened. Only Myra, who is naively happy in her religious belief, is an exception. She blunders into an exposure of the affair between Richard and Jan that everybody has preferred to ignore, but the others "save" the situation, and to the end they continue to uphold social conventions. Nevertheless the external conditions have worsened; the picnic spot, at one time a place for contact with nature, is now encroached upon by commercial building projects, and the old stone cross, the symbol of an intact relationship with the past, has been removed. What is worse, the two youngsters who in act 1 embodied the hope for a different, if utopian, future have been caught in the net of social conventions and bourgeois morality. Leonard's view is, therefore, deeply pessimistic, despite an occasional outburst of altruism or spontaneous feeling.

Leonard returned to the milieu of *Da* with *A Life*, his 1979 contribution to the Dublin Theatre Festival that was subsequently transferred to the London Old Vic. The play is about the life of Mr. Drumm, a civil servant with whom the young John Keyes Byrne seems to have had a love-hate relationship ever since Drumm helped him to get into the land commission, where he became Byrne's immediate superior. Drumm, as he appears in *Home Before Night*, was bitterly sarcastic and disillusioned. *A Life* shows how he may have reached this stage, with Drumm, who is dying of cancer, looking back on the many missed opportunities of his youth. *A Life* is an exercise in the bittersweet mood that seems to have become dominant in Leonard's recent plays.

For the past few years, Leonard has been program director of the Dublin Theatre Festival and as such has been partly responsible for the excellence of the festival and its emphasis on new plays and new playwrights, which entails a great deal of risk. In 1976-1977 he was also literary editor of the Abbey Theatre. To the average Irishman, he is perhaps even better known for his weekly column in *Hibernia* (1973-1976) and the *Sunday Independent* (since 1977) that is in the best tradition of Irish satirical and polemical writing. Some of these columns have been collected in *Leonard's Last Book* (1978) and *A Peculiar People and Other Foibles* (1979).

The adjective most frequently used to characterize Leonard's dramatic work is *professional*, a description that carries connotations of criticism as well as admiration. Leonard is highly conscious of a play's effectiveness onstage, and not infrequently he seems to employ effects for their own sake rather than out of any deeper necessity. He is well aware of changing fashions in modern drama, and he follows these fashions rather than creating them. Leonard is professional also in the mastery of technical requirements and in the sheer quantity of his output. But in comic invention and witty dialogue he is comparable to the best of those Irish writers who have had such a large share in the history of English stage comedy, and the underlying seriousness of his themes, as well as the variety of genres he employs to express them, ranks him with Brian Friel as one of the two most important living playwrights of Ireland.

Source: Heinz Kosok, "Hugh Leonard," in *Dictionary of Literary Biography*, Vol. 13, *British Dramatists Since World War II*, edited by Stanley Weintraub, Gale Research, 1982, pp. 284–91.

SOURCES

Billington, Michael, "Satire with Little Bite," in *Times* (London), April 24, 1969, p. 15.

"Fiendishly Clever Frolic," in *Time*, January 7, 1974, http://www.time.com/time/magazine/article/0,9171,910978,00.html (accessed September 20, 2006).

Gallagher, S. F., "Introduction," in *Selected Plays of Hugh Leonard*, Colin Smythe, 1992, p. 7.

Glover, William, "Leonard Offering in Irish Tradition," in *Los Angeles Times*, December 31, 1973, p. B11.

Leonard, Hugh, *The Au Pair Man*, in *Selected Plays of Hugh Leonard*, chosen and with an introduction by S. F. Gallagher, Colin Smythe, 1992, pp. 13–86.

The Oxford Dictionary of Quotations, edited by Geoffrey Cumberlege, Oxford University Press, 1954, p. 490.

Richards, David, Review of *The Au Pair Man*, in *New York Times*, February 16, 1994, http://theater2.nytimes.com/mem/theater/treview.html?_r=1&res=9C03E2DB163BF935A25751C0A962958260&oref=slogin (accessed September 20, 2006).

FURTHER READING

Delaney, Frank, *Ireland*, Avon, 2006.
   This novel is a fictionalized history of Ireland, told in a series of tales of kings, warriors, and supernatural beings by a wandering storyteller to a young boy. When the boy's mother banishes the storyteller for blasphemy, the boy sets off in a quest to find him.

Glassie, Henry, *The Stars of Ballymenone*, Indiana University Press, 2006.
   In 1972, during the height of the Troubles, Henry Glassie traveled to the farming village of Ballymenone in Northern Ireland. He listened to people talk and collected the stories and songs that make up an oral history of the region from the sixth century to the 1970s. This book provides a unique record of a vanished world and comes with a CD, so that the people's voices can once again be heard.

Leonard, Hugh, *Home before Night*, Andre Deutsch, 1979.
   This book is the first part of Leonard's autobiography, giving his vivid, moving, and often funny recollections of growing up in Dalkey, Dublin, in the 1930s and 1940s. It was reprinted, along with the second part, *Out after Dark*, by Methuen in 2002.

———, *Out after Dark*, Andre Deutsch, 1989.
   This book forms the second part of Leonard's autobiography, covering his later years, living in Dalkey, Dublin. It was reprinted, along with the first part, *Home before Night*, by Methuen in 2002.

McKittrick, David, and David McVea, *Making Sense of the Troubles: The Story of the Conflict in Northern Ireland*, Penguin, 2001.
   This book provides a clear, balanced, and accessible overview of the Troubles during the twentieth century.

Dirty Blonde

CLAUDIA SHEAR
2000

Dirty Blonde, a play by Claudia Shear, was first performed off-Broadway, at the New York Theater Workshop, in January 2000. It was a box-office success and moved to the Helen Hayes Theater on Broadway later that year. The play was published in 2002 by Samuel French, Inc., and as of 2006 was in print.

Dirty Blonde is at once a contemporary love story and a re-creation of key incidents in the life of Mae West, the legendary stage and screen star famous for her uninhibited sexuality, provocative double entendres, and lines such as "Why don't ya come up sometime and see me." As the play interweaves the growing romance between Jo and Charlie, two Mae West fans in New York—Charlie met Mae West in her old age—with scenes from West's career, the audience gets to see how carefully and confidently Mae West developed the extravagant, sexy, taboo-breaking public persona that was the hallmark of her fame. *Dirty Blonde* also hints at the personal price Mae West paid for her need to constantly maintain her public image and explores issues related to cross-dressing, homosexuality, and the need for self-discovery and self-acceptance.

AUTHOR BIOGRAPHY

Though her exact birth date is not provided in on-line sources that give biographical information, it is believed that playwright and actress Claudia

Claudia Shear   Photo by Lawrence Lucier. © Lawrence
Lucier/Corbis.

Shear was born about 1963. She is the daughter of
a deputy chief of the New York City Fire Department and an Italian mother who worked for a cosmetics company. Shear's father left her mother
soon after Shear was born. Shear grew up in Brooklyn, where she hung out with a crowd of tough girls:
"We broke bottles and made out in alleyways and
hid our cigarettes in bushes near our houses only
to retrieve them the next day, crushing leaves between our fingers to mask the smell of smoke," she
wrote in *Blown Sideways Through Life* (1995).
When she was twelve she got her first job, working in a hardware store in the Bronx, New York,
in the 1970s. She also spent time working on a dairy
farm in upstate New York. Shear was a voracious
reader, devouring everything from Dante's *Divine
Comedy* to the Book-of-the-Month Selections. "I
read anything I could get my hands on," she wrote.

As a young woman, Shear moved from one
low-status, menial job to the next. By 1995, as she
writes in *Blown Sideways Through Life*, she had
held sixty-five jobs. She had been a makeup artist
for Helena Rubenstein at Bloomingdale's, a bartender, a proofreader at a law firm, a takeout cook,
a "fake secretary for a guy pulling a con involving
pens," a room service waitress in a hotel, a phone
girl in a whorehouse on New York's East Forty-ninth

Street, and a nude model for a painter. The best job
she ever had, she wrote, was when, as a teenager,
she worked in a variety of positions at Joseph
Papp's New York Shakespeare Festival.

While she worked these jobs, she was also developing her talent as an actress and writer. *Blown
Sideways Through Life* made its first appearance as
a play staged at the New York Theater Workshop
in 1993. It received a favorable review from Frank
Rich in the *New York Times* and ran for eighty-nine
performances before transferring to the Cherry
Lane Theater, where it ran from January to July
1994. The play won the 1993–1994 OBIE Award,
with Special Citation for Claudia Shear.

Shear then wrote *Dirty Blonde*, a musical play
which explores the life of the twentieth-century
American cultural icon, Mae West, through the
eyes of two of her devoted fans. *Dirty Blonde*, with
Shear in the starring role, opened at the New York
Theater Workshop on January 10, 2000, moved to
Broadway later in the same year, and was also produced in London's West End. The play was nominated for five Tony awards and was also
nominated for Drama Desk awards. It received the
Drama League Award for Best Play.

Shear's credits as an actress include *The One
with the Fake Monica*. Her film credits include *The
Opportunists*, *Earthly Possessions*, and *It Could
Happen to You*.

PLOT SUMMARY

Dirty Blonde begins with Jo, a young would-be actress and her friend Charlie, both Mae West fans,
enthusiastically talking about how they admire a
"tough girl," a girl "who doesn't care if you're
shocked," and who says and does exactly what she
wants. (Tough girl was a phrase in vogue in the
1910s and 1920s. It was used to describe raucous,
assertive women like Mae West.)

Charlie recalls the dull conformity of his upbringing in the Midwest, while Jo remembers when
she first heard the Mae West song, "I'm No Angel," sung by a Catholic high school friend of hers
named Darla, who then promptly gave a full-blown
impersonation of West. Charlie recalls when he
first saw the Mae West film, *I'm No Angel*, when
he was still in high school. He was so captivated
he went to see the film every day for a week.

The next scene takes place in Poli's Theater, in
New Haven, Connecticut, in 1912. Jo, now dressed

as nineteen-year-old Mae West, is arguing with Harry (the same actor who plays Charlie), her partner in her traveling vaudeville act. (Vaudeville was a variety stage show made up of songs, dances, dramatic sketches, pantomime, juggling, and the like.) Harry is worried that Mr. Poli, the theater owner, will object to the sexual suggestiveness of Mae's act.

They do their act together. Mae addresses the young men in the audience ("you Yale boys") and then sings "Cuddle Up and Cling to Me." She moves vigorously to the music as Harry accompanies her on the piano. Her dress strap breaks, revealing a bare breast. She looks down, cups her breast, and the curtain falls. (This was a deliberate, well-established routine that Mae West went through in her early days in vaudeville.)

Harry then stands by the piano and explains to the *Dirty Blonde* audience that every week it was a different stunt, with Mae doing outrageous, sexy things on stage. He toured with Mae for thirty-two weeks. Finally he had sex with her, after which she fired him.

Jo enters and tells how in August of the current year she went to visit Mae West's grave. She enters the Cypress Hills Mausoleum in Brooklyn and on the second floor finds the West family. Mae is buried next to her mother.

The lights then go up on Charlie, who tells of a trip he made to Los Angeles to meet Mae when he was seventeen. He hung around in the lobby of the apartment house, until a man named Joe Frisco, a former vaudeville comedian famous for his jazz dance, arranged for him to go up to Mae's apartment.

The scene switches to Ravenswood, Mae's apartment. Part of the scene is a reenactment of Charlie's first meeting with Mae, and part of it is Charlie's later recollection of the event. He shows her the scrapbook he has been keeping of her, and they look at it together, page by page. Mae invites him to go to dinner with her and Joe Frisco at a Chinese restaurant. At the dinner, Mae tells Charlie how to stay healthy with regular enemas. He is embarrassed. He then makes the mistake of noticing another movie star in the restaurant. Mae glares at him; she does not like competition. She continues to talk frankly, this time about her sexual experiences as a young girl. She is interested in what Charlie says only if it is about her.

Charlie says he never forgot his week in Los Angeles. After her death, he visited her grave every year.

Jo and Charlie meet for the first time, at Mae's grave. It is August 17, Mae's birthday. Charlie says

Jo looks like Mae. As they leave the mausoleum, they get sandwiches and sit on a park bench, where they share their enthusiasm for Mae. Jo reveals that her ambition is to succeed as an actress, and Mae is her inspiration. Charlie reveals that he works in the film archives at the public library; he invites her to stop by some time. A tentative feeling of friendship grows between them.

At the Variety Vaudeville House in New York in January 1911, Mae confidently informs vaudeville star Frank Wallace that she is to be his partner. A month later, at Rehearsal Hall, they are seen rehearsing a dance step, and then in March of the same year they dance together at a theater in Chicago. At a theater in Milwaukee in April, Frank worries that they may be fired because they are not married. He persuades her to marry him, but soon Mae tires of their joint act, arranges for Frank to tour somewhere else, and strikes out on her own again. The audience boos her, and she gets poor reviews.

Jo visits the film archives, where Charlie shows her some photos of Mae and her family and associates. They briefly discuss their own families— Charlie's parents are both dead—and there is a brief moment of intimacy when they look at each other.

Frank Wallace recalls how he encountered Mae and her new lover, Jim Timony, on Broadway in 1920. Timony says he will be sending Frank divorce papers to sign. Frank goes home and cries.

In the film archives, Charlie recalls again his trip to Los Angeles. On his second day he returns to her apartment and they look at his scrapbook again, as Mae talks about incidents in her life and gives her opinions about some of the famous names of the day. Then she compliments Charlie on his physique and makes a sexual overture to him, but he does not respond. She then shows him some of her expensive gowns and even gives one of them to him.

Back at the archives, Charlie tells Jo that he took the gown back to his motel and tried it on.

In the next scene, Mae meets Edward Elsner, a successful theater director. Elsner has a formal manner and is sexually repressed. He is rather disconcerted but also entranced by Mae as she tells him about the play she has written, titled *Sex*, which she wants him to direct. He agrees.

At Daly's Theater, Mae is rehearsing her role as the prostitute, Margy Lamont, with a character named Lt. Gregg. Elsner interrupts and tells Mae she is acting too much. She does not need to act at all; rather, since she is naturally sexy, she should just be herself. They play the sexually suggestive scene again, with more instruction from Elsner. Elsner is delighted with the result and is turned on by the whole scene.

The scene switches to a courtroom, where Mae is appearing on a charge of public indecency because of the lewd content of the play. Mae spars with the judge, who fines her and sentences her to ten days in prison.

Jo and Charlie are smoking marijuana in Charlie's apartment and watching Mae's final movie, *Sextette*, made when she was eighty-five years old. Jo does not like the movie, but Charlie defends it. He also comments that the sad thing about Mae was that she never let herself love anyone other than herself.

As they talk, Charlie mentions that he was a wrestler in high school and was once district champion. Jo seems to be impressed and asks him to wrestle her. He refuses at first but after she shoves him, he agrees to show her a few moves. He soon pins her, and she says he is very strong.

They exit, and Ed Hearn enters. Ed was a female impersonator in vaudeville. Mae gave him a job backstage when her play *Sex* was running. In a reenactment, the two of them are shown talking at her dressing table. Mae learns from Ed that one of her admirers, a man named DuPont, is a homosexual. She had not realized this before, and it gives her an idea for a play called *The Drag*, which she envisions as a homosexual comedy. The Duchess, another female impersonator, enters, and he and Ed together sing a song, "*Oh My! How We Pose.*" They sashay around, showing Mae all the right moves and then move downstage together and continue singing. Ed and the Duchess then report how when they appeared in *The Drag*, they were arrested for indecency.

Jo enters and admits that men frighten her, but she likes being with Charlie. She knows he likes her. Charlie, who has entered during Jo's speech, recalls how he always loved to get dressed up as a vampire for Halloween. He hints that that is how "it started out," but he gives no details.

In the next scene, which takes place in mid-October, Jo and Charlie are sitting in the film archives. As they both eat candy bars, Jo talks about how she loves dressing up. Charlie tells her there will be a Halloween costume party at the archives the following week. He encourages her to go as Mae West but says he will not dress up. He refuses to tell her why.

At Charlie's apartment, Jo finds a large white satin skirt in a box in the bedroom. She assumes that it is intended for her, but when she shows it to him, he freezes. She assumes then that Charlie is not only gay, he also likes to dress up in women's clothes.

Charlie speaks directly to the audience, reproaching himself for letting his secret be found out.

As Jo goes behind a dressing screen and undresses, Ed Hearn enters, explaining how Mae's mother had insisted that he dress Mae like "a real woman," not in the fashionable style of the time. Ed and Charlie then assist Mae (Jo) to put on the whole Mae West outfit and to walk with the right swagger. Jo is thrilled. The crowning moment occurs when Charlie hands her the dirty blonde wig. Then Ed hands her a hat made out of willow, a few feathers and a diamond bracelet. Ed recalls that he attended the opening night of Mae's play, *Diamond Lil*, and this time the critics loved it. Jo, as Mae, sings a song, "A GUY WHAT TAKES HIS TIME." With Jo still in her Mae outfit, she and Charlie go to a club and dance. They also get drunk and have a wonderful time. In a taxi after they leave the club, Charlie tries to kiss her, but she rejects him, thinking that he is only doing it because he is drunk.

After Charlie gets out of the taxi, Jo wonders whether he may not be gay after all. But she is not ready to become involved with him. She does not even care for men who wear cologne, let alone— she implies—those who dress up as women.

She calls Charlie later on to tell him she had a great time. Charlie knows she is hesitant regarding him but convinces himself that the problem is hers, not his.

Ed Hearn enters, recalling Mae's first appearance in a movie, which was such a success that a movie was then made of *Diamond Lil*. He also recalls Mae's first meeting with Cary Grant and her first years of fame and success. He says she did not hang around with the Hollywood crowd, but with gays, blacks, and boxers. One boxer, Kid Moreno, recalls how Mae used to enjoy watching a bloody fight and how she would befriend the boxers.

The next scene is of a film set. Ed recalls how Mae would give him a part in all her movies. Mae is shown rehearsing Kid Moreno for the one line he has to say, but he still manages to get it wrong. Mae does a witty ad lib to save the day.

Ed recalls how Mae's movies declined in quality, and she had trouble with censors. But Ed also says that part of the decline was Mae's fault because she would not listen to good advice. She always had to be in charge. Ed mentions her disastrous collaboration with W. C. Fields in the Universal movie, *My Little Chickadee*. After Paramount dropped her in the late 1930s, Mae changed, says Ed.

The scene switches to Ravenswood in the late 1940s. Mae, now in her mid-fifties, refuses a part in Billy Wilder's film, *Sunset Boulevard*, because she does not want to play a has-been.

Charlie visits Jo at eleven o'clock at night. He confesses to her that he dresses up as Mae and only Mae. Jo says that is fine, but Charlie senses it is not. It is not even fine with him. She asks him to dress up for her, but he refuses.

Frank Wallace enters, talking about his divorce from Mae. He recalls that he last saw Mae in Las Vegas, on stage, surrounded by young musclemen, and singing full out.

The next scene is set in Las Vegas. Mae, seated on a chair as two musclemen pose, sings "Dirty Blonde."

After the lights change, Charlie recalls when he saw Mae's final movie, *Sextette*, which was made in 1978, when Mae was eighty-five years old. He was in Los Angeles at the time, so he went to see her. Mae remembers him and tells him how her fans wait on the corner of the street, hoping to get a glimpse of her. But she is too old to oblige them now. Instead, she says, her friends help her out sometimes. She and Joe Frisco persuade Charlie to dress up like her and go outside so the fans can get a glimpse of her in the shadow of a hedge. Charlie puts on gown, lipstick and eyelashes, diamond necklace, wig, hat, and boa. When a tour bus comes, Charlie steps out of the house and walks up and down in the shadow of the hedge, to the delight of the tourists.

In Charlie's apartment at Halloween, Charlie is dressed as Mae. Then Jo enters, also dressed as Mae. After her initial surprise, Jo says he makes a good Mae. As the music, "Closing Rant," plays, Jo and Charlie exchange a series of Mae West one-liners, after which Charlie grabs her and they kiss.

CHARACTERS

Armando

Armando is an Italian man who drives Jo to the cemetery where Mae West is buried.

Charlie

Charlie is rather lonely and isolated. He works in the film archives at the public library. He is a film buff and a huge Mae West fan; he even visits her grave every year on her birthday. When he was

seventeen and "very geeky and serious," he traveled to Los Angeles to meet Mae and spent some time with her in her apartment and at a restaurant. No date is given for this encounter, but Mae was well advanced in years at the time.

Charlie was raised in what sounds like a rather repressive, conformist manner in the Midwest: "You wore khaki trousers, blue oxford button-down shirts, Bass Weejuns, white socks. Your Daddy dressed like that and that's what your Momma dressed *you* like." He has been a Mae West fan since he was in high school, when he saw her film *I'm No Angel* for the first time.

As Charlie strikes up a tentative friendship with Jo, she thinks at first he is gay. This turns out to incorrect, but Charlie does like to dress up as Mae West. He first experienced the thrill of dressing up at Halloween when he was a child, but he insists to Jo that he is not like the normal cross-dresser who simply likes wearing women's clothes. He only dresses up as Mae West. That is all. Partly through his friendship with Jo, he learns to accept himself and his quirky habit without self-reproach.

Duchess

Duchess is a female impersonator. He says to Mae, "I'm just the type that men crave." Duchess sings and dances with Ed Hearn and Mae. He also appears in Mae's play, *The Drag*, and is arrested along with Mae.

Edward Elsner

Edward Elsner, a well-known director, producer, performer, and writer, directed many plays on Broadway between 1912 and 1929, including Mae West's *Sex*. In the play, he is presented as cerebral and repressed, but fascinated by Mae's sexual allure. He speaks formally to her but is clearly excited by the sexual suggestiveness of the scene she rehearses with Lt. Gregg.

W. C. Fields

W. C. Fields was a famous comedian of the early and mid-twentieth century. Mae West starred with him in the film *My Little Chickadee*, but the two of them did not get along well. Ed Hearn says that was because Mae always thought she had to run the show, but in this case, W. C. Fields was also an established star who was used to being in charge.

Joe Frisco

Joe Frisco was a former vaudeville comedian famous in his day for his jazz dancing. He became a friend of Mae West and knew her well. In the play, it is Joe who invites young Charlie up to Mae's apartment to meet her.

Lt. Gregg

Lt. Gregg is a character in the play *The Drag*. He rehearses a scene with Mae that takes place in a brothel. Edward Elsner tells him to remember that he has come to see a whore, "not to play bridge with [his] maiden auntie."

Harry

Harry is a piano player who is Mae West's vaudeville partner. He toured with her for thirty-two weeks in 1912. Everyone urged him not to sleep with Mae because then she would fire him, but in the end he succumbed to her sexual allure. Sure enough, a week later, in Pittsburgh, Mae fired him.

Ed Hearn

Ed Hearn is a female impersonator in vaudeville. He met Mae West when they were on the same bill together. Later, when he was broke, Mae took pity on him and gave him a job.

Jo

Jo is an enthusiastic, talkative young woman who works as an office temp but aspires to being an actress. She identifies strongly with Mae West because West was also from Brooklyn and succeeded in her career against all the odds. Jo is inspired to emulate her. "The first time I saw Mae West, a door opened up in my life," she says. When this happened she was filled with a sense of new possibilities and tried out for a part in the school play, even though she was the type of person who would normally be expected to occupy a more low-key position such as stage manager rather than being the star.

Jo is conscious of the fact that she does not really fit in her own family. No one else shares her interest in the arts. She has two married sisters, but she is unmarried. In the eyes of her family, she is "the weirdo," she says, and she seems very aware of her mother's disapproval of her lifestyle, including that fact that she does not keep her apartment tidy. Jo is also, until she meets Charlie, uncomfortable with men. Her father left home when she was little, she had no brothers, and she went to a Catholic girls' school. She explains, "Men were like foreign creatures to me—they frightened me. They frighten me now."

Judge

The judge presides over the City Magistrates Court, Tenth District, when Mae appears on a charge of public indecency after she performs in her play, *The Drag*. He speaks to Mae in an officious tone, fines her, and sentences her to ten days in prison.

Kid Moreno

Kid Moreno was a boxer, one of many who were befriended by Mae. She gave him a part in one of her movies, but he managed to fluff his one line.

Jim Timony

Jim Timony is Mae West's manager in 1920. He is a big Irishman. Frank Wallace describes him as "Face like a plate with a big derby stuck on top of his head."

Frank Wallace

Frank Wallace was a vaudeville performer who became Mae West's partner. In the play they are shown dancing together as they tour New York, Chicago, and Milwaukee in 1911. They secretly get married, although no one is sure about when or where. But in 1920, Mae leaves Frank and takes up with Jim Timony. Frank is distressed by his loss.

Mae West

Mae West was an actress, playwright, and film star during the first half of the twentieth century, famous for her brazen sexual allure and her risqué, bawdy wit. "When caught between two evils, I always pick the one I never tried before," is one of her well-known lines, which is quoted by Jo. In the play, Mae is seen at various stages in her career as a magnetic, forceful, but self-centered figure. Charlie, who observed her at firsthand, says, "she never let herself really learn how to love—anyone other than herself." It is as if Mae West is always playing the part of Mae West. She is also a woman who knows what she wants and persists until she gets it. In the scenes presented in the play, she dominates the men around her (with the single exception of W. C. Fields). She fires Harry, her accompanist, when she feels like it. She casts Frank Wallace, her husband, aside when he is no longer useful to her. Men like Joe Frisco are hangers-on. She does not bow to authority, and she makes her own rules. However, she can also be kind, as when she gives Ed Hearn a job when he is down and out and later sets him up in business.

THEMES

The Price of Stardom

Mae West worked long and hard to achieve success and to perfect the persona by which the world remembers her. She had some early failures, as shown in the play when she is booed off the vaudeville stage at the Albee Theater in Milwaukee

TOPICS FOR FURTHER STUDY

- Explain what scholars mean when they stress the difference between sex and gender. To what extent are gender roles determined by culture and to what extent are they rooted in biology? Describe how gender roles have changed since Mae West's heyday in the 1920s and 1930s. Write an essay in which you report on your findings.

- Examine the issue of gay rights. Trace the origins and growth of the gay rights movement since the Stonewall riots in 1969. Make a chart with the main points laid out clearly, and use it as part of a class presentation. Consider whether gays are still discriminated against in the United States and whether gay people should be allowed to marry.

- Compare Mae West to other screen legends of the period, such as Greta Garbo, Marlene Dietrich, and Jean Harlow. What was the distinctive appeal of each? Read some authoritative accounts of these stars, watch any of their movies you can obtain, and then write an essay which combines your own subjective opinions with objective research.

- Watch Mae West in any movie available to you. Watch her closely and analyze her style, how she delivers her lines, how she walks and her general demeanor. Make a class presentation, using the DVD or VHS tape, in which you examine her performance and the nature of her appeal. Does she appeal to you or are you mystified by the allure she held for so many?

- Compare Mae West to Madonna or any other female cultural icon today. Do such performers succeed because of talent and ability or through their gift for self-promotion combined with their desire to shock their audiences, to stretch the boundaries of what is considered acceptable? Make a class presentation with video clips to illustrate your points.

---

in 1911, and the reviewer for *Variety* has this to say about her: "her new single act is the same old rough stuff, an act too coarse for this two dollar audience." But the play also shows that Mae refused to allow such setbacks to affect her self-confidence. When *Diamond Lil* was an immediate success, she was not surprised, as Ed Hearn reports that Mae said: "I just never thought it would take this long."

However, the play also shows that West paid a price for her stardom. Having others admire, adore, and even worship her fed her vanity and narcissism. She could relate to others only when she herself was the subject. This is shown early in the play, in the scene in which young Charlie, visiting the aged Mae in her Ravenswood apartment, ventures the remark that he studies film and plans to work in a museum. The stage directions indicate that Mae immediately stops listening to him—they had previously been discussing one of her plays—turns to Joe Frisco and tells him what she wants for dessert. The point is clearly made: anything that is not about Mae West bores Mae West.

When she and Joe take Charlie to lunch, Mae sits alone in the back of the car, and Charlie observes her sink back into her seat, "staring straight ahead, like a doll on a pillow." This depiction shows how Mae always needed an audience; left to herself, it appears that she would simply disengage from life. She surrounded herself with people who did not question the fact that she was in control and set the terms of their relationship. She could not tolerate equals, as shone in the scene with W. C. Fields. Joe Frisco is a trusted companion because he is content to let Mae be in charge.

The Mae West of the play is a woman who refuses to grow and change. "She found what worked, what she was supposed to be, and she froze it, never let it go," says Charlie. This statement means that Mae tries as hard as she can to defy the passage of time. When Billy Wilder approaches her about a film role as a has-been, she refuses, claiming that she looks like a woman of twenty-six. (At the time, she was in her mid-fifties.) She calls to her maid to pull down the shades because the sun is too strong and she has to take care of her skin. This is a visual demonstration of Mae's need to deflect the real world and live only in the world she has constructed for herself.

Self-Discovery, Self-Acceptance, and Love

Jo and Charlie are oddballs, two people who feel, at the beginning of the play, that they do not really fit into ordinary life. Jo feels like the odd one out in her family. Her two sisters are married but she is not, and no one in the family understands her interest in the arts. She is working as an office temp, but she really wants to be an actress. Jo is a person who is not yet fully formed, but she is very clear that she owes a lot to Mae West. It is through Mae that she first awakens to the possibilities for her life—what she might be able to do that would most perfectly express who she is. Jo is never happier or more excited than when she is dressed up as Mae, as when she and Charlie go to the disco together. Allowing herself to dress up liberates something inside her, and she becomes more herself as a result.

Charlie is somewhat of a loner, a quiet man, a film-lover who has an abiding interest in, one might even say obsession with, Mae West. Like Jo, Charlie is not close to his family. Both his parents are dead, and he relates a story about how, on one occasion when he arranged a special screening of a Mae West film for his cousins, one cousin, Shirley, did not like Mae's act. Shirley says, "I don't get her at *all*."

As the friendship between Jo and Charlie grows, they learn together about self-discovery and self-acceptance. Charlie is timid at first, but it is clear that he likes Jo and feels that they might become friends. Jo has her doubts at first. She thinks Charlie is gay, and she learns about his cross-dressing habit. She says to herself about Charlie, "The longer I'm alone the more I know what I don't want." But eventually, when she knows more about Charlie, she realizes she has found someone with whom she can share a deep, authentic side of herself.

Charlie has some personal growth to do as well. He is troubled by his habit of dressing as Mae, but at first he is unwilling to admit it. He tries to convince himself that Jo's resistance to his attempts to kiss her after the dance reveals her problem rather than his. He assures himself: "'Cause you know what's wrong with you, Charlie? *Nothing*." But later, something inside tells him that this new relationship with Jo is important and that he must be authentic in it; he must share himself more fully,

especially as they both have such an interest in Mae West. When he goes to Jo's apartment late at night, determined to tell Jo the truth, he half-expects her scorn and rejection. When instead he finds acceptance, he is not sure how to react. At first he does not really believe what he is hearing ("You'll pretend everything is okay"), but then he finally admits being uncomfortable with his habit of dressing up as Mae: "It's not '*fine*' with me and *I'm the one who does it!*" He also admits that he wants change in his life and is ready to take action to achieve it. That is part of why he has turned up at Jo's apartment late at night and uninvited. He says, "It wasn't easy for me to come here—but I did it because I want my life to be different." Part of that change is to be more authentic about who he is, and the last scene shows that he has succeeded. It is Halloween, and Charlie is dressed up as Mae. When he modestly says that he does not make a good Mae, Jo reassures him by saying, "But you make a very good you." This sets up the conclusion, in which it is clear as they kiss that love is growing between them. By learning about and accepting each other they have also learned to be themselves, and in this acceptance love can find a way in.

STYLE

Economy of Resources

Although it contains many characters, performance of the play requires only one actress and two actors. The actress plays Jo and Mae; the first actor plays Charlie, Harry, Jim Timony, Lt. Gregg, Judge, Duchess, Kid Moreno, W. C. Fields, and a Muscleman. The second actor plays Armando, Joe Frisco, Frank Wallace, Edward Elsner, Ed Hearn, and a second Muscleman. The fact that so few actors can create so many characters is in keeping with the theme of impersonation.

The play is also notable for its rapid changes of scene and period, from the present-day encounters between Jo and Charlie to scenes set in the 1910s, 1920s, 1930s, 1940s, and probably 1970s. There are a total of twenty-eight short scenes. But in spite of these many changes, when the play was produced in New York, the set remained simple throughout. The scene changes were created mostly by period costumes and artful use of lighting. In the original production at the New York Theater Workshop, for example, the director used what Ben Brantley in the *New York Times* for January 11, 2000, called "the film-noir-style Venetian blind effect . . . for the scenes of Charlie's encounters with the ancient Mae." Lighting was also used to good effect in creating other scenes, enabling, for example, a pair of chairs to be transformed into a taxicab.

HISTORICAL CONTEXT

The Incomparable Mae West

Mae West was born on August 17, 1893, in Brooklyn, New York. Her father was a prizefighter and her mother a former fashion model (for corsets). Her mother had a major influence on Mae's career, taking her as a child to the theater, encouraging her to practice, and supporting her emerging ambitions in every way she could. Mae West first performed in vaudeville at the age of about eight. She also spent much of her childhood closely observing the great vaudeville acts, including the biggest star of the day, Eva Tanguay, and the many female impersonators. West learned from vaudeville how to develop her own stage and later screen personality, complete with suggestive lyrics and double meanings and glamorous, often outrageous costumes.

Known throughout her life for her sexual bravado, West had her first lover at the age of thirteen, when she willingly allowed her twenty-one-year-old music teacher to seduce her. Over the years, West made no secret of the fact that she had many lovers. In an age in which sex was not discussed as openly as it is in the early 2000s, she completely accepted her sexuality as natural, not something that she should deny or be ashamed of. For West, sex was as natural as eating.

West met song-and-dance man Frank Wallace on tour in 1909, and they teamed up. Urged by a friend to marry in order to protect herself from scandal, West secretly married Wallace in Milwaukee in April 1911. However, she did not like the constraints marriage imposed and separated from her husband within months with the excuse that her mother wanted her to do a single rather than a double act. Wallace kept their marriage a secret until 1935.

In an act Mae West put on in 1912 in New Haven, Connecticut, her dancing was so erotic that it almost provoked a riot. Six years later, in 1918, she played the lead in the musical *Sometimes*, in which she introduced the famous and sexy shimmy dance, which she had learned in a nightclub in Chicago frequented by African Americans. As Charlie in *Dirty Blonde* puts it, "she would plant herself in one spot and just *shake*—stopped the show."

In 1922, West hired Harry Richman, who was then an unknown piano player, as an accompanist. Their partnership was highly successful; between them they generated an exciting atmosphere on stage as they went through their routine of songs and skits, much of it written by West. However, Richman ignored a warning not to have an affair with West because it would cost him his job, and West subsequently fired him. After this, from 1923 to 1925, West's career slumped. Her decline was caused by poor decisions, a need always to be in charge, and some bad luck. Back on the vaudeville traveling circuit, she could no longer command top-of-the-bill status or the high salaries to which she had grown accustomed.

But in 1926, success returned when she starred in *Sex*, a play that she wrote herself. *Sex*, in which West plays a prostitute named Margy Lamont, ran at Daly's Theater on Broadway for three hundred and eighty-three performances. Critics disliked it, but that did not matter to West. However, the play also aroused the moral ire of the police, who raided the theater in February 1927 and arrested West and her fellow actors. West treated the trial as another role, wearing a different outfit in court every day. She was convicted of producing an immoral play, fined, and sentenced to ten days in prison. She served eight days and was given preferential treatment, even lunching with the warden in his home. When she was released, she donated some money to the prison library.

Her next play, *The Drag*, was about homosexuality, at the time an even more controversial subject than prostitution. West always had a sympathetic view of male homosexuals, although she disliked lesbians. The play opened in Bridgeport, Connecticut, in January 1927, but was banned from New York.

After appearing in another play, *The Wicked Age* (1927), West starred in *Diamond Lil*, which opened at the Royale Theater on Broadway in April 1928. Based on stories West heard about a woman in the 1890s who had captured the heart of every man in her neighborhood but who valued only the diamonds they gave her, the play was a huge box-office success, running for almost a year. Many critics were won over by West's magnetic performance.

In the 1930s, West conquered Hollywood. For her first movie with Paramount, *Night after Night*,

COMPARE & CONTRAST

- **1920s:** Mae West challenges conventional notions about decency in women's dress by sometimes revealing her breasts or legs on stage. In her thirties, West becomes full-figured and curvy and helps to set the fashion for the type of female body that is considered attractive.

  Today: The type of female body held up as the ideal is slim rather than full-figured. Thin models adorn the front pages of women's magazines and fashion magazines. Athletic, toned bodies are also considered attractive, and there are few restrictions about how little clothing women may wear in public or on stage.

- **1920s:** Growing affluence, methods of mass production, and the emergence of chain stores (known as dime stores) ensure that a range of cosmetics for women become generally available for the first time. These include face powder, lipstick, rouge, eyebrow pencil, eye shadow, and various creams, tonics, and lotions. Helena Rubenstein develops creams to protect the face from the sun.

In 1927, permanent waving is invented, enabling women with straight hair to have wavy hair.

  Today: The U.S. cosmetics and beauty industry accounts for over twenty billion dollars in sales per year. It is dominated by hair and skin care products. Women also turn to new methods of enhancing their youthful appearances, including facelifts and other types of cosmetic surgery, such as liposuction.

- **1920s:** Movies become a popular mass form of entertainment. Silent movies feature such stars as Rudolph Valentino. The first talking picture is made in 1926, and the first Oscars are given in 1927. Theater on Broadway reaches its peak. In 1927, two hundred and sixty-eight plays are offered in New York City.

  Today: In the United States, movies are the primary form of mass entertainment. It is estimated that over 70 percent of the U.S. population rents or goes to movies regularly. Revenue from a single hit feature film can be over one billion dollars.

---

starring George Raft, she was given only a small role, but she enhanced it by writing the line that became famous. This was her response, quoted in *Dirty Blonde*, to the hatcheck girl's remark, "Goodness, what beautiful diamonds!": "Goodness had nothing to do with it dearie."

The following year, West selected Cary Grant for his first leading role, in *She Done Him Wrong*, a screen version of *Diamond Lil*. The film was an outstanding success, and West became Hollywood's biggest star. *I'm No Angel*, released by Paramount the same year and in which West was again paired with Grant, enhanced her new status. From 1934 to 1938, West starred in five more Paramount films, but then Paramount dropped her. The reasons appear to have been many: her stock with critics had fallen, she made enemies with her licentious sexual behavior, and she was generally regarded as a low-class outsider in Hollywood.

In 1940, West co-starred in Universal's *My Little Chickadee*, but she disliked the role she was given and did not get along with W. C. Fields. Universal offered her two more pictures with Fields, but she declined.

In 1944, West played the title role in *Catherine Was Great* on Broadway, and in the 1950s, she developed her own stage show in Las Vegas, in which she was flanked on stage by eight musclemen, dressed only in loincloths. In the late-1960s, West, then in her seventies but still remarkably youthful in appearance, recorded two rock-and-roll albums, *Way Out West* and *Wild Christmas*. In 1970, West appeared in the movie, *Myra Breckinridge*, with John Huston, Raquel Welch, Rex Reed, Farrah Fawcett, and Tom Selleck. The movie sparked a new wave of interest in West. She made her final movie appearance eight years later, in *Sextette* (1978).

West died of a stroke in 1980, at the age of eighty-seven.

CRITICAL OVERVIEW

Dirty Blonde received mixed reviews from critics. Ben Brantley, in the *New York Times*, was enthusiastic. In his January 11, 2000, review, he wrote after the play's opening night off-Broadway that *Dirty Blonde* was a "wonderfully warmblooded . . . smart, tough and tenderhearted comedy," which makes a "persuasive and entertaining case for stargazing as healthy exercise."

Brantley points out that the characters Jo and Charlie use their obsessions not to take them away from reality but to understand themselves and to connect with each other. Jo and Charlie also understand the nature of their idol. They are not merely star-struck; they see the "woman, both monstrous and human, behind the gloriously vulgar screen siren." According to Brantley, it is this double focus—on Mae West and on her two twenty-first century fans—that gives the play its strength and raises it above the usual theater fare about a dead celebrity.

Brantley concludes that the play "demonstrates that this immortal sinner, who started life with little traditional beauty or classic talent, is a worthy saint for those seeking the divinity in their own mortal clay."

However, John Simon, in *New York*, was not quite so convinced of the play's merits, although he acknowledges that it is amusing: "If you like low camp, you'll find much of this highly amusing. If you don't, you'll still get some chuckles." Simon notes that Shear, who played Mae West, does not look like the screen idol and is also a "poor actress," although "a droll writer." Simon's conclusion points to what he feels is the play's superficiality; it is "a silly-sweet confection that will be enshrined in the annals of fluff."

When *Dirty Blonde* opened on Broadway on May 1, 2000, at the Helen Hayes Theater, *Time* magazine's Richard Zoglin was not overly impressed. He writes:

> Cleverly interweaving an odd-couple romance with a recap of West's career, the play rises above typical stage biodrama—but not far enough. Shear's nifty West impression aside, this sentimental trifle seems a pretty self-indulgent way to justify a playwright's old-movie obsessions.

Charles Isherwood, in *Variety* is more charitable, describing the play as a "genial, funny, crowd-pleasing riff on the life of Mae West and the inspiration it provides for a pair of square pegs in contemporary New York." Although like Zoglin he

Mae West, the bawdy legend of stage and screen, is the subject of this play Library of Congress

regards the play as "small potatoes," he pays tribute to the charm it exerted on the audience. He also comments that as an actress, Claudia Shear was more effective when she portrayed the aged Mae rather than her youthful self.

Brantley revisited the play in January 2001, when Kathy Najimy took over the leading role from Claudia Shear. This was a challenge for Najimy, Brantley notes, because Shear wrote the play with herself in mind, and the character of Jo is "clearly only a small fraction away from the author's real self." But Brantley was full of praise for Najimy's very different interpretation of the role. If the change of cast resulted in the play losing some of its "brassier highlights," it had, according to Brantley, gained "a new, gentler shimmer." He writes:

> Ms. Najimy doesn't have Ms. Shear's forthrightness or her shining armor of confidence. Where Ms. Shear's Jo seemed always to leap—eyes closed—before she looked, Ms. Najimy's version of the same character is more self-conscious and reflective, questioning events as they happen rather than after the fact.

Although many critics argued that the play was a slight offering, there was also some comment that it had brought the legend of Mae West to life again for a new generation born after her death.

CRITICISM

Bryan Aubrey

Aubrey holds a Ph.D. in English and has published many essays on drama. In the following essay, he discusses the themes of female impersonation and homosexuality in Dirty Blonde *and shows how they contributed to the development of Mae West's own performances.*

Female impersonation and homosexuality are prominent themes in *Dirty Blonde*: Charlie loves to dress up as Mae West; one of the most spectacular scenes in the play involves the female impersonators Duchess and Ed Hearn; West's play, *The Drag* is about homosexuals, and act 2 of that play contains a drag party. Both themes occur in period settings (the 1910s and 1920s) and in the present. When these themes are understood in context they help to explain the success and appeal of Mae West as an enduring cultural icon.

As far as the present-day setting is concerned, these two themes underlie the emerging relationship between Jo and Charlie. Soon after they meet, they walk to the subway together. After Charlie exits, Jo remarks to the audience that Charlie seems interested in her. But she quickly dismisses any notion that they might have a romance together: "Well, never mind. I mean the whole Mae West thing was a tip-off." She is referring to the fact that many of Mae West's fans, both during her lifetime and in the early 2000s were and are gay men, and she makes the assumption that Charlie is gay. This possibility is hinted at again a short while later, when seventeen-year-old Charlie is visiting Mae at her Ravenswood apartment, and Mae, who has found out that Charlie is a wrestler and has been feeling his arm, puts her hand between his legs. Charlie does not respond sexually, merely looking down at his scrapbook and then making an innocuous comment about Mae's gown. (More likely, Charlie is embarrassed and simply does not know what to do after being approached in this manner, but the playwright uses the opportunity to reinforce the notion already planted in the audience's mind that Charlie may be gay.)

Later, when Jo discovers the skirt in Charlie's apartment, she sees it as confirmation that Charlie is gay: "So, he's not just gay *as* a handbag, he's gay *with* a handbag." By the end of the play, though, she discovers that Charlie is not gay at all, but he likes to dress up as Mae West. Jo's assumptions about a man who cross-dresses turn out to be false. Although Jo does not know it, the

understanding she reaches is in line with modern studies of the phenomenon of cross-dressing by males in contemporary Western society. It appears that those who indulge in this practice, also known as transvestitism, are not necessarily homosexual. They simply find that dressing in women's clothes nourishes or gives expression to another side of their personality, and they feel more complete and whole as a result. The attraction to cross-dressing usually makes itself known in childhood; it is rarer for this desire and behavior to appear for the first time in adulthood. Charlie in *Dirty Blonde* appears to bear out this point, when he confesses to Jo that the first time he felt the attraction of cross-dressing was as a child at Halloween, when he dressed up as a vampire. The key part of the process, the part that conveyed the thrill for him, was a purely female aspect. As he puts it, he was "shivering with excitement as my mother leaned over me with her golden tube of lipstick, me looking at her, her looking at me, her mouth pouting a little, mirroring mine."

Charlie's small moment of insight about the origin of his unusual interest is a link to the theme of female impersonation in the parts of *Dirty Blonde* that are set in the 1910s and 1920s. In those decades, female impersonators were far more popular, and their acts far more mainstream, than they are in the early 2000s. There were many female impersonators on the vaudeville circuit, and as Marybeth Hamilton notes in *When I'm Bad, I'm Better: Mae West, Sex, and American Entertainment*, some of the best had national reputations. Their acts were considered entirely respectable, good wholesome entertainment suitable for middle-class families, including women and children. Such performances upheld cultural ideas about the ideal of womanhood, that women were graceful, delicate, and refined. One famous female impersonator of the period, Julian Eltinge, was reportedly so convincing on stage as a woman that it seemed almost impossible to audiences that he was really a man. As Hamilton explains, such entertainers were "lauded as magicians, able to conjure themselves across gender boundaries that their audience believed to be fixed and immutable."

Although there was no overt association in vaudeville between female impersonation and homosexuality, Hamilton notes that there were also female impersonators, largely confined to the less reputable saloons in New York City, who were quite open about being homosexual. Known as fairies, they deliberately "adopted female dress and mannerisms to suggest an illicit sexual identity." One of these was a man named Bert Savoy, who is mentioned by Ed Hearn in the play as being the favorite among all the other female impersonators. Savoy, according to Hamilton, was "an overt fairy who specialized in raunchy female mimicry that delighted a cult following of urban sophisticates." Savoy's career, as Hearn relates, came to a sudden end when in 1923 he was killed by lightning while walking during a thunderstorm.

Hamilton also reports that during the first decades of the twentieth century, this link between female impersonation and homosexuality was beginning to be felt at the margins of vaudeville respectability. Middle-class people were becoming aware of it. Part of this new awareness, Hamilton suggests, may have been due to the increasing visibility of the gay subculture in New York, fueled by police raids, press exposés, and the like. Another factor was that the medical profession at the time believed that cross-dressing was one of the symptoms of homosexuality, and homosexuality was regarded as a medical disorder. Yet this did not stop the enthusiasm in New York during the 1920s for openly gay performers and female impersonators. Observers even declared that Manhattan was "in the grip of a 'pansy craze'" during this time (as Jill Watts notes in her book, *Mae West: An Icon in Black and White*).

It was into this social climate that Mae West stepped in the late 1920s, when her plays *The Drag* (1927) and *Pleasure Man* (1928) were performed. In *The Drag*, the character Clair is unhappily married to Rolly, a gay man, although Clair is unaware of his sexual orientation. Rolly falls in love with Allen, a business associate who turns out to be in love with Clair. In the end, Rolly is murdered by David, his gay former lover who had sought help from Clair's physician father. David had expressed to the doctor his anguish over his condition, pleading that society should understand he was born homosexual and that he should not be called a degenerate or a leper because of it. David also alludes to the societal pressures on gay men to hide their true natures and marry, only to live in a loveless situation. The compassionate physician understands David, telling him he must learn self-acceptance; there should be no need for self-hatred or self-rejection. It is this aspect of the play, in which sympathetic understanding of gay people is shown, that prompts the comment from Ed Hearn in *Dirty Blonde*, who says, "Mae was a real pioneer," meaning that she accepted gay men when it was not fashionable to do so and brought their case to the theater-going public.

> THE CAMP ELEMENT IN WEST'S PERFORMANCE HELPS TO EXPLAIN HER ENDURING MYSTERY AND SUBTLE APPEAL, SINCE HER ACT WORKED AT SEVERAL DIFFERENT LEVELS."

However, West's attitude toward homosexuality was more complex than that. She was sympathetic to gay men, but she also believed that homosexuality was a threat to the social system. Prefiguring a debate that continues in the twenty-first century, she also divided homosexuals into two categories, those who were born with a biological predisposition to homosexuality and, therefore, could not be otherwise, and those who made a choice to indulge in same-sex practices. West believed the latter were, as Watts puts it, "secretive degenerates driven by acquired urges for unnatural sexual thrills." Indeed, some interpreters have seen in *The Drag* an anti-homosexual message, since the gay men are presented as unhappy misfits. Others claim that West's motivation in writing such a play was largely commercial; she saw an opportunity to cash in on an issue that was becoming lively in the public consciousness. In *Dirty Blonde*, this point of view is expressed by the female impersonator, Duchess, who scoffs at Ed Hearn's more idealistic view of West's purpose, saying, "She just wanted to be famous." Pointedly, Ed responds, "Well, that too." In other words, West's motivations were probably mixed.

Whatever her personal attitude toward homosexuality may have been, *The Drag* was notable for the fact that the gay characters were played by gay actors, which was not common at the time. Also, West made a point of consulting gay community leaders in connection with the play. The Duchess, for example, was a drag queen and activist for gay causes who taught other drag queens how to dress, speak, and carry themselves in their acts. Although it is not clear from the dialogue in *Dirty Blonde*, Duchess is in fact quoting from *The Drag* when he says: "I'm just the type that men crave. The type

WHAT DO I READ NEXT?

- *Three Plays by Mae West* (1997 edition), edited by Lillian Schlissel, contains three of the plays West wrote in the 1920s: *Sex* (1926), *The Drag* (1927), and *Pleasure Man* (1928). Schlissel's introduction discusses West's career and the theater of her day.

- *Master Class* (1995), a play by Terrence McNally, is about Maria Callas, the legendary twentieth-century opera diva. Like Mae West, Callas was adored by her fans worldwide and subject to constant media attention and gossip. The play is based on a series of master classes given by Callas in New York in the early 1970s and reveals the full range of her restless and tempestuous personality.

- Marlene Dietrich (1901–1992), a blond, German-born Hollywood actress and sex symbol during the 1930s and 1940s, was one of Mae West's rivals. Glamorous and mysterious, she became almost a legend in her own time. Dietrich's daughter, Maria Riva, wrote *Marlene Dietrich* (1994), a biography of her mother. Riva was Dietrich's close companion and confidant, and with much use of diaries and letters, she gives a unique portrait of the movie star at all stages of her long life.

- *Desperately Seeking Madonna: In Search of the Meaning of the World's Most Famous Woman* (1992), edited by Adam Sexton, includes a wide range of articles about the star who fills a role in contemporary popular culture not unlike the one played by Mae West in her day.

---

that burns them up. Why, when I just walk up Tenth Avenue, you can smell the meat sizzling in Hell's Kitchen."

This piece of dialogue gives a clue to the kind of language and attitude, ripe with double meanings, that typified the performances of drag queens and "fairies" that would appear again in West's play *Pleasure Man*, which made an explicit connection between female impersonators and homosexuality. Mae West herself adopted elements of this "fairy" style, also known as camp, in her own carefully cultivated stage and later film persona, the tough-talking, street-wise, seductive temptress Diamond Lil, a character who remained visible in all West's later guises. The camp element in West's performance helps to explain her enduring mystery and subtle appeal, since her act worked at several different levels. She was herself a female impersonator. Hamilton explains:

> She performed an impersonation at several removes: an authentic tough girl mimicking fairy impersonators mimicking the flamboyance of working-class women. What resulted was a baffling hall of mirrors that fascinated and bewildered nearly all who saw it, providing West with an enduring foundation on which she would build her career.

It is that enduring element of Mae West, the personification of camp, that is captured and celebrated in *Dirty Blonde*. It is heard throughout the play, but never more so than in the barrage of West one-liners with which it closes, including the immortal observation, "When I'm good, I'm very good, and when I'm bad I'm better."

Source: Bryan Aubrey, Critical Essay on *Dirty Blonde*, in *Drama for Students*, Thomson Gale, 2007.

Joyce Hart

Hart is a freelance writer and published author. In the following essay, she examines the play's definitions of what makes a girl tough and how Mae West does or does not fulfill those descriptions and how the characters Jo and Charlie try to emulate that toughness.

In Claudia Shear's *Dirty Blonde*, the characters Jo and Charlie open the play with statements of what they believe makes a girl tough. A tough girl is someone who does not care what other people think about what she does, how she talks, where she goes, they say. She does what she wants to do. She "doesn't sit like a lady or laugh like a little girl," Charlie says. Rather, she wants to "dress up" and "*go out*." And when she goes out, she wants to dance, but not just stepping to the music, she wants to dance "close and tight and hot." This is the introduction, in the play, to Mae West, the actress with whom Jo and Charlie are obsessed. Their shared attraction to Mae West brings Jo and Charlie together, keeps them interested in one another, and helps them to get to know and love each other. It is only appropriate that the life and personality of Mae West is developed in Shear's play, so the audience comes to appreciate the actress's life and rise to stardom and so the strange relationship between Jo and Charlie is better understood.

After describing some of the personality traits that Jo and Charlie believe Mae West had, they then relate some of those characteristics to their own lives. Charlie's version is that he wore a Madras shirt when he was young. This seems like a fairly mild form of rebellion or an attempt to stand out in a crowd, especially compared to some of the antics that Mae West pulled off to get attention, but for Charlie, a young Midwestern boy, it was a defiant stance of being tough. While everyone else was dressing in shades of white and khaki, he wore a plaid shirt of deep blues, purples, and red, colors that were so unsettled that when the shirt got wet, its colors bled. Although Charlie's connection to Mae West seems rather tenuous, Jo's in many ways is even more tangential. She has no claim to rebellion. Rather she lived through someone else who rebelled. She had a school friend who stood up in front of her study hall one day and belted out a song with sexual overtones. That was enough for Jo. When she found out that this song had been performed by Mae West, Jo was hooked on the actress. From these mild beginnings, both Jo's and Charlie's obsessions with Mae West developed, or at least that is what they claim. These were their early samplings of being tough.

The scene then switches to the historical Mae West and her early start in show business, which was almost as innocent as Jo and Charlie's beginnings. One of Mae West's first stage shows is filled with sexual innuendoes but not much else, especially in comparison to what she would do in the future. For example, she talks about her partner Harry's piano playing as a woman might talk about a lover. And she wiggles a lot across the stage. Then she ends the act with a risqué move: the strap of her dress accidentally breaks revealing a breast. According to the stage directions, Mae West does not immediately cover herself as any other woman

> " AS STRANGE AS IT MIGHT APPEAR TO THE AUDIENCE, THE PLAY ENDS WITH MAE WEST KISSING MAE WEST. ONE OF THEM IS JO AND THE OTHER IS CHARLIE—TOUGH WOMAN TO TOUGH MAN."

might have done were it truly an accident. Instead she pauses, looks down at her chest, says what will become a definitive exclamation of hers—"Oh!"—and then "slowly" covers herself. Jo and Charlie are right. Mae West is tough. She does exactly what she wants to do.

Charlie then describes something he did that was rather gutsy, showing that as he grew older he became a little more intense in his toughness. He travels to Los Angeles to fulfill his dream to meet Mae West. She is an old woman by now, but Charlie has brought an album of pictures taken when West was at the top of her career. This is a gentle touch by someone who wants to be tough, but it turns out to be just what Charlie needs to get to meet the aging actress. Charlie is persistent; he waits for several days outside Mae West's apartment. He has no clue that the odds are against his seeing her. He does not care. Like Mae West in this respect, he is going to do what he wants to do, even if it means lying to his parents. Charlie is not standing on stage and provocatively arousing his audience, but he is taking a chance. He has not resigned himself, as most other fans have, to sitting in an air-conditioned bus, driving by Mae West's apartment and hoping to gain a small glimpse of the actress. No, Charlie is much more daring than that. Because of both his innocence and his enterprise, Charlie achieves his wish, proving that Charlie is tough too, in his own way.

Mae West may be tough, just like Jo and Charlie believe, but even Mae West has her soft spots. When Charlie first meets her, he realizes that Mae West is not the immortal beauty that he had imagined. Even in his youth, or maybe especially because of his youth, and in his innocence, he realizes that the well-known actress is old enough to be his grandmother. For a grandmother, Mae West looks good. But Charlie stumbles in trying to say this to the actress, and Mae West proves she is incapable of accepting the fact that she has aged. When Charlie refers to a marble statue as an antique, Mae West is visibly hurt. "It's *me*, can't you tell, it looks just like me!" she says. The strength that Mae West once found in her youthful body is disappearing with age. Unlike the marble statue, her body is subject to a much more rapid rate of decay, and Mae West cannot face this fact. On this topic, she is far from tough. If she were truly a tough woman, she would have developed an inner strength that would have carried her into old age, a toughness that goes beyond the physical. If Mae West truly does not care what other people think, then why does she worry about her appearance? Joe Frisco, a boxer friend of hers, the guy who takes young Charlie up to meet Mae West, gives a more realistic impression of who the actress really is. Joe tells Charlie that what makes Mae West feel good is a really loyal fan, especially if that fan is a young man, and a bunch of flattering photographs of her. She thrives on a young man's adoration, but she also tears up pictures that do not make her look good. Joe paints a less flattering picture of Mae West. In his eyes, the audience sees an insecure woman. Joe knows that Mae West needs to be bolstered by a young, good-looking stranger who is enamored of her. She needs to see herself either through the young fan's eyes or through the softening lens of a camera. She wants to be told how good she is, how pretty she is, how adored she is. She even asks Charlie to dress up in her clothes so that tourists who drive by will think they have caught a glimpse of her. Well, not really her, but a hint of her, through Charlie's younger body. Even from a distance and through the branches of her hedge, Mae West does not want her public to see who and what she has become. She wants the myth of everlasting youth to continue.

When the play switches back to Mae West's younger days, the audiences sees the tough side of the actress again, such as when Mae West walks up to Frank Wallace and tells him she is his new partner, even though Wallace does not even know who she is. At this point, Mae West is still pushing to be recognized. She figures that she has nothing to lose. So she is confident in herself. Even after she marries Frank, Mae West does not change. That is a sign of toughness, too, especially back in her day. Neither her audiences nor the newspaper reviewers approve of her being too

tough, such as when she pushes Wallace off the stage and tries to perform solo. But her audience's boos do not stop Mae West. Shortly after, she files for divorce. She truly did not care what people thought of her. She ignored boos from the audience and found other audiences that appreciated her more. That kind of toughness made her a hit.

When Charlie receives one of Mae West's dresses, it is his turn to demonstrate how tough he is, how he does not care what anyone thinks of him. He tries the dress on in the privacy of his home. But at least he does it and admits to the audience how good it felt. "When I slid it over my head, it was so heavy and smooth that I just closed my eyes," he confesses. Then he adds: "I imagined myself blonde, of course, blonde and tough and ready for sex." Despite the fact that Charlie is obviously a male, something inside of him wants to feel what it was like to be Mae West, as much as he possibly can, that is. He wants to know what that kind of toughness is all about. He believes that if he makes himself up to look like her, he will find out. He does not share this information with Jo, at least not at first. He actually tries to hide it from her. He states that he hides the clothes in the closet so that no one will know. However, when Jo comes to visit, she finds a skirt, one that she first thinks Charlie has bought for her. But the skirt is way too big for her, and she is insulted that he thinks she looks that big. It takes a while for her to realize that the skirt belongs to Charlie. Jo, who professes to admire Mae West for not being afraid of who she is, is not quite as enthusiastic about Charlie's quirks. Although Charlie is strong enough to face himself, Jo is not ready to face this new aspect of Charlie.

As the play continues and switches back to Mae West, the actress once again proves her strength when she confronts Edward Elsner, a man she has heard about but has never met. She walks up to him and asks him to produce a movie she has written. At first, Elsner is not impressed with this request. This does not stop Mae West. She knows she is on a path that leads to success. She can feel it in her blood. Sure enough, not too much later, she stars in her own movie. Elsner tells her, "You have an unusual quality, Miss West," just before he decides to make her a movie star. One could argue that by this line, Elsner is referring to the quality that Jo and Charlie like in the actress—her toughness. That toughness works a little longer for Mae West, even when it lands her in court. As Charlie points out: "A tough girl knows that to be bad news is good business." And Jo responds: "The hotter the scandal . . . the hotter the ticket." As long as she is young, the tougher Mae West gets, the more her audience seems to like it. It is almost as if they like her in spite of themselves. "Tough girls go to Broadway anyway. And they watch as the limos line up," Jo stays. Charlie adds: "She knows that what they say afterwards doesn't count." Then Jo and Charlie say in unison: "What counts is that they came." It seems fans are stuck on the actress not so much because they like everything that Mae West does but because she does them.

But as she ages, Mae West's toughness changes. Even Jo and Charlie have to face this fact. They watch one of the actress's late-in-life movies and think that she is weird. "She's eight-five years old and she's wearing a wedding gown," Jo says. Charlie tends to agree with Jo, although he still holds out some reservations. He gives Mae West credit for continuing to be so tough that she tries her best to play young roles even in her old age. But even Charlie has to concede in the end. He thinks about Mae West and wonders if maybe all that toughness kept everyone out of the actress's life. Maybe she was too tough for her own good. "That's the sad thing," Charlie says. "She never let herself really learn how to love—anyone other than herself."

With this thought stirring inside of him, Charlie makes his move on Jo. It is as if Charlie wants to make sure that he does not make the same mistake. He tells Jo that he loves her, but Jo cannot handle it. She tells him that he really just loves her skirts, thus putting him down by making fun of his feelings. When Jo is alone, she admits that she does not know where to put Charlie or what to do with the feelings he wants to share with her. She has an image of what a man should be, and Charlie does not fit it. Jo gives no credit to Charlie for being strong enough to admit who he truly is. So this makes Charlie appear to be tougher than Jo.

Charlie further demonstrates his strength when he is alone, talking to his image in the mirror. Dressed as Mae West, he speaks about Jo's denouncement of him. He bolsters his confidence by stating that Jo does not know what is good for her and that her rejection of him is her problem, not his. But the play does not end here. Jo is given one more chance, and she rises to the occasion. She is tough enough to admit that she is not comfortable with Charlie dressed up in women's clothing, but

she surprises him by asking Charlie to let her see him like that. Charlie might not meet her preconceptions of an ideal mate, at least not on the superficial level. However, Jo does live up to her definition of a tough woman. She sees past the superficial and in the end does not care what anyone else thinks. Deep down, she loves Charlie for what he is, because deep down Jo loves, and is comfortable with, herself. As strange as it might appear to the audience, the play ends with Mae West kissing Mae West. One of them is Jo and the other is Charlie—tough woman to tough man.

Source: Joyce Hart, Critical Essay on *Dirty Blonde*, in *Drama for Students*, Thomson Gale, 2007.

Misha Berson

In the following review, Berson praises Shear's play as "delicious Broadway comedy" and asserts that "Dirty Blonde is also shrewd in its sophisticated approach to pop-culture biography."

It is one thing to imitate the inimitable film siren Mae West. It is another to capture her essence.

The latter feat occurs, gloriously, in *Dirty Blonde*, Claudia Shear's delicious Broadway comedy now making its Seattle debut at ACT Theatre.

Rather than just run through the high- and lowlights of West's fascinating saga, from vaudeville cooch dancer to Hollywood goddess, the show adroitly parallels Mae's saga with a sweet, offbeat romance between two contemporary misfits.

And it salts and peppers the dish with scattered vaudeville-style interludes, tidbits from Mae's lusty films and plays, and some spicy West epigrams—including the one that inspired the play's title: "I made myself platinum. I was born a dirty blonde."

That the central, dual role here is tailored perfectly to Shear's own stage personality is no problem in the ACT production. I can attest that Shear gave a terrific performance in the Broadway version of *Dirty Blonde*. But Seattle's Julie Briskman is delectably entertaining and compelling, too, switching seamlessly between the personas of Mae (at various points in her colorful life), and Jo, a tough-tender, motormouth New Yorker with a West fixation.

It don't hurt (as Mae might put it) that Briskman plays opposite Michael Winters, an expert Seattle actor who is just a natural for Charlie, a shy, endearingly shlumpy film librarian and West fan with a major crush on Jo—and an odd penchant for selective cross-dressing.

And completing the cast is versatile Mark Anders, a nimble utility player who serves as house pianist and appears as a half dozen consorts in Mae's life—mentors, lovers, co-workers and her quickly discarded husband, Frank.

The three are cannily directed in this 95-minute show by Jeff Steitzer, who has mostly (if not entirely) met the challenge of staging *Dirty Blonde* in the round in ACT's Allen Arena. One hurdle is that Shear, a seasoned solo performer, makes a lot of use of first-person narration in her script.

Charlie tells us (and re-enacts, with Briskman) the very funny, poignant story of forming an unlikely friendship with the elderly but still foxy Mae, when he was just a teenager.

Jo, a struggling New York actress ("when I'm not a temp"), lets us in on her private doubts about Charlie as they grow closer. ("So he's not gay as a handbag—he's straight with a handbag!") And various cronies of Mae have their say, including that hapless hubby Frank—whom the sexually cavalier star dumps for a shady Tammany Hall lawyer (Winters).

But even with the actors needing to shift positions constantly to give every patron some face time, and mime actions that we don't all see, their various characterizations are specific and wryly comic, and their presto costume changes are remarkable. (Costume designer Carolyn Keim and whoever is helping dress the actors deserve rounds of applause.)

Dirty Blonde is also shrewd in its sophisticated approach to pop-culture biography. West is a talisman for the modern characters because her unabashed bawdiness and bravado run counter to Jo's shaky self-esteem and Charlie's sexual insecurity. Mae's also an inspiration in the way she borrows, begs and steals from influences to invent her own archetype.

But she's no angel. Shear wisely references West's narcissism and ruthlessness too, forging a portrait that's both iconic and human.

Apart from an unsteady Brooklyn accent, Briskman masters all the notes and transitions in *Dirty Blonde*, and does so with style, heart and (when called for) a wicked sashay and shimmy. This is a breakout performance for her, in a show that is a welcome, dishy delight.

Source: Misha Berson, "*Dirty Blonde* Puts Life in Mae West and Her Men, ACT Tribute Fleshes Out Sex Symbol," in *Seattle Times*, June 10, 2002, p. E8.

New York Post

In the following review, the reviewer comments that "The famous one-lines that have become encrusted onto the iconic Mae West almost as much as the grotesquely corseted hourglass figure, cascading blonde wig and disgracefully imitable drag-queen purr of a voice, were all out there, twice as large as life."

Was there life for Claudia Shear's *Dirty Blonde* after Claudia Shear (and, for that matter, one of her co-stars, Kevin Chamberlin) left the production?

Frankly, I doubted it. Frankly, I was wrong.

This funny, witty, sweet and intermittently naughty play round and about the legendary Mae West, was clearly conceived by Shear as a vehicle for herself, and she rode it like a triumphant chariot.

All the same, would the chariot be sturdy enough to support another charioteer? It seemed a reasonable enough doubt.

Yet the play is sturdier than might be thought. When Kathy Najimy gave her own slant (or curve) on the inimitable Mae at the Helen Hayes Theatre, she provided a triumphant object lesson in how the West was won. With sheer gusto!

Shear has written a lovely and very clever play in which, over the years, many a Mae will bloom. Its cleverness comes in its structure—this is no mere bio-homage to Mae West, star and sex symbol of the silver screen.

Rather it is a love story for two losers who learn how to win. Jo (Najimy) and Charlie (newcomer to the cast, Tom Riis Farrell) meet, by chance, as fans both visiting West's grave on the anniversary of her birthday.

Jo is a semi-successful (with the accent on the semi), rather overweight, cutely hard-bitten actress, while a geeklike Charlie is a librarian at a theater library.

Both are obsessed with the immortal Mae, and they strike up a friendship. Slowly—despite a strange revelation on Charlie's part—the friendship develops into love.

Now for the cleverness. For playwright Shear and director James Lapine, who are jointly credited with the play's conception, have seamlessly interleaved this love story with vignettes from West's life and career.

So the actress playing Jo also plays Mae. All the other roles in Mae's life (apart from a soundtrack excerpt of the voice of Cary Grant) are given by the actor playing Charlie, and the third member of this protean cast, and the only original member left, Bob Stillman.

When I first saw *Dirty Blonde* in its original off-Broadway incarnation, I wrote of my impression of real Mac West on stage, for having seen West's longtime hit *Diamond Lil*, I was overwhelmed by how skillfully that real West had been captured.

When I saw her, she was then very much the wrong side of 50, her film career was well in its crumpled past, and she had become a blowsier parody of a blowsy parody.

Yet—weirdly—she was outrageously wonderful. Camp before people knew camp, yet she exuded a sensibility which insisted on you laughing with her rather than at her.

The famous one-liners that have become encrusted onto the iconic Mae West almost as much as the grotesquely corseted hourglass figure, cascading blonde wig and disgracefully imitable drag-queen purr of a voice, were all out there, twice as large as life. It was burlesque-style innuendo raised artlessly to art.

Najimy's image-take on West is certainly as viable as Shear's own—it is a little more open and vulgar, but retains the essential innocence caught so well by the play and eloquently conveyed by Shear and Najimy both.

If Najimy is the equal of Shear, I must admit Farrell is the clumsy, charming equal to Chamberlin. As for the also admirable Stillman, who plays the piano and as well as giving three or four incisive cameos, he is as splendid as ever.

This is a marvelously entertaining night out—as terrific for fans of Kathy Najimy as fans of Mae West—not to mention fans of Claudia Shear, who has now gone off to give *Dirty Blonde* to London.

Source: New York Post, "New York Pulse: Still Sheer Delight," in *New York Post*, January 30, 2001, p. 48.

Charles Isherwood

In the following review, Isherwood praises the set design, but comments: "It's bravura work that's rarely matched by the quality of the writing, however. The play's docudrama aspects are fairly pedestrian, despite the crips and attractive staging."

Mae West, the central character in Claudia Shear's *Dirty Blonde*, is not the most ravishing thing in the production, a misfortune that would probably have gravely disappointed the assiduously narcissistic performer. That prize goes to the ace work of set designer Douglas Stein and lighting designer David Lander, who together create a stunningly handsome, economical and elegant frame for this warmhearted tribute to the voluptuous star who is still the ultimate personification of sex on the silver screen.

A theatrical curio conceived by Shear and vet director James Lapine, *Dirty Blonde* combines a bio-play that traces the highlights of West's career with a contemporary romance between two misfits who idolize her. Neither half is particularly distinguished, but they are threaded together under Lapine's astute directorial hand to crate a genial evening of theater that also serves as an informative primer on the life and career of a one-of-a-kind showbiz personality.

Shear, best known for her hit solo show *Blown Sideways Through Life*, plays Mae at various ages as well as a young woman with suspiciously Shear-ish infections and attitudes who strikes up a complicated friendship with a man she meets while on a pilgrimage to West's grave. Kevin Chamberlain portrays this reclusive cinephile, Charlie Konner, whose recollections of his teenage encounters with the aged Mae captivate Shear's Jo, an aspiring actress who is heartened by West's career to see the potential in her own life.

"She was from Brooklyn, she was short, she certainly wasn't young or thin, and it took her 30 years but she made it anyway," as Jo tells Charlie. She was also an utter original, as Jo elsewhere observes ("She's the movie start equivalent of Venice"), and therein lies an obstacle the play cannot overcome. As with various other distinctive and oft-impersonated stars, it's easy to adopt Mae West's mannerisms but well nigh impossible to re-create her essence. Shear's performance as Mae registers as a less than perfect impression, and inevitably seems flat when compared to memories of the real thing—and those memories are often evoked, since the script draws on much of West's original material.

Lapine's artful direction keeps the pace brisk, and the turning points in West's life are staged with colorful vaudevillian panache. Chamberlin and Bob Stillman play all the men in Mae's life, bringing to each character a nicely calibrated dose of old-fashioned stage ham as well as occasional humanizing touches. They're aided by the flavorful costumes of Susan Hilferty, and period piano music often provided by Stillman himself.

The appeal of the production is enhanced to a remarkable degree by the beautiful stage pictures conjured by Lapine and designers Stein and Lander through the use of some very simple effects. The set is simply a large white box surrounded by darkness and lit with an array of softly saturated colors. Merely by manipulating chairs or adding or subtracting a few evocative details—a chandelier, a square of neon tubing, a theater curtain, a shaft of light in the distinctive shape of a car window—the designers move us among a wide variety of locales with astonishing ease and swiftness.

It's bravura work that's rarely matched by the quality of the writing, however. The play's docudrama aspects are fairly pedestrian, despite the crips and attractive staging, and Jo and Charlie don't acquire much more depth as contemporary characters than the more broadly depicted figures from Mae's life. Nor is the odd-ball romance between them—let's just say Charlie takes his identification with Mae to interesting extremes—particularly convincing.

The best-written scenes in the play are the encounters between the young Charlie and the aged Mae, which have a pungent, real pathos. Shear is in fact eerily convincing as the late, decrepit star, perhaps because by then West had in fact become a ghoulish caricature of her younger self.

In seclusion in Hollywood, visited by the occasional former admirer and yet all too eager to entertain a new one, West is entombed by her past, and Stein's enclosed cube set becomes a metaphor for the cosseting trap of celebrity. West's fame, which had cast such a bright light on the lives of Jo and Charlie, ultimately leaves the star herself in isolation, living in an insular, artificial world created to preserve her ego from the depredations of the real one.

Source: Charles Isherwood, Review of *Dirty Blonde*, in *Variety*, Vol. 377, No. 10, January 24, 2000, p. 68.

Charles Isherwood

In the following review, Isherwood comments that "the performances of its cast of three have now been polished to a fine sheen, with each bit of innuendo and double entendre—both West's classics and Shear's equally bawdy additions—popping brightly across the old-fashioned footlights."

The Helen Hayes Theater may at long last have a buxom B.O. tenant in *Dirty Blonde*, Claudia Shear's genial, funny, crowd-pleasing riff on the life of Mae West and the inspiration it provides for a pair of square pegs in contemporary New York.

James Lapine's bewitchingly pretty production looks just as chic on a Broadway stage as it did downtown at New York Theater Workshop, and the performances of its cast of three have now been polished to a fine comic sheen, with each bit of innuendo and double entendre—both West's classics and Shear's equally bawdy additions—popping brightly across the old-fashioned footlights.

As a piece of dramatic literature, *Dirty Blonde* is strictly small potatoes. It's like a segment of A&E's *Biography* combined with a semi-poignant episode of a wisecracking urban sitcom. These elements are, however, very deftly blended into a vaudevillian whole by director Lapine and author Shear. They conceived the show together, and Lapine's light-handed, fleet-of-foot direction perfectly complements Shear's snappy script. *Dirty Blonde* never digs deep, but it covers a lot of colorful territory in its brief running time.

Shear plays Jo, an aspiring actress who admires West for her determination to beat the odds in showbiz, which were (and still are) stacked against stacked women from Brooklyn with attitudes to match their ample proportions. Visiting West's grave one day, Jo meets a fellow West fanatic. Charlie (Kevin Chamberlin), who regales a fascinated Jo with recollections of his brief friendship with the aged Mae, entombed in her ego and a plush Hollywood apartment.

They form a two-member fan club, and as their friendship blossoms, it begins to take some surprising turns. These are played out against a re-enactment of the sometimes equally strange turns of West's showbiz career, with Shear playing Mae. Chamberlin and Bob Stillman, the third member of the hard-working cast, embodying the various men in Mae's life.

At one point Shear's Jo describes Mae as "the movie star equivalent of Venice"—an utter original that's impossible to approximate. She has a point, and Shear is better at evoking the late West, a ghoulish caricature of her former serf, than the younger Mae, who still flickers vividly in our memory banks. Truth to tell, even as Jo, presumably a variation on herself, Shear isn't the most dramatically convincing actress, but she has a connection to the material and the audience that gives her performance an undeniable, ingratiating appeal.

Chamberlin is sweetly pathetic as the scared-of-his-shadow Charlie, who harbors a strange secret that partially explains his timidity. He looks like a turtle who's always on the verge of pulling his head under his shell. Stillman is entirely first-rate and wonderfully adept at the quick-change artistry that's required of him. He transforms himself with a few physical and vocal adjustments from the gravel-voiced, cigar-chomping old-timer who pays court to the late Mae to the genteel drag queen who helped create the image of the young one.

Douglas Stein's set, and David Lander's lighting of it, are also major components of the show's overall charm. Most of the play is performed inside a giant white cube, with the back wall consisting of various simple backdrops that quickly set the scene: a theater curtain, a bank of office building windows. Lander's extraordinarily clever lighting does some of its own scene-setting, magically turning the stage into a disco or a pair of chairs into a taxicab. And Dan Moses Schreier's excellent sound design is also noteworthy, even more so in the Helen Hayes, a deeper space than New York Theater Workshop.

Dirty Blonde's charms are modest, and indeed its modesty is rather charming. But this means it will need a strong new set of reviews to compete for Broadway audiences at the height of the spring season, just before the summer swan dive at the B.O. It's already been the subject of much coverage in the *New York Times*, which has run a remarkable number of features about the show's performers and creators. The paper may next have to profile the player piano.

Source: Charles Isherwood, Review of *Dirty Blonde*, in *Variety*, Vol. 378, No. 12, May 8, 2000, p. 86.

SOURCES

Brantley, Ben, "Smitten by a Goddess, but She's No Angel," in *New York Times*, January 11, 2000, http://theater2.ny-times.com/mem/theater/treview.html?res=9B06E0D91E3B F932A25752C0A9669C8B63 (accessed September 22, 2006).

———, "Watching a New Mae Try On That Sashay," in *New York Times*, January 26, 2001, http://theater2.nytimes.com/ mem/theater/treview.html?_r=1&res=9C0DE3DA173FF935A 15752C0A9679C8B63&oref=slogin (accessed September 22, 2006).

Hamilton, Marybeth, *When I'm Bad, I'm Better: Mae West, Sex, and American Entertainment*, HarperCollins, 1995, pp. 141, 144, 151.

Isherwood, Charles, Review of *Dirty Blonde*, in *Variety*, Vol. 378, No. 2, May 8, 2000, p. 86.

Shear, Claudia, *Blown Sideways Through Life*, Dial Press, 1995, pp. 6, 8, 17.

———, *Dirty Blonde*, Samuel French, 2002.

Simon, John, Review of *Dirty Blonde*, in *New York*, Vol. 33, No. 7, February 21, 2000, p. 102.

Watts, Jill, *Mae West: An Icon in Black and White*, Oxford University Press, 2001, pp. 82–83.

Zoglin, Richard, Review of *Dirty Blonde*, in *Time*, Vol. 155, No. 20, May 15, 2000, p. 88.

FURTHER READING

Baker, Roger, *Drag: A History of Female Impersonation in the Performing Arts*, New York University Press, 1995.
This well-documented book, written in a lively, engaging style by a British journalist, describes female impersonation in the performing arts, going back to Elizabethan times when women were not allowed on the stage and all female parts were played by men and boys. The book includes a chapter on Japanese and Chinese female impersonators.

Bullough, Vern L., and Bonnie Bullough, *Cross Dressing, Sex, and Gender*, University of Pennsylvania Press, 1993.
In this culmination of thirty years of research, the authors survey cross dressing and gender impersonation throughout history and in a variety of cultures. They also examine the medical, biological, psychological, and sociological findings that have been presented in modern scientific literature.

Leider, Emily Wortis, *Becoming Mae West*, Farrar, Straus Giroux, 1997.
This biography emphasizes how West developed her distinctive persona. Leider argues that of all the stage and screen stars of the early twentieth century, West is the most enduring and the most relevant for today because of her interest in stretching and crossing rigid boundaries of gender.

Ward, Carol M., *Mae West: A Bio-Bibliography*, Greenwood Press, 1989.
In separate chapters, Ward includes an objective biography of West and an examination of how West created the myth about herself that is the core of her enduring appeal. Ward also analyzes many of the interviews West gave, and reprints two of them in their entirety. She surveys works by and about West and includes a bibliographical checklist of sources.

The Exonerated

JESSICA BLANK

ERIK JENSEN

2002

The Exonerated, a play by Jessica Blank and Erik Jensen, was first performed in Los Angeles by the Actors' Gang, on April 19, 2002, directed by the playwrights. The play premiered in New York City on October 10, 2002, at 45 Bleecker Theater, directed by Bob Balaban. It was first published in 2004.

The play tells the true story of five American men and one American woman who were convicted and sentenced to death for crimes they did not commit. Between them these six people spent over one hundred years on death row before the criminal justice system finally corrected its errors and freed them.

Blank and Jensen constructed the play entirely out of interviews they conducted with the former prisoners and from various court documents and case files. The lines of the play spoken by the characters are the actual words used by the exonerated prisoners. They tell their stories plainly, and the result is a shocking exposure of police and prosecutorial misconduct that led to the conviction and condemnation of the innocent. The stories are mini-chronicles of lives destroyed and precious time wasted—one man spent twenty-two years on death row—but the play also has its moments of humor as well as being a testimony to the fact that hope and faith can survive in even the bleakest of situations.

The Exonerated was highly successful, running off-Broadway for two years and over six hundred performances. Celebrity actors, including Richard

Dreyfuss, Jill Clayburgh, and many others, all accepted roles in the play at various times in its run. Illinois governor George Ryan attended a special performance of the play and later said it was a factor in his decision only a month later to grant clemency to all inmates of death row in Illinois.

AUTHOR BIOGRAPHY

Jessica Blank was born in 1975. Her mother is a movement educator with a background in modern dance; her father, Arthur Blank, is a psychoanalyst. In the 1960s, her parents were political activists who protested against the Vietnam War. Her father was an influential member of Vietnam Veterans Against the War.

The family moved to Washington, D.C., in the early 1980s, where Jessica's father worked at the Veterans Administration. Jessica grew up listening to political discussions at the dinner table; by seventh grade she was a vegetarian and feminist.

After graduating from college in Minnesota, Blank moved to New York City where she spent her time training at an acting studio, doing political organizing, attending auditions, and going to poetry slams.

When she met Erik Jensen in 2000, he had already been in New York City for almost a decade. Although there are few public sources that give much information about Jensen's family background, it is known that he grew up in rural and suburban Minnesota and after graduation from college attended an East Coast acting school. His career began in the early 1990s, and he made a living acting in independent films and television.

Blank and Jensen's interest in the death penalty began when they attended an anti-death penalty conference in 2000 held at Columbia University in New York. They heard about the group known as the Death Row Ten in Illinois who were falsely convicted following confessions extracted from them by a police commander using torture he had learned during the Vietnam War. The organizers of the workshop had arranged for one of the ten prisoners, Leonard Kidd, to call and speak directly to the audience. Blank and Jensen were moved by his story and resolved to write a play that would bring to a wider audience the issue of innocent people condemned to execution. After much discussion and research, the result was *The Exonerated*, which tells the story of six people who served time on

Jessica Blank and Erik Jensen AP Images

death row before being cleared of the crimes for which they were falsely convicted.

The Exonerated was first performed in Los Angeles by the Actors' Gang, on April 19, 2002, directed by Blank and Jensen. The play premiered in New York City on October 10, 2002, at 45 Bleecker, directed by Bob Balaban. During the course of the run, many big-name actors, including Richard Dreyfuss, Mia Farrow, Gabriel Byrne, Jill Clayburgh, and Sara Gilbert, appeared in the play. Susan Sarandon, Danny Glover, Brian Dennehy, Aidan Quinn, and Delroy Lindo starred in the adaptation of the play for Court TV. *The Exonerated* was awarded the 2003 Outer Critics Circle Award for Best Off-Broadway play, the Drama Desk and Lucille Lortel Awards for Unique Theatrical Experience, and the L.A. Ovation Award for Best World Premiere Play. It also received the Defender of Justice Award from the National Association of Criminal Defense Lawyers and Court TV's Scales of Justice Award.

As of 2006, Blank had an established career as an actor and writer; her television credits include *Law & Order*, *Criminal Intent*, *Rescue Me*, and *One Life to Live*; her film credits include *The Namesake*, directed by Mira Nair, *Undermind*, and *A Bird in Hand*. Blank's first novel, *Home*, was anticipated to be published in 2007.

As of 2006, Jensen had co-starred in more than a dozen feature films, including *The Love Letter* and *Black Knight*, and such television shows as *Love Monkey*, *Alias*, *CSI*, and *Law & Order*. His stage credits include Arthur Kopit's *Y2K* and Terrence McNally's *Corpus Christi*. He played the character Jeff in the 2005 Court TV version of *The Exonerated*.

As of 2006, Jessica Blank and Eric Jensen were married and living in Brooklyn, New York.

PLOT SUMMARY

The Exonerated takes place on a bare stage. The actors sit on armless chairs with their scripts on music stands in front of them. There are no sets or special costumes. The play is seamless; there are no blackouts and no intermission.

The first character to speak is Delbert, who acts as a kind of chorus, fading in and out of the action. He speaks in poetic phrases and spells out a warning: "It is dangerous to dwell too much on things: / to wonder who or why or when, to wonder how, is dangerous." He thinks out loud about the best way to approach the problem. Could he emulate Richard and Ralph and Langston? He is referring to African American authors who speak out boldly in their works about racism: Richard Wright, author of *Native Son* (1940) and *Black Boy* (1945); Ralph Ellison, who wrote *The Invisible Man* (1952); and Langston Hughes, one of the leading poets of the Harlem Renaissance in the 1920s and 1930s. It is not easy to be a poet, Delbert says, "Yet I sing."

After this somber beginning, the lights go up on Sue and her husband Gary. Gary tells his story. One day he went as usual to the motorcycle shop at his parents' farm. They were not there, but he thought nothing of it, since they had been planning a trip. When they had not returned the next morning, he called the police. He then found his father's body in a back room. About an hour and a half later, the police found the body of Gary's mother in a trailer in front of the house. Her throat had been slashed. Within hours, Gary had been arrested.

After some more poetic lines from Delbert, the lights go up on Robert and his wife Georgia. Robert was working as a groom at a racetrack where a white girl was raped and killed. A short scene is then acted out behind Robert, in which he is interviewed by two white policemen, who claim they know that he killed the girl.

Robert then continues. He says he had dated the murdered girl, and at his trial he knew he would be convicted, since there were eleven whites and only one black on the jury. He makes a reference to the celebrated case of O. J. Simpson in 1995, suggesting that Simpson did not commit the murder for which he was charged. He was put on trial because he was a black man and the murdered woman was white. Robert's wife, Georgia, disagrees with him, suggesting that Simpson was guilty.

The next story is told by Kerry, with his wife Sandra. In the 1970s, he was working at an apartment complex in Texas. He was walking to the swimming pool when he saw a gorgeous nude girl in a window. Two days later, he saw the same girl lying out by the pool, and they started talking. He told her he was a bartender in Dallas. They went back to her apartment and made out. He never saw her again, but three months later he was arrested for her murder.

A scene follows from Kerry's trial, in which the prosecutor explains that a fingerprint belonging to Kerry was found on the door frame of the dead girl's apartment. Kerry's defense counsel points out that it cannot be proved what time the fingerprints were made, but the prosecution continues to claim that the prints were left at the time of the murder. Kerry then explains that part of the case had been hidden for twenty years. This was the fact that Linda, the victim, had been having an affair with a professor at the university. The affair had been discovered, and he had been fired from his job. Linda's roommate, Paula, had seen a man fitting the description of the professor in Linda's apartment the night of the murder. At the trial, however, Paula identified Kerry as the man who was in the apartment.

The next story is told by David. He was still in high school when one day he was interrogated by police about a robbery at a grocery store. He repeatedly said that he knew nothing about it, but the police kept telling him what happened and trying to get him to describe it.

Sheriff Carroll is then seen explaining what happened. When he entered the store with a fellow officer, he saw three young black men. Five or six customers were tied down. The robbers demanded money from the officers and told them to lie down. But when the men tried to tie the officers up with pantyhose, the officers fought back. In the chaos that followed, eighteen or twenty bullets were fired.

Carroll was wounded, and his fellow officer was killed. The robbers disappeared.

During the interrogation, David was so frightened that he confessed to the crime, even though he did not do it. He fully expected the truth to come out.

Sunny is the next character to speak. In 1976, she had just given birth to a baby girl, fathered by her boyfriend, Jesse. She also had a nine-year old son, Eric. She drove to Florida to collect Jesse, who had no money and had no way of getting home. When she arrived, they both stayed with a friend of Jesse's named Walter Rhodes, who appeared to be involved in criminal activities. Rhodes agreed to take them to a friend's house in Broward County, but something terrible happened on the journey.

Delbert returns and tells his story. He had just dropped out of seminary and was hitch-hiking around the country. He happened to be in Florida when a man was killed and a girl raped. He was stopped and questioned by the Florida Highway Patrol, and the patrolman wrote him a note saying he was satisfied Delbert was not the man wanted in connection with the crimes. However, two weeks later Delbert was arrested in Mississippi and charged with the murder and rape, even though he fitted the description given by the victim in only one respect: he is black.

After a brief scene in which Robert and Georgia discuss racism amongst the police, the narrative returns to Sunny. Rhodes, Jesse, and she pulled off the road late at night at a rest area. The police arrived for a routine check, saw a gun at Rhode's feet, and found out that he was on parole. Possession of a gun is a parole violation. One of the policemen drew his gun; there were four shots, and the two policemen were killed. With a gun in his hand, Rhodes told Jesse and Sunny to get in the police car. They drove off, and Sunny felt as if she had been kidnapped. When they were apprehended at a roadblock, they were arrested, and Sunny was quickly charged with first-degree murder.

The play returns to Gary. He was interrogated by the police, who were convinced of his guilt. He was exhausted and confused and even began to think he might have had a blackout and actually committed the murders. Under pressure, he gave the police a hypothetical statement about what he would have done had he killed his parents. One of the policemen supplied much of the story himself, and Gary's statement was later used incorrectly as a confession, even though he stated that he had no memory of such events happening.

In the interrogation room, Sunny denied shooting anyone. They continued to question her in an

MEDIA ADAPTATIONS

- The Court TV version of *The Exonerated* (2005) was as of 2006 available on DVD. It was produced by Monterey Video and directed by Bob Balaban, and it stars Susan Sarandon, Danny Glover, Brian Dennehy, Aidan Quinn, Delroy Lindo, and David Brown Jr.

---

aggressive manner, and she said she wanted to cooperate with the investigation. Later she learned that Rhodes had negotiated a deal with the authorities. He claimed that Sunny and Jesse shot the two policemen.

Next is a scene from Sunny's trial, in which Rhodes testified that Sunny fired two or three shots at the first policeman and that Jesse then grabbed the gun, shot the policeman again, and then twice shot the second policeman. Then Rhodes said it was Jesse's decision to take the police car.

Delbert takes up his story. He voluntarily agreed to be extradited from Texas to Florida. Even though there was no evidence to tie him to the crime, he was convicted by a white jury.

After a brief scene in which Robert is appointed a public defender and Dilbert comments on how people are predisposed to see others in a certain way, the story returns to Kerry, who was presented by the prosecutors as a homosexual who hated women, even though his alleged homosexuality had nothing to do with the case against him. (In fact, Kerry was not a homosexual; he merely worked in a gay bar.) The prosecutor made a lurid, fervent speech to the jury, calling for the death penalty against Kerry.

Sunny returns. She tells of how Jesse was tried first and convicted. Sunny expected to be acquitted, but she was not. She speaks of prosecutorial misconduct, the hiding of evidence that would have proved she did not commit the murder.

The lights go down on Sunny, and up on David, the prosecuting counsel and his defense counsel. The defense counsel points out some of the misconduct in the case. David was questioned without counsel, for example, and did not hear the charges against him for five days, in spite of the fact that according to the law a defendant has the right to be taken without delay and have the charges read in open court.

Sunny recalls the moment in which the judge handed down the sentence of death, and then Delbert tells a story of how when he was at the University of Chicago, he took part in a lab experiment on the content of dreams. He remembers that they placed electrodes by his ears, the same thing that happens when a prisoner is about to be executed.

Sunny recalls the oppressive nature of the prison cell she occupied, and then David recalls how when he entered prison he had a relationship with God, but he lost it and is trying to get it back. Kerry recalls how during his time on Texas's death row, one hundred and forty-one inmates were executed. He knew every man personally. He also points out that he was not a thug but came from a good family. If it can happen to him, he says, it can happen to anyone.

Gary tells of how he kept to himself a lot because he had no gang protection. He found a sewing needle stuck in a concrete wall. It had been smuggled in, and he used it to teach himself embroidery. He even managed to use extra clothing to make himself a tote bag.

Robert shares a memory about how every week the authorities would test the electric chair, and he would hear it buzz. The guards were bullies. After Robert once agreed to sign a statement by another inmate claiming harassment by a guard, Robert found himself being harassed by the same guard. He wrote to a judge and complained about the guard, asking for a court order that would keep him away from the guard. He said in the letter that he would not submit to the harassment any longer.

Kerry reports that because he had been declared to be a homosexual, he was raped in prison. He lived in fear of his life and tried twice to commit suicide.

Delbert says that he has faith, and he refused to internalize all the anger he felt. He knew that if he did that, he would already in effect be dead.

David reports that while he was in prison, he felt the love of God for His people and was filled with religious spirit. One day when the prisoners were outside and it was raining, he commanded the rain, in the name of Jesus, to stop. The rain stopped. After it started again, David repeated the instruction to stop, and the rain stopped again. This happened three times in all. Another inmate, watching this, was amazed.

Sunny recalls the fifteen years in which she and Jesse communicated by letters. She saved them all. Jesse appears and reads a letter he wrote to Sunny in 1976, including code words in Japanese referring to sex. This exchange of letters sustained Sunny during her incarceration.

Kerry was sustained by his desire to hold on for his older brother, Doyle, who had always defended him. Doyle visited, saw Kerry's black eyes, and wanted to talk to the warden about it. But Kerry would not let him, because snitching is the worst thing a man can do in prison. So Doyle could not help him. He started drinking, his life went downhill, and in 1997, he was shot and killed outside a club in Tyler, Texas, after an earlier incident involving his friend, Jeff, and two other men. The murderer was convicted but served only three years in prison.

Sunny reports on how she refused to let her situation defeat her spirit. She found some faith, knowing there was a greater power than that which was imprisoning her and that she could appeal to that higher power.

Robert always dreamed he would get a new trial, and one day he did. At the trial, it emerged that all along the police had in their possession a sixteen-inch strand of red hair found in the dead girl's hand. The hair clearly belonged to the girl's ex-boyfriend, not to Robert.

Kerry reports that after twenty-two years on death row, he was released on DNA evidence that showed it was the victim's former boyfriend, the professor, who was the murderer. The professor was never charged.

Gary reports how a lawyer at Northwestern University took on his case. The lawyer found out that in 1995 the government got a videotaped confession from a member of a motorcycle gang that he killed Gary's parents. Gary says that two men have now been convicted of that crime, but he is adamant that they should not receive the death penalty.

Sunny reports that in 1979 Rhodes wrote to the judge. Rhodes then appears, reading his letter, in which he confesses that he was the man who shot the two policemen. Sunny points out that she was not released until 1992.

Delbert says that when he was released, he was numb and did not sleep for the first three days. Then a pastor prayed for him, and since then he has had no difficulty in sleeping. But he has had to learn how to feel again, how to be human again.

David reports that after he was released, he would lock his door at home after he returned from work, as if he were still in prison. Prison did something to him, he says, and now he is trying to find out who he really is. Sometimes he smokes marijuana and writes poetry, just as he used to do. He wants to recover his lost spirituality.

Kerry's wife, Sandra, is next. She tells of how she first met Kerry after his release, when as a member of the Dallas Peace Center she helped him reenter society. They soon married. Kerry reports that he still has nightmares as a result of his incarceration.

Robert and Georgia report that he has been out of prison for nearly four years, and they have been married for two years. He tries not to think of what he might have achieved in his life had he not been wrongly imprisoned. He is frustrated that he has been unable to get his license back for working at the racetrack.

Next, it is Sue and Gary's turn. Sue reports an incident at the market, in which a farmer implied that Gary might be guilty after all. Gary comments that everyone sees things in their own way, so it is hard to know what reality is.

Sunny explains that she got another chance because she sought it. Then she tells the horrific story of Jesse's botched execution, in which three long jolts of electricity were used, and it took thirteen and a half minutes for Jesse to die.

Delbert speaks about how a man cannot afford to give in to fear, and people should not blame all white people for what happened. He also says that in spite of the fact that the criminal justice system is broken, he thinks the United States is a great country. But people must still ask what is wrong with it and try to remedy it.

Sunny says she wants to be a living memorial, a testimony to the fact that she did not allow her experience of being wrongly convicted and condemned crush her.

The last words are given to Delbert, who repeats the words with which he began the play. In spite of the difficulty, still he sings, like a poet. As the sound of rain fades in, he tells David to sing. David raises his hand and the rain stops.

CHARACTERS

David

David is an African American man of about forty. He is described in the character notes as "A gentle, sad man." Born and raised in Florida, he is only eighteen when he is falsely convicted of murdering a policeman during a grocery store robbery. When he was a child, David had strongly developed religious feelings. He wanted to channel the power of God to cure the illness of a woman who lived across the street. In prison, he lost his sense of possessing a relationship with God and is still trying to recover it. He believes that the Kingdom of Heaven lies within, even though people tend to seek it in outer things.

David is based on the real life David Keaton.

Delbert

Delbert is a sixty-year-old African American man, a radical and a poet. According the authors' character notes, "His whole personality is like an old soul song: smooth, mellow, and with an underlying rhythm that never lets up." He is a serious, philosophical man who thinks deeply about the issues facing American society, such as racism. Delbert dropped out of a seminary and was hitchhiking across Texas, getting rides from white people and not experiencing any trouble at all until he was arrested and wrongly convicted of a murder and rape that took place in Florida.

Delbert is based on the real life Delbert Tibbs.

Doyle

Doyle is Kerry's older brother. He is murdered following an incident at a club.

Gary

Gary is a forty-five-year-old white man. He comes from the Midwest and is now an organic farmer, married to Sue. He is described in the character notes as a "hippie," who was at home in the 1960s and 1970s, and as "generally good natured, friendly, and quite smart." Gary was subjected to ruthless interrogation, and in a state of physical exhaustion and emotional distress, he confessed to killing his parents. After he is freed, he seems to remain optimistic and does not harbor feelings of revenge. He does not even advocate the death penalty for the two men who murdered his parents. He seems to have faith in God, in miracles, and in the power of DNA to establish guilt or innocence.

Gary is based on the real life Gary Gauger.

Georgia

Georgia is Robert's African American wife. She is from the South and is described in the authors' notes on the characters as "loudmouthed, outspoken, and extremely warm." She and Robert are very lively together and tend to finish each other's sentences.

Jeff

Jeff worked at a McDonald's restaurant in downtown Jacksonville. He became friends with Doyle, Kerry's brother, and witnessed Doyle's murder.

Kerry

Kerry is a forty-five-year-old white man from Texas. In 1977, at the age of nineteen, he was working as a bartender when he was arrested, tried, and convicted for a murder he did not commit. Kerry spent twenty-two years in prison and now wants to rediscover the world. The character notes state that he "always wants to make sure he connects with whomever he is talking to." Kerry married Sandra after he was released. She remarks that he is "really nineteen at heart."

Kerry's case is based on the actual case of Kerry Cook.

Robert

Robert is an African American man in his thirties. He was a horse groomer in the Deep South when he was wrongly convicted of murdering a white girl whom he had dated. Described as "hardened but not lacking a sense of humor," he is married to Georgia. He expresses optimism that there is less racism in the United States now than there was when he was convicted by a jury consisting of eleven white men and only one black man.

Robert is based on the real life Robert Earl Hayes.

Sandra

Sandra, a forty-year-old white woman, is married to Kerry. She is described as "sweet, nurturing," with a great sense of humor about her husband. Before she met Kerry, she says, she was "very conservative." She had a family member murdered and is a firm believer in capital punishment. But when she heard Kerry's story after he had been released, she wondered how such a thing could happen.

Sue

Sue is Gary's wife. She is a solid, reliable woman who speaks with a strong upper-Midwest accent.

Sunny

Sunny is a fifty-year-old white woman who is now a yoga teacher, living in California. The authors'

character notes state that Sunny's "lightness and positivity contrast with moments of great depth and clarity." She was wrongly convicted in 1976 of killing a policeman and was not freed until 1992. She shows courage and optimism during her long ordeal, in spite of the fact that during her incarceration her parents died, her two children grew up without her, and her husband Jesse Tefero, who was also wrongly convicted, was executed.

Sunny is based on the real life Sonia Jacobs.

THEMES

Faith and Hope

Although the play is a somber one, several of the characters give expression to their faith and hope. Sunny, for example, tells of how, during her imprisonment, she resolved not to feel sorry for herself. She had a great realization:

> I wasn't just a little lump of flesh that they could put in a cage. And I decided that I would have faith, that there was some power out there greater than them, to which I could make my appeal.

This faith gave her the strength to carry on.

Robert clings to hope because of a dream he had before he went to prison, in which he saw himself on death row and also saw himself released from it. "And 'cause a that dream, I always said, I'm gonna get a new trial." Sure enough, this is exactly what happened.

Delbert comes across as a strong man who has always been able to cope with whatever happened to him. He also mentions faith, although he acknowledges that sometimes it is not easy to maintain it:

> I don't know if I have the patience of Job—but I hope I have his faith. Even if you got a teeny-weeny bit, it's big. The s——is hard to come by, you know what I'm saying?

Sunny, Robert, and Delbert do not use their faith to gloss over what happened to them. They remain clear-eyed and realistic about the harm they suffered as a result of their wrongful incarceration. But they are also clear about what helped them through it.

By contrast, David, who had always had strong religious feelings, lost his faith while he was in prison. He has not forgotten that such a thing exists, however, and says, "I guess I'm still reachin' out to find it." He still knows in his heart that "the kingdom of God is within you," but there is no escaping the fact that his story is one not of hope but

TOPICS FOR FURTHER STUDY

- Do you support capital punishment? Write an essay in which you examine the arguments for and against the death penalty. Give reasons for the position you take.

- Make a class presentation in which you advocate for or against the death penalty. Take a poll before and afterwards to see if your presentation has caused any of your classmates to change his or her opinion.

- Since 1976, about 34 percent of people executed in the United States have been African American, three times the proportion of African Americans in the population. Almost 42 percent of current inmates on death row are African American. Investigate the influence of race on death penalty cases and make a class presentation with your findings.

- Create a courtroom scene in class. A defendant has been found guilty of murder and may face the death penalty. Describe the basic facts of the crime and the defendant. Choose whether you want to play the role of defense lawyer, pleading for your client's life, or the prosecutor, calling for the death penalty. The rest of the class acts as jury and votes on the sentence.

---

of loss. Near the end of the play, he talks about pictures of himself taken when he was in high school. In the photograph, he is smiling, but now "that's somethin' that people round here don't see me do too much, smile."

Racism

Racism in the criminal justice system is a recurring theme. Three of the exonerated characters are African American, and in at least two of their cases, racism is a factor in their arrest and conviction. Delbert knew all about racism when he attended the seminary, where it is "so pervasive you could cut it with a knife." He notes that the only way he resembled the descriptions of the suspect in the murder and rape case was that they were both black. He also points out the imbalance in jury selection, since juries are selected from voting rolls, and in 1974, black people in Florida had only had the right to vote since passage of the Voting Rights Act in 1965, so they were underrepresented on any jury in the "backwater town" in which he was tried. He alludes also to presumption of guilt that lay upon any black defendant in his situation: "If you're accused of a sex crime in the South and you're black, you probably shoulda done it, you know, 'cause your ass is gonna be guilty." But Delbert also stresses, as does Georgia, that not all whites should be regarded as racist.

Robert is also aware of the racism that helped to produce the miscarriage of justice in which he was a victim. He comments on the fact that he dated the white girl who was later murdered and that did not go down well with people in Mississippi, who did not approve of interracial couples. He says, "I might as well be wearin' a sign that says ARREST ME. I'M BLACK." Robert also knows he is going to be convicted when he sees that the jury is composed of eleven whites and only one black. In addition, he mentions a significant incident not directly related to his arrest. He was sitting talking with a white man at a gas station when a white policeman approached and asked the white man if he was having a problem. The policeman did not pose the question the other way round; he just assumed that Robert, being black, was harassing the white man. Robert's wife, Georgia, comments that racism is one of those things that are passed down from generation to generation and will never go away.

STYLE

Documentary Theater

The play belongs to the genre known as documentary theater, in which contemporary social issues are explored, often from a leftist or liberal standpoint, by the artful use of nonfiction materials, such as interview and court trial transcripts, speeches, articles, public hearings, and the like. The purpose of documentary theater is to challenge the audience to examine a particular social issue, such as an inequitable political system or social structure, abuse of power by those in authority, or other issues relating to class, race, gender, or sexual orientation.

The authors of *The Exonerated* interviewed many former death row prisoners and recorded hundreds of hours of audio tapes, which they then converted into typed transcripts. They also studied court transcripts and case files. As they write in the introduction to the play, "We spent countless hours in dusty courthouse record rooms, pawing through thousands of microfiche files and cardboard boxes full of affidavits, depositions, police interrogations, and courtroom testimony." Then they shaped and edited these voluminous and unwieldy documents into a ninety-minute play. Almost every word comes from the public record or from an interview the authors conducted. The result is a dramatic work that uses everyday language as spoken by real people, the stories of real people having been shaped by the dramatists into a theatrical form.

Although modern documentary theater was pioneered by German dramatists Bertolt Brecht and Erwin Piscator in the 1920s, the genre is as old as theater itself and can be dated back to 492 B.C.E., when the ancient Greek playwright Phrynichus wrote *The Capture of Miletus*, a play about the Persian War. Contemporary American dramatists who work in this genre include Mark Wolf, Emily Mann, Anna Deavere Smith, and Eve Ensler.

HISTORICAL CONTEXT

The Death Penalty in the United States

Historically, application of the death penalty has waxed and waned in the United States. In the 1930s, there was an average of one hundred and sixty-seven executions a year. But by the 1960s, opinion worldwide had shifted in favor of the abolition of capital punishment. In the period from 1960 to 1976, the number of executions in the United States fell to an average of between twelve and thirteen per year. In 1972, the Supreme Court ruled that death penalty statutes in forty states were unconstitutional. The Court also commuted the sentence of six hundred and twenty-nine prisoners on death row. However, Florida, Georgia, and Texas,

states in which the death penalty had been firmly entrenched, rewrote their laws, and in 1976, the Supreme Court upheld them. The Court also declared that capital punishment was not in itself unconstitutional. This set the stage for the resumption of executions in 1977, and the number of executions grew steadily. In the 1980s, one hundred and seventeen people were executed in the United States. In the 1990s, the figure rose sharply to four hundred and seventy-eight. The most executions were in Texas, Virginia, Oklahoma, Missouri, and Florida.

However, during this period, the Supreme Court established some limitations on capital punishment. In 1986, the Court banned the execution of insane people. In 2002, in *Atkins v. Virginia*, the Court declared that execution of mentally retarded people amounted to cruel and unusual punishment and was, therefore, in violation of the Eighth Amendment. This constituted a reversal of a 1989 Supreme Court ruling that had upheld the constitutionality of the execution of retarded persons.

Several rulings in the 1980s dealt with the execution of juveniles. In 1989, the Supreme Court held that the Eighth Amendment does not prohibit the death penalty for crimes committed at the age of sixteen or seventeen. Between 1985 and 2002, twenty-one men who were seventeen or under at the time they committed the crime were executed. It was not until 2005 that the Supreme Court, in *Roper v. Simmons*, struck down the death penalty for juveniles.

However, during the 1990s and beyond, there were growing doubts in the United States about the fairness of the death penalty and the validity of the process by which defendants are tried and convicted. Such doubts were created by the fact that between 1973 and 2002, according to the Death Penalty Information Center in Washington, D.C., one hundred and three people were freed from death row where they had been incarcerated for crimes they did not commit. Many of these cases, particularly in the later years, involved the use of DNA evidence, in which it was demonstrated beyond doubt that the convicted individual did not commit the crime.

In 1998, Northwestern University School of Law held a National Conference on Wrongful Convictions and the Death Penalty. The conference was attended by twenty-eight former prisoners freed from death row. In January 2000, Illinois governor George Ryan, concerned about the fact that thirteen men had been released from death row in Illinois over the previous few years, declared a moratorium on executions and appointed a blue-ribbon Commission on Capital Punishment to study the issue.

In 2002, the commission reported that the state's justice system concerning the death penalty was badly flawed. The commission made eighty-five recommendations for reform, including guaranteed access to DNA testing, mandatory videotaping of the interrogation of murder suspects, and improved training for defense lawyers. However, over the following months, the Illinois legislature made no progress in putting these changes into law.

In mid-December, there was a special performance of *The Exonerated* in Chicago, Illinois, in the context of a conference about death row inmates who had been released, sponsored by the Center on Wrongful Convictions. The performance was attended by Governor Ryan.

Blank and Jensen, in their book *Living Justice*, which tells the story of how *The Exonerated* came to be written, describe their reactions when they heard that Governor Ryan would be attending a performance of their play:

> We were blown away, honored, and totally humbled. Governor Ryan was in the midst of making a decision that would affect the lives of hundreds of people. He had opened up a dialogue with thousands of experts on both sides. And now *we* were going to get to be a part of that conversation?

After the play ended that night, Jensen introduced Governor Ryan to the audience and read a statement imploring him to "err on the side of life."

A month later, just before he left office, Governor Ryan granted clemency to all of the one hundred and sixty-seven death row inmates in Illinois. He commuted the sentences to life imprisonment. Governor Ryan made a statement, quoted in Stanley Cohen's book, *The Wrong Men*, that all the cases

> raised questions not only about the innocence of people on death row, but about the fairness of the death-penalty system as a whole. Our capital system is haunted by the demon of error: error in determining guilt and error in determining who among the guilty deserves to die.

Governor Ryan also granted full pardons to six men, including Gary Gauger, one of the characters featured in *The Exonerated*.

CRITICAL OVERVIEW

Reviewers were unanimous in praise of *The Exonerated* when it opened at New York's 45 Bleecker

Theater in 2002. Ben Brantley in the *New York Times* describes the play as "intense and deeply affecting." Commenting on the fact that the purpose of the play was obviously to shake the complacency of those who believed that such things could not happen in the United States, Brantley adds that in spite of this clear mission

> There is no reek of piety or creak of didacticism about *The Exonerated.* . . . It is, on its own terms, thoroughly involving theater, while reminding you that real life has a way of coming up with resonant metaphors, grotesque ironies and cruel coincidences that no dramatist would dare invent.

In *Newsweek*, Marc Peyser drew attention to the perhaps surprising success of such a no-frills, somber play at the box office. *The Exonerated*, he writes, "has become one of the hottest tickets in New York, even though its artfully woven testimonials of people freed from death row is hardly your light evening out."

John Lahr, in the *New Yorker*, was also appreciative of what he called the "harrowing stories" told in the play. He writes that *The Exonerated* "bear[s] witness both to the ineptness of the American judicial system and to the poetry of ordinary citizens. . . . Its stories are stark and riveting and cunningly orchestrated." Charles Isherwood, writing in *Variety*, expressed a similar verdict. He writes that the play is "disturbing and even grueling"; it amply fulfills one of the purposes of art, which is "bearing witness to human suffering." Isherwood argues that the early part of the play, in which the arrests and convictions are presented, is not as strong as it might be. With its collection of "mendacious lawyers, benighted judges and corrupt police officers, the show tips inevitably into caricature," he writes. The strongest portions of the play come later, the "plain-spoken reflections from the wrongfully imprisoned." Isherwood concludes:

> The play is a devastating memorial to injustice, but it also pays handsome tribute to the resilience of human hearts and minds. Having endured misfortunes it might be more comfortable to forget, the people depicted here chose to tell their stories, in the hope that one day there will be no more such stories to tell. The least we can do is listen.

As of 2006, four years after the first performance, the theater-going public was still listening; a new production of the play was performed at Theater Works in Hartford, Connecticut, from February to March, 2006. It seemed likely that audiences would be listening to these disturbing stories for some years to come.

Delroy Lindo, Susan Sarandon and Aidan Quinn, who portray the real-life subjects of The Exonerated, *are shown with Kerry Max Cook, one of the people depicted in the play* AP Images

CRITICISM

Bryan Aubrey

Aubrey holds a Ph.D. in English and has published many essays on drama. In the following essay, he discusses the ways in which the operation of the criminal justice system may result in innocent people being convicted.

Although over half the countries in the world have abolished capital punishment, the United States continues to use it, and a consistent majority of Americans support it. A 2004 Harris poll found that 69 percent favored the use of capital punishment, even though only 41 percent thought it was a deterrent. Thirty-six percent favored an increase in the number of executions. However, few people who have investigated the issue in depth can remain quite so sanguine about the criminal justice system in capital cases. The problems with the system, which are dramatized so effectively in *The Exonerated*, fall broadly into six main categories, as described in Stanley Cohen's book, *The Wrong Men: America's Epidemic of Wrongful Death Row Convictions*: eyewitness error; corrupt practices within the legal system; jailhouse informants who lie; false confessions; inadequate or poorly applied science (often known as "junk science"); and lack of evidence.

Eyewitness error is a common cause of invalid convictions. Although most jurors tend to believe eyewitness testimony, studies have shown that it is accurate in only about 50 percent of cases. It turns out that people do not have very accurate recall of people they may have seen for just a few fleeting seconds, often from a fair distance away, and sometimes in darkness. Also, people remember information less well when they are in stressful situations, such as witnessing a violent incident or a murder. An analysis of wrongful convictions since the restoration of capital punishment in 1976, conducted in 2001 by the Center on Wrongful Convictions at Northwestern University, concluded that erroneous eyewitness testimony, whether offered in good faith or perjured, was the most frequent cause of wrongful convictions in the U.S. criminal justice system. The center analyzed the cases of eighty-six defendants who had been sentenced to death but legally exonerated based on strong claims of innocence. Of those eighty-six, eyewitness testimony played a role in the convictions of forty-six—over half of the total. In thirty-two of those forty-six cases, only one eyewitness testified.

Also, eyewitness testimony was the only evidence against thirty-three defendants (38.4 percent).

Eyewitness error was a factor in the conviction of Delbert Tibbs, one of the characters in *The Exonerated*. The rape victim, Cynthia Nadeau, identified Tibbs from a Polaroid photo shown to her by police, even though Tibbs did not match the original description she gave. She also picked Tibbs out of a police lineup. But as both the play and Stanley Cohen point out, nothing else about the case supported Nadeau's story. There was no physical evidence against Tibbs, and no witnesses could place him anywhere near the place where the crime took place. The case against Robert Earl Hayes (Robert in *The Exonerated*) was also boosted by eyewitness testimony that later turned out to be false. Ironically, one of the characters in the play, David, who was only eighteen at the time and still in high school, shows a naïve faith in eye witness testimony. When he is coerced into confessing, he reassures himself that the eye witnesses to the crime will know he did not do it "'cause I just wasn't there and they would have seen that." He assumes that these witnesses will testify in court that he was not the robber. Unfortunately for David Keaton, the system did not work quite like that. Not a single eyewitness said at the trial that David was not the man they had seen.

According to Cohen, the second category of error that produces false convictions, corrupt practices, includes such factors as police perjury, prosecutors who withhold evidence that might benefit the defense, and incompetent defense counsel. Prosecutorial misconduct was the major factor in the false conviction of Kerry Cook. After Cook's conviction was overturned in 1991 and his retrial in 1992 had resulted in a hung jury, a state district judge ruled in 1993 that prosecutors had suppressed key evidence. This made no difference to the outcome of his third trial in 1994, when he was convicted and again sentenced to death. In 1996, the Texas Court of Criminal Appeals reversed the conviction, citing prosecutorial and police misconduct. The case against Cook rested largely on a fingerprint of his found on the door of the victim's home. A fingerprint expert testified that the print had been left only twelve hours before the body was discovered. However, it is not scientifically possible to date a fingerprint, and the expert later admitted that he had been coerced by the district attorney's office to testify otherwise.

Cook also had poor legal representation. In *The Exonerated*, the character Kerry points out that when a witness who had originally said she had seen someone else in the victim's apartment on the

> **MOST JURIES WILL CONVICT A DEFENDANT IF HE HAS CONFESSED TO THE CRIME, EVEN IF THERE IS COMPELLING EVIDENCE TO THE CONTRARY. PEOPLE MAY CONFESS TO SOMETHING THEY DID NOT DO FOR A VARIETY OF REASONS, BUT SOMETIMES SUCH CONFESSIONS RESULT FROM PSYCHOLOGICAL COERCION TACTICS USED DURING POLICE INTERROGATIONS."**

night of the crime, changed her testimony and points in the courtroom at Kerry as the man who was there, his lawyer did not even challenge her statement. He adds, "My court-appointed attorney was the former DA who jailed me twice before. He was paid five hundred dollars by the state, and in Texas you get what you pay for." Such things happen not only in Texas. Most defendants in capital cases cannot afford a lawyer, so the court provides one for them. These cases are complex and require much expertise and experience on the part of the defense counsel, but states provide little in the way of compensation. The result is that people on trial for their lives frequently are represented by inexperienced and sometimes incompetent lawyers. In one notorious case in 1989, a court-appointed lawyer in Alabama was found to be drunk during a capital trial. He was held in contempt and jailed.

The case of Robert Earl Hayes also contains an example of corrupt practices. Blank and Jensen, in their book *Living Justice*, discuss this case in more detail than they were able to do in the play. "Evidence was lost, mishandled, contaminated— and investigated incorrectly," they write. In their own investigations, Blank and Jensen found sworn testimony from one of the investigators at the crime scene that "they had been instructed to look only for 'Negro hairs.'" Because of this, the police ignored the fact that the victim was clutching in her hand

WHAT DO I READ NEXT?

- *Twelve Angry Men* (1955), by Richard Rose, takes place entirely within a jury room in New York City. Eleven jurors believe that the defendant in a capital murder case is guilty, but the twelfth juror is not convinced. Eventually he brings the others round to his way of thinking. The play is particularly interesting for what it reveals about the fallibility of eyewitness testimony, an issue that is also relevant in *The Exonerated*.

- Marc Wolf is an American dramatist who writes documentary plays. His *Another American: Asking and Telling* is about gays and the military. The title refers to the "don't ask, don't tell" policy in the U.S. military regarding homosexuality. Wolf interviewed dozens of military personnel, and the play tells of their experiences. He also includes some opinions of anti-gay people. The play can be found in *Political Stages: Plays that Shaped a Century*, edited by Emily Mann and David Roessel and published by Applause Books in 2002.

- Emily Mann is an American playwright known for her documentary plays that explore issues of social justice. Her book *Testimonies: Four Plays* (1996) contains *Annulla*, a play about the Holocaust; *Still Life*, about the Vietnam War; *Execution of Justice*, based on the assassination of Harvey Milk, mayor of San Francisco, and an openly gay supervisor; and *Greensboro: A Requiem*, based on the 1979 North Carolina riot in which an anti-Klan rally turned into a Klan killing spree.

- *Voicings: Ten Plays from the Documentary Theater* (1995), edited by Attilio Favorini, professor of theater arts at the University of Pittsburgh, is a collection of the most important twentieth-century documentary plays, some published here for the first time. The book also features a thirty-thousand-word history of documentary theater.

- The Death Penalty Information Center, with its headquarters in Washington, D.C., maintains a comprehensive, up-to-date website at http://www.deathpenaltyinfo.org that covers many issues associated with capital punishment.

---

clumps of sixteen-inch long Caucasian hair, which presumably she had torn from the head of her attacker. But this vital piece of evidence was ignored by police and was never tested. The tireless work by Hayes's lawyer, a public defender named Barbara Heyer, won him a new trial in 1997; at that trial, the sixteen-inch-long hair was found to belong to a man named Scott, who was already in prison for another rape and murder committed at a racetrack. Hayes was acquitted.

The third category of error identified by Cohen, jailhouse informants who have a motive to present false information, applies to the case of Sonia Jacobs (Sunny in the play). Cohen describes how the process works with these "jailhouse snitches," who are more formally known as "incentivised witnesses":

> They offer courtroom testimony for the prosecution in exchange for an incentive, usually the dropping of a criminal charge or its reduction to a lesser charge.

> If the witness is already incarcerated, he is likely to have his sentence reduced or his parole accelerated.

The Center on Wrongful Convictions has conducted a study on the one hundred and eleven people who were released from death row since capital punishment was resumed in 1977. The center found that fifty-one of those people (45.9 percent) had been convicted on the basis of incentivised witnesses. That makes snitches the leading cause of wrongful convictions in U.S. capital cases.

In the case of Sonia Jacobs, as well as her husband Jesse Tafero, the incentivised witness was Walter Rhodes, a man with a prison record who knew how to manipulate the system. He arranged for a plea bargain in which he would receive three life sentences and immunity from the death penalty in exchange for testifying against Jacobs and Tafero. Later, in 1979, he recanted his testimony—his letter doing so became part of *The Exonerated*—and admitted that he was the person who fired the fatal shots at the two policemen. Over the years, Rhodes recanted his story, then reiterated it, and told several different versions of what happened that day. In 1981, Jacobs's sentence was commuted to life imprisonment, but the unreliability of Rhodes's testimony did nothing to save Tafero, who was executed in 1990. Jacobs was more fortunate. As Cohen reports in *The Wrong Men*, a childhood friend of Jacobs named Micki Dickoff took an interest in the case and did some research. She found that Rhodes had failed a polygraph test but the result had been withheld from the defense. A federal appeals court had determined that only Rhodes could have fired the gun. Also, "The testimony of the state's witnesses was found to be false. The prosecution had suppressed the statement of a prison guard that corroborated Rhodes's recantation of his original testimony."

False confessions are another source of error in capital cases. According to Cohen, of convictions that have been reversed using infallible DNA evidence, 20 percent involved false confessions. Most juries will convict a defendant if he has confessed to the crime, even if there is compelling evidence to the contrary. People may confess to something they did not do for a variety of reasons, but sometimes such confessions result from psychological coercion tactics used during police interrogations. One technique is known as "hypothetical questioning," in which the police ask the suspect questions such as, "If you were going to do the crime, what method would you have used?" The suspect's answers are then manipulated to make it appear that he is confessing to actually having committed the crime. This method is clearly demonstrated in *The Exonerated* in the interrogation of Gary Gauger. He was put under extreme pressure, not being allowed to sleep or lie down. After some hours, during which the interrogators repeatedly said they knew he committed the murders, Gauger started to think that maybe he had had a blackout and was indeed guilty. He agreed to give what the police called a "'vision statement'— a hypothetical account of what I would have done if I had killed my parents." That account was then used as a confession, and nothing Gauger said in denial of it made any difference, even though, as he states in the play, his "vision statement" was not recorded or written down.

Despite the fact that there was no physical evidence linking Gauger to the crime, he was charged with a double murder, convicted, and sentenced to death in January 1994. The sentence was reduced on appeal to life in prison. In 1996, the Second

District Illinois Appellate Court ordered a new trial, holding that Gauger's so-called confession resulted from an arrest made without probable cause and, therefore, should not have been admitted at the trial. Since without the "confession" there was no evidence against Gauger, the charges were dropped and he was freed.

The Exonerated contains a second example of a false confession, that of David Keaton. In 1971, Keaton was interrogated for nearly a week without access to an attorney. He was not even allowed to call his mother. He claimed in an interview with Blank and Jensen that his interrogators threatened to kill him: "They said I could die right there. Or they'd put me in prison so far I'd never get out." He eventually confessed just as a way to get out of the situation he was in, naively believing that the truth would come out at the trial. He was wrong. He spent two years on death row before the Florida Supreme Court reversed the conviction on appeal, on the grounds that exculpatory evidence had been withheld by the prosecution. Three other men were later convicted of the crime for which Keaton had been incarcerated.

Cohen's next category of errors relates to "junk science," in which a defendant is convicted on the basis of scientific conclusions that do not hold up under close, objective examination. This can include, according to Cohen, "faulty ballistics technology, inaccurate medical diagnoses, and testimony induced under hypnosis." *The Exonerated* contains a textbook example of junk science in the case of Robert (Robert Earl Hayes). Hayes was convicted in part on a DNA test, but in 1995, the Florida Supreme Court ruled, as Cohen writes, "that the band-shifting technique used to identify the DNA had failed to reach the level of scientific acceptance." New DNA testing established that Hayes's DNA did not match the DNA found at the crime scene.

The last category Cohen identifies, which overlaps with the others, includes the cases in which there is insufficient evidence to prove a defendant's guilt beyond a reasonable doubt, which is the standard required in a criminal case. Cohen argues that in these cases, the justice system has lost sight of the fact that the burden of proof rests on the prosecution; the defendant is presumed innocent until proven guilty. Cohen fears that in many cases a jury has convicted on the basis of reasonable suspicion rather than reasonable doubt.

All the cases in *The Exonerated* fit into this category of lack of evidence. Since the six people represented in the play did not commit the crimes for which they were convicted, it almost goes without saying that there was no evidence against them that would stand up to full and fair scrutiny. That the justice system finally corrected its errors and freed them seems small compensation for the many years of unnecessary suffering they endured.

Source: Bryan Aubrey, Critical Essay on *The Exonerated*, in *Drama for Students*, Thomson Gale, 2007.

Klay Dyer

Dyer holds a Ph.D. in English literature and has published extensively on literature, film, and television. He is also a freelance university teacher, writer, and educational consultant. In the following essay, he analyzes The Exonerated *in terms of philosopher Michel Foucault's discussion of imprisonment and capital punishment in* Discipline and Punish: The Birth of the Prison *(1975).*

In his seminal study *Discipline and Punish: The Birth of the Prison* (1975), Michel Foucault discusses the transition within Western culture from what he describes as a social model of punishment toward a more subtle, and ultimately more powerful, model of discipline. In a culture shaped by a philosophy of punishment, Foucault argues, those individuals found guilty of crimes were subject to very public penalties, ranging from floggings through the spectacle of public execution by hanging or beheading.

Within the later, ostensibly more civil model, the criminal's body is kept whole but is at the same time wholly isolated within a labyrinthine system of incarceration, the early versions of the modern prison. Rather than punishing the body directly for the crimes that have been charged against it, this disciplinary system repositioned the incarcerated body within a new economy that saw the suspension of freedom as the most effective treatment of the transgressive spirit.

But as Blank and Jensen's documentary play *The Exonerated* shows, the movement toward a more private model of discipline did not erase the theatrics of punishment totally from the cultural stage. Rather the new model revised the terms by which the criminalized body would be manipulated and, eventually, put to death. Removed from the fields of public vision, executions of Death Row inmates have become orchestrated events overseen by doctors, chaplains, psychiatrists, media representatives, and invited guests. There is, Foucault argues throughout his study, a new morality to the act of execution, and it is one, ironically, that has erased not only the spectacle of the punishment but

the opportunity for a final sounding of the victim's voice. Hidden deep within the walls of the prison or removed to a designated outbuilding, the person to be executed body is both silenced and killed. Gone is the opportunity for a final protest or for making amends to the crowd, or for confronting the ironies of the execution proper. All that is left is the official proclamation of the death of the incarcerated body.

It is this echoing silence that *The Exonerated* seeks to address as it traces the arrest, imprisonment, and eventual exoneration and release of five men and one woman. Presented as a stage reading, with actors seated in a row on stools, their bodies visible behind music stands that hold their scripts, the staging of the play is eerily regimented. Each character's body is carefully partitioned, with each individual in his or her own place, and each place with its own individual. Audience members are positioned, in part, as wardens of this theatrical site, given the power to recognize and monitor the effects of imprecise distributions, sudden movements or disappearances, and to signal breaches of the imagined barriers separating one cell from the next.

Discomforting, too, is the recognition that the audience is sitting in judgment of the bodies themselves, assessing the movements of each individual and calculating its qualities and merits. The functionality of the theatrical space leads organically to the analytical, quasi-judicial organization that positions the audience as watcher, warden, and judge. This unsettling relationship is underscored in some productions by the use of spotlights and the sounds of shots ringing out, cell doors clanging open and shut, and helicopters circling as if in search of an escaping prisoner.

Drawn to the spectacle of the play itself, the audience is cast in an ambiguous role, not unlike those who centuries earlier had assembled to witness the public hangings or listen for the clatter of the guillotine. The audience witnesses the confinements and tortures inscribed in the name of the common good, and they confront the humanity of such measures with their own eyes. They *see* the bodies of the incarcerated once again raised upon the scaffold of a stage rather than hidden away in Death Row. Whereas hidden executions are, in a sense, privileged executions, this restaging of the incarcerated body forces the audience to take part in both the injustices of the imprisonment and the revolutions of the exoneration. But above all, the audience is drawn closer than ever before to those who have paid the ultimate penalty, to those who have given over their bodies to a system implemented to guarantee the safety of those sitting in the seats looking in.

This staging is a reminder of the physical nature of the punishment weighing in upon the characters of five men and one woman, three of whom are African American and three of whom are Caucasian. The regimentation of space is subverted as each person responds emotionally. In one scene, for instance, the character of Sunny Jacobs is delighted when an ensemble actor reads a letter in which her inmate husband Jesse Tafero uses their private coded words to express intimate thoughts. Her reactions are much darker when she recounts the details of Tafero's execution in 1990, two years before the evidence proving his innocence was uncovered.

But as Delbert Tibbs reminds the audience, although bodies are imprisoned, voices are not. Arrested in 1974 and convicted of the murder of a white man and the rape of his young girlfriend in Florida, Tibbs was sentenced to death despite the fact that even his physical description did not match what turned out to be the fabricated story of the female victim. He was, put simply, a body in the wrong place at the wrong time in a punishing culture in which color blindness is a promise yet unfulfilled. A poet in both voice and spirit, Tibbs provides a foundational voice to the various narratives that emerge and blend in the play.

As the stories unfold, the evidence accumulates, exposing both the injustices of the U.S. penal system and the failings of those carcerated. In remembering the judicial proceedings raised against them, many of the exonerated speak, for instance, of the ambiguous physical evidence used against them. Kerry Max Cook, for instance, was the longest tenured Death Row inmate to be freed. Exonerated by conclusive DNA evidence, he carried with him the bodily reminders of prison rapes and suicide attempts. (As he recounts in graphic detail, following one such assault, Cook's attackers carved obscenities deep into his buttocks.) Robert Earl Hayes (convicted of rape and murder) was convicted on the basis of faulty science and was exonerated when suppressed evidence of the assailant's hair was taken into consideration.

As the play moves to its emotional close, the incarcerated bodies of *The Exonerated* are reimagined as a metaphor of emergence, a resistance to the theatrics of punishment and the regimentation of space that defines the stage. It is a reimagining that collapses the cells that have marked the stage

> " AS THE PLAY MOVES TO ITS EMOTIONAL CLOSE, THE INCARCERATED BODIES OF *THE EXONERATED* ARE REIMAGINED AS A METAPHOR OF EMERGENCE, A RESISTANCE TO THE THEATRICS OF PUNISHMENT AND THE REGIMENTATION OF SPACE THAT DEFINES THE STAGE."

and makes each member of the audience accountable both politically and emotionally for the stories that have been shared and the scars that remain as reminders of the dangerous legacy of punishment.

Source: Klay Dyer, Critical Essay on *The Exonerated*, in *Drama for Students*, Thomson Gale, 2007.

Brian Gilmore

In the following review, Gilmore comments on the docu-style presentation and the "relentless first-person testimony" that engulfs observers in The Exonerated, *forcing them to examine the play's controversial topic.*

After appearing in a recent performance of Jessica Blank and Erik Jensen's documentary drama *The Exonerated*, actor Ben Vereen signed poetry books in the lobby of New York City's Bleecker Theater. Vereen hadn't written the books himself. The author was the person he portrays in the play, Delbert Tibbs, who spent years on death row. When I bought my copy of Tibbs' *Songs Singing Songs*, I asked Vereen why he took the role.

"The message is so important," he stated emphatically.

Vereen is not the only famous actor who feels that way. Since *The Exonerated* began its New York run in October 2002, Tim Robbins, Robert Vaughn, Susan Sarandon, Connie Britton, Brian Dennehy, and Peter Gallagher have all appeared on the Bleecker Theater stage.

Over the past three decades, at least 111 individuals on death row in America have been found to be innocent. These men and women weren't freed on legal technicalities or because of lost evidence. They were freed because they didn't commit the crimes that landed them there. Yet somehow, they were arrested, convicted, and sentenced to die, and some came awfully close to execution. Some lost more than 20 years of their lives.

This fall, people across the country will finally be able to see *The Exonerated* for themselves when the play begins a multicity U.S. tour. Stops include Orlando, New Orleans, Seattle, and even Fort Worth, in the heart of the most efficient state-sponsored killing zone of all, Texas.

The Exonerated is a simple play consisting of six independent stories told in documentary style. Five men. One woman. All were on death row in the United States at one time. Their own words make up the play's script.

"Every word you hear comes from the people represented on stage," a voice announces, and the play begins. Ten high black chairs that look like bar stools are sitting on a dark stage. Eight of them sit in a line flanked by two other chairs elevated on each end of the stage. Ten actors take the seats— some have dual parts—and recount their journeys through life, death, justice, and then back into the world as free Americans. Except for occasional sounds (music, gunshots, jail bars slamming), this is the show. But that hardly suggests the emotional experience that awaits many in the audience.

Playwrights Jessica Blank and Erik Jensen, now married, insist they are actors and not writers. But these two New Yorkers have managed to succeed at the literary genre often described as the most difficult to master.

"We were at a conference at Columbia University in the spring of 2000 in a workshop about the Death Row 10," Blank says, referring to a group of people in Illinois who had been tortured by Chicago police into confessing to crimes they hadn't committed. "We were at the workshop on those cases, and one of the guys on death row calls by phone and begins to tell his story."

In the middle of the call, the prison guards cut the caller off. "It was a very emotional moment," she says. "The whole room was crying."

Inspired to share this wrenching experience with those who might not normally care about such issues, Blank and Jensen began corresponding with former death row prisoners. A few months later, they went on the road to interview 20 former death row inmates who had been exonerated. By October 2000, they

had written enough text to try out an early version of the play. They pushed themselves through 17-hour days to offer a series of readings over three nights in New York, but despite a lot of positive feedback, they knew they still had more work to do.

"We realized we had to tell the story more fully," Blank says. Which meant researching the actual trials. She estimates that they read 250,000 pages of court transcripts all over the country. "Every place we visited, everyone thought we were law students," she says. With help from various defense attorneys and others connected to the cases, they eventually spliced together a free-flowing, highly emotional saga detailing the destruction of six ordinary lives.

Aesthetically, the key to *The Exonerated* is the relentless first-person testimony. Except for the lack of a narrator, the feel of it is like something you'd see on PBS's *Frontline* documentary series. The stage lights shine upon an actor, who begins to speak, and the knowledge that the words are taken from an interview with a living, breathing person engulfs you.

Given the play's compelling nature, you're apt to quickly forget that the actor is Ben Vereen; you are meeting Delbert Tibbs. Robert Vaughn is Gary Gauger, sentenced to death in 1994 for killing his parents, then exonerated in 1996. Connie Britton is Sunny Jacobs, sentenced to death in 1976, exonerated and released in 1992. As each person's story fades, another resumes, until you're left wondering how the justice system could have broken down so many times.

And the answer is there on the stage as well: overzealous prosecutors, ruthless law enforcement officers, lying witnesses, the deliberate withholding of evidence, coerced confessions, and public hysteria. But in one case after another, the most important source of injustice reveals itself to be the lack of resources needed to provide a proper defense for these hapless people accused of capital crimes.

Eventually, *The Exonerated* reaches that joyous part where the people portrayed explain how they finally won their freedom. The play stands as a symbol of how America's system of capital punishment is slowly losing its credibility. Death-penalty defense projects around the country are taking on new cases and finding all kinds of problems. DNA technology has freed a number of wrongly imprisoned people. Meanwhile, rising public concern is leading to greater scrutiny, forcing lawmakers and political leaders to move cautiously before they allow someone to be put to death.

The Exonerated accomplishes what a newspaper op-ed piece rarely if ever does: It gets people talking to each other about capital punishment. Blank and Jensen report that death-penalty supporters who have seen the play have come up to them afterwards to say they are rethinking their position.

Blank has given some thought to the play's upcoming performance in Texas. She is acutely aware that this is the state where President Bush presided over 152 executions when he was governor.

"It will be interesting to see," she says, "what will happen when the play goes to Fort Worth."

Source: Brian Gilmore, "Spotlight on the Death Penalty: A New Play Sheds Dramatic Light on Death Row Tragedies," in *Utne*, November–December 2003, pp. 51–53.

Terry Stoller

In the following review, Stoller notes that audiences were emotionally aroused by the "deeply affecting material" presented by the cast of The Exonerated, *a play that exposed the injustices that resulted in the imprisonment and near execution of innocent people.*

For their new documentary play, *The Exonerated*, writers Jessica Blank and Erik Jensen interviewed sixty people who had spent anywhere from two to twenty-two years on death row. Incorporating six of those interviews with court testimony, police interrogation, and personal correspondence, Blank and Jensen have crafted a powerful indictment against the criminal justice system and capital punishment.

The narrative spans the arrest, imprisonment and eventual exoneration and release of five men and one woman—three of whom are African American and three Caucasian. The cases include coercion of suspects to make misleading statements, representation by attorneys who were not disinterested parties, and inconclusive fingerprint evidence. Prison life is presented as treacherous: when one prisoner was assaulted by his fellow inmates, they carved the words 'good p——' on his buttocks. Prison held other horrors: exercise had to be taken in a yard where the electric chair was in full sight. After release, some had trouble adjusting: one needed to lock himself in to feel safe, another resorted to drugs to cope with the loss of self. But others were able to form new alliances as well as draw on inner resources to appreciate the riches of life on the outside.

The Exonerated is presented as a staged reading. The primary players are seated in a row on stools behind music stands that hold their scripts. Two ensemble actors who play, among other characters, police interrogators and courtroom lawyers, sit on raised platforms on either side of the group of ex-prisoners and their mates. Although the production apparatus was, of necessity, minimal, director Bob Balaban used light and sound to good effect: creating scenes via spotlights; using sounds of shots ringing out, helicopters circling their prey, and cell doors clanging shut to drive home the fear and terror that these people had lived through. A number of well-known actors, such as Richard Dreyfuss and Jill Clayburgh, appeared in the opening weeks of the play. Susan Sarandon, Tim Robbins, Harry Belafonte, and Gabriel Byrne are reported as being part of a roster of celebrities who will join the cast. By the second week of the production, there were already new luminaries in the lineup.

The Exonerated explains how individuals came to be falsely accused of a capital crime and describes how they coped with years of imprisonment. A would-be poet/philosopher, embodied with great dignity by the sonorous-voiced Charles Brown, says that although "it ain't easy to be a poet here . . . I sing." In a particularly moving passage, we hear the correspondence between Sunny (in an excellent performance by Jill Clayburgh) and her common-law husband Jessie Tafero, both of whom were wrongfully convicted for murdering two law officers. Their letters to each other, Sunny says, had to be delivered unsealed so that prison authorities could make sure they were not plotting an escape. Using Japanese words, the two develop a code in which they can express their more intimate thoughts. An ensemble actor reads Jessie's letter aloud, and we see Sunny's delighted reactions. She takes what little pleasure she can in jail, because, she says, she's not a lump of flesh you can put in a cage. Sunny eventually shares the horrific details of Jessie's botched electrocution in 1990. David Brown, Jr. and April Yvette Thompson, playing man and wife, provide some comic relief with their repartee. The husband admits that now that he is out of prison, he is restless and reluctant to go home at night, much to the dismay of his mate.

Both the program and an announcement at the top of the show remind the audience that the words of *The Exonerated* are from real people. Having celebrities portray characters in the play means their past performances and public personas "haunt" the stage, to use Marvin Carlson's term. This creates a distance between performer and character, so that the audience is always aware that the actor is giving voice to the testimony of real people. In a curtain speech the afternoon I saw the play, Richard Dreyfuss made a financial appeal for the six ex-prisoners, who were not compensated by the state upon their release. The deeply affecting material had roused the audience's emotions, and as people exited the auditorium they acted upon their empathy, dropping five- and one-dollar bills into a collection basket. Perhaps upon reflection of the issues of injustice that the play had addressed, they will also be roused to take political action.

Source: Terry Stoller, Review of *The Exonerated*, in *Theatre Journal*, Vol. 55, No. 2, May 2003, pp. 345–47.

Stanley Cohen

In the following essay, Cohen focuses on Delbert Tibbs, a man wrongly accused and sentenced to death, and his struggle with the legal system and the weak evidence against him.

Few victims of the capital justice system have roused public support the way Delbert Tibbs did when he was sentenced to death in 1974 for killing a hitchhiker and raping the man's sixteen-year-old traveling companion. Tibbs, a young black theology student, was celebrated in song by Pete Seeger and Joan Baez and was made a cause célèbre by the 1960s black activist Angela Davis.

Tibbs's travails began innocently enough when he was hitchhiking his way from Florida back to his Chicago home earlier that year. Nearing Leesburg, he was stopped by a Highway Patrol trooper who said he fit the description of a man who was wanted in Fort Myers. The officer questioned Tibbs and, satisfied that he was not the man they were looking for, let him go. Before releasing him, however, he photographed Tibbs with a Polaroid camera.

A few days later, on February 3, two white hitchhikers, Terry Milroy and Cynthia Nadeau, were picked up by a black man driving a green truck just south of Fort Myers. Milroy was on his way to a job in the Florida Keys and Nadeau was a teenage runaway from Rhode Island. As Cynthia later told it, after a brief ride the driver pulled off the road into a vacant field and stopped the truck. He asked Milroy to come out and help him with something. When Nadeau followed, she saw the driver pointing a gun at Milroy. The driver ordered her to undress, then shot Milroy and raped her.

Police showed her the Polaroid photo of Tibbs, and Nadeau identified him as the man who had raped her and shot Milroy, although he did not fit her original description of the killer. A regional search by police found Tibbs hitchhiking in Mississippi. He was brought back to Fort Myers, and Nadeau picked him out of a police lineup.

Tibbs was tried before an all-white jury. Nadeau's testimony was the guts of the prosecution's case, and it was woefully weak. There were too many questions that had no answers and virtually nothing that would support Nadeau's story. No physical evidence was offered, the murder weapon had not been found, and no witnesses could place Tibbs anywhere near Fort Myers at the time of the crime. Then there was the matter of the truck that was central to Nadeau's account. Where was the truck and how did it figure in the odyssey of a man who apparently had spent much of the past week hitchhiking from Florida to Mississippi? If he had access to the truck, why was he thumbing rides along the highway? The only corroboration of Nadeau's story was delivered by Tibbs's cellmate, who testified that Tibbs had confessed to him while awaiting trial.

Tibbs structured his defense around what appeared to be an airtight alibi: he was in Daytona Beach on February 2 and 3, in Leesburg on the sixth and Ocala on the seventh—each location a long distance from Fort Myers—and he had the documentation to prove it. The defense also sought to impeach Nadeau's testimony, noting that at age sixteen she was already a heavy drug user and had admitted to getting high on marijuana shortly before the crime was committed. It was of no avail. The trial was over in less than three days; the verdict was in an hour and a half later: Tibbs was found guilty of murder and rape. The jury recommended death as the penalty for the murder, and a life sentence was added for the rape.

The appeal process began, and so did the drumbeat of protest and support that came from up north. Tibbs was, after all, not a likely suspect for the random murder and rape of a pair of wayward hitchhikers. He was well educated, an aspiring poet, a veteran of the civil rights struggles of the sixties, and when arrested he was in the midst of a coast-to-coast journey "to experience firsthand the woes and wonders of the world," as a newspaper reporter put it. When he returned, he had planned to finish studying for his degree at the Chicago Theological Seminary.

The basis for Tibbs's appeal to the Florida Supreme Court was that there was insufficient evidence to place him at the scene of the crime. Florida law requires close scrutiny of the victim's testimony if she is the only witness for the prosecution. (The jailhouse snitch, himself a convicted rapist, had already admitted that his testimony was false and was given in the hope of receiving consideration in return.) In reviewing the trial court's record, the judges found several weaknesses in Nadeau's story: all available evidence other than the witness's testimony seemed to place Tibbs far from the scene at the time of the crime; a car and helicopter search of the area failed to locate the green truck; the gun was never found and Tibbs had no car keys in his possession when he was picked up; Tibbs had been stopped by police more than once as he hitchhiked his way north, he cooperated each time, and none of the officers who questioned him found cause to suspect his credibility; finally, since the crime took place at night and Nadeau had been high on marijuana, her ability to identify her attacker was diminished. The state supreme court reversed the conviction and ordered a new trial.

The question then raised was whether a new trial would subject Tibbs to double jeopardy, which is prohibited by the Fifth Amendment. Tibbs filed a motion to dismiss the indictment on those grounds. The trial court agreed that retrying the case would violate the defendant's Fifth Amendment protection. The state took the case to the Florida Court of Appeals, which ruled that double jeopardy would not apply since the reversal of the conviction was based on the *weight* of the evidence presented, not its *insufficiency*. Had the court decided that the evidence offered, even if unchallenged, was not sufficient to support a conviction, the case against Tibbs would have been dismissed. The legal proceedings moved through the judicial machinery for five years. In June 1982, when the U.S. Supreme Court affirmed the decision of the court of appeals, it appeared Tibbs was headed for a new trial.

Two months later, however, the state decided not to retry Tibbs. The prosecution's case had, in the past five years, evaporated. Cynthia Nadeau had become a confirmed drug addict, making her useless as a witness, and there was no other evidence to be presented to a jury. What's more, James Long, who had prosecuted the case, announced that the original investigation had been "tainted from the beginning" and that if there was a retrial he would testify for the defense.

Since his release, Tibbs has campaigned actively against the death penalty, giving public lectures and testifying at legislative hearings. "It's quite easy," he tells listeners, "to build a case against an innocent man."

Source: Stanley Cohen, "Eyewitness Error," in *The Wrong Men: America's Epidemic of Wrongful Death Row Convictions*, Avalon Publishing Group, Carroll & Graf Publishers, 2003, pp. 55–59.

SOURCES

Blank, Jessica, and Erik Jensen, *The Exonerated: A Play*, Faber and Faber, 2004.

———, *Living Justice: Love, Freedom, and the Making of "The Exonerated,"* Atria Books, 2005, pp. 141, 150, 291, 296.

Brantley, Ben, "Someone Else Committed Their Crimes," in *New York Times*, October 11, 2002, http://theater2 .nytimes.com/mem/theater/treview.html?_r=2&res=990 6E4DC173AF932A25753C1A9649C8B63&oref=slogin &oref=slogin (accessed September 3, 2006).

Center on Wrongful Convictions, "The Snitch System," http://www.law.northwestern.edu/depts/clinic/wrongful/ Causes/Snitches.htm (accessed September 7, 2006).

Cohen, Stanley, *The Wrong Men: America's Epidemic of Wrongful Death Row Convictions*, Avalon Publishing Group, Carroll & Graf Publishers, 2003, pp. 147, 152–53, 196, 221–23, 265.

Isherwood, Charles, Review of *The Exonerated*, in *Variety*, Vol. 388, No. 10, October 21, 2002, p. 43.

Lahr, John, Review of *The Exonerated*, in *New Yorker*, Vol. 78, No. 32, October 28, 2002, p. 88.

Peyser, Marc, "Death Becomes Them, Even Off-Broadway," in *Newsweek*, December 2, 2002, p. 14.

Warden, Rob, "How Mistaken and Perjured Eyewitness Identification Testimony Put 46 Innocent Americans on Death Row," Center on Wrongful Convictions, http://www .law.northwestern.edu/depts/clinic/wrongful/Causes/eye witnessstudy01.htm (accessed September 7, 2006).

FURTHER READING

Arriens, Jan, ed., *Welcome to Hell: Letters & Writings from Death Row*, Northeastern University Press, 1997.
> This book is in two parts. The first is a case history of a man named Edward Johnson, who was executed in 1987 in spite of serious doubts about whether he was guilty. The second part is a collection of letters, written to members of the Lifeline organization, in which inmates tell their stories and describe their lives on death row.

Dawson, Gary Fisher, *Documentary Theatre in the United States: An Historical Survey and Analysis of Its Content, Form, and Stagecraft*, Greenwood Press, 1999.
> This is a historical and critical survey of documentary theater in the United States. It defines the genre as a dramatic representation of societal forces using a close reexamination of events, individuals, or situations. Dawson demonstrates that documentary theater is steeped in the oral history tradition and is an alternative to conventional journalism.

Jackson, Joe, and William F. Burke Jr., *Dead Run: The Shocking Story of Dennis Stockton and Life on Death Row in America*, Walker Publishing Company, 2000.
> This is the story of Dennis Stockton, who was executed in 1995 for a murder which, the authors demonstrate,

he did not commit. The authors draw on extensive interviews, as well as Stockton's own diaries, to reveal rampant corruption within the prison system.

Prejean, Helen, *The Death of Innocents: An Eyewitness Account of Wrongful Executions*, Random House, 2004.
Prejean is the author of the memoir *Dead Man Walking* that inspired the Oscar-winning film released in 1995. A long-standing opponent of the death penalty, Prejean tells the story of two men whom she believes were wrongly executed. Dobie Williams received inadequate legal representation at his trial and was convicted of murder even though there was no hard evidence against him. Joseph O'Dell was convicted and later executed as a result of false testimony by another inmate who stood to gain by lying.

Rossi, Richard, *Waiting to Die: Life on Death Row*, Vision, 2004.
Rossi has been an inmate of Arizona's death row since 1983. In this book, he examines every aspect of life on death row, including medical neglect, inadequate food, and psychological abuse by prison officials.

The Forc'd Marriage

The Forc'd Marriage, or the Jealous Bridegroom was first performed in 1670, at the Duke's Theatre in London's Lincoln's Inn Fields. It belongs in the category of Restoration drama, which refers to drama written between 1660, when the monarchy was restored, and 1688. The play, a tragicomedy, was Aphra Behn's first and one of the first plays by a woman to be presented on the English stage. Behn went on to write many more plays and was the first woman to make her living as a writer.

In *The Forc'd Marriage*, the heroine, Erminia, is forced by her father and the king to marry Alcippus, a young warrior whom she does not love. The man she loves, and who loves her, is Prince Philander, the king's son, while the king's daughter, Galatea, is in love with Alcippus. In time-honored comic fashion, the tangle eventually gets sorted out and true love wins in the end.

The text of *The Forc'd Marriage* used in this chapter is taken from the edition by Montague Summers published in 1915. It was reprinted by Phaeton Press in 1967 but, as of 2006, was out of print. A more recent edition can be found in *The Works of Aphra Behn: The Plays 1671–1677*, edited by Janet Todd and published by Ohio State University Press in 1996. As of 2006, a less expensive edition was available from Kessinger Publishing, but unfortunately this edition omits both the prologue and the epilogue of the play.

APHRA BEHN

1670

Aphra Behn   Library of Congress

AUTHOR BIOGRAPHY

Many of the facts about the early life of the dramatist, poet, and novelist Aphra Behn are matters of conjecture. It is likely that she was born in the village of Harbledown, near Canterbury, Kent, England in 1640, the second daughter of Bartholomew and Elizabeth Johnson. When Aphra was three, the family went to live in the West Indies. Her father died during the journey, but his wife and two children lived in Surinam, which was then a British colony. Behn returned to England in 1664 and married a Dutch merchant. Thereafter, she was known as Mrs. Behn, although the exact name of her husband is not known. Her husband died in 1665, which left Behn without any means of financial support. Out of necessity, the following year, Behn went to Antwerp in the Netherlands as a spy for King Charles II, gathering information about Dutch military and political activity. However, the English government made no use of the information she sent back and also failed to pay her. Behn had to borrow money to get back to England, and her financial problems continued. She was put in debtors' prison in 1668 because of debts accumulated during her service to the king.

The circumstances surrounding Behn's release from prison are unknown, but apparently she decided that from then on she would make her living as a writer. She appears to have had no desire to remarry or to otherwise depend upon a man. She had already been writing poetry, but she turned to drama, which offered more lucrative opportunities. From that point until her death, Behn made a living solely from her writing, the first woman ever to do so in England. Her first play was *The Forc'd Marriage*, which was produced at Lincoln's Inn Fields by the Duke's Company in 1670. Over the following seventeen years, Behn had seventeen plays produced. Some of her most popular comedies are: *The Town Fop* (1676), *The Rover* (1677), *Sir Patient Fancy* (1678), *The Rover, Part 2* (1681), *The Roundheads* (1681), *The City Heiress* (1682), *The Lucky Chance* (1686), and *The Emperor of the Moon* (1687). So successful was Behn that the male literary establishment was forced to acknowledge her as an equal. However, throughout her career she was a controversial figure. She was an early feminist who argued for equality between the sexes and for education for women. She also pushed the boundaries of what might be presented on the stage, and some of her plays were regarded as scandalous. *The Lucky Chance*, for example, was denounced as lewd, but Behn claimed the charge was made only because she was a woman.

Behn also published poetry and novels. *Poems Upon Several Occasions* appeared in 1684; the novella *Oroonoko*, based on her experience in Surinam and detailing the horrors of slavery, was published in 1688.

Behn died on April 16, 1689, and was buried in Westminster Abbey.

PLOT SUMMARY

Prologue
The Forc'd Marriage begins with a prologue spoken by an actor and then an actress directly to the audience. It identifies the playwright as a woman and appeals to the audience to give the play a good reception.

Act 1, Scene 1
The warrior Alcippus has just returned from a battle in which he distinguished himself in the command of twenty thousand men. The king has to decide whether to honor Alcippus or his own son, Philander, who has also shown valor. He decides to promote Alcippus to the rank of general, pointing out that the former general, Orgulius, had asked

to be relieved of his post, since he is getting old. The grateful but surprised Alcippus requests the hand of Orgulius's daughter Erminia in marriage. With Orgulius's approval, the king grants him his wish, to the consternation of Philander, who is also in love with Erminia.

Everyone exits, except for Alcander, Pisaro, and Falatius. Alcander is annoyed to see Alcippus promoted above him. He thinks that he himself fought in the battle with equal valor. He is also unhappy that his friend Philander, the prince, has lost his chance to wed Erminia. Pisaro, a friend of Alcippus, tries to mollify Alcander by saying that Alcippus did not know Philander was in love with Erminia. Pisaro also reveals that Erminia does not return Alcippus's love. Talk then turns to Aminta, Pisaro's sister, who is being courted, without, he believes, much success, by Alcander. After Alcander and Pisaro exit, Falatius reveals that he is also romantically interested in Aminta. He sends Labree to tell Aminta about the wounds he received in battle. In truth, he received none, but he plans to wear patches on his face so the ladies will think he has been wounded.

Act 1, Scene 2

Galatea, the king's daughter, talks with Olinda, her maid, and Aminta. She learns that Erminia is horrified at the thought of marrying Alcippus. Aminta confesses that she herself has been in love many times and is currently in love with Alcander. Erminia enters and speaks of her sorrow, since she is in love with Philander. Her grief is matched by that of Galatea, who is in love with Alcippus. Erminia vows not to let Alcippus into her bed. The two women attempt to console each other.

Act 1, Scene 3

A weeping Erminia protests to her father, saying that she loves Alcippus as a brother but no more. She confesses that she is in love with Philander, who returns her affections. Orgulius rebukes her, saying that the king would never agree to her marrying the prince and that she should accept Alcippus instead. He wants to bring forward the time of the wedding to that night. Erminia reluctantly agrees, saying she will do her duty, but after her father exits, she rails at her situation, saying that only death will set her free.

Act 1, Scene 4

Philander tells Alcander that he wants Erminia, whom he loves, to defy her father. He claims that Orgulius cannot claim that he was ignorant of their feelings for each other, since everyone knew about their love. He plans to go to the king to win his sympathy, and if that does not work, he will settle matters with his sword.

Act 2, Scene 1

After the wedding is represented on stage, Philander and his sister Galatea enter. They are both angry. Philander feels that he has suffered a humiliation, having to watch the woman he loves being married to someone else against her will. He vows to kill Alcippus, which horrifies Galatea, who is in love with Alcippus. She tries to dissuade him, but succeeds only in getting him to temporarily postpone his vengeance. She responds by saying that if he kills Alcippus, she will kill Erminia. Knowing that neither of these events is likely to happen, she suggests that at the wedding banquet, Philander should make Alcippus a little jealous, and she will do the rest. It appears that she has a plan.

Act 2, Scene 2

Olinda, Alcander's sister, tells Aminta about how deeply her brother is in love with her. Aminta at first pretends she is not interested in Alcander, but she soon admits that she is in love with him, but she wants to keep it a secret. Falatius enters, with patches on his face and tries to convince Aminta of his heroism. Alcander enters and is annoyed to see Aminta with Falatius. He tells Aminta about his love for her. After Alcander exits, Aminta shows her pleasure at his words, which disappoints Falatius, who realizes that Alcander is his rival.

Act 2, Scene 3

In the bedroom at night, Alcippus realizes that Erminia does not wish to sleep in his bed. She confesses what Alcippus seems already to know, that she is in love with Philander. Her heart belonged to the prince before Alcippus asked for it. She says she married Alcippus only to please the king and her father. Angry, he seizes her by the arm and shows her a dagger. She manages to pacify him by speaking about the power of love, and he says that in time he hopes to win her love. He tries once more to persuade her to share his bed, but she is firm in her resolve.

Act 2, Scene 4

At midnight, the sleepless Philander confesses to Alcander his grief at losing Erminia. He accuses her of breaking her vow to him. Alcander urges him not to give up but to possess Erminia and not worry about the sin of taking another man's wife. He tries to convince the prince that this is what Erminia is expecting him to do. Philander decides that he and Alcander should serenade the bride that very night.

Act 2, Scene 5

Pisaro reveals that he has been watching the wedding feast closely. He has observed the looks of love given by Galatea to Alcippus and also the obvious love between Philander and Erminia. He has also noticed the growing hostility between Philander and Alcippus. Pisaro is disturbed by the situation because he also wants to win Galatea's love. He is conflicted because Alcippus is his friend.

Act 2, Scene 6

At the door of Erminia's chamber, while Philander and Alcander look on, a page sings a song about the cruelties of love. Pisaro enters, and he and Philander quarrel. Alcander intervenes, and he and Pisaro fight. Pisaro falls. Alcander and Philander exit, and Alcippus, aroused by the commotion, enters. He helps Pisaro, who says he is not wounded.

Act 2, Scene 7

Philander and Alcander return and encounter Erminia in her nightgown. Erminia demands to know where Alcippus is, since she is concerned for his safety. Philander speaks scornfully to her, but she tells him that she has kept her vow to him. He rejoices at hearing this report. Alcippus enters, sees Philander and Erminia together, and suspects the worse. Alcippus and Philander draw their swords and fight. Alcippus is wounded. Erminia and Alcippus exit together, and Philander wants to chase after them. Alcander convinces him that justice is on his side and that his time to possess Erminia will come.

Act 3, Scene 1

Pisaro explains to Alcippus why he quarreled with Philander. Alcippus hints to his friend of his fear of Erminia's unfaithfulness to him, but Pisaro says he knows nothing about Alcippus being wronged. Pisaro confesses that he is in love with Galatea and that Galatea is in love with Alcippus. Alcippus is amazed at this information, which he had not suspected. He does not know what to do and asks Pisaro for his advice. Pisaro tells him that he should choose Galatea, since he will then inherit half a kingdom, rather than wasting his time on Erminia who does not love him. He offers to act as a spy for Alcippus, who has to go away to a military camp that day.

Act 3, Scene 2

Falatius encounters Cleontius, Philander's servant. They quarrel over Issilia, Cleontius's sister, and agree to fight a duel. Aminta enters and Falatius protests that she loves Alcander, even though she disguises it, more than she loves him. Alcander enters, offers Aminta his sword and asks her to kill him. He says he thinks he has killed her brother Pisaro. Aminta collapses in the arms of Olinda, Alcander's sister, and then tells Falatius to take revenge against Alcander. After Aminta exits, Alcander tells Falatius to kill him to fulfill Aminta's wish, but he is too cowardly to do so. Alcander exits, and Aminta returns with Pisaro. She asks Falatius if he has killed Alcander yet. Falatius is overjoyed to see that Pisaro is alive, which means he does not have to choose between disobeying the woman he loves and committing murder. Aminta directs him not to tell Alcander that Pisaro is alive. After Pisaro exits, Alcander enters. Aminta informs him that Pisaro is not dead, and she returns his sword. She and Alcander continue their verbal sparring. He admits he loves her but says he will leave her to Falatius. She replies that she can do without both of them.

Act 3, Scene 3

Thinking that Erminia is too puffed up with pride, Galatea reminds her of her humble origins. Erminia seems to say that she has a duty to return Alcippus's love, which produces an angry outburst from Galatea. Erminia weeps and confesses that, in truth, she hates Alcippus. Galatea tells her to remember that Philander loves her and that she should yield herself to his desire. When Erminia asks her how she may conceal such an act from Alcippus, Galatea tells her to trust her; she will arrange it. Alcippus, who is about to go to camp, and Pisaro enter. Alcippus talks about his grief and accuses Galatea of having taught Erminia how to be cruel. Galatea denies it, and Alcippus apologizes. He turns to Erminia and pleads with her to give him some hope. In an aside to Erminia, Galatea tells her to soften her attitude toward Alcippus. After Galatea exits, Erminia speaks more kindly to Alcippus and weeps. Alcippus is touched and encouraged by what he thinks is her new attitude toward him. But as the scene ends, she insists that when they meet again, it must be as friends, not lovers.

Act 4, Scene 1

Galatea and Aminta are met by Philander and Alcander. Philander is planning to see Erminia while Alcippus is away, and Aminta encourages him. Philander asks Galatea to use her charm to get the king on her side, and, by implication, on his. After Galatea and Philander exit, Alcander once again tells Aminta he is in love with her, but she continues to resist him, reminding him of all the women he has loved in the past. But when he decides to leave, she is more forthcoming, and Alcander realizes her true feelings. After he leaves, Aminta regrets she has let her passion for him be known and thinks she has lost her power as a result.

Act 4, Scene 2

Alcippus tells Pisaro he is distressed and jealous because he knows Erminia does not really love him, in spite of the gentle words she spoke to him. He decides that he will not go to the camp. Instead, he will return to visit Erminia, even though Pisaro tells him that if he finds Philander there he may fly into a rage and do something that will ruin his life. Pisaro makes him promise to remain calm.

Act 4, Scene 3

When it is dark, Philander and Alcander call at the lodgings of Erminia. Isillia, Erminia's maid, lets them in.

Act 4, Scene 4

Philander kneels at the feet of a surprised Erminia and tells her how much he loves her. But he breaks off suddenly, telling her he is unwell. Erminia takes him into an inner room where he can rest.

Act 4, Scene 5

Alcippus knocks at the door, and Alcander realizes to his horror who it is. Alcander steps outside, and there is an argument that leads to a fight. Alcander manages to grab Alcippus's sword, but Alcippus succeeds in getting inside the building. Alcander, who is wounded, follows him in.

Act 4, Scene 6

Isillia informs Erminia that Alcippus is approaching the bed chamber, and Erminia tells Philander to hide. He hides behind the bed but leaves his sword and hat on the table. Alcippus does not take long to notice them. Erminia pretends they belong to her father, but Alcippus knows this is untrue, and he accuses her of treachery. Philander emerges from his hiding place and confronts Alcippus. A violent encounter seems imminent, but Erminia steps between the two men, preventing Alcippus from attacking the unarmed Philander. Philander agrees to leave. Left alone with Erminia,

Alcippus accuses her of adultery and strangles her. He throws her on the bed, thinking she may be dead. Pisaro enters, sees Erminia, and, thinking she is dead, rebukes Alcippus. Alcippus says she deserved her fate. Pisaro speaks of some messages that Galatea had sent to him through Philander. At the mention of the names of Galatea and Philander, Alcippus feels conflicting emotions and gives way to a longing for death.

Act 4, Scene 7

Falatius informs Galatea that Erminia is dead. Stunned at this news, Philander falls into the arms of Alcander. The king and Orgulius enter. Orgulius calls for revenge against Alcippus. Galatea says that if Alcippus dies, she will, too. She has that night already explained to the king that she loves Alcippus. She tries to defend Alcippus, saying that the murder would not have happened had Erminia not been forced to marry a man she did not love. The king says that had he known Philander was in love with Erminia, he would have allowed them to marry. The king inquires about Philander, and Galatea thinks he could not bear to live once he found out about Erminia's death. The king says that if Philander is dead, Alcippus too shall die.

Act 4, Scene 8

Falatius and Labree enter. As they speak, a veiled Erminia enters. The men think she is a ghost and fall shaking to the ground.

Act 4, Scene 9

Philander plans to take vengeance on Alcippus by killing him, after which he plans to kill himself. Erminia enters, calling his name, saying she is a soul from Elysium come to visit him. Philander is amazed and frightened. Alcander enters, and Erminia glides away. Philander insists that his vision of her was not a dream. Alcander does not believe him, but then Erminia returns. They are both frightened, not knowing whether she is a ghost, but she soon reveals that she is the living, flesh-and-blood Erminia. Erminia worries that the whole court is alarmed since both Aminta and Falatius have seen her and thought they were seeing a ghost. Aminta and Galatea enter. They have heard the rumors, but Philander leads Erminia out to them. Philander has a plan that involves keeping secret the fact that Erminia is alive. He speaks some tender words to Erminia.

Act 5, Scene 1

Pisaro reports to Galatea that he has seen Alcippus, full of remorse, sitting by a fountain. Galatea asks if Alcippus has mentioned her, and Pisaro replies that he has spoken about her with shame and passion. Pisaro did his best to cheer him up and left him sleeping on a couch.

Act 5, Scene 2

Alcippus awakes and weeps, still full of grief and remorse over his actions. Pisaro and Erminia enter, the latter dressed like an angel with wings. Alcippus, who is looking into a mirror, sees Erminia, who has stolen up behind him, in the mirror. He is frightened, and as he turns around Erminia speaks to him like a disembodied spirit, saying that she is living in a blessed place and is as happy as a god. She hopes this will end his woe. Galatea enters as a spirit, bows to Alcippus, and exits. Erminia tells him it is she whom he must possess. She continues to instruct him as various figures, representing Glory, Honor, Mars, Pallas, Fortune, and Cupid, cross the stage, bow, and exit. Then they return and dance, making an offering to the figure in the middle, that represents love. Erminia exists, leaving Alcippus speechless. When Pisaro enters, Alcippus tells him he just had a fine dream in which he saw Erminia's spirit in glorious form. Pisaro tells him that Philander has persuaded the king to pardon him.

Act 5, Scene 3

The king meets with Philander and tacitly agrees that his son should marry the one he loves. Philander expresses his gratitude.

Act 5, Scene 4

Alcander pleads with Aminta to show him some love, while Aminta asks him to prove that he really does love her. Alcander is disappointed that she should question his commitment to her, and they exit without having reached an agreement.

Act 5, Scene 5

In a black-draped room, Alcippus weeps before the coffin that supposedly contains the dead Erminia. Philander enters, and there is a tense exchange between the two men. They draw their swords and begin to fight, until Pisaro gets between them. Alcander enters, followed shortly by Galatea and Aminta. Galatea reproaches both men for their quarreling. The king enters and speaks harshly to Alcippus for threatening the prince. Philander and Alcippus then both try to accept the blame for their quarrel, and the king agrees to forgive Alcippus. After the king exits, Philander speaks warmly to Alcippus and bestows on him Galatea as his wife.

Alcippus is amazed at the prince's generosity. Philander goes out and returns with Erminia. Alcippus, after he has recovered from the shock, kneels and asks her forgiveness, which she grants. The king enters, with Orgulius, who bestows his daughter Erminia on Philander. The king then gives Galatea to Alcippus. Two more betrothals follow: Falatius to Isillia and Aminta to Alcander. The king makes a final speech in which he wishes the new couples long and happy lives.

Epilogue

The short epilogue is given by a woman, who speaks self-deprecatingly on behalf of her sex, admitting the superiority of men as far as wit is concerned and saying that women can conquer only through their beauty.

CHARACTERS

Alcander

Alcander is a friend of Philander. As the prince's confidant, he plays the same role with Philander as Pisaro does with Alcippus. He listens to Philander's woes and gives him advice, telling him to ignore the marriage of Erminia and Alcippus and continue to seek Erminia. He insists that Philander is in the right and that his time will come—a prediction that proves accurate. Alcander is himself a brave soldier, and he is slightly wounded trying to prevent Alcippus entering the room and finding Erminia and Philander together. Alcander is in love with Aminta, who for most of the play pretends that she has no interest in him. It appears that Alcander has something of a reputation as a lover, and Aminta cruelly reminds him of the names of his previous loves.

Alcippus

Alcippus is a valiant young warrior who has just returned from a battle in which he successfully led an army of twenty thousand men. No one disputes his bravery or his right to be elevated to the rank of general. He is also immediately granted his wish to marry Erminia. He appears to be set for a happy life, but his troubles begin when he discovers that Erminia does not love him and refuses to come to his bed. He feels humiliated by this snub and is jealous of Philander. On the wedding night, he gets into a quarrel with the prince, and there is a fight, during which Alcippus is slightly wounded. Later, when he suspects Erminia of infidelity with

Philander, he flies into a rage and strangles her. He is then filled with remorse about his actions, because he thinks he has killed her. When he learns the truth, he asks Erminia to forgive him, and he is willing to accept the hand of Galatea in marriage.

Aminta

Aminta, Pisaro's sister, is in love with Alcander, but she makes a pretense of scorning him as a way of testing his love. The two lovers are united at the end of the play.

Cleontius

Cleontius is Isillia's brother and a servant to Philander.

Erminia

Erminia is the beautiful daughter of Orgulius. Since she came to the court, she and Philander have been in love. She is, therefore, horrified when her father and the king give her in marriage to Alcippus, whom she does not love. On their wedding night, she treats her new husband with respect but refuses to share his bed. Torn between her love for Philander and her duty to her husband and father, she chooses love. When Alcippus discovers that Philander has been to visit her, he accuses her of treachery and strangles her. He thinks she is dead, and she appears to him pretending to be a spirit, telling him not to grieve for her death but to accept the love of Galatea. Thus, she prepares the way for the final resolution. Her stand for love is rewarded when Philander persuades the king to endorse his claim to her hand.

Falatius

Falatius is a cowardly courtier who pretends to have been wounded in battle in order to impress the ladies at the court. He is courting Aminta, with no success, and at the end of the play, the king orders him to marry Isillia.

Galatea

Galatea is the daughter of the king and sister of Philander. The princess is in love with Alcippus and is heartbroken when she hears that he is to wed Erminia. There are more shocks in store for her. She is aghast when she hears her brother threaten to kill Alcippus and says that if he does so, she will kill Erminia. At one point, the two women quarrel, and Galatea accuses Erminia of possessing too much pride. Although her position seems unpromising, Galatea persists in believing that the wrong can be undone. She tells Erminia that she

should have Philander, since he is the man she desires. Galatea finally explains to her father that she is in love with Alcippus, and she persuades the king to accede to her desire to marry the young warrior.

Isillia

Isillia is Cleontius's sister and a maid to Erminia. She is eventually betrothed to Falatius.

King

The king is an old man who wants to behave honorably. He appears to be a strong ruler with a sense of justice tempered with mercy; he once banished, but did not execute, Orgulius for leading a rebellion against him. But the king appears to have no idea of who is in love with whom at his court, and he makes the mistake of marrying Erminia to Alcippus even though his own son Philander is passionately in love with Erminia. However, the king does have the ability to forgive and to acknowledge his mistakes, and this is one reason that the play can end happily.

Labree

Labree is the servant of Falatius.

Olinda

Olinda is Alcander's sister and maid of honor to Galatea.

Orgulius

Orgulius is the king's general who asks to be relieved of his position because of his advancing age. He is also the father of Erminia who willingly gives his daughter in marriage to Alcippus. In act 3, scene 3, Galatea supplies more information about Orgulius. It transpires that many years earlier, before Erminia was born, Orgulius led the army in a bid to overthrow the king. For that crime, he was banished to some remote spot, and Erminia was born in a humble cottage. When Erminia's beauty captured Philander's heart, that also elevated her father's fortunes, and he was restored by the king to his former position.

Philander

Philander is the son of the king. He is in love with Erminia and fully expects to marry her. He is furious when Erminia is bestowed on Alcippus because he thought it was general knowledge at the court that he and Erminia were in love. He refuses to accept the new situation, which sours his previous good relationship with Alcippus. He goes to the king to plead his case, telling his sister that if he does not get what he wants, he will settle the matter with his sword. He also tells Galatea that he will kill Alcippus. On two occasions the two rivals draw their swords against each other and begin to fight. He finally manages to persuade the king to grant his desire, and he marries Erminia.

Pisaro

Pisaro is a friend of Alcippus and brother of Aminta. Alcippus trusts him and treats him as his confidant, and Pisaro responds by giving Alcippus sound advice and calming him down at key moments. At one point, Pisaro quarrels with Philander, who calls him a spy, and then fights with Alcander. Pisaro also offers to act as a spy for Alcippus while the latter is away at camp. In the last scene, Pisaro is brave enough to step between the quarreling Alcippus and Philander. Like Alcippus, Pisaro is in love with Galatea, but nothing comes of it.

THEMES

Conflict between Love and Honor

The central theme of the play is the conflict in the heroine, Erminia, between love and honor. She loves Philander, but she has been married against her will to Alcippus. She therefore finds herself in an acutely painful emotional situation, with apparently no power to alter it. She cannot simply stop loving Philander, even if she were to decide to do so, because the heart will not give way to the dictates of reason. Yet she clearly has a need to behave honorably and obey the moral codes of her society. She must honor the king, who bestowed her upon Alcippus as part of his reward for prowess in battle, and her father, who agreed to the match. To disobey them would be to rebel against the basic order of this patriarchal society. This conflict in Erminia between duty and desire is so intense that she cannot imagine anything worse happening to her, as she explains to Galatea in act 1, scene 2: "Fate has bestow'd the worst she had to give." Erminia feels that her whole soul is dying because of what has happened. She cannot conceive of loving anyone other than Philander, and her knowledge that Philander is also experiencing torment, seeing the woman he loves given to someone else, adds to her distress.

The situation is similar for Philander. He too feels a conflict between duty and desire. He holds his love for Erminia sacred; he tells Alcander that they are like twin flames in love: "Our Souls then met, and so grew up together, / Like sympathizing Twins." But like Erminia, Philander is duty-bound to obey the king, who also happens to be his father. He feels betrayed and dishonored by what has happened. He thinks that the whole court knew about his love for Erminia and that the reason Orgulius, her father, had been recalled as general was so Erminia could have a place at the court. Philander tries to recast his sense of duty by convincing himself that the honorable thing to do is to kill Alcippus. He tells his sister Galatea that even the gods sanction revenge in certain situations. (Galatea manages to talk him out of his desire to kill Alcippus, at least temporarily.)

In this painful dilemma, both Erminia and Philander choose love rather than duty. Philander does not appear to think twice about it. He tells his friend Alcander he plans to tell Erminia to disobey her father, and Alcander encourages him in this desire to consummate his love for Erminia regardless of the fact that she has just been married to someone else.

For her part, Erminia refuses to budge in her commitment to love. Showing great courage, she tells Alcippus that she can offer him friendship but no more. As far as love is concerned, she must remain true to the one who has captured her heart. She also shows that she is willing to defy her father and the king by putting aside all scruples and accepting Philander as a secret lover even though she is married to Alcippus.

In the end, honor and love, desire and duty are reconciled. The king is persuaded to allow Philander and Erminia to marry, and Orgulius consents to the new pairing as well. Harmony is therefore restored.

Subjection of Women

Although the setting of the play cannot be located in any particular time or place, the society depicted is one in which women are almost entirely powerless. This is a society run by men for the convenience of men. When the play begins there are eight male characters on stage, as well as certain male "officers." There is not a woman in sight. The opening speeches reveal a society which places the highest value on the manly arts of war and conquest. It is Alcippus's valor as a warrior that earns him not only the title of general but also the woman of his choice. In this society, a woman appears to be a piece of property owned by her father or her husband. Marriage is arranged by men, and the women are pawns in the exchange. Having received

TOPICS FOR FURTHER STUDY

- Research divorce trends in the United States. Is divorce becoming more common? What might explain changes in the rate of divorce? What are the social consequences of divorce? How does it affect children? Write a paper in which you describe your findings.

- Read *The Rover*, Behn's most popular play, and write a paper in which you compare it to *The Forc'd Marriage*. Why is *The Rover* universally regarded as a superior play to the earlier one? You might want to think in terms of plot and characterization.

- Imagine you are an actress who wants to play the part of Erminia in a production of *The Forc'd Marriage*. Write to a theater director arguing the case for a revival of the play. Tell the director why you think a modern production might succeed.

- Although in the United States, there is less inequality between men and women than there was in Behn's day in England, inequalities still exist. Make a class presentation in which you describe some social inequalities based on gender and what might be done to solve the problem.

Alcippus's request for Erminia, the king says simply, "*Alcippus*, with her Father's leave, she's thine." The entire business is conducted in Erminia's absence. The women do not appear until act 1, scene 2, when Erminia and Galatea have to deal with the emotional turmoil and pain inflicted on them by the male world in their absence.

When Erminia arranges an interview with her father to protest what has been done to her, Orgulius dismisses her as weak and foolish. His argument is that she is young and cannot see what a fine thing it is to be married to a great warrior. When she tells her father the truth about her love for Philander, she is told, "Destroy it, or expect to hear of me." In this society, women are rewarded by keeping quiet. Orgulius's affection for his daughter, for example, is conditional upon her doing what he wants. When she finally says she will obey his will, he says, "This duty has regain'd me, and you'll find / A just return: I shall be always kind."

In act 5, scene 5, after the love tangle is resolved, the king affirms once more the masculine nature of the kingdom he rules. His final speech, in which he addresses his "brave Youths," evokes once more a picture of a warlike society:

When you remember even in heat of Battle,
That after all your Victories and Spoil,
You'll meet calm Peace at home in soft Embraces.

It appears that the real business of life for this unnamed society is battle, victory, and the spoils of war; women are playthings whose job it is to provide the men with some moments of calm and physical love before the next battle begins.

STYLE

Rhyming Couplets and Blank Verse

The play is written almost entirely in either blank verse or rhyming couplets. Blank verse is unrhymed verse written in predominantly iambic feet. An iambic foot consists of two syllables, in which the stress falls on the second syllable. Blank verse is usually written in iambic pentameters. A pentameter is a ten-syllable line with five stresses. In act 1, scene I, for example, Alcippus's line, "To lead on twenty thousand fighting Men," is an iambic pentameter, as is his "Those Eyes that gave this speaking life to thine," in act 5, scene 2. However, Behn writes with a great deal of variation, and much of the blank verse in the play does not follow strict iambic pentameter or any regular metrical pattern. Shorter lines are common.

Much of the play is written in rhyming couplets, a pair of rhymed lines. For example, the two lovers Aminta and Alcander often speak in rhyming couplets. These are Aminta's lines in act 5, scene 4:

Alcander, you so many Vows have paid,
So many Sighs and Tears to many a Maid,
That should I credit give to what you say,
I merit being undone as well as they.

The couplets can consist of single lines by different speakers, as in

Gal. *Aminta*, wilt thou this Humour lose?
Am. Faith, never, if I might my Humour chuse.

Behn frequently makes use of imperfect or partial rhymes in her couplets, as in the following example from act 5, scene 1, spoken by Pisaro:

Then speak as if *Erminia* still did live,
And that Belief made him forget to grieve.
—The Marble Statue *Venus*, he mistook,
For fair *Erminia*, and such things he spoke,
Such unheard passionate things, as e'en wou'd
    move,
The marble Statue's self to fall in love.

In this quotation, "live" and "grieve," as well as "mistook" and "spoke," are imperfect rhymes, since the vowel sounds in each pair are different. The final couplet is an example to a modern audience of "eye-rhyme," in which the words are spelled alike and look similar on the page but are now pronounced differently. Often in such cases, the two words ("move" and "love" in this case) were once pronounced similarly, so the eye-rhyme has developed over the course of time as pronunciation has changed.

Tragicomedy

Tragicomedy is a genre that began in Elizabethan and Jacobean drama and was revived during the drama of the Restoration period (post-1660). Tragicomedy mingles comedy and tragedy. The comic action often involves young people in love who are wanting to marry. However, some unforeseen obstacle results in a romantic tangle that seems impossible to unravel, so much so that the plot appears to be leading to tragedy until a reversal of circumstances ensures a comic (i.e. happy) ending. *The Forc'd Marriage* is a comedy in the sense that a father or other authority figure (in this case Orgulius) obstructs the course of happy love by imposing an unwanted marriage. The play moves toward tragedy when Alcippus strangles Erminia, after which for several scenes the characters believe that Erminia is dead and the audience is unsure about the truth of the matter. The audience also wonders what penalty Alcippus will pay for his crime. The play returns to comedy with the discovery that Erminia is alive, the king's acceptance

of Philander's desire to marry her, and the pairing of Alcippus with Galatea.

HISTORICAL CONTEXT

Women and Restoration Drama

After English drama had risen to new heights in the Elizabethan and Jacobean era, the theaters were closed in 1642 with the outbreak of the English Civil War. In 1649, King Charles I was executed, and the monarchy was abolished. England became a republic, known as the Commonwealth of England, and later the Protectorate. In 1660, parliament restored the monarchy, and Charles II was installed as king. The drama written during the period that followed is, therefore, known as Restoration drama.

One major change from the Elizabethan and Jacobean ages was that in the Restoration age, women were allowed to perform on stage. In the earlier eras, all female parts were played by men and boys. The first woman to appear as a regular professional actress was Margaret Hughes, who played the role of Desdemona in Shakespeare's *Othello* on December 8, 1660. One of the most famous of the new actresses was the illiterate Nell Gwyn (1650–1687), who first appeared on the stage in 1665 and in 1668 became the mistress of Charles II. Said to possess a remarkable comic talent, Gwyn was also a friend of Aphra Behn. The leading dramatist of the day, John Dryden, paid Gwyn the compliment of writing leading parts in his plays specifically for her. Her career spanned a seven-year period, ending in 1671 when she was only twenty-one years old. Another actress, Elizabeth Barry (1658–1713), became the most successful tragic actress of the period, noted for her ability to move the audience to tears and to bring even mediocre roles to vivid life. From 1675 to 1682, Barry worked for the Duke's Theatre at Dorset Gardens, the most luxurious theater in London. This was the same company that staged all Behn's plays up to 1681. Another leading actress was Mary Saunderson, commonly known as Mrs. Thomas Betterton (c.1637–1712). It was Mrs. Betterton who played Erminia in the first performance of *The Forc'd Marriage*, at the Duke's Theatre in 1670.

Male members of the audience for Restoration drama enjoyed the novelty of seeing women on the stage, who sometimes were required to act in sexually suggestive scenes. Plays were often written

COMPARE & CONTRAST

- **Late 1600s:** In 1665, an outbreak of the deadly bubonic plague ravages London. The theaters are closed. The Great Fire of London begins on September 2, 1666, and rages for four days and nights. It destroys two-thirds of the city within the walls, including St. Paul's Cathedral, and leaves a hundred thousand people homeless.

  Today: Londoners worry more about being attacked by terrorists than catching diseases or enduring natural disasters. On July 7, 2005, suicide bombers attack London's public transport system, killing fifty-two people and injuring seven hundred.

- **Late 1600s:** The coffee shop, first introduced to the city in 1652, is the center of London's social life. It is a gathering place where, for a small admission fee, men may socialize, smoke, drink coffee, and read the newsletters.

  Today: Coffee shops can be found all over London, offering a huge variety of coffee. The U.S. company Starbucks offers coffee and espresso beverages at many locations. It claims on its website that in London, no one is never more than five minutes away from a Starbucks shop.

- **Late 1600s:** The official doctrine of the Catholic Church and the Anglican Church is that marriage is indissoluble; however, the concept is under increasing strain as married couples seek legal ways to end unhappy relationships. The practice of arranging private separation deeds increases, as a first step towards divorce.

  Today: Divorce in the United Kingdom is more easily obtainable than formerly. It can be granted on the basis of the irretrievable breakdown of a marriage as a result of adultery; unreasonable behavior; desertion for two years; and living apart for two years (with consent) or living apart for five years. However, divorce rates are declining. Between 2004 and 2005, the number of divorces granted in the UK decreases by 7 percent from 167,138 to 155,052. This is the lowest number of divorces since 2000, and the first annual decrease since 1999–2000. The 2004–2005 figure is 14 percent lower than the highest number of divorces, which peaked in 1993.

to include "breeches roles," which refers to roles in which a female character dresses in male clothes as part of the intrigue and complications of a plot. The men in the audience relished the opportunity of seeing women dressed in the more form-fitting male attire.

Women also took part in theater management. In 1668, after the death of Sir William Davenant, control of the Duke of York's theater company passed to his widow, Lady Davenant. She proved to be an able administrator with a practical knowledge of the theater, and it was under her management that the Duke's company staged Behn's *The Forc'd Marriage*. It was Lady Davenant who noticed the talent of the young Elizabeth Barry and guided her acting career. Barry eventually occupied a position in theater management, as did Mrs. Betterton.

Female Playwrights

During the Restoration, female playwrights wrote for the public stage for the first time. In 1663, a translation of Corneille's *La Mort de Pompée*, by Katherine Phillips, became the first work by a woman, either as author or translator, to be professionally produced on the English stage. In 1670, a female playwright, Frances Boothby, had her tragedy, *Marcelia*, performed at the Theatre Royal, Drury Lane, and later that year, Behn's *The Forc'd Marriage* was staged at the rival Duke's Theatre. During the 1670s and 1680s, however, Behn was a lone female voice amongst the ranks of playwrights. In the prologues to her plays, she sometimes brought attention to the fact that the author of the play was a woman. In *The Forc'd Marriage*, for example, the actor who speaks the prologue says that women are about to add "wit" to beauty and invade a domain formerly occupied solely by men, that is, the art of writing plays. He appeals to the audience not to be alarmed by this but to give the female-authored play a good reception:

> To day one of their Party ventures out
> Not with design to conquer, but to scout.
> Discourage but this first attempt, and then
> They'll hardly dare to sally out again.

Audiences did not always heed this appeal. After *The Dutch Lover* (1687) met a hostile reception, Behn wrote in a preface to the published version that criticism was directed at her by men solely because she was a "defenceless Woman." She argued that had her comedies been published under a man's name, the general verdict would have been that they were as good as any plays written in her time.

In the decade following Behn's death, more female playwrights emerged. In late December 1695 or January 1696, sixteen-year-old Catherine Trotter had her first play, an adaptation of a French short story translated by Behn, produced at Drury Lane Theatre. In 1698, her tragedy, *The Fatal Friendship*, elicited an extremely favorable reception. During the same decade, another playwright, Mary Pix, had ten of her plays produced in as many years. These playwrights were followed by Susanna Centlivre, who produced nineteen plays between 1700 and 1724 and was the most successful female playwright of the century. Some of her plays were still being performed in the nineteenth century.

According to Paddy Lyons and Fidelis Morgan, in their introduction to *Female Playwrights of the Restoration*, in the half-century from 1660 to 1710, over fifty plays by female playwrights were published. Since publishers only brought into print plays that had been successful, the chances are that a far greater number of plays by women were performed but not published, or published anonymously.

CRITICAL OVERVIEW

The first recorded response to *The Forc'd Marriage* was by John Downes, the prompter for the Duke's Theatre in Lincoln's Inn Fields in London where the first performance took place in December 1670. Downes wrote that the play was "a good play and lasted six days" (quoted in the theatrical history note in Montague Summers's edition of the play). Six nights was a respectable run in those days, since the audience pool was relatively small and a large number of plays had to be produced. However,

Arranged marriages, common during the period of this play, did not always please the bride and groom © Mary Evans Picture Library/The Image Works

another contemporary comment was not so favorable. In *The Rehearsal* (1671), a satirical work on the drama ascribed to George Villiers, the second Duke of Buckingham, Villiers mocks *The Forc'd Marriage* as well as Behn's second play, *The Amorous Prince* (1671). In particular, Villiers pokes fun at the scenes in which Philander serenades Erminia and the later scene in which a fake funeral is provided for Erminia.

Critical opinion since then has not warmed to *The Forc'd Marriage*, which is regarded as one of Behn's weakest plays. Critics have commented on its shallow characterization, conventional plot, and poorly integrated sub-plot. Annette Kreis-Schinck, in *Women, Writing, and the Theater in the Early Modern Period* notes that the dramatic turnaround in the play, in which the forced marriage is ended, is achieved without any elaboration. Kreis-Schinck explains that at this very early stage of her career, Behn "has not yet found a verbal concept for the process of separating the wrong partners. All the dramatist is able to do in her first play is to leave a gesture, a linguistic blank, an absence to be made up in a number of her later plays."

Some scholars, however, have drawn attention to the importance of the play's prologue. In *The Passionate Shepherdess: Aphra Behn (1640–1689)*, Maureen Duffy writes that in the prologue, "Behn claimed the right to deal with sex as outspokenly as the male playwrights did. It must have brought down the house with its daring." For Catherine Gallagher, in "Who Was That Masked Woman?: The Prostitute and the Playwright in the Comedies of Aphra Behn," Behn's prologue "announces her epoch-making appearance in the ranks of the playwrights. She presents her attainment, however, not as a daring achievement of self-expression, but as a new proof of the necessary obscurity of the 'public' woman."

After its initial run, there was at least one further performance of *The Forc'd Marriage*, in January 1671. However, in his edition of the works of Behn first published in 1915, Summers stated that there had been no revival of the play since its first production. Although a number of Behn's plays, especially *The Rover*, are staged quite frequently in the English-speaking world, it appears that Summers's remark made nearly a hundred years ago remains valid; as of 2006, *The Forc'd Marriage* had not been revived.

CRITICISM

Bryan Aubrey

Aubrey holds a Ph.D. in English and has published many essays on drama. In the following essay, he discusses The Forc'd Marriage *in terms of the subjection of women and the divorce practices of the day.*

Given that she was writing plays in a male-dominated profession and society, it is perhaps not surprising that Behn would be concerned with issues such as the status of women and the gender inequalities in social institutions such as marriage. Many of her plays, including *The Forc'd Marriage*, deal with the topic of unsuitable, unhappy marriages and how they might be ended. During the Restoration era in England, a divorce was not easily attained, but Behn writes with an awareness of the legal practices of the time.

Notably, the play is set not in Behn's own time but in an unspecified time and place, apparently an ancient warrior culture in which men hold all the power, masculine values of courage are lauded, and women are given away as the rewards for valor in battle. This is significant because, according to Derek Hughes in *The Theatre of Aphra Behn*, the idea underlying many of Behn's plays is that "the subjection of women is an irrational survival from archaic societies which depended upon military strength." Hughes continues, commenting on the fact that at the time it was men who controlled the

> BEHN WAS ALSO AWARE THAT SHE HAD TO PRESENT TO HER AUDIENCE A PLAUSIBLE SCENARIO WHEREBY ERMINIA, WHO IS MARRIED TO ALCIPPUS, MIGHT BECOME FREE TO MARRY PHILANDER. HOW WAS THIS MARRIAGE TO BE DISSOLVED?"

writing of history: "Men exercise the power of the word because it is always underwritten by that of the sword. The source and continuing support of men's supremacy is in their capacity for violence. . . . For Behn, civilization is . . . founded on violence."

Hughes's point is amply demonstrated in the play. In this society, men wield the power and cannot imagine things being any other way. The plot is propelled solely by the forced marriage of Erminia to Alcippus and the determination of Erminia and her true love Philander to circumvent it. Erminia, since she is officially powerless, relies on her strength of character and her determination to honor her true feelings when she stands up to Alcippus and refuses to submit to him sexually on their wedding night. She does this in spite of the aggression that Alcippus shows against her. On the wedding night (act 2, scene 3), for example, when Erminia insists that she is an unwilling partner and will never give her heart to Alcippus, he reacts as if he is on the battlefield rather than in the bedroom. Flying into a rage, he grabs her arm, pulls a dagger, and threatens to kill her, neatly inverting the values of good and evil as he does so: "Recal that Folly, or by all that's good, / I'll free the Soul that wantons in thy Blood." Masculine virtues may serve this anonymous kingdom well when war and conquest are called for, but they serve Alcippus poorly at this moment. It does not seem to occur to him that threatening to kill his wife might not be the best way to win her love. Puffed up with righteous indignation, he implies that if he were to kill her right then, her "ungrateful Soul" would go to hell. Erminia holds her nerve, keeps talking, and manages to mollify the supposedly noble warrior—the

WHAT DO I READ NEXT?

- *The Rover and Other Plays*, edited by Jane Spenser and published in 1998 by Oxford University Press in the Oxford World Classics series, contains four of Behn's most popular and important comedies: *The Rover*; *The Feigned Courtesans*; *The Lucky Chance*; and *The Emperor of the Moon*.

- *The First English Actresses: Women and Drama, 1660–1700* (1992), by Elizabeth Howe, is a book for general readers about how and why women were allowed for the first time to act on the public stage after 1660. Howe explains the treatment received by the actresses and addresses issues such as the extent to which the arrival of female actresses altered dramatic portrayals of women and encouraged equality between the sexes.

- *The Meridian Anthology of Restoration and Eighteenth-Century Plays by Women* (1994), edited by Katherine M. Rogers, contains seven plays, by Behn (*Sir Patient Fancy*), Frances Burney, Susanna Centlivre, Hannah Cowley, Elizabeth Inchbald, Mary Griffith Pix, and Mercy Otis Warren. Rogers's introduction discusses the changing status of female playwrights during the period.

- William Congreve's *The Way of the World* is one of the greatest of all Restoration comedies. It was first acted in 1700. It includes a brilliant marriage-bargain scene, common to many Restoration comedies, in which each partner duels for an advantageous marriage contract. The play is available in a 2006 Penguin edition, *The Way of the World and Other Plays*, edited by Eric S. Rump.

"generous Youth," whose virtues Orgulius cannot stop talking about in the first scene—who is in the grip of a homicidal rage because his will has been thwarted by a woman. Erminia knows she must keep talking to save her own life.

To be fair to Alcippus, however, one might say that he is limited by the warrior code of his society, which emphasizes the need for glory on the battlefield and the upholding of male honor. If the thought of having sexual relations with Alcippus offends Erminia's honor, he perceives her refusal as an affront to his own sense of honor—his legitimate expectation of what is due to a husband from a wife. This is why he reacts violently to her words. It is also clear that the fierce emotions simmering below the surface are not going to be subdued for long, and when in act 4 the plot veers toward tragedy, it can hardly be a surprise. When Alcippus finally does strangle Erminia, suspecting her of adultery with Philander, he resembles another more famous warrior in drama, Shakespeare's Othello, who kills his wife Desdemona when he incorrectly believes that she has been unfaithful to him.

This moment, when Alcippus, full of a sense of righteousness and justice and believing that the gods are smiling at his actions, throws the apparently lifeless Erminia on the bed presents a visually effective climax of raw male aggression in the play. The heroine lies still and apparently dead; masculine honor has been satisfied. Behn then engineers a happy ending partly through employing a device that Shakespeare had used in *Much Ado about Nothing* and *The Winter's Tale*—the heroine who only appears to be dead. The revived Erminia has a chance to exert some power for the first time in the play, although it is a different kind of power than that wielded by the men. When she appears as a spirit, she is able to help prepare Alcippus for his marriage to Galatea, and she also manages to frighten all the men. As Hughes has noted, when Erminia is an ethereal, spiritual presence rather than a flesh-and-blood woman, the men are quite unnerved by her presence and fall down in fear. She is empowered. But as soon as she becomes Erminia once again, the situation returns to how it was in the beginning. She becomes once more an object to be given away by the king and her father. The only difference is that this time the authority figures have managed to identify the correct recipient of the "gift."

Behn was also aware that she had to present to her audience a plausible scenario whereby Erminia, who is married to Alcippus, might become free to marry Philander. How was this marriage to be dissolved? As Annette Kreis-Schinck points out in her book, *Women, Writing, and the Theater in the Early Modern Period*, there were during Behn's time only two official ways in which a marriage could be dissolved. The first was a decree of nullity issued by a church court which declared the marriage to have been invalid in the first place. The reasons for granting such a decree were consanguinity (i.e. the two partners were related by blood), impotence (which would mean the marriage was never consummated), or pre-contract (one or other of the partners was contracted to marry someone else). After a decree of nullity had been issued, both parties were free to marry someone else, and it was considered that they were marrying for the first time. It was also possible to obtain a legal separation on the grounds of adultery or cruelty. In 1670, the same year that *The Forc'd Marriage* was first performed, it became possible for the first time to obtain a divorce by a private act of Parliament rather than through a decree issued by an ecclesiastical court.

The topic of divorce was, therefore, a lively one at the time, so it is not surprising that it features prominently in a number of Behn's plays. In *The Forc'd Marriage*, the reasons for the annulment of the marriage between Erminia and Alcippus are in keeping with the laws of England at the time: nonconsummation and the existence of a pre-contract. Erminia's refusal to have sexual intercourse with Alcippus, then, is not only a means of creating tension in the play, it is also vital to the final resolution of the plot. This is why it is emphasized again in act 2, scene 7, when Erminia tells Philander, to his great relief, that she has kept her word and has not had physical relations with Alcippus. This creates the possibility that the marriage might be declared invalid. The second reason for the annulment is that there was, in effect, a pre-contract between Erminia and Philander. This is repeatedly emphasized. Philander lays it out in act 1, scene 4, to his friend Alcander: "I offer'd her a Crown, with her *Philander*, / And she was once pleas'd to accept of it." He goes on to explain that there was nothing secret about their love. It was the reason that Orgulius, Erminia's father, was recalled from exile, put in charge of the army, and given a salary of twenty thousand crowns a year, so that Erminia could live at the court and be near Philander, the prince. "The world was full on't," Philander says, meaning that everyone knew about it. This pre-contract makes Erminia's willingness

to receive Philander after she was given to Alcippus blameless. Because of the pre-contract, she was not really married to him. In the final scene, Alcippus himself acknowledges the validity of Philander's contract with Erminia: "But, Madam, you were Wife to my Prince," which means he also acknowledges the invalidity of his marriage to her. The play offers no explanation of why the king and Orgulius were so ignorant of what everyone else knew, a mystery that can perhaps be attributed to the lack of skill in the dramatist, in this her first produced play. But Behn did succeed in writing a play that ended with the traditional comic resolution of multiple marriages in a way that her contemporaries could recognize as valid and believable.

Source: Bryan Aubrey, Critical Essay on *The Forc'd Marriage*, in *Drama for Students*, Thomson Gale, 2007.

Derek Hughes

In the following essay, Hughes comments on the male invasion of "female autonomy" and the female body in The Forc'd Marriage.

The Young King was the first play Behn wrote, but the first to be performed was *The Forc'd Marriage* (September 1670). Strikingly, it begins where *The Young King* had ended, with a king rewarding a warrior with a bride: the heroine, Erminia, is given as prize to the victorious warrior Alcippus, but she does not wish the match, since she and the king's son, Phillander, are in love; the king's daughter, Galatea, in turn secretly loves Alcippus. The emotional asymmetries are eventually resolved, but not before Alcippus has become so blindly jealous as, apparently, to murder Erminia. Further components are the tensely bantering courtship of the witty Aminta and the heroic warrior Alcander, and the altruistic love of her brother Pisaro for Galatea, whom he self-sacrificingly unites with Alcippus.

The Forc'd Marriage has no known single source, but it is clearly influenced by several earlier plays, all (inevitably) by men: as she had done with *Life is a Dream*, Behn appropriates and transforms male texts for her own distinctive woman's agenda. The most obvious influence is *Othello*, which was popular on the Restoration stage. The return of the heroine from death may recall Shakespeare's earlier and non-tragic study of jealousy, *Much Ado about Nothing*. Beyond Shakespeare, there are debts to two more recent plays. One is to a play which constitutes Behn's earliest documented contact with the Restoration stage, *The Indian Queen* (1664) by John Dryden and Sir Robert

> ❞ THE FORC'D MARRIAGE
> VISUALLY SIGNALS THE
> SUBORDINATION OF WOMEN
> BEFORE A WORD IS SPOKEN, FOR
> THE INITIAL SPECTACLE IS OF A
> STAGE DOMINATED BY MEN. . . ."

Howard, for which Behn (as she claims in her novel *Oroonoko*) provided feathers brought from Surinam. At the beginning of *The Indian Queen*, the Ynca of Peru offers his victorious general, Montezuma, any reward he cares to name, but banishes him when he requests the hand of his daughter. Here, it is the daughter who is willing and the king who is opposed. Behn's reversal of this situation—with the king now willing the marriage and the woman resisting—creates an entirely new perspective upon military heroism: Dryden's Ynca is unjust because he contravenes the rules of his society, breaking his promise to the soldier on whom he depends; Behn's king, by contrast, is unjust because he obeys the rules and rewards the hero. Her simple switch—with the hero's marriage opposed not by the king but by the heroine—turns civilization into a male conspiracy. In *The Indian Queen*, individual merit and affection are oppressed by unjust patriarchal power; in *The Forc'd Marrige*, the hero and the patriarchal ruler join forces to oppress the woman, and her own father very quickly supports them.

The other debt is to an incident in a play which is now understandably forgotten, but which marked an important stage in the development of Restoration serious drama: *The Generall* (1661), by the Earl of Orrery. In each case, the focus of the incident is the female body, but in Orrery the significance of the body is completely determined by the patriarchal and militaristic context in which it is set, whereas Behn entirely reverses Orrery's social vision of femininity, showing instead the invasion of a female order by disordered male force. Towards the end of *The Forc'd Marriage* the two men who love the heroine jealously duel as her seemingly lifeless body lies on its bier. The heroine of *The Generall* similarly undergoes apparent death, and lies insensible during no less than three duels,

but these duels are not mere explosions of male sexual aggression. On the contrary, the first two bring decisive moral and political victories, including the killing of a Cromwell-like usurper by the true king. Indeed, Orrery's heroine partially symbolizes the land over which they are fighting, so that her corpse is almost necessarily present during the duel. Although she is an elevating moral force, her body is significant because it can symbolize a system of patriarchal power, and it is never described as a thing in itself, but only as a moral sign: the pallor of the seeming corpse is, for example, a 'pale Emblem of her Innocence.' In Behn, however, the body of the seemingly murdered woman is initially placed in a predominantly female order: it is surrounded by mourners who (apart from the penitent Alcippus) are chiefly women. But the scene of female community is then disrupted by male violence, as Phillander (Erminia's true love) enters, the men draw, and the women mourners are put to flight, their ceremonial garb of grief being lost and disordered in the process. In Orrery, the woman's body serves as an image of a male political order; in Behn, it illustrates the way in which male values invade female autonomy.

Both *The Generall* and *The Indian Queen* celebrate Charles II's return. *The Generall* a clear allegory of the Restoration, as (at a greater and more critical distance) is *The Indian Queen*. We need not assume that Behn synthesized these influences because of their political connotations—most serious drama of the 1660s alluded in some way to Charles II—but she certainly altered the political meaning which the men gave to their material. They show rebellion being followed by the return of the old order and the triumph of justice; an exemplary status quo is disturbed and then reinstated. In *The Forc'd Marriage*, however, justice requires change: a determined female challenge to a status quo in which sexual and political power are indivisibly vested in men. It is remarkable that the heroine's father is a former traitor: all customary differences in political virtue are overshadowed by a unanimous interest in controlling and exchanging women.

The Forc'd Marriage visually signals the subordination of women before a word is spoken, for the initial spectacle is of a stage dominated by men: all the important male characters are there, plus '*Officers*', yet there is not a woman to be seen. This is not only a gathering of men but a ritual of masculinity: the honouring of the heroic warrior Alcippus in a society whose values and structures of power are clearly militaristic. The cult of virile strength is encoded even in the Greek meanings or associations of the characters' names, over which Behn took some trouble (it may have included the trouble of consulting a classically educated male friend): Alcander (man-strength), Alcippus (horse-strength), Philander (loving masculinity), Orgulius (from *orgê*, anger), Cleontius (from *kleos*, glory). When the men start to speak, they at once establish an economic system of exchange in which the primary scale of value is male strength, a feudal economy, whose foundation is the warrior's duty to his king. The question is by what sort of exchange the warrior is to be rewarded for his performance, and in the event he receives two rewards, military power and a woman. The woman, however, is a powerless cipher, erased in the linguistic transaction in which her body is transferred:

> KING Name her, and here thy King engages for her . . .
> *Alcippus*, with her fathers leave, she's thine.
>
> (I. i. 114–18)

From the outset of her career, Behn thought in terms of the tangible, visible and spatial aspects of theatre as well as the purely textual. Her ability to shape plays visually as well as textually is illustrated by this opening ceremony of masculinity, which lays bare the basis and distribution of power, and which acts as a repeated visual point of reference at later stages of the play. For example, the second act opens with another ceremonial scene:

The REPRESENTATION of the *WEDDING*.

> *The Curtain must be let down; and soft Musick must play: the Curtain being drawn up, discovers a Scene of a Temple: The King sitting on a Throne, bowing down to join the hands of* Alcippus *and* Erminia, *who kneel on the steps of the Throne; the Officers of the Court and Clergy standing in order by, with* Orgulius. *This within the Scene. Without on the Stage,* Phillander *with his sword half-drawn, held by* Galatea, *who looks ever on* Alcippus: Erminia *still fixing her Eyes on* Phillander; Pisaro *passionately gazing on* Galatea: Aminta *on* Falatius, *and he on her:* Alcander, Isillia, Cleontius, *in other several postures, with the rest, all remaining without motion, whilst the Musick softly plays; this continues a while till the Curtain falls; and then the Musick plays aloud till the Act begins.*

The scene is pure dumbshow, separated from the surrounding action (unusually) by the rising and falling of the curtain. The characters are reduced to voiceless, paralysed prisoners in a spatially choreographed system of power. This system repeats and redisplays that which was visible in the first scene, with the wedding being visibly and directly an action of royal power, but it also highlights the plight of the unfulfilled and emotionally isolated individuals who are trapped in the hierarchies of power.

This is a ceremonial exercise of authority which manifestly overrides the lives and aspirations of those who are forced to participate in its choreography, and by using the proscenium arch to separate the desirers from the objects of desire Behn creates a great fissure within the ceremony itself. The ritual is a composite sign, radiating from the will and person of the king, in which the individual persons are allowed no local or personal significance. The final scene of the play shows a reconciliation between the rituals of authority and individual desire, in that true lovers are finally united by royal action, but the rituals are still explicitly male. Those of women are far less powerful. Although women predominate in the scene of ceremonial mourning for Erminia, they are in a passive and victimized role, and the ritual is in any case disrupted when Erminia's lovers start fighting over her corpse.

The public rituals of the opening scene are followed by a scene of privacy, involving most of the female characters. At first, it seems to promise an alternative economy to that of the previous scene: a feminine economy of empathetically shared sensation rather than competitive violence. When Erminia talks with the Princess Galatea, who is tormented by undeclared love for Alcippus, there is no bitterness or rivalry: merely a sense of the equality of sorrow enforced by their different situations:

> Your cause of grief too much like mine appears,
> Not to oblige my eyes to double tears.
>
> (I. ii. 75–6)

This alternative feminine economy is never, however, allowed to develop, for one of the recurrent points of the play is the degree to which the women become complicit in the warrior cult from which, in the first scene, they had been visually excluded. Galatea, for example, very quickly switches from feminine empathy with Erminia to a moment of aggressive hostility: restraining Phillander's desire to kill Alcippus, whom she loves, she threatens to kill Erminia in retaliation. As she makes the threat, she draws a dagger: a recurrently used emblem of male violence.

The appeal of the warrior cult to women is foreshadowed even in the closing stages of the opening scene. As the warriors successively leave, attention is increasingly focused on the cowardly courtier Falatius (i.e. Fallacious: false) and his unrealistic sexual rivalry for Aminta with the warrior Alcander. The falsity declared by his name is his fraudulent pretence to courage, as is indicated when, in a half-feminine act, he sticks patches on his face to create the appearance of battle-scars, and in doing so plays upon the meaning of his own name:

> I'le wear a patch or two there . . .
> And who, you fool, shall know the *fallacie* [?]
>
> (I. i. 259–61; italics added)

Virility is written into the names of all the other male principals; the falsity that is written into Falatius's name is the absence of virility. The cult of the warrior may constrain and obliterate the autonomy of women, yet its opposites seem irremediably marginal. Falatius is contemptible, and there is no love or reward for the more admirably unaggressive character of Pisaro, Aminta's brother, who loves Galatea but selflessly schemes to unite her with Alcippus.

Ignominious as he always is in his lack of macho courage, however, Falatius nevertheless increasingly exposes the problems of manliness itself. After Aminta's suitor Alcander has seemingly killed Pisaro in a scuffle outside Erminia's lodgings, it is to Falatius, her other suitor, that she turns for vengeance, appealing to his virility in a fortunately unsuccessful attempt to incite him to murder:

> I care not who thou beest, but *if a man*
> Revenge me on *Alcander.*
>
> (III. ii. 104–5; first italics added)

Falatius's inability to meet the challenge of manhood here averts disaster, yet the incident also shows how uneasily complicit women can be in the cult of violence. The moment at which Aminta demands her lover's death is the darkest moment in what is in general a very dark love duel, featuring an intelligent, articulate woman who is apprehensive of her infatuation with a war machine. Conventional though their amorous sparring is, it is unconventionally conditioned by the violence of the male.

The greatest eruption of erotic violence occurs when Alcippus seemingly murders Erminia, believing that she has cuckolded him with Philander. As in many of Shakespeare's plays (including *Othello*), the heroic aggression which sustains the state on the battlefield proves dangerous and uncontainable in peaceful life. The centrality of war to civilization creates fissures and contradictions within the nature of civilization itself and, like many Shakespeare characters, the national hero becomes an alien and barbarian within the very state that he has saved: 'A strange wild thing' (IV. ii. 5), and a traitor who fights against his prince. Thersander had also been a 'Stranger', and had also nearly killed the woman he loved, and in Behn's late play *The Widdow Ranter* the hero does inadvertently kill his beloved, the queen of an alien enemy race (she is an American Indian, he an invading European). Time and again, there is a fearful alienness in sexual relationships.

Erminia, however, survives the murder attempt. Whereas Hero in *Much Ado* (and Hermione in *The Winter's Tale*) eventually return from apparent death in a climactic surprise of which the audience has had no prior warning, Behn takes the aesthetically risky course of having Erminia repeatedly appear to other characters as, seemingly, a ghost. The first character to whom she appears is the cowardly Falatius, who reacts according to type, falling on the ground and trembling; but, when she appears to Phillander, Alcander and Alcippus, they are frightened too, if less ludicrously. In her period as a ghost, Erminia suspends the distinction between the heroes and cowards, virile and non-virile, but she has the power to do so because she seems to lack a body: to lack that which disqualifies her from participation in the heroic world of war, and which has rendered her a mere object of exchange and possession. Whereas Shakespeare merely presents the heroine's resurrection as a joyful *fait accompli*, Erminia must create circumstances in which she can repossess her body on new terms, and no longer be the cipher whom the King presented to Alcippus.

When Alcippus's remorse for the death of Erminia is described at the beginning of Act V, he is said to have embraced a marble statue of Venus and mistaken her for his wife. The woman is here reduced to a lifeless and passive sign, without interior essence or autonomy of her own. There is obviously, however, an allusion to the myth of Pygmalion, who had fallen in love with a statue of his own creation, and successfully prayed Venus to bring the statue to life, so that the story concludes with the dead icon of femininity gaining a consciousness and independence of its own. (When Shakespeare represents Hermione's return to life and motherhood at the end of *The Winter's Tale*, he varies the Pygmalion story, having her first appear to her husband as an apparent statue.) The name of Pygmalion's statue was Galatea—the name of the woman Alcippus eventually marries—and succeeding events show Erminia recapitulating the myth of the statue, ascending from sign to personal presence: immediately after hearing about Alcippus and the statue, we see him directly, holding a portrait of Erminia with a mirror on the reverse, their conjunction literally reducing the woman to a sign reflecting the male; then, for the first time since her seeming death, Erminia appears to Alcippus, standing behind him in the guise of an angel, so that her reflection appears alongside his, claiming that women have a separate and autonomous significance.

This is followed by the one occasion on which women do take command of the stage in a ceremony. With her seeming angelic powers, Erminia presents

Alcippus with, apparently, a prophetic dream of his future: of the woman he is truly destined to marry, and the victories he is to win. Disguised as a spirit, Galatea passes over the stage. Then come Aminta and Alcander as Glory and Honour, two further characters as Mars and Pallas, and Alcander's sister Olinda as Fortune. Here, women appear as the equals of men, even in the representation of war, but they can only do so because they seem disembodied: symbol rather than flesh, dream rather than waking. The return to the body brings a return to subjection. The quarrel over the corpse is still to come, and when affections are redistributed at the end—when the marble statue turns into Galatea rather than Erminia—it is in a ritualized sequence of giving where the men are the donors and the women the objects. As soon as Erminia has publicly returned from the dead, she is promptly given to her father: '*receive* the welcom Present which I *promis'd*' (V. v. 195; italics added) says Phillander to Orgulius, and '*Gives him Erminia*' (V. v. 195). Orgulius then '*resign[s]*' her to Phillander, who gladly '*receive[s]*' the '*gift*' (V. v. 205–8). This is a recapitulation of the giving ritual of the opening scene. It lacks the conflicts between the design of the whole and the wishes of the parts that were so visibly delineated in the wedding ceremony, but it is an order in which men are the active disposers. They remain so in all Behn's plays. Nevertheless, the rituals of power now acknowledge the woman instead of erasing her.

Unlike most of Behn's early plays, *The Forc'd Marriage* was published with a cast list. Falatius was played by Edward Angel, one of the Duke's Company's two best comic actors, who often played more broadly buffoonish roles, and the parts of Alcippus and Phillander were, as one might expect, taken by the company's two leading men, Thomas Betterton and William Smith, Alcippus drawing on Betterton's talent for conveying sexual danger and ruthlessness. Erminia was played by Betterton's wife Mary, an important actress who excelled as Lady Macbeth, but who was often provided with roles which, like that of Erminia, suggest sexual vulnerability (Ophelia, for example). An actress who was to be a more consistently fiery star, Mary Lee, took the small part of Olinda.

The text of *The Forc'd Marriage* gives very sparse indication of settings. Outdoor spaces are alluded to—the battlefield, the camp to which Alcippus plans to fly after the seeming murder, the fountain by which he weeps—but it is not clear that the characters are ever seen in the outside world. If not, the consistent constriction of the indoor setting would emphasize one of Behn's major points: that the codes

of the battlefield have been turned in against the domestic and the civic. What is even more clear than in *The Young King* is Behn's interest in the sexual control of space: men can possess and dominate the entire stage in a way that is possible for women only when they are attenuated into fleshless symbols in a seeming dream. She also shows immense care in prescribing the language and actions of the body, and their extension through manual props: whereas *The Young King* had created a significant interplay between the weapon and the document, characters in this play hold almost nothing but weapons (apart from the mirror, which disembodies and equates the images of Alcippus and Erminia). The great marriage tableau, where Phillander stands '*with his sword half-drawn, held by* Galatea', and where other characters are frozen in expressions of despairing unfulfilment, is the most elaborate expression of a general concern with the body and its adjuncts. The prominence of swords and daggers is certainly not unique to Behn, but it is distinctive of her, and constantly renders visible the ultimate sign and basis of male authority: women hold weapons on only two occasions, and on neither are they used.

The language of the body itself is a language of domination and subjection, weakness and strength, with far greater range than the repeated kneeling of *The Young King*: characters still kneel, but they also bow, weep, fall down, embrace and pull each other; after he has seemingly killed Erminia, Alcippus throws her body on to the bed. Like the great tableau at the beginning of Act II, these gestures of force, equality, vulnerability and submission, show the implication of the body in systems of power, sometimes institutional and ritualized, sometimes spontaneous acts of domination and surrender which recapitulate the official systems of power. For only in special cases are women recipients of the bow or the bent knee. When Alcippus bows and kneels to Princess Galatea, he is coldly keeping the relationship at a distant and formal level, and refusing to take notice of her hints that she loves him. The only woman who systematically receives gestures of bodily submission is Erminia in her apparently disembodied and ghostly state: here men fall down, kneel, look frighted, and bow. But the submission of the male body ceases with Erminia's re-entry into a female one. When her 'ghost' first appears to Phillander, he '*goes back in great amaze*' (IV. ix. 29a), kneels, and seems '*frighted*' (IV. ix. 27), as do both he and Alcander (IV. ix. 64). The two men at first refuse her invitation to touch her hands, since they are too terrified. Once they have touched her and discovered her corporeality, however, they manipulate her with confident superiority, Alcander leading her out and Phillander shortly afterwards leading her back in. Then, at the moment at which Erminia publicly re-emerges as an embodied being, Alcippus kneels to her. But this moment of recognition and submission is also the moment at which her power ends: shortly afterwards, she kneels to her father, and enters the play's final ritual, of the giving and taking of women, and the bowing by grateful men to the king (women only perform the male gesture of the bow during the masque of spirits).

In his invaluable and entertaining memoirs, John Downes, the Duke's Company prompter, records that *The Forc'd Marriage*, 'a good play', had a run of six days but then 'made its Exit.' (We know, however, that it was again performed in 9 January 1671.) Downes also records that Thomas Otway, who was to be one of the greatest playwrights of the Restoration, made his début as an actor in the role of the king: 'but he being not us'd to the Stage; the full House put him to such a Sweat and Tremendous Agony, being dash't, spoilt him for an Actor.' This was not an experience to be easily forgotten, but Otway remembered it in a rather unexpected way. Towards the end of the play Galatea begs the king, her father, to spare Alcippus, despite his apparent murder of Erminia, and works on his feelings by stressing her resemblance to her dead mother:

> If the remembrance of those charmes remain,
> Whose weak resemblance you have found in me;
> For which you oft have said you lov'd me dearly . . .
> (IV. vii. 36–7)

At the end of Otway's greatest play, *Venice Preserv'd* (1682), a daughter similarly pleads with her father for the life of the man she loves, and in writing her speech Otway clearly remembered the speech to which he had listened all those years before:

> in my face behold
> The lineaments of hers y'have kiss'd so often . . .
> And y'have oft told me
> With smiles of love and chaste paternal kisses,
> I'd much resemblance of my mother.

The echo provides a glimpse of the mutually supportive friendship and regard between Behn and many of the leading male dramatists among whom she worked; and it reminds us that one such friendship existed on the first night of her first play.

Source: Derek Hughes, "First Impact: *The Forc'd Marriage*," in *The Theatre of Aphra Behn*, Palgrave, 2001, pp. 30–39.

SOURCES

Behn, Aphra, *The Forc'd Marriage; or, the Jealous Bridegroom*, in *The Works of Aphra Behn*, edited by Montague Summers, Vol. 3, Benjamin Bloom, 1967, pp. 187, 281–381.

———, "Preface" to *The Lucky Chance*, in *The Works of Aphra Behn*, edited by Montague Summers, Vol. 3, Benjamin Bloom, 1967, p. 187.

Duffy, Maureen, *The Passionate Shepherdess: Aphra Behn, 1640–89*, Jonathan Cape, 1977, p. 99.

Gallagher, Catherine, "Who Was That Masked Woman?: The Prostitute and the Playwright in the Comedies of Aphra Behn," in *Rereading Aphra Behn: History, Theory, and Criticism*, edited by Heidi Hunter, University Press of Virginia, 1993, p. 66.

Hughes, Derek, *The Theatre of Aphra Behn*, Palgrave, 2001, pp. 8, 10.

Kreis-Schinck, Annette, *Women, Writing, and the Theater in the Early Modern Period: The Plays of Aphra Behn and Suzanne Centlivre*, Associated University Presses, 2001, p. 95.

Lyons, Paddy, and Fidelis Morgan, eds., *Female Playwrights of the Restoration: Five Comedies*, J. M. Dent, 1991, p. xi.

FURTHER READING

Aughterson, Kate, *Aphra Behn: The Comedies*, Palgrave, 2003.
    Aughterson shows how Behn employs comic and dramatic conventions to radical ends and how she forces her audience to engage with issues about gender and sexuality while retaining a witty and accessible style.

Fraser, Antonia, *The Weaker Vessel*, Weidenfeld & Nicholson, 2002.
    Historian Fraser presents an engaging account of the lives of women of all classes in seventeenth-century England, from heiresses to prostitutes and actresses. She examines issues relevant to many of Behn's plays, such as marriage and divorce.

Roberts, David, *The Ladies: Female Patronage of Restoration Drama, 1660–1700*, Oxford University Press, 1989.
    This is a study of the female audience for Restoration drama. Roberts examines why women went to the theater and how their attendance shaped the kind of plays that were presented. Many plays, for example, exhibited a concern for women's rights.

Todd, Janet, *The Secret Life of Aphra Behn*, Pandora, 2000.
    This biography of Behn examines some of the mysteries and contradictions in her life, including sexual intrigues. Todd has done extensive research and makes use of previously unexamined documents from England and Holland. She also discusses Behn's works.

Inadmissible Evidence

JOHN OSBORNE
1964

The first performance of *Inadmissible Evidence* at the Royal Court Theatre in London on September 9, 1964, by the English Stage Company, was a resounding critical and popular success. It also reinforced John Osborne's status as England's most important post–World War II dramatist. The play chronicles the mental disintegration of middle-aged, London solicitor Bill Maitland over the course of two days as he experiences the breakdown of his professional and personal life. Osborne combines elements of realism and theater of the absurd as he illustrates Bill's nightmarish world that ironically Bill has constructed himself. It results from his inability to face up to his own failures as well as to the pain he has caused those who have tried to save him. In this poignant study of one man's struggle to avoid harsh truths about himself and his relationships with those closest to him, Osborne presents a compelling portrait of the devastating causes for spiritual and emotional bankruptcy.

AUTHOR BIOGRAPHY

John James Osborne was born December 12, 1929, in London, England, to Thomas Godfrey Osborne, a commercial artist and copywriter, and Nellie Grove Osborne, a barmaid. Much of his childhood was spent in ill health and in poverty, especially after his father died of tuberculosis in 1941. Osborne earned a General School Certificate from

John Osborne © Hulton-Deutsch Collection/Corbis. Reproduced by permission

St. Michael's, a boarding school in Devon, but never went further with his education, which made him feel like an outsider among the intellectual group of playwrights with whom he was grouped in the 1950s.

After graduating, he wrote for trade journals for a few years but left to take a position as a tutor for child actors in a touring company. He worked his way up in the troupe to assistant stage manager, and in 1948, he began acting in their productions. Osborne toured the country with the troupe for the next seven years, during which time he began writing plays, including *The Devil Inside Him*, with Stella Linden, first performed in 1950, and *Personal Enemy*, with Anthony Creighton, produced in 1955. Osborne, however, could get neither play published and ran into trouble with the Lord Chamberlain's Office concerning the latter play, which deals with homosexuality, forcing Osborne to delete key scenes.

While his *Look Back in Anger*, which premiered on May 8, 1956, earned mixed reviews, the impact the play had on the theater became legendary due to its biting commentary on postwar England and the status of the British working class, as well as to its influence on an entire generation

of playwrights. Osborne, who like *Anger*'s Jimmy Porter came to be known as an angry young man, gained a reputation as a result of this and other plays, as well as in the press, as a controversial figure who spoke his mind about political and social issues of the age, including the Lord Chamberlain's Office's censorship power over the theater. His personal life became as tumultuous as that of his characters: he married five times and was estranged from his daughter for a long time.

Osborne enjoyed a long, successful career in the theater, penning over twenty plays, as well as several television dramas and screenplays, including one for the celebrated film *Tom Jones*. He received several awards during his career, including the Evening Standard Drama Award for the most promising playwright of the year for *A Patriot for Me* in 1965 and for *The Hotel in Amsterdam* in 1968; the New York Drama Critics Circle Award for *Look Back in Anger*, and for *Luther* (1961); a Tony Award in 1964 for *Luther*; an Academy Award for best adapted screenplay in 1963 for *Tom Jones*; the Plays and Players Best New Play Award in 1964 for *Inadmissible Evidence*, and in 1968 for *The Hotel in Amsterdam*; and the Award for Lifetime Achievement from the Writers' Guild of Great Britain, 1992, the same year his final play, *Dèjávu*, was staged. *Inadmissible Evidence* was published by Faber and Faber in 1965.

Osborne wrote two autobiographies, *A Better Class of Person* (1981) and *Almost a Gentleman* (1991). Osborne, a diabetic, died of heart failure on December 24, 1994.

PLOT SUMMARY

Act 1

Inadmissible Evidence opens with a dream sequence in a solicitor's office, involving the main character, Bill Maitland, and his trial for "having unlawfully and wickedly published . . . a wicked, bawdy and scandalous object. . . . Intending to vitiate and corrupt the morals of the liege subjects of our Lady the Queen." The object is Bill Maitland himself. Bill pleads not guilty and insists that since he is a lawyer, he will defend himself. He tries to begin his defense, but random thoughts keep breaking in, and he ultimately admits, "I'm incapable of making decisions." The session is interrupted by Bill searching for his tranquilizers, noting that he has a headache brought on by too much drinking the night before.

Bill then begins a brief summary of his personal history, ending with his admission that he is "irredeemably mediocre." After losing his train of thought, he thinks he sees his ex-wife, his father, and daughter, all there in the room. He then offers a character analysis of himself, ending with his assertion that he has never wanted anything more than good friendship and the love of women but has failed at both. The light then fades, and the judge becomes Hudson, Bill's managing clerk, and the court clerk becomes Jones, Bill's clerk as Bill emerges from the dream into reality.

In the next scene in Bill's law office, Hudson and Jones chat about the latter's upcoming marriage as Bill arrives. Bill criticizes Shirley, his secretary, for not wearing any makeup and makes lewd comments to her about her fiancé, which she throws right back at him. Jones announces that Shirley is going to quit her job because "she's fed up with the place" and especially with Bill, who insists, "I haven't touched that girl for months."

Bill then begins another series of lewd comments directed toward Jones, concerning his fiancée and Shirley, which embarrasses the clerk. Later, he criticizes Shirley's fiancé and Jones, insisting that they are too cautious and boring. Another secretary, Joy, brings Bill a glass of water after Shirley ignores his request, and he flirts with her as Hudson tries to focus Bill's attention on a client's divorce case. Bill admits that something seems a bit odd this morning: he was not able to get a taxi and now he cannot concentrate on his cases.

Bill complains of his headache, brought on by too much drinking the previous night, and searches for his pills. He tells Hudson that he needs to get out of a weekend planned by his wife, Anna, to celebrate their daughter's birthday so that he can spend the time instead with Liz, his current mistress. Bill believes that Anna planned the weekend because she discovered his arrangement with Liz.

As he discusses with Hudson the juggling he must accomplish with his wife and mistress, he wonders whether his sexual escapades are worth the trouble and admits that he has never found anything that gives him a sense of meaning. Hudson tells him that the key is to not expect too much out of life. The two talk about Mrs. Garnsey's divorce case, Bill's recent inability to remember anything, and his marital situation until they are interrupted by a phone call from Anna. Bill tries to get out of the weekend, but the situation is left unresolved.

MEDIA ADAPTATIONS

- A film version of *Inadmissible Evidence* was produced by Woodfall Films (United Kingdom) in 1968. The screenplay was written by Osborne and starred Nicol Williamson, who had played Bill to rave reviews on the British and U.S. stage. As of 2006, this film was not available.

Later, Shirley tells Bill that she is leaving because she is pregnant and is getting married soon. When Bill tries to show concern for her situation, assuming that the baby is his, and asks her to stay, noting their past relationship, Shirley gets angry and declares that she is leaving immediately. Bill, visibly shaken, asks Joy to ask Mrs. Garnsey, who has just arrived, to wait. He then calls in Hudson and asks him to become a partner in the firm. Hudson does not give him an answer, admitting that he has received several other offers, but he agrees to think about it. Bill phones Liz about Anna's plans for the weekend and complains about his lack of connection with his family. He ends the call by exacting a promise from her that she will see him that evening.

As Bill interviews Mrs. Garnsey about her husband's infidelities, she begins to feel sorry for her husband who has been rejected by her and their children. When Bill tries to comfort her, he cannot move and so calls Joy to bring her a drink. After Mrs. Garnsey leaves, Joy tells Bill that he does not look well. Bill asks her to stay late that evening and to call Liz and tell her "to expect [him] when she sees [him]."

Act 2

The next morning, as Bill is lying on the sofa in his office having slept there through the night, Liz calls, angry about his not coming over. After excusing himself to throw up, he returns to the phone and tells her that he loves her and that yesterday was a bad day for him. He begins to ramble, which he does during every conversation that he has during the day, to the point that the audience does not know whether he is really speaking to someone or is only dreaming.

Bill continues his ramblings about his wife and her boring friends and about his daughter, Jane, whom he criticizes as well. He pauses periodically to ask if Liz is still there. At the end of the conversation, he gets her to promise that she will wait at home for his call. He then speaks with Anna on the phone, telling her that he will be spending the weekend with Liz and that Jane would not care whether he attended her birthday. When Jane gets on the phone, he asks her to come see him that afternoon so he can explain about the weekend. After speaking briefly again with Anna, he tells her that he loves her and ends the conversation.

Hudson arrives and tells Bill that he still has not made up his mind about the partnership offer. Joy calls Mrs. Garnsey to set up another appointment and learns that Mrs. Garnsey has decided to call off the divorce. Joy and Bill discuss the previous evening, which apparently included sexual activity between the two in the office. He gets her to promise that she will not leave as Shirley has done.

Bill asks Jones whether he would take Hudson's place as managing clerk if Hudson leaves, but Jones will not commit. Bill accuses Jones of thinking that Bill will soon have to defend himself against charges of unprofessional conduct brought on by the Law Society. He then admits that he lost Mrs. Garnsey as a client and that he is "the wrong man for these things." Bill reads the divorce papers for Maureen Sheila Tonks, whom he claims he used to date.

Mrs. Tonks, who is played by the same actress as Mrs. Garnsey, arrives and begins to discuss her petition against her husband, who, she insists, made inordinate sexual demands upon her. As she presents the details of her case, Bill counters with her husband's written claims, but eventually, he begins responding to her charges with accounts of his own marital behavior. He has trouble defending that behavior and often admits to his shortcomings. When Joy interrupts, announcing the arrival of Mrs. Anderson, Bill passes Mrs. Tonks off to Jones.

As he waits for Mrs. Anderson, Bill remembers having an affair with her as well, and when she enters, the audience sees that she is played by the same actress as Mrs. Tonks and Mrs. Garnsey. As Mrs. Anderson begins to describe the details of her divorce case, Bill struggles to keep focused but again adopts the role of the client's husband, providing details of his own personal life. Since Mrs. Anderson does not directly respond to Bill's comments, he may be voicing them only in his head, or Mrs. Anderson could be a part of a dream. Bill rambles about the details of his funeral and speculates about what it would be like if Anna died. Mrs. Anderson ends her statement with painful account of her husband's lack of feeling for her, but Bill shows no compassion, not having paid any attention to what she has said.

When Bill sends Mrs. Anderson out, Joy tells him that Mr. Hudson has left. He tries to get his colleagues on the phone, but they refuse to talk to him. He then phones Liz and admits that no one will speak to him and that he fears that they are all laughing at him. He pleads with her not to go out so he can call her later and insists that they will spend the weekend together.

The next client, Mr. Maples, who is played by the same actor as Jones, arrives to give his statement to Bill concerning his arrest for indecency but also includes personal information about his homosexuality and the effect that had on his marriage. Bill actually appears to be listening to this client as he asks Maple questions about his relationships with his wife and his lovers, but he does not take any notes. When Maple realizes this, he leaves.

When his daughter comes into his office, Bill begins a long rambling monologue outlining all of his troubles: "there isn't any place for me . . . in the law, in the country, or indeed, in any place in this city." He grows increasingly agitated until he demands, "Do you want to get rid of me? . . . Because I want to get rid of you." Bill tells Jane that he feels only "distaste" for her as he does for all of her generation whom he considers unfeeling and apathetic. During the monologue, Jane does not respond but gets increasingly distressed. Finally, Bill tells her to leave, and she does without a word.

Joy tells Bill that the Law Society is investigating him and admits that she does not like him either. After Bill insists that he is "packed with spite and twitching with revenge" and that he would like "to see people die for their errors," Liz arrives, and Joy leaves. Angry that Bill never came to see her, Liz tells him that he is "a dishonest little creep" but that she still loves him. Liz shows real concern for Bill's deteriorating condition, but he refuses to allow her to comfort him and so she leaves him. At the end of the play, Bill calls Anna, noting that his vision is fading and telling her that he has decided to stay in his office. Bill hangs up and waits for something that is not identified.

CHARACTERS

Liz Eaves

Liz Eaves is having an affair with Bill Maitland. She appears at the end of the play, worried about Bill's mental state but willing to confront him about his repeated broken promises to her. Although she tries to get him to face up to his bad behavior, she shows patience and concern, repeatedly telling him that she loves him. When she cannot get Bill to commit to their relationship, she decides to leave him.

Wally Hudson

Wally Hudson, Bill's patient office manager, tries to offer sound advice to Bill but it is ignored. His sense of responsibility and loyalty emerges as he continually takes cases that Bill cannot handle. His loyalty, however, has its limits. Realizing that Bill is being investigated for misconduct and that he is losing his grip on reality, Hudson decides to think of his own future and accepts another position.

Joy

Joy, a young, attractive office worker, appears rather shallow when she is flattered by Bill's attention that has shifted from Shirley to her. She initially plays along with his flirtatious games and has sex with him, but she soon grows tired of his self-involvement and determines that she will quit as well.

Bill Maitland

Bill Maitland is an egotistical, self-centered lawyer who eventually alienates all those close to him. He tries to manipulate others into feeling sorry for him by providing them with a long list of perceived injustices that he has endured as well as his mental and physical ailments, which makes him appear pathetic. In an effort to retain his wife's and mistress's loyalty, he insists that he loves them, but his lack of consideration for them proves that he is incapable of that emotion. Unable to face his shortcomings, he blames others for his failures in order to deflect attention from them.

As Bill refuses to recognize the needs of others, he withdraws further into his world until he becomes unable to separate illusion from reality. The only perspective he acknowledges is his own, but his judgment becomes clouded by self-centeredness and by his alcohol and drug consumption. His inability to form satisfying relationships with others results in his complete isolation and mental breakdown.

Shirley

Shirley, Bill's young, attractive secretary, is pregnant with his child. Her coldness toward Bill is a result of her anger with him for not taking responsibility for her pregnancy. She tries to deflect his attacks by ignoring him or by firing back with flip responses, but she cannot endure his ill treatment of her, and she quits by the end of the day.

THEMES

Objectification as a Defense Mechanism

The play explores how objectification, which occurs when someone is regarded as a type or object rather than a distinct person, can be used as a defense mechanism. Bill objectifies his secretary and daughter in order to dismiss them as individuals so he will not need to feel any responsibility toward them. He places Shirley initially in the category of "sexy" and then when she does not speak to him, he lumps her together with all modern "girls" who no longer wear makeup. When he orders her to put on some lipstick, he is trying to push her back into the "sexy" category, a type that he knows how to deal with. He keeps her in this category by making lewd comments about her having sex with her boyfriend so that he will not have to see her as a woman who is pregnant with his child.

Bill regards his daughter only as a part of a generation that he feels has dismissed him. Since he insists that he knows what her responses will be, he never allows her to voice her own opinions. He claims that she is not upset but merely bored by his relationship with his mistress as "any of those who are more and more like you" feel about any personal attachments. He groups her with all of those he sees "in the streets," inflicting "wounds," without shame and "unimpressed, contemptuous of ambition but good and pushy all the same." Since women are only types, not flesh and blood humans who can be damaged by his actions, Bill absolves himself from any sense of blame in an effort to protect his fragile psyche. Ironically his objectification of others pushes them further away, which eventually leads to his mental collapse.

Search for Meaning

Another factor that leads to Bill's mental collapse is his inability to find meaning in his life. Bill no longer has any respect for the law that he feels has exploited him, and he has in essence abandoned his family because he feels useless to them. He claims that he tries to "take an interest in all kinds of things,"

TOPICS FOR FURTHER STUDY

- Read Osborne's *Look Back in Anger* and compare its "angry young man" to that of *Inadmissible Evidence*. Determine what has caused each man to be angry and compare how each vents that anger and the consequences of that venting. Prepare a PowerPoint presentation comparing and contrasting the two men and be prepared to discuss what point you think Osborne makes about the nature and/or the consequences of anger in these two plays.

- If you can get a copy of the film version of the play, be prepared to lead a discussion on how the filmmaker depicts Bill's mental collapse.

If you cannot get a copy of the film, write a section of a screenplay that reflects the audience's inability to determine whether Bill is speaking to real people. How would you cast doubts in a film version on the reality of certain characters?

- Research the tensions that were emerging in the 1960s between British parents and teenagers and prepare to lead a discussion on whether these tensions were similar to the ones that arose in the United States during this period.

- Write a poem or short story that traces someone's descent into madness.

---

but "the circle just seems to get smaller." Left in the circle at this point are his affairs with other women, but he recognizes that his attractiveness is waning along with his interest in them. In his self-absorbed universe, Bill ascribes meaning only to experiences that buoy his ego. When others refuse to excuse his selfishness, he turns on them and searches elsewhere for a sense of contentment. By the end of the play there is no where else for him to look. Osborne here suggests that the absence of a clear sense of meaning can cause spiritual and psychological bankruptcy.

STYLE

Theater of the Absurd

Theater of the absurd is drama that communicates a sense of the fundamental meaninglessness of the human condition by employing surreal or unrealistic techniques. Playwrights in this genre abandon the clear sequential scenes that are logically connected for disjointed and illogical scenes and moments. Osborne uses elements of the absurd throughout the play to suggest Bill's disconnection from his world and his growing confusion about his relation to it. This focus emerges in the opening dream sequence when Bill struggles to defend himself and his actions in

front of an imaginary court. Osborne combines realism with absurdism in the rest of the play as he depicts Bill's interactions with his family, his mistress, and his colleagues. Some scenes, especially the early ones, contain actual dialogue between two people, as the conversations between Bill and Hudson and Bill and his secretaries. But at other points, it becomes unclear whether Bill is talking to an actual person or addressing a figment of his imagination, as when he speaks on the phone to his wife and mistress and continually asks whether anyone is there. Reality is further confused when one actor takes on different roles as in the case with the woman who plays all of Bill's female clients. Osborne's use of absurdist elements reflects Bill's unhealthy mental state as the lawyer descends deeper into a world of his own making.

HISTORICAL CONTEXT

British Theater in the 1950s and 1960s

In the early 1950s, British audiences watched imported American musicals; sentimental plots involving the middle class and their traditional, moral standards of behavior; and drawing-room comedies. The British theater offered nothing, in

COMPARE
&
CONTRAST

- **Mid 1960s:** *The Feminine Mystique* (1963), by Betty Friedan, chronicles the growing sense of dissatisfaction women feel about the unequal treatment they are receiving in the home, the workplace, and in other institutions.

  Today: Women have made major gains in their fight for equality. Discrimination against women is against the law in England and in the United States. Yet while women hold prominent positions in Parliament (20 percent) and in Congress (15 percent), as a population, they are underrepresented as is the case with corporate CEOs in both countries.

- **Mid 1960s:** A group of playwrights come into prominence as creators of a new school of drama, the theater of the absurd, which has a great impact on theatrical conventions. These playwrights adapt existentialist theories from philosophers such as Jean-Paul Sartre and Albert Camus, creating

individual views on the essential meaninglessness of life and the absurdity of the human condition. Playwrights included in this group are Edward Albee and Arthur Kopit (American), Eugene Ionesco and Samuel Beckett (French), and Harold Pinter (British).

  Today: Musicals, such as *The Producers* and *Phantom of the Opera*, and reality-based plays, such as *Proof*, dominate Broadway and the London stage.

- **Mid 1960s:** Fed up with social mores and government policies that reinforce the status quo, the youth in Britain and the United States hold protest rallies for civil rights, especially for minorities, and against the Vietnam War.

  Today: Young people are often accused of being politically and socially apathetic as their main pursuits become materialistic.

---

short, that was connected to the social and political realities of the age. Then on May 8, 1956, John Osborne brought new life to the London stage with his play *Look Back in Anger*, a work that focuses on the British working class and its sense of being betrayed by political and social institutions. This new type of realism urged a generation of British playwrights such as Arnold Wesker (*Chicken Soup with Barley*, 1958, and *The Kitchen*, 1959) and Edward Bond (*Saved*, 1965)) to recreate on stage cottages in dirty industrial towns in the north of England as well as rented one-room flats in London. In these plays that came to be known as kitchen sink dramas, angry young men like Osborne's Jimmy Porter offered caustic attacks on society as they struggled to survive economically as well as emotionally in a world that offered them no real purpose.

In the late 1950s, Harold Pinter, in plays such as *The Room* and *The Dumb Waiter*, both produced in 1957, combined the realism of the kitchen sink

dramas with the absurdism of Samuel Becket, creating often claustrophobic works that focus on the difficulties of communication in an incomprehensible world. In 1964, Osborne experimented with structural and stylistic combinations in *Inadmissible Evidence*, retaining the same gritty realism of *Look Back in Anger* but adding absurdist elements, such as the play's opening dream sequence, which externalizes his conscience. His angry, middle-aged hero, while firmly in the middle class, struggles, like Jimmy and the other heroes of this generation of playwrights, to find meaning in his life.

CRITICAL OVERVIEW

Inadmissible Evidence was a commercial and critical success in London, especially with Nicol Williamson in the lead, but it did not fair as well with U.S. audiences. Many critics conclude that the play

Nicol Williamson as Bill Maitland and Clive Swift as Hudson in a 1978 production of Inadmissible Evidence © Donald Cooper/Photostage

is appreciated more by British audiences because of its essentially British character. Harold Clurman, in his review of the play, explains: "The English see in Maitland a 'hero' of their day, the present archetype of the educated middle-class Britisher," who has withdrawn from the world due to a sense of personal despair. He notes that several English critics found the play to be more "profound" than Osborne's famous *Look Back in Anger* because it is "the more universal play—a modern tragedy." Clurman finds that British audiences see themselves in Maitland, and in this, along with the author's "extraordinary faculty for derision in passages of coruscating rhetoric, lies the strength of Osborne's play." Clurman determines that American audiences want a sense of hope in the theater and so tend not to identify with Maitland as readily as those in England.

Many critics praised the structure and themes of the play, including Simon Trussler, in his article on British neo-naturalism, who writes that "Osborne has found his happiest medium so far in the solipsistic" play, and Benedict Nightingale, who declares it is "maybe his finest play."

Others, however, have found fault with its structure and bleakness. Robert Brustein, in his

article on the English stage, determines that if Osborne does not "put his wonderful eloquence at the service of consistently worked-out themes, he will remain a playwright of the second rank." Brustein concludes that "after a brilliant first act, [the play] collapses completely into structural chaos as the author introduces rhetorical essays on subjects only remotely related to his theme." In his review of the play, John Gassner wonders "whether, so to speak, Osborne's ingenious game is worth the candle," as he criticizes the play's "essential lack of conflict." While he praises the characterization of Mr. Maple, Gassner insists "that it gives us not much else," which becomes "the mark of its intrinsic failure." Clurman notes that "it crackles with sharp phrases which startle us to a guffaw" but criticizes its negativity and lack of compassion.

Frank Rich, in his review for the *New York Times*, finds its themes compelling, however, concluding that if the play presents "an evening of almost pure pain, it is honest pain, truthful pain." While he finds the play "by no means flawless" with its "overlong Act II," Rich argues that "one cannot take away the tough-mindedness that Mr. Osborne has brought to the creation of Bill Maitland"

and for finding "a common ground where the audience and his hero can meet." Rich insists that "it is Mr. Osborne's achievement that *Inadmissible Evidence* takes us right up to the edge of that darkest of voids . . . the sweaty fear that we may, in the end, be completely alone in the world."

CRITICISM

Wendy Perkins

Perkins is a professor of twentieth-century American and British literature and film. In the following essay, she traces the causes and consequences of the main character's mental breakdown.

John Osborne's *Inadmissible Evidence* opens with a dream or rather a nightmare in which Bill Maitland struggles to defend himself in court against charges that he has "unlawfully and wickedly published . . . a wicked, bawdy and scandalous object": himself. When Bill claims in this opening scene that he is innocent of these charges, the audience assumes that during the rest of the play, he will try to defend that innocence. Yet after Bill emerges from his dream, he spends the next two days proving the opposite as he alienates his family, colleagues, clients, office workers, and mistress. The growing sense of his inability to establish strong connections with anyone and thus to find some kind of moral stability throws him into a state of confusion and despair that ultimately leads to a complete mental breakdown.

In his defense during the dream sequence, Bill insists upon "the ever increasing need . . . for, the stable ties of modern family life," and his desire to face "up realistically [to] the issues that are important." Yet in the next two days, he severs those ties as he alienates his wife and daughter by ignoring, betraying, exploiting, and belittling them as he does others. Bill has created a solipsistic world, aided and enhanced by tranquilizers and alcohol, in which all his failures are perceived by him to result from others letting him down. Since he is the center of that world, he is unable to respond to the needs of others, lashing out instead at them for their "errors" against him, which ultimately compound his isolation.

Bill admits truths in his dream that he refuses to recognize in his conscious state. He realizes that he is "*only* tolerably bright . . . and irredeemably mediocre." He declares, "I have never made a decision which I didn't either regret, or suspect was just plain commonplace or shifty or scamped and

> " IRONICALLY, BILL'S EFFORT TO CONSTRUCT A PROTECTIVE WORLD IN WHICH HE DOES NOT HAVE TO FACE REALITY INEVITABLY COMPOUNDS HIS ISOLATION AND THREATENS HIS SANITY."

indulgent or mildly stupid or undistinguished." Only in the dream does he acknowledge that in his relationships with women, he "succeeded in inflicting . . . more pain than pleasure." He insists that he cannot escape the truth of his actions. Ironically, in this dream state, he is more aware of the reality of his relationships with others and the damaging effects he has had on them. When he emerges from his dream, this evidence becomes "inadmissible" because of his inability to face it, and so he begins to create his own world, one he refuses to allow others to penetrate.

Bill's solipsism is illustrated by his repeated insistence that he cannot see or hear clearly. This becomes evident when he is unwilling to recognize his abhorrent behavior toward his wife, Anna, and the effect that it has on her. Bill does not try to hide the fact that he has a mistress or that he will not be attending his daughter's birthday weekend so that he can spend the time with his lover. Although he calls Anna "darling" and often professes his love for her, his conversations with her center exclusively on his own difficulties, and when Anna brings up the birthday weekend, he refuses to acknowledge the pain he is causing her except for muttering a quick and feeble "sorry," before he hangs up. Later he tries to blame his wife for his predicament when he tells his mistress that Anna cooked up the weekend just to thwart their plans.

Bill employs similar tactics with his daughter, Jane, in an effort to justify his bad behavior toward her. In explaining why he will not be attending her birthday celebration, he attempts to gain Jane's sympathy by insisting that his colleagues and family are ignoring him and that there no longer is a place for him in the world. When that comment

WHAT DO I READ NEXT?

- Osborne's *The Entertainer* (1957) chronicles the downfall of music hall performer Archie Rice in a period when that venue had become practically obsolete. Osborne parallels Rice's decline with that of Britain in a scathing attack on what he considered to be his country's moral bankruptcy.

- Osborne's *Look Back in Anger* (1956) is often said to have inspired a revolution in the theater due to its reaction against the sentimental, middle-class plays of the previous decade. The play focuses on Jimmy Porter, an "angry young man" who has turned his back on his middle-class roots and on the society that he feels has failed him.

- Doris Lessing's "To Room Nineteen," one of the collected stories in her *A Man and Two*

Women (1963), centers on a middle-aged English woman who embarks on a journey of self-discovery that ultimately becomes a descent into madness. The story is set against the backdrop of early 1960s London, when women were caught in the social conservatism of the past and unable to see the promise of a future that would encourage choice, fulfillment, and personal freedom.

- Samuel Beckett's *Endgame* (1957) is set on a bare stage that represents a partially underground room where Hamm the master, Clov his servant, and Hamm's parents, who live in trash cans, alternatively try to humiliate each other as they wait for something to occur.

does not elicit a sympathetic response from her, he switches to an attack on her character in an effort to justify and deflect attention from his actions. Bill suggests that she is not worthy of his love and support, and he objectifies her as part of a generation of "unfeeling things" who regard their elders with "distaste." Then he abruptly tells her to leave without having listened to her concerns or asked her to respond to any of his charges.

Bill also treats the women in the office as sexual objects that are there solely for his pleasure. For example, when Shirley, his secretary, snubs him, he retaliates, criticizing her for not wearing makeup and insisting that she must not be getting enough sex. After Jones tells him that she is quitting because of him, he declares, "*I've* done no harm to her. If she's unhappy it's not my fault," refusing to recognize that she is angry because he is the father of her unborn child and has taken no responsibility for it.

Ironically, Bill's effort to construct a protective world in which he does not have to face reality inevitably compounds his isolation and threatens his sanity. The subconscious recognition in his dream of his responsibility for alienating his family causes him to take more pills and drink more alcohol to

the point that he becomes incapable of making decisions and of remembering important details about his work. This pattern in turn negatively affects his relationship with his colleagues as he insists that they handle his workload and as he loses clients because of his inability to focus on their cases. His inability, along with that of the audience, to determine whether he is speaking to real people on the other end of the phone or real clients in his office or just to himself as his state of confusion and resulting agitation increases signals his impending breakdown.

By the end of the play, after his office manager and secretary have quit their jobs and his last client has been lost, Bill's only connection to reality and possible salvation is his mistress, Liz, who appears at his office, trying to find out why he has been avoiding her. She offers him a last chance to forge a connection with another human being and so save himself from moral and psychic collapse. When she begs Bill to trust her, he insists, "it isn't easy to trust someone you're busily betraying." This moment of clarity is short lived, however, as he begins to attack her for scrutinizing and assessing him.

Liz tries to compel him to face reality when she declares: "You pretend to be ill and ignorant just so you can escape reproach. You beggar and belittle yourself just to get out of the game." Ironically, though, at this point, Bill is not pretending. After Liz gives up trying to force him to establish a real connection with her and leaves, Bill's vision fades as he suffers a complete breakdown, determining that he will stay in the office until something happens, although he has no idea what that might be.

Bill's inability to find meaning and significance in relationships with others causes him to repeatedly betray people until he is left morally and psychologically bankrupt. Osborne offers no hope for Bill, which has prompted some critics to determine that the play is too bleak. When Osborne refuses to rescue Bill from the solipsistic world of his own creation, he forces his audience to acknowledge through his poignant and harrowing portrait of this man that the recognition of complete and utter isolation is too much for the human mind and heart to bear.

Source: Wendy Perkins, Critical Essay on *Inadmissible Evidence*, in *Drama for Students*, Thomson Gale, 2007.

Klay Dyer

Dyer holds a Ph.D. in English literature and has published extensively on literature, film, and television. He is also a freelance university teacher, writer, and educational consultant. In the following essay, he discusses Osborne's use of the metaphor of marriage to represent the breakdown of civility and reason in the world of the play.

The opening stage directions to John Osborne's *Inadmissible Evidence* establish this play as "*A site of helplessness, of oppression and polemic*." It is a site that Osborne mines with virtuosity, as he had in the groundbreaking, autobiographical *Look Back in Anger* (1956), a play that explores the emotions of the prototypical angry young man. In both plays, angry men are forced to confront the failings of their marriages and their respective will to live a life guided by intellect and honesty, what Bill Maitland calls "an ethic of frankness." Over his career, Osborne repeatedly focused on these themes, on the unforgiving retrospection that focuses on the disintegration of marriages and decay of family and other personal relationships.

Whereas Osborne's earlier plays feel at times almost claustrophobic in their compressions of language and emotions, in *Inadmissible Evidence* the metaphors of decay expand ruthlessly to map Bill Maitland's spiral away from civility into a chaotic nightmare world of vicious mutterings. At once a

> DESPITE THE THICK VENEER OF MISANTHROPY, MAITLAND IS FORCED TO CONFRONT THE IRREDEEMABLE MEDIOCRITY OF HIS LIFE. . . ."

tragic figure in a world that increasingly presses its citizens to adapt to "different conditions . . . and . . . rapid change," Maitland barely contains his anger. On trial in the courtroom of his own mind, Maitland is forced to acknowledge his own metaphoric divorce from the world in which he lives. He is, as he admits, a man "more packed with spite and twitching with revenge" than anyone he knows.

Despite the thick veneer of misanthropy, Maitland is forced to confront the irredeemable mediocrity of his life and his pathological inability to change the trajectory of his decline. As he admits in his opening statement, Maitland is naturally "indecisive," has never made a move in his life that he did not regret, and has lived in fear of "being found out" and exposed.

Indeed, Maitland's day on stage is a monotonous litany of divorce cases, musings on the monotony of his own extramarital affairs, and misogynistic ranting about sex and women. When the telephonist Joy enters his office, for instance, Maitland comments casually about opportunities for group sex. Full of such comments and more tellingly with discussions of couples in various stages of dissolution, the play emphasizes marriage as a metaphor, as a figurative strategy for making meanings or, alternatively, for creating a framework of connotations through which new connections between ideas might be explored. In this sense, Osborne's marriage metaphor *creates* for the audience an uncomfortable sense of familiarity with Maitland's world.

If members of the audience do not know this world personally, they have seen it before in the plays of Harold Pinter, Edward Albee, and Tennessee Williams. But in this play, Osborne's marriage breakdown radiates outwards, extending beyond the intimacy of coupled lives into a cloud of ambiguities and multiple meanings that accumulate during the play. Marriage as a kind of sustained balancing act, a negotiation of mutual respect and compassion, becomes reconfigured through the language of this play into an illogical game in which no one wins and the measure of success ultimately seems to be based on a prowess for inflicting pain both verbally and physically. The metaphoric implications of marriage, then, becomes martial rather than marital, grounded more in the language of divisiveness (separation) and battle than in the vocabulary of honeymoons and happy endings.

The broader problem is that over time, even the most powerful of cultural metaphors become stagnant, less meaningful, even unsupported assumptions. In the world of *Inadmissible Evidence*, the metaphor of marriage has lost its value, in the same way that guilt has been reduced to "a real peasant's pleasure. . . . For people without a sliver of self-knowledge or courage." As Maitland argues frequently in addressing his clients, one way or another misfortune looms over marital relationships, which inevitably end badly or approach the impasse of reticence and resentment. Maitland's business day is telling in its routine: the termination of union is negotiated, divorce papers are signed, and new hopes are born. But as the stagnation of the office and the world weariness of his colleagues attest, failure of even this burgeoning hopefulness is soon to follow, and the routine will go on.

Yet, as Maitland illustrates, marriage is a metaphor that the audience cannot escape, either as a social contract into which he and his clients seem destined to enter or as a set of memories (the failed, the failing) that inevitably crash into the present tense of the play. As Maitland observes during his conversation with his client Audrey Jane Anderson: "Our marriage. What a phrase." It is a phrase and an idea that cannot be avoided when discussing Osborne's play or when considering Maitland's defense of his own life, in which repeated failed unions are inevitably unmasked.

Glimpses into his past show Maitland to be a character drawn more in the tradition of Albee's venomous husband George (*Who's Afraid of Virginia Woolf*, 1962) than of Eliot's tragically passive Prufrock ("The Love Song of J. Alfred Prufrock," 1915). Maitland has "succeeded," as he admits, in "quite certainly inflicting, more pain than pleasure" in those marriages, both literal and metaphoric, that have come to define his life. At the point in this internalized trial that frames the play, he lives on pills and alcohol, totally dependent on what Tennessee Williams would call the kindness of strangers, or as Maitland knows it, on "the goodwill of others." But in Maitland's world kindness and goodwill are anathema, and the middle-aged solicitor is forced to watch as his much-abused ex-wife Sheila and daughter Jane desert him, setting a path that will be followed by law associates, mistresses, and a variety of other women.

His daughter's ghostly figure, hovering in memory and at the edge of the stage, reminds Maitland poignantly of his failed marriages. "But, and this is the but," he admits to her, "I still don't think what you're doing will ever, even, even, even, approach the fibbing, mumping, pinched little worm of energy eating away in this me, of mine, I mean." Fumbling for the language that will bring his thought to expression, Maitland steps into the fullest light of his own drama, acknowledging that he has sunk "slowly into an unremarkable, gummy little hole" of a world, "outside the care or consciousness of anyone."

The play illuminates the vitriol and wastefulness of a life lived in anger. Relationships dissolve and language unravels, neither able to provide the meaning to which Maitland might cling in one final desperate attempt to make sense of his world. He is forced to admit that when "you feel you are gradually being deserted, and isolated, it becomes elusive, more than ever, one can grasp so little, trust nothing." Trapped in self-pity and divorced from any reassuring sense of who he is and what he believes in, he declares late in the play: "[I]t's inhuman to be expected to be capable of giving a decent account of oneself." It is inhuman, Maitland concludes, to be able to articulate clearly the depth and breadth of one's own humanity. As the stage lights fade and Maitland dissolves into shadows, he struggles towards the final separation, divorcing himself from his own life, stepping aside to view himself as a man guilty of a life energized only with a "spluttering and spilling and hardening" spirit.

Source: Klay Dyer, Critical Essay on *Inadmissible Evidence*, in *Drama for Students*, Thomson Gale, 2007.

Thomson Gale

In the following essay, the critic gives an overview of John (James) Osborne's work.

Prior to John Osborne's arrival on the scene, the British theater consisted mainly of classics, melodramas, and drawing-room comedies. But in 1956, Osborne's third play and first London-produced drama, *Look Back in Anger*, shocked audiences and "wiped the smugness off the frivolous face of English theatre," as John Lahr put it in a *New York Times Book Review* article. "Strangely enough," commented John Mortimer in the *New York Times*, "*Look Back in Anger* was, in shape, a conventional well-made play of the sort that might have been constructed by Noel Coward or Terence Rattigan." Yet, as Mortimer explained, "What made it different was that Jimmy Porter, the play's antihero, was the first young voice to cry out for a new generation that had forgotten the war, mistrusted the welfare state and mocked its established rulers with boredom, anger and disgust." As a result, Mortimer observed, "The age of revivals was over. A new and memorable period in the British theater began."

Look Back in Anger established the struggling actor and playwright as a leading writer for theater, television, and film. And, while his later works may not have created as great a stir as his London debut, as Richard Corliss wrote in *Time*, "The acid tone, at once comic and desperate, sustained Osborne throughout a volatile career." Perhaps more important than its effect on Osborne's personal career, however, was the impact that *Look Back in Anger* had on British culture. In Corliss's opinion, the play not only changed British theater, directly influencing playwrights such as Joe Orton and Edward Albee, but it also "stoked a ferment in a then sleepy popular culture." All manner of writers, actors, artists, and musicians (including the Beatles) soon reflected the influence of Osborne's "angry young man."

As *Look Back in Anger* begins, Jimmy Porter is a twenty-five-year-old working-class youth with a provincial university education and bleak hopes for the future. He frequently clashes with his wife, Alison, who comes from a more privileged background. The couple share their tiny flat with Cliff, Jimmy's partner in the sweet-shop business. A triangle forms—Jimmy, Alison, and Alison's friend Helena, who alerts Alison's parents to the squalor their now-pregnant daughter is living in and helps convince Alison to leave Jimmy. Helena, however, stays on and becomes Jimmy's mistress. As time goes on, Alison miscarries and, realizing her love for Jimmy, returns to the flat. Helena decides that she cannot come between Jimmy and his wife any longer and withdraws. Meanwhile, Cliff also leaves the flat in an attempt to better his lot. "And Alison's baby which could have taken Cliff's place in their triangular relationship will never be," Arthur Nicholas Athanason explained in a *Dictionary of Literary Biography* article. "Jimmy and Alison

> ATHANASON DESCRIBED THE PLAY AS OPENING IN A 'KAFKAESQUE DREAM SEQUENCE SET IN A COURTROOM THAT FORESHADOWS THE FATE OF [MAITLAND,] ON TRIAL BEFORE HIS OWN CONSCIENCE FOR "HAVING UNLAWFULLY AND WICKEDLY PUBLISHED AND MADE KNOWN A WICKED, BAWDY AND SCANDALOUS OBJECT"—HIMSELF.' "

must depend more than ever now on fantasy games to fill this void and to achieve what moments of intimacy and peaceful coexistence they can in their precarious marriage."

With the immediate and controversial success of *Look Back in Anger*, continued Athanason, the author "found himself, overnight, regarded as a critic of society or, more precisely, a reflector of his generation's attitudes toward society. Needless to say, the concern and feeling for intimate personal relationships that are displayed in *Look Back in Anger* may indeed have social and moral implications. But what really moves Osborne in this play seems to be the inability of people to understand and express care for each other better—particularly in their language and their emotional responsiveness. What is new and experimental in British drama about [the play] is the explosive character of Jimmy Porter and his brilliant and dazzling vituperative tirades, in which a renewed delight in a Shavian vigor and vitality of language and ideas is displayed with virtuoso command." Noting a resemblance to Tennessee Williams's play *A Streetcar Named Desire*, Athanason labeled *Look Back in Anger* "an intimate portrait of an extremely troubled working-class marriage (riddled with psychological problems and sexual frustrations), which was, in its way, a theatrical first for British drama."

When *Look Back in Anger* opened in London in 1956, few critics showed enthusiasm for the play.

Kenneth Tynan, in a review for the *Observer*, was the most notable exception. He found that Osborne had skillfully captured the character of British youth, "the drift towards anarchy, the instinctive leftishness, the automatic rejection of 'official' attitudes, the surrealist sense of humour." Tynan conceded that because disillusioned youth was at the play's center, it might have been narrowly cast at a youthful audience. "I agree that *Look Back in Anger* is a minority taste," he wrote. "What matters, however, is the size of the minority. I estimate it at roughly 6,733,000, which is the number of people in this country between twenty and thirty."

Most other critics could not see beyond Jimmy's explosive character to examine the themes underlying the fury he directed against the social mores of the day. More recent critics have been able to look back with greater objectivity on the merits and impact of the play. "Osborne, through Jimmy Porter, was voicing the natural uncertainties of the young, their frustrations at being denied power, their eventual expectations of power and their fears of abusing it, either in running a country or a family," noted John Elsom in his book *Post-War British Theatre*. For this reason, Elsom suggested, Osborne was not guilty, as some critics maintained, of simply using Jimmy's anger as a ploy to create shock and sensationalism. Nor was he guilty of portraying the angry young man as cool. "Osborne made no attempt to glamorise the anger," Elsom wrote. "Jimmy was not just the critic of his society, he was also the object for criticism. He was the chief example of the social malaise which he was attacking. Through Jimmy Porter, Osborne had opened up a much wider subject than rebelliousness or youthful anger, that of social alienation, the feeling of being trapped in a world of meaningless codes and customs."

So impressed was Laurence Olivier with *Look Back in Anger* that the actor commissioned Osborne to write a play for him. The result was a drama—*The Entertainer*—which featured a leading role that is considered one of the greatest and most challenging parts in late twentieth-century drama. In chronicling the life of wilting, third-rate music-hall comedian Archie Rice, Osborne was acknowledged to be reflecting in *The Entertainer* the fate of post-war Britain, an island suffering recession and unemployment, losing its status as an empire. "Archie is of a piece with the angry Osborne antiheroes of *Look Back in Anger* and [the author's later play] *Inadmissible Evidence*," noted Frank Rich in a *New York Times* review of a revival of *The Entertainer*. "He's a repulsive, unscrupulous skunk, baiting

everyone around him (the audience included); he's also a somewhat tragic victim of both his own self-contempt and of a declining England. If it's impossible to love Archie, we should be electrified or at least antagonized by his pure hostility and his raw instinct for survival. Mr. Osborne has a way of making us give his devils their pitiful due."

The drama's allegory of fading Britain and Olivier's compelling portrayal of Archie made *The Entertainer* a remarkable success in its first production. However, when it was revived on Broadway in 1983 with Nicol Williamson as Archie, *New York Times* reviewer Walter Kerr observed that in the play Osborne "has first shown us, at tedious, now cliche-ridden lengths how dreary the real world has become—what with blacks moving in upstairs, sons being sent off to Suez, and everyone else sitting limply about complaining of it all." Kerr added, "He has then had the drummer hit the rim of the snare as a signal that we're leaping over into music-hall make-believe—only to show us that it is exactly as dreary, exactly as deflated, exactly as dead as the onetime promise in the parlor. There is limpness in the living room and there is limpness before the footlights. . . . There is no transfusion of 'vitality,' no theatrical contrasts."

As Athanason explained, the author "owes a particular indebtedness to the turns and stock-character types of the English music-hall tradition, and, in *The Entertainer* particularly, he set out to capitalize on the dramatic as well as the comic potential of these values. For example, by conceiving each scene of this play as a music-hall turn, Osborne enables the audience to see both the 'public' Archie performing his trite patter before his 'dead behind the eyes' audience and the 'private' Archie performing a different comic role of seeming nonchalance before his own family."

Inadmissible Evidence presents another Osborne type in Bill Maitland, a contemporary London attorney who finds that his lusts for power, money, and women do little to fill the emotional voids in his life. Athanason described the play as opening in a "Kafkaesque dream sequence set in a courtroom that foreshadows the fate of [Maitland,] on trial before his own conscience for 'having unlawfully and wickedly published and made known a wicked, bawdy and scandalous object'—himself." Although he pleads not guilty to the court's indictment of him, his life is presumably the inadmissible evidence that he dares not produce in mitigation.

"Essentially a journey through the static spiritual hell of Maitland's mind, *Inadmissible Evidence* dramatizes a living, mental nightmare that culminates, as Maitland's alienation is pushed to its inevitable end, in a complete nervous breakdown," continued Athanason. "The play is principally a tour de force monologue for one actor, for its secondary characters are mere dream figures and metaphors that externalize the intense conflict going on within Maitland's disintegrating mind." The critic also felt that in this drama Osborne demonstrated his finest writing to date.

Osborne wrote other notable plays, including *A Patriot for Me*, a fictional telling of the trial and last days of Hungary's infamous Captain Redl, who was framed for his homosexuality and pronounced an enemy of the state; and *Luther*, a biography of religious reformist Martin Luther, an antihero in his time. But the works that garnered Osborne perhaps the widest notice after the mid-1960s were not plays but autobiographies: *A Better Class of Person: An Autobiography, 1929-1956*, and *Almost a Gentleman, Volume II: An Autobiography, 1955-1966*.

In relating his life story through the age of twenty-six in *A Better Class of Person*, Osborne caught the attention of critics for his caustic, even bitter, descriptions of his home life, especially his relationship with his parents. Osborne's father, who worked intermittently in advertising, was a sickly figure who spent his last years in a sanitarium. His mother, a bartender, seems to be the focal point of the author's harshest remarks. Osborne "looks back, of course, in anger," remarked John Leonard in a *New York Times* article. "In general, he is angry at England's lower middle class, of which he is the vengeful child. In particular, he reviles his mother, who is still alive. Class and mother, in this fascinating yet unpleasant book, sometimes seem to be the same mean thing, a blacking factory." Through his harsh view of family and society, Osborne captured the essence of his time and place. David Hare maintained in the *New Statesman*, "He understands better than any modern writer that emotion repressed in the bricked-up lives of the suburb-dweller does not disappear, but that instead it leaks, distorted, through every pore of the life: in whining, in meanness, in stubbornness, in secrecy."

If Osborne's memories were more bitter than sweet, a number of critics found that the author's hard-bitten style made for an interesting set of memoirs. *Washington Post Book World* reviewer David Richards did not, indicating that "like the male characters in his plays, who fulminate against the sordidness of life, Osborne is probably a romantic *manque*. But it is often difficult to feel the real anguish under the relentless invective of his writing.

A Better Class of Person is the least likeable of autobiographies, although it should, no doubt, be pointed out that affability has never been one of Osborne's goals." More often, however, critics had praise for the book. Hilary Mantel commented in the *London Review of Books*, "*A Better Class of Person* is written with the tautness and power of a well-organized novel. It is a ferociously sulky, rancorous book." Hare was impressed by Osborne's style: "His prose is so supple, so enviably clear that you realise how many choices he has always had as a writer."

Other reviewers were taken, as John Russell Taylor put it in *Plays and Players*, by "not the sense of what he is saying, but the sheer force with which he says it." In the words of *Newsweek*'s Ray Sawhill, Osborne "has an explosive gift for denunciation and invective, and what he's written is—deliberately, nakedly—a tantrum. . . . He can blow meanness and pettiness up so large that they acquire a looming sensuality, like a slow-motion movie scene. His savage relish can be so palpable that you share his enjoyment of the dynamics of rage." Osborne's memoirs constitute "the best piece of writing [the author] has done since *Inadmissible Evidence*," according to John Lahr in his *New York Times Book Review* piece. "After [that play,] his verbal barrages became grapeshot instead of sharpshooting. He neither revised his scripts nor moderated his cranky outbursts. His plays, like his pronouncements about an England he could no longer fathom, became second-rate and self-indulgent. But *A Better Class of Person* takes its energy from looking backward to the source of his pain before fame softened him. [The work proves that] John Osborne once again is making a gorgeous fuss."

Some readers of *A Better Class of Person* expected more insights into the playwright's writing process; instead, Osborne offered only insights into the playwright. As *Los Angeles Times* critic Charles Champlin pointed out, "There is nothing about stagecraft in *A Better Class of Person*, but everything about the making of the playwright. The [author's *Look Back in Anger*] was abrasive and so is the autobiography. It is also, like the play, savagely well-written, vividly detailed, and corrosively honest, unique as autobiography in its refusal to touch up the author's image. He encourages us to find him impossible and absolutely authentic." The self-portrait that Osborne paints, observed Benedict Nightingale in *Encounter*, "is of a young man of strong likes and (and more often) dislikes, capable of passion but also, as he himself wryly recognizes, of a disconcerting pettiness; a dedicated rebel, though mainly in the sense of not hesitating to make himself objectionable to the dull, drab or conventional. Interestingly, he seems to be without social or political convictions."

Osborne continued his autobiography—his exploration into the people, places, and events that made him the caustic king of the British theater—in *Almost a Gentleman*. In Hilary Mantel's view, Osborne's first volume of autobiography "bears witness to the grown man's failure to separate himself emotionally from a woman he despises [his mother].... The consequences of this failure are played out in the second volume: they are a disabling misogyny, a series of failed and painful relationships, a grim determination to spit in the world's eye. He is not lovable, he knows; very well, he'll be hateful then." By the second volume, critics were not surprised by the force of Osborne's hatefulness, so they were able to look beyond it to the writing, its stories and style. As Alan Brien wrote in the *New Statesman*, "Few practitioners provide twin barrels fired at once so often as John Osborne. However, after the initial splutter, there are still a few anecdotes that leave this reader dissatisfied." Brien also found Osborne's writing uneven. "His language comes in two modes. Rather too often his use is slapdash and approximate, at once confusing and surreal." *Times Literary Supplement* contributor Jeremy Treglown faulted the book for disintegrating "into a sad jumble of diary entries, fan-letters, bits of Osborne's journalism and occasional drenching of sentimentality or bile." Yet, Brien admitted, "Almost equally often, he wields his pen like a blow-torch, melting down banalities and cliches into new-minted inventions of his own that sting and sizzle."

In the early 1990s, Osborne looked back on *Look Back in Anger*, writing a sequel entitled *Dejavu*. This episode in the life of Jimmy Porter, the angry young man, finds a twice-divorced Jimmy living with his grown daughter Alison in a large country home. His buddy Cliff still spends a lot of time and shares a lot of drinks with Jimmy. The fourth character is a friend of Alison's and Jimmy's soon-to-be lover. "Some of the targets inevitably have changed, and the bile is now more elegantly expressed," observed Jack Pitman in *Variety*, "but otherwise hardly a beat has been missed in the 36 years since 'Anger' rocked the Brits." The biggest change is that Osborne's angry young man has become an angry old man. A reviewer in the *Economist* characterized the result: "For much of the first act Jimmy Porter sounds like an educated Alf Garnett—or, for Americans, an educated Archie Bunker." He rails against his past and how it has brought him to his current station. He failed before and he continues to fail. Suggested the *Economist* review, "He fails in life because he is not willing to make the compromises to his social superiors that are necessary for success in England."

Osborne had a great deal of difficulty having his final play staged, and it was not widely reviewed. The playwright's difficulties at finding success at the end of his career seemed to parallel the difficulties portrayed in this episode of Jimmy Porter's life. *Time* reviewer Richard Corliss called *Dejavu* "a glum sequel to *Anger*. In it [Osborne] described himself as 'a churling, grating note, a spokesman for no one but myself; with deadening effect, cruelly abusive, unable to be coherent about my despair.'" Still, critics found merit in Osborne's ability to turn his critical, mocking eye on himself. Wrote Matt Wolf in the *Chicago Tribune*, "Unendurable as *Dejavu* seems as if it's going to be, it is that rare play which really does improve, and by the last half hour or so, both it—and its superb star, Peter Egan—have long since exerted a rather macabre fascination." Pitman admitted that the play is long and without a coherent plot but acknowledged that "the show takes on an emotional depth as the raging misfit Porter gradually concedes the failure of his life."

John Osborne's anger may not have inspired the same following later in his career as it did with the debut of *Look Back in Anger* in 1956. Yet, his impact on the theater remains indisputable. "Few dramatists tried to mimic the Osborne style in the way in which [Harold] Pinter was imitated," Elsom commented. "The success of *Look Back in Anger*, however, destroyed several inhibiting myths about plays: that the theatre had to be genteel, that heroes were stoical and lofty creatures, that audiences needed nice people with whom to identify." John Mortimer maintained that the positive power of Osborne's anger was also beyond dispute. "Osborne's anger was in defense of old values of courage and honor. It was often unreasonable, wonderfully ill considered and always, as he wrote of Tennessee Williams's plays, 'full of private fires and personal visions worth a thousand statements of a thousand politicians.'"

Source: Thomson Gale, "John (James) Osborne," in *Contemporary Authors Online*, The Gale Group, 2002.

Peter Kemp

In the following review, Kemp comments on the "self-testimony" and "special pleading for a character who seems his author's alter ego." He praises several of the cast but finds that Inadmissible Evidence *is a "solo turn."*

Di Trevis's production of *Inadmissible Evidence* makes one notable addition to the play; a closing tableau in which most of the cast are seen sitting in a jury-box and staring accusingly at the protagonist, Bill Maitland. While in keeping with the judicial atmosphere of the work—which opens with a fantasy courtroom sequence and spotlights the personal and professional trials of a solicitor— it's an incorporation that is not altogether judicious. For, as the rest of the evening has exhibited, *Inadmissible Evidence* is a play that puts a man in the dock, only to let him slip out of it and don the robes of prosecuting counsel, stabbing the finger of indictment at everyone and everything around him.

Almost three decades on from its first production in 1964, *Inadmissible Evidence*—its scabrous directness no longer a novelty—shows itself more clearly as an exercise in special pleading for a character who seems his author's *alter ego*. Though it shifts from opening phantasmagoria into something closer to naturalism, the drama stays intensely solipsistic—as the set at the Lyttelton, with its see-through walls and weird fades, suggests. True to the seething, drink-muzzed consciousness the play dramatizes, scenes elliptically blur, people swim into sharp, momentary prominence, then float away.

Around the sneering, snarling figure at the heart of the drama, occurrences are far from varied. Such plot as the play possesses consists of clients, colleagues, secretary, switchboard-girl, daughter, mistress and wife parting company with Maitland. Emphasizing this escalating breaking-off of communication, there's repeated trouble with telephones: missed or cut-off calls, engaged lines. But the only connection Maitland really seems interested in establishing is with his inner self.

As always in Osborne, monologue is the preferred mode. Significantly, the first utterance of any length not made by Maitland—a woman's deposition for divorce—describes a man whose predicament replicates his. Other tales of woe recited by visitors to Maitland's office are likewise transformed into projections and reflections of his own malaise.

As the embodiment of the septic sensibility taking up most of the play, Trevor Eve puts in a portrayal that is younger and more vigorous than the legendarily fetid figure Nicol Williamson made of the role in 1964 and again in 1978. Vitality vibrates through Eve's fleshing-out of Maitland's rebarbative lineaments: the frantic fumblings for pills and whisky, the flickerings of the sour tongue round the stale mouth, the swivellings of the jaundiced eyes in search of some fresh target to abuse, the spitting tirades of derision.

A result of this more youthful-seeming playing of the part is to highlight the arrested immaturity of Maitland, shown especially in his callow assumption that strident truculence is the only alternative to mealy-mouthed hypocrisy. Mixed up with this is the notion that vehemence of feeling somehow excuses vileness of behaviour. Through Maitland's diatribes of disgust, Osborne strives to convince you that he is a man tortured by a craving for the "good fortune of friendship" and the "comfort of love", tormented by thwarted "energy".

This is most clamorously expressed in an encapsulating scene where Maitland's daughter—here emblematically got up in Carnaby Street plastic mac, suede knee-boots, mini-shift and beads—is required to stand totally mute while he berates her and her generation for their affectless poise and cool hedonism. As against her "swinging indifference", you gather, he represents swingeing concern. His rage, it is intimated as a plea of mitigation, stems from outrage. Laced with the play's invective is sedulous self-advocacy. Along with the depiction of a breakdown goes a kind of build-up.

One hindrance to this effort to elevate Maitland's fulminations is that he appears most disturbed by mere aesthetic shortcomings. Decrying people's dress sense, fondness for the Christmas lights in Regent Street or liking for mascots in their car's rear window, his aggrieved outbursts carry as much moral impact as the peeves of a ratty, jeering style-journalist.

Though the subsidiary characters mainly function as grouting around the grousing, Trevis's cast work wonders with what's available. Lynn Farleigh nicely differentiates three wives, each petitioning for divorce in language that pathetically mingles the domestic and the legalistic. As a dapper homosexual who has been entrapped by the police, Jason Watkins—at once courageous and rather campily comfy—is excellent. And Matilda Zeigler is perkily effective as the sexy butt of Maitland's sexism.

Essentially, though, *Inadmissible Evidence* is a solo turn: a self-testimony which, despite the final tableau this production sets up, is far from designed to bring in an unequivocal verdict of guilty. Opening as if it might be an unwavering X-ray of a confused psyche, the play swivels into a flatteringly angled mirror in which inflamed narcissism can contemplate itself.

Source: Peter Kemp, "The Mirror and the Lump," in *Times Literary Supplement*, July 2, 1993, p. 20.

John Gassner

In the following review, Gassner asserts that Osborne's main character in Inadmissible Evidence *is "mediocre," expresses himself minimally and with total indifference to others. He also reproaches Osborne's writing as lacking insight and feeling.*

On Broadway, as has been recently the case with embarrassing frequency, the most distinguished productions were of European, mainly English, provenance—most notably Peter Weiss's *Marat/Sade*, Peter Shaffer's *The Royal Hunt of the Sun*, John Osborne's *Inadmissible Evidence*, and John Whiting's *The Devils* . . .

Concerning *Inadmissible Evidence*, much as one may be grateful for seeing another play by this gifted writer, I can only wonder whether, so to speak, Osborne's ingenious game is worth the candle. The game includes such departures from tight, realistic, and "well-made" structure as starting the action backward, deliberately making the scenes repetitive, depriving the story of a conclusion other than letting the central solicitor-character Bill Maitland drop his tired head on his desk, and requiring one actress to play three different women as if to say tell us that the desperately sated, emotionally drained debauchee and failure Maitland sees all women in the same impersonal way. A related intention reveals itself first in a long monologue that isolates the alienated middle-aged lawyer Maitland for the audience and also makes the play-structure as lopsided as the character's life and as febrile (in a somewhat expressionistic manner) as his state of mind. It is only a slight exaggeration to say that the entire play is a monologue even after the bizarre prologue. The central character is morbidly involved only with his own ego, and so nobody else actually matters to him, neither his wife nor his mistresses nor his employees. He seeks to hold on to an office girl with whom he has had a pallid affair, but he has hurt her too much to be able to repair the relationship. He makes one belated effort to attach his legal associate to himself by offering him a partnership. He makes a lame attempt to win the affection or at least the attention of his long-neglected daughter in one fine scene played by her entirely in pantomime, and he gets not a syllable of response from her. He doesn't even get a good fight out of the mostly cardboard figures with whom he has such unsavory relationships or casual dealings; and this fact, this essential lack of conflict, tells heavily against the play. In the end he is left alone, a fading egotist mired in his own quicksand of unstable relationships, a morbid romanticist *manqué,* a mouldy Don Juan with a sharp mind that sputters apt phrases to signalize disillusion with himself and others.

That there is no genuine story after the prologue in which he gives "inadmissible evidence" against himself in the privacy of his chambers is easily apparent. There is only a swirl of rapid recollection and confrontations that occasionally constitute an episode; the visis of a hopelessly homosexual client makes an especially strong scene. That the play supplies a remarkably incisive character portrait is its main, perhaps its *only* virtue. That it gives us not much else is the mark of its intrinsic failure, disguised by its theatricality of the structure and the opportunity it affords the gifted young British actor Nicol Williamson for an unforgettable *tour-de-force* performance. It would be certainly unforgettable if it were not such a relief for some of us to forget the insufferable character he impersonates. In England, the omnipresence of this "person" on the stage must have been appreciated as an exposé, and the public and the reviewers in London (where *Inadmissible Evidence* ran half an hour longer) could endure even more of him than the New York management dared entrust to the mercies of American playgoers, who evinced no eagerness to storm the box-office. Here it seems to me Bill Maitland is mostly a bore. In portraying a corruptible, if supercilious weakling, John Osborne was far more successful when he collaborated with the actor Anthony Creighton on *Epitaph for George Dillon;* even if this role was much less theatrically striking than that of Maitland, George Dillon was involved in greater depth with other and more richly drawn characters. His failure while less spectacular was also more meaningful because the earlier written play developed a natural process of decline in the case of a character who succumbs to a commonplace marriage and a career of hack-writing after pretensions to superiority. It is, in sum, altogether possible to tire of magnified exposure, no matter how brilliantly accomplished, of a third-rate Hamlet of the professional classes like Maitland even while Osborn remains an admittedly vigorous and fortunately still "angry" man. The very magnification of the presentation of this character by Osborne's showmanship, the very theatricalization of the exposé, calls attention to the waste of effort in exposing him at a greater length than a one-act-play.

If this review, too, may seem to have exceeded a justifiable length, my justification is the fact that *Inadmissible Evidence* came here with the enthusiastic endorsement of London critics, one of whom acclaimed it as "Mr. Osborne's best play to date." Some New York reviewers were also greatly impressed with it. Henry Hewes of *The Saturday Review* wrote that the play was a theatrical statement "naked and shattering yet ultimately soaring above the desperation it so relentlessly presents." I wish I could agree with a former student and a tireless friend of the stage on two continents instead of agreeing with Robert Brustein of the *New Republic* that except in the George Dillon play, "Osborne's writing has always lacked a magnetic core around which particles of insight and feeling might collect"—here especially in the case of a mediocre character whose action, if one can call it such, is from the beginning an exercise in "solipsism." . . .

Source: John Gassner, "Broadway in Review," in *Educational Theatre Journal*, Vol. 18, No. 1, March 1966, pp. 55, 59–60.

SOURCES

Brustein, Robert, "The English Stage," in *Tulane Drama Review*, Vol. 10, No. 3, Spring 1966, p. 132.

Clurman, Harold, Review of *Inadmissible Evidence*, in *Nation*, December 20, 1965, p. 508.

Gassner, John, "Broadway in Review," in *Educational Theatre Journal*, Vol. 18, No. 1, March 1966, p. 59.

Nightingale, Benedict, "Critic's Choice," in *Times* (London), May 6, 2006, p. 19.

Osborne, John, *Inadmissible Evidence*, Faber and Faber, 1965.

———, *Inadmissible Evidence: Plays Three*, Faber and Faber, 1998, pp. 177–264.

Rich, Frank, "The Stage: *Inadmissible Evidence*," in *New York Times*, February 24, 1981, p. C18.

Trussler, Simon, "British Neo-Naturalism," in *Drama Review*, Vol. 13, No. 2, Winter 1968, p. 138.

FURTHER READING

Denison, Patricia D., ed., *John Osborne: A Casebook*, Garland, 1997.

Denison has collected a wide range of useful articles on Osborne, such as analyses of individual plays, including *Inadmissible Evidence*; an examination of the plays' reflection of their historical moments; a commentary by Osborne's contemporary in British theater, Arnold Wesker; and a comprehensive bibliography.

Gilleman, Luc, *John Osborne: Vituperative Artist*, Routledge, 2002.

Gilleman focuses on the themes of power and sexual politics in Osborne's plays, analyzing their destructive effects on his characters.

Heilpern, John, *John Osborne: The Many Lives of the Angry Young Man*, Knopf, 2007.

Heilpern provides a fascinating account of Osborne's life and uncovers the autobiographical elements in his plays, especially those that deal with the psychology of his characters.

Shellard, Dominic, *British Theater since the War*, Yale University Press, 2000.

Shellard presents a comprehensive view of trends in British theater in the latter half of the twentieth century, examining political and social influences and successful exports, as well as the development of the National Theatre.

Indians

ARTHUR KOPIT

1968

Indians, by Arthur Kopit, was first staged at the Aldwych Theatre in London on July 4, 1968. It is a long one-act play that is about the genocide of the American Indians and the legendary figure of Buffalo Bill who is both sacrificial hero and sly showman. *Indians* is an experimental, absurdist piece that eschews conventional plotting and characterization. These qualities brought *Indians* a fair amount of criticism of the play's structure. Nevertheless, the power of this play's message and the new presentation that it attempts garnered Kopit admiration, launching his career as a playwright from collegiate productions to the professional realm.

The late 1960s, when *Indians* was first produced, was a tumultuous time in the history of the United States. Minority groups, including the American Indians, were fighting for equal civil rights, which were legally granted by the Civil Rights Act of 1964. Abroad, the U.S. government had involved itself in the Vietnam War against which many U.S. citizens protested. Kopit was inspired to write *Indians* after reading that the deaths of innocent people killed in the Vietnam War were viewed as the "inevitable consequences of war," reports Lewis Funke in the *New York Times*. *Indians* is a critical look at a brutal period in U.S. history—the consequences of which Americans were still trying to face and acknowledge in the early 2000s.

Arthur Kopit AP Images

on another continent," Don Shewey wrote in the *New York Times. Indians* was the inspiration for the 1976 Robert Altman film, *Buffalo Bill and the Indians, or Sitting Bull's History Lesson*, starring Paul Newman as Buffalo Bill. The play was published in 1969 by Hill and Wang. Kopit received a Guggenheim Fellowship in 1969 and spent ten years experimenting with avant-garde theater before his next major play was produced. *Wings* (1978) is one of Kopit's most avant-garde plays and was inspired by his father who lost his ability to speak from a stroke in 1976.

The semi-autobiographical *End of the World* (1984) is drawn from the playwright's experience of being hired to write a play about nuclear weapons, a subject Kopit found very difficult to handle. The turn-of-the-century success, *Y2K* (2000), delves into fears about computers, security, and identity theft, themes which remained relevant even as technology continued to evolve.

Kopit married Leslie Garis in 1968. He has taught playwriting at Wesleyan University, Yale University, and the City University of New York. As of 2006, Kopit lived in Connecticut.

AUTHOR BIOGRAPHY

Arthur Lee Koenig was born May 10, 1937, in New York City, but his mother, Maxine, divorced his father when he was very young, and she then married George Kopit, a jewelry salesman. Kopit grew up on Long Island in New York and graduated from high school in 1955. He attended Harvard University on an engineering scholarship but discovered theater while there and spent a lot of time writing and directing plays. Kopit had seven of his own plays produced at Harvard's Dunster House Drama Workshop, six of which he directed. He graduated from Harvard cum laude in 1959 with a bachelor's degree in engineering. While traveling Europe the following year, Kopit wrote *Oh Dad, Poor Dad, Mamma's Hung You in the Closet and I'm Feeling So Sad* in five days for a small contest at Harvard, which he won. The play was a wild success, eventually making its way to Broadway in 1963. Kopit also won the Outer Critics Circle Award and the Vernon Rice Award in 1962 for *Oh Dad*.

Kopit's accidental career in playwriting continued with *Indians* (1968), which was inspired by the Vietnam War. He saw what was happening in Vietnam as "a continuation of cowboys-and-Indians

PLOT SUMMARY

Scene 1

Indians opens with three glass cases displaying an effigy of Buffalo Bill, an effigy of Sitting Bull, and, in the last case, a buffalo skull, a blood-stained Indian shirt, and an old rifle. Buffalo Bill himself appears on stage, riding an artificial horse and his Wild West Show coalesces around him. He starts off speaking with confidence about his Wild West Show until a Voice interrupts him, telling him that it is time to start. Buffalo Bill is distraught. Indians appear and the Voice continues to urge him to start. Buffalo Bill goes on the defensive, declaring, "My life is an open book." He calls himself a hero and the scene ends.

Scene 2

Sitting Bull and his people are starving on the reservation where they have been relocated. The president (the Great Father) sends three senators out to investigate their complaints, and they bring Buffalo Bill along to help them. Buffalo Bill promised Sitting Bull that the Great Father himself would come, and Sitting Bull and his people do not understand why the Great Father did not come. They are very angry. Buffalo Bill tries to keep

MEDIA ADAPTATIONS

- *Indians* was loosely adapted into the major motion picture, *Buffalo Bill and the Indians, or Sitting Bull's History Lesson*, directed by Robert Altman and starring Paul Newman. It was released in 1976 by MGM Studios and as of 2006 was available on VHS tape and DVD.

relations calm between the Indians and the senators. John Grass speaks first for the Indians; he tells the story of how the Great Father convinced them to take up farming but gave them poor farmland. The Great Father also sent Christian missionaries who beat the Indians. Now they are starving and the buffalo are all gone, and the Great Father has yet to fulfill his promises to give them clothing, food, and money. All they want is what they have been promised—and for the buffalo to return.

Scene 3

In a flashback, Buffalo Bill is shooting buffalo for sport, to impress the grand duke of Russia. He is thrilled with his success and then comments to himself that the buffalo are getting harder to find. His enthusiasm turns solemn. Spotted Tail, who has been watching from afar, confronts Buffalo Bill about shooting so many buffalo. Bill invites Spotted Tail to help himself to the meat and talks about how things are changing. He seems to feel some guilt but confesses to Spotted Tail that he hopes to be famous someday. The grand duke appears with his entourage, including reporter Ned Buntline. The grand duke gives Buffalo Bill a medal and asks him to come back to Russia. Buffalo Bill declines. Encouraged by Buntline, Buffalo Bill launches into a fantastical story of how he got into a fight with fifty Comanches and killed their chief. The grand duke declares that he wants to be like Buffalo Bill and kill a Comanche also. Buffalo Bill tries to explain that the Comanches are in Texas, and he is in Missouri. The grand duke fires into the darkness and kills Spotted Tail. Buffalo Bill is stunned, saddened. Buntline and the grand duke are thrilled.

Scene 4

This scene returns to the discussion between the senators and Sitting Bull's people. Buffalo Bill pleas with the senators to understand how important it is that Sitting Bull's Indians' lives are saved. "For it is we, alone, who have put them on this strip of arid land. And what becomes of them is . . . our responsibility."

Scene 5

The scene shifts to Buffalo Bill's Wild West Show. Geronimo is announced and appears crawling through a tunnel. He is prodded by two cowboys into a cage. Geronimo shouts about his conquests over white people. Buffalo Bill enters his cage, walks up to him, turns his back, and then walks out. Geronimo is worked up to a fighting frenzy but does nothing to Buffalo Bill.

Scene 6

At the Senate Committee, Senator Logan asks John Grass to be more specific about the Great Father's promises. The senators deny knowledge of any promises. They discuss a treaty in which Sitting Bull's Indians sold the Black Hills to the U.S. government. The money from the sale is supposedly held in trust at a bank, and the senators will not give it to the Indians. Frustrated, Grass keeps trying to walk away, but the senators and Buffalo Bill make him come back. Grass describes where the treaties were signed and what was promised to them. The senators point out that the Indians do not know how to read and cannot be sure of the content of the treaties. Grass is confused and appeals to Buffalo Bill, asking him why he could not get his friend, the Great Father, to come himself.

Scene 7

Scouts of the Plains, a play about Buffalo Bill written by Buntline, is being performed at the White House for the Ol' Time President and the First Lady. Buffalo Bills plays himself, as does Wild Bill Hickok. They are on a mission to stop the Pawnee tribe's "dreadful" Festival of the Moon and rescue the maiden Teskanjavila. Hickok is not really interested in acting and quickly abandons his lines. He argues with Buffalo Bill and then stabs and kills Buntline because he feels humiliated "'[b]out havin' to impersonate myself." Hickok then lustfully goes after Teskanjavila, hiding with her half-naked behind the curtain. Throughout the fumbled production, the Ol' Time President and the First Lady are blissfully unaware of the reality of what is happening in front of them. They think the play is fantastic. Buffalo Bill is left alone on stage, in a daze, spinning in circles.

Scene 8

At the Senate Committee hearing, Senator Logan challenges John Grass, insisting that it was the Indians who did not fulfill their terms of the Fort Lyon Treaty. Grass insists that the Indians did not know they were giving up their land in exchange for twenty-five thousand cows; the Indians thought the cows were a gift. The Indians understood the white people wanted to take the land, but they also seemed to think they could stay there. Grass tells the senators that they were intimidated into signing the treaty. When pressed by the senators, Grass says that he and his people prefer to live like Indians, not white people—and they want their promised money. Senator Dawes refuses because Indians only spend money on alcohol. Grass retorts that the Indians are only imitating white people, making all the Indians laugh and irritating the senators.

Scene 9

At the Wild West Show, Buffalo Bill is introducing his performers when the Voice returns, reminding him to include the Indians. Buffalo Bill is uncomfortable but complies. Indians set up for a recreation of their sacred Sun Dance while a very old Chief Joseph recites his surrender speech for the audience. Then Buffalo Bill introduces the Sun Dance. It is a gruesome and brave ritual particular to the tribes of the Plains, and Buffalo Bill's Indians are only imitating it because it has been outlawed by the government. John Grass appears, affixes the barbs to his chest, and goes through the ritual in the traditional fashion. At the end, he collapses and dies from loss of blood.

Scene 10

Buffalo Bill goes to visit the Ol' Time President and ask him to come to Sitting Bull's reservation and speak with the Indians personally. The Ol' Time President is riding a mechanical horse. He refuses to go to the reservation, saying that the Indians are beyond his help. Buffalo Bill pleads with him, and the Ol' Time President agrees to send a committee since he is so grateful to Buffalo Bill for his Wild West Show. Buffalo Bill knows that a committee is useless but cannot change the president's mind.

Scene 11

At the Senate Committee hearing, Sitting Bull is upset with Buffalo Bill that the Great Father (the president) did not come himself and sent stupid men instead. Buffalo Bill sees a fundamental, cultural misunderstanding between Sitting Bull's Indians and the senators. He tries to explain the Indian point of view to the senators: that plowing land to farm is harmful to their sacred earth and land ownership is a concept that does not exist in Indian culture. Senator Logan invites Sitting Bull to speak, and Sitting Bull tells them of the depravation his people are experiencing. He says he wants to live as white people do since the old way of life is gone. This stuns his Indians, but he continues by asking the senators to send enough animals, tools, and other material items for them to set up life as farmers. On the surface his demands are not unreasonable because he is only asking for what white people have, but his request is so enormous that it underlines how little the Indians have by comparison. Sitting Bull is also insulted that the senators do not recognize his authority as chief. Senator Logan belittles Sitting Bull, denies him any further speech before the committee, and closes the hearing for the day. Sitting Bull gets in the last word: "If a man is the chief of a great people, and has lived only for those people, and has done many great things for them, *of course he should be proud!*"

Scene 12

In a saloon full of cowboys, Jesse James is singing a song about a dead man. Buffalo Bill enters, asking for Wild Bill Hickok. Suddenly Buffalo Bill is involved in a stand-off against Billy the Kid and Jesse James. Hickok enters and he and Buffalo Bill go off to a corner to talk in private. Buffalo Bill is consumed with guilt for killing the buffalo and driving the Indians to starvation. But he does not believe he is responsible because he was only doing his job, while working for the government. He tells Hickok that Sitting Bull's Senate Committee hearing went poorly, and the government had Sitting Bull murdered. Buffalo Bill wants Hickok's help to know who he is so that he does not die wrong, in the middle of his show. Hickok calls forth a group of Buffalo Bill look-a-likes. Buffalo Bill tries to shoot them down and begs for the show to close, but the Voice says, "Not *yet*" and reports that the rest of Sitting Bull's tribe were also murdered.

Scene 13

The bodies of Indians lay in heaps in the center of the stage. Colonel Forsyth tells two reporters that he and his men wiped out all the Indians in this tribe, making up for Custer's slaughter. He describes it as "an overwhelming victory" and an end to the "Indian Wars," although some call it a massacre. The colonel, his lieutenant, and the two reporters leave for the barracks, and Buffalo Bill stays behind to honor Sitting Bull. Sitting Bull's ghost appears, and Buffalo Bill yells at him for not listening. Sitting Bull points out that although Buffalo Bill was trying to help the Indians with his Wild West Show, he was also exploiting and humiliating them. Buffalo Bill reiterates his fear of dying in the middle of his show. Sitting Bull, just before he leaves, tells Buffalo Bill "how terrible it would be if we finally owe to the white man not only our destruction, but also our glory." Alone with the Voice, Buffalo Bill is excited to almost be done. He delivers a prepared speech about how Indian tribes across the United States were decimated by the government in various ways, but his speech is sympathetic to the government's position. While he is speaking, the dead Indians rise and surround him. Other Indians appear onstage as well. Individual Indians announce their names and that they are dying while Buffalo Bill is speaking. Buffalo Bill denounces any responsibility on his part or the government's for the termination of the Indian way of life. He cuts himself short and pulls Indian artifacts out of his bag and shows them to the audience. Buffalo Bill sits by his display of trinkets and falls silent. Chief Joseph repeats his surrender speech. The stage gradually fades to dark and then comes back to full light with the Roughriders circling. Buffalo Bill enters on a white stallion. Indians lurk in the shadows and move toward him as the lights fade again. When lights are restored, the stage is set with three glass boxes as seen at the beginning of the play.

CHARACTERS

Grand Duke Alexis

Grand Duke Alexis of Russia visits the United States, and Buffalo Bill escorts him on a tour of the wild west. The grand duke is excited by Buffalo Bill's cowboy lifestyle and kills Spotted Tail in an effort to be more like Buffalo Bill. The grand duke's simple-minded view of the Indians is similar to that of the Ol' Time President.

Billy the Kid

Billy the Kid is a famous outlaw who appears near the end of the play at the Dodge City saloon.

Buffalo Bill

Buffalo Bill is the central character of *Indians*. He is a cowboy, a scout, a showman, and a humanitarian. Wild Bill Hickok is Buffalo Bill's foil: whereas Hickok is hard-edged, dangerous, and interested in immediate satisfaction, Buffalo Bill is easy-going and hopes to be famous. Buffalo Bill's name, like his Wild West Show, is a mockery of American Indian naming conventions. The irony of his name is that it does not refer to a reverence for the natural world but instead Buffalo Bill's slaughter of enormous numbers of buffalo. Buffalo Bill, as a young man, tells Spotted Tail that his people must assimilate to survive. He also declares that he wants to help people and become famous. This sentiment sets the tone for the play. Buffalo Bill believes that in helping people, he is a good person and deserves accolades and fame. So when the American Indians continue to die despite Buffalo Bill's efforts to help them, he is demoralized and wracked with guilt. He believes the Indians are going about things all wrong and perhaps deserve what is coming to them. But he also has compassion for them as suffering humans and wants to help. Guilt and compassion do not seem to be enough to absolve Buffalo Bill of his mixed involvement in the decimation of the American Indians. Buffalo Bill wants to absolve himself of responsibility, but his monologue at the end of the play underlines his basic hypocrisy, which has been apparent since the beginning but clouded by Buffalo Bill's good intentions and clumsy follow-through. After the death of Sitting Bull and Buffalo Bill's monologue of self-absolution, Bill is reduced to pathetic peddling of American Indian trinkets—all *he* has left of his Indian friends.

Ned Buntline

Ned Buntline is a writer who chooses Buffalo Bill as the subject of his work. He wants to make Buffalo Bill famous, which the cowboy finds intoxicating. Buntline urges Buffalo Bill toward tall tales and unnatural behavior to improve his stories. Buntline's play *Scouts of the Plains* is performed at the White House, starring Buffalo Bill and Wild Bill Hickok as themselves. Like Buffalo Bill's Wild West Show, Buntline's play is a sad caricature of the real experience. Buntline is stabbed and killed when Hickok realizes the humiliation Buntline's play is attempting to put him through. Like the American Indians, Buntline dies with Buffalo Bill standing there, doing nothing, unsure of whom to please next.

William Frederick Cody

See Buffalo Bill

Senator Dawes

Senator Dawes is one of three senators sent by the Ol' Time President to host a Senate Congressional hearing with Sitting Bull's tribe.

First Lady

The First Lady is married to the Ol' Time President. She is as delighted as her husband is with Buntline's play, which is performed by Buffalo Bill, Buntline, and Wild Bill Hickok. In true absurdist fashion, the First Lady does not seem to realize that Buntline's death and Tenskajavila's rape are real and not part of the script of Buntline's play.

First Reporter

First Reporter gathers information from Colonel Forsyth about the death of Sitting Bull.

Colonel Forsyth

Colonel Forsyth is responsible for the slaughter of Sitting Bull and his tribe. He does not see what he has done is a massacre even though many of the people killed were women and children. Instead, the colonel sees the attack as a victory that wins the U.S. government the war against the American Indians. He has not bothered to count the dead Indians, and they are left on the ground, being covered by snow, while the colonel goes inside the barracks for warmth and conversation.

Geronimo

Geronimo, an Apache leader, was renowned for his fierceness in fighting back against white aggressors. He appears in the play as a caged animal in Buffalo Bill's Wild West Show. It is unclear whether Geronimo is acting for benefit of the show or is actually imprisoned.

John Grass

Grass is an articulate Indian belonging to Sitting Bull's tribe. Grass is supposed to understand white people better than many in his tribe because he attended a white school. Grass even has a name that sounds more white than American Indian. Sitting Bull asks Grass to be the first to speak for the tribe at the Senate Congressional hearing, but Grass is unable to successfully negotiate an agreement. He states his tribe's grievances over promises made to them and signed in treaties, but the senators refute these claims, saying that these things they were promised were not actually detailed in the treaties and that the American Indians have not behaved in good faith toward their agreement. Frustrated, Grass makes fun of the senators which angers them and effectively ends the day's hearing. Grass next appears at the Sun Dance imitation going on at Buffalo Bill's Wild West Show. He interrupts the performance and does the Sun Dance the traditional way with barbs through his chest, which is illegal according to the U.S. government. Although the Sun Dance does not have to be lethal, Grass pushes himself until he tears free of the barbs and falls to the ground, bleeding to death. Traditionally the Sun Dance is for penitence so this is probably not intended as suicide.

James Butler Hickok

See Wild Bill Hickok

Interpreter

The interpreter works for Grand Duke Alexis of Russia. He translates Russian and English between his duke and the American hosts.

Jesse James

Jesse James is a famous western outlaw whom Buffalo Bill meets briefly at the Dodge City saloon near the end of the play.

Chief Joseph

Chief Joseph appears in Buffalo Bill's Wild West Show, a shadow of the powerful man he once was. Chief Joseph of the Nez Perce is famous for helping his tribe escape and evade U.S. soldiers for years in the Pacific Northwest. His eventual surrender, when his people were starving and greatly diminished in number, was considered a significant victory by the government. Chief Joseph, weak and defeated, recites his surrender speech at Buffalo Bill's Wild West Show as a way to earn some money. He now lives a half-life.

Lieutenant

The lieutenant serves Colonel Forsyth.

Senator Logan

Senator Logan is one of the three senators sent by the Ol' Time President to host a Senate Congressional hearing with Sitting Bull's tribe.

Senator Morgan

Senator Morgan is the lead senator sent by the Ol' Time President to host a Senate Congressional hearing with Sitting Bull's tribe.

Ol' Time President

The Ol' Time President is a foolish man, caught up in the romantic view of the wild west as full of adventure, romance, and cowboys fighting Indians. He has no compassion for the American Indians and refuses to personally meet with Sitting Bull in case it would send the wrong message to other American Indian tribes.

Poncho

Poncho is at the Dodge City saloon near the end of the play.

Second Reporter

Second Reporter is gathering information from Colonel Forsyth about the death of Sitting Bull. Second Reporter is more outraged than the first over the slaughter of Sitting Bull's tribe.

Sitting Bull

Sitting Bull is the leader of a Sioux tribe of displaced American Indians. Originally living in the Black Hills, Sitting Bull's tribe was displaced by the U.S. government when gold was discovered there. Sitting Bull spent some time working for Buffalo Bill in his Wild West Show. He appears to foresee his tribe's fate and tries to make the senators see the errors in their understanding of native ways, particularly in relation to ownership. The senators are rude to him, perhaps because they feel threatened. Sitting Bull and his people are killed in a raid commanded by Colonel Forsyth. His ghost visits Buffalo Bill soon thereafter and will not absolve the cowboy of his guilt. Sitting Bull's greatest sorrow is the thought of "how terrible it would be if we finally owe to the white man not only our destruction, but also our glory."

Spotted Tail

Spotted Tail is a Sioux Indian who is shot and killed by the Grand Duke Alexis for sport. Buffalo Bill pretends, for the sake of the grand duke and Buntline, that Spotted Tail was actually a dangerous Comanche warrior—from Texas.

Teskanjavila

Teskanjavila is the so-called Indian princess created by Buntline for his play *Scouts of the Plains*, which is performed at the White House. She is played by an Italian actress.

Uncas

Uncas is the evil Indian chief created by Buntline for his play, which is performed at the White House for the Ol' Time President and the First Lady.

Wild Bill Hickok

Wild Bill Hickok is an unapologetic, classic cowboy and scofflaw. Hickok, because of his straightforward nature, is uncomfortable with Buntline's play in which he is supposed to perform as himself. He finds this to be shameful—just like the Indians in Buffalo Bill's Wild West Show—and refuses to go on. Hickok kills the writer and makes off with the buxom actress. Buffalo Bill seeks Hickok out at the end of *Indians* to ask him for help in identifying Bill's true self.

THEMES

Genocide

Kopit's primary theme in *Indians* is genocide (mass murder). Genocide is usually motivated by racial, ethnic, or nationalistic prejudices. Kopit was motivated to write about the U.S. government's genocide of American Indians because of the U.S. involvement in Vietnam, in which he saw a similar arrogance. In this play, Kopit unabashedly points out the unethical treatment, dispossession, suffering, and death brought upon the American Indians by the U.S. government. Bolstered by greed, nationalism, and presumed ethnic superiority, white Americans of European descent in the U.S. government of the nineteenth century repeatedly lied, cheated, coerced, and murdered the native inhabitants of North America. They perpetrated these crimes in an effort to gain fertile or otherwise rich land and to eliminate a culture that they saw as obstructing this appropriation. *Indians* represents some of the ways in which the U.S. government brought harm to native tribes people: the futile Senate Committee hearing, the wasteful hunting of buffalo, the surprise-attack slaughter of entire tribes, and even Buffalo Bill's Wild West Show. Buffalo Bill tries to bridge the gap between his government and the American Indians, but although he understands the Indians more than many white people, he does not understand them well enough to find a solution amenable to both sides. Genocide has occurred throughout human history and includes events in the twentieth and twenty-first centuries, such as those in World War II Europe, in Rwanda, and in Darfur.

Guilt and Responsibility

Buffalo Bill feels guilty about his role in harming the native way of life. As a young man in the

TOPICS FOR FURTHER STUDY

- In his play, Kopit explores the genocide of the American Indians at the hands of the U.S. government. Research another instance of genocide from world history and prepare a fifteen-minute presentation. Tell your classmates what the background of the genocide is, how and why it was carried out, and what, if anything, was done to stop it. When the presentations are complete, hold a roundtable discussion about what can be done to prevent future genocides from happening, using your collective knowledge to inform your ideas.

- Buffalo Bill was a man of conflicting interests. He worked for the U.S. government but was also sympathetic to American Indians. Research the life of Buffalo Bill (whose real name was William Frederick Cody) and write an essay that compares his life to Kopit's presentation of him. Is Kopit's version accurate in fact and emotion? Explain.

- Write a fifteen-minute monologue from the point of view of an American Indian, a settler, or a U.S. soldier. What problems does your character face and how is he or she dealing with them? Be as specific and detailed as possible. Perform your monologue for your class. Discuss as a class how the characters you have each created would interact with one another.

- There are hundreds of different American Indian tribes across North America, from the Abenaki of the northeastern United States to the Hopi of Arizona. Although all of these tribes are recognized as native people and as such called American Indians or Native Americans, their customs vary dramatically. Choose two geographically separate tribes and research their customs and history. Create a visual aid such as a poster or diorama that exhibits these differences and put it up in your classroom or school hallway to share what you have learned with others.

- There are food traditions particular to American Indians, although they can vary widely among tribes and across geography. Research dishes of an American Indian tribe. What unique ingredients do they use? How are they similar or different from foods eaten in the United States today? Select a dish to prepare and make it for your class. Have a potluck party and taste the different foods of native tribes of North America. Let everyone choose a favorite and explain why this choice appeals.

- Which U.S. presidents held office during the nineteenth century? What were their policies toward American Indians? Who was the most sympathetic and who was the harshest? Write a report that examines the influence of the U.S. president on the treatment of American Indians. What responsibility do the presidents bear for the genocide of the American Indians? Can you imagine other ways in which this cultural clash between American Indians and European settlers could have been resolved? Explain.

- Buffalo Bill's Wild West Show was very popular. It traveled around the country claiming to educate and entertain audiences about the wild west. It toured for more than twenty years and at its peak employed over twelve hundred performers. In small groups, investigate the details of the Wild West Show and select a portion of it to recreate for your class. Use costumes, music, props, and sets as needed to establish the tone—but remember that the Wild West Show was a traveling production.

- Research two incidents of genocide and write an essay that compares them. Explain why these genocides happened, who were the parties involved, and what (if anything) was done to curtail them. How did they end? Was anyone held responsible? What are the similarities and the differences between these two instances of genocide?

- Write a play or story about a frontier. A frontier is a border land between what is familiar and what is not. Your frontier can be the Wild West, outer space, or uncharted island—use your imagination. For extra credit, incorporate some of the themes or stylistic devices used by Kopit in *Indians*.

employ of the U.S. Army, Buffalo Bill slaughtered thousands of buffalo, driving the species to near extinction. He is undeniably responsible, in part, for the destruction of the Indians although he did not directly lay his hand against them and even actively tried to help them. Buffalo Bill's guilt drives him to find ways to help the American Indians adapt to their new neighbors. He also wants to be famous. Joining these disparate ambitions, he starts up a traveling Wild West Show, which is hugely popular and even exhibits some famous American Indians such as Geronimo, Sitting Bull, and Chief Joseph. Buffalo Bill's efforts to help and support the American Indians are finally ineffective in holding off the grim determination of the U.S. government to clear American Indians from the land they occupy. His solution, assimilation, is a different, slower death which also causes the American Indian culture to break down.

The Ol' Time President and Colonel Forsyth, in contrast to Buffalo Bill, actively and consciously participate in the destruction of the American Indians and feel no remorse because they have objectified the Indians as the so-called bad guys while they identify themselves as the good guys. This binary, us/them approach dehumanizes the opponent as the other. The only responsibility the president and the colonel feel is toward their own government, which, they believe, is threatened by the native way of life.

Wild Bill Hickok is portrayed as the stereotypical cowboy—brash and fiercely independent. He is so straight-forward that he never behaves contrary to his nature. He suffers no guilt because he does not second-guess himself and is not introspective. Near the end of the play, Buffalo Bill feels he has lost himself and asks Hickok for help, but Hickok's twisted solution of multiple Buffalo Bills only exacerbates Bill's guilty conscience. Consumed by remorse and yet confused because he believes he is a good man, Buffalo Bill is the one left suffering at the end of *Indians*; he is the most human and humane of the white people in the play.

Ownership versus Stewardship

The difference between the concepts of ownership and stewardship define the difference between white people and American Indians in Kopit's play. Western white people believe in individuality and property. One's success is intrinsically tied to one's wealth, which may be measured in possessions, property, and land. American Indians, by contrast, have a communal lifestyle in which property is shared collectively but not owned personally. American Indians see themselves as stewards of the land, responsible

for its care. The land is a gift to them from the Great Spirit, and they see the land as a living entity which cannot be bought, sold, or traded but instead belongs to everyone. As Kopit expresses in his play, the Indians are baffled by the white men's request to buy their land, such as in the Laramie Treaty. The Indians accept the offer, seeing it as a type of gift since of course the land cannot actually be transferred from one person to other; however, the white men are offended that the American Indians are not upholding their side of the agreement, uneven as it was, because they understand the treaties to be legally binding documents. This misunderstanding fuels the arguments that American Indians are not as smart as white people and not as honorable.

STYLE

Plot

Kopit uses a non-linear plot structure to build dramatic tension in this play which is largely based on historical events and is thus a story with which audience members are already familiar. At the center of action is Buffalo Bill and throughout the play, viewers see events from his youth, from the recent past, and the present time of the telling of his story which takes place toward the end of his life. Throughout the play, Buffalo Bill feels varying levels of guilt over his involvement in the genocide of the Indians, and this guilt seems to increase as he grows older. The non-linear plot may also be an acknowledgement of an American Indian world view, where history is perceived as cyclical. Kopit combines several threads of Buffalo Bill's life, but the image finally depicted is not of a humanitarian. Buffalo Bill has tried to connect with the American Indians but failed to be a hero or their friend.

Absurdism

Absurdism is a literary style that emphasizes the disconnection and meaninglessness in human experience. When the style is used in drama, the plays do not provide rational sequences or realistic portrayals of action, and these plays may collectively be referred to as theater of the absurd. Characters in absurdist plays are often disorientated and feel threatened, like Buffalo Bill. In *Indians*, Kopit shows how Buffalo Bill is overcome by guilt and cannot come to terms with what has happened to the American Indians. He is jumpy and rubs his head and squints often as if he has a headache. The other white men in the play are absurdist in their unreal, over-the-top behavior.

Theater of the absurd is highly unconventional and purposefully strives to keep the audience off balance. Kopit achieves this effect with his grotesque presentation of the Wild West Show and direct look at the brutality perpetrated against Indians. Theater of the absurd rejects language as a reliable means of communication and seeks to evoke myth and allegory to find alternative meaning. Buffalo Bill's attempts to serve as an interpreter between the senators and the Indians, between Hickok and Buntline, between the grand duke of Russia and the Indians, all underline a breakdown in language as an effective means of communication. The allegory of *Indians* is in its similarity in theme and outcome to the Vietnam War, which was contemporary with the first production of the play.

Tone

Tone is the writer or narrator's attitude toward the story, which helps to set the mood. Tone influences how readers feel about the characters and what happens to them. The tone of *Indians* is one of anxiety, outrage, and futility. Kopit knows there is nothing that can be done to change what has already come to pass, but if his message can be communicated to audiences, then perhaps genocide may be averted in the future. Kopit communicates his frustration and anger through Buffalo Bill's quiet desperation, the irresponsible behavior of the other white men in the story, and the edgy resignation of the American Indians. *Indians* is a play of difficult emotions, but Kopit avoids heavy-handed badgering by making Buffalo Bill a flawed yet somewhat sympathetic character.

HISTORICAL CONTEXT

Vietnam War

The Vietnam War was a protracted military conflict between North and South Vietnam, lasting from 1957 until 1975. Vietnam was a proxy war for the cold war going on between communist and democratic nations. The United States was involved in Vietnam on the side of the South Vietnamese starting in 1955, but it was not until the appointment of General William Westmoreland in 1964 that the numbers of U.S. troops engaged there rose significantly. It quickly became apparent that the U.S. military was unprepared for the guerilla style of fighting used by the North Vietnamese. Guerilla warfare is a decentralized approach that works well for defending against foreign invaders. U.S. soldiers, never knowing who was friend or foe, were demoralized. Their fear contributed to their perpetrating crimes against civilians. Many Vietnam War veterans suffered from psychological trauma as a result. In the United States, many people were outraged by what they learned from daily news reports. Large numbers of citizens, especially young people immediately affected by the involuntary draft, began to protest publicly against the war. These protests polarized public opinion, causing sharp division between those who disapproved of U.S. involvement in Vietnam and those who accepted the government's argument that the United States was defending democracy against communism. By the end of the Vietnam War, two to four million people—military and civilian and of all nationalities—were dead and South Vietnam, along with her allies including the United States, had lost the war.

American Indian Rights

American Indians, along with other minorities, gained civil rights protection with the passage of the Civil Rights Act in 1964. But the Bureau of Indian Affairs was still trying to bring American Indians into mainstream U.S. culture in order to do away with reservations. In the 1970s, a group called the American Indian Movement (AIM) staged several highly publicized protests to bring further awareness to the rights of native peoples. Their goals included improving living conditions, protecting Indians from police brutality, and working to remove Indian caricatures from sports. Their methods were sometimes dramatic, but AIM overall made progress in raising awareness and respect for the cultures of American Indians. At the beginning of the twenty-first century, American Indian tribes have federal rights of self-government, much like states have. Almost three million American Indians live in the United States, divided into 563 tribal governments. Efforts to disenfranchise some tribal governments continued in the early 2000s as their land was sought for the valuable resources it contains. Other areas of the country resist permitting the formation of tribal governments because of concerns over gambling and casinos, which are often built and run by tribes to generate revenue.

Theater of the Absurd

The term, theater of the absurd, was coined by Martin Esslin in his 1962 book of the same name.

COMPARE
&
CONTRAST

- **1860s:** Buffalo Bill is a famous showman and western hero in his own time, having created the widely popular Buffalo Bill's Wild West Show.

  1960s: John Wayne and Clint Eastwood are actors known for their performances as cowboys in western movies.

  Today: Clint Eastwood is still a figure readily identified with westerns, although his career is diverse. Genre blending of science fiction, anime, and westerns is popular.

- **1860s:** Approximately fifty million buffalo (American bison) roam the plains of North America but are being killed in large numbers for their hides and to protect farms and settlements and to remove a source of food from nomadic tribes of Native Americans.

  1960s: Buffalo slowly recover from their near extinction in the late 1800s when only twenty-three wild buffalo remained.

  Today: The National Bison Association estimates that there are four hundred thousand buffalo in North America.

- **1860s:** American Indians have no civil rights and are not considered citizens according to the U.S. government. Treaties between the Indians and the government are often misunderstood and betrayed.

  1960s: A movement grows to improve the civil rights of American Indians, who have been struggling against assimilation since they were made U.S. citizens in 1924. The American Indian Movement (AIM) organization is formed.

  Today: Tribes are autonomous entities within the federal government, much like states. Many tribes run casinos to generate revenue, but some feel that casinos contribute to the further destruction of their culture. American Indians are protected by the same anti-discrimination laws that shield other minority groups, but fights over land, resources, and sovereignty continue.

It refers to existential playwriting that asserts the meaninglessness of life. Esslin formulated his theory of the theater of the absurd after reading Albert Camus's essay, "The Myth of Sisyphus," in which the meaninglessness of life is a central idea. The four playwrights Esslin identified as being the forerunners of the absurdist movement are Samuel Beckett, Jean Genet, Eugene Ionesco, and Arthur Adamov. Theater of the absurd is, in essence, a type of avant-garde presentation. It employs unconventional and unrealistic settings, characters, plot development, and dialogue. Experimental literature has been written for centuries. Avant-garde was coined in Paris in 1861 to refer to those works that test conventions and initiate change. Avant-garde works such as those produced by surrealist poets and cubist painters were especially popular in the early twentieth century, paving the way for the rise of theater of the absurd in the 1950s and 1960s.

CRITICAL OVERVIEW

The 1968 opening of *Indians* in London was greeted with a mixture of puzzlement and guarded praise. People wondered why a show that was so thoroughly American would first be staged in Britain. Irving Wardle, reviewing for the London *Times* proclaims: "the play is one of the few necessary works to have appeared from the America of the sixties. Whatever holes you care to pick, it is a work of high ambition." Stateside, drama critic Clive Barnes, also reviewing the London production, writes that Kopit's play is "only partially successful" and that "the play is at its best at its most serious, when it is making substantial and documented charges against the Government." British critic Martin Esslin, writing for the *New York Times*, considers *Indians* to be both "moving" and "amusing."

Buffalo Bill Cody shown with Native American chiefs in 1891 Library of Congress

When *Indians* was restaged in Washington, D.C., a year later, Julius Novick found it to be "more annoying than satisfying" and "not yet a good play," while acknowledging that the merits of this play establish Kopit as more than a one-hit wonder. Barnes also reviewed the D.C. production and found it to be greatly improved, structurally, over the London production. While Barnes is over-all positive about the show, he tempers his review by observing that "there is still an odd strain of facetiousness in the play, although not nearly so much as before." In October 1969, *Indians* moved to Broadway where Barnes reviewed this third production, summarizing his position: "It is not the greatest play ever written—far from it. But it does, even by the freedoms of dramatic form it grandiloquently permits itself, extend our theater."

Lewis Funke, in the *New York Times*, takes a far more positive position, declaring that *Indians* is "one of the most theatrically spectacular productions to reach Broadway in years." But Walter Kerr's review of the Broadway production was more harsh: "Everywhere substance has been skimped. Sometimes the skimpiness is covered over by attitudinizing, sometimes it is covered over by moralizing (because we are guilty, must we accept weak dramaturgy?)." *Indians* was restaged twenty-two years later and received an even more

negative review from Alvin Klein, who found the play to be shapeless and polemical. He writes in the *New York Times* that *Indians* "comes off as more diatribe than drama" and that it is "perhaps most unsettling for being so relentlessly penitential and uninvolving."

CRITICISM

Carol Ullmann

Ullmann is a freelance writer and editor. In the following essay, she discusses Kopit's characterization of Buffalo Bill and whether the character's efforts to help the American Indians are disingenuous.

Indians, by Arthur Kopit, is a difficult play to absorb because the message about the genocide of American Indians at the hands of the U.S. government is frank and unavoidably accurate. Buffalo Bill was a unique figure in this conflict historically because he had a foot in both camps. Advancements in civil rights since the 1960s have reduced the shock of Kopit's message, which was also intended to comment on the U.S. role in Vietnam. Critic Lewis Funke quotes Kopit as explaining his inspiration for *Indians*: "I was reading a newspaper in which General Westmoreland expressed regret for the accidental killing and wounding of innocent people in Vietnam. These, he said, were the inevitable consequence of war." This sentiment is repeated in the last scene of *Indians* when Colonel Forsyth congratulates himself on his so-called victory against Sitting Bull and his tribe.

> One can always find someone who'll call an overwhelming victory a massacre. . . . Of course innocent people have been killed. In war they always are. . . . In the long run I believe what happened here at this reservation yesterday will be justified.

The fact is Colonel Forsyth's hope for justification never came. Buffalo Bill pursues justification even as he tries to help the American Indians survive, but to no avail. Throughout *Indians*, Buffalo Bill wants to be understood and forgiven; therefore, he seeks justification as a means toward understanding. The horror of what has happened to the American Indians at the hands of white people is too painful for a single person to contain. Buffalo Bill seems to be the only white person at the time who is taking in the whole of this experience, and his conscience is tearing him apart as a result.

The title of Kopit's play is deceiving because the focus is actually Buffalo Bill and not the Indians. The Indians, some named and many nameless, come and go throughout Buffalo Bill's story, already ghosts of their true selves. Even John Grass and Sitting Bull, who are the most animated of the Indians, seem to have seen their fates and know that they are going through the motions in a history that has long since become inevitable. It is this inevitability that Buffalo Bill cannot face because it means he has lost control—or never had any control to begin with. It means that his good intentions were not good enough.

Indians is not about *what* happened in the United States in the late nineteenth century, but *why* it happened. *Indians* is based on historical figures and events, so the audience already knows the basic plot. Kopit, an avant-guard, absurdist playwright, has elected to use a non-linear structure, weaving together several episodes in time without conventional regard to chronology. The play is framed by Buffalo Bill's public face, his Wild West Show. It is grotesque and opaque, repulsive in its unreality. The Wild West Show also appears near the middle of the play, both before and after the central three scenes which feature John Grass's testimony at the Senate congressional hearing and Buntline's play at the White House. These two Wild West Show exhibitions feature American Indians: Geronimo as a caged animal, Chief Joseph blandly reciting his surrender speech, and an imitation of the American Indians' sacred Sun Dance. In the scenes of the Wild West Show, beneath the bravado, one can see Buffalo Bill's nervousness. His nervousness stems from his guilt over the suffering of the American Indians, but Buffalo Bill also worries about his identity. He is afraid of dying onstage and being lost to history as a mockery of his true self. He is scared because he is no longer sure what his true nature is.

Buffalo Bill has only wanted to help others. The main, repeating episode in *Indians* is the Senate congressional hearing which makes up five out of thirteen scenes. In these scenes, no agreement or solution is achieved, no resolution even attempted between the government and Sitting Bull's Sioux. The senators, John Grass, and Sitting Bull, all speak their parts and seem incapable of understanding one another's point of view. They do not even try. Buffalo Bill intervenes, first begging the Indians for cooperation and later trying to explain each side's position to the other. But his pleas for middle ground are ignored. The Indians are stubborn, sad, and resigned. The senators are stubborn and ruthless. Buffalo Bill is thus defeated in his not-quite selfless quest to help. He can give jobs, money, and supplies to the American Indians, but he is incapable of changing history. Buffalo Bill is, by increasing degrees, hypocritical because although he wants to help American Indians, he believes more strongly in assimilation than in finding a way to live as neighbors. He does not understand the gravity of what he asks when he presses the American Indians to assimilate. Hickok senses it when he refuses to perform in Buntline's play. The American Indians performing in the Wild West Show also understand the humiliation of assimilation.

In scene 3, Buffalo Bill is seen at his youngest, shooting buffalo for sport and to entertain the grand duke of Russia. His infectious enthusiasm engages the duke, who takes up a gun and shoots the nearest Indian—Buffalo Bill's friend Spotted Tail. To bolster his career and reputation, Buffalo Bill barely reacts to Spotted Tail's death, staying in showman form. It is his first step down a long path of self-aggrandizement at the expense of his Indian friends. When Buffalo Bill employs American Indians to perform in his Wild West Show, so that they might have jobs and more easily assimilate to white culture, he fails to recognize the humiliation his show costs them.

Ned Buntline's *Scouts of the Plains* extends this humiliation to Buffalo Bill and Wild Bill Hickok. Hickok recognizes the exploitation right away and refuses to perform. Although he is a scofflaw who kills Buntline and rapes the Indian princess Teskanjavila, Hickok never pretends to be anything different. He knows himself and is content with his life. Buffalo Bill, as he grows older and more confused about his role in history, yearns for Hickok's surety and goes to the saloon in Dodge City to find himself, with Hickok's aid. Hickok shows him a group of Buffalo Bills, declaring that now he can help more people because he can be in more than one place at once. This idea horrifies Buffalo Bill because he has grown to hate himself. He does not want to discover his true identity; he wants to become something else.

Buffalo Bill is a proud man with a troubled conscience. Through the various scenes, we see increasingly into his heart. He is disturbed by the harsh treatment of American Indians, which the audience sees when Buffalo Bill argues with the senators about their responsibility for the livelihood of Indians they have displaced. He even appears to understand something of the Indian worldview when he tries to convince the senators that the American Indians do not understand ownership the way white people do. But Buffalo Bill is haunted by the faces of dead Indians.

Buffalo Bill's sincerity is ultimately undermined in the final scene when, in a passionate, almost angry monologue, he argues the government's view that the American Indians were difficult to deal with and fought unfairly: "I am sick and tired of these sentimental humanitarians," he says in ironic reference to himself. All around Buffalo Bill American Indians are dying, and he, having failed at being greater than the sum of his parts, is reduced to selling Indian trinkets. He is a shadow of the great man he envisioned himself as being, reduced to arguing his own innocence with himself.

Buffalo Bill, as characterized by Kopit, is earnest but hypocritical. While he proclaims concern for American Indians, he believes that their only salvation lay in cooperation and assimilation, which assumes the supremacy of white culture over Indian culture. Early in Kopit's play, Buffalo Bill says to Spotted Tail, "things're changin' out here. . . . So if you wanna be *part* o' these things, an' not left behind somewhere, you jus' plain hafta get *used* to 'em. . . . you've got to *adjust*." His viewpoint of assimilation was one held by many

> " ALL AROUND BUFFALO
> BILL AMERICAN INDIANS ARE
> DYING, AND HE, HAVING FAILED
> AT BEING GREATER THAN THE
> SUM OF HIS PARTS, IS REDUCED
> TO SELLING INDIAN TRINKETS."

Americans and was actively practiced by the U.S. government through the 1970s.

"No one who is a white man can be a fool," Spotted Tail says to Buffalo Bill after Buffalo Bill has slaughtered a hundred buffalo for sport. Spotted Tail's statement, as understood in the context of Kopit's play, is ironic: Buffalo Bill, at the center of this tale, is king of all fools.

Source: Carol Ullmann, Critical Essay on *Indians*, in *Drama for Students*, Thomson Gale, 2007.

Vera M. Jiji

In the following review, Jiji explores four main theatrical conventions that Kopit employs in Indians.

Indians, Arthur Kopit's first major serious play was, in the words of one London reviewer, "one of the few necessary works to have appeared from the America of the sixties." It is not difficult to see why it merited such praise.

The play takes place on what Peter Brook would call "holy ground." Brook was speaking of that common groundwork of community feeling when he instanced "the great Kazan-Williams-Miller hits, Albee's *Virginia Woolf*, [plays which] summoned audiences that met in the true shared territory of theme and concern—and they were powerful events, the circle of performance was riveting and complete." In *Indians*, the true shared territory of theme and concern is not merely white America's guilt about its treatment of the red man, but of the black man, the yellow man, the native of Vietnam.

Kopit conceived of *Indians* when he heard General Westmoreland express regret for the accidental

FOR *INDIANS* TO 'WORK,'
THE AUDIENCE MUST SYMPATHIZE
WITH BUFFALO BILL EVEN AS IT
SEES HIS WEAKNESSES."

killing in Vietnam. Although the Vietnamese are never mentioned in the play, every spectator can identify as contemporary the press conference in which the victor rationalizes his sword—the U.S. Colonel who exterminated Sitting Bull and his tribe, justifying the measure on the ground that no more skirmishes between Indians and whites would now occur: "in the long run I believe what happened here at this reservation yesterday will be justified."

Kopit's choice of the Indian Massacres for his theme was most apt. Most white Americans are still unaware of the terrible events which led to the Indians' incarceration. On the simplest level, Kopit wanted to inform the audience as to how it had happened. But more than that, as the audience mourned for the dead Indians, they were to feel that no massacre could ever "be justified." Thus Kopit hoped to build from the sympathy Americans can now feel for the slain warriors whose remains adorn Museums of Natural (sic) History, to a sympathy for those still being slain. The bridge was to be the play's central character: William Cody, also known as Buffalo Bill.

It was a brilliant idea for a play. Cody had seen himself as the Indians' friend. But through his exploits as Buffalo Bill he had contributed significantly to the Indians' defeat. In the gradual loss of Cody's integrity, Kopit saw a ready-made mythic symbol of all ignorant exploiters. The Wild West Show, which converted slaughter and warfare to entertainment, was a documented symbol of American hypocrisy. As the audience watched Cody's impotent grief over deaths he had hastened, they were to be moved to alter their behavior lest the callous disregard of human life, the cruelty, self-justification, cowardice, and complacency shown by the white Americans toward another weaker people be unchecked. The play is all but too timely in its treatment of its flawed, guilt-ridden central character.

Kopit's desire to share his concern with his fellow Americans was shaped, however, by a sophisticated and ironic view of the limitations of propaganda art as a vehicle for expressing a message. That Kopit felt a direct political statement would not do is clear from the comments about the "value" of art built into the play itself, as we shall see. Since the oblique treatment of the theme seemed necessary to Kopit, the form was burdened with carrying much of the play's message.

Kopit had conceived of the form along with the theme. At the moment of hearing Westmoreland's statement, he happened to be listening to a symphony by Charles Ives in which chamber music is played against distorted marching band music. In the contemporary symphony, the grave, sweet, measured assonance of the chamber music clashed ironically with the harsh dissonance of the military band. Kopit intended to create the same irony in his play, the same discomfort with the dissonances of American military policy in the minds of his audience as the music created in his ears. Thus was the form dictated: in Kopit's words, "a mosaic, a counterpoint of memory and reality."

Kopit's form, then, is "a mosaic," in which various theatrical styles are employed: sometimes in alternation, sometimes simultaneously. This article is in two sections, for I intend to show first how Kopit counterposed four disparate kinds of theatrical conventions in the play, and second, why that "riveting circle of performance" remains incomplete.

The play is written in thirteen scenes. The first and last scenes use three presentational conventions: the theatre of fact, the Brechtian theatre of alienation (which derives, of course, from Shakespeare's theatre), and the expressionist theatre. Scenes Two, Four, Six, Eight, and Eleven actually constitute one long representational, naturalistic scene in which the protagonist appears as William Cody, a sensitive man who loves the Indians and is trying to intercede on their behalf with a Senate committee. In contrast, in Scenes Three, Five, Seven, and Nine, which are in the ironic Brechtian mode, William Cody is shown in his fictionalized persona as the opportunistic Buffalo Bill. Scene Ten is representational again, but is a flashback to action which is antecedent to Scene Two. Here Cody visits the President to plead for the Indians, but the President is willing to see him only because he had been entertained (in Scene Seven) by the nonsense of Buffalo Bill. Now the two sides of Cody's

WHAT DO I READ NEXT?

- *The End of the World* (1984), by Arthur Kopit, is a semi-fictional dramatization of the author's struggle to write about nuclear bombs.

- *Waiting for Godot* (1954) is a two-act absurdist play by Samuel Beckett. Two characters, outside a specific definition of time and space, await the arrival of a third person, named Godot, who never arrives, which illustrates the difficulty and essential meaninglessness of life, a tenet important in existentialist philosophy.

- *The Bald Soprano* (1950) is Eugène Ionesco's first play, written when he was in his forties. It is loosely based on Ionesco's experience learning English by using an unusual method of memorizing whole sentences. Ionesco was one of the earliest of the theater of the absurd playwrights, and *The Bald Soprano* shows the breakdown of language to the point of dysfunctionality and the inability of people to relate to each other.

- *Waterlily* (1988), by Ella Cara Deloria, is a novel that follows the life of a Sioux woman during the nineteenth century. Deloria, born at the end of the nineteenth century, was of mixed blood but was born and lived her life on Indian reservations in North and South Dakota. She was intimately aware of traditional Sioux life and filled her book with astonishing detail.

- *Who's Afraid of Virginia Woolf?* (1962), by Edward Albee, is a Tony Award-winning play about an unhappy couple, George and Martha, who invite another couple, Nick and Honey, over to dinner. George and Martha attack each other verbally, flirt with and insult their guests, and argue about a son who does not exist.

- *Rosencrantz and Guildenstern Are Dead* (1967), by Tom Stoppard, is an absurdist play reminiscent of Beckett's *Waiting for Godot*. In this play, two minor characters from Shakespeare's *Hamlet* are seen drifting through the events of Shakespeare's plot, unable to change their situation.

- *Theater of the Absurd* (1962), by Martin Esslin, is the defining text for absurdist, experimental theater in the 1960s. Esslin identifies four playwrights as being at the vanguard of the absurdist theater movement: Ionesco, Beckett, Genet, and Adamov.

- In the title essay collected in *The Myth of Sisyphus and Other Essays* (1955), Albert Camus examines the importance of life and the possibility of suicide. It is from this essay that Esslin adapted the phrase "theater of the absurd."

- *Oh Dad, Poor Dad, Mama's Hung You in the Closet and I'm Feeling So Sad* (1963) is Kopit's first professionally produced play. It is a wacky, farcical one-act play that he wrote in a just a few days. This play initially caused Kopit to be labeled as an absurdist playwright, though his later work showed that he was capable of presenting a wide range of theatrical models.

- *Century of Genocide: Eyewitness Accounts and Critical Views* (2004), edited by Samuel Totten, William S. Parsons, and Israel W. Charny, is a collection of essays that examine the history of genocide in the twentieth century as well as how and why these genocides occurred. The purpose of the contributors is to bring awareness to a topic often marginalized by those who choose to remake history.

---

personality are being seen together. In Scene Twelve, Cody's conscience torments him for what Buffalo Bill has done; the scene is pure expressionism and leads to the ultimate *agon* of Scene Thirteen. There, William Cody—Buffalo Bill expresses his anguish and ours. We have, then, a musical or rondo form, in which the themes and conventions are introduced in an overture, developed in ironic juxtaposition throughout the work, and recapitulated in a coda. Let us examine this process in Scene One in detail (using the New York production, for that is the basis of the published script).

As the audience comes into the theatre, it hears "strange music coming from all about" and finds itself facing three museum cases holding larger-than-life-size effigies of Sitting Bull, Buffalo Bill and Indian relics. The setting is contemporary (the figures represent the past) and documentary: there is no curtain, no realistic reproduction of a recognizable "set" or locale. Thus, the conventions are of the theatre of fact. These conventions are commonly understood to mean that the author has done massive research on his subject, and that what is shown onstage conforms to the demands of historical accuracy. Thus, the audience, clued in by the play's title and its antiseptic setting, prepares its collective mind to receive the facts—straight.

But then a "voice over" is heard calling "Cody, Cody;" Wild West music is played; spotlights crisscross the stage, and Buffalo Bill prances in on an artificial white horse, "a great smile on his face . . . proudly waving his big Stetson to the unseen surrounding crowd" (Scene 1). A great shift in the audience's relation to the play is thus quickly achieved.

When Buffalo Bill canters in, the audience faces a new set of conventions. Buffalo Bill is "acting" as the showman. From the first speech of Scene One, "Yessir, BACK AGAIN," to the last one of that scene, "I dunno what you folks know 'bout show business, but le' me tell you, there is nothin' more depressin' than playin' two-a-day in a goddam ghost town," he presents himself as a narrator about to start his own story: confidential, gossipy, at ease with his audience.

But his posture of self-confidence is undercut in several ways. First, the audience is placed in a false relationship to the event onstage. From the contemporary theatre-of-fact setting, the actor's entry has transported the audience into the past. Moreover, the audience is no "unseen surrounding crowd" come to see a Wild West Show. Its awareness that the play is forcing it into an unreal position already creates a sense of irony and Brechtian alienation. Then too, when Buffalo Bill begins to speak, the patently false relationship between his Wild West persona and his real personality is emphasized. After the solemn brooding silence of the effigies, his cheerful show-biz manner sounds a false note. The voice-over urges him on: "And now to start . . ." He replies by getting out of character as Buffalo Bill, showman, and losing his temper: "WHAT'S THE RUSH? *WAIT A SECOND* !" (Scene 1). Thus the character is introduced on two levels simultaneously: as William Cody, the man who can lose his temper, acting as Buffalo Bill, the cheerful performer.

Buffalo Bill's reference to a ghost town is followed immediately by the sudden appearance of some ghostly Indians "around the outside of the ring. The horse senses their presence and shies; Buffalo Bill, as if realizing what it means, turns in terror" (Scene 1). Thus, the third theatrical convention, expressionism, is introduced.

These Indians derive from Bill's imagination. They loom out of the darkness, embodying his guilty conscience. As he explains later, "I see them everywhere. . . . Took a drink from a river yesterday 'an they were even there, beneath the water, their hands reachin' up, I dunno whether beggin,' or t' . . . drag me under" (Scene 12).

By the end of Scene One, then, the audience has been introduced to three of the play's four themes: first, the play has reminded us, through the theatre-of-fact framework, of the death of the Indian culture in this country; second, through Buffalo Bill's appearance and speeches, it has offered an ironic, even burlesque commentary on part of the West's history; third, through the silent appearance of the ghostly Indians, it depicts Cody's inner struggle with the forces of his conscience, showing his degradation and remorse.

And Kopit introduces a fourth convention and fourth theme in the play's second scene. The transition to the naturalistic convention is handled by an actor in Indian regalia using direct address to the audience. "I am Sitting Bull." He explains the reason for the meeting with the Senate committee, which the audience is about to see, and introduces "William Cody," who enters on the cue line. When Cody addresses the Indians directly, the audience becomes invisible and the naturalistic convention has been established. From this point on in the play, Kopit will use the naturalistic convention exclusively to reveal the history of Sitting Bull's tribe. He has chosen a penultimate moment of high tension for his setting: a meeting between the tribe and a Senate committee which could, if it chose, save the Indians.

The audience's attention has been captured in this scene by the impending conflict. It knows that the Indians will lose, but it wants to see that fate realized theatrically. Primed by Cody's guilty response to the apparitions at the end of Scene One, and by its prior knowledge of Indian affairs, the audience finds John Grass' speech detailing the Indians' cause against the government very convincing. There is no reason to doubt that this is an imaginative recreation of what actually occurred during that historic meeting. In fact, John Grass' statement that "the buffalo had gone away" while the Indians had been learning to farm will be illustrated in Scene Three where Cody is seen again, at an earlier time of his life, shooting the buffalo for sport.

Why, when Kopit has begun picking up some narrative interest in the dramatic confrontation between Sitting Bull and the Senate committee, does he drop it in favor of returning Cody to center stage? Because the destruction of Cody's character must also be detailed. Thus Cody makes a significant choice in Scene Three. While the slaughter of a hundred buffalo with a hundred bullets to win a bet may be regarded with displeasure by the audience, it is probably forgivable. But when the Grand Duke of Russia shoots an Indian in the same cavalier spirit, Cody stifles his desire to protest the senseless murder. Instead, he spouts nonsense to the Grand Duke while Ned Buntline writes it all down.

Now Kopit, in Scene Three, has returned to Brechtian conventions. Thus the "buffaloes" are not handled realistically, but are "played by" Indians. When the Grand Duke shoots the Indian, the latter falls dead and immediately rises to tell the audience that it is a case of mistaken identity before he falls down again. The Duke, not astounded by this Ascension, merely wants to know what the fellow said. And Cody lies.

We should assume that in this scene Kopit is enlightening the audience through the Brechtian "Verfremdungseffekt." He is showing how "history" is made of lies, and how a foolish boy's head can be turned by publicity. Pretty soon, Cody will be believing the myth of himself as Buffalo Bill as distorted by Buntline. But there is a problem here. The burlesque elements in the scene, the obviously mock buffalo and obviously mock death, prevent the audience from taking Cody's moral turpitude seriously. In each of the first three scenes we have had to orient ourselves to differing conventions. Assuming that we are sufficiently entertained by the prospect of gore and anguish to give the play our full attention, we have had to turn from a suffering (and therefore sympathetic) Cody in Scene One to a weak raisonneur of a Cody in Scene Two, to a callow opportunist in Scene Three. When Scenes Four, Five and Six rotate rapidly between the meeting and a scene from Cody's life as Buffalo Bill which shows him at his most cowardly, the audience's detachment from the protagonist has gone very far. It is not retrieved until Scene Nine

In the meantime, in Scenes Six and Eight, John Grass is emerging as the play's "hero." Humiliated

by the Senators for having signed the false treaty which he now wants to repudiate, he is sufficiently flawed to be human and sympathetic. To our anti-heroic age, his is the noblest available response: to protest, though it be only with his own death that he may speak. These scenes are powerfully, effectively written.

But between them, in ironic juxtaposition, is a key scene: the play within the play, and this produces another problem. What is wrong about Scene Seven is not necessarily that it abrogates the tension building in the alternating representational committee scenes. Scenes Six and Eight are strong enough to bind audience interest right through. What is wrong is that the burlesque of Seven is simply too farcical, too silly, too inconsequential to be occupying our attention while important affairs are going on elsewhere.

Some telling ironic points *are* made in Scene Seven. For example, the President is shown enjoying "the girl. Note her legs. How white they are. For an Indian." The First Lady is pleasantly stimulated by Hickok's genuine violence. When Hickok stabs Buntline (whose collapse is ignored by everyone except Buffalo Bill) and proceeds to undress the "Indian maiden," only Buffalo Bill is concerned. In fact, he is left "in a daze" at the President's final comment: "Good show, Cody! *Good Show* !"

This scene has shown Buffalo Bill's increasing complicity in his own prostitution. In his quarrel with Hickok he remarks, "Ya see, Bill, what you fail to understand is that I'm not being false to what I *was*. I'm simply *drawin'* on what I was . . . [pause in script] and raisin' it to a higher level" (Scene 7).

More important, the play-within-the-play shows that the President is eager to swallow any cheap melodrama about the Indians. He is no more anxious to learn the truth than any other customer for the Wild West Show. There is a guilty partnership between Buffalo Bill who purveys such nonsense and the President who stands ready to accept it.

Last, the playlet offers an ironic comment on the worthlessness of any straight-forward propaganda play. Had the President been the least bit open to seeing what was before him, he would have found Hickok's senseless violence repellent. But Hickok stabs Buntline and prepares to rape the actress (who turns out to be compliant) and the President and First Lady merely applaud the show.

Kopit's construction of his play here has been hampered, perhaps, by the rich ore of his factual material. Certainly Buffalo Bill's life did have many such unsympathetic aspects. As William Coleman has recently shown, even the employment of "the beautiful Indian maiden with an Italian accent and a weakness for scouts" is historically accurate. When Hickok appeared with Cody's show, the latter said, "I could not do much with him as he was not an easy man to handle, and would insist on shooting the supers in the legs with powder, just to see them jump." The change from gun powder to the stabbing of Buntline is both poetically and artistically justified. Kopit's point here, that the meaningless violence of the Wild West stereotype fed into and encouraged an equal real-life violence which had actual consequences, is an important aspect of his theme. The indifference of the President, the Italian actress and the First Lady (despite her remark that Buntline "looks kind of dead") are also important.

However, the playlet is already so bad that the additional twists of the Italian and German accents and the "seduction," while they may be historically accurate, are unjustified artistically. They distract the audience and provide another level of alienation when it is hardly needed. Since Buffalo Bill is responsible for the show, we lose any remaining sympathy for him as well as for his burlesque production. This is not to say that the play is ineffective at this point. As the measurement of the human pulse can indicate health or sickness, so the measurement of a play's rhythm and intensity can indicate much of its condition.

There is an effective beat of intensity which picks up from Scene Six when the audience begins to be strongly involved in the committee meeting. Scene Seven, though burlesque, has a second death onstage, a bit more serious than the first (insofar as Buffalo Bill's "dazed" condition indicates that the stabbing is real to one person of the half dozen or so on stage at the time). In Scene Eight, the earlier candor and dignity of the Indians gives way to exasperation and insults, culminating in a highly effective, angry exchange. The Indians, having demanded the cash that the government is "holding in trust" for them, are told that they would only use it to get drunk if they had it. John Grass retorts that, if this is so, "when an Indian gets drunk, he is only imitating the white men he's observed!" It is this retort, called forth by his personal humiliation, which engenders the vindictiveness of the Senators.

Scene Nine returns to the Wild West Show. As Scene Eight raised the tension of the committee meeting scenes, this scene too raises the tension of the Wild West scenes. But more importantly, Buffalo Bill's inner conflict becomes dramatized effectively for the first time in the play.

In Scene Nine, the manipulation of the Indians' courage into a source of audience titillation is continued. Chief Joseph repeats his heart-rending speech of surrender, explaining that he does so "twice a day, three times on Sunday," because Buffalo Bill has promised that, in exchange, his people will receive food. He distances the speech by "exaggerated and inappropriate gestures," and his comment: "after which, the audience always applauded me." After Chief Joseph's "act," the Wild West Show Indians are to perform an imitation of a religious rite involving self-mutilation. They "take the barbed ends of long leather thongs . . . and hook them through plainly visible chest harnesses" while Buffalo Bill explains that no one will be hurt.

Now John Grass appears. By the time he comes onto the scene, the audience's concern and sympathy for the Indians is strongly focused in him. Few people in the theatre will note that his appearance in Scene Nine is anachronistic, the Wild West scene in progress presumably occurring well before the committee meeting. He begins to perform the rite authentically. He "pulls the Indians out of their harnesses, rips open his shirt, and sticks the barbs through his chest muscles. He chants and dances. The other Indians, realizing what he's doing, blow on reed whistles, urge him on. Finally he collapses, blood pouring from his chest." Thus in this scene, the play's two strands are joined for the first time in the person of John Grass. He attempts to express the extremity of his need to be authentic as an Indian brave in the face of the show's whoopdedoodle.

Again Cody, seen as Buffalo Bill, must react silently to an onstage mutilation. But now, for the first time, as the actor gathers the fallen Indian tenderly in his arms, the audience can feel that Cody has taken the Indians' agony into himself. It is a physical, a corporeal and thus truly theatrical gesture: a feint, I would call it, in that the audience's gut sympathy moves from Grass' self-mutilated, physically heavy body to Cody, as Cody takes the weight of the body.

It is with that weight and sympathy behind him that the audience watches his vain appeal to the President in Scene Ten. The furious ending of the committee meeting in Scene Eleven is almost anti-climactic. The play is then over; the history is unfolded. What remains is only the agony of the protagonist, who has, at last, earned the audience's sympathetic hearing.

As the focus has shifted to Cody's inner conflict, the conventions shift again to pure expressionism. Thus Scene Twelve takes place in a ghostly saloon whose customers include Jesse James and Billy the Kid. Wanting to ease his conscience, Bill confesses his failure to warn Sitting Bull and begs Hickok to teach him to be authentic as Hickok was in the playlet scene. But Hickok has meanwhile adopted Buffalo Bill's solution; he brings on a group of apparitions, copies of Buffalo Bill personified in "a group of men . . . their faces . . . covered by masks of *his* face." Buffalo Bill tries to shoot them but, in true expressionist fashion, "they fall and immediately rise again. They slowly surround him. He screams as he shoots. They disappear" (Scene 12).

The psychological conflict between Cody's idealism and Buffalo Bill's callousness to the consequences of his actions has been one of Kopit's main themes, since he introduced the dual aspects of Cody's personality and his weak self-justification in the first scene. But after that, he has split the aspects in two.

This division of the main character into his contrasting aspects would appear on paper to be a brilliant notion, much more viable here than was, say, Eugene O'Neill's similar attempt in *The Great God Brown* and *Days Without End*. But the confusion which had vitiated *The Great God Brown* is still produced in *Indians*. Not only did Walter Kerr, for example, call the conflict undramatized, but Julius Novick, reviewing the Washington production, remarked that the play was half over before he knew it had a plot. When the personality is already split in two, it is very difficult to dramatize the agonizing attempt to harmonize its warring elements. The fact that Kopit almost succeeded is a tribute to his ingenuity. But the expressionism carried a good thing too far.

That the expressionism is a weak crutch here can be seen in that Kopit treats ghosts and apparitions differently, depending on whether the scene is expressionist or Brechtian. If the convention is Brechtian, Buffalo Bill has no fear of the ghosts. Thus he "translates" the ghost's remarks in Scene Three, reacts emotionally but without fear to the possibly dead Buntline and John Grass in Scenes Seven and Nine respectively, and talks to the dead Sitting Bull in Scene Thirteen with love. But he turns to the ghostly Indians in Scene One with horror. In the expressionist Scene Twelve he is terrified of the copies which have been made of him.

Kopit has structured Scene Thirteen as a reprise, in an attempt to bring the themes and disparate conventions together in consanguinity. There are Brechtian elements: "The Indians cover the center area with the huge white sheet, then lie down upon it in piles" (to represent their massacre). Buffalo Bill and Sitting Bull have a philosophical discussion of their relationship in which both talk as if they were dead:

BUFFALO BILL:
Oh, God. Imagine. For a while, I actually thought my Wild West Show would *help*. I could give you money. Food. Clothing. And also make people *understand* things . . . better.

(He laughs to himself.)
That was my reasoning. Or, anyway, *part* . . .
(Pause.)
of my reasoning.

SITTING BULL:
(Slight smile)
Your show was very popular.
(Pause.)

BUFFALO BILL:
We had . . . *fun*, though, you and I.
(Pause.)
Didn't we?

SITTING BULL:
Oh, yes. And that's the terrible thing. We had all surrendered. We were on reservations. We could not fight or hunt. We could do nothing. Then you came and allowed us to imitate our glory. . . . It was humiliating! For sometimes, we could almost imagine it was *real*.

Thus we have the ghost of a real Indian describing himself and other real Indians playing fake Indians in order to feel like real Indians.

The "interview" between Colonel Forsythe and the reporters also works on several levels. It is supposed to be about the Indian massacre, but the tone and diction are strongly contemporary as the Colonel says, "Of course innocent people have been killed. In war they always are." The reporters enter in 1970's clothing. Thus the events of the play are "distanced" forward to our involvement in Vietnam.

The expressionist elements also appear briefly in the last scene. The Indian apparitions reappear, as do the "Roughriders of the World." Chief Joseph reprises his speech. (The use of another expressionist device, the bloody plastic masks, was Stacy Keach's idea, rather than Kopit's. Kopit—rightly, I think—would have preferred not to have them, for the play is moving, at the end, towards a simpler resolution.) The factual material, the philosophical query as to the nature of their existence,

Paul Newman portraying Cody in the film adaptation, Buffalo Bill and the Indians United Artists/The Kobal Collection

the emotional response of anguish to the sense of guilt are to be heard and seen at the end in the context of the audience's recognition that a subject of great human significance has been explored "in the round," so that all its aspects have been voiced, and so that the play corresponds deeply to man's experience. Thus in Scene Thirteen various figures: the military, the "liberal" press, the government as quoted by Cody, express their views about the Indians' death. Cody meets the dead souls, Sitting Bull's at length, and expresses his sorrow in an ambivalent, highly moving, lyrical coda.

As I have shown, one of Kopit's purposes has been to teach the audience a lesson from history. Thus Buffalo Bill's recital of the facts of U.S. Indian policy in Scene Thirteen, deriving from the theater of fact, provides the outermost framework. At the beginning and end, we contemplate the remains: the museum cases and the trivial junk of Indian tourist trade. But we are expected to remember that the entire work represents a mosaic of Cody's memories, and is therefore as factual as memory can be. How factual is that?

Despite my great admiration for this play, I have shown why it failed to arrive at that riveting circle of performance for many of its audiences. The reasons are easy to see. Reviewers noted many of them. Stanley Kauffmann felt Kopit's language was inadequate. This objection, I feel, is valid, insofar as the substitutes for eloquence used in the play, except in Scene Nine, are external to the character and thus comparatively weak. Walter Kerr found the "argument unorganized, the conflict undramatized." But we have seen how carefully the argument is organized. However Kerr is right in saying that *the* conflict is undramatized, because the play has, as we saw, four distinct themes.

On the simplest level, Kopit uses the naturalistic convention for the committee scenes. As he allows John Grass and Sitting Bull to argue with the Senators, the audience may interject or accept uncritically Kopit's view of the Indians' suffering at the hands of the whites. But Kopit has not intended to write a propaganda play about the Indians which will have no more effect than the play-within-the-play had upon the sensibilities of the President. For he knows how easily people can turn any onstage horrors into "entertainment." Thus he has used the Brechtian techniques of alienation for his second aim; to force the audience to think critically about the material of the play.

The use of the voice-over narrator, the deliberate alienation of the audience from the play through the many distancing devices of the various other narrators (Cody, Sitting Bull, Chief Joseph who narrates his own performance rather than putting on such a performance), the play-within-the-play for the President inside the Wild West framework inside the museum-theatre-of-fact framework, are all very complex alienation techniques.

To make the audience think, to make them appreciate the ironies of the situation, Kopit also uses many reversals of pretense and reality. The meeting between the Senators and the Indians appears real, but Scene Ten tells us that it too is but a meaningless performance, for the committee's visit is only a "gesture." The Indians have been condemned already. Which is real—the William Cody of the committee scenes who loved the Indians and played Buffalo Bill, or the Buffalo Bill of the Wild West show who played into the false myth of manifest destiny and destroyed the Indian way of life? Cody pretends to ride a prancing stallion; the Indians pretend to be wounded buffalo. The Wild West Show pretends the Sun Dance, but John

Grass "really" performs it. The White House playlet pretends the rescue of a maiden by a Western Scout, but the Scout "really" knifes a comrade instead. Cody pretends a defense of his government's policy in Scene Thirteen, but embodies the living hell of the white man's guilt. The Brechtian method, with its refusal to allow the audience to fall into the complaisant position that it is being entertained by a fantasy, is heavily relied on. However, as the acerbic John Simon said, "now it may be right and desirable to make the audience temporarily lose its intellectual bearings, but it is risky, indeed unwise, to play games with its emotional responses, ceaselessly inflating, undercutting, manipulating, till assimiliation becomes impossible on any level."

As this example illustrates again, the Brechtian convention has never worked, per se. People do not learn from "facts." They learn only from facts tied to cases, examples, instances which may have captured their sympathetic attention. Brecht's plays work in spite of him, because he failed to alienate his audiences from the characters as he had wished to do. For example, Brecht wanted his audiences to see Mother Courage as stupid—to learn that one who ties herself to the war machine is bound to be mangled by its operation. Yet audiences continue to admire this foolish, persistent creature.

For *Indians* to "work," the audience must sympathize with Buffalo Bill even as it sees his weaknesses. Yet with all the brilliance with which Kopit has manipulated the manifold conflicts and conventions of the play, it fails to develop an organic forward motion until the split personality of Cody coalesces into one struggling human being. While the alternating structure is perfectly appreciable upon analysis, its effect in the theatre is to halt the flow of the audience's involvement and excitement. It is as if the play must begin all over again in Scenes Two, Three, and Five. Unlike the Ives' symphony in which two sets of conventions are simulaneously heard, the play's sets alternate here.

Kopit has done some interesting work before *Indians*, but there has always been an imitative element in his work which threatens to overwhelm it, so it loses its own structural autonomy in favor of a schematic imitation. *Oh Dad, Poor Dad* took off on Tennessee Williams. *Chamber Music* was an impressionist exercise. *The Day the Whores Came Out to Play Tennis* was a parody on *The Cherry Orchard*, with the tarts' farts as the Ra-

belaisian counterpart of Chekov's delicate broken string. *Indians* was a major theatrical achievement, but Kopit was still too closely tied to the Brechtian conventions for the play to be completely authentic on its own terms. Perhaps in his next play, he will sever his dependence on authorial models and produce an authentic masterwork of his own.

Source: Vera M. Jiji, "*Indians*: A Mosaic of Memories and Methodologies," in *Players: The Magazine of American Theatre*, Vol. 47, No. 5, June–July 1972, pp. 230–36.

SOURCES

Barnes, Clive, "The Theater: 'Indians' in Washington," in *New York Times*, May 27, 1969, p. 43.

———, "Theater: Irreverence on London Stage," in *New York Times*, July 9, 1968, p. 30.

———, "Theater: Kopit's 'Indians,'" in *New York Times*, October 14, 1969, p. 51.

Esslin, Martin, "Osborne's Author and Kopit's Indians," in *New York Times*, July 21, 1968, p. D12.

Funke, Lewis, "Origin of 'Indians' Recalled by Kopit," in *New York Times*, October 15, 1969, p. 37.

Kerr, Walter, "But If the Play Is Sick at Heart," in *New York Times*, October 19, 1969, p. D1.

Klein, Alvin, "'Indians,' an Echo of Vietnam," in *New York Times*, October 20, 1991, p. NJ13.

Kopit, Arthur, *Indians*, Hill & Wang, 1969.

Novick, Julius, "'Liberty and Justice'—for Indians?" in *New York Times*, May 18, 1969, p. D3.

Shewey, Don, "Arthur Kopit: A Life on Broadway," in *New York Times*, April 29, 1984, p. 91.

Wardle, Irving, "Moral Pageantry from the West," in *Times* (London), No. 57295, July 5, 1968, Arts, p. 7.

FURTHER READING

Adams, Alexander B., *Sitting Bull: An Epic of the Plains*, Putnam's Sons, 1973.
    Adams's popular biography of the Sioux chief explores the complex relationships of Sitting Bull and his contemporaries, such as Crazy Horse, Buffalo Bill, Spotted Tail, and General Custer.

Brown, Dee Alexander, *Bury My Heart at Wounded Knee: An Indian History of the American West*, Holt, Rinehart, and Winston, 1970.
    Brown's book was a breakthrough in historical interpretation at the time that it was published. Using primary sources, the author showed white

Americans the Indian side of what happened in the late 1800s.

Cody, William Frederick, *An Autobiography of Buffalo Bill (Colonel W. F. Cody)*, Cosmopolitan Book, 1920.
  Buffalo Bill revised his autobiography until his death in 1917. The story of his life reads like a novel in some parts, with dialogue and action. Buffalo Bill's romanticized interpretation of the events of his life are reminiscent of Kopit's characterization.

Young Joseph, Chief of the Nez Perce, "An Indian's Views of Indian Affairs," in *North American Review*, Vol. 128, No. 269, April 1879: 412–33, http://cdl.library.cornell.edu/cgi-bin/moa/moa-cgi?notisid=ABQ7578–0128-41 (accessed September 21, 2006).
  Chief Joseph's essay explains the culture and laws of American Indians to white people who have been taught that North America's native inhabitants are savage and barely human.

Indiscretions

JEAN COCTEAU

1938

Indiscretions is the English translation of *Les Parents Terribles*, by the French playwright and poet Jean Cocteau, which was written and first performed in 1938. The play is available as *Les Parents Terribles (Indiscretions)*, translated into English by Jeremy Sams (1995). When it was first produced in Paris, the play scandalized audiences with its portrayal of diseased love infecting a bourgeois family in 1930s Paris, and it was subsequently banned from the publicly owned theater by the city authorities. It still retains its power to shock. In the play, Cocteau returns to the theme of incest, which he previously explored in the play *La Machine Infernale*, produced and published in 1934.

To show a young man's attempts to escape the suffocating love of his mother, *Indiscretions* draws upon the ancient Greek story of Oedipus, who unknowingly killed his father and married his mother. While Cocteau's play shares the tragic inevitability and melodrama of the Oedipus story, its elements of farce, sense of the absurd, and hilariously comic dialog cause the audience often to laugh at the most emotionally fraught moments.

AUTHOR BIOGRAPHY

The French poet, playwright, novelist, artist, and film maker Jean Maurice Eugene Clement Cocteau was born to a wealthy family on July 5, 1889, in the small town of Maisons-Lafitte near Paris,

Jean Cocteau Everett Collection

France. His father committed suicide when Cocteau was ten years old. Cocteau was attracted to the theater at an early age. He loved to see his mother dressed for the theater, created toy theaters, and staged productions with his siblings. He briefly attended school, but was expelled.

By 1916, Cocteau was associating with an avant-garde group in Paris which included the painters Amedeo Modigliani and Pablo Picasso; the writers Marcel Proust, André Gide, and Guillaume Apollinaire; and the Russian ballet master Sergei Diaghilev. Diaghilev challenged Cocteau to write a scenario for a ballet, and the result was the ballet *Parade* (1917). The music was composed by Erik Satie, and the sets and costumes were by Picasso. The first performance caused a scandal because of its modernist nature. The audience rioted, and Cocteau commented that had it not been for the presence of Apollinaire, who was dressed in his military uniform and had a war wound, the authors of the ballet would have been attacked.

Though Cocteau was exempted from military service in World War I, he went to the front as a volunteer and drove ambulances. His reputation for frivolity was not helped by the fact that he had an outfit designed by a couturier for him to wear there, but the war made a deep impression on him. He wrote about his experiences in his novel *Thomas l'Imposteur* (Thomas the Imposter, 1923). A friendship he formed during the war with the aviator Roland Garros inspired Cocteau's first acclaimed book of poems, *Le Cap de Bonne-Espérance* (Cape of Good Hope, 1919).

Cocteau openly said he was a homosexual, though he also had relationships with women. In 1918, he formed a close relationship with the fifteen-year-old writer, Raymond Radiguet. When Radiguet died from typhoid in 1923, a traumatized Cocteau took refuge in opium, to which he remained addicted for most of his life.

Cocteau rejected naturalism and saw almost all his work as poetry. In the preface to his play, *Les Mariés de la tour Eiffel* (The Eiffel Tower Wedding Party, produced 1921), a satire on bourgeois values, he announced that he was trying to create a poetry of the theater, where meaning was not in the text but the action of the play. None of the actors speaks; they dance and mime their roles. However, in subsequent plays, Cocteau turned to traditional text-based forms. In *Antigone* (produced 1922), Cocteau updated Sophocles's tragedy, initiating a lifelong preoccupation with contemporizing Greek myths. *Orphée* (Orpheus, produced 1926), based on the ancient Greek story of Orpheus, is among Cocteau's most admired works. It explores the role of the poet and his relationship to inspiration.

Cocteau also wrote several adaptations of the Oedipus myth. *Oedipus-Rex* (Oedipus the King, produced 1927) is an opera-oratorio on which he collaborated with composer Igor Stravinsky. The play *Oedipe-Roi* (produced 1937) combines many performing arts to evoke tragedy. Cocteau's most respected reworking of the Oedipus story is the play *La Machine Infernale* (The Infernal Machine, produced 1934).

In 1930, Cocteau's first film, *Le Sang d'un Poéte* (Blood of a Poet) was released. It created another scandal because of its surrealistic strangeness.

After the composition of *La Machine Infernale*, Cocteau's financial difficulties led him to produce work that was less original and more commercial. Doing so damaged his reputation with critics, but his fame continued to grow. Two plays were especially successful: *Les Chevaliers de la Table Ronde* (The Knights of the Round Table, produced 1937) and *Les Parents Terribles* (produced 1938; translated as *Intimate Relations*, 1961, and as *Indiscretions*, 1995). Both plays starred the actor Jean Marais, who became Cocteau's lover and muse.

Published as *Les Parents Terribles (Indiscretions)* (1998), this play is available from Nick Hern Books.

In the 1940s, Cocteau moved away from classical sources toward contemporary issues. His play *La Machine à Écrire* (The Typewriter, produced 1941) became the second of his plays (*Les Parents Terribles* being the first) to be shut down by the Nazi-collaborationist Vichy government. The reason was not the content of the play but the fact that the playwright was a homosexual and a drug addict.

By the late 1940s, Cocteau had shifted his attention to cinema. After *La Belle et la Bête* (The Beauty and the Beast, 1946), Cocteau produced a film version of *Les Parents Terribles* (1948). In 1950, he produced arguably his greatest film, *Orphée*, which won prizes at the 1950 Venice Film Festival and the 1951 Cannes Film Festival.

Cocteau never aligned himself with any artistic movement, though he was influenced by dadaism and surrealism. Both movements set out to shock and bewilder observers and to challenge bourgeois values, including rationality.

Cocteau was elected to the Académie Française in 1956. He died of a heart attack on October 11, 1963, in Milly-la-Foret, Essone, France, after hearing about the death of his friend, the singer Édith Piaf.

MEDIA ADAPTATIONS

- *Indiscretions*, under its original title *Les Parents Terribles*, was adapted as a French-language film in 1948. Jean Cocteau wrote the script and directed. The film stars Jean Marais as Michael, Yvonne de Bray as Yvonne, Gabrielle Dorziat as Leo, Marcel André as Georges, and Josette Day as Madeleine.

- A second French-language television adaptation was released in 2003. This version was directed by Josée Dayan and stars Jeanne Moreau as Leo, Nicole Garcia as Yvonne, François Berléand as Georges, Cyrille Thouvenin as Michael, and Ariadna Gil as Madeleine.

- As of 2006, the 1948 version (with English subtitles) was available from www.inetvideo.com. The 2003 version, in French, was available from www.glowria.fr.

PLOT SUMMARY

Act 1

Indiscretions opens on a scene of panic in Yvonne's chaotic bedroom. Yvonne, a diabetic, looks close to death. Her husband George thinks she has taken an overdose of insulin. Yvonne's sister Leo and George guess that Yvonne has been driven to desperation by the failure of Michael, the son of George and Yvonne, to return home the previous night. Yvonne explains that she forgot to eat or take sugar to balance her insulin dose as she was worried about Michael. Leo gives her sugar dissolved in water, and she recovers.

Yvonne and Leo discuss their family. Leo says that an uncle left his fortune to her because she is the only orderly member of the family among a group of "raggle-taggle gypsies." She is happy to support them all, even George, whose fruitless research on an underwater machine gun she claims to admire.

Leo tells Yvonne that she suspects that Michael spent the night with a woman and suggests

that he is glad to escape the mess of Yvonne's "gypsy camp." She adds that George, too, has sought refuge with another woman, and this is hardly surprising, as Yvonne gives all her love and attention to Michael. Yvonne cannot believe that Michael would have an affair because she still thinks of him as a child, but she shows no concern at the news that her husband is straying. Leo recalls that George was originally her fiancé, but she pushed him and Yvonne together as she believed they were better suited. Leo points out that Michael is not a child, despite Yvonne's attempts to keep him dependent upon her, for example, by preventing him from taking a job.

Michael comes home to a grilling from Yvonne and George, who want to know where he has been. Michael decides to tell his mother on her own first, and the two snuggle up on her bed. He says that he has met a girl called Madeleine. She works as a bookbinder and has helped Michael financially. She is involved with an older man but has decided to break off the relationship to be with Michael. Yvonne, furious, accuses the girl of being a scheming older woman who is exploiting Michael. She makes a terrible scene and demands that he break off his romance.

Leo rushes in to calm Yvonne, who hits her. George summons Michael to his room, and they leave. Yvonne tells Leo that her suspicions were right: Michael has fallen in love with a woman, and he no longer loves his mother. Leo rebukes Yvonne for her selfishness. She advises Yvonne to keep control of her feelings. She says that she herself has had to do this, since she has always loved George. Leo has sacrificed her life to stay near George. Again, Yvonne is unconcerned about this revelation about her husband.

George enters, looking shocked. Left alone with Leo, George reveals that he has discovered that Michael's girlfriend, Madeleine, is the same woman with whom he has been having an affair. What is more, he has lied to Madeleine, using a false name and claiming that he is a widower who has lost a daughter who looks like her. Recently, Madeleine had claimed that her strict married sister had come to live with her, so she could no longer see George at her flat. George had borrowed money from Leo to rent a flat so that he could continue to see Madeleine. George realizes that the story about the sister was an excuse not to see him. Madeleine had arranged to meet George that evening; he realizes that this was to break with him so that she could pursue her relationship with Michael.

George feels hurt. Leo, feeling sorry for him, suggests that they all go to visit Madeleine, as Michael wishes. There, George must take revenge on her by threatening Madeleine that if she refuses to break it off with Michael, he will reveal all about her affair with him (George). George agrees that he will arrange to see Madeleine in private at the beginning of the visit and issue his threat. George and Leo rejoin Yvonne, who reluctantly agrees to accompany them to Madeleine's. Michael, unaware of Leo and George's plan, is delighted that they will meet his girlfriend.

Act 2

Act 2 opens in Madeleine's tidy flat. Madeleine is nervous about meeting Michael's family. Michael reassures her but wishes that she had first managed to break off her relationship with the older man (actually George). She says that she was about to, but the man called and postponed the meeting. She admits that she still loves this man, but not as she loves Michael.

Leo arrives at Madeleine's flat and admires its tidiness. She has come in advance of George and Yvonne to warn Madeleine and Michael that George wants to see Madeleine on her own first. Yvonne and George arrive. Madeleine is shocked to recognize George as her older lover, but says nothing. George asks Yvonne, Leo, and Michael to leave so that he can speak to Madeleine alone.

Left alone with Madeleine, George reflects bitterly that this coincidence is like something out of the books that Madeleine binds, except that the books are mostly tragedies, and this is a comedy. He accuses Madeleine of lying to him, but she replies that he also lied to her about his situation, claiming he was a widower. She says that she lied to protect him, because she cares about his feelings. She adds that she only realized what real love was when she met Michael. She expects George to stand aside for the sake of Michael's happiness, but George says he has no intention of doing so. George orders her to break off her relationship with Michael, using a made-up story of a third man (not George) with whom she is having an affair. If she refuses, George will tell Michael about Madeleine's affair with George. Madeleine is shocked that George would try to stand in the way of her and Michael. She believes that Yvonne and George have only taught Michael how to be idle; she means to change him and put him to work. George claims that he only has his son's future happiness at heart. Madeleine cannot bear the thought of Michael knowing the truth about her and George, so she reluctantly agrees to do as George wants.

George tells Yvonne, Leo, and Michael that Madeleine has confessed that she is involved with another man and cannot marry Michael. Michael at first does not believe him, but when Madeleine does not deny the story, he tells his mother that she was right about her. Yvonne is relieved that she has her son back in her clutches. Madeleine tells Michael to leave and collapses on the stairs. George leaves.

Leo sends Michael home with Yvonne and stays to look after Madeleine. Leo tells Madeleine that she has guessed that the third man is an invention and that George forced her to lie. Leo admits that before she met Madeleine, she had little confidence in George or Michael's choice in women. But now that she has met her, she likes her. She suggests that she and Madeleine join forces to fight Yvonne and George. Madeleine is not confident, but she agrees to try. Leo tells her to come to visit them at five o'clock the next day, when she will clean up the "mess" that George has made.

Act 3

At Yvonne and George's house, George and Leo discuss Michael and Yvonne's responses to the catastrophe. Michael is distraught and Yvonne is triumphant, as she thinks she has won Michael back. George has told Yvonne about his affair with Madeleine, but she was not interested, caring only about any effects on Michael if he should find out. Leo tells George that what he did to Madeleine was unforgivable. George reminds Leo that it was her plot, and he merely did what she told him. Leo orders him never to repeat that to anyone. She adds that she was wrong about Madeleine and wrong to do what she did, but now she is going to put everything right. George is unwilling, but Leo tells him that he must make a sacrifice, as she did. She tells him that she has always loved him, but sacrificed herself to ensure his happiness. She now knows that it was the wrong decision. George warns Leo that Yvonne will never agree to Leo's new plan to reconcile the lovers, now that she has Michael back.

Leo explains her plan to George: they will tell Yvonne and Michael that Madeleine did not feel worthy of him and that she invented the third man to set Michael free. She says that their family is "a wreck" but that she is determined to salvage something before it is too late. George, ashamed, agrees that she is right.

Yvonne reports that Michael is in such despair that she is almost ready to give Madeleine to him, but she cannot do this because the girl is morally loose. George tells Yvonne that Madeleine is innocent and that the third man does not exist. He confesses that he forced Madeleine to lie and that he was motivated by revenge. Yvonne rebukes George for endangering Michael. George says that they have all nearly killed Michael and Madeleine out of selfishness, but it is not too late to save them. Yvonne cannot bear the thought of allowing the marriage to go ahead, saying that Madeleine is not in their class. George reminds Yvonne that there is nothing admirable about their family, whereas Madeleine offers Michael "real possibilities and fresh air and open space." Yvonne is unwilling to agree to Leo and George's plan. Leo and George tell her that Madeleine is coming to visit soon and that she, Yvonne, must tell Michael the truth. Yvonne is plunged into fear and confusion.

Michael enters, apologizes to Yvonne for sending her away, and tells George that he plans to accept the job he offered him in Morocco. Yvonne, faced with the terrible prospect of losing Michael, is now eager to tell him to truth so that he has no reason to leave Europe and her. George announces that Madeleine is innocent and that she invented the story of the third man to set Michael free because she thought she was not worthy of their class. Michael says they must find Madeleine, and Leo reveals that she has been concealing the girl in her room. Michael faints.

Madeleine enters and is joyfully reconciled with Michael, who has recovered from his faint. George and Leo notice that Yvonne has vanished. Yvonne shouts from the bathroom that she is just doing her insulin injections. She stumbles in and collapses on the bed. As Michael is about to take Madeleine to see his room, Yvonne calls out in terror. Leo says that she has poisoned herself. Yvonne explains that she had seen Michael and Madeleine, and George and Leo, all together. She felt she was an encumbrance and wanted to die. But now, she regrets her action. She wants to live and see Michael happy. She even feels that she will grow to love Madeleine. Madeleine tries to leave, but Leo says that Michael will need her, just as George will need her (Leo). Yvonne overhears Leo and curses them all, saying that she will poison them just as she poisoned herself.

As Yvonne is dying, she threatens to tell Michael that George was Madeleine's lover. George tries to silence her by kissing her on the lips, and Leo ushers Michael and Madeleine out on the pretense that she needs them to telephone the doctor again. Yvonne veers between wanting revenge by telling Madeleine the whole truth and wanting to live and see the couple happy. Then she dies. When George tells Michael to pay attention to his mother, Michael stamps his foot like a child and denies that she is his mother; she is, he says, his best friend. Madeleine, horrified, exclaims that Michael is mad. Michael breaks down by the bed, and Madeleine comforts him. The doorbell rings. It is the cleaner. Leo tells her that there is nothing for her to do, as everything is in order.

CHARACTERS

George

George is the patriarch of the family, the husband of Yvonne, and the father of Michael. He is an ineffectual and immature man—Leo calls him "an overgrown schoolboy"—who reads comics and spends much of his time in his study working on a useless invention, an underwater machine gun. Ignored by his wife, he is, figuratively speaking, the archetypal castrated male. Perhaps in an attempt to rediscover a sense of manhood, George has an affair with Madeleine before she becomes involved with Michael. His tragedy is that he loses both of the women in his life, Yvonne and Madeleine, to Michael. George's tendency toward petty-mindedness is shown in his readiness to break up his son's relationship with Madeleine by forcing her to invent an imaginary lover. He does this out of a desire for revenge against Madeleine and jealousy of Michael. However, under pressure from his sister-in-law Leo, he redeems himself by admitting that he did wrong and declaring Madeleine innocent, thereby enabling the young lovers to be together. These actions make clear that he has an element of honesty and generosity that Yvonne lacks.

Leo

Leo is Yvonne's cool and calculating sister, who lives with her and George. She was previously George's fiancée before she pushed him and Yvonne together, as she thought her feelings for him were too cerebral to make him happy. She is, however, still in love with him. Leo is sensible, practical, and devoted to order. She was left the family fortune by a rich uncle and uses it to support George's family. She spends much of her time cleaning up after the messy Yvonne, George, and Michael, and rescuing Yvonne from various crises. Leo's motivation is not at first pure, in that she is driven by her illicit love for George. To make his life easier, she concocts a plan, which George carries out under her orders, to destroy the romance between Michael and Madeleine. However, when she meets Madeleine, she recognizes a kindred spirit of orderliness and realizes that the love between Madeleine and Michael must be supported. She admits that she was wrong to try to divide them and goes on to put right all the wrongs that have been done to the young couple by George (albeit under her direction) and Yvonne. In this respect, she becomes the family's figurative as well as literal cleaner. Her actions show that there is one thing that is more important to her than her love for George, and that is love itself.

Throughout the play, Leo acts as a foil to the other characters, in that she is the sane, grown-up one with whom the audience can identify. She is a wise and sardonic commentator on the actions and motivations of the other characters.

Madeleine

Madeleine is a beautiful young woman with whom Michael falls in love. She is three years older than Michael and is much more practical than he is, earning her own living as a bookbinder and living in her own very tidy flat. Unknown to Michael, she is also his father's mistress. Madeleine hates disorder and lies, and she contrasts with Michael's chaotic family. In the spirit of honesty, she tells Michael the truth about her older lover from the start, but he does not recognize his father in her description because George has lied to Madeleine about his name and situation. It is Madeleine's tragedy that though she has a pure motivation, she is forced to lie by George, who makes her invent a third lover in order to break off her relationship with Michael. Madeleine is saved by Leo, who, out of respect for her orderliness, becomes her ally. Through Leo's intervention, Madeleine is in the end joyfully reconciled with Michael. Signs that their future is bright include Madeleine's remark to George that she intends to put Michael to work, which meshes well with Michael's determination to break away from his mother and take up a job, even at a point when he thinks he has lost Madeleine.

Michael

Michael is the twenty-two-year-old son George and Yvonne. He is dominated by his mother and suffocated by her all-consuming passion for him. Yvonne treats him as a child whom she can mold to her will, but at the same time, as her lover. She has never let him get a job because she wants to keep him dependent on her, and this has made him impractical, idle, and immature. Madeleine refers to him as "a child." Nevertheless, Michael is relatively untainted by his mother's dark obsession. He is an innocent character whose motivation is pure: he wants to break away from his mother and marry Madeleine, whom he loves, and he pursues this goal honestly. He welcomes Madeleine's ethos of orderliness and hard work, which suggests that he will cast aside his mother's influence and become an adult.

Yvonne

Yvonne is the darkest character in the play and the center of its disorder and uncleanness, both on the physical and psychological levels. She is primarily responsible for the "gypsy camp" quality of the family's existence. She is as emotionally dependent upon her savage and all-consuming passion for her son as she is physically dependent on her insulin (she is a diabetic). She lives in a darkened, gloomy, messy atmosphere, seldom rising from her bed. She ignores her husband and is unconcerned about Leo's revelations that he is having an affair and that Leo is in love with him: all she cares about is Michael.

Yvonne opposes the romance between Michael and Madeleine from the start because it threatens her ownership of him. Selfishly, she threatens suicide and verbally attacks Madeleine, whom she views as a rival. She is the most dishonest of all the characters, never intentionally admitting her true motives. This is shown in the absurd reasons she gives for disapproving of Madeleine as a match for Michael: throughout the play, she claims that Madeleine is a scheming old woman, but after she meets her, she changes her story, saying "she's too young . . . compared to me." Unwittingly, she has revealed her true conviction: that only she can be the lover of her son.

Yvonne's inability to face the truth about herself makes her irredeemable, in that the only way that the right order can be restored and the young couple marry is for Yvonne to die. Her near-suicide at the beginning of the play foreshadows her actual suicide at the end. What would be a tragic event in one of the ancient Greek plays to which Cocteau was referring in his borrowing of the Oedipus story, however, is undermined by absurd farce. Yvonne keeps changing her mind about whether she wants to die or live to see the young couple be happy, and Leo and George frantically try to silence her in any way they can as she tries to tell Michael that Madeleine was George's mistress. It seems emblematic of Yvonne's disorderly nature that her death is the final mess that her long-suffering family is forced to clean up.

THEMES

Perverted Love

Indiscretions explores the chaos and confusion of destructive family relationships in 1930s Paris. In his introduction to Jeremy Sams's translation of the play, Simon Callow quotes Cocteau as writing in the program of the original production: "Here . . . is the Rolls-Royce of families, uncomfortable and ruinous." In the play, Leo comments:

> this family is a wreck, a hopeless, hypocritical, middleclass mess, hanging on desperately to its false values as it rolls inexorably to its inevitable doom, like some dreadful juggernaut, crushing everything in its path—hopes, dreams, possibilities, everything."

The relationship between Yvonne and Michael is based on a lie, a refusal to see the reality of the situation, as the two do not acknowledge each other as mother and son. Michael hardly ever calls Yvonne mother, but uses a pet name, Sophie. Yvonne,

for her part, does not treat Michael as a son, but as a lover. She has ejected her husband George from his rightful role and is unconcerned about revelations of his infidelity except insofar as it could affect Michael. The sexual element of the relationship between Yvonne and Michael is never made explicit. It cannot be said with certainty that physical incest occurs, though it is suggested: she cuddles up with Michael on her bed and touches up her makeup when she hears him coming home. The abuse that Yvonne perpetrates on Michael is emotional. She creates a terrible scene when Michael tells her of his love for Madeleine and sets herself up as a rival to Madeleine, implying that Michael has to choose between them. In a revealing turnabout, Yvonne claims during the first two acts that Madeleine is unsuitable for Michael because she is a scheming old woman, but in act 3, scene 2, as honesty begins to permeate the family, she changes her story to "she's too young . . . compared to me." In fact, Madeleine is just three years older than Michael, whereas Yvonne is over twice his age. In Yvonne's unnatural, ingrown world, only the mother is a fit lover for the son.

The diseased nature of this relationship infects others in the family. The sidelined husband George has an affair, which happens to be with Madeleine, which in turn makes George and Michael into rivals and leads to a determination on George's part to end Michael's romance with Madeleine. Michael is less tainted by this unhealthy love than Yvonne. He is protected by his natural innocence, which prompts him to want to break away from his mother to live with the orderly, honest, and psychologically healthy Madeleine. In all of these twists on family relationships and sexuality, Cocteau explores the oedipal connections between parent and child and how these are threatened as the adult child turns outward to the world to find an appropriate sexual partner.

Order and Disorder

Throughout the play, the external disorder and order associated with the characters reflects their psychological state and their effect on other people. Yvonne is the center and source of disorderliness, living in a darkened room amid piles of dirty linen and other mess. Leo, in contrast, is "obsessive about order" and is constantly cleaning up the mess made by Yvonne, of both the literal and figurative sorts. Madeleine is also a force for order, as is obvious from her tidy flat. Michael, though superficially tainted by Yvonne's disorderly ways, has a fundamental "cleanness," to which Madeleine is attracted. She means to clean him up even further by

TOPICS FOR FURTHER STUDY

- Choose an ancient story, myth, or legend from any culture and create a short story, mini-play, poem, film, or dance that updates it to the present time. Whichever art form or mixture of art forms you choose, this assignment should culminate in your reciting aloud or performing your work in front of a group. Make some written notes for your audience about which aspects of your source story were easy to carry over into the modern age, which were more difficult, and why.

- Create an original work of art for performance that uses two or more different art forms. Possible forms include poetry, narrative, drama, painting, costume design, dance, film, and mime.

- Research the work of an artist or writer who lived and worked in Paris at any time between 1900 and 1945. Trace the development of his or her work during a time period of your choice, identifying any influences from certain artistic movements or other artists or intellectuals.

- Write a short story, poem, or play about a destructive relationship.

- Research an aspect of incest and write a report on your findings.

- Watch one of Cocteau's films and write a review of it. Give reasons for your responses, whether positive or negative, or a mixture of both.

---

encouraging him to work and make something of himself. George stands between disorder and order, in that he becomes drawn into Yvonne's disorder when she is determined to split up the young lovers, but finally he is persuaded by Leo to become her ally in the restoration of order and the union of the lovers.

Purity of Motive

In her book *French Drama of the Inter-War Years*, Dorothy Knowles quotes Cocteau's comments on *Indiscretions*: "Two of the roles create the balance of the order and of the disorder which motivate the play. The young man whose disorder is pure, and his aunt whose order is not pure." Cocteau means that though superficially Michael has acquired some of his mother's disorderly living habits, he is at his center innocent. His motive, to marry Madeleine, remains clear, and he is honest about it.

In contrast, while Leo is the personification of order, her motivation is not pure because she has long been secretly in love with George. Her plot to separate the lovers stems from a hidden desire to make George's life easier and her lack of faith that George or Michael would make a good partner. While she redeems herself in her rapid realization that Michael's union with Madeleine must go forward, the question

of whether Leo could have prevented Yvonne's suicide remains unanswered. An even darker question is hidden beneath Leo's calm exterior: is her determination to reconcile the lovers at all motivated by the knowledge that doing so will destroy Yvonne, enabling Leo to unite with George? When George asks Leo whether she loves Yvonne, she only replies, "Don't dig too deep in anyone's heart." She warns Madeleine, too: "Don't try and understand me. Don't look too deep; God alone knows what lurks in the rag and bone shop of the heart." It is clear that Leo believes that her motivations are not fit to be examined. Nevertheless, she is instrumental in restoring the right order of things, thus becoming a positive force that transcends the twists and turns of her personal motivation.

STYLE

Symbols

Indiscretions is rich in symbols that serve to draw attention to the family dynamics. Images of outward disorder at Yvonne's house, such as the blocked bath and piles of dirty linen, symbolize her emotional stagnation and chaos, as well as the disordered and unnatural relationships that she generates. Leo calls the house "a gypsy camp," a metaphor that to Cocteau's audience would suggest messiness and a lack of responsibility, as well as pointing to the tendency of this family to live outside the general social norms. Leo cleans up Yvonne and George's mess, both literally and figuratively (when she reconciles the lovers he has separated). Madeleine's tidy and well-functioning apartment, in contrast, shows her healthy and honest approach to life.

Cocteau uses sound, too. Stage directions indicate doors are slammed, symbolizing the indirect and nonverbal expression of anger within this family. The effect on the audience may be jarring, just as the interactions between the family members are emotionally jarring.

Darkness and light are used symbolically to indicate the degree of psychological health or sickness of the characters and the degree of truth that they can tolerate. Yvonne lives in a claustrophobic atmosphere of darkness, suggesting a womb-like or sinister state in which she tries to envelop Michael. The fact that George seeks a lighter and healthier atmosphere is symbolized by his attempt to turn on the lights in act 1, scene 3, though he is prevented by Yvonne, who says, "I like the darkness." This shows that Yvonne has no interest in changing or in facing the truth. It is no surprise that George flees to the "real possibilities and fresh air and open space" offered by Madeleine. When Madeleine is about to arrive at Yvonne's house, a stage direction mentions that it is getting lighter, a reference to Madeleine's positive influence on the family. After George's lies about Madeleine having another lover take hold of Michael, he lies face down in the dark, symbolizing that he is (temporarily at least) back in Yvonne's grasp. When he finally emerges from his room, it is no accident that he has decided to take a job in the sunny country of Morocco, a sign that he is not prepared to retreat into the darkness of his mother's womb once again but has chosen the light. This is also a sign that he truly deserves Madeleine, a creature of the light.

The underwater machine gun that George works on alone in his study is an obvious and comic phallic symbol. The fact that it is a useless invention that will never leave the drawing board symbolizes his castration by his wife, whose object of passion is her son not her husband.

Yvonne's diabetic dependency upon insulin, and her inability to manage even this vital aspect of her life efficiently, is a symbolic reference to her dependency upon Michael and the emotional disorder that this causes. Her relationship with Michael is as much an illness as her diabetes.

Boulevard Theater

In the program of the original production of the play, as Simon Callow quotes in his introduction to Jeremy Sams's translation of *Indiscretions*, Cocteau wrote, "with this play, I'm resuming the tradition of boulevard theatre." The boulevard theater movement sprang from the popular plays that were performed in the theaters of the Boulevard du Temple, a street in Paris, from the last half of the eighteenth century. The boulevard theater became known for crime stories and melodramas, as well as farces and comedies based on the conventions of infidelities and mistaken identity, and the location of these theaters provided the name to an entire subgenre of drama. Cocteau consciously used boulevard traditions in *Indiscretions*. The melodrama is seen in Yvonne's excessive responses to Michael and her suicide. The boulevard comedic conventions are exactly reflected in Cocteau's plot. George's discovery that his mistress is also his son's fiancée is the obvious example. George himself comments to Leo, "My God, you could put it in the silliest Boulevard farce and it would be dismissed as being a little far-fetched." But where Cocteau's play differs from conventional farce is that George's discovery is marked as much by pathos and tragedy as by humor. George says, "It'll break my heart." Similarly, Cocteau subverts the expected tragedy of Yvonne's suicide with the farcical element of having George and Leo use desperate tricks to try to stop the dying Yvonne from revealing the truth about George and Madeleine to Michael.

Cocteau's major innovation in this play was to combine a boulevard dramatic style with the tragic inevitability of the ancient Greek Oedipus story. The combination enables him to draw attention to the tragedy within the absurd and the absurd within tragedy.

Distancing

In this play, Cocteau makes use of a dramatic technique known as *Verfremdungseffekt* (translated as distancing effect or alienation effect). The technique formed an important part of epic theater, a theory about theater that was pioneered by the influential German playwright and poet Bertold Brecht (1898–1956). Brecht was a communist. He believed that a play should not cause spectators to identify with the characters and action on stage or to undergo an emotional catharsis (purging). Instead, a play should encourage spectators to retain a critical distance that enables them objectively to identify social problems highlighted in the play, reflect on them, and then take action to change the world for the better. He tried to achieve this aim through various methods, including having the actors hold up explanatory signs to the audience or address the audience directly. The effect was to remind the audience that the play is a construct and can be changed, just as society can be changed.

One Brechtian distancing method taken up by Cocteau in *Indiscretions* is a reminder to spectators that they are watching a play. In act 2, scene 3, after Leo has recited a melodramatic passage from one of Madeleine's books in order to test whether people upstairs can hear people downstairs, Michael tells Leo that she could have been an actress. The audience will pick up on the irony that the woman playing Leo is indeed an actress. There is an additional, deeper message that Leo is lying about her reasons for checking the soundproofing in the flat: she does not want George's attempts to persuade Madeleine to lie to be overheard. Thus, the character Leo is also an actress. While Cocteau is not primarily trying, in the political sense, to encourage the audience to criticize social ills, the effect of the distancing technique in this case is to encourage the audience to stand apart from Leo and to remember that at this point, her motivation is not pure. Like an actress in a play, she is trying to create an effect. In this way, Cocteau deconstructs the illusion of reality which the stage presents.

Dramatic Irony

Cocteau uses irony to draw attention to the gap between normal family relationships and the twisted relationships in this play. For example, In act 2, scene 1, Madeleine tells Michael about her older lover: "I was as fond of George as I would be of your father, as I will be of your father when I meet him." Neither she nor Michael knows that her lover, in fact, is Michael's father, but the audience knows. This technique, where the audience knows something of which the character is unaware and which would transform his or her attitude if he or she did know, is known as dramatic irony. There is another example of dramatic irony in the same scene. Michael tells Madeleine about his mother, "Sophie's told me so often that she's my best friend, I could hardly hide anything from her, could I?" Michael's innocence is both amusing and touching, as the audience is aware that Yvonne is acting as his bitterest enemy. Dramatic irony permeates Sophocles's play,

Oedipus Rex, and the technique here is a fitting parallel.

HISTORICAL CONTEXT

The Parisian Artistic Community between the World Wars

In the period from 1918 to 1939, between World War I and World War II, Paris was famous for its cultural and artistic communities. The city became a vibrant meeting place for artists from other European countries and the United States, including exiled Russian composer Igor Stravinsky, Spanish painters Pablo Picasso and Salvador Dalí, and various writers, such as the Irish James Joyce and the Americans Ernest Hemingway and F. Scott Fitzgerald. Cocteau was at the center of this group of artists and formed many fruitful collaborations. For example, with Picasso, the Russian ballet master Sergei Diaghilev, and the French composer Erik Satie, Cocteau produced the revolutionary new ballet *Parade* (1917).

Many aspects of this artistic community were characterized as *bohemian*, a term derived from the French word for *gypsy*. The term comes from the association of gypsies with Bohemia, which during these years was the westernmost province of Czechoslovakia, later redrawn as the Czech Republic. From the mid-nineteenth century, the term was used for certain artists, intellectuals, and writers who rejected social conventions and chose nontraditional lifestyles. Bohemian communities formed in places where people could live cheaply, such as the Montmartre in Paris. This village within the city of Paris is on its highest hill and was a gathering place for painters and other artists in the 1920s and 1930s. Bohemians gained a reputation for unorthodox marital relations, lack of cleanliness, and a tendency toward drug use, as well as literary and artistic creativity and innovation. The term carries a suggestion of privileged knowledge or extraordinary artistic ability.

In *Indiscretions*, Cocteau satirizes pretensions to bohemianism in the character of Yvonne and her family. Yvonne, as Leo points out in act 1, scene 2, has all the less admirable aspects of bohemianism—the messiness and confused family relationships—yet none of the artistic distinction. Leo calls the family "The middle class gypsies. 'Cos, let's face it, we're not artists, we're not bohemians, not remotely." She points out that at the first sign of independence on Michael's part, the bohemian façade

COMPARE
&
CONTRAST

- **1930s:** Paris is the hub of a vibrant artistic and intellectual community, many members of which are expatriates from other countries, including the United States and Russia. Cocteau is at the center of this community, interacting with writers, painters, composers, and ballet choreographers, with whom he sometimes collaborates.

  Today: Increased global mobility and technologies, such as the Internet and television, enable artists from many different cultures to interact and exchange ideas without gathering necessarily in one location.

- **1930s:** Performed in the original French, *Les Parents Terribles* shocks Paris audiences with its portrayal of an incestuous family relationship and is banned, in part because it is perceived as immoral.

  Today: While artistic works dealing with previously taboo subjects such as incest and child abuse are relatively common and widely accepted, some works of art continue to be censored. Reasons given are more often a fear of giving offense to certain religious or ethnic groups than immorality. Works that are thought to encourage pedophilia because of the way they present children are still vulnerable to censorship.

- **1930s:** Sexual and covert or non-sexual incest are taboo. On the rare occasions when victims speak out, they are frequently ignored or vilified; often they are not believed. Incest is not considered acceptable subject matter for artists and writers, though this taboo is broken within the safer genre of pagan myth, by the German composer Richard Wagner in his opera *The Ring Cycle*. In most industrialized countries, incest is forbidden by law, though a surprising number of incest laws only cover sexual penetration of a minor. Covert incest is impossible to restrict by legislation.

  Today: Incest is taboo, though it does form the subject matter of various works of art. Twentieth-century novels which feature incest include Vladimir Nabokov's *Ada or Ardor: A Family Chronicle* (1969) and J. R. R. Tolkein's *Silmarillion* (1977). Many support groups exist to help victims and perpetrators of incest, though they frequently have to overcome the wall of silence that surrounds the practice.

- **1930s:** Freud popularizes his concept of the Oedipus complex, claiming that it is universal and applies to girls (in whom it is called the Electra complex) as well as boys.

  Today: Many modern psychologists question the universal application of the Oedipus complex. Some contend that the sex drive is not as important a factor in childhood development as Freud believed.

---

falls away, exposing Yvonne's narrow bourgeois (property-owning middle-class) values and petty snobbery.

The Oedipus Story and the Oedipus Complex

The Oedipus complex is a theory developed by the Austrian founder of psychoanalysis, Sigmund Freud (1856–1939). Freud believed that young boys go through a developmental stage in which they unconsciously wish for the exclusive love of their mother. Since they see their father as a rival for their mother's love, they feel jealous of him and unconsciously wish for his death. Freud named this pattern of behavior the Oedipus complex after the ancient Greek story of Oedipus, who unknowingly kills his father and marries his mother.

The Oedipus story held a great fascination for Cocteau, who revisited it in various works. The story gave him the opportunity to explore one of his favorite themes, the devouring female who suffocates a man with her love and impedes his maturation or artistic development. Another attraction of the story for Cocteau is that it portrays man as fate's plaything, helpless in the face of destiny and doomed to suffering. This sense of tragic inevitability is never far from the surface in Cocteau's works. In *Indiscretions*, Yvonne's fate is marked out from the play's first scene—featuring her failed suicide attempt.

Decadence and the Rise of Communism

The French Communist Party (*Parti communiste français*, or PCF) was founded in 1920 and attracted many intellectuals and artists in the 1920s and 1930s. The growth of communism and socialism in Europe drew strength from the Wall Street stock market crash in 1929 and the subsequent economic depression. It was thought that economic liberalism had failed, and alternatives were sought.

It should be noted that Cocteau was not a communist. He believed that poets, among whom he numbered himself, existed in a realm apart from politics, and he criticized other artists, including André Breton, the leader of the surrealist movement, for allying themselves with communism. However, the growing disapproval of the bourgeois class, which was perceived as self-absorbed and non-productive, was part of the *zeitgeist*, or spirit of the age, and was picked up by political and artistic thinkers alike. This was partly an effect of World War I (1914–1918), in which whole sections of society who had never done manual labor were mobilized into the workforce, laborers were seen as heroes who helped win the war, and the value to society of inherited wealth and nobility was increasingly questioned. In *Indiscretions*, Cocteau satirizes pretensions to nobility in Yvonne's hypocritical contempt of Madeleine for not having a maid, when Yvonne herself does not have one, and in her references to the supposed inferiority of Madeleine's family, when Yvonne's only claim to family distinction is a grandfather who counted the semi-colons in the work of a great writer.

The disorder, idleness, and chaos that characterize Yvonne's family would have been seen by the many communists among Cocteau's artistic Parisian contemporaries as symptoms of the decline into decadence of the bourgeoisie. In his review of *Indiscretions* for the *New York Times*, Vincent Canby notes that "the play is . . . a spookily revealing artifact from a society grown soft and corrupt." He points out that when the play was written, the Nazis were occupying France, and "Frenchmen willingly assisted the Germans in rounding up other Frenchmen and sending them off to the camps." The character of Madeleine represents the capacity for honest hard work that was viewed as the mainstay of a well-functioning society by the communist and socialist movements.

CRITICAL OVERVIEW

Indiscretions, under its original title *Les Parents Terribles*, was first produced in 1938 at the Théatre des Ambassadeurs, which was owned by the Municipal Council of Paris. Though the play was popular with the public, it was accused of immorality due to its portrayal of an incestuous family relationship and was banned by the Municipal Council from the city-owned theater. It reopened the following year at the Théatre des Bouffes-Parisiens, where it continued to play to packed houses. By the time the play was revived in 1941, the Nazis had occupied Paris, and France's Vichy government was collaborating with them. Attacks on the play's supposed immorality escalated, and members of France's fascist party, the *Parti Populaire Francais*, threw tear gas at the actors. The Germans closed the play.

Critic Raymond Bach, in his "Cocteau and Vichy: Family Disconnections" (1993), argues that the play's portrayal of disorderly and diseased family relationships threatened the model of the ideal family propagandized by the Vichy government. In particular, the play was at odds with the public image of the head of state, Marshal Pétain, who was portrayed as a hero and father of the nation.

Critics tend to be divided on Cocteau's work in general, and their views on *Indiscretions* are no exception, despite its popularity with the theater-going public. Some critics have attacked the rhetoric and melodrama of the piece, and the caricatured quality of the characters, while others object to its reliance on what they consider to be a discredited theory, Freud's Oedipus complex. Supporters of the work point to the innovative concept of updating an ancient Greek tragedy to shock and surprise modern audiences. The perceptiveness with which the dynamics of the "terrible parents" are drawn, the tightness of construction, and the ebullient wit and humor of the play have also been praised.

Jeremy Sams's translation of the play was first performed at London's National Theater in 1994. The production, directed by Sean Mathias, was so successful that it was moved to the Barrymore Theater on Broadway the following year. The role of Michael made an overnight star of the actor Jude Law, who made headlines with his leisurely nude

Gabrielle Dorziat and Jean Marais in a 1948 production of Les Parents Terrible (Indiscretions)
Sirius/The Kobal Collection

entrance. The production ended in a spectacular effect whereby the entire set fell into rubble, reflecting the collapse of the family under the onslaught of truth. The production was enthusiastically received and earned Tony nominations for the director, designer, and most of the actors.

Eileen Blumenthal, reviewing the production for *American Theater*, notes the juxtaposition of tragedy and farce in the play, though she sells Cocteau short when she writes, "The triumph of Sean Mathias's direction is that he realizes—even more, it would seem, than Cocteau himself did—

how fundamentally this tragedy is a farce." Writing in the *New York Times*, Vincent Canby calls the play Cocteau's "remarkable, brilliantly bent boulevard comedy," and a "lethal if often hilarious farce about the darkest neuroses of familiar comic characters." He also hails Mathias's production's "breathtaking panache." Referring to the fact that Cocteau wrote the play in just eight opium-fuelled days, Canby notes that it has "the eerie seamlessness, the tight construction and the density of a work composed in one spontaneous rush of the imagination."

Mathias's production, according to Robert Hurwitt in the *San Francisco Chronicle*, "played for over-the-top outrageousness," which, however, "tended to mute some of the play's darker themes." In her 2001 production at the Marin Theater in Mill Valley, California, director Amy Glazer downplayed the more farcical elements in favor of clarity. This, Hurwitt remarks, highlighted the shallowness of the characters and produced a plodding effect in places. He comments that "Glazer's version could use more of the same febrile energy" as the production done by Mathias. On the other hand, Glazer's production succeeded in retaining the play's "fever of sharp spikes of comedy and tragedy" and "delivers a darker, more disturbing impact in the end" than Mathias's production.

CRITICISM

Claire Robinson

Robinson has a Master of Arts in English. She is a writer and editor and a former teacher of English literature and creative writing. In the following essay, Robinson examines the journey from disorder to order in Jean Cocteau's Indiscretions.

Indiscretions explores the chaos engendered in a bourgeois family by a mother's obsessive love for her son. The mother, Yvonne, is determined to keep her son, Michael, for herself and so seeks to destroy his burgeoning romance with the young Madeleine. The destructive nature of the love that Yvonne feels for her son is summed up by her husband George when he says, "She'd rather hold his corpse than see her son in someone else's arms." This is a love that is more allied with death than with life.

Yvonne's internal disorder is reflected in the external disorder she creates, both on the literal and emotional levels. As far as the literal level is concerned, she lives in a darkened room amid piles of dirty linen, lounging on her messy bed and creating dramas of various kinds. On the emotional level, Yvonne manufactures life-or-death crises out of what should be the everyday business of life. She is diabetic and depends upon timely doses of insulin and sugar for survival but cannot manage even this vital aspect of her life. The play opens with her narrow escape from death after forgetting to take sugar to balance her insulin; this fit of distraction stems from Michael's failure to come home the previous night. Yvonne repeatedly has to be rescued from her manufactured crises, and in a normal family, this task would fall to her husband, George. But Yvonne has shut George out of her life; she lavishes all her passion and attention on her son. George is emotionally and physically absent, sequestered in his study. Therefore, Yvonne is rescued, time and again, by her sensible sister Leo.

From the point of view of dramatic convention, too, Yvonne is the enemy of order. The natural order of comedies, which *Indiscretions* follows, demands that the young fertile couple marry and have children. The role of older people is to support them in this process, not to oppose them. But Yvonne disrupts this natural order. She tries to prevent the marriage between Michael and Madeleine. What is more, her neglect of George drives him to seek affection from a mistress, who happens to be Madeleine, a woman who is young enough to be his daughter and who intends to marry George's son. George, his feelings hurt by Madeleine's desertion, joins his wife in opposing the marriage. In the context of drama, these confused relationships are perversions of the natural order and must be put right before order can be restored. All of them have their origin in Yvonne's diseased and disorderly passion. When George tells Yvonne that it is the natural order of things that children grow up and take the place of older people like them, Yvonne replies, "I wouldn't know—order's not my forte."

The great force of order in the play is Leo. Her character is diametrically opposite to Yvonne's. She is "obsessive about order" and spends much of her life cleaning up Yvonne's mess on both external and internal levels. It is Leo who rescues Yvonne from her initial overdose of insulin, and Leo who, from the start, tries to persuade Yvonne not to oppose the marriage of Michael and Madeleine. Her passion for order is only overshadowed, temporarily, by her long-hidden love for George. When George discovers that his son's girlfriend is also his own mistress, he feels hurt and vengeful and wants to separate the young lovers. Faced with the prospect of losing both of the women in his life to his son, George begins to express something of his wife's destructive and suffocatingly possessive passions. Leo too is drawn into George's desire for vengeance, for a brief moment, because she feels sorry for him. But once she meets Madeleine, she is struck by the tidiness and order of her flat and her life and recognizes a kindred spirit of order. (In this play, the stage sets elucidate character and tell a story.) Leo's loyalty to order proves stronger than her loyalty to George. She forms a new alliance with Madeleine— "let's call it order versus disorder"—and hatches another plot to reconcile the lovers. Leo draws attention to the symbolic link between external and internal disorder when she insists that she is helping Madeleine primarily because "the mess made here today, by George, offends me. A horrid heap of dirty linen."

Madeleine's role as a force for order is underlined by the symbolism of the audience's first sight of her. Michael has a bath at her flat as the bath at his home is blocked up—a symbolic reference to the unhealthy stagnating emotions generated by Yvonne's influence. Madeleine's bath, naturally, is never blocked. Furthermore, her cleansing influence will save Michael from following his mother into decadence and regression. When she tells Michael that she loves his cleanness and that he is not really dirty but "grubby, like kids are grubby," symbolically, she is saying that he has picked up his mother's disorderly ways but that he is pure and innocent at heart and, therefore, redeemable.

The theme of order and disorder is reflected in the carefully planned structure of the play. In her book *The Esthetic of Jean Cocteau*, Lydia Crowson points out that the play is constructed on three triangular relationships. While in the visual arts, triangular forms may create harmony, they generally do the opposite in human relationships, as *Indiscretions* graphically proves. The first triangle consists of George, his wife Yvonne, and Leo, who has always loved George. This triangle generates the action of the play, since Yvonne has separated herself from George, enabling George and Leo to become allies. Leo's devotion to George makes her plot with him to separate Madeleine from Michael, but subsequently she changes her allegiance to the young lovers, whom she unites. The second triangle is the tragic Oedipal one of George, Yvonne, and their son, Michael. Yvonne's suffocating love for Michael excludes everyone else, even her husband. The third triangle, involving George, Michael, and Madeleine, builds on the other two and precipitates a crisis in the family. George takes a mistress, Madeleine, who, unknown to him, is also his son's girlfriend. This triangle involves the sexual mix-ups typical of farce. It also has Oedipal echoes, because George is soon to be the father-in-law of his mistress, Madeleine, and also, though Michael does not marry his mother, he marries someone who occupies his mother's place in his father's life.

For order to be restored, these unruly triangles must be destroyed and a rightful order of couples established—a young couple and an older couple. This is in line with the comedic tradition in which

> WHILE IN THE VISUAL ARTS, TRIANGULAR FORMS MAY CREATE HARMONY, THEY GENERALLY DO THE OPPOSITE IN HUMAN RELATIONSHIPS, AS *INDISCRETIONS* GRAPHICALLY PROVES."

older people must stand aside and allow a young couple in love to marry.

Adults behaving like children is part of the theme of disorder that runs through the play. It is against the natural order of things and, in Leo's terminology, a mess that has to be cleaned up. As may be expected, it is another perversion of the natural order in which Yvonne and her family excel. Early in the play, Leo tells Yvonne:

> There are two distinct tribes in this world, children, and grown-ups. I, alas, fall into the latter category . . . you . . . George . . . and Michael . . . you belong to the former. Children who will always be children, and as children do, commit the most appalling crimes, apparently thoughtlessly.

Leo is a grown-up because she does not get involved in the childish antics of the rest of her family. She stands apart, cleaning up their messes and advising them on the right thing to do.

Yvonne is childish in that she is too bound up in her own obsessive world to consider others, leading to irresponsible behavior. Leo tells her, "you do damage without even noticing." George, faced with Yvonne's inability to treat him like a man, behaves like a small boy, playing with useless inventions and reading comic books and science fiction. When he tells Madeleine that he has no intention of allowing her to marry Michael, Madeleine tells him that he is "a child": "Someone's broken your nice toy, so you want to break theirs." Madeleine also recognizes that Michael is a child, but he is partially excused by his youth. Moreover, he is eager to change, and she intends to encourage him to grow up and shake off his immature irresponsibility, just as he washes off his grubbiness in her bath.

Through Leo's intervention in pushing forward the marriage, all but one of the childish characters

WHAT DO I READ NEXT?

- Cocteau revisited the Oedipus story and the theme of incest in several works. The greatest among these is widely considered to be his play *La Machine Infernale*, first produced and published in 1934.

- The source for Cocteau's Oedipus works is the ancient Greek play *Oedipus Rex*, written in 428 B.C.E. by the tragedian Sophocles. It is well worth reading for its compelling story, emotional power, and extraordinary influence on writers and thinkers up to the present day. The 2006 Cambridge University Press *Sophocles: Oedipus Rex*, edited by R. D. Dawes, gives readers lots of support in its excellent introduction and analyses of the play's language.

- Thomas Mann's novel *The Holy Sinner* (1951) is a story based on the medieval legend of St. Gregory. It highlights the spiritual consequences of incest and describes redemption through forgiveness.

- The novel *The God of Small Things* (1997), by Indian author Arundhati Roy, features a set of twins who have a cathartic sexual experience. The novel shows how the small things in life build into bigger things that govern the fate of individuals.

- *Silently Seduced: When Parents Make Their Children Partners—Understanding Covert Incest* (1991), by clinical psychologist Kenneth Adams, explores the problem of covert parent-child emotional incest, as opposed to overt sexual incest. Adams argues that covert incest, while seldom identified, is deeply harmful to children, as it denies them proper parenting, betrays their innocence, and places unfair demands on them to deal with their parents' needs.

---

grow up. Michael is able to take his place beside the already adult Madeleine (though, with an ambivalence typical of Cocteau, in her desire to change Michael, she is also acting like a parent to Michael's child—albeit a far more benign and healthy parent than Yvonne). Only Yvonne, unable to mature, continues her childish selfishness in the ultimate destructive act, suicide. This act, prompted by Leo's plot to enable the reconciliation of the lovers, frees George, or so the audience can speculate, to enter an equal relationship with Leo.

The process of restoring order depends upon the revelation of certain truths. These include Michael's announcement that he is in love with Madeleine; George's discovery that she is also his own mistress; and Michael's discovery, brought to light by Leo, that the story about Madeleine's having another lover is false. George and Leo both change during this process, adapting their attitudes and motivations as they acknowledge the rightful order of things (Michael's union with Madeleine) and the injustice of their obstructing it. But Yvonne

is not sufficiently self-aware or mature to adapt to the new climate of truth, so order can only be restored by her death. It is significant that after she dies, the cleaner rings the doorbell but is sent away by Leo: "I told her that there was nothing for her to do . . . that everything was in order."

Source: Claire Robinson, Critical Essay on *Indiscretions*, in *Drama for Students*, Thomson Gale, 2007.

Eileen Blumenthal

In the following review, Blumenthal identifies the mythical, fantastical and neurotic in the sexual relations in Cocteau's play Indiscretions. *She also notes that the play is less about the male adolescent view of the world and more about "a homosexual male vision of heterosexual coming of age."*

"Unbelievable!" the characters in *Les Parents Terribles* pronounce at each preposterous turn of events. And they're right. Yet, from a tangle of impossible coincidence and illogic, Jean Cocteau has spun a persuasive tale. *Les Parents Terribles*, in its current Broadway incarnation, *Indiscretions*, presents the world according to 22-year-old Michael—that is, the subjective, half-baked, narcissistic reality of a boy belatedly careening into adolescence. Like most adolescents, Michael suffers as his rightful happiness is stymied at every turn. Mom will kill herself before relinquishing exclusive title to his love. Dad will stop at nothing to usurp Michael's youth and vitality. In short, the very forces of the cosmos conspire against Michael. The stakes are life and death. And it's all his parents' fault.

Anyone who has been an adolescent can recognize the felt truth of Michael's agony. And anyone who has survived adolescence can see the ridiculousness in the bathos. The triumph of Sean Mathias's direction is that he realizes—even more, it would seem, than Cocteau himself did—how fundamentally this tragedy is a farce.

Jocasta, Phaedra and Medea

The "unbelievable" plot goes like this: Michael—handsome, passionate, adored by everyone—has fallen in love. This throws the stable pathology of his family into pandemonium. His incestuously doting mother, Yvonne, who subsists in a dimly lit, disorderly bedroom, instantly becomes a bourgeois Freudian cliché—Jocasta, Phaedra and Medea rolled into one. Meanwhile, George, the doofus inventor husband Yvonne has ignored since Michael's birth, realizes to his horror that his son's beloved is none other than his own secret paramour—that Michael is the castrating Zeus to his Kronos. Yvonne's sensible, competent sister Léonie, who has long carried a torch for George, concocts a rescue plot (which makes no sense): the family will visit Madeleine together, as Michael wishes them to, and George will blackmail the young woman to end her affair with Michael. Then, after the nasty scheme has worked, Léonie about-faces and (implausibly) convinces George to set things right. But in this funhouse-Freudian world, the mother scorned knows no such generosity. The distraught Yvonne promptly kills herself.

Like much of Cocteau's theatre—including *Beauty and the Beast*, *Orpheus* and *The Infernal Machine* (and his sundry other versions of *Oedipus*)—*Indiscretions* gives concrete form to myth, fantasy and neurosis. Speaking about his film version of the play, Cocteau once said, "*Les Parents Terribles* is not a realistic film, for I have never known a family that lives like that. It is the most imaginary painting you can conceive." But, he said, the play captured a certain claustrophobia, showing "the thunder-laden corridors which had haunted my childhood." It attempted "to approach not *the* truth which objectively doesn't exist, but *a* truth which is subjectively ours."

The broad, vaudevillian style of Sean Mathias's direction rises to meet the play's idiosyncratic reality. The actors play in bold strokes. Roger Rees's George is the eternal bumbler, unable to master his goggles and hoses, his own limbs or his ill-fitting role of *pater familias*; inept and creepy, this George embodies the meanness (in both senses) of one with no real role in life. Jude Law's Michael lurches, gushes, crumples and stirs back to life—precisely the right emotional repertory for a bursting sex-urge, a walking ejaculation. And Eileen Atkins's crisp, smart Léonie sets the emotional and physical messiness of the others in high relief, as she sculpts the airspace with a turn of her head or the contour of a phrase. Interestingly, while the three English actors can produce intense emotion with stylization, the two Americans—Kathleen Turner, as Yvonne, and Cynthia Nixon, as Madeleine—maintain the chiseled edges of their performance only when the character is not spewing heavy emotion. Americans, misled by Method acting's apotheosis of "inner truth," apparently permit feelings to squelch form.

A Gerbil-Ramp for Farce

The physical production also projects the skewed preciseness of a cartoon. Yvonne's lair is a cornucopia of disorder, spilling out its plentiful clutter of clothes, linens and household paraphernalia. An endless spiral staircase in Madeleine's apartment becomes a gerbil-ramp for farce. Costumes and props define characters—whether the silly gear of George's inventions, the ecru lace negligee and ragg socks of Yvonne's boudoir attire, or proper Léonie's telltale scarlet nail lacquer.

Mathias's farcical tone is, in fact, quite different from that set by Cocteau in his own treatment of the play—at least as preserved in his 1948 film version. There, melodrama prevails, breaking through into comedy only in flashes. Apparently, Cocteau was not quite ready to laugh at the *sturm und drang* of his haunted youth.

But both versions of Cocteau's play share another quirk: this "subjective reality" about a boy's heterosexual coming of age is remarkably unhetero-erotic. Such sexual energy as exists in this work about boy-mom incest comes mainly from the older women. In the current *Indescretions*, Kathleen Turner's Yvonne projects a sloshy sexuality, and Eileen Atkins's Léonie clearly knows the nature of the impulses she represses. But any eroticism to be found in the clean-white-collar femininity of Madeleine—as written by Cocteau and played by Cynthia Nixon—is, let's say, a figment of Michael's subjective reality. Nor is there any sexual spark in Roger Rees's George to lend credibility either to his affair with Madeleine or to Léonie's ongoing attraction to him.

Stewed, Sticky Possessiveness

In fact, Michael's world is consistent with Cocteau's direction—and probably built into the play. In Cocteau's film—where the older generation looks 60-something rather than 40-something— the boy-and-adult relationships make emotional sense. Yvonne De Bray, as the mother, oozes a kind of stewed, sticky possessiveness that her son might well fear would entrap, or at least besmear, him. Léonie seems a proper school-marm whose carnal appeal, if any, is unreadable to a young man. And George has the aging asexuality one attributes to parents. But Josette Day's starched perfectness gives Madeleine about as much eroticism as Barbie. And Jean Marais's Michael is clearly enamored mainly of his own dazzling smile, not of Madeline or Yvonne. I doubt any woman would believe this man ever generated a heterosexual spark.

In life, of course, Marais was Cocteau's gorgeous 24-years-younger lover (who was, nonetheless, 10 years too old for the film role of Michael). And Cocteau's play, in all its incarnations, while purporting to expose the shocking, unspeakable "truth" of mother/son incest, actually captures a quite different "truth" not often called by its name: *Les Parents Terribles* is less a generic male adolescent vision of the world than a homosexual male vision of heterosexual coming of age. And that assuredly is, as Cocteau himself said, not "realistic" but "*a truth* which is subjectively" his.

Source: Eileen Blumenthal, "Sexual Relations," in *American Theatre*, Vol. 12, No. 6, July–August 1995, pp. 16–17.

Lydia Crowson

In the following essay, Crowson states that the characters in Les Parents Terribles (Indiscretions) *give themselves over to the play, reacting to their circumstances as the play governs their actions.*

The mechanisms that direct Cocteau's later plays are much more complex than those of his first attempts at dramatic creation. Whereas *La Voix humaine*, for example, unfolded in a strictly linear fashion, *Les Parents terribles*, *Renaud et Armide*, and *L'Aigle à deux têtes* depend on a conflict of archetypes and motifs. The logic of *Les Chevaliers de la*

Table Ronde and *Bacchus* derives in part from the author's personal mythology but belong also to a larger, more accessible system. In the later plays, though characters remain mechanical dolls, they are not homogeneous and they are caught in intricate situations which force their "givens" toward crisis. Each work, therefore, groups and contrasts predefined forces that struggle toward resolution.

Les Parents terribles is constructed on three triangular relationships, each of which operates according to well-established theatrical conventions. The triangle which generates the play itself is that of Georges, his wife Yvonne, and his former fiancée Léo, who is also his sister-in-law and who lives with the couple. Having decided that, since she lives more abstractly than concretely, she could not give Georges the deep love he needed, Léo brought him and her sister together. Although she and Georges have never had an affair (as they would have done in a Boulevard play), Léo is still in love with him. Through the years she has done everything she can to protect him and to make his life easier. Therefore, even if her affection, because of her character, can never manifest itself physically, her emotions are nevertheless alive. Her only allegiance stronger than the one to Georges is the one she has for love itself, the idealized love she and he could never have.

The second triangle is the essentially tragic one composed of Georges, Yvonne, and their son Michel. Yvonne has a savage, possessive love for her child that excludes everyone else. On the other hand, it appears that Michel has a normal relationship with her. Like many little boys, he once expressed the desire to marry his mother, but then he naturally passed beyond this stage and fell in love with someone his own age. Just as there is no adultery between Léo and Georges, there is no incest between Michel and Yvonne, but in both cases strong emotions lie close to the surface.

The third triangle which, because of the other two, precipitates a crisis in the family is a deflected Oedipal relationship which, resulting from a *quiproquo*, takes the form of a vaudeville episode or, in Georges' words, a "a play by Labiche" (Crowson's translation, footnote 38). Ignored by his wife, who is interested only in her child, Georges takes a mistress, Madeleine, who is much younger than he. After spending a night away from home, Michel returns to announce that he intends to marry a young woman who happens to be, unknown to him, his father's mistress. Coupled with the second triangle, the third has an ambiguous quality—of an Oedipal tragedy and of a farce—which Cocteau developed simultaneously. For example, one confrontation between Georges and Madeleine summarizes the misunderstanding at the base of *Oedipe-Roi:*

> MADELEINE: If you had told me your real name . . .
> GEORGE: You would have met Michael anyway.
> MADELEINE: I would have avoided him.
>   [Crowson's translation, footnote 39]

Moreover, Madeleine is three years older than her fiancée, she is much more mature than he, and she has a job and the responsibilities of an adult where he has none, because he is a child. In addition, she is his father's mistress. Not marrying his mother, Michel has nevertheless found someone who virtually occupies her position in his father's life. On the other hand, these circumstances are also in the tradition of Molière's *Ecole des femmes*, in which the older man in love with a younger woman is ridiculed and repulsed. It must be remembered that Cocteau highlighted the vaudeville, boulevard aspects of *La Machine in fernale*. As Taladoire has pointed out, Cocteau was able to balance the tragic and vaudeville aspects of *Les Parents terribles* by drawing upon the structural characteristics common to both genres of theater:

> the miracle of this play is that it is a vaudeville piece and a tragedy at one and the same time. . . . The two are tightly linked by a double-edged fatality whose elements are coincidence and the sequence of events. A poet is capable of perceiving the meaning of these coincidences, which are not routine, when, like Cocteau, he is both humorist and playwright. Therefore, the vaudeville-like aspects of a subject can unfold at exactly the same time as the tragic ones.
>   [Crowson's translation, footnote 40]

However complicated these interlocking series of events may be, they are premises that entail an inevitable conclusion. As we have indicated, Yvonne's attachment to her son is not reciprocated in like manner. He loves her, but not as she loves him; he maintains a close but ordinary mother-child attachment. Similarly, his attraction to Madeleine is "natural," whereas the relation of his father to the girl, like that of Arnolphe and his ward Agnès, is not. It is the order of the world, at least on the stage, that sons leave their mothers to marry and that an older man loses in love to a younger one. Therefore, Michel and Madeleine will be united at the end of the play. The only momentary obstacle is Leonie, who, anxious to help George, plans a drama to separate them. However, her passion for order, for the ideal of love, is *a priori* stronger than her affections for her former fiancé (or she would have married him herself), and she corrects her mistake. Consequently, everything falls into place. Because of her impetuous, emotional nature, Yvonne commits suicide, although she really does not want to. She simply reacts without thinking, as usual, because she understand the inevitability of what is about to take place—Michel's marriage. Thus ends the tragic thread of the play.

What Cocteau meant when he said of *Les Parents terribles* that "The roles should be sacrificed to the play and should serve it rather than use it," (Crowson's translation, footnote 41) now becomes clear. At every stage of the action, at every decision they make, the characters are in fact reacting to their circumstances instead of creating new circumstances. They have no power over what is being accomplished: after the machine is set in motion, they are only the material it shapes. In turn, the effect it has on them is determined by what they are, by the preexistent mechanism of their own personalities. It is the unfolding of the various motifs which represent the forces at work in the universe that governs the action.

Source: Lydia Crowson, "The Nature of the Real," in *The Esthetic of Jean Cocteau*, Published for The University of New Hampshire by The University Press of New England, 1978, pp. 74–78.

Lydia Crowson

In the following essay, Crowson focuses on the moral codes formed by Cocteau's characters' own "desire or inclination" to see themselves free from societal laws, a trait common in children, and in Indiscretions *all the characters are "children, regardless of age."*

Perhaps no play of Cocteau has been as controversial as *Les Parents terribles*. The problem is one of definition, and the resulting confusion strengthens Cocteau's claims of the deforming tendencies of conventional morality. Man's narrow systems make him blind to everything except what he wants to see he said, and he predicted many outraged reactions to his work. In fact, he intended to shock the public. He described his play in the following terms:

> To me, *The Terrible Parents* is purity itself. There is a closed atmosphere where evil does not enter, where the question of good and evil isn't even asked. This is what links the play to the novel *The Terrible Children*.
>   [Crowson's translation, footnote 28]

As he explains, the work is not concerned with good or evil; rather, it depicts a family in which the moral code of each member is personal and dependent upon his own desires or inclinations. In a sense, then, it is a return to nature.

The only character in *Les Parents terribles* who is not impulsive and pure is Léonie, the adult. She represents the existence of an order imposed arbitrarily on life. As a detached observer of the rest of her family, she plays a role that hides her emotions. Even her stylish clothing contrasts with the others' lack of concern for appearances.

Georges, Michel, and Yvonne are children. They live without pretense and expect the same of those around them. Like Cocteau's *angéliques*, they are selfish and disinterested at the same time. From the point of view of society, they are amoral. The distinction between the adults and the children of the play is made in the first act:

> LEO: I am not mean. I have been observing you since yesterday, Yvonne, and I congratulate myself for having brought some order into the trailer. In this world, there are children and adults. Unfortunately, I'm one of the adults and you others belong to the race of children who never stop being children and who would commit crimes . . .
> [Crowson's translation, footnote 29]

Leo is the only adult in a child's *roulotte*, which is Yvonne's pet term for the apartment and which evokes the freedom and independence of gypsies. Such people exist outside of society's laws because they refuse to be part of a larger, more regimented system. Therefore, Georges, Yvonne, and their son lead an unstructured life. Georges invents gadgets that never work, Yvonne rarely leaves her bed, and Michel drifts from interest to interest.

Although Michel's fiancée Madeleine represents order, she, unlike Léo, is true to herself and therefore pure. She and Léonie resemble each other superficially by their passion for neatness, which in the aunt is imposed upon her character without resulting from it. On a deep level, then, Madeleine, like Esther, like any of Cocteau's "angels," belongs to the children's realm, since she refuses to compromise her "line" at the same time that she admits her amorality:

> MADELEINE: I hate lies. The smallest lie makes me sick. I accept the fact that someone might be quiet so that things work out with as few complications as possible. But real lying . . . a lie that is a simple luxury! I am not really being moral, because, in fact, I am quite amoral. I intuit that lies upset processes which transcend us and that they upset waves, that they get everything out of joint.
> [Crowson's translation, footnote 30]

What threatens Yvonne's way of life is not so much an antagonistic society as a natural relationship challenging her position. The very animal nature of the mother is such that she cannot accommodate herself to anything but her own desires; she is compelled to follow her emotions even

if they destroy her. When she sees the new family composed of Madeleine, Michel, Georges, and Léo, she feels that there is no longer a place for her, that she has lost all that mattered to her in the world, and she takes an overdose of insulin. Capable of analyzing her objectively, Léo understands that her sister could never live a compromised existence in which she would be prevented from being completely herself and in which she could not totally dominate the life of her son.

Like *Les Enfants terribles*, *Les Parents terribles* is one of Cocteau's most personal works. In both the novel and the play the characters are children, regardless of age. They live according to their own ethic in a game which, to them, is reality. They dwell in a dimly lit, primeval world outside the realm of societal laws: "There are houses and lives whose existence would stupify reasonable people" (Crowson's translation, footnote 31). Unlike the novel, however, where "The spirit of the room was watching" (Crowson's translation, footnote 32) and Elizabeth's husband is killed before he can contaminate the purity of the household, Yvonne's world is destroyed by the presence of an outsider: the mother has no means of preventing her child from becoming an adult. Instead of choosing conformity, as Esther does, she chooses death, for she is much more impetuous than the actress, much closer to nature's savagery and to that of the very young child. Unable to have her way, she becomes spiteful, but she has no chance to reverse her decision. This *pureté farouche* which tolerates no compromise is unique to Cocteau's theater, since it is almost impossible to present such a hermetic universe on the stage. Yet it does not approach the brutality of *Les Enfants terribles*, where mythological child-gods drive each other to an inevitable death, and where the world of play excludes everything outside itself.

Source: Lydia Crowson, "The Role of Myth," in *The Esthetic of Jean Cocteau*, published for The University of New Hampshire by The University Press of New England, 1978, pp. 143–46.

Jacques Guicharnaud and June Guicharnaud

In the following essay, the critics discuss Cocteau's use of tragedy and the victimization of the hero in his plays. They also comment on the playwright's theme of isolation.

Almost all of Cocteau's plays lead toward the same resolution. They are often directed toward a violent death, and the hero generally more like a victim of the drama than the tragic master of his fate. Victims of either magic spells or very special circumstances, Cocteau's heroes submit to action more than they direct it. In *Les Parents terribles* it is not Yvonne who is responsible for Madeleine's lie, but Georges and Léo; in *Les Chevaliers* many of the characters are replaced by a demon who takes on their appearances; and particularly in *La Machine infernale* such stress is put on the caprices of the gods and destiny that Oedipus' heroism disappears. Oedipus did not solve the Sphinx' riddle: she gave him the answer out of love; and although he puts out his eyes at the end, it is not so much his own act as it is in Sophocles' version. During Cocteau's play the weapons themselves (Jocasta's brooch and scarf), from the very beginning, are impatient to put out Oedipus' eyes and strangle Jocasta. Moreover in the third act there is a kind of rehearsal of Oedipus becoming blind when he looks into Tiresias' eyes and thinks he is blinded by pepper. In short, Cocteau emphasized Oedipus' mechanical victimization more than his tragic heroism.

Here Cocteau is eminently representative of modern drama, which draws as near to tragedy as possible, yet most often remains on this side of it. Tragic heroism for the Greeks consisted in going all the way through an ordeal, to the point of giving any final acceptance the value of a challenge and finding true grandeur in the catastrophe itself. Today this conception is replaced by a taste for victimization that is still colored by Romanticism.

Cocteau uses the basic elements of tragedy in his dramas: the misunderstanding, a source of tragic irony, and the play of supernatural forces or obscure powers. Yvonne is mistaken about the meaning of her love for Mik, just as Oedipus is mistaken about the oracle and the encounters in his life, while the interiorization of fate and its expression in psychological terms detract nothing from its transcendency. But either the characters, following in the path of fate, stop just on the edge of the revelation that might have elevated them (Yvonne, in *Les Parents terribles*, dies without having really got to know herself), or the development of the action remains outside the character, who is victimized and then liberated, without having had any determining effect on the drama (King Arthur, in *Les Chevaliers*, does no more than talk about the forces that "intoxicate" and then "disintoxicate" him), or, as is most frequently the case, the characters accelerate the final movement and precipitate their own deaths in gestures that are more evasive than fulfilling (Solange's suicide in *La Machine à écrire*, the anticipation of Hans, who kills himself, in *Bacchus*).

> **COCTEAU'S HEROES—
> PURE, STILL NOT DISILLUSIONED,
> AND PREYS TO CIRCUMSTANCE—
> ARE VICTIMS OF CHANCE, OF A
> *FATALITAS* OFTEN SIMILAR TO
> THAT OF MELODRAMA."**

Although the precipitated denouements are far from classical tragedy, they have two great merits. First of all, their theatricalism is effective. The foreshortening, the elements of spectacle, and the effects of surprise and shock do create an unquestionable climate of finality. The spectacle is carried away by an increasingly rapid whirlpool of scenic movements and at the end death is imposed, so to speak, on the spectator's nerves. Secondly they suggest a conception of freedom which is Cocteau's own. In the preface to *Les Mariés de la Tour Eiffel*, he wrote:

> One of the photographer's lines could be used on the title page: *Since these mysteries are beyond us, let's pretend to be their organizer.* It is our line par excellence. The conceited man always finds refuge in responsibility. Thus, for example, he prolongs a war after the phenomenon that had been its deciding factor is over.

Freedom would then be shown in the acceleration or slowing down of the necessary developments, in their foreshortening or extension. Freedom is Cocteau's "pretense" and the others' "conceit." And Cocteau has no illusions about his own characters. When at the end of *Bacchus* Hans cries out, "Free . . . ," his way of dying should be seen not as "tragic death par excellence, both fated and chosen," but as a pretense, a voluntary illusion. Hans' final freedom is in fact abstract. It consists only in anticipating an already determined event. Similarly, the Queen's command, "Say that I wanted it," in the third act of *L'Aigle à deux têtes* seems merely a verbal claim, for Stanislas' suicide—the very reason for her own—was not part of her plans.

What Cocteau's plays reveal, then, is not a traditional tragic vision but a particular conception of destiny very near to fatalism, wherein the best man can do is to live "as if" he were capable of controlling his fate. That "as if" can be found in all the eloquent affirmations, costumes, grand gestures, and, at the extreme limit, art itself. In *La Machine à écrire* many inhabitants of the city claim, at one point or another, to have written the anonymous letters. The play explains that in making the claim they hope to escape from the mediocrity in which they are imprisoned. They want to be recognized even in crime, and their desire is so powerful that they end by believing their own lies. Actually, their mythomania picks up the "pretense" and "conceit" of the preface to *Les Mariés*. Caught in a development of events that is beyond them and for which they are not responsible, they want to have themselves put in prison so that everything will happen *as if* the scandal was their own work. In short, the only escape from fare is in the lie, and the game of lying must be played to the very end—that is, until total illusion is achieved, until the mask of freedom is seen as the very flesh of man—for man's only recourse is to deceive himself and others.

Death by suicide, in Cocteau's works, is the highest form of human pretense. By precipitating death, it often appears as an escape. The character disappears before the last illuminations of his ordeal. He wants to testify before it is too late and thus makes himself the martyr of certain values (poetry, love, grandeur, humanity) at the very moment that these values may be shown as impossible. As soon as the character realizes that the world has tricked him, he answers with the definitive trickery of suicide. He neither triumphs nor makes his peace: he retires. The deep and despairing cry of Cocteau's works is in the agitation of man who is caught and either ignores the fact or succeeds only in reconstructing a higher ignorance in the form of illusion. But although gilded by language and adorned with all the devices of mind and imagination, the trap remains merciless. By means of theatrical devices Cocteau has invented a masked ball, and he is the first to proclaim its vanity.

Cocteau's heroes—pure, still not disillusioned, and preys to circumstance—are victims of chance, of a *fatalitas* often similar to that of melodrama. They believe that they benefit from it until, having gone too far in the game, they are seized with an unbearable mistrust which leads to a voluntary illusion. Cocteau's universe is one not of tragedy but of danger. The cosmos surrounding the characters is not that of a great moral order in the Greek manner, in conflict with man's affirmation of himself; it is a Coney Island contraption, a layout of pitfalls: in *Les Chevaliers* the characters are deceived by a

demon who takes on the appearances of several of them, and the Grail that appears is a false Grail; in *Les Parents terribles* mother love hides incest; in *La Machine infernale* everything is a trap or a threat, from Jocasta's scarf to the young girl who is a mask of the Sphinx. Those who fall into the traps—and who are marked out for them—are the naïve and the pure in heart: poets, idealized adolescents, dewy-eyed revolutionaries—whence the melodramatic aspect of Cocteau's theatre.

Parallel to the hero of Byronic gloom or the fated Romantic, his hero can be recognized by a sign, a coincidence, or phrases with double meanings that he utters without quite knowing their significance. One might cry out *Fatalitas!* during *La Machine infernale,* in which ghosts and ambiguous dialogue transform the *Tyrannos,* caught by Sophocles at the height of his glory, into the hero of an adventure novel; or when during a storm in *L'Aigle* a young revolutionary, who just happens to be the dead King's double, takes refuge in the Queen's room; or during *Les Parents terribles,* when Mik, a good son and good lover, finds himself not only the object of incestuous love but his own father's rival. Characterized by adolescence—a state of both grace and malediction, and a combination of impulsive acts, ignorance, purity, disorder, and youth—Cocteau's heroes are to a certain extent "going forces" in the Romantic manner, and they are "going" in a treacherous universe filled with every danger. Actually, "Romantic" does somehow describe Cocteau's works. The variety of forms, the aesthetic debates surrounding the plays, and the justifying abstractions of the subject matter (poetry, youth, impure order, pure disorder) only partially disguise the underlying theme of isolation—an isolation of the individual destined for better and for worse.

Source: Jacques Guicharnaud and June Guicharnaud, "The Double Game," in *Modern French Theatre: From Giraudoux to Genet,* Yale University Press, 1967, pp. 52–59.

Dorothy Knowles

In the following essay, Knowles comments on the "interplay of human affections" and tragedy in Indiscretions. *She explains that the text was a "pretext," that Cocteau wanted the setting to drive his plays, and that "all concrete details" were "subordinated to the theme."*

The series of modern plays of which the matter is the interplay of human affections, and which derive none of their interest from mere scenic effects, is continued by *Les Parents terribles,* first performed on November 14th, 1938, at the Ambassadeurs. Cocteau had been made temporary director of this theatre by the Municipal Council of Paris, but had to resign after an argument with the Council and the Ministry of Education over an ill-advised invitation sent to Paris schools by the star Alice Cocéa. The play was transferred to the Bouffes-Parisiens, where it had a successful run. It was revived at the Gymnase on October 23rd, 1941, but was banned by the Occupation authorities after German troops had thrown teargas bombs in the auditorium. It was revived again on February 8th, 1946, when it was clear that what had been an *avant-garde* play had become a very great Boulevard success. In the preface to *La Machine à écrire* Cocteau states that *Les Parents terribles* was a tragedy which touched the masses on the raw by its attack on the disorders of a decadent *bourgeoisie*. It was this attack which provoked the early violent opposition to the play. Such an attack actually ran counter to Cocteau's own theory that a playwright must not take sides, but must concentrate on achieving "style", though not "fine writing." It is a powerful play and Cocteau's best.

Cocteau made another interesting statement regarding this play in an interview reported in the *Œuvre* (October 11th, 1938). "I was the first playwright", he said, "to take an intense interest in settings and to proclaim that a text was only a pretext for creating settings and showing them off on a lavish scale. I put on *Antigone*, *Roméo*, *Orphée*, and *La Machine infernale* for the sake of the setting, for the pictorial framework, in short for everything which now seems to me to be irrelevant . . . I have written this play solely for the sake of the actors. Nothing shall occur to distract the spectator's attention from the acting, or from the text. There shall be nothing in the setting which is not absolutely necessary, not a chair which has not some special function. There will be no cigarettes, no telephone, no maids, no accessories to fill up any gap, or any silence. . . . The theatre must be more real than reality, more real than life. It is life intensified and concentrated." In a subsequent interview reported in the *Figaro* of November 8th, 1938, Cocteau said that when he wrote *Les Parents terribles* he was in a small hotel in Montargis, where he had no books except *Britannicus* and *Le Misanthrope*. The repeated reading of these plays inspired him with a desire to emulate the artistic economy of Racine and Molière. "It seems to me that I must make every single gesture a cog in the machine, as it were, and never admit any expression of feeling which is purely decorative for fear of unnecessary elaboration." This economy of concentration, according to

Cocteau, removes the possibility of even momentary relaxation of the spectator's nerves. The actor is the instrument by which the playwright magnetizes his audience.

Cocteau was here putting forward the classical notion according to which all concrete details must be subordinated to the theme. The merely accessory is irrelevant. Emphasis is laid on the work of the author and of the actor, and there is no place for "business", such as the use of the telephone. For his characters Cocteau did not envisage any "monolithic" creations, such as Corneille's Horace or Rodrigue, but rather characters subject to dual or multiple enthusiasms and conflicting emotions, in a manner more typical of Racine. "Two of the rôles", Cocteau writes, "create the balance of the order and of the disorder which motivate the play. The young man whose disorder is pure, and his aunt whose order is not pure." Here, in a very different setting, Cocteau treats the theme already developed in *Les Chevaliers de la Table Ronde*—namely, the establishment of a new order after truth has been brought to light. Here, too, appears the theme, later to be exemplified in Hans and the Cardinal in *Bacchus*, of the purity of the disorder of the impulsive mind and the impurity of the order of the calculating mind. For Michel, a spoilt child and a mother's boy, order is established only after his mother's death, which he unwittingly brings about in his desire to escape her jealous affection. This mother, a slovenly creature who spends the day amid piles of dirty linen, going to and fro in a dressing-gown covered with cigarette burns, between her unmade bed and an untidy dressing-room, is a powerful force of disorder, albeit pure. Her well-groomed but embittered sister Léo, the only really grown-up person in the play, brings truth to light and order—a new order—into the home at the price of her sister's suicide, which she does nothing to prevent. Whether her feelings for her sister's husband, her ex-fiancé, in any way affect her attitude it is hard to say; in any case, Léo herself does not know, nor does she care to know. The whole action, which moves forward inexorably to the mother's death, is set in motion by the son's failure to return home one night. In an admirable first act the characters face up to reality for the first time in twenty years, and say what they have on their minds. The father learns that he and his son have the same mistress, but the situation, current in Boulevard comedy, here has a poignancy not to be found on the Boulevard. The second act shows the attempt of the father, in his monstrous egoism, and of the mother, in her monstrous possessiveness, to prevent the son's engagement to the girl. The third act is given to the torment of the mother, who cannot accept to share her son with any other. Her passion, as absolute as any child's—there is not the slightest hint of any subconscious incest in her attitude—raises her to the level of a figure of tragedy. She is like one possessed. Beside her, Léo, statuesque, stands like destiny itself. There is no mistaking the Greek inspiration of the play despite the "Boulevard" elements, to which Cocteau himself drew attention by making the father compare himself to a character in a Labiche play. Little wonder that the critics of the first performance referred to the flat of the Atrides, spoke of beslippered Labdacides, and conjured up the shades of Clytemnestra, Electra, Jocasta, and Creon. *Les Parents terribles* is a tragedy, but in it the characters bellow out their passions without classical restraint, and when Michel learns that his father is his rival he throws himself upon a pile of dirty linen on the floor in a fit of jealous rage. In 1948, with the complete text as a scenario and almost the same cast as he had had in the stage production, Gabrielle Dorziat, Jean Marais, and Yvonne de Bray, who had inspired the play but whose part had been taken by Germaine Dermoz because of her illness, Cocteau undertook the difficult task of making a film from his play. In the film he limits himself to the two settings used in the play, but his camera picks out significant objects and gestures for their visual as well as for their psychological value, and the film is far from being "canned theatre" ; it is a fine example of the art of the cinema.

Source: Dorothy Knowles, "Studio Theatre: Cocteau and Company," in *French Drama of the Inter-War Years, 1918–39*, George G. Harrap, 1967, pp. 56–61.

SOURCES

Bach, Raymond, "Cocteau and Vichy: Family Disconnections," in *L'Esprit Createur*, Vol. 33, No. 1, Spring 1993, pp. 29–37.

Blumenthal, Eileen, "Sexual Relations," in *American Theater*, Vol. 12, No. 6, July–August 1995, pp. 16–17.

Callow, Simon, "Introduction," in *Les Parents Terribles (Indiscretions)*, by Jean Cocteau, translated by Jeremy Sams, Royal National Theatre and Nick Hern Books, 1994, p. viii.

Canby, Vincent, "*Indiscretions*: Cocteau's Ferocious View of the Rolls-Royce of Families," in *New York Times*, April 28, 1995, http://theater2.nytimes.com/mem/theater/treview .html?res=990CEEDE1139F93BA15757C0A963958260 (accessed October 25, 2006).

Cocteau, Jean, *Les Parents Terribles (Indiscretions)*, translated by Jeremy Sams, Nick Hern Books, 1994.

Hurwitt, Robert, "Marin Theatre's *Parents* Is a Little Too Discreet: Toned-down Version of Cocteau Tragic Farce," in *San Francisco Chronicle*, January 18, 2001, p. E1.

Knowles, Dorothy, *French Drama of the Inter-War Years, 1918–39*, George C. Harrap, 1967, p. 59.

FURTHER READING

Paini, Dominique, and others, *Cocteau*, Center Pompidou, 2004.
    This book is a collection of fascinating essays on Cocteau's life and art. The authors, some of whom knew Cocteau personally, argue that he has been severely undervalued because of his overt homosexuality and his involvement in many art forms, including plays, poetry, novels, drawing, painting, scenery design, film, and ballet (leading some to brand him a dilettante).

Seigel, Jerrold, *Bohemian Paris: Culture, Politics, and the Boundaries of Bourgeois Life, 1830–1930*, Johns Hopkins University Press, 1999.
    This book examines the part played by artists, writers, and intellectuals in the development of the bohemian counterculture in Paris. Featured figures include Cocteau, Émile Zola, Édouard Manet, and Arthur Rimbaud.

Steegmuller, Francis, *Cocteau: A Biography*, David R. Godine, 1992.
    This popular and well-written biography makes clear why Cocteau is one of the most influential people in French art and literature. The book also gives a sense of Paris during Cocteau's lifetime.

Van Derbur, Marilyn, *Triumph over Darkness: Understanding and Healing the Trauma of Childhood Sexual Abuse*, Beyond Words, 1991.
    This book is a collection of writings and drawings that provide first-person accounts of incest, rape, and other forms of abuse. Seventy women share their experiences and describe how they overcame their trauma.

A Lesson from Aloes

ATHOL FUGARD

1978

Athol Fugard's *A Lesson from Aloes* was first performed at the Market Theatre in Johannesburg in 1978. In 1980, it was performed at the Yale Repertory Theater, starring James Earl Jones. Later that year, the play opened on Broadway, gaining an enthusiastic public and critical response. This play, as is the case with many of Fugard's other works, focuses on the tensions that arose between whites and blacks living under the system of apartheid in South Africa. The plot of *A Lesson from Aloes* centers on a farewell dinner in 1963 given by a white Afrikaner for his good friend, a black activist who has given up the cause. During the course of the evening, the two friends confront issues of loyalty and betrayal and sanity and madness, as they struggle to make sense of their experience in an oppressive and divisive world and of the effect that experience has on human relationships.

AUTHOR BIOGRAPHY

Athol Harold Lannagan Fugard was born in the Karoo village of Middleburg, South Africa, on June 11, 1932, and grew up in nearby Port Elizabeth with his Polish Irish father and Afrikaner mother. He studied for two years at the University of Cape Town in South Africa before signing on as a merchant sailor. A few years later, he worked as a freelance journalist and law clerk. In 1959, he relocated to London where he became involved in the theater

Athol Fugard © Bettmann/Corbis. Reproduced by permission

there, acting and writing plays that focused on racial tensions in South Africa. His first play, *Blood Knot*, was produced there in 1961. In 1962, after returning to Cape Town, he wrote a letter supporting a boycott of segregated theaters in South Africa, which, along with the controversial nature of his plays, resulted in the confiscation of his passport and the harassment of his family. He then involved himself in South African theater, and in 1973, he and his wife, Sheila, founded the Space Theatre there.

By 1982, his plays began to enjoy an international audience and have since been produced in South Africa, London, and New York. *A Lesson from Aloes* was published in 1979 and first produced in the United States in 1980. Published by Theatre Communications Group in 1981, this play won the New York Drama Critics' Circle Award. Fugard's *Master Harold . . . . and the Boys* premiered in Johannesburg, South Africa, in 1983, and was another big success.

In the last two decades of the twentieth century, Fugard continued his successful career as a playwright and also became involved in film. He acted in the film versions of some of his plays, including *Boesman and Lena* (1976) and in other films, such as *Gandhi* (1982) and *The Killing Fields*

(1984). In 1992, he directed the film version of his play *The Road to Mecca*, and in 2006, the film version of his 1980 novel, *Tsotsi*, won an Academy Award for the Best Foreign Language Film.

PLOT SUMMARY

Act 1, Scene 1

A Lesson From Aloes opens in the backyard of Piet and Gladys Bezuidenhout's home in South Africa in 1963. Piet is seated in front of an aloe plant, reading aloud from a book on the subject, trying to identify his specific plant but not having any luck. Gladys sits nearby. After he tells her that if this is a new species, he will name it after her, he then begins a brief monologue on the importance of names, quoting from Shakespeare's *Romeo and Juliet* to help prove his point.

Gladys claims that time is passing slowly that afternoon as they wait for their friend Steve and his family to come for dinner. Piet asks if everything is ready in the kitchen for them, and Gladys tells him it is. He tells her to relax then and enjoy the lovely autumn weather, but she is worried about getting sunburned. When Piet returns with her sun hat, she appears anxious and goes into the house to confirm that she put away her diary.

Piet again turns his attention to his aloe, insisting that he must not neglect it. He asks Gladys whether they have enough food, noting that Steve is bringing his wife and four children. Her response that food is "not going to be the problem" reveals her apprehension about their arrival. When Piet tries to calm her by reminding her that they are friends, Gladys claims that she is "out of practice" and is worried about coming up with conversation, noting that they have been the first visitors since she has been back from the mental hospital.

Piet turns his attention to his plant again and reasserts the importance of naming, explaining that a name is the first thing people give a newborn and someone met for a first time. He is frustrated that he cannot find the right name for his plant and then discusses its qualities, describing its ability to survive in harsh terrain. Piet suggests that there may be a lesson in the plant's survival mechanisms for all of them, but Gladys refuses to identify herself with it and begins to get upset by their discussion. She claims that conversation with him always turns political, "a catalogue of South African disasters" because he "seem[s] to have a perverse need to dwell on what is cruel and ugly about this country." She insists that she wants more out of life than just to survive. Although she is afraid of the country and the effect it can have on her, she is determined not to let it pass on its "violence" to her. In an effort to lighten the mood, Piet shifts the conversation to the upcoming dinner.

Act 1, Scene 2

As they get ready for the dinner, Gladys tell Piet that she feels isolated there while he is at work since no one is nearby. She notes that during the almost seven months that she has been back from the hospital, not one of their friends has come to visit. When she wonders whether they are avoiding her, Piet declares, "it's a dangerous time and people are frightened," citing all of the political and social unrest that has been occurring. Gladys insists that his explanation is too simple; she complains about people's "lack of courage and faith," alluding to the political activism in which they are no longer involved. Piet admits that he is frightened, too.

Later, Gladys proudly recalls every word from a quote by Thoreau about finding and following a purpose in life that Piet had recited to her on their first date. When he admits that he still believes in the sentiment, Gladys declares that she envies him that. She insists that she would be lost without her diary, which keeps her secrets. When she brings up the fact that her diaries were stolen from her, Piet tells her to try to forget, but she cannot. As she remembers the government officials coming into her room, she gets increasingly angry and agitated. Piet tries to reassure her that they will not come again, but she is not sure that she believes him.

When Gladys discovers that Piet still has the receipt the men gave him for the diaries, she demands that he rip it up so she can cancel those years. After Piet tears up the receipt, she calms down a bit, explaining how important the diaries were to her. But her hysteria returns when she thinks about how her trust in herself and in life has been shattered and declares that there is no safe place to hide her diary. She begins to attack Piet, blaming him for her "condition" but then pulls back and apologizes. When Piet offers to cancel the dinner, she tells him that she will be all right and that she does not want to hide anything anymore. The scene ends with her telling Pier, "I am trying," suggesting that she is struggling to cope with her fragile emotional state.

Act 1, Scene 3

Piet declares that he owes Steve "more than anybody else in this world," since his friend gave him

a sense of purpose. He explains that when he worked as a bus driver, he had no interest in politics. On the morning of a bus boycott, he was reassigned into the "Coloured area" where he saw people "full of defiance" over the penny increase the government demanded for bus fares. He wondered why they made such an issue over a penny, but then started listening to a man who was handing out pamphlets and speaking to a crowd on a street corner. Steve was that man, and he was soon arrested by the police, but the next day he was back on the corner.

Piet decided that he should hear what the man had to say and was surprised that the crowd welcomed him, which became, as he describes, "the most moving thing that has ever happened to me." Piet quit work that day, and a week later, he was handing out pamphlets with Steve on the same corner. Even though the bus company got their penny raise, Piet saw the boycott as a success since it "had raised the political consciousness of the people." Political activism like this, he was certain, could "make this a better world to live in."

Piet then tells Gladys that Steve and his family are leaving for England and will not be able to come back. Although she is surprised, Gladys declares that they are very lucky to be leaving. She knows that she could never convince Piet to leave and becomes cynical about the fight against apartheid that Piet and Steve were both so committed to now that it seems to have failed. She admits that she could never become as devoted to their cause because some of their goals, such as overthrowing the government, frightened her.

When Piet argues that the movement's slogans were not empty, that they, not their dreams, failed, Gladys notes that just one person, the informer, failed. Someone apparently told the police that Steve was going to break the order that banned him from meeting with his friends, and so he was arrested. Piet insists that he does not know the identity of the informer and tries to change the subject to the upcoming dinner, but Gladys presses the point, asking him if other people think that he is the informer. Piet admits that it appears that they do, but that Steve does not believe it was him. After Piet tells her how horrible it is to be considered an informer, Gladys asks, "it's not true, is it?" Piet does not respond and turns away. Later, he announces that Steve and his family should be arriving soon.

Act 2

Two hours later, Steve arrives without his family, claiming that one of his daughters is ill. Piet is thrilled that Steve has arrived, sure that "he wouldn't have come if everything wasn't all right." When he and Steve toast the "good old days," Piet recites the quotation he found for the occasion. Piet later declares that he has been thinking a lot about his days on the farm when he had to help bury the child of a family that had worked for him. The child died of a stomach ailment since there had been no clean water on the farm. On that day, Piet admits, "a sense of deep, personal failure overwhelmed me," as the family waited for him to say a few words, and he was too overcome with emotion to speak. Three months later, he left the farm.

Gladys tells Steve that he is fortunate to get out of the country, and he asks her what England is like, thinking from her manners, that she has lived there. Gladys at first denies this, but then admits, "In a way I suppose I am from England," referring to Fort England Clinic, the mental hospital where she received treatment. Steve then shows Piet an old snapshot of him and his father on the day the latter caught a big fish, "the biggest moment in the old man's life." Soon after, however, the family was kicked out of their home, which had been declared a white area, after losing all of their money trying to fight the relocation. Steve notes that it "finished" his father.

Steve wants Piet to admit that he understands why Steve is leaving, but Piet does not want to talk about the subject. Trying to justify his decision, Steve explains that he has not been allowed to work for four years and that he has to get his family out so that they can survive, insisting that he does not want to be a martyr to the cause. He asks Piet to name one thing they accomplished and to admit that they fought for a lost cause, but Piet cannot agree. Steve tells Piet to get out while he can and come to England with him.

When Gladys tells Steve that everyone thinks that Piet is the informer and asks Steve if he thinks so too, Piet tries unsuccessfully to stop her, which causes her to grow agitated. She declares that enough lies have been told and that Piet is the informer. After Piet refuses to defend himself, Steve tells about the mental torture he endured while incarcerated, and that eventually, he told them everything he knew about the group's political activities, information, ironically, that the police already had. Steve then asks Piet if he is the informer, noting that Steve's wife thinks that he is, but Piet still refuses to respond.

Gladys declares that she admires Piet's faith in himself and admits that she lied about his being the informer. When Steve asks her why she lied, she becomes angry and argues that he is not the only victim

of their country and rails against Piet for not protecting her from the police and from the doctors who gave her shock treatments. She becomes hysterical when she remembers the treatments, insisting that they "burned my brain as brown as yours, Steven."

After Gladys escapes into the house, Piet explains how after the police took her diaries, she became paranoid and thought that he was one of them. Piet then tells Steve that he did not deny her charge because there would have been no point if Steve had believed it. After Steve leaves, Piet goes in to Gladys, who admits that she tried to wreck his friendship with Steve and that she wanted to destroy the goodness in Pier, just like the country has done to its people. She decides that she has to go back to the clinic but will "go quietly this time." Piet gives her pills to help her sleep and goes into the backyard where he sits with his aloe.

CHARACTERS

Gladys Bezuidenhout

Gladys Bezuidenhout is a middle-aged white woman, living with her husband in South Africa. She spends the entire evening trying to hold onto her sanity, but by the end of the play, she recognizes that she will need to go back to the mental hospital. Gladys is eventually overcome by her fears about her safety amid the racial tensions of South Africa. These fears carry over into other areas as well, as when she gets nervous about whether she will be able to make conversation with Steve's wife, whether his son's boisterousness will upset her, and whether people are avoiding her. Her fears also transfer into an obsession with where to hide her diary so that no one can read it, although by the end of the play, Piet discovers that she has not been writing in it.

Gladys insists on setting herself apart from black Africans, which suggests that she has racist attitudes. She obsesses about getting sun burnt, although it is now autumn. When she explains, "Mommy was terrified that I was going to end up with a brown skin," she is speaking about her own fears as well. Her desire to protect herself from the sun so that she would not turn brown has been thwarted, however, by the shock treatments she received in the mental hospital, which, as she tells Steve, have "burned [her] brain as brown as [his]," an admission that helps speed her descent into madness. Another way Gladys tries to keep herself separate is through her language. Steve notes that she talks like an Englishwoman, and she always uses a formal address for her husband and Steve, referring to them only as "Peter" and "Steven."

Piet Bezuidenhout

Piet feels a strong identification to his heritage and to his home. That identification, however, is problematic since Afrikaners are part of the apartheid movement in South Africa. Piet devotes himself completely to whatever he becomes involved in, farming, political activism, or raising aloes. He needs a clear sense of purpose, even if it is directed toward naming aloes. When he fails at one enterprise, such as his farm and his fight for the cause, he quickly finds another project, refusing to be consumed by a sense of defeat.

Sometimes that adaptability causes him to ignore reality, as is the case with his wife's emotional instability. He is accommodating of her needs, assuring her that what she has prepared for dinner will be fine and getting her a sunhat to alleviate her fears that she will be burnt. Yet he continually sidesteps the reality of her mental health, turning to his aloes rather than discussing the cause of her fears. He values his friendship with Steve but avoids the reality of the racial tensions that have affected it. He also does not comment on Steve's descriptions of the torture he endured or the fact that, as a result, he told the police all that he knew about his and his friends illegal activities. When he ignores painful realities, Piet tries to sustain his comforting vision of his homeland and his place in it.

Steve Daniels

When Steve comes to dinner without his wife, who believes that Piet is the informer, he proves his loyalty to Piet and his trust in him. He shows his good humor when he first arrives, as he jokes with his old friend. Steve is honest enough to admit that he broke under torture, that he became an informant, and that he has "had enough" of his difficult life in South Africa. He was devoted to the fight for equal rights in his country, but when he can no longer support his family, he decides to move to England for their sakes, even though it is difficult to leave his homeland.

THEMES

Sanity and Madness

During the course of the play, Gladys struggles to maintain her sanity by pushing back her fears that she is not safe. At one point, she admits to Piet that she is even afraid of his aloes because, she claims: "they're turgid with violence, like everything else in this country. And they're trying to pass it on to me." Her mental state results from the governmental officials reading and confiscating her diaries, which made her feel "violated." Piet explains to Steve that after that incident, she became more and more paranoid to the point that she thought her own husband was a spy, and, as a result, she was sent to a mental institution.

In an effort to try to maintain her sanity, Gladys redirects her fear into anger, and Piet is her target. She insists that he is to blame for her "condition" since he is the one who convinced her to trust in herself and in life, and now she does not trust in anything, not even his ability to protect her. Gladys declares that the diaries contain intimate information that a woman addresses only in private dialogue with herself. Her loss of trust causes her to obsess about where to hide her diary so that no one will find it, but she cannot find any safe place, for her or her diary.

Her anger also causes her to accuse Piet of being the informer who was responsible for Steve's incarceration. But when Piet refuses to respond to her accusations, her anger is deflected and her fears return as she recognizes that Piet feels safer in their environment than she does. This recognition reinforces her own fears that by the end of the evening become so severe that she feels herself slipping back into madness. Gladys's inability to maintain her sanity reveals the profound effect that an insane political realm can have on the personal one.

The Consequences of Isolation

Both Gladys and Piet feel isolated in their home and community although Gladys is the only one to admit it. The streets around their community are relatively empty, due most likely to the racial tension that surrounds them. Also, their friends, who suspect Piet of informing on Steve, have been noticeably absent. Using avoidance as a coping mechanism, Piet fills his time tending to his aloes so that he will not dwell on the failure of his cause to which he has devoted himself so completely. The isolation, however, has had greater effect on Gladys, which is evident in her response to Steve's coming over for dinner. She exclaims: "I won't have any trouble finding something to write in my diary tonight. At last! Other people! Just when it was beginning to feel as if Peter and I were the last two left in the world." She tells Piet that during the day "it's hard sometimes to believe

TOPICS FOR FURTHER STUDY

- Read Fugard's *Master Harold . . . and the Boys* and compare its treatment of race relations in South Africa to those in *A Lesson from Aloes*. Does Fugard raise any new points in *Master Harold* about the tensions that arose between blacks and whites living under apartheid? Write a comparison and contrast paper on the two plays.

- Fugard reveals the incident when the police took Gladys's diaries only as a memory. Write a new scene that could be added to the play that would depict this important event, noting Gladys's

sense of betrayal and the beginning of her descent into madness.

- Research the subject of race relations in the United States during the 1960s and compare your findings to conditions in South Africa during the same period. What do you think accounted for the differences? Present a PowerPoint presentation on your findings.

- Write a poem or short story that focuses on the interaction between two people of different races.

there is a world out there full of other people." The isolation helps push her further from sanity since she becomes more afraid when no one is home and when she has no one to help her face reality. Gladys's response to isolation illustrates that the social as well as the political can have a great impact on emotional and psychological stability.

STYLE

Symbolism

The aloes in the play's title become symbolic of the situation of each of the main characters in the sense that they all must struggle to survive their harsh environment. The one "nameless" aloe that Piet keeps returning to throughout the evening becomes especially symbolic of the characters' situation due to its anonymity. Piet notes that since the aloe is confined in a tin, its roots are "going to crawl around inside . . . . and tie themselves into knots looking for the space creation intended for them." Africa has become a tin for Piet, Gladys, and Steve, confining each of them in different ways. Steve's tin is created by the oppression of apartheid, which ultimately causes him to take his family and leave his country. Gladys's is formed by the fear generated by her husband's involvement in the cause to overthrow the system, which is brought to a peak when government officials raid their house and

steal her diaries. Piet is restricted by the failure of his cause, which removed his sense of purpose and limited his activities to tending plants.

Fugard suggests that extra care must be taken with aloes and people alike when they are confined by their environment. Piet notes that the aloes will not survive if he neglects them. Gladys also will not survive if Piet does not stay vigilant in his attempts to reassure her that she is safe, and Piet will not survive unless he has the distraction of his plants, which takes his mind off of his failed cause and damaged relationship with his wife and best friend. Perhaps, Piet has the best chance of survival since he, like the plant, has developed a thick skin, a lesson he has learned well. Ultimately, however, the play illustrates how apartheid confines and isolates, an unhealthy, even dangerous system, against nature. Adapting and coping within the confines of this unequal system cannot be called living.

HISTORICAL CONTEXT

The Colonization of South Africa

Dutch colonists were an early group of outsiders to settle in South Africa. Calling themselves Afrikaners, they established Cape Town colony in 1652 and set up a rigid social and political hierarchy that gave them complete control of the government and the power to force most Africans into

COMPARE
&
CONTRAST

- **1960s:** The government of South Africa, in its second decade of the enforcement of apartheid, begins to crack down on protesters. During one protest near Johannesburg in 1960, police gun down sixty-seven Africans and wound nearly two hundred others.

  Late 1970s and early 1980s: In 1982, the newly established Internal Securities Act attempts to contain escalating opposition to the government.

  Today: The government under President Mandela desegregates schools and prohibits discrimination in the workplace.

- **1960s:** The Pan Africanist Congress, a multiracial organization in South Africa, holds successful demonstrations against the government in the form of work stoppages.

  Late 1970s and early 1980s: All levels of society, including Afrikaner business leaders, begin to recognize the failure of apartheid and to denounce the system. In 1983, six hundred South African organizations come together to form the United Democratic Front, which openly opposes the policies of apartheid.

  Today: Protests against the government are ended but social problems, such as the lack of health care for AIDS sufferers, have not been adequately addressed.

- **1960s:** In 1961, Nelson Mandela becomes one of the leaders of the African National Congress (ANC), a political group that forms to fight Apartheid. A year later, he is arrested and thrown in prison where he is to spend the next eighteen years.

  Late 1970s and early 1980s: In 1980, Mandela issues a statement from prison, urging his supporters to continue the fight against apartheid.

  Today: Mandela is released from prison in 1990. He is elected president in 1994 and serves until 1999, when he retires from the office. After that he continues his advocacy work for human rights organizations.

---

slavery. When the British seized control of the colony in 1795, they continued the system of racial segregation set up by the Afrikaners, appropriating land from South Africans and encouraging large groups of immigrants from Europe and Britain to settle there. Although Britain outlawed slavery in 1830, the South African government continued to enforce racial segregation. In 1910, the white minority institutionalized policies that disenfranchised Africans and legalized racial discrimination and segregation. A few years later, British troops forced hundreds of thousands of Africans off of their land, which was confiscated by the government; these displaced people were moved into restricted, separate communities that did not have adequate living facilities.

Some colonists suffered under this system as rural Africans were forced to urban settlements. Afrikaners, who were only one rung below the British in the established hierarchy, were especially hard hit as their farmers lost many of their cheap laborers. They feared that growing unrest in the black communities would further jeopardize their economic status if reforms were enacted that enabled blacks to gain political power. The Afrikaner Nationalist Alliance was subsequently formed in order to assist blacks in gaining a voice in the government. The alliance proposed a political and social system that would address the growing concerns of the white minority, which they called apartheid, an Afrikaner word for apartness.

Apartheid

The system of apartheid was based on the division of South Africa into four racial groups: the whites, predominantly British and Dutch descendants; the Africans, black descendents of indigenous Africans; the Indians, immigrants from Asia

This South African playground shows the separation between races that serves as the backdrop for A Lesson from Aloes. *The park benches were "For Whites Only" and the black African women had to sit on the ground while they watched their charges play* AP Images

and India; and the Coloreds, South Africans of mixed race. The ideology of apartheid asserted the dominance of the white race because of its perceived racial superiority and granted it the power of governance in all areas. To ensure the effective control of the country, racial segregation was enforced. This system was adopted and put into effect in South Africa in 1950, after Afrikaners aligned themselves with the National Party, which won control of the country in 1948. The government passed the Group Areas Act, which restricted all persons of color to segregated living and work areas with substandard facilities.

In the 1950s and 1960s, black Africans, often aided by sympathetic whites, formed political groups that began to protest government policies through strikes, boycotts, demonstrations, and riots. In the 1960s, some members of the international community also protested, which resulted in South Africa's withdrawal from the British Commonwealth. In 1985, Britain, along with the United States, imposed economic sanctions on the country in response to its apartheid policies. By the 1990s, the South African government, led by President F. W. de Klerk, began

to reform the system, legalizing black political groups and releasing black political prisoners. By 1994, the system of apartheid was dismantled, and the country held for the first time, free general elections that resulted in Nelson Mandela becoming South Africa's first black president.

CRITICAL OVERVIEW

The play received mostly positive reviews that applauded its treatment of race relations in South Africa as well as its dramatic structure. In his essay on Fugard's plays, Michael J. Collins insists that while *A Lesson from Aloes* lacks "the immediate political relevance" of his earlier work, it manages "without ever ignoring or mitigating the horrors of life in South Africa, to move beyond the particulars of place and affirm, in a world of cruelty and suffering, the value and dignity of human life everywhere." He especially praises act 2, which he claims "is beautifully written, exquisitely paced and inordinately moving."

Joel G. Fink, in his review in *Theatre Journal* of this "important" play, echoes Collins's sentiments regarding act 2, arguing that "with the arrival of Steve, ... the evening's dramatic conflicts are truly engaged." He finds fault, however, with act 1 in which, he claims, "too much effort is focused on the introduction of poetic symbols." Overall, Fink concludes that "the play's theme and literary textures are strikingly and surprisingly akin to those of Chekov" and that it "confirms that Athol Fugard continues to grow and mature as a dramatist." Gerard Molyneaux, in his review of the play for *Library Journal*, found it to be "honest" but "not altogether dramatic."

Sheila Roberts, in her article on Fugard, does not find the thematic import of the play compelling enough, suggesting that "no lessons are learnt." She concludes, "The aloes can only teach Piet to wait. But for what? The play doesn't tell us."

> " HIS NAME AND HIS CLASSIFICATION AS AN AFRIKANER GIVE HIM HIS IDENTITY BUT APPEAR AT ODDS WITH THE CAUSE OF RACIAL EQUALITY TO WHICH HE IS DEVOTED, WHICH INCLUDES THE FIGHT TO OVERTHROW THE SOUTH AFRICAN GOVERNMENT AND ESTABLISH CIVIL RIGHTS FOR ALL THE COUNTRY'S INHABITANTS."

CRITICISM

Wendy Perkins

Perkins is a professor of twentieth-century American and British literature and film. In the following essay, she considers the importance of language in the play.

At the beginning of Athol Fugard's play, *A Lesson from Aloes*, Piet Bezuidenhout, an Afrikaner living in South Africa with his wife, Gladys, searches a book on plant species in an effort to discover the name of an aloe plant that he is growing. When Gladys questions his determination, Piet insists on the importance of the task, noting that a child is given a name as soon as it is born and the first thing people do when they meet is to exchange names. Adam, he claims, named his world as soon as he was created. Consequently, he declares, "there is no rest for me until I've identified this." Not finding an exact match for his "Aloe Anonymous" frustrates him because, he admits, knowing its name would make him feel "that little bit more at home in [his] world." Having the right name or words for an object or an occasion has become important for Piet, since they also provide him with a sense of order and meaning, which are lacking in this world of great racial conflict. During the course of the evening, Piet uses the power of language to try to impose an order onto his world, but he ultimately discovers that there are some aspects of human experience that cannot be so easily named or understood.

Piet considers his aloe plant "a stranger in our midst." Naming it would immediately forge a connection between him and the plant and between him and the terrain of South Africa, where the species thrives. Establishing connections with the indigenous forms of life in this country is important to Piet because he knows the difficulties of living in a world of racial segregation and has been caught up in the fight to end apartheid. However, he hints at the complications he will face in his determination to use language as a connecting device when he quotes lines from *Romeo and Juliet*, a play about prejudice and the perceived need to keep opposing factions separate. He says, "'What's in a name? That which we call a rose / By any other name would smell as sweet.'" The stage direction notes, *"These lines, and all his other quotations, although delivered with a heavy Afrikaans accent, are said with a sincere appreciation of the words involved."* Yet when Piet declares, "Alas, it's not as simple as that, is it?" he recognizes that naming does not necessarily bridge separations.

Piet has tried to impose a sense of order on his world by naming his home Xanadu, which means a place of beauty and contentment. Yet neither he nor Gladys has been content there as they are caught in tensions between blacks and whites in their country. Piet tries to make his home a safe place for himself and his wife, but the outside world, in the form of government officials who

WHAT DO I READ NEXT?

- Ian Barry's *Living Apart: South Africa under Apartheid* (1996) examines the history of the implementation of the racist policies under apartheid and the effect that they had on black Africans.

- Fugard's *Master Harold . . . and the Boys* (1982), another of his semi-autobiographical plays that condemns the racist policies of apartheid, centers on seventeen-year-old Hally, who is white, and his relationship with two middle-aged black men who work in his parents' tea room in Port Elizabeth, South Africa.

- *South Africa in Pictures* (2003), by Janice Hamilton, includes photographs of the landscapes and people of South Africa throughout its troubled history.

- *The Poisonwood Bible* (1998), by Barbara Kingsolver, focuses on the experiences of the Price family, who arrive in the Congo in 1959, emissaries of the Southern Baptist Mission League. The family struggles to adapt to and to survive in the harsh conditions in the Congo as their beliefs about racial relationships are challenged.

conduct raids on whites sympathetic to black causes, has invaded their home, leaving Gladys feeling violated and on the brink of insanity and Piet afraid for both of them. Their home is also the place where the tensions between Piet and his friend Steve erupt, damaging a relationship that had given both a sense of meaning and purpose.

Piet, however, insists that "names are more than just labels," as he struggles to maintain a sense of order and gain a clear understanding of his world and his relationship to it. At one point, he paraphrases another part of Juliet's speech to Romeo, thinking about his own name, "trying to hear it as others do." He insists that there is a clear connection between his name and who he is. His name identifies his "face" and his "story." While it may seem easier for Italians like Juliet to "deny thy father and refuse thy name," Piet declares that this would be a difficult task for Afrikaners: "No. For better or for worse, I will remain positively identified as Petrus Jacobus Bezuidenhout . . . . and accept the consequences." The consequences can be problematic for a member of a group of immigrants that exploited black Africans during their colonization of the country and helped the government establish the repressive system of apartheid. His name and his classification as an Afrikaner give him his identity but appear at odds with the cause of racial equality to which he is devoted, which includes the fight to overthrow the South African

government and establish civil rights for all the country's inhabitants.

In conjunction with the function of naming, Piet uses words in the form of quotations to provide meaning to his experience. As he tries to impress on Gladys the importance of naming, he quotes Shakespeare to give his view more authority. Later, he finds what he considers to be the perfect quotation to express his feelings about Steve and their dinner together. Reciting quotations, however, can also be an avoidance strategy; he attempts to reestablish order when he reads the quotation for Steve, in effect trying to shift the conversation away from discussion of the informer. The reestablishment of order also becomes his motive when he repeatedly returns to his aloe during the evening. Gladys insists that the aloes give him a purpose, which he denies, claiming that they are only a pleasure to him. But Gladys understands his actions at times more than he does, declaring, "with your aloes, quoting your poetry . . . . in spite of all that has happened, you've still got a whole world intact."

Piet discovers, however, that no words can offer meaning and comfort in certain situations, such as when a child dies on his farm. At the grave, he became so emotional that the words would not come, and eventually he had to walk away. He spent the next three months reading a book of poetry and stories, "looking for something [he] could have said out there in the veld," but he never found anything.

Piet also learns that words can create chaos. The word, informer, changes in the play. First, it is applied as innuendo to Piet by others, including Steve's wife, who think that he betrayed Steve to the authorities. Gladys then uses the word as a lie and a tool for revenge when she tells Steve that Piet is the informer. Ironically, this accusation causes Steve to confess that he informed on members of their group when he was tortured in prison.

By the end of the play, Piet and Steve have exposed the breakdown of their relationship with each other as well as the failure of the political cause that brought them together. Steve admits to Gladys that he and Piet have nothing left to say to each other by the end of the evening, so Steve leaves with no parting words. Yet Piet still clings to his belief that language can have a great deal of significance, and so turns at the end of the play to his unnamed aloe as Gladys drifts off to a troubled, drugged sleep. Instead of thinking about her return to the mental clinic, Piet tries to reestablish a sense of order and comfort by continuing his search for a name for the plant that he is nurturing, working to ensure its survival in its inhospitable environment, along with his own survival in a harsh political one.

Source: Wendy Perkins, Critical Essay on *A Lesson from Aloes*, in *Drama for Students*, Thomson Gale, 2007.

Thomson Gale

In the following essay, the critic gives an overview of (Harold) Athol Fugard's work.

As a white child growing up in segregated South Africa, Athol Fugard resisted the racist upbringing society offered him. Nevertheless, the boy who would become, in the words of Gillian MacKay of *Maclean's*, "perhaps South Africa's most renowned literary figure, and its most eloquent anti-apartheid crusader abroad" did not completely escape apartheid's influence—he insisted that the family's black servants call him Master Harold, and he even spat at one of them. Fugard told MacKay that the servant, an "extraordinary" man who had always treated him as a close friend, "grieved for the state" of Fugard's soul and forgave him instead of beating him "to a pulp."

Fugard never forgot this incident, which he transformed into a powerful scene in the play, *"Master Harold" . . . and the Boys*. He told Lloyd Richards of *Paris Review* that the event is like a deep stain which has "soaked into the fabric" of his life. In Fugard's career as a playwright, director, and actor, he has forced himself and his audiences to consider their own "stains." As Frank Rich remarked in a

> FUGARD EXPLAINED THAT HE WANTED TO DEMONSTRATE THE 'COMPLEXITY' OF THE AFRIKANER IN *A LESSON FROM ALOES*. HE TOLD RICHARDS IN HIS *PARIS REVIEW* INTERVIEW, '[WE WILL] NEVER UNDERSTAND HOW WE LANDED IN THE PRESENT SITUATION OR WHAT'S GOING TO COME OUT OF IT' IF WE 'SIMPLY DISPOSE OF THE AFRIKANER AS THE VILLAIN IN THE SOUTH AFRICAN SITUATION.'"

1985 *New York Times* review of *The Blood Knot*, "Mr. Fugard doesn't allow anyone, least of all himself, to escape without examining the ugliest capabilities of the soul."

Despite Fugard's insistence that he is not a political writer and that he speaks for no one but himself, his controversial works featuring black and white characters have found favor with critics of apartheid. According to Brendan Gill of the *New Yorker*, *The Blood Knot*, the play that made Fugard famous, "altered the history of twentieth-century theatre throughout the world" as well as the world's "political history." Not all critics of apartheid, however, have appreciated Fugard's works. Some "see a white man being a spokesman for what has happened to black people and they are naturally intolerant," Fugard explained to Paul Allen in *New Statesman and Society*.

Whether Fugard's theatrical explorations of passion, violence, and guilt played a role in undermining apartheid or not, it is clear that he was involved in breaking physical and symbolic barriers to integration. He defied the apartheid system by founding the first enduring black theater company in South Africa, by collaborating with black writers, and by presenting black and white actors on stage together for integrated audiences. He insisted upon performing plays for local audiences in South Africa as well as for those in New York City and London; his plays carried messages that people around the world needed to hear. Even after the government took Fugard's passport and banned his work, he refused to consider himself an exile or to renounce his country. Love, and not hate for South Africa, Fugard maintained, would help it break the chains of apartheid. "Wouldn't it be ironic if South Africa could teach the world something about harmony?," he asked MacKay.

Fugard is highly regarded by literary and theater critics. Stephen Gray of *New Theatre Quarterly* noted that the author has been called "the greatest active playwright in English." His works are renowned for their multifaceted, marginalized characters, realistic yet lyrical dialogue, and carefully crafted, symbolic plots. Critics have also praised Fugard's ability to write scenes which elicit emotion without declining into melodrama. Fugard has forged new paths in theater by directing and acting in many of his own plays and by writing and composing plays with the actors who perform in them.

Fugard credits his parents with shaping his insights about South African society. As a child, he developed close relationships with both his English-speaking South African father, Harold, and his mother, Elizabeth, the daughter of Dutch-speaking Afrikaners. Harold, a jazz musician and amputee who spent a great deal of time in bed, amused the boy with fantastic stories and confused him with his unabashed bigotry. Fugard's mother Elizabeth supported the family by efficiently managing their tea room. In an interview with Jamaica Kincaid for *Interview*, Fugard described his mother as "an extraordinary woman" who could "barely read and write." In Fugard's words, she was "a *monument* of decency and principle and just anger" who encouraged Fugard to view South African society with a thoughtful and critical eye.

If Fugard learned the power of words from his father, and if he discovered how to question society from his mother, he gained an understanding of the complexity of human nature from both parents. Like Fugard's characters, his parents were neither entirely good or evil. Nevertheless, as Fugard explained to Kincaid, "I think at a fairly early age I became suspicious of what the system was trying to do to me. . . . I became conscious of what attitudes it was trying to implant in me and what *prejudices* it was trying to pass on to me." Fugard fed his intellectual appetite with conversations with his mother and daily trips to the local library. By the

time he began college, he knew he wanted to be a writer. He accepted a scholarship at the University of Cape Town and studied philosophy, but he left school before graduating to journey around the Far East on a steamer ship.

At this time in his life, Fugard entertained notions of writing a great South African novel. Yet his first attempt at writing a novel, as he saw it, was a failure, and he destroyed it. After Fugard met and married Sheila Meiring, an out-of-work South African actress, he developed an interest in writing plays. *The Cell* and *Klaas and the Devil* were the first results of this ambition.

Not until after Fugard began to keep company with a community of black writers and actors near Johannesburg did he experience a revelation in his work. During this time, he witnessed the frustration of the black writers and learned the intricacies of a system which shrewdly and cruelly thwarted their efforts to live and work freely. The plays he penned at this time, *No-Good Friday* and *Nongogo*, were performed by Fugard and his black actor friends for private audiences.

In 1959 Fugard moved to England to write. His work received little attention there, and Fugard began to realize that he needed to be in South Africa to follow his muse. Upon his return home in 1961, Fugard wrote a second novel. Although he tried to destroy this work, a pair of graduate students later found the only surviving copy, and it was published in 1981. Critics have noticed the presence of many of the elements which would re-emerge in Fugard's more famous plays in this novel, *Tsotsi*.

Tsotsi portrays the life of David, a young black man whose nickname, "Tsotsi," means "hoodlum." Tsotsi spends his time with his gang of thieving, murderous friends. He has no family and cannot remember his childhood. It is not until a woman he is about to attack gives him a box with a baby in it, and David gives the baby his name, that he begins to experience sympathy and compassion, and to recall his childhood. When David is about to kill a crippled old man he has been pursuing, he suddenly remembers how his mother was arrested and never came home, and how he began to rove with a pack of abandoned children. It is not long before he recalls the trauma that led to his violent life on the streets. Fugard does not allow David's character to revel in his newly discovered emotions or to continue his search for God: at the novel's end, David is crushed under a bulldozer in an attempt to save David, the baby.

Critics appreciate *Tsotsi* for the insight it provides into the lives of even minor characters. Fugard did not allow his readers to categorize characters as "good" or "bad"; instead, he forced readers to understand their complexity. In the *New York Times Book Review*, Ivan Gold called *Tsotsi* "a moving and untendentious book" which demonstrates Fugard's ability to "uncannily insinuate himself into the skins of the oppressed majority and articulate its rage and misery and hope." Although Barbara A. Bannon in *Publishers Weekly* commented that *Tsotsi* is "altogether different in tone" from some of his plays, she also observed that the "milieu is much the same as the one that has made Fugard . . . the literary conscience of South Africa."

While Fugard generally works on one project at a time (typically writing with pens instead of word processors), he wrote *Tsotsi* and *The Blood Knot* simultaneously. The inspiration for *The Blood Knot* came when the author walked into a room and saw his brother asleep in bed one night. His brother had lived a difficult life, and his pain was apparent in his face and body. Realizing that there was nothing he could do to save his brother from suffering, Fugard experienced guilt. By writing *The Blood Knot*, Fugard recalled to Richards in *Paris Review*, he "was trying to examine a guilt more profound than racial guilt—the existential guilt that I feel when another person suffers, is victimized, and I can do nothing about it. South Africa afforded me the most perfect device for examining this guilt."

The Blood Knot is the story of two brothers born to the same mother. Morris, who has light-skin, can "pass" for white; he confronts the truth about his identity when he returns home to live with his dark-skinned brother, Zachariah. Although the opening scene of the play finds Morris preparing a bath for hard-working Zachariah's feet, it soon becomes clear that the brothers' relationship is a tenuous one. The tension between the brothers is heightened when Zach's white pen pal (a woman who thinks Zach is white) wants to meet him, and Morris must pretend to be the white man with whom she has been corresponding.

Morris's attempts to look and sound white are painful for both brothers: To convincingly portray a white man, Morris must treat his black brother with the cruelty of a racist. In his role as a white man, Morris sits in the park and calls insults at his brother, who chases black children from the presence of his "white" brother. By the last scene, the "game" is out of control, and Zach tries to kill Morris. According to Robert M. Post in *Ariel*, the brothers in *The Blood Knot* "are typical victims of the system of apartheid and bigotry" and "personify the racial conflict of South Africa."

Fugard had little support in producing the play; it was not until actor Zakes Mokae joined the project that the production emerged. As a result of this collaboration, the first production of *The Blood Knot* was controversial not only for its content, but also because it featured a black actor and a white actor on stage together. Fugard played the light-skinned brother who "passes" for a white man, while Mokae played the darker-skinned brother. *The Blood Knot* opened in front of a mixed-race, invitation-only audience in a run-down theatre. As Derek Cohen noted in *Canadian Drama*, this first production of *The Blood Knot* "sent shock waves" through South Africa. "Those who saw the initial performance knew instinctively that something of a revolution had taken place in the stodgily Angloid cultural world of South Africa," he wrote. "Whites, faced boldly with some inescapable truths about what their repressive culture and history had wrought, were compelled to take notice."

Responses to *The Blood Knot* varied. As Cohen notes, some Afrikaners believed that the play's message was that blacks and whites could not live together in peace, and some black critics called the work racist. Many now accept the interpretation of the play as a sad commentary on the way racism has twisted and tangled our understanding of brotherhood and humanity. More specifically, according to Cohen, *The Blood Knot* is "about the hatred which South African life feeds on."

According to Dennis Walder in his book *Athol Fugard*, many of Fugard's plays "approximate . . . the same basic model established by *The Blood Knot*: a small cast of 'marginal' characters is presented in a passionately close relationship embodying the tensions current in their society, the whole first performed by actors directly involved in its creation, in a makeshift, 'fringe' or 'unofficial' venue." Since the first production of *The Blood Knot*, the substance of Fugard's plays as well as the means of their production have reflected the historical circumstances in which they evolved. Fugard insists that individual performances of each of his plays represent the legitimate play; he personally selects the actors and also continues to direct and act in them himself.

Boesman and Lena, produced in 1969, was Fugard's next great success; Cohen called it "possibly the finest of Fugard's plays." This work develops around the image of an old, homeless woman Fugard once saw, presenting a homeless couple (both "colored") who wander without respite. According to Cohen, it is a "drama of unrelieved and immitigable suffering" which becomes "more intense as the characters, impotent against the civilization of which they are outcasts, turn their fury against each other."

Fugard suffered from writer's block after he wrote *Boesman and Lena*, but went on to work in collaboration with actors to create *Orestes* in 1971. *Orestes* developed as a collection of images which, Walder remarked, "defies translation into a script" and explores "the effect of violence upon those who carry it out."

Fugard's next project began after two amateur actors, John Kani and Winston Ntshona, asked Fugard to help them become professional actors. As Fugard explained to Richards in his *Paris Review* interview, "at that point in South Africa's theater history . . . the notion that a black man could earn a living being an actor in South Africa was just the height of conceit." Nevertheless, the trio decided to create their own play. Three plays eventually emerged from this plan in 1972—*The Island, Sizwe Banzi Is Dead*, and *Statements after an Arrest under the Immorality Act*, also known as *The Statements Trilogy* or *The Political Trilogy*.

In these plays, personal experiences, along with the direction of Fugard, combine to provoke audiences. Post commented that *The Island* and *Statements* share "the basic conflict of the individual versus the government." In *The Island*, prisoners (portrayed by John and Winston) in a South African jail stage Sophocles's *Antigone;* the play within the play suggests that, according to Post, the "conflict between individual conscience and individual rights . . . and governmental decrees . . . corresponds to the conflict between the individual conscience and the rights of black prisoners and white government." *Statements* follows the relationship between a white librarian and a black teacher who become lovers despite their fear of being caught and castigated; eventually, their "illegal" love is uncovered by the police.

The development of *Sizwe Banzi Is Dead* began with an image of a black man in a new suit, seated and smiling, that Fugard saw in a photographer's store. Speculation about why the man was smiling led to a story about the passbook that blacks had to carry around with them under the apartheid system. Before Sizwe Banzi can get his passbook in order, he must symbolically die by trading his identity for another. The play was performed "underground" until, as Fugard told Richards, it "had

played in London and New York" and earned a reputation that "protected" its writers and cast. In 1974, Kani won a Tony Award for his New York performance in *Sizwe Banzi Is Dead*.

Fugard unveiled *A Lesson from Aloes* in 1978. Like his other works, this play demonstrates the extent to which apartheid effects everyone in South African society. Piet, a Dutch Afrikaner living in Port Elizabeth in 1963, tends his collection of hardy, bitter aloe plants and joins a group of political activists. When the group's bus boycott is disrupted by the police and Piet's only friend Steve is found to have mixed blood and sent away, Piet is blamed. Even Piet's wife, whose diaries have been read by the police, believes he betrayed Steve.

Instead of defending himself, Piet isolates himself in his quiet aloe garden, and even the audience is unsure of his innocence. At the same time, Gladys, his wife, laments the violation of her diaries and goes insane. Fugard explained that he wanted to demonstrate the "complexity" of the Afrikaner in *A Lesson from Aloes*. He told Richards in his *Paris Review* interview, "[we will] never understand how we landed in the present situation or what's going to come out of it" if we "simply dispose of the Afrikaner as the villain in the South African situation."

"Master Harold" . . . and the Boys communicates similar notions. Hallie, whose childhood parallels Fugard's, is troubled by his father's thoughtless and unthinking attitude. Although he has a close relationship with his family's black servants, Sam and Willie, even he is not immune to the evil of apartheid; at one point in the play, the boy spits in Willie's face. Fugard tells Richards how the relationship shared by Hallie, Sam, and Willie is autobiographical, and how he really did spit in Willie's face. He felt that it was "necessary" to deal with what he'd done by writing *"Master Harold" . . . and the Boys*.

"Master Harold" . . . and the Boys was the second of Fugard's plays to open in the United States, where it earned critical acclaim. Despite this American success, the play provoked criticism from individuals and groups who, as Jeanne Colleran noted in *Modern Drama*, either asserted that characters like Sam exhibit "Uncle Tom-ism," or demanded that Fugard present his plays in South Africa instead of abroad, in "languages of the black majority." Colleran suggested that because of this criticism, "Fugard cannot write of Johannesburg or of township suffering without incurring the wrath of Black South Africans who regard him as a self-appointed

and presumptuous spokesman; nor can he claim value for the position previously held by white liberals without being assailed by the more powerful and vociferous radical left. . . . Ironically . . . Fugard has been forced to practice a kind of self-censorship by those whose cause he shared."

"Master Harold" . . . and the Boys also received negative attention from the South African government, which claimed that it was subversive. The government proclaimed it illegal to import or distribute copies of the play. Fugard later managed to present "Master Harold" . . . and the Boys in Johannesburg, because the government did not forbid the play's performance.

The publication of Notebooks, 1960-1977 reinforced Fugard's growing popularity in the United States. This book provides what Pico Iyer of Time calls "the random scraps out of which Fugard fashioned his plays" and "a trail of haunting questions." Richard Eder of the Los Angeles Times Book Review asserted that, in addition to providing "the most vivid possible picture of an artist striving to shape his material even as it was detonating all around him," the Notebooks are "an illuminating, painful and beguiling record of a life lived in one of those tortured societies where everything refers back, sooner or later, to the situation that torments it."

When The Road to Mecca opened in 1984 at the Yale Repertory Theatre, American audiences were captivated by Fugard's mastery once again. Nevertheless, this play reinforced Fugard's reputation as a regional writer by reconstructing the character and life of a woman who lived in Karoo, where Fugard kept his South African home. Unable to take comfort from the Karoo community, Helen Martins isolates herself at home; there, she produces sculpture after sculpture from cement and wire. Benedict Nightingale noted in New Statesman that while Helen Martins actually committed suicide by "burning out her stomach with caustic soda," Fugard recreates her as "a docile old widow" with a beautiful life; "that paranoia, that suicide are ignored" by the playwright. The central problem in the play consists of the local pastor's attempts to get Helen to enter a home for the elderly to hide his secret love for her. As Jack Kroll observed in Newsweek, although The Road to Mecca "doesn't seem to be a political play at all," it "concerns love and freedom, and for Fugard that is the germ cell of the South African problem."

With some exceptions, The Road to Mecca was lauded by critics. While Nightingale appreciates the presentation of the Afrikaner pastor "in the round,

from his own point of view as much as that from the liberal outsider," he also finds the play to be "exasperatingly uneven, as unreal and real a play as Fugard has ever yet penned." According to Colleran, The Road to Mecca was "extraordinarily well received," playing at Britain's National Theatre and on Broadway. Graham Leach asserted in Listener that The Road to Mecca is "universal" and "a major piece of theatre. . . . Many people here believe it may well end up being judged Fugard's finest work."

A Place with the Pigs, as Colleran recounted in Modern Drama, is a personal parable "concerning the forty years spent in a pigsty" by a "Red Army deserter." It premiered at the Yale Repertory Theatre in 1987 with Fugard in the leading role. Unlike The Road to Mecca, A Place with the Pigs did not receive critical acclaim. Colleran suggested that the play may have failed to gain positive attention because it "simply does not conform to the audience's expectations of what a work by Athol Fugard should be like." In her opinion, the "dismissal" of A Place with the Pigs is unfortunate, in part because this "parable of one segment of South African society—the white South African who is committed both to dismantling apartheid and to remaining in his homeland—it adds a new voice, an authentic one, to those clamoring to decide the future of South Africa."

My Children! My Africa! was the first of Fugard's plays to premiere in South Africa in years. According to Gray in New Theatre Quarterly, Fugard believed that "South African audiences should have this play first." Fugard ensured that many audiences were exposed to this work: After a long run at the Market Theatre in Johannesburg, My Children! My Africa! was performed for six weeks in a tour of black townships in South Africa in 1989 with Lisa Fugard, Fugard's daughter, and John Kani in starring roles.

Like "Master Harold" . . . and the Boys, My Children! My Africa! portrays the struggles of youths to live with or confront the division between races in South Africa. Yet, as Allen of New Statesman and Society observed, the play marks "the first time Fugard . . . put the struggle itself on stage." Fugard was inspired by the story of a black teacher who refused to participate in a school boycott and was later murdered in Port Elizabeth by a group that believed he was a police informer.

Playland was the first of Fugard's plays to appear after the fall of apartheid. It is set on New Year's Eve in a traveling amusement park in Karoo. Here, a black night watchman painting a bumper car and a white South African whose car has broken down meet, discuss their lives, and reveal their darkest secrets: the white man tells how he killed blacks in a border war, and the black man confesses that he killed a white man who tried to force his fiancée (who was working as the white man's servant) to have sexual intercourse with him. John Simon of *New York* criticized the play: "There is hardly a situation, a snatch of dialogue, an object that isn't, or doesn't become, a symbol." But, according to Edith Oliver in a *New Yorker* review of the play, the spell cast by the actors' performances "is rooted in Mr. Fugard's moral passion." She concluded: "I have rarely seen an audience so mesmerized, or been so mesmerized myself."

Set after Nelson Mandela's election as South Africa's new president, *Valley Song* portrays four "colored" characters as they prepare to face the challenges of the future. Fugard was happy to premiere *Valley Song* at the Market Theatre in Johannesburg. As Donald G. McNeil, Jr., of the *New York Times* reported, Fugard was also optimistic about the future of South Africa: "We're pulling off a political miracle here." In a *World Literature Today* article, Harold A. Waters stated: "*Valley Song* is a paean to post-apartheid."

Fugard published an autobiography in 1997, entitled *Cousins: A Memoir*. In it, the playwright describes his relationship to Johnnie, his cousin of Afrikaner descent, and Garth, his English cousin. Fugard considers that as different as the two men's characters may have been, each served as an important inspiration to him in his literary work. This memoir also includes some hints of autobiographical events that appear in his plays. "A readable gem of a memoir," wrote Katherine K. Koenig in *Library Journal*. In a *Booklist* review, Jack Helbig commented that *Cousins* is a "warmhearted memoir." A reviewer for *Publishers Weekly* called the book "an excellent complement to [Fugard's] plays."

Cousins was followed by a dramatic memoir, *The Captain's Tiger: A Memoir for the Stage*, which first appeared in Johannesburg and Pretoria. This play is concerned with the twenty-year-old writer as he travels from Africa to Japan on a steamer. During his sea journey, the young man makes an inner journey through his attempt to recount the story of his mother's life. "Athol Fugard has cooked up a rare feast for theatergoers," wrote David Sheward in *Back Stage*. In a *Variety* review, Charles Isherwood voiced conflicting sentiments about the play. "It's suffused with a tenderly evoked sympathy for [Fugard's] mother," said Isherwood, but, he

continued, "it's a minor-key and ultimately rather uninvolving play." Later in the article, the critic stated: "The play feels like a piece of prose only half transformed into stage material." Robert L. Daniels called *The Captain's Tiger* "a sweetly autobiographical memory play" that demonstrates Fugard's "lyrical sense of storytelling." Daniels remarked in his article in *Variety:* "Fugard is delightfully feisty and impish" in his role as the ship's steward. The critic concluded that the co-directors (Fugard and Susan Hilferty) had directed *The Captain's Tiger* "with tasteful simplicity."

Sorrows and Rejoicings is yet another drama in Fugard's series of post-apartheid plays. It involves an Afrikaner poet, David Olivier, who goes into exile in England when his writings are banned in South Africa. He returns to his homeland, along with his wife, Allison, shortly before his death. As the play begins, David has already died, and his story is recounted by his wife, his "colored" mistress, and his illegitimate daughter. The ghost of David appears onstage to interact with the women in his life.

Critics greeted this play with mixed reviews. "Fugard's sparsely populated and sparely plotted tone poems are an advanced model of the most literary kind," said Sean Mitchell in a *Los Angeles Times* review. He also noted that the writer's words "fail to gather much steam as drama," despite the fact that they "offer enduring images of a beautiful, cruel land." Charles Isherwood called *Sorrows and Rejoicings* an "eloquent, moving and piercingly sad new play. . .which has been sensitively staged." "The play does not succeed so well as most of [Fugard's] earlier work," commented Robert L. King in *North American Review*. In a *Variety* article, Robert L. Daniels stated that *Sorrows and Rejoicings* is "a romantic memory play heightened by the playwright's poetic storytelling gifts." Ed Kaufman praised Fugard as "a writer-poet with power and passion." In his *Hollywood Reporter* review, the critic considered the play to be Fugard's "most personal statement about the political, social and moral dynamics within South Africa."

Twenty-eight years after its premiere, a revival of *The Island* appeared in London in 2002, featuring the original actors, Kani and Ntshona. Since the play was written and staged during the apartheid period, it might well have seemed outdated; the theater critics, however, did not find that to be the case. "The production makes the prisoners' experience seem vividly of-the-moment as well as universal in application," wrote Dominic Cavendish in *Daily Telegraph*. Michael Billington of the *Guardian* praised Fugard's "astonishing collaborative play" that is staged with "sheer theatrical intelligence."

In an interview with Simon Hattenstone, Athol Fugard considered his work in the light of post-apartheid. When apartheid first ended, Fugard thought he might become "South Africa's first literary redundancy." After further reflection, however, he considered "that the new complicated South Africa needs more vigilance than ever before." Although the country's politics have changed, Fugard finds himself faced with a challenge: "What do I do now? That is the question and I'm trying to answer that question. . .by way of the three post-apartheid plays I've written."

Source: Thomson Gale, "(Harold) Athol Fugard," in *Contemporary Authors Online*, Thomson Gale, 2004.

Gerald Weales

In the following excerpt, Weales points out that Fugard writes about what he knows. As a South African, glimpses of Fugard can be found in his character Piet in A Lesson from Aloes *and the characters in the play "are necessarily South African."*

"A man's scenery is other men," Fugard wrote in November 1966 (*Notebooks* 141), contemplating the final image of the Piet-Gladys-Steve story that would become *A Lesson from Aloes* in 1978. The men and women on Fugard's human landscape are necessarily South African. "I stand on a street in Port Elizabeth or Johannesburg or a small South African town, and in terms of the life that passes me I've mastered the code," he told Mel Gussow, and he gives a sample portrait of a black woman carrying shopping bags. "If I stood on a corner in London or New York, I couldn't put that sort of biography behind *any* of the people walking past me. Mastering the code of a place has been necessary to me as a writer." The three characters in *Aloes*—distantly based on people mentioned in *Notebooks* as early as 1961—are veterans of the struggles in a cause that—for two of them at least—has come to seem false, a kind of ideological self-delusion that made their idealism and their sense of community appear to be politically important. Piet, the Afrikaner, driven by drought from the farm he loved, found new meaning as a political activist. He still believes that man-made inequities "can be unmade by men", but he is isolated, shunned by his old colleagues, who think he is an informer. There is a kind of stolidity in Piet which allows him to withstand the attacks/demands on him by Gladys and Steve and which incidentally makes him a difficult character for an actor to play. Gladys, in

response to a police raid in which her private diaries were read ("They violated me, Peter"), has been in and out of mental hospitals. Even though she knows better (her hysteria frequently breaks through her quiescent mask during the play), she blames Piet for what has happened, for luring her from the safety of her middle-class English home with his siren song, "Trust, Gladys. Trust yourself. Trust life." She not only accuses him, but tries to punish him by destroying the no longer existing closeness between him and Steve, the "coloured" friend whose eloquence brought him into the movement. "There was nothing left to wreck", Piet says. As for Steve, just out of prison and on his way to voluntary exile in England, he has come to Piet because he believes, with the others in their group, that Piet is an informer, and it is a flawed Piet that he needs. The most interesting thing about Steve is the way in which he transfers his own feelings onto Piet, at first attacking him for accusations that Piet never makes about his decision to leave South Africa and then, presumably in search of a fellow sinner, by revealing that he turned informer in prison.

At the end of the play with Steve gone and Gladys inside packing for her return to the hospital, Piet is left alone in the backyard with his collection of aloes. The metaphor of the aloes is explained, perhaps too obviously, in the exchange between him and Gladys in Act One, in which he describes the power of aloes to withstand drought, but the lesson is somewhat ambiguous. "Is that the price of survival in this country?" she asks. "Thorns and bitterness." Those words do not describe the Piet we see in the play, but he does find "some sort of lesson" in aloes, insisting, "We need survival mechanisms as well." The aloes in the play, however, are not "the veritable forest of scarlet spikes" he remembers from the farm, but captive plants, and "An aloe isn't seen to its best advantage in a jam tin in a little backyard." Gladys rejects the survival lesson. "If that's what your expectations have shrunk to, it's your business, but God has not planted me in a jam tin." That she may have a jam tin of her own—her recurring madness—does not alter the validity of her statement. God may not have planted Piet in a jam tin either, but at the end he crawls into one, joins the other potted plants in the backyard. "I wasn't writing about a *hero*," Fugard told Gussow. "I was writing about a *victim*. I've never written about a hero. I don't understand heroism. Piet is a very simple man, saying, 'I've lived through one drought. I'll try to survive this one as well.'" Of course, he lived through the drought by leaving the land which, in the present context, would be a Steve solution which is impossible for Piet. A positive negative end, then, in the best Fugard tradition.

There are a great many set pieces in *Aloes*— Piet on aloes, Piet on the drought, Piet on the bus strike and his conversion, Steve on his father's fish and his decay after losing his home, Steve on his prison experience, even Gladys on the diary and the raid. Sometimes these appear to be information-giving speeches, for the audience not the other characters, but at their best they work dramatically. Piet uses his to deflect Gladys's anger, Steve uses his to elicit Piet's presumed complicity, and Gladys's are both weapons against Piet and indications of her increasing instability. Fugard has always used such devices, although at times he seems to disapprove of them. . . .

Source: Gerald Weales, "Fugard Masters the Code," in *Twentieth Century Literature*, Vol. 39, No. 4, Winter 1993, pp. 505–506.

Errol Durbach

In the following excerpt, Durbach explores the Afrikaner characters in A Lesson from Aloes *who want to "create a world of sustaining order" amid the chaos in South Africa in the 1960s, like the "miraculous" aloe plant which springs forth from seemingly deficient and hostile land.*

When *A Lesson from Aloes* premiered in Johannesburg, Fugard himself played the role of Steve Daniels. When it opened in New Haven, James Earl Jones was cast as Steve. The role, clearly, is ambiguously "Coloured"; but it would be a mistake to regard Steve Daniels as a representative of the Black South African community (which has its own story, its own peculiar hell, and a very different history). The significant fact about the three million Coloureds in the Cape Province is that they are the racially mixed children of predominantly Afrikaner parentage—

> Damned from birth by the great disgrace,
> A touch of the tar-brush in his face (Butler 102)

—and denied by their Afrikaner father as shameful evidence of his "immorality." They speak the same language as the Afrikaner (which the Black people do not), belong in large numbers to the Dutch Reformed Church (which the Black people do not), and share in the Afrikaners' gene-pool (which the Black people do not). The very names of Afrikaner and Coloured—"Willem Gerhardus Daniels," "Petrus Jacobus Bezuitenhout"—resonate with a Dutch sonority which bears witness to their common heritage. The Coloureds, in other words,

have no racial origins apart from those shared with the Afrikaners, no country beyond South Africa, no "homeland" to which they may be summarily banished (like the Black people). They are the reef on which all rational arguments for apartheid smashes and sinks, living evidence that its basis is racist and not cultural, that its politics are those of blood-purity and not the much vaunted integrity of the Afrikaner language and faith. The history of the Coloured people of South Africa has been one of systematic deprivation, a tragedy of dispossession, disinheritance and disenfranchisement unmatched in the fate of any other racial group: humiliated by the Immorality Amendment Act (1950) which extended the prohibition against interracial sexual contact to White/Coloured relationships, racially classified (or reclassified) under the Population Registration Act (1950), segregated from their White neighbours under the Group Areas Act (1950) and forcibly removed where necessary, and struck—after five years of constitutional wrangling—from the voters' roll in the Cape by the Separate Representation of Voters Act (1956). The Coloured experience of the 1950s is captured in Steve's fragmented recollection of his father, the fisherman expelled under the Group Areas legislation from his "home" in racially reclassified "White" area, and excluded by distance from the sea. Two memories dominate: the old man's Bible-curse on the little bit of ground after the legal battle to save his land, and his Job-like despair in the face of his nation's destiny under apartheid: "Ons geslag is verkeerd" ["Our generation . . . our race is a mistake"]—an image of the Coloured as an error on the White genetic map. It is this very despair that impels his son to decisive action in the 1960s, that drives him to countermand his fate as a racial "mistake" in the history of humankind.

The "Cause" begins in a non-violent, optimistic alliance of White and Coloured interests and there is a vivid lived-through quality to Piet's recollection of a Xanadu of hope and solidarity: the boycott of the Port Elizabeth buses which, for the first time, impels the Coloured community into political action; the sensation, "like rain after a long drought," of being welcomed by the non-White brotherhood; and the lessons in Liberal philosophy, learned from Steve Daniels, that an evil system is not a natural disaster and that men have it in their power to correct social injustice and reform the world. But the rhetoric, restated in 1963, rings trite and hollow—like the first inspiring utterances of faith and purpose in Gladys's diary, and their gradual fading into blankness and silence. It was the

Sharpeville massacre in 1960 and the banning of the African National Congress, as Margaret Munro suggests (473–74), that decisively terminated all inter-racial alliances in South Africa. But Liberalism had begun to die even before Sharpeville. The growing militancy of ANC splinter-groups, like POQO with its "Africa for the Africans" slogan, redefined the "Cause" in terms of a Black nationalism which had lost all patience with White Liberal purpose and its evolutionary dream of political change. White participation in the Black struggle is no longer welcome, and Liberalism of any hue becomes a counter-revolutionary betrayal of the "Cause."

The response of the Nationalist Government to Black Nationalism, civil disobedience and political dissidence was to declare a State of Emergency and enact the Unlawful Organisations Act (1960) to ban political groups. Individual banning had been made possible under the Suppression of Communism Act (1950, 1954)—which defined one of the aims of Communism as "a belief in racial equality" (Brookes 204)—and it is possible under a banning order to restrict mobility, effectively silence a dissident, forbid communication, and preclude him from belonging to any political organisation. The only alternative to the banning order is "voluntary expatriation" under an Exit Permit which prohibits any return without the Government's permission. And to make assurance doubly sure, the General Law Amendment Act (1963) licensed the South African police to arrest without warrant or charge, and detain for up to ninety days, anyone suspected of committing or knowing about certain specified types of political offences. There is no appeal to the Courts, and many detainees (as Edgar Brookes discreetly puts it) "were subjected to solitary confinement, with, in some cases, marked psychological results."

This is the massive reactionary backlash in which Steve Daniels is ensnared and to which he has fallen victim "with marked psychological results." His experiences are loosely based on those of the exiled Coloured poet, Dennis Brutus, whose career is coupled in Fugard's *Notebooks* with that of Piet V.—the prototype of the Liberal Afrikaner. There is a passage in the September 1963 entry (99–100) about the wounding of Brutus who had taken a stand against apartheid in sport, had been banned, arrested for breaking his banning order, then captured by the Security Police and shot in the stomach. No lead smashes into Steve Daniel's stomach, but the violence inflicted by the police is no less devastating. He, too, is arrested for breaking his banning order, and under police interrogation is

> IF ONE OF THE PLAY'S POLITICAL 'LESSONS' ADVOCATES A COUNTER-REVOLUTIONARY PHILOSOPHY OF STOICAL ENDURANCE, ANOTHER SURELY CELEBRATES NATURE'S RESISTANCE TO THE FETTERS AND SHACKLES OF MAN-MADE SYSTEMS."

driven to the brink of suicide. Finally, his nerve broken and his defences smashed in prison, he is pressured to provide whatever information—real or fictitious—the police demand. But his breakdown is merely an occasion for mockery and derision. They know it all already. Some unknown traitor to the "Cause" has already leaked its secrets, most probably the same informer who had betrayed Steve's violation of his banning order to the authorities. His world, devastated of trust, becomes merely uninhabitable. Half-fearing that his visit to Xanadu may be a trap, his courage boosted by liquor, Steve Daniels is shamefully prepared to believe the worst of his staunchest ally.

Joseph Lelyveld, in *Move Your Shadow*, provides a useful gloss on the "exorbitant price of trust" in South Africa. Visiting Port Elizabeth for the POQO trial, he meets two Black friends at Athol Fugard's cottage and asks them why Black policemen and state witnesses in political trials are never assaulted in the townships.

> "To do something like that," one of the men said, "you would want at least two men, wouldn't you?" Pausing to indicate that my question was hypothetical and not intended as incitement, I gestured towards the only other person in the room, the man's best friend. "How do I know," came the mumbled reply, "that he is not an *impimpi* [informer]?" No one who was not in jail or house arrest under what was called a banning order could ever be immune from that suspicion. So pervasive was it then that the authorities could compromise stalwart black nationalists by seeming to ignore them. (9–10)

This is more insidious than a bullet in the guts. It strikes not at the individual, but at his relationship with a world of men; it undermines the Universal Brotherhood more effectively than an Act of Parliament; and it infects even the most apparently unassailable relationship with a corrosive suspicion. "Your beautiful friendship?" cries Gladys. "Can't you see it's rotten with doubt?" For if Steve can suspect Piet as *impimpi* then nothing remains of Xanadu, the Liberal domain whose inhabitants must now engage in a charade of friendship with others who may (or may not) be fee'd servants of the Special Branch. The clandestine meeting of two old comrades in the back yard of Xanadu merely underscores the interlocking tragedies of cunningly programmed alienation and disillusionment in a country where *not* to be imprisoned is as heinous a penalty as banishment. One exile leaves his "home," shamed by his betrayal of fellowship and trust. The other remains "at home," exiled forever in an ice cave of suspicion and fear.

Gladys's story and her history have little in common with Steve's. She is a visitor to Xanadu, rather than a founding member, one temporarily inspired by the rhetoric of a "Cause" which now leaves her fundamentally indifferent, and involved in the violent aftermath of its collapse only as an apathetic bystander. She is the rose in a garden of uprooted and rootbound aloes searching, in their jam-tins, for the space nature intended for them and seeking to survive the South African drought. But the price of survival, "thorns and bitterness," is too much to pay in a country which she resolutely refuses to acknowledge as her "home." "I know I was born here," she says, "but I will never call it that." Her allegiance remains with a land she has never seen, a climate she has never known, a culture absorbed at second-hand. But she clings to her "Englishness" as a drowning woman to a spar, Anglicizes her world in a futile endeavour to deny its Africanness (Piet is called "Peter" in her domestic vocabulary), and dissociates herself from God's unspecified curse on the Afrikaner nation. South Africa, with its sun and its politics and its violence, has scarred her; and her Anglo-African attitude of sentimental nostalgia for a world of English rose-gardens and sunny spots of greenery barely conceals the fear that she is as "homeless" and "roofless" as Steve Daniels. It might have been possible, before the 1960s, for the English-speaking South African to cherish an illusion of England as some primary "home," and domicile in Africa as a temporary visit of the uncommitted; but in 1961 South Africa withdrew from the Commonwealth, severed its cultural ties with Great Britain and declared itself a Republic. The psychological effect upon the Anglo-Africans

was to spoil the illusion of the alternative "home" and the myth of a temporary sojourn; and the symptoms of this shock of cultural redefinition are clearly manifest in Gladys's depression, her dissociation from the catalogue of South African disasters, and her sense of almost apocalyptic isolation in an alien universe:

> Do you know they've got a date worked out for the end of the world? It's not far off, either. I almost told him there are times when I think it has already happened . . . it's hard sometimes to believe there is a world out there full of other people. Just you and me. That's all that's left. The streets are empty and I imagine you wandering around looking for another survivor.

The great irony in the life of this existentially displaced person is that "England" is, indeed, her final "home"—not the country to which Steve is exiled, but the Fort England Clinic in Grahamstown where she has been treated before, and to which she will retreat again. Persecuted for a political "Cause" she has never really believed in, violated by the confiscation of her diaries by the Special Branch (she experiences it as rape), Gladys's descent into madness reduces her to another item in the catalogue of South African disasters. For merely to *live* in South Africa is to be incriminated, either by indifference or complicity or chance, in the violence of apartheid and the misery of others; and the notion of a refuge in some other "home" is as illusionary as the myth of Xanadu. "England"—the only England she knows—is a Romantic cliche on the wall of a Mental Hospital, a composite of greenery and soft mist and thatched roofed cottages glowing in the twilight of Somerset. She is sane enough to dismiss it as a futile distraction from the reality of her situation. For her, there is finally no hope, no faith, and no trust left in the world—nothing but the absolute goodness of her Afrikaner husband, which is a terrible provocation to her desire to violate it. Her lesson in survival has been the bitterness and the turgid violence which she associates with the aloe-garden of Xanadu. And to save herself from what she most hates and fears, she packs her bags for voluntary exile, "home" to the protective custody of the Fort England Clinic.

"The aloe," writes Perseus Adams in his poem "The Woman and the Aloe," "talks truly only to those who have endured her wait"—the seasons of drought, the silence, the loneliness:

> Nothing else can so quickly, and with such pure art
> Raise up my thorn-riddled love for this place
> Hard as banishment—yet lit with wild
>   sweetness too.
> A neighbour to stones am I, a sister to a priceless
>   gift.

"The aloe," writes Vandenbroucke in his stringent criticism of the image, "is too simple a symbol to bear the weight expected of it since it has no meaning outside of its ability to survive a harsh environment. Instead of being evocative it is demonstrative." Maybe so, for the reader who has not had to endure her wait. But few images evoke more breath-catchingly the South Africanness of the icon, that pervasive poetic tradition in which, as J. M. Coetzee puts it in *White Writing*, "the stony truth of Africa emerges in the form of a flower." In a tradition stretching from the early Afrikaner verse of van den Heever to the poetry of Roy Campbell—whose lines on the "glory" bred from "thirsty rocks" clearly establish the context of Piet's miraculous vision—the aloe reasserts her hold on the poetic imagination and affirms once more the poet's faith in the "living heart" beneath the rocky and unpromising surface of Africa (Coetzee 168). To Gladys, who rejects the wild sweetness of the aloe, the "lesson" it teaches is the appalling cost of survival—thorns, bitterness, a turgid violence. She knows nothing of the scarlet spikes of *aloe aborescens* with its nectar-filled cups for the *suikerbekkie* birds, or the defiant flowering of *aloe ferox* in the desolate veld, or *aloe ciliaris* pushing through the undergrowth to find the sun. Over and against the demonstrative lesson in survival is a wonderfully evocative image of uncommon beauty and defiance and a miracle of natural variation and difference which resists man's habitual attempts to codify, and classify, and separate. If one of the play's political "lessons" advocates a counter-revolutionary philosophy of stoical endurance, another surely celebrates Nature's resistance to the fetters and shackles of man-made systems. But beyond all the didactic "messages" spoken in the play, there is a peculiarly South African Romanticism in Piet's sympathetic affinity with the aloe, the kinship (in Perseus Adams's words) that "carries the undertow of twelve deep / Seasons together":

> What a bane it must be to the cold heart of Death
> That beauty could rise and be stronger than this
>   heat.

Survival is not merely a matter of weathering the "dry white season" of the Nationalist regime, naively trusting in a change of heart and political climate. It inheres in the one quality Piet shares with Gladys's mother: "a terrible determination not to die," not to succumb to the congealment of spirit in the ice-cave of apartheid. The cold heart of Death has already claimed Steve Daniels and Gladys. What they cannot understand in Piet is his determination to endure the futility of his commitment to a politically uninhabitable country. What can "home" possibly mean to a socially displaced and ideologically suspect Afrikaner? His condition at the end of the play, as Fugard describes it, is one he shares with Beckett's lonely protagonists: "face-to-face with himself . . . the absurdity of himself, *alone*." It is, again, a peculiarly South African variation on a European existential theme.

Piet's identity would seem, initially, unassailable. He knows who he is and, like an aloe, finds himself "at home" in the South African landscape:

> For better or for worse, I will remain positively identified as Petrus Jacobus Bezuitenhout; Species, Afrikaner; Habitat, Algoa Park, Port Elizabeth, in this year of our Lord, 1963 . . . and accept the consequences.

This sounds unappealingly like the sort of South African bloody-mindedness that one associates with Afrikaner Nationalism—the defiant political arrogance, contemptuous of consequence, that typified the Nationalist Party triumphs of 1963: the smashing of resistance movements under the Sabotage Act, the abrogation of *habeas corpus* under the Detention laws, the imposition of stringent censorship controls under the Publications and Entertainment Act, and the arrest and imprison-ment of Mandela and other White, Black and Indian dissidents. But the early 1960s were also witness to the emergence of a radically alternative form of Afrikanerdom: the "Sestigers" who resisted censorship of their writing and were denounced as traitors, ostracized from the community, their books publicly burned and their publishers threatened (Brink and Coetzee 10); a courageous group of Dutch Reformed Churchmen and intellectuals—among them Professor Geyser and Beyers Naude—incapable of reconciling Scripture and Apartheid, and consequently denounced as apostates and heretics (Lelyveld 277–314); and an indeterminate number of "ordinary, good-natured, harmless, unre-markable" Afrikaners (Brink 9), like Fugard's Piet or André Brink's Ben Du Toit, whose humanity is outraged by the system, and whose defection from the Tribe brands them as *kafferboeties* ["n———-lovers"] and *hensoppers* ["Boer War traitors"]. It soon becomes manifestly clear that Piet Bezuitenhout is just such a dissident Afrikaner, and that "accepting the consequences" of his betrayal of the *volk* is the defining aspect of his absurd endurance—clinging to an idea of "home" in a country "harsh as banishment," expending his "thorn-riddled love" in a land where his roots no longer find the space creation intended for them, confident of his own integrity on a political stage where others cast him in the role of an *impimpi*. In a world devoid of trust, all human action suddenly becomes absurd—a cautious playing of parts in relationships riddled with uncertainty and doubt. In the final analysis, it is Piet who is betrayed by the appalling failure of others to recognize his essential goodness.

Piet's story is that of the grass-roots Afrikaner, politically naive and unsophisticated, whose consciousness is raised by his own humanitarian response to the harsh circumstances of South African life and the misery of the Black and Coloured people. The death of a child on his drought-stricken farm, the defiant dignity of the Coloureds who refuse to ride the Cadles buses, the discovery that "politics" begins in human sympathy and solidarity: the discontinuous narrative sections of the play trace the unexceptional history of an Afrikaner "common man," a simple farmer, whose tragedy is inseparable from the tragedies of the other racial groups in the 1960s. In a sense, it is the African farm that fosters both the humanity and the naïveté. Race relations, as Piet V. puts it in Fugard's *Notebooks* have no place on a farm where Black and White children play together in friendship, and where the old Afrikaner tradition of household prayers takes place in a gathering which recognizes no racial differences. Piet's Xanadu is, in some ways, an anachronistic urban replication of this aspect of the South African farm, sharing with it the same isolation from rough "boer-boy" politics, the same unworldliness of Liberal idealism which Piet has pieced together from a Palgrave's Golden Treasury of Political Thought. Like his impassioned recitation of Longfel-low's "The Slave's Dream," his aspirations and ideas are simultaneously comic, pathetic, and deeply moving.

They are also contradictory, confused, and "banal" (Vandenbroucke 175) to those who demand that political drama advocate political solutions to the South African predicament. If an evil system is not a natural disaster and men can make this a better world to live in, how can Piet's stoical determination to endure change the situation? "What sort of significant action is that," asks Nadine Gordimer, "in terms of the contest of our country?" (Seidenspinner 339). The point, however, is that Piet's attitudes are challenged consistently throughout the play in an attempt to define the absurdity of his final resolution. "I am . . . surprised," says Gladys, voicing the single most insistent objection to the play's politics, "at how easily you

accept the situation." To which he replies, "I don't accept it easily, but there is nothing else to do. I can't change human nature." For the Marxist "significant action"—through revolutionary violence, if necessary—will alter the situation and make a better world in which human nature can flourish. But for Fugard, if bad laws and social injustice are to be unmade by men, it may be necessary to change human nature as precondition for significant action. We can make a better world, he would seem to imply, by being better people; but insofar as "human nature" has been conditioned by the psychopathology of apartheid to deny love and trust and faith as the only strategies for resistance against the "cold heart of Death," what *political* solution can there be? Even Gladys, in her irresistible urge to violate the "goodness" of her husband, succumbs to deadly thoughts. Did he collude in the police raid on her private property? Is he one of the Special Branch? It is not only Steve Daniels whom she deliberately infects with such suspicion, but the audience as well. The deadliest moment in the play is Gladys's response, at the end of Act One, to the shame and humiliation that overwhelm Piet at the thought of being branded an *impimpi*. "It's not true, is it?" she asks. His answer is a shocked silence. If wife and friend can believe such outrage, what point is there in denial? And what possible action can be taken when the greatest contest of the country is the havoc wreaked on human nature by the operation of the Nationalist Party regime on human connections?

Can a writer so passionately identified with his country, clinging so vainly to an outmoded Liberal ethic, and bound by his own Afrikaner heritage into such sympathy with his protagonist ever provide a viable alternative to the South African predicament? Many of his critics point to a career of failure and despair, withdrawal from action, and guilt. "He has dreamt of a 'superman'," writes Margarete Seidenspinner, "but has finally identified with Piet Bezuitenhout, the 'victim' of the system whose only wish is to survive, a notion whose pessimism has created a very strong antipathy in many South African spectators." It is a curious "victim," however, who refuses to compromise his humanity, who *chooses* his mode of survival—neither compelled by the State into exile, nor driven ineluctably into insanity—and whose pessimism is held in a delicate balance with an absurd form of hope. At the end of the play, Piet Bezuitenhout is left contemplating the same unidentifiable aloe that eluded categorization at the beginning. Aloe Anonymous? Some improbable new species, like nothing else in South African botanical records? The final sympathetic affinity that binds the Man and the Aloe is their anomalous and mutant identity—unnamable first specimens in an evolutionary, grassroots change that begins with one ordinary and unremarkable individual finding his "home" in a world not programmed for his survival. Is there, finally, a *name* that fits a subversive Afrikaner who refuses to relinquish his drought-stricken tradition, whose defection from Afrikanerdom has left him without tribal connections, rejected and ostracized by a Brotherhood of which he is the conscience of the tribe? To the Afrikaner majority he is "kafferboetie" and "hensopper." To the Liberal minority he is "impimpi." To the political Left he is a compromising counter-revolutionary evasionary. To Fugard he is an absurdly courageous pessimist, an answer to the death of spirit in the South African ice-cave, and an indomitable survivor like Perseus Adams's Aloe-woman: . . . "Though the silence and loneliness have beaten / The walls of my identity and failed." The hope, in 1963, was that the species would take root and spread and that a new generation of "Verligte" [Enlightened] Liberal Afrikaners would engage in the dialectics of South African history. It would be naive to claim any validity for this prophetic expectation when the "Verligte" movement in Afrikanerdom has been so brutally offset by an extreme Right wing backlash—the "Verkramptes," whose electoral victory has made them the official parliamentary opposition. But the Piet Bezuitenhouts are an undeniable term in the South African political argument, as indigenous a species, now, as the Aloe Aborescens. Their survival may be tenuous and endangered (Ben Du Toit in Brink's novel is murdered by the Special Branch); but Fugard's play, "in celebration" of his Afrikaner mother, Elizabeth Magdalena Potgieter, also celebrates the "absurd" goodness and decency which remain the Liberal's weapons against all attempts to destroy him.

Source: Errol Durbach, "Surviving in Xanadu: Athol Fugard's *Lesson from Aloes*," in *Ariel: A Review of International English Literature*, Vol. 20, No. 1, January 1989, pp. 9–21.

SOURCES

Collins, Michael J., "The Sabotage of Love: Athol Fugard's Recent Plays," in *World Literature Today*, Vol. 57, No. 3, Summer 1983, pp. 369, 370.

Fink, Joel G., Review of *A Lesson from Aloes*, in *Theatre Journal*, Vol. 33, No. 3, October 1981, pp. 398, 399.

Fugard, Athol, *A Lesson from Aloes*, Theatre Communications Group, 1981.

Molyneaux, Gerard, Review of *A Lesson from Aloes*, in *Library Journal*, June 15, 1981, p. 1319.

Roberts, Sheila, "'No Lessons Learnt': Reading the Texts of Fugard's *A Lesson from Aloes* and *Master Harold . . . and the Boys*," in *English in Africa*, Vol. 9, No. 2, October 1982, p. 33.

FURTHER READING

Colleran, Jeanne, "Athol Fugard and the Problematics of the Liberal Critique," in *Modern Drama*, Vol. 38, 1995, pp. 389–407.
> Colleran examines Fugard's depiction of liberalism in South Africa, including an analysis of its failure as depicted in *A Lesson from Aloes*.

Fugard, Athol, *Notebooks 1960–1977*, Knopf, 1984.
> In these notebooks, Athol records autobiographical information, including his experience with people who inspired *A Lesson from Aloes*.

Mshengu, "Political Theatre in South African and the Work of Athol Fugard," in *Theater Research International*, Vol. 7, No. 3, 1982, pp. 160–79.
> In this article, Mshengu argues that Fugard's whiteness and privileged class have caused him to ignore in his plays certain realities of Africans' experience in South Africa.

Von Staden, Heinrich, "An Interview with Athol Fugard," in *Theater*, Vol. 14, No. 1, 1982, pp. 41–46.
> In this interview, Fugard talks about his ambivalent feelings toward South Africa and how those feelings emerge in his plays.

Wilderson, Frank, III, *Incognegro: From Black Power to Apartheid and Back*, Beacon Press, 2007.
> The literary memoir of a revolutionary, this book tells the thrilling story of an African American who lived a double life during the years from 1991 to 1996, teaching in universities in Johannesburg and Soweto during the day, and at night participating in the armed branch of the African National Congress. The book gives one view of the political intrigue that marked the final years of apartheid.

The Prisoner of
Second Avenue

NEIL SIMON

1973

Neil Simon, one of the most popular of twentieth-century American dramatists, is known for his comedies that often examine the tensions that can arise among family members or between men and women living in New York. In his play, *The Prisoner of Second Avenue*, which ran on Broadway for 788 performances beginning in 1973, Simon's comedy turns darker as he explores the devastating effect that city life can have on a middle-aged couple. In early 1970s, when the play takes place, New York City was beset by financial problems, high crime, and strikes that made daily life often inconvenient and sometimes dangerous. The play chronicles Mel and Edna's struggle to survive city life, coupled with noisy neighbors, faulty plumbing, and the loss of employment, and to maintain a measure of dignity in the process.

AUTHOR BIOGRAPHY

Neil Simon was born on July 4, 1927, in the Bronx, New York, to Irving, a garment salesman, and Mamie Simon. He grew up in Washington Heights, Manhattan, during the Great Depression. After he graduated from high school, Simon joined the army and wrote for military publications while he took classes at New York University and the University of Denver.

After his discharge in 1946, "Doc" Simon, a nickname he earned as a child from impersonating

Neil Simon   © Bettman/Corbis. Reproduced by permission

the family doctor, began a career as a comedy writer for several television shows, including *The Phil Silvers Show* and Sid Caesar's *Your Show of Shows*. In 1961, when his first play, *Come Blow Your Horn*, appeared on Broadway, Simon turned his talents to playwriting.

Several of Simon's plays have autobiographical elements taken from his childhood as well as his relationships with his four wives, including dancer Joan Baim, who died while they married, an event that inspired Simon's *Chapter Two*, and actress Marsha Mason, who starred in several stage and film versions of his plays. Plays influenced by events in his childhood often involve coming-of-age stories, while those that reflect his marriages explore the tensions that can develop between men and women in relationships.

Simon has received Emmy Awards for his television work, the Tony Award for Best Play for *The Odd Couple* in 1965, for *Barefoot in the Park* in 1966, for *Sweet Charity* in 1968, for *Plaza Suite* in 1969, for *Promises, Promises* in 1970, for *Last of the Red Hot Lovers* in 1972, for *The Prisoner of Second Avenue* in 1973, and for *The Sunshine Boys* in 1978. In 1975, he was awarded a special Tony Award for his overall contributions to the theater. He has earned several other writing and drama

awards as well as Oscar nominations. He was elected to the Theater Hall of Fame in 1983 and received a Pulitzer Prize for Drama in 1991 for *Lost in Yonkers*. Simon was honored at the Kennedy Center in 1995, and in 2006, he received the Mark Twain Prize for American Humor. *The Prisoner of Second Avenue* is available in *The Collected Plays of Neil Simon*, volume two, which was published by Plume in 1979.

PLOT SUMMARY

Act 1, Scene 1

The Prisoner of Second Avenue takes place in a Manhattan apartment from midsummer to December, most likely in 1971. Mel and Edna Edison have been living on the fourteenth floor in this small apartment for six years. When the play opens, Mel is sitting alone anxiously in the dark at 2:30 a.m., moaning "Ohhh, Christ Almighty," which wakes up Edna. When she asks him what is wrong, he replies, "Nothing," and tells her to go back to bed, but then he keeps moaning. She soon gets him to admit that he cannot sleep because it is freezing in the apartment due to the broken air conditioner and asks what she can do to make him feel more comfortable. She notes that he has been tense for a week.

Mel then complains about the ugly pillows on the couch and declares that he is tired of the apartment, the building, and the entire city as they listen to the jarring street noises. He claims that he is more sensitive to noise, including the ones emanating from the apartment next door, where two German stewardesses entertain nightly guests. As he bangs on the wall, yelling at them to be quiet, he cracks it. Mel then orders Edna to call the superintendent in the morning and demand that the crack be fixed, along with the air conditioning and running toilet, insisting that he will not pay for any of it.

When Mel admits that tranquilizers no longer help calm him down, Edna begins to worry about him, which sets him off on a rant about everything that is wrong with the city and the world, including the lack of safe, good tasting food and the smell of garbage that permeates the air. Edna argues that he has to accept city life or leave Manhattan, but Mel insists that he will stay and exercise his right to protest. After he yells at a barking dog from his terrace, voices from above tell him to be quiet, but he just hollers back at them.

When Edna tries to get him to calm down, he screams at her. After he finally starts to relax a bit, he admits that he has not been sleeping well and

MEDIA ADAPTATIONS

- Melvin Frank directed a film version of the play in 1975, starring Jack Lemmon and Anne Bancroft, with a screenplay by Simon. Bancroft subsequently received a BAFTA Film Award nomination, and Simon was nominated for a WGA Screen Award. The film was available as of 2006.

- L. A. Theatre Works's unabridged cassette version, produced in 2001 and read by Richard Dreyfuss and Marsha Mason, was available as of 2006.

that he feels he is losing control. Edna tries to reassure him that everyone is feeling that way in the city and suggests that he go back to his analyst. Mel tells her though that the doctor is dead and that therapists cost too much anyway.

When Mel declares that he is worried about losing his job, Edna says that they could move somewhere that does not cost as much, but Mel refuses to take her advice seriously. Then the stewardesses from next door call and complain about the noise, which sets Mel off on a tirade again, insisting that Edna "bang back" on the wall. The scene ends with the voice of news commentator Roger Keating, reporting on the long list of the city's problems.

Act 1, Scene 2

A few days later, Edna has come into the apartment and discovered that they have been robbed. When Mel comes home, she explains that she went to the store for a short while, and since she lost the door key, she left the apartment unlocked. The robbers took everything, including the liquor and Mel's suits. Edna is frightened, while Mel fumes to the point where he loses control, screaming and throwing ashtrays on the floor. He then admits that he was fired four days earlier but did not tell her because he hoped that he could find a new job. As he promises that he will find something, Edna insists that she has confidence in him.

Mel gets increasingly agitated about their lack of money as Edna tries to calm him down, telling him that they will get by. As he rants about the money that they have spent on useless things and about how he was mistreated by his company, a voice from an above apartment calls down to him to quiet down. When he refuses and yells back at the voice as he is standing on his terrace, he gets hit with a bucket of water from above, which drenches him. The scene closes with Edna wiping him off, trying to assure him that everything will work out.

Act 2, Scene 1

Approximately six weeks later in mid-September, Mel is wandering around the apartment in his bathrobe, grimmer and angrier than in the first act. When Edna comes home from her job as a secretary to make him lunch, she rushes, since she only has half an hour. She has a difficult time getting Mel to talk to her. He admits that he is frustrated by his failed attempts to find a job and humiliated by the fact that Edna is working.

He then begins to explain to Edna that "the social-economical-and-political-plot-to-undermine-the-working-classes-in-this-country" is preventing him from finding a job. He has heard this on the radio talk shows and believes that "the human race" has hatched this "very sophisticated, almost invisible" plot "to destroy the status quo" and insists that he is a victim of it.

Edna gets increasingly agitated during this rant to the point where she determines that he needs to see a therapist. While Mel ignores her and begins to plan his revenge, which involves burying those trying to destroy him with snow, Edna calls the doctor, insisting that her husband must see him as soon as possible. The scene closes again with the voice of Roger Keating, reporting that the governor has been mugged and that city workers are on strike.

Act 2, Scene 2

Two weeks later, Mel's brother Harry and three sisters, Pauline, Pearl, and Jessie, meet at Mel's to discuss his situation and how they can help. The sisters talk about Mel's childhood while Harry tries to get them focused on Mel's financial troubles. He proposes that they all chip in to pay for Mel's doctor bills, but the sisters are reluctant to finance them if they last more than a few months. Harry, however, insists that Mel is their responsibility and deserves their help for as long as he needs it.

When Edna arrives, Harry proposes his plan, and she is deeply touched but asks if they could buy a summer camp for him instead. Edna is certain that if Mel gets out of the city and into the country, he will regain his mental health. After Harry rejects the plan, arguing that Mel does not have any business sense, a heavily sedated Mel appears after just having taken a walk. The scene ends with the voice of Stan Jennings, who has taken over reporting duties from Roger Keating after the latter was mugged.

Act 2, Scene 3

Six weeks later, in mid-December, Edna is on the phone, trying to get someone to restore the water and electricity to the apartment. When Mel arrives, he declares that he is not going back to his incompetent doctor and will instead work out his problems himself. Edna, who is getting increasingly upset about the lack of water and electricity, tearfully tells Mel that her company has gone bankrupt, and she is out of a job. Like Mel had done at the beginning of the play, Edna begins to rant about all of the city's problems, claiming that all she wants is to be able to take a bath. She implores Mel to bang on the pipes as she banged on the wall for him to try to get someone to pay attention to her. In order to calm her, Mel agrees to move with her out of the city.

Harry arrives, offering Mel money for the summer camp. When Mel refuses, Harry leaves, and he and Edna argue about Harry's offer. Their shouts prompt a voice from above to tell them to shut up. As Mel tries to apologize to his neighbor, he is hit again with a bucket of water. As he stands on the terrace in a state of shock, it starts to snow. Edna and Mel look at each other, and he goes to the closet and takes out his shovel. The play closes with Roger Keating's voice, warning residents of the upcoming snow storm and asking them to work together to shovel everyone out.

CHARACTERS

Edna Edison

Edna Edison is a loving, supportive wife whose main concern is her husband's welfare. She has adopted a traditional role in marriage, taking care of the household while her husband works outside of the home. When he becomes agitated about their living conditions, she tries to offer alternatives that she thinks will benefit both of them and continually tries to revitalize his confidence in himself. She is not a dishrag, however. When Mel gets verbally

abusive, she stands her ground, insisting that he treat her with respect.

When Edna is forced to switch roles with Mel, she tries to devote herself to her job while maintaining her steadfast support of her husband. She rushes home to prepare his lunch and check up on his emotional state, running herself ragged in the process. As a result, she experiences the same level of frustration as Mel has endured and so ends up collaborating with his plans for vengeance by the end of the play.

Harry Edison

Harry Edison, Mel's older brother, generously offers to pay for Mel's therapy, even amid the protests of his sisters who are worried about how long it will take to cure him. Harry is confident of his own judgment that Mel has no business sense and so initially refuses to give him money for a summer camp. Yet his loyalty to his brother eventually supersedes his concerns, and he decides to give the money unconditionally. Simon suggests that Harry could be motivated by his desire to be the favorite in the family, a position, he claims, he never achieved.

Jessie Edison

Jessie Edison criticizes her brother Mel but insists that, since he is the baby of the family, his behavior must be excused. She does not want to think about the implications of his present behavior and tries to comfort Mel when he arrives at the apartment. Her tears betray her concerns about him, yet she would rather go shopping than face the reality of his situation.

Mel Edison

Since Mel Edison has adopted the traditional role of head of the household, his ego takes a major blow when he loses his job and can no longer support himself and his wife. At that point, the tensions that he has lived with for six years become overwhelming and cause him to harbor paranoid notions that he is the victim of a conspiracy to undermine the working class in the United States. He tries to maintain his sanity by venting his emotions and lashing out to those closest to him, including his wife and his neighbors.

His inability to cope with the pressures he faces causes a mental breakdown. Simon glosses over the details behind his recovery but suggests that his departure from corporate America helps to restore his self esteem and his sanity. He reveals the magnanimous side of his nature when he is ready

TOPICS FOR FURTHER STUDY

- Neil Simon wrote the screenplay for *The Out of Towners*, a film about a young Ohio couple vacationing in New York who are forced to face many of the same problems that drive Mel and Edna to the brink of insanity. View the film and compare and contrast the couples and their response to the chaos of the city. How do you account for the differences? Prepare a PowerPoint demonstration comparing *The Prisoner of Second Avenue* and this film.

- After researching the subject of coping mechanisms, prepare to lead a discussion of how Mel

and Edna could have found healthier ways to remedy their situation.

- Determine if all of the events announced by the reporter at the end of most scenes in the play really happened. Prepare a report that presents an in-depth look at the problems New York City faced in the late 1960s and 1970s. Include a discussion of whether those problems were resolved.

- Write a story or autobiographical essay that focuses on the frustrations of urban living.

---

to forgive his neighbor for her slanderous assault on Edna, but when he is humiliated a second time by her, his need for revenge overtakes his humanity, and he plots her destruction.

Pauline Edison

Pauline Edison defends her brother Mel against her sisters' attacks. She has always found excuses for his behavior. She also seems more grounded in reality than her two sisters, consistently correcting their memories about him.

Pearl Edison

Pearl Edison is the most practical sister and tries to control all of her siblings, insisting to Edna, "We just want to do the right thing."

THEMES

Male and Female Roles

Simon characterizes Mel as a traditional man who is devastated when he loses his job because that is what defines him. He has tolerated all of the irritations of daily city life for six years until he is fired, which causes him to feel worthless. His wife becomes an outlet for his anger and frustration as well as those nearby who threaten his peace. Edna also plays a traditional role at the beginning of the play as she suffers with Mel through the troubles

that arise, remaining supportive by continually trying to assure Mel that everything will work out for them. However, there is a limit to the abuse that she will take. Proving herself to be more rational than her husband, Edna tries to get him to recognize that she is living in the same situation with the same set of problems and that "you either live with it or you get out."

Their roles reverse, however, along with their temperaments, when Edna gets a job. Mel then becomes the more passive member of the family, caused in part by his medication, taking long walks around the city and beginning to work through his problems. This time, when the neighbor yells down to them to be quiet, Mel apologizes rather than feeling that he has to stand up to her. Ironically, Edna adopts this role, baiting the woman regarding the water she threw down previously at Mel. The tensions of working in the city, coupled with the other indignities of life there, have made her as tense and irritable as Mel has been, especially when she is fired as well. By reversing traditional roles for men and women and creating similar consequences for each, Simon illustrates the damaging effects that living in an urban jungle can have on an individual, male or female.

Imprisonment

Mel feels imprisoned by his world, surrounded by nameless, faceless tormentors who compound

COMPARE & CONTRAST

- **1971:** Between 1965 and 1971, reported crime rates in New York City rise by 91 percent.

  Today: Violent crime rates go down in the United States and in New York during the first years of the twenty-first century, but in 2005, they start to rise again.

- **1971:** On January 14, twenty-five thousand members of Patrolmen's Benevolent Association in New York City go on strike.

Today: Labor unions are weakened by plant closings, especially those in the auto industry and in job outsourcing to overseas companies where labor is cheaper.

- **1971:** On June 13, racists attack a Puerto Rican Day Parade in New York City, which results in hundreds being injured.

  Today: Minorities have gained prominent positions in business and government, including former secretary of state Colin Powell and Hispanic senator Jon Corzine.

---

his misery. After he loses his job, the walls of the small apartment close in on him as he paces back and forth into every corner. The apartment becomes a microcosm of the city. Whether he is inside freezing or outside roasting, "Either way," Mel claims, "they're going to get me." Mel sees no exit from this prison, eventually acknowledging that he is too old to play baseball or begin a new career running a summer camp. By the end of the play, the city has defeated Mel, who is reduced to fantasizing about revenge plots. In all, the play seems darkly about how an individual is powerless to create change in a certain kind of urban landscape fraught with its own difficulties.

STYLE

Black Humor

C. Hugh Holman and William Harmon define "black humor" as "the use of the morbid and the absurd for darkly comic purposes in modern fiction and drama." Simon uses both verbal and situational black humor to express Mel's bitter response to his situation as well as its absurdity. Mel uses verbal humor in the form of sarcasm and self-deprecation as a defense mechanism. He tries to alleviate his own sense of failure by belittling his

wife, when, for example, Edna suggests that they move to another country where the cost of living is cheaper, Mel responds: "All right, call a travel agency. Get two economy seats to Bolivia. We'll go to Abercrombie's tomorrow, get a couple of pith helmets and a spear gun." He tries to poke fun at his own situation and thereby lighten it when, after Edna demands, "Don't talk to me like I'm insane," he responds, "I'm halfway there, you might as well catch up."

Situational black humor occurs throughout the play, most notably at the end of each act when Mel is drenched with the water. Both instances provide comic relief in the form of slapstick comedy, but they also are moments of intense humiliation for Mel that heighten his angst, revealing the uselessness of his attempts to fight back against the injustices of his world.

HISTORICAL CONTEXT

New York City in the Early 1970s

Sheridan Morley, in his review of the play for *Spectator*, writes that *The Prisoner of Second Avenue* "deals with a moment in history when not only the central character but Manhattan itself was on the brink of a total nervous collapse." The events that occurred in 1971, the probable year in

Anne Bancroft and Jack Lemmon in the film version of Neil Simon's The Prisoner of Second Avenue
The Kobal Collection

which the action of the play takes place, illustrate this pervasive deterioration. City police went on strike along with eight thousand state, county, and municipal employees and local members of the Communications Workers of America. Crime rates soared while two city policemen were murdered and participants in a Puerto Rican Day Parade were attacked. In September, riots broke out in New York State's Attica Prison, which lasted for several days. When order was restored, thirty-two prisoners and eleven guards and police were dead.

Social institutions were strained to the breaking point in the 1970s. Rising rates of inner city poverty, drug use, and youth crime overwhelmed police and social services. Many residents, especially the white middle class, fled the city, eroding the tax base. By the end of the decade, almost a million people had left the city, a population loss that would not be regained for twenty years. All of these factors contributed to the fiscal crisis that emerged in the 1970s, which pushed New York to the edge of financial collapse. Mayor John Lindsey feared that he would have to declare the city bankrupt. Initially, President Gerald Ford refused to provide federal money for the city, but after

severe criticism from the New York City press, he eventually approved a loan.

CRITICAL OVERVIEW

While some of Neil Simon's plays are not well received by critics, audiences love just about all of them. *The Prisoner of Second Avenue*, however, earned some strong reviews like the one from Cliff Glaviano in the *Library Journal*, who writes, "Simon takes a good look at apartment life, career and role reversals, a nervous breakdown, and the love, torture, care, or inertia that somehow keeps a couple in a relationship for many years." He praises both the style of this "classic American comedy" that "at points" is "laugh-out-loud funny" and filled with "fast-moving dialog with nonstop Simon quips and jokes" as well as its themes, claiming that "it offers sensitive insight into the human condition."

In his review for the *Los Angeles Times*, Philip Brandes criticizes "dramatic ironies so broad you could drive a truck through." He also finds fault with "those relentless one-liners, capping dialogue that predictably opts for cleverness at the expense of truth," as when "a Simonized breakdown polishes the rough edges of schizophrenia to more comfortable contours." Yet he concludes, "while the production has its problems, it works in unexpected ways," especially in the darkness of its comedy.

Sheridan Morley, in his review for *Spectator*, finds "a couple of rather uneasy comic turns in a curiously and uncharacteristically clumsy construction," noting that four of the play's characters appear only at the end of act 2.

Reviewers disagree over whether the play is dated. Brandes claims that it is, along with Morley who calls it "a time-warped slice of urban history." Yet Glaviano insists that if the audience can "add a cellular phone or two, . . . it's life in 2000."

CRITICISM

Wendy Perkins

Perkins is a professor of twentieth-century American and British literature and film. In the following essay, she examines the play's theme of urban survival.

Neil Simon's *The Prisoner of Second Avenue* is set in Manhattan during the early 1970s, a time of great turmoil for New York City as it struggled to deal with a fiscal crisis, high crime rates, and population loss. In his article, "The Ominous Apple," Peter Tietzman notes that the play was a response to Simon's negative view of the city during that period. As quoted by Tietzman, Simon claims: "people were so alienated and so fearful that they were separating themselves from contact. And not without cause." The play is his "statement about those urban ills" as well as his exploration of how the system's failures can cause an erosion of humanity as each individual's primary motive becomes survival.

When the play opens, middle-aged Mel Edison is beset by problems in his small, overpriced, Manhattan apartment. When he and Edna moved in six years ago, Simon explains in the stage directions, *"they thought they were getting . . . all the modern luxuries and comforts of the smart, chic East Side. What they got is paper-thin walls and a view of five taller buildings from their terrace."* They also acquired a broken air conditioner that refuses to go above twelve degrees and music coming through the walls from the apartment next

> BY THE END OF THE PLAY, MEL HAS SURVIVED HIS NERVOUS BREAKDOWN, BUT EDNA'S LOSS OF EMPLOYMENT CAUSES TENSIONS TO RISE AGAIN AS THE TWO BEGIN ARGUING ABOUT ACCEPTING MONEY FROM HIS BROTHER."

door where German airline stewardesses nightly entertain a steady stream of men. Any attempts to relieve the annoyances inevitably fail: when Edna tried to get the superintendent to fix the air conditioner, he could not find anything wrong with it, and when Mel tries to quiet down the stewardesses, he bangs on the wall, cracking it but getting no other response.

Mel's troubles are not confined to his apartment. The city itself seems to be conspiring against him. The temperature outside is a sweltering eighty-nine degrees at 2:30 in the morning, and traffic noise and the stink from uncollected garbage seep in even with the windows closed. Inside or out, Mel claims, "Either way they're going to get me."

The noise and the stink and the freezing temperature, however, are not the primary reasons Mel cannot sleep. He paces his apartment in the middle of the night because he has lost his job. After revenues declined three million dollars that year, his company fired forty-three people in one afternoon. Mel understands how difficult it will be to find another job at age forty-seven in a city that is facing fiscal crisis. Although he declares to Edna, "I still have value, I still have worth," Mel later admits that his situation has begun to scare him. He tells her, "I'm unraveling . . . I'm losing touch . . . I don't know where I am half the time . . . or who I am any more. I'm disappearing."

Mel's frustrations and fears cause him to lash out at everyone in his immediate vicinity, including Edna, repeatedly blaming others for his misery. He faults her for the broken air conditioner and toilet that will not stop running, insisting, "I asked you a million times to call that office" and then attacks her decorating skills, berating her for keeping "ugly little pillows" on the couch. As Edna tries to find remedies to their situation, suggesting that they could move out of the city, Mel becomes sarcastic and ridicules her ideas to the point where Edna declares, "Don't talk to me like I'm insane." His attacks on her increase in intensity until he ends up screaming at her.

Edna tries to deflect her husband's verbal assaults, arguing, "Mel, I'm a human being the same as you. I get hot, I get cold, I smell garbage, I hear noise," and declaring, "I'm not going to stand here and let you take it out on me." Yet Mel insists, "If you're a human being you reserve the right to complain, to protest. When you give up that right, you don't exist any more." His protests, in the form of rants against the city and outbursts directed toward his wife and his neighbors, work as a defense mechanism and so help him cope to a degree with his situation. Mel, however, has become a part of the problem, intensifying the angst of those around him, which inevitably redoubles his own.

The newscasts at the end of most scenes link Mel's troubles to those of other beleaguered New Yorkers who, like him, face municipal strikes, muggings, robberies, and unsanitary conditions. In his efforts to retain a measure of sanity, Mel lashes out at his neighbors, trying to exact revenge for the nuisances and humiliations he has suffered. They, however, are tormented by their own city-bred annoyances and so give it right back to him, which only increases his misery. At the end of the first act, after his rantings have prompted angry voices from the apartment above to insist that he lower his voice to prevent the children from waking up, Mel merely screams louder to the point where he is drenched with a bucket of water, the ultimate humiliation. He struggles to cope by fantasizing about burying the neighbors in a foot of snow in retaliation for the injustice.

The city's failure to improve living conditions for its citizens soon begins to drive Edna to the breaking point as well. She must endure her husband's tirades, his insistence that she keep banging on the walls to quiet the neighbors, and a significant loss when everything is stolen from their apartment. She faces the same pressures Mel had at work, when she accepts a secretarial position. She also worries each day about how to help Mel regain his mental health. When she eventually is fired, she wonders whether "the whole world [is] going out of business," and when the apartment loses electricity and water, Edna adopts Mel's tactics, insisting

that he bang on the pipes until the super restores the water so that she can take a bath.

By the end of the play, Mel has survived his nervous breakdown, but Edna's loss of employment causes tensions to rise again as the two begin arguing about accepting money from his brother. Their voices once more prompt other tenants to call down to them, but this time with a much more vitriolic tone, which generates a war of words between Edna and her neighbors. It appears though that Mel has learned to cope with the indignities of life in an urban jungle when he offers his apologies to the voice from above. Unfortunately, he only gets another bucket of water dumped on him for his troubles.

The play's final irony comes in the newscaster's call at the end of the play for New Yorkers to "live together and work together in a common cause" as a snowstorm threatens the city. While they watch the snow increasing in intensity, Mel, with Edna's silent approval, grabs the snow shovel from the closet, preparing for his revenge. Ultimately, through this final act of humiliation and subsequent plan for vengeance, Simon promotes a grudging respect for Mel and Edna in their refusal to be defeated by the city as they return to their survivors' mentality, determined to fight back in the urban warfare that has made them prisoners of Second Avenue.

Source: Wendy Perkins, Critical Essay on *The Prisoner of Second Avenue*, in *Drama for Students*, Thomson Gale, 2007.

Jackson R. Bryer

In the following interview, Simon discusses his work, how his playwrighting emerged from TV and radio writing, the plays and playwrights that impressed him, his writing process, and his evolution as a writer.

A critic has described Neil Simon as "relentlessly prolific." By virtually any accepted standard, he is the most successful playwright in the history of the American theatre. In thirty years, his 26 Broadway shows (including revivals of *Little Me* and *The Odd Couple*) have played a total of well over 15,000 performances. When *The Star-Spangled Girl* opened in December 1966, Simon had four Broadway productions running simultaneously. Despite this popular success and general critical approval, Simon did not win his first Tony Award for Best Play until 1985 (*Biloxi Blues*), although he had won the Tony for Best Author of a Play for *The Odd Couple* in 1965. His most recent play, *Lost in Yonkers*,

WHAT DO I READ NEXT?

- In Simon's romantic comedy *Barefoot in the Park* (1963), a young man and woman, whom the author claims are the younger version of Mel and Edna, struggle to cope with life in New York as they learn to adapt to each other's personality and temperament.

- Simon's autobiographical *Chapter Two* (1977) explores the pain a middle-aged New Yorker experiences after the death of his wife and the guilt he feels when he remarries soon after. That guilt causes major problems in his new relationship.

- *New York: An Illustrated History*, by Ric Burns, James Sanders, and Lisa Ades, was published in 2003 as a companion to Burns's popular PBS series. The authors supplement a comprehensive social and political history of the city with photographs, paintings, and newspaper headlines.

- Jane Mushabac and Angela Wigan's *A Short and Remarkable History of New York City* (1999) offers a brief but comprehensive overview of the city and a timeline of its development. The book is an excellent resource for those beginning a study of the city.

---

won both the Pulitzer Prize for Drama and the Tony Award for Best Play in 1991.

Simon's Broadway productions include the plays *Come Blow Your Horn* (1961), *Barefoot in the Park* (1963), *The Odd Couple* (1965), *The Star-Spangled Girl* (1966), *Plaza Suite* (1968), *Last of the Red-Hot Lovers* (1969), *The Gingerbread Lady* (1970), *The Prisoner of Second Avenue* (1971), *The Sunshine Boys* (1972), *The Good Doctor* (1973), *God's Favorite* (1974), *California Suite* (1977), *Chapter Two* (1977), *I Ought to Be in Pictures* (1980), *Fools* (1981), *Brighton Beach Memoirs* (1983), *Biloxi Blues* (1985), *Broadway Bound* (1986), *Rumors* (1988), and *Lost in Yonkers* (1991). His 1990 play, *Jake's Women*, closed before reaching New York. He has written the books for the musicals *Little Me* (1962), *Sweet Charity* (1966), *Promises, Promises* (1968), and *They're Playing Our Song* (1979). Besides the adaptations of several of his plays for the movies, his screenplays are *The Out-of-Towners*, *The Heartbreak Kid*, *Murder By Death*, *The Goodbye Girl*, *The Cheap Detective*, *Seems Like Old Times*, *Only When I Laugh*, *Max Dugan Returns*, *The Slugger's Wife*, and *The Marrying Man*.

Born, like George M. Cohan, on the Fourth of July, in 1927 in the Bronx, New York, he grew up there and in the Washington Heights section of Manhattan with his only sibling, his brother Danny.

He early received the nickname "Doc" for his ability to mimic the family doctor. When their parents, Irving (a garment salesman) and Mamie (who often worked at department stores to support the family during her husband's frequent absences), divorced, the two boys went to live with relatives in Forest Hills, Queens, and Simon attended high school there and at DeWitt Clinton in Manhattan. After brief military service at the end of World War II, he worked for several years with his brother as a comedy writer for radio and television. In 1953, he married Joan Baim, a dancer, who died of cancer in 1973. His second wife was actress Marsha Mason; he is now married to Diane Lander. He has two grown daughters and a step-daughter.

This interview was conducted on January 23, 1991, in Simon's suite at the Willard Hotel in Washington, DC, while he was preparing *Lost in Yonkers* (then playing at Washington's National Theatre) for its Broadway opening. The interview was transcribed by Drew Eisenhauer.

[*Bryer:*] *You always say that very early on you knew you wanted to be a playwright.*

[Simon:] I wanted to be a writer very early on. It's not quite true about the playwrighting thing. I started writing the first play when I was thirty and got it on when I was thirty-three, so that's fairly old to be starting as a playwright.

Most young people want to write poetry or want to write novels. When you knew you wanted to be a writer, was it always writing plays that you wanted to do?

I started out with different aims and ambitions. I grew up in the world of radio so the first couple of jobs I had were in radio and then television. I think I was setting my sights for film. I'm not quite sure when I decided to do plays. I know when I actually did so which was after years of working on *Your Show of Shows* with Sid Caesar, and *The Bilko Show*. I said I didn't want to spend the rest of my life doing this—writing for someone else— I wanted to do my own work. So I started writing the first play, *Come Blow Your Horn,* and it took me almost three years to do the twenty-some complete new versions before I got it on. When I did get it on, I said, "My God, three years!" and I was exhausted. I had only taken other little jobs just to make a living, since I had a wife and two children. But once the play hit, *Come Blow Your Horn* subsidized the next one which was a musical, *Little Me,* and that subsidized writing *Barefoot in the Park,* and then I was making enough money so I could do this full-time.

So, in a sense, your playwrighting grew out of writing for TV and radio in that writing for TV and radio was basically working within a dramatic form? That's what really led to the playwrighting.

Right. I started off just writing jokes for newspaper columns and things and then working on *Your Show of Shows* and *Bilko*. *Your Show of Shows* was writing sketches and *Bilko* was like a half-hour movie; so I was learning the dramatic form. Then I worked for about two years with Max Liebman, who was the producer of *Your Show of Shows*, doing specials. It was a very good education for me because we were updating pretty famous musical books of the past—*Best Foot Forward* and *Knickerbocker Holiday*. We would throw the book out completely and use the score; we would sort of follow the story line but use our own dialogue. So I was able to step in the footprints of previous writers and learn about the construction from them.

What was the purpose of those? Were they for television?

Yes. We did about twenty of them, two shows a month. One show would be a book show. A couple of them were originals; one was *The Adventures of Marco Polo*, and we used the music of Rimsky-Korsakoff. So I was really learning a lot about construction. I had made a few abortive attempts to write plays during that time—one with another writer on *The Bilko Show*—and it was going nowhere. I always had my summers off because in those days we did 39 shows a year on television in consecutive weeks and you had something like thirteen weeks off in the summer in which I would try to write plays; and I would say, "Wow, this is tough!" Finally, I went to California to do a television special—for Jerry Lewis of all people. I had quit *Your Show of Shows*—it had finally gone off the air—and so I was free-lancing. I went out there for six weeks. In about ten days I wrote the whole show and I said to Jerry Lewis, "What'll I do, I've got all this time?" He said, "I've got other things to do. Just do what you want until we go into rehearsal." And I started to write *Come Blow Your Horn*, which was almost a satirical or a farcical look at my upbringing with my parents. I was on the way but it took three years to do that, as I said.

As a child, and as a young adult, did you read plays and did you go to the theatre?

I went to the theatre. I read quite a good deal. I went to the library; I used to take out about three books a week, but they weren't about the theatre. It wasn't until I was about fourteen or fifteen that I saw my very first play, *Native Son*, the Richard Wright book and play.

A strange thing for a fourteen or fifteen year-old to go see, wasn't it?

There was a local theatre in upper Manhattan, in Washington Heights where I lived. It was called the Audubon Theatre. It used to be a movie house and then they used it for acts—sort of vaudeville acts but I wouldn't really call it vaudeville. They started doing that all over New York at the time when the theatre was truly flourishing. You not only played Broadway, you could go to Brooklyn and Manhattan and the Bronx and there were theatres that did their versions of plays that had closed on Broadway. So I went to this local theatre and saw *Native Son* and was mesmerized by what the theatre could do. I had also acted in plays in public school and in junior high school, so I had a little glimpse of that; but acting is a lot different from writing. I think that slowly, as my parents started to take me to the theatre more, mostly musicals (I remember seeing *Oklahoma!* ; it was—for its time—so innovative and so original), in the back of my mind I thought about that. But all during those years I was working with my brother and I thought that the only way to write a play was to do it by yourself, because one needed an individual point of view. Even if we were to write about our own family background, his point of view would be completely different from mine, and so it would get diminished somehow and watered down. When I wrote *Come Blow Your Horn,* I never even told him about it. It meant that I would have to make a break with him after ten years of writing together. The break was pretty traumatic. It was worse than leaving home because one expects that, but this was breaking up a partnership that he started because he was looking for a partner. He doesn't like to work by himself, and he always noticed and encouraged the sense of humor I had. I didn't have a sense of construction; he had that, and I was wonderful with lines and with the comedy concepts. Finally, when I did *Come Blow Your Horn,* I knew I had to step away. Partly I think it had to do with my being married; I began to feel my own oats and wanted the separation.

Can you speak at all about plays or playwrights that impressed you, influenced you, early or late?

Well, it was any good playwright. I didn't have favorites. In terms of comedy, I guess maybe Moss Hart and George S. Kaufman. A play that neither one of them wrote, Garson Kanin's *Born Yesterday,* I thought was a wonderful comedy, and I liked *Mr. Roberts* too; but I was as intrigued by the dramas as I was by the comedies. It wasn't until sometime later that I decided what I wanted to write was drama and tell it as comedy. I was such an avid theatregoer, especially when I first married Joan. You could go to the theatre then twice a week and not catch the whole season on Broadway and even off-Broadway. *Streetcar Named Desire* probably made the greatest impression on me, that and *Death of a Salesman.* These are not comedies. Although I knew I was not up to writing a drama as yet, I thought when I wrote something it would be from a comedy point of view.

If you could have written one play that was written by somebody else, what would that play be?

The question has been asked a lot and I generally say *A Streetcar Named Desire.* I have a certain affinity for that play; so does everyone else in America for that matter, I think. *Death of a Salesman* I thought was maybe the best American play I've ever seen—but it lacked humor. The humor that I saw in *Streetcar Named Desire* came out of a new place for humor. It came out of the character of Stanley Kowalski saying, "I have this lawyer acquaintance of mine" and talking about the Napoleonic Code. It was the way he talked that got huge laughs, and I knew that this was not comedy; it was character comedy and that's what I aimed for later on. If I were able to write a play, an American play, I would say it would be *Streetcar.*

The same quality is present in The Glass Menagerie, *too. That play also has some very funny moments in it, but they grow very organically out of Amanda and out of her situation.*

Yes. Even in Eugene O'Neill, who really lacks humor, I found humor in *Long Day's Journey,* in James Tyrone's meanness with money—turning out the light bulbs all the time and being so cheap. That was a play that I said to myself when I saw it, "I could never write that but I would love to write like that," to write my own *Long Day's Journey.* I have an oblique sense of humor; I see comedy—or humor, not comedy (there's a difference)—in almost everything that I've gone through in life, I'd say, with the exception of my wife's illness and death. Humor has become so wide open today that it's almost uncensored on television. It's all part of the game now. As I said, *Long Day's Journey* impressed me very much early on, and the writings of August Wilson impress me very much today. There's great humor in them and great sense of character and story-telling; it's almost old-fashioned playwrighting, in a way. There are not many playwrights who write like he does.

I think some of the humor in O'Neill comes from the Irish quality in those plays, the whole Sean O'Casey tradition of Irish drama where the humor and the seriouness are very closely juxtaposed; and I wonder whether there isn't something similar in the Jewish idiom, with humor coming out of serious situations. Do you feel that is a factor in your own plays?

I'm sure it is, but I find it a very difficult thing to talk about because I'm unaware of anything being particularly Jewish. This present play, *Lost in Yonkers,* is about a Jewish family but rarely is it mentioned or brought up. But the humor comes out of the Jewish culture as I know it. It's fatalistic; everything bad is going to happen. In the opening scene, the father talks about his troubles with his wife dying, being at a loss about what to do with the boys and so worried about how they're going to look well and be presented well to the grandmother. It's all out of fear; there's no sense of confidence, because he knows what he's up against. The mother is, I think, more German than Jew, because she was brought up in Germany, and her culture is German. So one doesn't ever get a picture that she was brought up in a Jewish home in which they paid attention to the services. I would doubt very much if they were Orthodox Jews. But it's there someplace, and it's so deeply embedded in me and so inherent in me that I am unaware of its quality. When I write something I don't think, "Oh, this is Jewish." At one time I thought I did, that I needed Jewish actors, but I found that people like Jack Lemmon or George C. Scott or Maureen Stapleton were equally at home with my material and they gave great performances. I rarely work with Jewish actors now; there are very few of them in *Lost in Yonkers.* However, in making the film of *Brighton Beach Memoirs,* when we did not get Jewish women to play the mother and the sister, it didn't sound right. Blythe Danner and Judith Ivey, as wonderful as they are, did not sound right. To the gentile ear it may not sound wrong, but still the audiences are aware that something is not quite organic. They don't know what it is; they can't name it. The difference came when Linda Lavin played in *Broadway Bound* and was right on the button and had the sense of truth. I think it's true too with O'Neill. He doesn't have to have Irish actors but Jewish actors playing O'Neill would have to have a very wide range to be able to do it well.

You have always said you stopped writing for TV because you wanted control, because you wanted to be on your own, not to have network executives and ad men running your creative life. But didn't the same sort of thing start to happen after a bit when you started to write for the stage, where producers like Saint-Subber wanted you to write a particular kind of play?

Saint used terms that no longer exist; they come from the turn of the century. He talked about "the carriage trade," those people, not necessarily Jewish, maybe New York society or wealthier people, who we wanted to appeal to as well. When I wrote *Barefoot in the Park* I think in an earlier version I made them a Jewish family without saying so. Saint said stay away from that because we're going to miss the carriage trade, so to speak; so maybe I was aware of it. Certainly it was in *The Odd Couple,* with Oscar Madison, only because Walter Matthau played it. I was aware of that in the beginning and then gradually got away from it until I got specifically Jewish when I was writing the autobiographical plays. In *Chapter Two,* something made me lean toward an actor like Judd Hirsch playing the leading character George because I knew the cadences and the attitudes came from me, so I thought that character had to be Jewish but I didn't call him Jewish. In these plays— I'm talking about "The Trilogy" (*Brighton Beach Memoirs, Biloxi Blues,* and *Broadway Bound*) and about *Lost in Yonkers*—they are Jewish families, you can't get away from it. Some plays are just not; *Barefoot in the Park* was not necessarily at all. *The*

Odd Couple has proven not to be because it's the most universal play I've written. They do it in Japan as often as they do it here now. It's done all over the world constantly because it is such a universal situation. Two people living together cannot get along all the time and it made it unique that it was two men. It seemed like such a simple idea that you thought surely someone would have written a play about it, but no one ever did up until that time. It was the idea or concept that made it so popular and then the execution.

Which of your plays gave you the most trouble and which was the easiest?

Rumors gave me the most trouble because of the necessities of farce. One has to get the audience to dispel their sense of truth, and they must believe in the premise even though we know it's about three feet off the ground. It has to be filled with surprises, and it has to move at a breakneck pace. People have to be in jeopardy constantly; the minute the jeopardy stops and they can sit back and relax, it's like a train that runs out of steam. And it has to be funny every minute. It was like constructing a murder mystery, an Agatha Christie mystery in which you are kept in suspense, only it had to go at a much greater pace than any of Agatha Christie's stories. I wanted to do it because I wanted to try the form. In a sense I was buoyed by watching an interview with Peter Shaffer, whom I respect enormously. I think he's a wonderful playwright. *Amadeus* is one of my favorite plays, again a play with a great concept—an original one—about professional jealousy. The interviewer said, "Why did you write *Black Comedy?*" And he said, "Well, it was a farce, and everyone wants to write one farce in their life." I had tried bits and pieces of it; the third act of *Plaza Suite,* with the father and mother trying to get the girl out of the locked bathroom, is a farce. But it only ran for thirty minutes and it wasn't a full-blown piece, so I wanted to try that. That was the most difficult. None of them come easy.

What happened with *Brighton Beach* was interesting. I wrote thirty-five pages and stopped and put it away for nine years; and when I came back to it, somehow the play had been written in my head over those nine years without thinking of it so I wrote it completely from beginning to end without stopping. But that's only the beginning of the process. You can never say any play is written easily because you write it once, and then you write it again, and then you write it again; then you have a reading of it, and then you go into rehearsal in which you write it ten more times. So they all present their difficulties. But I can't think of any one play where it was really easy, where I didn't have a difficult time with it.

Have your writing methods changed over the years? You say you wrote Come Blow Your Horn *twenty times. Is that still true, that you write a play over and over again, or do you find that you're getting better at it?*

If I do write it over and over and over again, it means that the play has some serious flaw. I wrote *Jake's Women* seven times, almost from beginning to end, before I put it on the stage; so I never really corrected the serious flaw. With this play, *Lost in Yonkers*, the first version was fairly close to what we have now. I did two more versions before we went into rehearsal but I had less trouble with the construction of the play. It just seemed to lead to the right thing. It has to do with the beginnings of the play, with how each of the characters is introduced and how each of them has his own problem. Manny Azenberg, our producer, has always said that if I reach page thirty-five it is almost always a "go" project. Sometimes I get to page twenty-five or so, and I start to look ahead and say, "What are you going to write about? What else could possibly happen?" I've come up with some wonderful beginnings of situations and don't always know where they're going but sort of know what they're going to be.

Billy Wilder, the director, once said to me (he was talking about a film but I think it applies to a play as well), "If you have four great scenes, you've got a hit." He says if you don't have those great scenes then you're not going to make it. When I wrote *The Sunshine Boys*, the whole play came to me at once in a sense. Since I fashioned it somewhat (even though I didn't know them) after the careers of Smith and Dale, and got the premise that they had not spoken to each other in eleven years and then they were being offered this job to work together and didn't want to speak to each other, I said, well, they've got to get together. That's the first funny interesting conflict, then the rehearsal, then the actual doing of the show on the air. I knew that they could cause great conflict and problems with each other, and then there would be the denouement of finally getting together. I said there's those four scenes. I don't think about that all the time, but that time I knew where it was going—there was a play there—so I sat down with some sense of confidence.

Others just unfold themselves. When I was writing *Lost in Yonkers*, I knew I had these four

characters in my mind. I had witnessed somebody who has this dysfunction of not being able to breathe properly and I never thought about using it; but it suddenly came to mind in this dysfunctional family which the mother has created. When you write you're always trying to catch up with your thoughts. They're ahead of you, like the carrot in front of the rabbit or the horse. If it's always there ahead of you then you know that each day that you go to work you will be able to write something. It's awful when you are writing a play and you get to page forty and you come to your office in the morning and say, "Well, what do I write today? Where does it go?" I want to leave it the night before saying to myself, "I know what that next scene is tomorrow" and I look forward to the next day.

How do you get started on a play? Do you usually start with an idea, or with a character?

First it starts with a desire, to write a play, and then the next desire is what kind of play do you want to write. When I finished *Broadway Bound*, I said I do not want to write another play like this right now. I've done a play that in degrees develops more seriously because I thought that *Broadway Bound* dealt more truthfully with my family and with the kind of writing I wanted to do than anything I had done in the past. I did not have an idea for the next one, and so sometimes you just play around with an idea. I said I wanted to write a farce, and I just sat down and thought of the opening premise. It literally started with how it looked. Most farces are about wealthy people. They're not about people who are poor because their lives are in conflict all the time. They must be satirical; you want to make jabs at them socially. These were all fairly prominent people, and I wanted them all to show up in black tie and their best gowns because I knew whatever it was that I was going to write they would be a mess at the end of the evening—either emotionally or physically—with their clothes tattered and torn. I thought of it as a mystery. I had no idea where it was going. The host had attempted suicide and was not able to tell them what happened, the hostess wasn't there, and there was no food: that's all I knew. I had read (I read a great deal of biographies of writers and artists) that Georges Simenon wrote most of his murder mysteries without knowing who was going to be murdered and who the murderer was. He picked a place, a set of situations, just something that intrigued him. I think almost anyone can sit down and write the first five pages of a murder mystery because you don't have to leave any clues. You just think of some wild situation that sounds interesting. It's only the really great mystery writers who know where to take it. *The Thin Man* is one of the most complicated books I've ever read. I don't think Dashiell Hammett is given enough credit. That's really literature, that book. What was your original question?

How you got the ideas for plays.

I never really can remember the moment, maybe with a few exceptions. *The Odd Couple* came out of watching my brother and the man he was living with at that time. They had both just gotten divorced, had decided to live together to cut down expenses, and they were dating girls. I said what an incredible idea for a play. *Barefoot* came out of my own experiences with my wife. Strangely enough, *Barefoot in the Park* started in Switzerland. The first version of it—this really happened—was when my wife and I went on our honeymoon to St. Moritz, Switzerland, met an elderly couple, and decided to go hiking with them. My wife then—Joan died in '73—was a wonderful athlete and she and the older man were practically jumping up this mountain while his wife and I staggered behind, and I was angry at Joan for being able to jump like a goat up this mountain. Then I realized that it had too exotic an atmosphere and I wanted to locate it in a place where one could relate to it more. I thought about that tiny apartment that we actually lived in that was five flights up and had a shower and no bath; it had a hole in the skylight in which it snowed. So I used all of those things. You don't know that when you're sitting down to write it. It's an adventure; it's really jumping into this big swimming pool and hoping there's going to be water when you hit.

How has the experience of writing musicals and writing films been different and why do you continue to do them when you don't need to? Why have you continued to write in collaborative situations and seemingly against the whole idea of wanting to be independent?

I do it because I think I have to keep writing all the time. Each year I want to be doing something. I wouldn't know how to take a year off and do nothing. I would feel it a wasted year of my life, unless I did something else productive that I love— but I haven't found anything. I think that even at this age I'm still growing and that I want to do as much as I can before I can't do it anymore. Again, I think, what do you want to do following what you have just done? I was about to start another play that I had in mind but I still haven't quite licked where it's going and I'm not ready to do it. It's not

that I won't have anything on next year, but I won't have anything to work on. So I'm toying with the idea of doing a musical now which is like a breather, even though the musical is a much more collaborative and a much more debilitating effort than anything else in the theatre could be. The movies have been in the past—some of them—such good experiences that I was usually eager to do one again. The movie industry has changed enormously. I did ten films with Ray Stark. Nine of them were successful and one was terrible. But for all of them, Ray Stark was the producer; he always got me a good director, always got a good cast, and was really the blocking back for me, the runner, with the studio. I almost never had to deal with the studio. This last experience I had, *The Marrying Man,* was enough to make me say I never want to do a film again.

I did have good experiences doing *The Heartbreak Kid* and *The Goodbye Girl,* even *Murder By Death. Murder By Death* is not a great work of art but it's great fun. In my reveries I used to wish that I were older in the Thirties and in the early Forties and could write for Cary Grant and Humphrey Bogart and Jimmy Stewart. One of the great thrills I had in Hollywood was when I met some of these people and they said, "Gee, I wish I could have done a picture with you!" When Cary Grant said that to me, I said, "Wow, what I've missed!" Those actors who were, I think, in some ways (the best of them) superior to some of the actors we have today, carried none of the weight that the actors do today. Now even a small star, a starlet, has something to say about the picture. I will deal with the director always, with the producer seldom but sometimes, the studio hardly ever, and with an actor never. I will listen to an actor's inabilities to find what he needs to accomplish in a part and try to accommodate that, but not because he wants to be portrayed in a certain way. On the stage Manny Azenberg and I must have fired eight to ten actors over the years because we found they were not fulfilling what we wanted. An actor's training is mostly with dead playwrights, so when they do the classics they don't expect any rewrites. I want them to feel the same thing. I rewrite more than anybody I know; I just do it over and over. I'm still giving pages and new lines on *Lost in Yonkers* and will do it until we open. But they'll always come to you and say, "I'm having trouble with this line. Can you think if there's another way of me saying it that makes it more comfortable?" I'll say, "I'll rewrite it if it makes it more comfortable for the character, not for you." When they understand that then we can find a way to do it.

To give you a really good example of the difference between films and plays for me, a director of a play will come to me and say, "What do you think about this section? I'm not so sure that this is working. Do you think you could find something else?" And I'll either agree with him or disagree with him and write it or rewrite it, but he does nothing about it until I rewrite it. He'll even come to me about a sentence or a couple of words. That play is sold to the films, and he becomes the director. He shoots the film, then invites me to the first cut, and three major scenes are missing. I say, "What happened to those scenes?" He says, "They didn't work for me." It now has become his script; it's not mine anymore. And the only way to control that is to direct your own films which I don't want to do. I'm not a director. I don't want to spend all that time. I love writing. I hate directing. I hate hanging around the rehearsals. I do it when I'm working and I need to do something, but just to stand there and watch—I don't want to do it. So I do the films, but I'm not really very happy with them. Musicals are something else, because when you work with some of the best people (I worked with Bob Fosse a number of times and I thought he was really a genius; I worked with Michael Bennett a few times, even a little bit on *Chorus Line*), that's great fun. That's like being invited to the party, so you just do it.

You talk about rewriting. When you're readying a play like Lost in Yonkers *and you're doing the rewriting, to whom are you responding when you do the rewrites? Is it purely your own responses when you're in the theatre? Or do you also respond to critics, or the director, or an actor?*

All of them. Not an actor so much, a director yes, a critic sometimes. If a critic says something that's valid, and especially if it's backed up by another critic who hits on the same point, I say, "I've got to address this." When you're writing it over and over again and then you're in rehearsal and you're out of town and you start to try it, you've lost all objectivity. Now you need the audience to be objective for you (and they are totally) and you listen to them. Sometimes the actor will come to me and say, "This line isn't getting a laugh." And I say, "I never intended it to." They assume that everything they should say when the situation is comic should get a laugh. I say, "No, no, no, this is character; it's pushing the story ahead." That never happens in any of the dramatic scenes in *Lost in Yonkers*. Very few of those lines were ever changed because they don't have the difficulty in expecting a reaction from the audience. I rewrite

just watching what it is that I hear wrong. And sometimes I can watch a play and after about eight or nine performances, I say, "I don't like that." There was a producer who once said to me, "Only look at the things that don't work in the play. The good things will take care of themselves, don't worry about that. Don't say, 'I know this stuff doesn't work but look at all the good things I have.'" He said, "The bad things'll do you in every time." So I concentrate on the bad things; and after I get whatever I think is unworthy of the play out, then I start to hear it more objectively. I stay away for two or three performances and come back and say, "We need something much better than that." When you first see that play up on a stage for the first time in front of an audience, all you care about is that the baby is delivered and is well and has all its arms and legs and moves. Then you say, "OK, now starts its education."

I teach a course in Modern American Drama, and many of the playwrights in the course, people like John Guare and Beth Henley, are considered by the "establishment" to be serious playwrights who write plays that contain comic moments. Neil Simon, on the other hand, is considered a writer of funny plays that are occasionally serious. That strikes me as unfair because, especially in the most recent of your plays, like "The Trilogy" and now Lost in Yonkers, *the proportion of humor to seriousness is if anything less comedy than in, say,* Crimes of the Heart.

Crimes of the Heart *is a comedy.*

Yes, but Henley is considered a serious playwright.

I don't consider it necessarily unfair. I just think it's inaccurate. Unfair means that I'm being picked on for not writing serious, which is better than comedy, which I don't hold to be true. For the most part, I think I have written, with the exception of *Rumors* and the musicals (starting even with *The Odd Couple*), a serious play which is told through my own comic point of view. There are no serious moments in *The Odd Couple*; but when I first sat down to write it, naive as this may be, I thought it was sort of a black comedy, because in most comedies up to that point, there were always women in the play and a romantic relationship. Here there were none; the relationship was between these two men. *Plaza Suite*, with a husband and wife getting a divorce after twenty-three years, was basically a serious play that had comedy in it. The audience at that time was so trained to laugh at what I wrote that, in Boston, Mike Nichols and I kept taking out all the funny lines in the first act—and they found other places to laugh.

I write with a sense of irony and even with lines that are not funny, sometimes the audience senses the irony when they are sophisticated enough and they see the humor. That's why I always need really good productions for the plays to work. I once met a woman who said, "You know, I've never been a fan of yours." and I said, "Oh, that's OK." and she said, "Now I'm a big fan!" and I said, "What happened?" She said, "Well, I come from"—it was either Wyoming or Montana—and she said, "I've only seen dinner theatre productions of your plays in which they would play all the plays on one superficial level. They played it all as comedy, and then I read the plays and I said, this isn't comedy at all." I remember people walking out of *Prisoner of Second Avenue* confused because some would say, "This wasn't funny." I didn't mean it to be funny; I thought it was a very serious subject, especially at that time. It was the beginning of people being so age-conscious with the man of forty-eight years old losing his job and finding it very difficult to start all over again which is true even today. That to me was a serious play that had a great deal of comedy.

I use the comedy in a way to get the audience's attention and then sort of pull the rug from underneath them. That's how I view life: things are wonderful, things are going along just great, and then a telephone call comes and just pulls the rug from under you. Some tragic thing, some tragic event, has happened in your life, and I say if it can happen in life I want to do that in the theatre. It took a long time to convince audiences and critics that one could write a play that way. I remember reading Lillian Hellman saying, "Never mix comedy and drama in the same play; the audiences won't understand it." They say to me, "What are you writing?" and I'll mention something, and they say, "Is it a comedy?" I say, "No it's a play." They say, "Is it a drama?" and I say, "It's a play. It has everything in it."

When you look back over your career to date, how has Neil Simon changed as a playwright? In other interviews you've mentioned the idea of the tapestry play, that you're now writing about more than two people as the focus of the plays. I assume that's one way, but are there other ways that you see your plays changing?

Well, in a glacier-like way. They move slowly; I don't make sudden overnight changes. I think back to *Chapter Two,* which was the story of the guilt a man feels who has lost a spouse and feels too guilty or is made to feel too guilty by his children or other relatives to go ahead in another relationship. There were people who spent the next fifteen or twenty years or the rest of their lives never moving on with it. In my own case, I was encouraged by my daughters to move on when I met somebody else. But still you get that kick of guilt, not a high kick, a kick in the gut, of guilt much like the survivors of the Holocaust when those who lived felt guilty all their lives. So the man in the play was not able to give himself the enjoyment and the latitude of exploring this new relationship without always pulling in the guilt of being alive and his wife being dead. Around that point, it's what I started to look for in almost every play. I think if there's any change it's that way. It's not necessary for me to be conceived of as a serious playwright because the word is so bandied about I think that it gets misinterpreted, serious meaning the intention is lofty. It isn't any loftier than comedy can be, but I don't write a pure comedy anymore, with the exception of *Rumors* where I intentionally did. I try to write plays about human emotions. I don't write plays about society. I find I can't. They become very current plays, and I like plays to be able to last for fifty or a hundred years or so. These are plays that contain serious subject matter. *Lost in Yonkers* is very well disguised, not that I meant it to be, but I couldn't open up the play showing the tragic side of Bella. It only came out when she was confronted with this chance to better her life and she didn't quite know how to do it and didn't get the permission of her mother who was the one who stunted her growth in the first place. That has to be built to, and I see how the audience is taken by surprise as it goes on. If they leave after that first act, they say, "It's nice, it's funny, it's cute." And then the second act just hits them so hard. It's what you leave the theatre with, not what's going on in the beginning of the play, that's important.

Perhaps this analogy will seem far-fetched to you, but one could say that it took O'Neill almost his whole creative life to write a play like Long Day's Journey, *where, as he said, he "faced his dead at last." He had started to do it with* Ah, Wilderness! *in a more light-hearted way.* Ah, Wilderness! *and* Long Day's Journey *are really the same play but one is weighted towards a comedic treatment and the other towards a more tragic approach. It seems to me that you could say the same thing about* Brighton Beach Memoirs *and* Broadway Bound: Brighton Beach Memoirs *is your* Ah, Wilderness!, *and* Broadway Bound *is your* Long

Day's Journey. *You started to confront your family directly in* Brighton Beach, *particularly through Eugene's narration in a comic way, and then in* Broadway Bound *you did so much more seriously.*

There was a really valid reason for that. With *Brighton Beach* my mother was still alive, so she could come and enjoy it and *Biloxi Blues* as well. She died after that so she never saw *Broadway Bound.* I would not have written *Broadway Bound* if my parents were alive. I couldn't have put them up on the stage that way. I don't think I put them in an unsympathetic light certainly, but in a truthful one in a way. I was probably harsher on my father than I was on my mother; at that time in our lives, I really think she was the one who caused the anguish in the family. But I have more of an understanding of him now having lived through some of the same things myself.

So you think it was basically the death of your mother that enabled you to write Broadway Bound *when you did?*

It freed me to do it. I reveal things about her, her inability to be close and emotional. I don't remember ever being hugged by my mother as far back as being a child. I always knew that she loved me, but she was unable to show emotion. I did talk about something that happened to my mother personally, that she was burned in a fire; the grandfather talks about that. I don't go into it in *Broadway Bound* but it must have affected their marriage very much—how she was scarred. She was actually scarred on the front, not on the back as in the play.

And you never could have done that if she'd still been alive?

No, I couldn't. When O'Neill wrote *Long Day's Journey* he put it in a drawer and said it couldn't be done until twenty-five years after his death, which didn't happen of course; his wife had it done. I sort of felt that way. *Chapter Two* was cathartic for me. It helped me get rid of my own guilt by sharing it with the world. But *Broadway Bound* was not cathartic. It was an attempt to try to understand my family and my own origins. It's a play of forgiveness, and I didn't realize it until somebody associated with the play—the set designer or a costume designer—said after the reading, "It's a love letter to his mother." I had a very up and down relationship with my mother. I used to get angry at her very often, and I loved her too, but there was no way for either one of us to show it—and so there it is on the stage. I remember in real life once I gave a surprise birthday party for my mother—she really was surprised—and we

brought out the cake. She couldn't smile or say, "This is wonderful." She just looked at me as she was about to cut the cake and said, "I'm still angry with you from last week when you did such and such." It was the only way she could deal with it. So when I wrote the play, what I had to do after listening to the first reading when I didn't have that scene about George Raft, I said I've got to show the other side of my mother, show her when she was happy. I like that when in the second act of a play, you begin to show what really is information that happened way before that, to give it late in the play.

Do you have a favorite among your own plays? The last one you wrote?

Yes, it's generally that. It suddenly becomes the one that you're working on; but when I think of my favorite, I think about what my experience was when I wrote it and put it on. Was that a good time in my life, in my personal life and in doing the play? With some of the plays I had terrible times doing the play yet the play came out very well; other times it was great fun doing it. I think the greatest kick I got on an opening night—when I knew I was sort of catapulted into another place in my life—was the opening night of *The Odd Couple.* It was accepted on such a high level by everyone. It was what you dream about—Moss Hart in *Act One*—the hottest ticket in town. That night was a terrific night!

What about as a craftsman? Which of the plays are you proudest of as a piece of writing?

Structurally I like *The Sunshine Boys,* and I like this one structurally.

The Sunshine Boys *is my favorite Simon play so far because of the integration of comedy and seriousness and because of the organic nature of that integration. Maybe it's an accident of the subject matter because you're dealing with comedians.*

You're dealing with comedians which gives you license for them to be funny. But the seriousness in the play was inherent too; it wasn't always written about because you knew that they were old, you knew they couldn't deal with things. One was really fighting for his way of life to continue, the other was quite satisfied to be retired and live in another way; so there was something classic about it. It just seems to hark back to another period in time. That play is done by more national theatres in Europe—in England or even Germany—because they relate to it in some part of their own culture, to the old vaudevillians and what's happened to them. They've died out. That's another play that sat in the drawer for six months after I wrote twenty-five pages of it until I had lunch with Mike Nichols and said, "I'm kind of stuck. I have a play." I started to tell him the idea and he said, "That sounds wonderful!" That's sometimes all I need; that's like a great review. "You really like that, Mike?" "Yes." And I went ahead and wrote the whole thing.

Can you think of plays that exceeded your expectations and plays that you had great expectations for that never reached them once you saw them on stage?

That's an interesting question because I think I always know what the reception is going to be. I'm rarely surprised. Sometimes I write a play knowing it's not going to succeed. There's a psychological subconscious will to fail after writing four or five hits—you don't deserve that much. I pick a subject matter that is so far out—something that I would not do right now. Not one that's more dangerous and that's taking more of a chance with an audience, but one that's almost guaranteed not to be commercially successful (not that I always know when it's going to be). *The Odd Couple* and *Barefoot in the Park* fooled me because they were so early in my career. I didn't know what to expect. When they were both such big hits, I was really shocked. But a play that I knew I wanted to write for a reason other than artistic or commercial success was something like *God's Favorite*.

God's Favorite was my way of dealing with my wife's death. It was *Waiting for Godot* for me; I could not understand the absurdity of a thirty-nine-year-old beautiful, energetic woman dying so young. It was railing at God to explain to me why He did this thing, so I used the *Book of Job*. One critic cried on television in his anger: "How dare you do this to the *Book of Job*!" Yet there were critics like Walter Kerr, a devout Catholic, who loved it, just adored it. And so I wasn't too surprised that we weren't a major success, but I learned in hindsight that it was not a Broadway play. It should have been done off-Broadway as *Fools* should have been. *Fools* I did in a way like *Rumors*. Again it was farce in a sense. I just loved the premise. It's almost Hebraic culturally like the towns written about by Sholem Aleichem in which there were stupid people (without ever going into the reasons why) and I had a curse in my town. I thought it was good. Mike Nichols came up and did it; we had a good time. If we had done it in a small theatre, it would have been fine—Playwrights Horizons or something like that—but not with the expectations of a Broadway audience

paying whatever it was at the time, expecting a certain kind of play.

I remember when we did *The Good Doctor*, which was another play written during my wife's illness when they discovered that she would not live. I was just sitting up in the country and I wanted to write to keep myself going and I read a short story by Chekhov called "The Sneeze" ; and, just to kill time, I dramatized it. And I said, "Gee, this would be fun, to do all Russian writers and do comic pieces—or non-comic pieces—by them." I couldn't find any, so in order to give unity to the evening I decided to do Chekhov because he had written so many newspaper pieces where he got paid by the word and I found as many of them as I could. Then when I tried them out of town some of them didn't work, so I wrote my own Chekhov pieces and some of the critics pointed them out and said, "This one is so Chekhovian." which wasn't his at all! I don't mean that as flattery to me but as not knowing by some of the critics. I remember a woman in New Haven coming up the aisle and she said to me, "This isn't Neil Simon." So I asked, "Do you like it or do you not like it?" She said, "I don't know. It's just not Neil Simon." I have to overcome their expectations of me so that they don't get to see what they want to see. It's like going to see Babe Ruth at a baseball game; if he hits two singles and drives in the winning run, it's not a Babe Ruth game.

How do you feel about the current relationship between the theatre and film and TV? It's a cliché that television is ruining the theatre, that we are a culture of filmgoers not theatregoers. Do you feel those are valid kinds of observations? You once said you thought the biggest obstacle to theatre was the price of theatre tickets. Do you think it's really that?

That's one of them. It's only one of them. No, there's enough money around, I think, for people to go to Broadway theatre. I think we've lost the writers more than anything. David Richards of the *New York Times* recently said to me, "Do you realize you may be the only one left around who repeatedly works for the Broadway theatre?" And I said, "Well, they're all gone." Edward Albee hardly writes at all. Arthur Miller has grown older and writes occasionally for the theatre but rarely for Broadway; it's usually for Lincoln Center or someplace else. David Mamet now would rather direct and write his own films. Sam Shepard was never a Broadway writer. There are no repeat writers—the Tennessee Williamses, the George S. Kaufmans, or even Jean Kerr in terms of comedy. You talk to anybody today, especially in California, and they will use writing as a stepping stone to becoming a director. They want to be directors; it has to be about control. Even a promising young writer like John Patrick Shanley has a big success with *Moonstruck* after he had small success in the theatre. We had said this is an interesting playwright, he does *Moonstruck*, and then he wants to direct—so he does *Joe Versus the Volcano* and I'm sure he just wants to keep on directing. Nora Ephron writes a couple of movies that are nice and now she wants to direct. I have no desire to direct at all. I see the soundness of it, in terms of movies. As I said before, I have no control over what goes on up on the screen or what's cut later. Between the director and the actors you lose all of that.

It's almost a mystery as to what's happened in the theatre. I think it's just changing. It's becoming regional theatre and the plays are in a sense getting smaller, not necessarily in their scope. *Six Degrees of Separation* is a wonderful play; I really like that play. I'm not so sure if it had opened on Broadway at the Plymouth Theatre that it would have gotten the kind of attention, the demands for seats. It's viewed from a different perspective when it's presented in an off-Broadway atmosphere. You see what happens when they transfer plays. One of the few that transferred fairly well was *The Heidi Chronicles,* but even when you're watching *The Heidi Chronicles,* you say this isn't really a Broadway play. That could be a misnomer too because it makes it sound crass and commercial, but *Amadeus* is a Broadway play and I think it's a great play. I think most of Peter Shaffer's plays are wonderful plays: *Five Finger Exercise* and the one about the Incas, *The Royal Hunt of the Sun.* Tennessee Williams didn't write off-Broadway plays except at the end of his career when the plays got smaller in their scope. *Cat on a Hot Tin Roof* is a beautiful play, but it's got size to it, and there is no one around who does that anymore. It's changed, I guess maybe the way painting has changed. I don't know who the great portrait painters are anymore if they exist at all. I think it's economics that changes it. In the theatre now they are catering to an international audience. Who comes to America now but the people who have money—the Japanese or the Germans? They don't all understand English but if they go see a musical like *Cats* they don't have to. Even *Phantom of the Opera*—if you don't understand it you can still enjoy it. If a play runs two years it is amazing. Most musical hits will run ten years now. You can't get *Cats* out of that theatre. *Phantom* will be there forever. It will be interesting to see what

happens with *Miss Saigon* because it has this amazing anti-American number. When I saw it in London, you could almost cheer it, but if when it opens in March this war is still going on there may be some repercussions.

One of the things that occurred to me when I was watching Lost in Yonkers *the other night is that you're one of the cleanest playwrights I know, even though you write about very intimate things.*

You write to what fits the play. There are all sorts of four-letter words in *Rumors* because these are very contemporary people. In *Lost in Yonkers,* you're dealing with the 1940's and you're not only trying to emulate a play that might have existed in that time, but certainly what life was like at that time. And that kind of language, street language, I at least didn't hear that much. I never heard it at home, except maybe in a violent argument between my mother and father. It's interesting to watch playwrights like Tennessee Williams and Arthur Miller who never resorted to that language but found another language that was more potent. In doing *The Marrying Man* with Kim Basinger and Alec Baldwin, which was just an awful experience, she did this scene in which she was sitting in a box at the opera in Boston. She used to be Bugsy Siegal's girlfriend but is found by this guy who's a multi-millionaire and they get married; they're forced to get married through no intention of their own. Later on, they fall in love and get remarried. She's sitting in Boston and a man in the box is annoying her as she's sort of kissing the ear of Alec Baldwin. He keeps shushing her and she says, "Oh, come on, this opera isn't even in English, you can't understand it" ; and it goes on and finally she adlibs, "Oh, go f——yourself." And I said, "Wait, you can't say that." It had nothing to with my thinking that the language is offensive; it's so wrong for the character and for the tone of the movie. It's a movie that takes place in 1948. It's OK when the Alec Baldwin character and his four cronies are in the car. They use all sorts of language; but for her to use it in that place seemed so wrong for me. So it wasn't being prudish about anything; you've just got to use it where it's got some weight. Sometimes I would use "f——you" or whatever it is once in a play, and it has much more impact than just using it all the way through. I like it when David Mamet does it sometimes like in *American Buffalo.* It is said so often that it is no longer offensive. It bothers some people I know; they don't want to hear it. But it never bothers me. I think he writes in such wonderful rhythms and cadences that the language is so important, so precise.

Linda Lavin once said à propos of Last of the Red-Hot Lovers, *in which she was then appearing: "People come to the theatre to see their lives verified. They haven't been offended. The life they lead hasn't been challenged, it's been reaffirmed." And I think you once said, "recognition" is what you'd like to see your plays be all about. Let me be a devil's advocate and say that one should come out of the theatre upset, as Edward Albee insists. I don't mean necessarily emotionally upset but something should have changed. You shouldn't have been patted on the head, you should have been disturbed.* Lost in Yonkers *can be a very disturbing play in that way.*

Oh, absolutely.

Do you think you've changed in that respect?

Yes. I remember that when I did *Plaza Suite* and I wrote the first act about the husband who's having the affair with the secretary, the general manager for the play read it and said, "You can't do this play." I said, "Why not?" He said, "Do you know how many men come from out of town and meet their secretary or somebody and come to this play. They'll be so embarrassed." I said, "Good, that's what I want to do. I want to shake people up." So I don't think I was trying to reaffirm middle-class values. In *Last of the Red-Hot Lovers,* the man was trying to have an affair. I found him sort of a pitiful character not even being able to break through that. I saw him as an Everyman in a way who finally had the courage to try to break out but didn't know how to do it. Sometimes those labels stick with you. But as I said it's a glacier. It moves along and it changes and it pulls along the debris with it. I don't think I write that way. I think why I get bandied about a lot by critics is because of the success ratio. There must be something wrong when it appeals to so many people around the world. They hate it that I've become a wealthy person from the plays.

You can't be any good if you're wealthy!

Yes. I remember at the time reading about Tennessee Williams's wealth, which was relative compared to today's market, but he was a fairly wealthy man because he was so successful. But he also took such chances with plays like *Camino Real.* He was a poet and he made his reputation on plays like *The Glass Menagerie* and *Streetcar Named Desire.* It's because I do write plays that for the most part are so popular. I never mind a bad review from a good critic who has liked some of the work in the past and then says, "No, you didn't do it this time." I say that's valid and I can accept it. I don't expect a rave from Frank Rich. Frank Rich always will find fault.

He's tough to figure out because he'll write a very middling review of *Brighton Beach* and talk about its faults and at the end of it say, "One hopes there will be a chapter two to *Brighton Beach*." He finds fault with the play yet he wants to see a sequel to it! I had no intention of writing a trilogy, I just wrote *Brighton Beach.* When I read his notice I said, well, I'll do another play. You still don't think about a trilogy because if the second play fails, who wants to see the sequel to a failure? So I wrote *Biloxi Blues,* which he loved. It won the Tony Award, and so I did the third one which he again then finds fault with by saying, "I missed it being a great play." He gives it a negative sounding review by saying it almost reaches great heights but doesn't.

You have to steel yourself. You become very thick-skinned after a while because you're out there naked and they are writing about you personally. They don't write about your work as much as who you are in the reviews. In a way I think the theatre has been changed a lot by critics who are now looking to make names for themselves. It bothers me that critics are hailed as personalities. Siskel and Ebert, good critics or bad critics it makes no difference to me, I hate that they are celebrities and have such power. Fortunately, there are so many people who write reviews for films, and people generally make up their mind to go see a film before they read the reviews. Not so with the theatre. The reviews mean everything. If you get a bad review in the *New York Times,* you can still exist but you've got to overcome it.

No, that's not exactly true. You can still exist. Neil Simon can still exist. A lot of other people can't with a bad review in the Times.

Well, it depends on the play. There have been a few that have existed without it, but it's very hard. Rich loved *Biloxi Blues* and the first day after *Biloxi Blues* opened we did an enormous amount of business, twice what we did on *Brighton Beach Memoirs.* But *Brighton Beach Memoirs* ran twice as long as *Biloxi Blues.* The audience seeks out what they want and *Brighton Beach,* next to *The Odd Couple,* is played more than any play I've ever done. There is something about the idealization of the family in that play that we all dream about. They know it's an idealization. It's like looking back on your family album and seeing it better than it was.

But it's not Ah, Wilderness! *It's not that sappy.*

Well, those were sappier days.

There's a lot of what happens in Broadway Bound *underneath the surface of* Brighton Beach.

Oh, yes—the mother's hurt when she finds out that the father has had this heart attack and that the boy has lost all the money.

What do you think you've done differently in Lost in Yonkers *? What would you say has inched the glacier forward with this play?*

I've written about much darker people than I ever have before. I've written about normal people in dark situations before—the death of spouses, the break-up of marriages (tragedies in proportion to their own lives at that time like in *Brighton Beach*), anti-semitism and anti-homosexuality in *Biloxi*. But in this play, I really wrote about dysfunctional people and the results of a woman who was beaten in Germany who in order to teach her children to survive teaches them only to survive and nothing else. That's much further than I've gone in any other play, so it's deeper. It's why I want to do a musical next year because I need really sure footing to go on to the next place. That doesn't mean I need to write about people even more dysfunctional, but as a matter of fact the play that I've been working on and haven't been able to lick quite yet is about two people in a sanitarium who have had breakdowns and find solace in each other almost more than in the doctor. I've written about thirty pages of it and I've had it there for two years and I'm anxious to write it, but each play comes when its time is ripe. Who knows if at some point I lose faith in the musical I'm working on, I'll probably go back and start to write that play. Right now, all I want to do is get out of Washington, go home, rest, come back, do the stuff in New York. Then I forget all about *Lost in Yonkers*. They all become a piece of the past for me. I've learned from them, and then they only come up in interviews like this when you talk about them. I don't think of the plays. I don't try to remember or go back or ever read them and see what I've done to see how I could do that again. I want to go to some other place. I'm just hoping that there'll even be a theatre enough around for people to want to go see these plays.

Source: Jackson R. Bryer, "An Interview with Neil Simon," in *Studies in American Drama, 1945–Present*, Vol. 6, No. 2, 1991, pp. 153–76.

SOURCES

Brandes, Philip, Review of *The Prisoner of Second Avenue*, in *Los Angeles Times*, September 17, 1992, p. 14.

Glaviano, Cliff, Review of *The Prisoner of Second Avenue*, in *Library Journal*, January 2001, pp. 184, 185.

Holman, C. Hugh, and William Harmon, *A Handbook to Literature*, 5th ed., Macmillan, 1986, p. 58.

Morley, Sheridan, "Tricks not Treats," in *Spectator*, April 10, 1999, pp. 46, 47.

Simon, Neil, *The Prisoner of Second Avenue*, in *The Collected Plays of Neil Simon*, Vol. 2, pp. 231–99.

Tietzman, Peter, "The Ominous Apple," in *Neil Simon: A Casebook*, edited by Gary Konas, Garland Publishing, 1997, p. 148.

FURTHER READING

Hischak, Thomas S., *American Theatre: A Chronicle of Comedy and Drama, 1969–2000*, Oxford University Press, 2001.
    Hischak examines the new trends in American theater that emerged during the last few decades of the twentieth century. He includes an analysis of *The Prisoner of Second Avenue*, as well as of Simon's later plays.

Koprince, Susan, *Understanding Neil Simon*, University of South Carolina Press, 2002.
    In this assessment of Simon's career as a playwright, Koprince provides detailed explications of the style and themes of several of his plays, concluding that Simon has often been wrongfully overlooked by scholars.

Simon, Neil, *Neil Simon Monologues: Speeches from the Works of America's Foremost Playwright*, Dramaline Publications, 1996.
    Simon collects his best monologues in this book, which range from the serious to the comic. The collection offers a valuable tool for actors preparing for the plays as well as for students since a summary and analysis of each monologue is included.

———, *Rewrites: A Memoir*, Simon and Schuster, 1998.
    Simon reflects on his career and his personal life, from his childhood through his early years as a television comedy writer, to his huge success as a playwright into the 1970s. He includes a discussion of his art and the influences on it as well as honest accounts of his problems with writer's block and personal relationships.

Take Me Out

RICHARD GREENBERG

2002

Take Me Out, Richard Greenberg's 2002 Broadway hit, explores with wit and compassion what might happen if a player on a major league baseball team were to announce that he is gay. Greenberg brings out many attitudes toward homosexuality by drawing his main character as a very specific, unique individual. Darren Lemming is *the* star player who has led his team to win two Worlds Series in a row. He comes from a middle-class, biracial family but has never faced any sort of racial prejudice. He is the ideal ballplayer on the ideal team, until the day he decides to announce his sexual orientation to his team: then his relationships change with his coach; his team-mates; his new business manager, who is gay; his best friend, who is devoutly religious; and especially with the homophobic pitcher recently up from the minors, who refers to Lemming by using an offensive slur during an interview. The play is full of insights about baseball, masculinity, and identity in the twenty-first century, told with humor, and ending in tragedy.

Greenberg was a constant presence in the Broadway theater after his first works were produced in the 1980s. He has won or been nominated for most major awards available to playwrights, including the Pulitzer Prize, Drama Desk, the Oppenheimer Award, and the PEN/Laura Pels Award. *Take Me Out* was the Tony Award for Best Play the year that it opened, along with garnering Tonys for best actor and best director, but it is also known for generating controversy for including male nudity on the legitimate stage. *Take Me Out* was published by Faber and Faber in 2003.

Richard Greenberg AP Images

AUTHOR BIOGRAPHY

Richard Greenberg was born in East Meadow, New York, on February 22, 1958 or 1959—official sources conflict. He was raised there in a middle-class household. His father, Leon, was an executive for the Century Theaters movie chain, and his mother, Shirley, was a housewife. After graduating from East Meadow High School in 1976, Greenberg attended Princeton University, graduating with a Bachelor of Arts degree in English in 1980; one of his instructors was the famed novelist Joyce Carol Oates. He went to graduate school at Harvard University from 1981 to 1982, studying fiction writing and finding that he did not like it as much as he did acting: at that point, he decided to try play writing. The play he wrote earned him acceptance to the Yale School of Drama, where he completed an M.F.A. in 1985.

Greenberg's first produced play, *The Bloodletters*, drew attention from critics when it was first produced in New York in 1985, and after that, Greenberg remained active in the theater world. By 2006, he had produced twenty-eight plays, almost always supported by critical raves. For a brief while in 2003, three of his plays were running on Broadway at once: *Take Me Out, The Violet Hour,*

and a revival of 1988's *Eastern Standard*. At one point in the early 2000s, he had five plays in production at one time.

Though he lived in New York City much of his adult life, Greenberg worked with directors across the country. He was a member of Ensemble Studio Theatre and an associate artist at South Coast Repertory in Costa Mesa, California. He won numerous awards, including the 2003 Tony Award for Best Play for *Take Me Out* and the George Oppenheimer Award and the Los Angeles Drama Critics' Circle Award, both for *Three Days of Rain*. He has also been a finalist for the Pulitzer Prize and a nominee for the Drama Desk Award, both for *Take Me Out*. In 1996, Greenberg and playwright Arthur Miller were the first recipients of the PEN/Laura Pels Award for Drama.

PLOT SUMMARY

Act 1

Take Me Out starts with Kippy Sunderstrom, shortstop for the fictional major league team the Empires, talking to the audience, trying to pinpoint exactly when "the whole mess" started. He explains that Darren Lemming, the team's star center fielder, was an audience favorite, encouraged by all. After the All-Star break, the team started losing and brought up a relief pitcher from the minor leagues, and *that* might have been the start of it all. Then he settles on the problem starting on a day when Darren gave a press conference: the stage lights come up on Darren surrounded by the other members of the team as he speaks to the public about his hope that his being gay will not change how people act toward him.

The setting changes to the clubhouse, where Kippy and Darren discuss what this announcement will mean. Kippy says that the other players are certain to feel a little uncomfortable about Darren's sexual preference and will be a little resentful about not having been told earlier. Darren counters that he did tell Skipper, who assured him that the team would support him, but Kippy's warning comes true when teammates Martinez and Rodriguez pass by, grunting something inaudible. Kippy says that he would like Darren and whoever he is dating to come to the house for dinner with his wife and three kids, but Darren has no particular love interest at the moment.

Jason Chenier, the team's new catcher, enters. He approaches Darren timidly to say that, though

MEDIA ADAPTATIONS

- *Take Me Out* premiered on June 21, 2002, at the Donmar Warehouse, London, produced by Donmar Warehouse, directed by Joe Montello.

- The play opened in New York at the Public Theater in New York City, produced by the Donmar Warehouse and the Public Theater. It moved to the Walter Kerr Theatre on Broadway on February 27, 2003.

---

he never felt comfortable talking to him, he feels all right about it now after the announcement. In trying to compliment homosexuals, he refers to a book that someone he knows once read; he associates ancient Greeks with homosexuality and then incorrectly attributes the Egyptian pyramids to the Greeks. Kippy and Darren laugh about his ineptitude, and Jason leaves, embarrassed.

The lights come up on the locker room. Darren is by his locker, undressing, when Toddy Koovitz comes in from a shower. When Toddy takes off his towel, he becomes angry that he now must be self-conscious about being naked in the locker room around Darren, despite Darren's assurance that he has no sexual interest in him at all. Toddy tells Darren that his importance to the team will not keep God from punishing him, and he gives examples of other ballplayers—Roberto Clemente, Thurman Munson, and Lou Gehrig—who he says were struck down by God. Darren dismisses him with bemusement.

Kippy returns to the spotlight as narrator, wondering why Darren chose to reveal his sexual orientation at that particular time, and the scene goes to a lounge where Darren and his best friend in baseball, Davey Battle, are drinking after a game in which the Empires defeated Davey's team. The two friends discuss their lives: Davey is a religious man with a wife and three kids, and Darren is mysterious and sarcastic, unwilling to talk about love. Their discussion ends with Davey telling Darren that he should want his true nature known to the world, and a week later Darren gives his press conference about being gay.

Mason Marzac comes onto the stage, introducing himself to the audience as a man who cared nothing about baseball until Darren made headlines with his announcement. Darren joins him onstage and the audience sees their first meeting, as Mason explains that he is the accountant assigned to handle Darren's finances now that his previous accountant, Abe, has retired to Florida. Darren notes that his commercials only run on late-night television since the announcement, assuming that his sexual identity is probably disturbing, and he implies that Mason is assigned to him because Mason is gay. Mason counters that he is, in fact, quite good at making money with the investments of people like Darren, celebrities who would like to make money for a time in the future when they will not be able to work. He asks Darren to select a charity to receive donations from him. When Mason tries to thank him on behalf of the gay community for being open about his sexuality, Darren counters that he does not feel like he is part of any community.

Kippy returns to the stage, explaining that, soon after, the team fell onto a slump and started losing games at an unprecedented rate. A relief pitcher, Shane Mungitt, was brought up from the minor leagues. Mason returns to the stage to list the philosophic things about baseball that he finds appealing: its symmetry, its democratic rules, and the leisurely pace it takes, as when a batter who has hit the ball out of the park is still required to take the time to trot around the infield, touching each base.

Shane comes onstage, and Darren and Kippy approach him, asking about his life. He was raised in orphanages after his father shot his mother and then himself, leaving the child Shane trapped with the bodies for three days. After telling them his story, Shane laughs maniacally. Kippy recognizes his problem as an inability to speak clearly and vows to help him. Before he gets a chance, though, Shane speaks out in a television interview, alienating himself from his team by talking about "colored people" and "gooks" and "spics" and "coons" on the team, saying that the worst thing is that he has to shower every night with a "*faggot.*" The team, watching him on television, is frozen with horror.

Act 2

The second act begins with the team's manager, William R. Danziger (or "Skipper") reading a formal letter that he has written to Darren, addressing him distantly as "Mr. Lemming" and stating his objection to Shane Mungitt's prejudiced remarks. The letter ends stating that, though he supports Darren, he wishes that he were not a baseball player.

Kippy enters and summarizes the situation: since Shane was so crass on television, most people have contacted Darren to express support, a situation that Darren finds degrading. Kippy points out that this incident has had a humanizing effect on the myth surrounding the team's best player, but Darren complains that going from godly to human is a demotion.

Because Shane has been suspended, the team starts to lose again. The resentment of the players is stated by Toddy Koovitz, who thinks that Darren planned for Shane to speak out against him, for the sake of gaining publicity. Kippy's theory is that the members of the Empires have become self-conscious, afraid of doing things that might make them look gay.

Shane returns to clean out his locker, and the teammates refuse to talk to him. Later, in the locker room, Martinez and Rodriguez speak to each other in Spanish, excluding their teammates: Kippy claims to recognize some of their discussion to be a criticism of Kawabata's pitching. He then claims to be able to translate Kawabata's reaction as a discussion of a classic Japanese film. As Kawabata speaks, Kippy translates his words as expressing his loneliness in America.

Shane talks about a letter that he wrote to the Skipper, apologizing for having offended Darren Lemming, explaining his own intellectual weakness and accepting the idea that he should be punished. The letter has become public, and the press soon reports the sordid details of his childhood, and he becomes a sympathetic figure in the fans' views.

Darren goes to Skipper to ask about the rumor that Shane will be allowed back on the team, registering his objection. Skipper tells him that the other team members would not mind Shane coming back if it means that they would start winning again, while Darren believes that it would be enough if Shane's return offended him, because he is the team's best player.

Darren calls Mason Marzac after the meeting and asks him to meet him at the stadium the following night. Mason narrates his thrill with being at the game, now that he has been following it and can appreciate baseball's subtleties. After the game, Darren meets him and explains that he is thinking of retiring from baseball the very next day. Mason tells him that he does not have enough invested to retire that early. He convinces Darren to stay with the game, at least until the next day's game against Davey Battle's team, which, Mason says, he has told the press is his favorite thing to do. Mason

implores him, both as a gay man and as a baseball fan, to reconsider. Darren ends the meeting promising not to retire the next day.

The following day marks Shane's return to the team. Davey comes to the Empires' clubhouse to talk with Darren for the first time since Darren's public announcement that he is gay. Kippy has a brief discussion with Davey while he is leaving. At the same time, Shane is taking a pre-game shower, and Darren joins him. Darren's presence makes him nervous, and Darren eggs him on, taunting him about his racism and homophobia. He ends up going to Shane, grabbing him, and kissing him, pretending that he and Shane are lovers, though Shane shouts at him throughout the experience.

The ballgame goes well for eight innings, with Kawabata pitching a perfect game for eight innings and two outs. With one out to go, the opposing team starts scoring, and Shane is sent in to pitch against Davey Battle. Shane's first pitch goes straight to Davey's head, killing him.

Act 3

Act 3 starts with Takeshi Kawabata talking to the audience, explaining the constant media coverage of Davey's death. Attention shifts to Mason taking a late-night phone call from Darren, who is sad and angry about the events. Kippy calls on Darren's other line to express his support and love for him. When he returns to his conversation with Mason, Mason asks Darren if Shane is going to be arrested. He says that some of the other players heard him coming out of the locker room before the game, muttering that he hates them all and vowing to kill somebody. Darren tells Mason that they should arrest Shane and that he should be arrested himself.

Kippy introduces the last meeting between Darren and Davey, in the clubhouse before the game. Davey is angry and sarcastic: At one point he asks if Darren is *fleering* at him, using an archaic word for smirking in derision. Davey finally confronts him directly, asking him if he has been thinking of him sexually over the eight years of their friendship. He also accuses Darren of using the public reputation that Davey has cultivated to hide his secret. They part angry with each other: Davey, to go on to the conversation with Kippy that is dramatized in act 2, and Darren to the scene in the shower with Shane.

At a Major League Baseball inquest about the fatal pitch, Shane refuses to talk, saying that he wants to speak with Kippy. Despite his reluctance, Kippy decides to go to him. But Darren decides to go along.

When they meet with him, they find that Shane mistakenly believes that there is a chance that he might be able to rejoin the team. At length, Kippy makes him see that he will never play baseball again. When he turns his attention to Darren, Shane refers to the attack in the shower. He also reveals the fact that he heard Darren and Davey cursing at each other when they parted before the game. When Kippy tries to find out whether the fatal pitch was on purpose, Shane says that Kippy could answer for him, just as Kippy wrote the letter that gained him enough sympathy to be let back on the team after he was thrown off for the offensive interview.

In narration, Kippy explains to the audience that the Empires won the World Series and that no charges were leveled against Shane, who returned to wherever he came from: one night Shane bought a shotgun and went from one store to another, shooting up all of the bottles of milk, and so he ended up in jail.

After the last game, Kippy talks with Darren, expressing his hope that they might someday be friends again. Before he leaves, Mason shows up. Being new to the game, Mason is enthusiastic about the team's win and only somewhat aware of the emotional trauma that the team has suffered. Darren begins to mention retiring again, but Mason stops him, feeling it inappropriate on the night of the World's Series win. Darren invites him to the party, giving him one if his World's Series rings to wear (though he admonishes Mason when he holds his hand up to look at the ring in an unmanly way, reminding him that "it's gonna be a roomful of *jocks* "). The play ends with Mason ruminating about what they will do until the next season starts in spring.

CHARACTERS

Davey Battle

Davey Battle, Darren Lemmings's best friend, is a star player, but the team that he plays for is not as good as the Empires, which, as Davey points out, allows him to stand out more. Darren chides Davey for his middle-class religious values: his happy marriage, his three children, his unwillingness to use God's name in vain. Davey encourages Darren to keep no secrets, to live his life publicly, which leads to Darren's announcement about his sexual orientation.

Davey comes into the Empires' clubhouse the night that Shane Mungitt returns from his suspension, flouting the rule that prohibits members of the opposing team from entering a team's quarters. He and Darren have an argument, during which it is revealed that he has refused to talk to Darren since his announcement about being gay. Having thought that Darren was just a wild, successful bachelor, Davey feels betrayed to find out that he harbored a secret about his sexual orientation. Darren feels betrayed by Davey's anger and tells him to drop dead. Shane overhears the end of the conversation, and his first pitch to Davey hits him in the head and kills him.

Jason Chenier

Jason Chenier is a catcher who has been with the Empires for three weeks. Since coming to the team, he has been too shy to talk to the star player, Darren Lemming. After Darren announces that he is gay, however, Jason feels that he can approach him. He awkwardly tries to compliment Darren by saying that the ancient Greeks, who are associated with homosexuality, did great things such as building the pyramids (which the ancient Egyptians actually built). Darren and Kippy laugh at his ignorance, though he does not seem to know he is being mocked.

In act 2, when Kippy is talking to his teammates about their "stray homosexual impulses," Jason mistakenly believes for a moment that Kippy is talking to him in particular.

William R. Danziger

See Skipper

Takeshi Kawabata

Takeshi Kawabata, the star pitcher for the Empires, started his first season on the team playing brilliantly, but in the second half, his game would go to pieces some time around the seventh inning. To make up for his slump, the team brings Shane Mungitt up from the minor leagues. In act 2, Kippy pretends to translate Kawabata's Japanese into English, giving his words meanings that fit an Asian stereotype, about his ancestors and honor and death. Kawabata speaks directly to the audience in imperfect English at the start of act 3, showing himself to be quite aware of what is going on around him and willfully ignoring it.

Toddy Koovitz

Toddy Koovitz, a member of the Empires, becomes belligerent after the announcement that Darren is gay. He feels uncomfortable about being nude in the locker room with Darren and resents the fact that he is made to feel this way. He warns

Darren that his importance to the team as a player will not save him from God's punishment, citing such examples as Roberto Clemente and Thurman Munson, who died in separate plane crashes, and Lou Gehrig, who died of amyotrophic lateral sclerosis.

Toddy is an illiterate man, given to pronouncing words incorrectly, such as saying "sanc-chewy" for "sanctuary" and "rackled" for "racked." Speaking of the fact that amyotrophic lateral sclerosis is commonly called Lou Gehrig's disease, he says "Gehrig's got a *fate* named after him," which leads Darren to note, "Ya got a real sorta poetry of the ignoramus goin' on." To prove his point about Toddy's lack of intelligence, Darren recalls a time, during a playoff game, when Toddy caught a fly ball and, thinking it the final out of the inning, handed it to a girl in the stands, while two runners from the opposing team scored.

After Shane Mungitt makes a public, very derogatory statement about Darren Lemming's sexual orientation, Toddy expresses the belief that Darren might have arranged the whole controversy to gain public sympathy.

Darren Lemming

Darren Lemming is the play's central character. He is the center fielder for the Empires, an excellent player on a team that has won the World Series twice in a row. Darren is biracial, with a white father and a black mother, and was raised in a stable middle-class environment, which, along with his talent as a ballplayer, has helped make him a favorite of the fans.

After a talk about authenticity with his friend and competitor Davey Battle, Darren holds a press conference, at which he announces that he is gay. His teammates are generally supportive: some, such as Jason Chenier, find him to be approachable in a way that he never was before, while others, such as Toddy Koovitz, resent the intrusion of sexuality into the private confines of the locker room. His public approval suffers some, with his television endorsements moved to late night hours.

When Shane Mungitt, a new player, bluntly refers to Darren as a "*faggot*" in an interview, public reaction supports Darren. Darren insists that Shane should be thrown off of the team because it is what he, as the star player, desires. The Skipper refuses, and Darren mulls over the idea of retiring that very night, but his accountant, Mason Marzac, talks him out of it. On the day of Shane's return, Darren goes to where he is showering alone, mocks and taunts him, then grabs him and kisses him.

The first time that he speaks with Davey after announcing that he is gay, Darren finds that he misunderstood his friend earlier. Davey was not encouraging him to live openly as a gay man, and, in fact, Darren's sexual orientation offends Davey's religious background. They part angrily, cursing at each other. Shane overhears this, which is one reason that he purposely throws the pitch that kills Davey.

Steeped with guilt, Darren goes on to play some of his best baseball, and the Empires win their third World Series. After the last game, he is depressed and thinking of leaving, but he is joined by Mason, whom he asks to attend the celebration dinner as his date, indicating what might be the start of a new love.

Martinez

One of the Spanish-speaking members of the Empires, Martinez is always with Rodriguez and is indistinguishable from him.

Mason Marzac

Mason Marzac is an investment counselor who is assigned to handle Darren Lemming's money when his predecessor retires. He admits to having been uninterested in baseball until Darren announced that he was gay. His business association with Darren, along with his personal interest in him, draws Mason to baseball, so that by the end of the play he is an avid fan.

Mason is, by his own admission, quite successful as an investor: "I have taken some clients with fairly modest portfolios and made them *rather* wealthy," he says after Darren suspects that he has been assigned to him only because he is gay. He is enthralled by Darren from their first meeting, captivated by him as a hero to gay people everywhere because he has talked publicly about his sexual orientation. Darren, who takes his own eminence for granted, is bemused by Mason's devotion.

As the play goes on, they become friends. Mason can look at baseball as a theorist, as an outsider, speculating on the abstractions of players' records or the social significance of the pointless trot around the base when a ball has been hit out of the park. Darren decides that, to be part of the baseball world, Mason needs a nickname, and he takes to calling him Mars.

When Shane is allowed back on the team after publicly complaining about having to shower with Darren, Darren threatens to quit, and he calls Mason, as his financial advisor, to find out if he can afford such a move. The day of Davey Battle's funeral, though, he calls Mason for solace. He asks to hear about Mason's life but is too distracted to pay attention.

After the Empires win the World Series, Mason joins Darren at the stadium, and Darren invites him to the celebratory party as his date. He gives Mason one of his World Series rings to wear.

Shane Mungitt

When he first introduces Shane Mungitt to the audience, Kippy, as narrator, points out what a good pitcher Shane is, though lacking intelligence, and then notes that "he didn't seem to like the game." From the start, it is clear that Shane's skill is tied to certain psychological problems carried over from childhood. He is aloof from the other players, and, when questioned by Darren and Kippy, explains the terrible trauma of his early life: his father shot Shane's mother and himself when Shane was just a little boy, and he was trapped with their decaying bodies for three days, dehydrated when he was finally found; after that, he spent the rest of his childhood in one orphanage after another. The only thing that he ever learned to do well is pitch. When he tells them this tragic story, Shane laughs, although he says it is not made up.

Shane has such poor communication skills that during an interview with a reporter he refers to his teammates with derogatory racial slurs. He calls them "a funny bunch of guys," apparently unaware that the words he is using are offensive, and then elaborates by calling them "the gooks an' spics an' the coons an' like that." What makes the biggest headlines, though, is when he refers to Darren Lemming, the star of the team who has recently gone public about his homosexuality, as "a *faggot*." After that, Shane is suspended from the Empires.

The letter that gets him reinstated to the team, despite its characteristic misspellings and twisted grammar, is found later to have been written by Kippy, without Shane's knowledge. The day that Shane comes back, he overhears Darren arguing with Davey Battle, who plays for the opposing team. Shane, who has a ritual of taking three showers before each game, is in the shower alone when Darren enters, bringing to life the very fear Shane had complained about to the interviewer. He starts out making fun of Shane, but soon becomes physical, grabbing Shane and kissing him. When Shane is brought into the game, he throws a pitch that kills the first batter he faces, Davey Battle.

In jail, Shane pathetically believes that he might be allowed to come back to the team, not realizing that his baseball career is over. Released without being charged, he fades into obscurity, until one night when he drinks too much and takes a gun from one store to another, shooting milk bottles. He ends up in prison.

Rodriguez

Rodriguez is never onstage without the other Spanish-speaking member of the Empires, Martinez. Their conversations together are a mystery to the other team members.

Skipper

Skipper is William R. Danziger, the manager of the Empires. He is known for his personal skills, his ability to be tough when he needs to be and gentle when it is called for. Although Darren Lemming is loved by his public and his teammates, he is particularly important to Skipper, who, as Kippy points out, "thinks he *invented* Darren."

After Darren surprises his teammates by publicly announcing that he is gay, and Shane Mungitt publicly insults him because of it, Skipper writes him a formal letter, expressing both his support and also his frustration. Referring to him as "Mr. Lemming," he tells Darren that he would be proud to have a son like him, would support him if he were gay, and in fact would be glad, if his son were gay, if he had a lover like Darren. He ends the letter by saying that his feelings are hurt that Darren has brought his sexuality into the game of baseball.

After the decision has been made to allow Shane back onto the team, Darren goes to Skipper to explain that, because he is the team's star player, his opinion about the matter should take precedence over other factors, but Skipper just tells him that he should be able to adjust to the changing situation. Darren notes that Skipper refers to his affection for him in the past tense, a point that Skipper does not deny.

Kippy Sunderstrom

Kippy serves often as the narrator of the play, speaking directly to the audience and giving background details.

He is Darren Lemming's closest friend on the Empires. Their conversations are philosophical. Darren describes him as "The most intelligent man in Major League baseball," but Kippy counters that he only seems intelligent because he is not as large as Swedes usually are. He is the person with whom Darren will joke about the intellectual weakness of the other team members such as Koovitz, Chenier, and especially Shane Mungitt. He is good at understanding the nuances of situations and explaining them to Darren and the other teammates. When Martinez and Rodriguez speak Spanish, and when Kawabata speaks Japanese, Kippy says that he can translate what they are saying, though his translations are vague and unconvincing.

When Shane has been thrown off of the team for speaking out offensively in public about Darren's sexual orientation, Kippy arranges to have him reinstated by writing an apologetic letter and signing his name to it, a fact that does not become public until after Shane has killed a batter. His secret is even more poignant because the batter who is killed, Davey Battle, is Darren's best friend off of the team, and Kippy shows a little jealousy because of it. His last words to Davey, said jokingly, are "We're gonna kill you."

The night of Davey's funeral, Kippy calls Darren and tells him that he may have been a little jealous of Davey's friendship with him. He tells Darren that he loves him, though he tries to take some of the seriousness out of the situation by saying "that's *fraught*, given the circumstances, but you know I mean it in an unfraught sort of way." At the end of the season, he confesses to Darren that he went to college on an academic scholarship, not an athletic one, but chose baseball over intellectual pursuits because playing is a celebration of life.

THEMES

Culture Clash

Take Me Out derives much of its dramatic tension from the contrast of two subcultures that have traditionally been kept separated: homosexuality and major league sports. Greenberg draws attention to the novelty of this situation by making Darren Lemming biracial, which his teammates and fans not only accept but actively support: as Kippy says in his introductory speech, baseball is "one of the few realms of American life in which people of color are routinely adulated by people of pallor," and Darren, being comfortable about his mixed heritage, is admired as someone who represents the best of both cultures.

Homosexuality is new to the world of baseball, though, and the play centers on Darren's teammates' struggle to adjust to it. Skipper, in a formal letter, expresses his wholehearted support for Darren as a gay man, but he also expresses his disappointment that Darren has openly brought homosexuality to

baseball. Jason Chenier, a new player, sees Darren's announcement about his sexual orientation as a weakness that brings Darren, the team's star player, down closer to his level: while he was previously too intimidated to approach Darren, after the announcement he adapts a somewhat patronizing attitude toward him, citing references to past achievements by homosexuals that appear to be aimed at making Darren feel good about himself. Toddy Koovitz, on the other hand, turns angry and suspicious about the news, unsure about how the knowledge about Darren's orientation might change the locker room dynamic and afraid that it might make him change his own comfortable habits. Davey Battle, who is Darren's best friend before the announcement, rejects him with hostility upon finding out he is gay: the religious Davey cannot reconcile Darren's sexuality with his own views on the subject.

Take Me Out also shows the reverse situation, with gay culture, represented by quiet intellectual Mason Marzac, being introduced to the culture of professional sports. Mason comes into Darren's life with very little knowledge of baseball, but grateful to Darren for being open about his homosexuality. Because of his involvement with Darren, though, he begins following the game and becomes engrossed in it. He spins elaborate, abstract theories about the hidden significance of many of the rituals surrounding the game that baseball's traditional fans might take for granted.

Social Classes

Although it may seem to some that Shane Mungitt is the villain of this play, Greenberg draws the character very carefully to show that Shane is not bad at heart but that he is instead a victim of the lower-class background from which he comes. Even though Shane uses insulting words to describe his teammates and speaks derisively about Darren's sexual orientation in public (unlike players like Toddy Koovitz, who are just as derisive, but not in public), he also shows that he is disappointed that he cannot socialize with those same teammates, showing that his problem is not one of hatred, but of being too poor at communication to effectively express what he means.

Shane is the opposite of Darren Lemming in almost every way. Being the product of a "triumphant yet cozy middle-class marriage" has given Darren the education that he needs to speak his mind and the self-assurance that he needs to do so. When things go poorly for Daren, such as when Shane publicly insults him, Darren is in a position to insist that

TOPICS FOR FURTHER STUDY

- Do some research on Jackie Robinson, who became the first black player in Major League Baseball in 1947. Make a list of the personal qualities that Robinson had that made him able to break baseball's color barrier. Then write a letter to Darren Lemming, the pitcher in *Take Me Out*, explaining how you think he should speak to the public about his sexual orientation.

- *Take Me Out* achieved some notoriety for the scenes that call for male nudity onstage. Divide into teams to debate whether nudity onstage is appropriate and whether male nudity should be handled differently than female nudity. Teams should use examples from previous Broadway productions to support their positions.

- Baseball players have long been known for their close sense of camaraderie. Watch the 1973 movie *Bang the Drum Slowly*, based on a famous baseball play by Mark Harris, and make a chart of the similarities that you see between the relationship between Wiggen and Pearson in the movie and Darren and Kippy in *Take Me Out*.

- As of 2006, laws existed that made homosexual behavior a crime in some places in the United States. Research some of these laws, and write an opinion that explains either why these laws should be allowed to continue or why they should be overturned.

- Every four years brings the International Gay Games, a competition that parallels the International Olympics. Make a chart of which athletic records have been broken at the Gay Games then research one of the record-breaking athletes, and explain how her or his life has or has not changed as a result of holding a world record in a non-mainstream competition.

- Read *The Boys in the Band*, a 1968 play that was the first big Broadway hit focused on the lives of gay men. Write a short story which shows how you think Darren Lemming would react if he somehow wandered into the long-ago world of that play.

---

his will be followed or to quit if it is not. Shane, on the other hand, was traumatized early on by his parents' deaths, and all of the anger that presumably came before it and followed in a succession of orphanages. He has not been raised to have the financial resources that Darren has, and more important, he lacks the emotional security to adapt to new situations. The one thing that Shane and Darren have in common is that they are both excellent baseball players: in putting such diverse characters into contact with each other, the play makes a point about how baseball transcends the ideas of social class that usually keep people separated in U.S. society.

Moral Confusion

When Davey Battle is introduced in the play, the audience is told that he is Darren Lemming's best friend. By the end, however, it turns out that Davey and Darren are the causes of each other's

destruction, due to misunderstandings that they both have about the other's moral perspective.

In their first scene together, Darren and Davey joke with each other good-naturedly about their differences while maintaining their basic affection. Darren does not recognize the depth of Davey's religious convictions, and Davey does not see just how far from his worldview Darren actually is. Darren jokes about Davey's willingness to use some swear words but not others and about the fact that Davey will drink beer in a bar: he thinks that Davey is using their friendship to convince the public that he is a regular person. Davey tells Darren that he believes, regardless of what Darren thinks about himself, that he is a good man at heart who will feel better about himself once he tries leading an open and honest life. He knows that Darren is not in a loving, committed relationship but has no idea that he is gay.

After Darren's sexual orientation is announced to the public, Davey approaches him with anger. He refers to homosexuality as a demon and to Darren's "ugliness," and says that he would never have encouraged Darren to be true to himself if he had known that he was "a pervert." His anger and confusion are so great that he even accuses Darren of pretending to be his friend in order to have sex with him. The Christian love that Davey showered on Darren earlier, when he thought that he just needed confidence, is pushed aside by intolerance.

STYLE

Equivocation

Greenberg's title phrase, *Take Me Out*, is an example of equivocation because it can be read or interpreted in different ways.

The title's most obvious reference, to a reader just approaching this play, is that the words "take me out" are the first words sung in baseball's unofficial anthem. At almost every baseball stadium throughout the country, each game has a seventh-inning stretch, when fans are invited to rise to their feet, stretch their limbs, and sing, "Take Me Out to the Ballgame." This song, written in 1908, is estimated to be the third most frequently sung song in the United States, after "The Star-Spangled Banner" and "Happy Birthday to You." It is an inextricable part of baseball culture.

But this play is also about romantic relations. When he first announces his sexual orientation to the world, Darren Lemming does not have a particular romantic interest in mind, a fact that he states emphatically to his friend Kippy Sunderstrom. By the end of the play, though, he has enough tentative connection to Mason Marzac for the audience to see a relationship starting to form, culminating is his asking Mason to be his "date" to the celebratory party after the last game. Although Mason never explicitly tells Daren to "take me out," the sense of going out and asking someone out is clearly implied in the title.

A third sense of the phrase is that it represents the opposite of what athletes usually request of their coaches. When watching from the bench and feeling enthused about being able to help the team, an athlete will often tell the coach to put him in: this phrase is highlighted in one of baseball's most famous songs, John Fogerty's 1985 tune "Centerfield," with its refrain, "Put me in coach, I'm ready to play today." Greenberg's use of the phrase in its negative form might be a reference to the fact that

Darren Lemming is a reluctant player, planning his retirement from baseball, or it could refer to the way that Shane Mungitt destroys his career, implicitly asking to be taken out of the game. Ominously the phrase also suggests an invitation to be murdered.

Dramatic Narration

Several times in *Take Me Out*, characters step away from the dramatic situation that is being acted onstage to talk directly to the audience. Kippy Sunderstrom does this most often, but it is also done by Mason Marzac and Takeshi Kawabata.

The idea of directly giving audiences information that they need, rather than working the information into the situation that the characters are dramatizing, is hardly a new one. It has its roots in the dramas of the great Greek playwrights Aeschylus (525–456 B.C.E..), Sophocles (496–406 B.C.E..), and Euripides (480–406 B.C.E..). Their plays relied on the use of a chorus of citizens to provide background information to the audience. As drama evolved, however, playwrights tended not to have characters directly tell background information, called exposition, to the audience. The usual method has been to let the action and dialogue that takes place between the characters onstage convey all of the information that audiences need to know. By having Kippy narrate the story in the way that he does, Greenberg relies on a device that goes back to the roots of Western drama.

The speech that Kawabata gives at the beginning of act 3 resembles a specific kind of narration, a soliloquy. Different than narration, the soliloquy reveals the speaker's internal thoughts and emotions. Mason's speech about baseball as "a perfect metaphor for hope in a democratic society" is also a soliloquy, though it does not look like one to the casual eye. The speech does not convey any information that is necessary to understanding the play's story but is instead meant to give Mason's personal perspective. While a soliloquy gives private thoughts and emotions, Mason's speech sounds more like a philosophy lecture. This is because he is an analytic, dispassionate character himself, whose personality thrives on developing new theories: what sounds like a lecture is an accurate reflection of his inner emotions.

HISTORICAL CONTEXT

Homosexuality in Organized Sports

When *Take Me Out* was produced, no players for any major league sports teams were openly homosexual. The first player in any team sport to come out about his sexual orientation was Dave Kopay, an NFL running back who was retired for several years before going public. The NFL also produced Roy Simmons, who played offensive guard for the Giants and Redskins from 1979 to 1983 and then revealed his orientation on the Phil Donahue talk show in 1992, and Esera Tuaolo, an offensive lineman who announced that he was gay and that he and his partner had two adopted children, but kept his private life a secret until 2002—three years after he left football.

Major League Baseball had only had two admittedly gay players and one gay umpire, and none of them came out to the public about their sexual orientation while their careers were going on. The first player was Glenn Burke, an outfielder for the Los Angeles Dodgers and the Oakland Athletics during the 1970s. Burke kept his life as a homosexual a secret from the public: at one point, the Dodgers offered to pay for an opulent honeymoon if he would participate in a sham marriage to a woman, but he refused. In 1980, after a brief retirement, he returned to the Oakland A's, and their manager at the time, Billy Martin, made disparaging remarks about not wanting gays in the clubhouse, although he named no names. Burke injured his knee that year and retired. He revealed his orientation during a 1982 interview with *Inside Sports*, and went on to be a participant in the 1982 and 1986 Gay Games. Although he was a barrier breaker, he died a forgotten man: after a car accident ruined his leg in 1987, he spiraled into drugs, which led to jail and then homelessness. He died of AIDS in 1995.

Billy Bean, who was an outfielder for the Tigers, Giants, and Padres from 1987 to 1995, came out publicly in 1999. His autobiography, *Going the Other Way*, tells of the jibes that he had to suffer from his teammates about his sexuality, including the fact that he felt compelled to skip the funeral of his domestic partner, who had died of AIDS, in order to keep their relationship a secret.

Dave Pallone was a major league umpire for eighteen years but was quietly dismissed in 1988 because of rumors about his sexual orientation. Later, he published an autobiography and traveled the country giving speeches about sexual orientation, diversity, and acceptance.

While there are still no openly gay players in the four most prominent team sports—baseball, football, basketball, and hockey—there are gay athletes in sports that compete on an individual basis. The most prominent of these are tennis superstar Martina Navratilova, who came out about her sexuality in 1981 after speculation about her relationship with author Rita Mae Brown, and Greg Louganis, one of the greatest Olympic divers in history, who went public about his orientation in 1994. In a *Sports Illustrated* poll published in March of 2006, a majority of players in each of the four major professional sports said that they would welcome an openly gay teammate, with 61 percent of major league baseball players responding positively, according to the Outsports.com website.

The John Rocker Controversy

A few years before *Take Me Out* was produced, John Rocker, a relief pitcher for the Atlanta Braves, became famous around the world for controversial comments similar to those made by Shane Mungitt in the play. In an interview with *Sports Illustrated* published in 2000, Rocker, who had been harassed by New York fans during the 1999 playoffs against the Mets, said that he would never be able to play in New York:

> It's the most hectic, nerve-racking city. Imagine having to take the [Number] 7 train to the ballpark, looking like you're [riding through] Beirut next to some kid with purple hair next to some queer with AIDS right next to some dude who just got out of jail for the fourth time right next to some 20-year-old mom with four kids. It's depressing.

An overwhelming public outcry followed, during which widely diverse fans all around the country called sports shows to voice their outrage. For weeks he was mocked on comedy shows such as *The Tonight Show*, *The Late Show*, and *Saturday Night Live*. He was suspended for the first twenty-eight games of the season, though his suspension was later revised to just fourteen games.

At Rocker's first game in New York after his suspension, Mets officials called on ten times the usual number of police for protection. Beer sales were limited, and a special protective cover was installed over the Braves' bullpen for protection. Before the game, a taped apology from Rocker was played on the stadium's giant television screen. Rocker was brought in to jeers and chants during the eighth inning and went on to win the game, but his career spiraled downward after that: in quick succession he was traded from Atlanta to Cleveland to Texas. He played only two games for the Tampa Bay Devil Rays at the start of the 2003 season before the team dismissed him. His last comeback was, ironically, in the New York metropolitan area, where he pitched for the Long Island Ducks in 2005, compiling a dismal 6.50 Earned Run Average in twenty-three games.

CRITICAL OVERVIEW

Critics have generally viewed *Take Me Out* as a heartfelt work that is clearly knowledgeable about both the game of baseball and what it is to be public about homosexuality in the United States of the twenty-first century; still, most critics have tempered their support for the play by expressing discomfort about Greenberg's two-dimensional handling of characters, particularly Shane, while giving other characters verbal abilities that seem quite unlikely to be found among ballplayers.

Some reviewers had nothing but praise for the play when it ran on Broadway in 2002. For instance, David Kaufman, writing in *Nation*, starts his review with a brief overview of how far theater has come in portraying gay issues onstage since the 1960s, determining that *Take Me Out* "is indeed one of the best gay plays in years," noting that "Greenberg seamlessly ties together matters of sex, race, multiculturalism, politics, political correctness, and celebrity." Stuart Miller's review in the *Sporting News* was also laudatory, but with reservations. "The plot falters with its climactic contrivances," Miller writes, "and the numerous nude shower scenes may turn off some, but the play stirs emotions on issues ranging from friendship to trust to hero worship. Score *Take Me Out* a stand-up double—it doesn't quite hit the ball out of the park, but it provides plenty to cheer about."

Elysa Gardner, the reviewer for *USA Today*, touches on the reservations that most reviewers had when praising the play. Gardner points out how the move from Off-Broadway to the Walter Kerr Theatre drew attention to the play's weaknesses: "The bright lights and bustling dialogue that dazzled in a smaller setting are now too flashy at times, and at other points reveal flaws in Greenberg's impressive text." She also notes the disparity between the verbal acumen of Kippy and Darren in the play, while the foreign players and, especially, Shane Mungitt, are left inarticulate, explaining that "the playwright's cavalier mockery of the others is self-defeating." In the end, though, the review characterizes the play as "a winner."

A few critics did not care for the play, such as Bill Hagerty, who reviewed the London production in 2002 for the *Hollywood Reporter*. His review notes that

> Greenberg never loses the audience's attention. . . . But if the writer is suggesting that big-time sport and homosexuality mix as happily as salt and sugar, it is a simplistic conclusion. If he is attempting to say more, it still hadn't emerged by the bottom of the ninth.

Frederick Weller playing Shane Mungitt along with Neal Huff as Kippy and Daniel Sunjata as Darren Lemming in a London production of Take Me Out © Donald Cooper/Photostage

This review, unique in its weak enthusiasm for the writing, credits the acting and directing but determines in the end, "This baseball saga sports a disappointing batting average."

CRITICISM

David Kelly

Kelly is an instructor of English literature and composition. In the following essay, he examines why Darren Lemming remains a sympathetic character, despite his behavior in the play.

In his play *Take Me Out*, Richard Greenberg imagines the day, which by all reasonable estimates cannot be long off, when a major league baseball player will publicly announce that he is gay. Of course, like most other persons who have successfully broken down invisible social barriers, Greenberg's fictional center fielder Darren Lemming is an extremely talented player, whose dominance of the game is widely accepted. This removes any question of whether gay players are as capable as

> WHILE LEMMING'S WIDESPREAD POPULARITY IS TAKEN AS A GIVEN AT THE BEGINNING OF THE PLAY, THE TRULY SURPRISING THING IS THAT IT HOLDS UP UNTIL THE END, REGARDLESS OF WHO HE SHOWS HIMSELF TO BE IN THE INTERVENING TIME."

straight players. The fact that Lemming is, in fact, a superstar earns him more freedom from his fans than a lesser player would enjoy.

The play illustrates how the world reacts to Lemming's sexual orientation when another player, Shane Mungitt, makes a harsh public reference to having "a *faggot* " on the team. Not only are those viewing the play left with dropped jaws by the disrespect shown to Lemming, but Greenberg makes it clear from Mungitt's immediate suspension from Major League Baseball that baseball fans in the world of the Greenberg's play side with Lemming. They continue to consider Lemming a hero and will not accept a verbal assault against him. Any ambivalence in how the fans feel about the opening of baseball to gays is mild and contained: one character mentions that Lemming's commercials have been shifted to late-night television, but that is a much more measured reaction than pulling them from the airwaves completely. Nothing is said of riots outside of stadiums, of increased violence against gays, or plummeting ticket sales, all of which conceivably might happen under such circumstances.

Greenberg establishes Lemming's popularity very early in the play, at the same time that he acknowledges the clear contrast between the way homosexuals have been excluded from professional sports and the ways that racial minorities have gained acceptance. Kippy Sunderstrom, the clubhouse intellectual who narrates much of the play's back story, explains within the first few lines that Lemming is the product of a white father and a black mother, noting, "Even in baseball—one of the few

realms of American life in which people of color are routinely adulated by people of pallor, he was something special: a black man who had obviously not suffered." These few lines set the tone of the play, and of the public's mood, in several ways.

For one thing, this line tells audiences, in case they did not know it, that the color line has been rendered all but irrelevant in the world of professional sports. It holds as true in the world of this play as it does in real life: there may be a few fans here and there who might hold back from supporting a player of a certain race, but expressing such a view would certainly mark one as an oddity among true sports fans.

Another thing the quotation reveals is Darren Lemming's complete dominance of the game of baseball. He is not just "adulated," which would be good enough for an ordinary sports hero, but he is "special" in addition to that. Lemming is established as being among the best of the best from the script's first page on.

The third and most unstable idea that comes out of Sunderstrom's sentence is the actual reason why Lemming is thought of so kindly by his fans. If this quotation is correct, several assumptions are running through the mind of a fan who accepts Lemming. One is the assumption that most black players have to suffer to reach the major leagues. Another is that audiences have heard so much about black players who have suffered that they find Lemming, with his happy, well-adjusted background, to be a refreshing change. The last is that Darren Lemming has had such a smooth life that the lack of suffering in his background is obvious.

While Lemming's widespread popularity is taken as a given at the beginning of the play, the truly surprising thing is that it holds up until the end, regardless of who he shows himself to be in the intervening time. Darren Lemming is not at all humble. He acts toward both his teammates and his fans as if he deserves every bit of honor given to him, plus more. He is disgusted with fans who have the nerve to offer him compassion after he has been publicly insulted, feeling that compassion brings him down to the level of a common person: they should envy him instead. He rails against people who try to understand him, pouts when his word alone is not enough to have Mungitt thrown out of baseball, and mocks the people who adore him. By all rights, Lemming should wear out his welcome with the theater audience by the time *Take Me Out* is over. When the final curtain falls, however, Greenberg leaves audiences feeling more sympathy

WHAT DO I READ NEXT?

- *The Changing Room*, by British novelist and playwright David Storey, won the New York Critics' Best Play of the Year Award for 1972. The play, drawn from Storey's own experiences, takes place in the clubhouse of a rugby team. It examines the competitive nature of sports and the camaraderie that exists among teammates and was a precursor to *Take Me Out* in its use of onstage male nudity. First published in 1971 by Jonathan Cape, it is available in *David Storey Plays: The Changing Room / Cromwell / Life Class*, published by Methuen in 1996.

- Peter Lefcourt's *The Dreyfus Affair* (1992) is an amusing novel about a very successful second baseman whose life starts unraveling when he finds that he is falling in love with the team's shortstop. When the men are caught kissing, they are banned from baseball for life.

- Glenn Burke was an African American center fielder, credited with being the player to invent the high five. He was also the first player in Major League Baseball history to go public about being a homosexual, a few years after his retirement. His autobiography, *Out at Home: The Glenn Burke Story* (1995), was published posthumously by Excel Publishing. It details the difficulties that Burke faced with drug addiction, a stint in San Quentin, and living with the AIDS virus, which eventually killed him.

- When a revival of Greenberg's 1997 *Three Days of Rain* opened in 2006, media attention focused on actress Julia Roberts, who was making her Broadway debut. But the play illustrates Greenberg's versatility, centering on three characters in the 1990s who cope with their own lives and the resurgence of their father's cryptic journal: in act 2, the same actors play their parents, in the 1960s. The play is available from Grove Press, in a 1999 edition that also includes Greenberg's *The American Plan*, *The Author's Voice*, and *Hurrah at Last*.

---

for Lemming than for Davey Battle, the character who was killed by a wild pitch, or for Mungitt, the character whose mental and emotional shortcomings lost him his chance to do the one thing that he really understands.

To some extent, empathy for Lemming is the natural outcome of the play, its only proper, satisfactory conclusion. The story starts out with a player who has everything he could want in his professional career but lacks the ability to love freely, so it is reasonable to feel that the play has reached its fulfillment once he finds someone to love. Audiences may have doubts about Lemming's hubris throughout the play, but, like the dramatic convention of bringing up a wedding at the play's end, no matter how contrived or remote, to signify a happy ending, the budding relationship between Lemming and Mason Marzac in the last scene lets everyone leave the theater feeling good.

Greenberg goes further than just providing a happy ending. He also makes it easier to sympathize

with Lemming, regardless of how the character might feel about such sympathy, by showing those characters who oppose him to be misguided, foolish, and even evil.

In this play, it is sadness, not anger, that dominates the clubhouse mood after Lemming's orientation is acknowledged. This is best expressed in the letter that the team's manager, William R. Danziger, sends to Lemming soon after Mungitt has humiliated him publicly. Danziger is not at all equivocal about his feelings for Lemming: he expresses his great regard for him as a player and as a man. By saying that he would wish that if his son were gay he would have a lover like Lemming, Danziger shows that he has no fear of homosexuality. Still, despite his respect, it distresses him that Lemming has introduced homosexuality into baseball. Danziger is a man who loves the game, and he regrets seeing things change. He does not speak with anger, but he clearly is not happy with this turn of events. His attitude seems to be like that of most baseball fans in the world of Greenberg's play: disappointment and acceptance.

Of course, the central relationship in the play is the one between Darren Lemming and Shane Mungitt. Mungitt is uneducated and was traumatized as a child; he has ended up the diametric opposite of Lemming. He is racist and homophobic, airing his anxieties in public. In the end he kills a man, probably intentionally. He is not a sympathetic character, but, once the story of his parents' murder/suicide is explained, it is also difficult to blame him for his ignorance. Greenberg does not make Mungitt an evil character, just one who is unable to behave well. He may be a victim of circumstances, but he is so lacking in the attributes that make Lemming admirable that his collapse is not even a moral issue.

The character who represents evil in the play is Davey Battle. Like Lemming, he is a star player, and he is Lemming's best friend, a fact that is told to the audience several times. Battle has all of the attributes that should make him sympathetic, but in the play's climax, he turns out to be missing what might be the most important element of all: empathy for Darren Lemming. He finds that he cannot tolerate the fact that Lemming is gay, which leads to an argument that Mungitt overhears, which results in Battle's death. Audiences can register how sad it is that a man has been killed over a simple misunderstanding, but in the play's larger moral sense, Battle's death is not a misunderstanding at all: his opposition to Lemming earns him his just reward. As a character, Davey Battle loses audience support because of his own intolerance, which turns out to be a more serious, punishable offense than Mungitt's ignorance or even Lemming's rage against Mungitt.

The main character of *Take Me Out* does not behave admirably. He is proud and arrogant to such an extent that he preys on the weak-minded Mungitt's fear of male intimacy, and he turns against fans and teammates who want to sympathize with him. Still, he is a sympathetic, even sweet character in the final scene. The play is crafted to keep audiences connected to Lemming, to take them as far as they can go with a fictional character whose behavior would probably be found unacceptable in real life.

Source: David Kelly, Critical Essay on *Take Me Out*, in *Drama for Students*, Thomson Gale, 2007.

Allen Ellenzweig

In the following review, Ellenzweig explains that Take Me Out *is about the quick turn to intolerance when a black baseball player announces he is gay. He also praises O'Hare's performance as Mason, Greenberg's "mouthpiece" for his obsession for baseball.*

When Richard Greenberg's play *Take Me Out* first played downtown at The Public Theater several months ago by way of London's Donmar Warehouse, much of the buzz concerned its lavish display of male nudity. Not since Mary Martin had to wash that man right out of her hair had the act of lathering up seemed so novel a theatrical idea. Now *Take Me Out* has been moved to Broadway in a two-act instead of a three-act version. Though I can't speak to that change, having missed the former production, I can assure interested parties that a chorus line of well-built men taking a shower on stage will not hurt its commercial fortunes.

The scene in question is not a cheap trick, however, occurring in a play about baseball that considers the consequences to a team of a star player coming out as gay. The athlete in question, one Darren Lemming, has the additional distinction of being half black and half white. Until his gay declaration, he has managed to attain iconic status and has prepared no one for his burst of candor. As played by Daniel Sunjata, Lemming is a brash, cocky, smug gay rake who has had enough of the duplicity of the closet.

While the play's narrative revolves around the various reactions of his fellow Empires in pinstripes (think New York Yankees), the emotional heart of the play lies elsewhere. Lemming takes on a new business manager in the person of Mason Marzac, a sober gay schlemiel who bones up on baseball the moment the young hunk becomes his financial charge. Here, in the impish performance of Denis O'Hare, the playwright finds his mouthpiece. Mason is a seriously controlled and hemmed-in personality, but his growing adoration for the game of baseball loosens his tether and releases the pixie inside. In O'Hare's alternately droll and intoxicating demeanor, we get the great pleasure of watching a gay nebbish bloom, his heart gone loopy over the numerological wonders of nine players arrayed around a diamond over the course of nine innings. In interviews, Greenberg has admitted to his own conversion to the great American pastime. He obviously has poured his new obsession into the character of Mason Marzac.

If Mason is the uptight gay man getting in touch with his inner jock, Shane Mungit is an inarticulate redneck pitcher (think John Rocker of the Atlanta Braves) who publicly reveals the breadth of his bigotry toward his fellow teammates, and thus propels the climactic drama of *Take Me Out*. In reaction to a sexual provocation by Lemming—aimed at forcing Mungit's homophobic response—the inchoate feelings of this white trash phenom find their way into a wild pitch aimed at Lemming's best friend, another African-American player on an opposing team. Frederick Weller brings a sense of inexpressible grievance to the mullet-haired Mungit, and doing so, he matches the three-dimensional rapture of O'Hare's baseball-smitten gay number-cruncher.

Take Me Out does better at bringing into view the fault lines of race and class in team sports than in developing a fully realized comedy-drama. Its weakness lies in a central character, Lemming, whose arrogance and self-love never reveal themselves as the armor of a gay black man struggling for a place in the pantheon of American heroes. The internal tensions in his plight might have played out in his relationship to the upright Davey Battle, his rigorously moral black colleague from another team. Lemming and Battle seem fully prepared to enact the loneliness of the African-American athlete in their one heated exchange, but by then it is too late. Greenberg has not prepared us sufficiently for this theme, although he drops hints throughout *Take Me Out* that his protagonist's race has never been a problem for him. For certainly to be black and gay demands of a young man a reckoning with his own heart and his twin communities.

There is much to admire in Greenberg's writing. His comic lines are full of sass, sometimes coming as fast and furious as those in a 1930's screwball comedy. And in the character of his play's narrator, the loquacious and thoughtful Kippy Sunderstrom, Greenberg proposes the device of the Stage Manager from *Our Town* or the memory guide such as Tom in *The Glass Menagerie*. In this, he achieves a direct line to the audience and a sense of intimacy. As a work of art, *Take Me Out* has more height than depth—a gorgeous surface veneer, like that line up of young bucks soaping up in a locker room shower.

Source: Allen Ellenzweig, "It Takes a Jock," in *The Gay & Lesbian Review*, Vol. 10, No. 3, May–June 2003, p. 50.

Steven Drukman

In the following review, Take Me Out *is described as a microcosm of the nation, "plagued" with the same "social issues" experienced during the twentieth century. The essay ends with an interview with Greenberg, and he discusses "the mix of homosexuality and baseball" in his play.*

Last century began tinged with an optimism alien to today's jaded baseball fans. To quote a 1901 issue of *Baseball Magazine*: "Thomas Jefferson, when he wrote the Declaration of Independence, made proper provision for baseball when he declared that all men are free and equal. That's why

RICHARD GREENBERG'S *TAKE ME OUT* . . . IS THE FIRST MAJOR PLAY TO GRAPPLE WITH HOMOSEXUALITY AND ITS UNEASY OVERLAP IN THE WORLD OF PROFESSIONAL BASEBALL."

they are at the ballgame, banker and bricklayer, lawyer and common laborer."

This sunny-sky view of the American polls has suffered its share of rain delays over the past 100 years. Whether at Ebbets Field or Camden Yards, decade after decade proved that all men were not always created equal, even in that most pastoral of settings. In fact, baseball struggled—in lockstep and in microcosmic form—with the same social issues that plagued the nation throughout the 20th century. Alongside the game's heroic tales there have been seamy stories of labor strife, corruption, gambling, racial prejudice and, now, drug use. The American experiment is far from over, and baseball—despite its geometric and algebraic perfection—is far from "perfect" in the sociopolitical realm.

Over the past two decades, a handful of "baseball plays" have grappled with social issues. Allen Meyer and Michael Nowak's *The Signal Season of Dummy Hoy*, about a deaf Chicago White Sox player in the 1910s, addressed disability on the diamond in its 1987 premiere at Chicago's Commons Theatre. That same year, August Wilson's Pulitzer-winning *Fences*—a stirring drama about the fictional Troy Maxson, who was kept from big league play because of the game's ban on black athletes—debuted on Broadway. In 1994, Eric Simonson's adaptation of Mark Harris's 1956 novel *Bang the Drum Slowly*—a play about a dying ballplayer that ran at Boston's Huntington Theatre—was, according to its author, "made relevant in the age of AIDS."

More recently, in 2000, Lee Blessing's *Cobb* (first staged by New York's Melting Pot Theatre Company) rose above the mere baseball bio-play by placing a decidedly politically incorrect athlete in proper cultural context. (Blessing's antihero, the bigoted Ty Cobb, is shown in Blessing's imagination to be haunted by Oscar Charleston, who played in the Negro Leagues and was known as the "black Cobb.") Last season, Ken LaZebnik's *League of Nations* (which premiered at Minneapolis's Mixed Blood Theatre in March) used one team's pitching rotation—which included a Korean, an African American, a Mexican and a hot new Japanese import—as a portrait in miniature of this country's roiling, sometimes boiling, melting pot. Still, despite these admirable efforts from socially conscious playwrights, the phrase "baseball play" usually conjures but one: *Damn Yankees*, Adler and Ross's 1955 Goethe-meets-Doubleday musical that dressed the Faust legend in cleats and made the Washington Senators sing "you gotta have heart."

Richard Greenberg's *Take Me Out* (which is currently having its U.S. premiere at New York's Public Theater) is the first major play to grapple with homosexuality and its uneasy overlap in the world of professional baseball. But Greenberg's play is about much more (and, in its true-to-baseball spirit, much *less*) than sexual politics: As the playwright himself explained, the real love story in *Take Me Out* is with the game, pure and simple. The play—concerning Darren, a young superstar who decides, in a mixture of hubris and candor, to "come out" to his adoring fans as a red-blooded, 100-percent homosexual (he doesn't even, uh, swing both ways)—premiered at London's Donmar Warehouse last June to mostly rave reviews. Writing in the *New Yorker*, critic John Lahr asserted that "if there's anything that confounds the British more than American optimism, it's baseball . . . a game—some would say a ritual—of hope." Nonetheless, the result of Greenberg's "mischievous ambition: to marry the old ballgame with gay politics" is "exhilarating." Lahr suggests that *Take Me Out* would win over even the most resistant Brit who might find the project not quite cricket.

Take Me Out's implicit message—that social issues sit like thorns in the manicured green fields of ballparks—may explain why professional baseball is sometimes a bit tentative in its approach to cultural politics. (And when it comes to professional *theatre*, why for every *Cobb* there will always be a hundred *Pride of the Yankees*—or, for that matter, *Damn Yankees*.) This has less to do with players, owners, sportswriters and, for that matter, playwrights-who-are-fans "being in denial" than it does with the ontology of the game: The panglossian spirit cannot be extracted from baseball's very essence (as the quote from *Baseball Magazine* attests). Darren doesn't believe his admission can hurt him because the fans will still come out, rosy-eyed and rooting to the end. That's baseball's way, and you see it in every game.

And this spirit pervades more than each *individual* game: For the true aficionado, there's always that irresistible force of optimism in the face of adversity that peppers the *larger* epic drama that stretches out over every season. Hope "springs" eternal (even for Cubs fans) in spring training, and "falls" for most by the end of October. Even if your team is showing you (as Casey Stengel said of his hapless Mets in 1962) "new ways to lose," with the right midseason trades and a little bit of luck . . . well, you never know how things will end up. Baseball—perennial, passed on to our kids and prone to extra innings—tends to play out as the theatre of American renewal.

To wit: This conversation took place when a baseball strike appeared imminent. But like fans down by two runs in the bottom of the ninth, both the interviewer and his subject seemed illogically, even desperately, hopeful. In baseball (like theatre), there's always next season.

[*Steven Drukman:*] *You know why I'm writing this piece, don't you?*

[Richard Greenberg:] Well, I never knew but just found out you were an incredible baseball fan.

I am, but we're on opposite sides of the fence, so to speak.

Oh, God, you're not from some place like Boston, are you? [*they both laugh*] Well, we can still talk.

Well, this launches us quite easily into what I've always believed: that baseball allows us to play out our particular geographical, social, ethnic (you name it) issues, but in the end, baseball itself is what's important. Red Sox fans like me love our pious Brahmin pessimism almost as much as we love our team.

It's true. You Red Sox fans—your misery concretizes all those New England virtues, that Protestant deferred gratification. And now, I guess, after 83 years of losing in the post season, that's a lot of deferral. And you guys are always complaining about the Yankees, blaming our payroll.

Oh, New Englanders are always crying poverty. We're thrifty.

You're martyrs. The Diamondbacks just played a series with the Red Sox—*and swept them*—but your fans didn't care: They just kept coming up to the Diamondbacks and thanking them for beating the Yankees in the World Series last year! That's nuts. And as I say in my play *Three Days of Rain*, "Boston isn't a city, Boston is a parish."

We finally agree. Now is Take Me Out *your first baseball play?*

I think it has to be my only one, don't you? After Tom Stoppard wrote *The Real Thing* he said, "Well, that's the love play." Which is odd, because love is a bigger subject than baseball—well, no, not really. Anyway, I think this is my baseball play.

Is this a "gay play"?

I don't want to make any of those disingenuous remarks like "What is a gay play?" Aren't all my plays "gay plays," in a way? Actually (and this is not enlightened as much as it is . . . blind): I don't remember if plays I've written have gay characters in them or not. Because you know how our lives are more multifarious than that? I just think of characters in the same way. I guess this one has a gay "angle."

Well, at any rate, the mix of homosexuality and baseball in a play is not old hat.

Funny, though: A publicist recently complained to me that it marginalized the play to call it a "gay play" because then baseball fans won't show up.

Or vice versa. We gay baseball fans are in the minority, Richard. But this play is really more tragic than the tag "gay baseball play" suggests. To me, it's not unlike [John Knowles's novel] A Separate Peace.

Oh, my God! You know, it's hilarious that you said that—nobody has said that. The narrator, that's part of it, sure, as is the crisis of masculinity, of course. But recently when I read the play I heard an echo of that book, and I haven't read it in 20 years, so that's very astute. And also it's a love story. Though I think that the love story in this play is really love for baseball. Because—okay, a confession: I have only been a fan since 1999. What happened was, I became a fan and instantly couldn't focus on anything else. I thought about baseball, and everything else came second. It possessed me. Eventually I could make room for the rest of my life, but only when I could see relationships, work, what have you, through the eyes of the game. Baseball is that large, though—it allows for metaphors, as you know.

It's bizarre that someone's induction to this game should come so late.

Which is why I am such a fanatic. I was so skeptical—I thought people who cared about baseball were ridiculous. I've never been a "fan" of anything, really. I was never one of those "Oh, Liza" people. So the experience of fan-dom was a new one, along with baseball. I went out and bought histories, and that Ken Burns documentary sits on my TV like a shrine, an altar. I'd read anything.

Now I feel like I'm spending a lot of time cramming. The history of this game isn't embedded. I'll read anyone—I enjoy George Will, for example, when he's writing about baseball, not politics. (I've gotten over that idea that someone has to be morally vetted before you can use or enjoy them.) It's why I can forgive [Yankees pitcher] David Wells if he made homophobic comments—he's just not evolved yet, is the way I prefer to think about it.

And, of course, he pitched a perfect game for the Yankees.

Well, that too.

But I prefer the sentiment of his teammate Mike Mussina, who, when asked how he would feel if he found out he was playing with a gay man, replied: "I assume I already have."

Good for him, yes. See, as I say, I'm a new fan, so I didn't know all that.

So in a way, the character Mason [a gay character who becomes an instant baseball fan in Take Me Out *] is standing in for you.*

Yes, the way he just fell in love with it right away is true of me. And now if there is a Yankee game I can possibly see, it's mandatory. I am watching it. That first season, when it ended so abruptly for me, I couldn't take it. I couldn't bear that feeling of loss—I would scan the upper reaches of cable TV, and discover Dominican winter baseball.

Well, there's always ESPN Sports Classics [a channel that broadcasts old sporting events].

Yes, but some of those years, in the '70s, when everyone had to be a hippie, and uniforms were fuchsia and orange—I can't take that.

But in a way, what's true for Mason in Take Me Out *is true for all of us, even those of us who loved the game from childhood. Nostalgia is part of baseball, I think.*

That sort of Wordsworthian experience of baseball being unconsciously lodged in us—it certainly happened to me. And that's what I uncovered writing this play. It was almost an enormous relief coming to baseball so late in my life—it conjured up these memories I didn't even know I had, but of course I did. It's like that closing sentence in Jim Bouton's *Ball Four*: "You spend a good piece of your life gripping a baseball, and in the end it turns out that it was the other way around all the time."

Well, it seems that there are other characters in Take Me Out *loosely based on real-life players.*

(Sarcastically) Oh, gee, ya' think so? Who could you be thinking of?

Darren—the half-black, half-white beloved star who admits his homosexuality—is a bit like Derek Jeter.

(*Mock surprise*) No!

And Shane Mungit, the bigoted relief pitcher, has a hint of John Rocker.

Wow! I never thought of that.

Okay, I'll stop. But it occurs to me that playwrights should make more of these eccentric characters in baseball. Especially the psycho/superstitious pitchers.

Oh, absolutely. Actually, when Rocker gave that bigoted interview to *Sports Illustrated*, I was really happy, because it suited my play quite nicely. And [Mets reliever] Turk Wendell, with that demeanor on the mound. But there was something appealing in him—just the courage to wear that necklace.

[Red Sox pitcher from the 1970s] Bill "Spaceman" Lee . . .

Oh, yeah, he was witty. Though he was the one guy in baseball that [Yankee coach] Don Zimmer said he wouldn't let in his living room. He hated him. That's all in Zimmer's affable but not-quite-compelling memoir.

You actually read that?

Of course! You don't see Zimmer very much this season. I wonder if it's age that is making him less appealing or if [Yankees owner] Steinbrenner is just punishing him for those hemorrhoid commercials!

Actually, speaking of the crisis of masculinity and baseball: You have to admire [Texas Ranger] Rafael Palmeiro doing those Viagra commercials.

Really? Do you? I guess. I admire Derek Jeter for doing those peanut butter commercials, actually. You know, let 'em have their endorsements. I don't care.

I'm amazed that you watch so much baseball and write so much. This year we'll also see The Violet Hour (*opening Nov. 3 at California's South Coast Repertory*), *and last year we had both* Everett Beekin *and* The Dazzle.

Think of it this way: What else do I do? I don't have a family to be responsible to, or have to support anyone beyond myself. And everything that has happened in the last couple of years represents work that goes back six or seven years. So we're talking an average of a play a year, and I don't think that is extraordinary output if that is actually your job. I'm steady more than prolific. Look at Philip Roth. He's writing novels, thick novels, and they are masterpieces. I find that astonishing. He's turned his entire life into writing. I admire that. I *do* try to do that—turn my life's moments, all of them, into writing.

What is The Violet Hour *about?*

It's about a young man who's starting an independent publishing firm, and he has to choose between publishing the first novel of a classmate and the memoir of a blues/jazz singer with whom he is actually having a clandestine affair. And a machine of indeterminate function and origin comes into the office and starts picking and changing everything.

And you used some baseball consultant on Take Me Out *?*

Well, we have a baseball-ographer (she doesn't want to be called a choreographer). She's coaching movement.

Okay, Richard, this piece is coming out in October. Any World Series predictions?

Uh, well . . . I'm Jewish. So, therefore, superstitious. I guess I can go ahead and name the National League winner because I don't care: the Diamondbacks. Again.

I'll pick the Braves in the NL because in addition to the Bosox, I'm a Mets fan, and, so, a pessimistic fatalist.

You're probably right. Poor Mets, especially last year after the Subway Series. I can't get over these teams who have great seasons and then fall precipitately, one season later. It's a tragedy; I love it.

Speaking of the Mets, this was the year that Mike Piazza had to "come out" and say, "Sorry, I'm not gay." So who do you think is the gay Met?

Oh, that's easy. I actually have a relative who runs with the sportswriters, and he has told me who it is.

Tell me!

Well, off the record . . .

Source: Steven Drukman, "Greenberg's Got Game: A Master Playwright Swings for the Fences with a Socially Conscious Baseball Play," in *American Theatre*, October 2002, pp. 24–28.

John Lahr

In the following essay, Lahr explains that Greenberg unites baseball with "gay politics." He also adds that the play "suggests" there are "unknown" consequences, good and bad, in coming out.

If there's anything that confounds the British more than American optimism, it's baseball, which brings together on one bright pastoral greensward those twin nineteenth-century American deliriums: industrialization and individualism. Baseball turns into fun the oppressions of industry—management, productivity, accounting, specialization, even stealing—and yet the pageant of winners and losers in this proto-corporate world also allows for goodness to be measured, made immutable, and, thanks to the eternal vigilance of statistics, kept alive.

Baseball is a game—some would say a ritual—of hope. Part of that hope lies in the clarity of the sport—a kind of mathematical absoluteness that spills over into moral absoluteness, and explains why the fantasy of all-American wholesomeness goes with the game like sauerkraut with hot dogs.

These thoughts came to mind two weeks ago as I listened to pundits on the BBC's *Newsnight Review* try to shout one another down over the American playwright Richard Greenberg's exhilarating *Take Me Out*, which premièred at London's Donmar Warehouse, co-produced by New York's Public Theatre (where it will appear in September). I hope that Greenberg, who spun his tall tale well, and his American director, Joe Mantello, who has mounted it with crisp, good-humored flair, didn't hear the dismissive showboating claptrap that the critic Germaine Greer was peddling as expertise. Among Greer's assertions were the claims that numbers don't matter in baseball; that no player would be called up from the minors to help a defending team win a championship; and that Mr. Greenberg was misguided in depicting the team's catcher—who is, after all, the anchor of the game—as a malaprop-prone ignoramus with as much brainpower as a radish. Paging Yogi Berra.

The play's mischievous title—at once a paean and a plea—hints at Greenberg's equally mischievous ambition: to marry "the old ballgame" with what you could call "the new ballgame": gay politics. *Take Me Out* is about a baseball colossus, a young African-American built to mythic size by both his extraordinary exploits on the field and his extraordinarily cheerful interracial upbringing: "Even in baseball—one of the few realms of American life in which people of color are routinely adulated by people of pallor—he was something special: a black man who had obviously never suffered," the white shortstop, Kippy Sunderstrom (the appealing Neal Huff), explains. The player in question, the aptly named Darren Lemming (Daniel Sunjata), is a center fielder for the champion New York Empires. Lemmings, we know, are small rodents famous for their sometimes suicidal habits of migration; Darren's particular way of going south is to announce to the press one day—for no good reason other than that it suits his sense of invulnerability to do so—that he's gay. The news creates an almost seismic disturbance. "This seems to be a bigger event in *your* life than it is in mine," Lemming says to Kippy, his liberal Stanford-educated best friend.

As Greenberg has wisely conceived Lemming, he is far from sexually rampant; he exists within the brilliant corona of his own glamour, which requires distance from others and encases him in a kind of

asexual solitude. His coming-out is only an incidental act of bravery, which neither defines him nor exorcises a hidden political agenda. "I don't *have* a secret," he says. "I *am* a secret." Superbly played by the handsome and self-contained Sunjata—so easy in his muscular body, so nonchalant in his sense of entitlement—Darren is turned on only by his own prowess. He is the apple of his eye, and he just about admits it. "If I'm gonna have sex—and I *am*, because I'm young and rich and famous and talented and handsome, so it's a *law*—I'd rather do it with a guy," he says. "But when all is said and done, Kippy? I'd rather just play ball."

In a series of tight, tart illustrative scenes, crosscut with ballplaying tableaux vivants and with Kippy delivering expository asides, like the narrator in "Casey at the Bat," Greenberg demonstrates how Lemming's sexual "mess," as Kippy calls it, seeps into his apparently straight teammates, not always to happy effect. A lot of the disturbance takes place in the showers, where the cast members lather their pecs and their penises and turn Scott Pask's clever set into a kind of well-hung homoerotic heaven. "You're not *getting* me, man," says a vacant teammate, Toddy Koovitz (Dominic Fumusa), apparently annoyed at having to wear a towel over his privates. "Why do I have to go around this room, which is, has been, which is this sancchewy, rackled with self-consciousness about my body?" When Darren responds to Toddy's misspoken sexual paranoia, his sang-froid broadcasts his superiority. "Well, 'cause if you have some hope of reëntering decent society, they make ya," he says. "They *insist* on it."

On the surface, the team seems to take its star's homosexuality in stride, but the victory hugs, the fanny pats, the shower-room larks are now no longer a carefree macho gambol. "What do we do with our stray homosexual impulses? We tamp them down, we frustrate them," Kippy says, trying in vain to be clubhouse psychologist to this crew of inarticulate and disgruntled players. Then, in a John Rocker moment, the Empires' lanky, monosyllabic, newly called-up closer, Shane Mungitt (the excellent Frederick Weller), emboldened by a string of big wins, finds his tongue in front of reporters. "I don't mind the colored people—the gooks an' the spics an' the coons an' like that," he says as the curtain falls on Act I. "But *every night* t' have t' take a shower with a *faggot!*"

In the prevailing politically correct climate, Lemming finds himself suddenly turned from an object of envy to an object of pity. His sense of grandiosity is more offended than his sense of justice. "I liked you before—*loved* you in a manly sort of way," Kippy tells him. "But now you're . . . more human." "Isn't that a *demotion*?" Lemming replies. Mungitt is suspended, then reinstated after apologizing, and at one point Lemming finds himself alone in the shower room with the pitcher, who, it seems, has "a cleanliness thing." "Cleanliness is next to godliness," Lemming jokes—a great line that is lost on his oafish teammate. Mungitt's failure to engage goads Lemming even further. "All these showers ya take. You just tryin' to scrub away the skin?" he asks. "You tryin' to get through all these layers 'f tissue an' organs 'n' stuff to get to where the real dirt lies?" Finally, in a moment that plays only partly as a joke, Lemming lunges at Mungitt and mortifies him with a kiss. "Our little secret," Lemming shouts after him. "You dumb cracker f——." "F——" is the word that Mungitt later reportedly mumbles to himself on the mound as he beans—and kills—an African-American star from another team, thereby transferring his murderous feelings for Lemming into the opposing player: an act, if you'll forgive the pun, of projectile identification.

What Greenberg's story suggests is that by coming out you risk letting in the unknown, both good and bad. Lemming's whim leads to his unwitting collusion in a murder, to the cooling of his friendship with Kippy, and to Mungitt's banishment from baseball. Against all these negatives, Greenberg counterposes the blessing of connection—between Lemming and his timid, closeted accountant, Mason Marzac (the scene-stealing Denis O'Hare), who is unexpectedly liberated by Lemming's revelations. Neither man starts out with a community; Lemming feels above everyone, while Marzac, as he admits, feels beneath everyone. In the course of befriending Lemming, Marzac falls in love with baseball, too. To Marzac, the home-run trot—the player rounding the bases and pausing for celebration—becomes profoundly poetic. "That's what we do in our ceremonies, isn't it?" he says. "Honor ourselves as we pass through time?"

At the finale, a Cinderella moment in the empty stadium after the World Series has ended, Lemming turns to Marzac just before he exits. "What a f—— of a season, huh?" he says. Marzac, in his Empires baseball cap and his giant "We're No. 1" foam glove, echoes his friend's sentiment. "It was . . . tragic," he says, then adds, "What will we do till spring?" Whether on the stage or in the stadium, Greenberg seems to be saying, play mediates tragedy because it kills time and answers woe with wonder. In this realm, as *Take Me Out* marvellously demonstrates, the spirit can be lost and sometimes found.

Source: John Lahr, "Play at the Plate: Losing It in the Locker Room," in *New Yorker*, Vol. 78, No. 20, July 22, 2002, pp. 80–81.

SOURCES

Buzinski, Peter, "Majority of Pros Would Welcome Gay Teammate," in *OutSports*, March 2, 2006, http://www.outsports.com/news/20060302gayteammatesurvey.htm (accessed October 22, 2006).

Gardner, Elysa, "Despite a Few Bad Hops: *Take Me Out* Looks like a Hit," in *USA Today*, March 4, 2003, "Life" section, p. 03d.

Greenberg, Richard, *Take Me Out*, Faber and Faber, 2003.

Hagerty, Bill, Review of *Take Me Out*, in *Hollywood Reporter*, Vol. 374, No. 19, July 19, 2002, p. 30.

Kaufman, David, "Playing the Field," in *Nation*, July 7, 2003, p. 30.

Miller, Stuart, "*Take Me Out*: A Play Worth Extra Bases," in *Sporting News*, March 10, 2003, p. 9.

Pearlman, Jeff, "At Full Blast," in *Sports Illustrated Online*, December 23, 1999, http://sportsillustrated.cnn.com/features/cover/news/1999/12/22/rocker/ (accessed October 22, 2006).

FURTHER READING

Anderson, Eric, *In the Game: Gay Athletes and the Cult of Masculinity*, State University of New York Press, 2005.
Anderson interviewed gay athletes at all levels of team play, from high school sports to professional teams, in order to document the prevailing attitudes toward homosexuality and how it fits with or clashes with the macho culture of competition.

Morgan, William J., "Baseball and the Search for an American Moral Identity," in *Baseball and Philosophy: Thinking Outside the Batter's Box*, edited by Eric Bronson, Open Court Publishing, 2004, pp. 157–68.
In *Take Me Out*, the character Mason Marzac learns to appreciate baseball from an intellectual standpoint, while other characters, particularly Kippy and Darren, discuss the moral issues surrounding the game. In this essay, Morgan examines what the game has to say about the American character.

Robinson, Jackie, *I Never Had It Made*, Harper Perennial, 1972.
This autobiography of the first African American in Major League Baseball recalls the struggles and taunts that Robinson had to endure as a trailblazer, foreshadowing the situations that the first openly gay player might face.

Woog, Daniel, *Jocks: True Stories of America's Gay Athletes*, Alyson Publications, 1998.
Woog, a soccer coach, provides profiles of over two dozen openly gay athletes and coaches, exploring how they deal with the public perception of them. This book is less scholarly, more anecdotal, than Anderson's *In the Game*.

Two Trains Running

AUGUST WILSON

1990

One of the leading playwrights of the late twentieth century, August Wilson brought African American culture and history to the stage with eloquence. His many awards, including two Pulitzer Prizes, together with his formidable critical reputation and the popularity of his plays, marked his status as perhaps the greatest black dramatist of his generation. Wilson is widely known for his ear for idiomatic African American dialogue, his gift for portraying political dilemmas and social turbulence in an immediate and compelling manner, and his deep knowledge of daily life among impoverished blacks living in U.S. cities.

Two Trains Running, one of Wilson's most overtly and pointedly political works, takes place during the heyday of the black power movement, at a moment of great upheaval in U.S. race relations. It is one of a series of plays dealing with African American culture and history in the twentieth century, and perhaps its central theme is the manner in which the poor urban black community reacted to legal victories of the civil rights movement. Wilson stresses that a sense of hopelessness went hand-in-hand with optimism and progress in places such as 1969 urban Pittsburgh, where equal rights applied to African Americans only in theory and many blacks struggled daily with meager wages and dismal prospects. As of 2007, the play was available in a 1993 paperback edition published by Plume Drama. It originally opened in 1990 and came to Broadway in 1992 with a cast that included Samuel L. Jackson and Laurence Fishburne.

August Wilson AP Images

AUTHOR BIOGRAPHY

Born in Pittsburgh, Pennsylvania, on April 27, 1945, August Wilson was the fourth of six children in a poor mixed-race family. He was named after his father Frederick August Kittel, a white German, but Kittel never lived with the family, and Wilson's mother Daisy Wilson, a cleaning woman, later married David Bedford, an ex-convict who had spent twenty-three years in prison after killing a man during a robbery. The character Troy Maxson of *Fences* is based on Bedford, and this play serves as an indication of the tense relationship between Wilson and his stepfather.

Wilson attended Catholic school but encountered severe racial abuse and changed schools twice. He quit public school after a history teacher accused him of plagiarizing a term paper. He began to read literature by various writers, including Langston Hughes, Ralph Ellison, and Dylan Thomas. Wilson briefly joined the U.S. Army and then, at age eighteen, returned to his Pittsburgh neighborhood where he took on a variety of jobs and began writing poetry.

When his biological father died in 1965, Wilson officially took his mother's maiden name and moved into his own apartment. He became interested in the blues singer Bessie Smith, the poet Amiri Baraka, and African American oral culture in general, and he became involved in the black power movement. In 1968, Wilson helped to open the Black Horizon Theater Company, which intended to promote black self-awareness. The next year he married a Muslim woman named Brenda Burton, and they had a daughter in 1970, but the marriage ended in 1972. In 1973, Wilson wrote a play about a troubled marriage entitled *Recycle*, and from then on Wilson's choice of subject matter as a dramatist was often influenced by his personal life, even though he consistently claimed in interviews that he did not write autobiographical plays.

In 1978, Wilson moved to St. Paul, Minnesota, to work as an educational scriptwriter for the Science Museum of Minnesota. His breakthrough as a playwright came in 1982, with the production of *Jitney*, a play about a Pittsburgh cab company, and the acceptance of *Ma Rainey's Black Bottom* for workshops at the Eugene O'Neill Theater Center in Waterford, Connecticut. The latter was produced on Broadway in 1984 to critical acclaim, and Wilson won a variety of prestigious fellowships and awards based on it. His next play, *Fences*, was produced on Broadway in 1987 and won the Pulitzer Prize. He also won a Pulitzer Prize in 1990 for *The Piano Lesson*. Wilson's plays continued to be produced through the 1990s, usually to considerable success, and he came to the conviction that each of his plays should portray a different period of twentieth-century African American history. Each play in his cycle takes on a different decade, including *Joe Turner's Come and Gone* (1986), which details an ex-convict's journey to find his wife in the 1910s, and *Two Trains Running* (1990), which is set in the 1960s and which won the American Theatre Critics' Award in 1992.

Wilson, who remarried twice and was survived by his third wife, Constanza Romero, continued to write plays until he died of liver cancer on October 2, 2005, in Seattle, Washington.

PLOT SUMMARY

Act 1, Scene 1

In a restaurant across the street from West's Funeral Home and Lutz's Meat Market, West talks on the phone about his job running numbers (taking bets for an illegal lottery). Memphis tells him to get off the phone, and Risa criticizes the numbers game. Memphis explains why his wife left him, and Holloway enters telling them about the people lining up at the funeral home to see Prophet Samuel. He says people were charging to see him until West stopped them, and the men declare that West must be very wealthy, in part (they say) because he robs corpses of their valuables before burying them. Memphis says that West has always wanted his land and that the city wants to tear down his restaurant. He says he will refuse to take less than twenty-five thousand dollars, and the men continue to talk about how West takes too much money from people.

Hambone enters, repeating "He gonna give me my ham" as usual, and Risa expresses sympathy for him. Sterling enters and chides them for having very little available to eat. He recognizes Risa as the sister of his old friend, flirts with her, and reveals that he has been in prison. The men give him some recommendations about finding a job, but Sterling has already tried most of them and found that it is very difficult to find work. They talk about how the people hope to become lucky by rubbing Prophet Samuel's head, and Holloway says it is better to go to see Aunt Ester. They explain to Sterling that Lutz promised Hambone a ham if he painted the fence well but gave him a chicken instead, and every morning for almost ten years Hambone has demanded the ham. Holloway discusses how Aunt Ester and Prophet Samuel earned the affections and trust of the community, and Sterling leaves in search of Aunt Ester.

Act 1, Scene 2

The men watch as Hambone confronts Lutz once again, and Holloway argues that Hambone might have more sense than any of them, since he refuses to accept "whatever the white man throw at him." Memphis tells about how white residents drove him out of Jackson, Mississippi, and expresses confusion about the fact that Risa cut her legs in order to distract attention from her beauty. Then Memphis says he found out that Sterling had robbed a bank, and Holloway argues that the problem is not that Sterling or black people in general are lazy, but that the money that black people make inevitably goes to white men. He says that white people have always "stacked" or exploited black people since the times of slavery.

West enters and defends his lucrative undertaking business. He offers to buy the restaurant for fifteen thousand dollars in cash and tells Memphis that the city will not give him more than ten thousand for it. Sterling enters saying that Aunt Ester was not available and inviting everyone to a rally celebrating the birthday of Malcolm X. They discuss

Malcolm X and the black power movement, and Memphis expresses frustration with such political movements. Hambone enters, and Memphis angrily kicks him out of the restaurant.

Act 1, Scene 3

Unable to find a job, Sterling talks with Risa about his past, invites her to a rally for Malcolm X, and claims that they will get married if the number she suggests wins the lottery. He tells Holloway that Hambone painted the fence very well and deserves his ham, and West enters with gifts for Risa and Memphis. Sterling asks to borrow money so he can bet on a number, and he and Wolf agree that the world is crazy and hopeless. Holloway tells him that he is headed for jail, and Sterling says that he will end up there anyway.

Wolf starts a collection to get Bubba Boy out of jail so he can attend his wife's funeral, and Sterling teaches Hambone the phrase "Black is beautiful." Memphis enters complaining that the city offered him fifteen thousand dollars for the restaurant, so he fired his black lawyer and hired a white one. He says he decided not to settle for anymore "draws" after he missed his mother's death because he could not borrow the money to travel down to Jackson, and he resolves to make the city meet his price.

Act 2, Scene 1

Sterling steals Risa flowers from Prophet Samuel's visitation room and seems to have stolen a can of gasoline as well. He tries to teach Hambone other black power slogans and starts hollering with him, then sells the gas to Memphis. Memphis starts to get irritated with his customers, and Wolf sells Sterling a gun on credit. Memphis hangs up on a caller trying to reach Wolf and says that Wolf cannot receive calls at the restaurant anymore.

West enters complaining that someone has broken the window to his funeral home, and someone tried to break in the basement. He offers Memphis twenty thousand dollars for the restaurant, with the catch that he withhold five thousand until after he sells it to the city. Memphis refuses and explains how the white community in Jackson confiscated his land, killed his mule, and set fire to his crop, all because he had found a way to irrigate his field. Sterling asks West for a job as a driver, but West refuses and tells about the time that he asked Aunt Ester whether his wife was in heaven. Holloway says that he went to see Aunt Ester because he wanted to kill his grandfather, who loved white men and helped them control other slaves. Sterling asks Memphis if he wants to form a partnership selling chicken to steel mill workers, but Memphis refuses.

Act 2, Scene 2

Holloway says that Hambone did not go to see Lutz that morning and describes Prophet Samuel's funeral. Wolf tells them that he has two women in Atlanta, but one of them thinks he is a rich man so he cannot go there unless he has money. Then Wolf says that Sterling won the numbers game yesterday, but the family who runs it cut the amount of the winnings. Holloway refuses to explain this to Sterling, and Memphis tears down a black power poster that Sterling has put on the wall. Sterling enters and describes Prophet Samuel's funeral, and Memphis says that Prophet Samuel used to cheat people out of their money. Sterling says he believes the world is coming to an end. Memphis pays Risa and asks Holloway where Aunt Ester lives.

Act 2, Scene 3

Holloway says that Hambone is dead, and Risa sweeps at Wolf with her broom. West enters describing how he retrieved Hambone's body, and Risa tells him that he should bury Hambone in a decent coffin. West says that this would be too expensive for him. Sterling enters and invites West to come gambling with him in Las Vegas, but West says he is no longer interested in this kind of life. West tells Sterling that his expectations for life are too high, but Sterling refuses to listen. Wolf enters and explains to Wolf that they cut the numbers in half, and Sterling says he is going to demand his money from the Alberts despite Wolf's and Risa's warnings.

Act 2, Scene 4

Sterling tells Risa how he confronted Old Man Albert but did not actually ask for his full winnings. He then went to see Aunt Ester and threw twenty dollars into the river on her advice. Sterling asks Risa why she cut up her legs and says that it is only natural that he wants to be with her. She tells him he would be an unreliable husband who will end up in jail, and he says they can kiss without marrying. Risa puts on the jukebox and they dance, then kiss.

Act 2, Scene 5

Holloway philosophizes that there is nothing in the world but love and death, and the men discuss the rally the previous night. A drug store was burned down, but Holloway thinks it was just a scam so that the owner could collect the insurance. Wolf tries to explain why he does not have a girlfriend,

and West agrees that he made Hambone's visitation look good. Wolf says that it is all right that Sterling is together with Risa, and Memphis enters slightly drunk. Memphis explains that he went to see Aunt Ester, threw twenty dollars into the river, and went to the courthouse where they awarded him thirty-five thousand dollars for his restaurant. His wife moved back in, but he moved out and says he plans to go down to Jackson and claim back his land. He gives Risa fifty dollars to buy flowers for Hambone, and Sterling enters with blood on his face and a ham he has stolen from Lutz, for Hambone's casket.

CHARACTERS

Bubba Boy

Bubba Boy is deeply in love with his wife. When she dies of a drug overdose, he steals a dress for her and is arrested.

Aunt Ester

Aunt Ester is an old black woman who tells fortunes and helps people find relief. Holloway claims that she is three hundred and twenty-two years old, which means that she is about as old as African slavery in North America, and this correspondence suggests that she may symbolize the black experience in the United States. She gives advice about how to cope with life rather than change circumstances, and she frequently advises black people to throw money into the river.

Hambone

Hambone is a mentally disturbed, or possibly mentally handicapped, man who repeats the same two phrases continually. He is in his late forties, and his character description terms him, "*self-contained and in a world of his own.*" A major source for his deterioration seems to be Lutz, the white owner of the meat market across the street from the restaurant, who promised to reward Hambone with a ham if he painted his fence well, but then agreed only to give him a chicken.

Hambone is of great symbolic importance to the play, and the main characters all come to feel an affinity with him and sadness at his death. West reveals that he had scars all over his body, and this image recalls flogging marks of blacks from the South, helping to depict Hambone as a symbol of the oppressed black man. Hambone's dogged insistence that the white man must give him his due seems pathetic and even ridiculous at first, but later it seems that he is not necessarily so different from the other characters. In some ways, Hambone is a foil, or a character whose purpose is to reveal something about another character, for Memphis, since they both make demands of white people with similar persistence, but seem to go about it in different ways.

Holloway

Holloway, a wise and philosophical man who has strong religious beliefs, voices "*his outrage at injustice with little effect.*" His character description indicates that he has come to "*accept his inability to effect change and continue to pursue life with zest and vigor,*" but he has not lost his fury with the oppression that African Americans continue to face at the end of the 1960s. Somewhat cynical about people's motives to make money and take advantage of others, Holloway's opinions are nevertheless justified by his experience.

Holloway was deeply affected by his grandfather's loyal and subservient relationship to white people and was ready to kill him until he came under the influence of the spiritual advisor Aunt Ester. After that, he was able to endure his troubles by believing that he can do little or nothing to make matters better for black people. Holloway serves as a valuable and articulate source of context and history for the audience; he is always probing for reasons for current problems and scolding blacks for failing to see the broader causes behind their desperation.

Lutz

Lutz is the white owner of the meat market across the street from the restaurant. The black characters despise him, particularly after Hambone's death, for refusing ever to give Hambone the ham that he promises him. They differ, however, in their opinion as to whether he will ever succumb to Hambone's persistence. Lutz himself never appears in the play, and there is no indication that he regrets refusing to satisfy Hambone for nine and a half years.

Mellon

Mellon is a rich white banker and speculator who may be exploitative of or racist toward blacks. Holloway indicates that Mellon had a shady alliance with Prophet Samuel.

Memphis

The central character of the play is the restaurateur Memphis, whose life comes to the brink of tragedy when his marriage breaks up, and the city moves forward with its plans to demolish his restaurant. His character description states that he is a "*self-made man whose values of hard work, diligence, persistence, and honesty have been consistently challenged by the circumstances of his life,*" and identifies "*impeccable logic* " as his best quality. Memphis is by no means a simple character, however, and his sense of rationality or logic is not always straightforward. For example, he strongly believes that individuals are born free and able to determine their own destiny, but he is limited in his ability to understand the ways in which black people are not exactly free in the United States due to continued racial oppression. He is also inept at maintaining and cultivating personal relationships, and he is unable to see why his wife is not satisfied simply because he supports her financially.

Memphis has a strong sense of justice and self-worth, and he is willing to fight violently and resourcefully for his own well-being. He continually makes demands of white people (such as twenty-five thousand dollars for his restaurant and the ownership of his farm in Jackson) based on his sense of entitlement. He fails, however, to address the broader, institutional forces working against him and other black people.

Old Man Albert

Old Man Albert is the head of the white family which runs the numbers game and is probably tied to organized crime.

Prophet Samuel

Prophet Samuel is a very popular preacher whose funeral attracts large numbers of supporters. Holloway and Memphis accuse him of cheating people and having corrupt ties to powerful businessmen, but Risa and Sterling support him. His political and religious position is never perfectly clear, but Risa explains that he was interested in justice for black people and talked about the end of the world approaching.

Risa

Risa is a resilient woman with deeply held convictions, the only female character in the male-dominated world of the play. Her character description indicates only that she cut herself with a razor in order to focus attention away from her good looks and towards her personality. Her personality remains something of a mystery, however, since she refuses to go into detail about her personal life, possibly because she remains disgusted by the fact that men think of her only as a sex object.

Risa is nevertheless outspoken about her convictions, and she makes no secret of her dedication to Prophet Samuel and her admiration for Hambone. She criticizes the men for wasting their money gambling and persists in asking West to provide a decent coffin for Hambone. She is attracted to Sterling in part because of their shared interest in the black power movement, but she refuses to see him as a potential marriage partner because she does not think he is reliable.

Sterling

A personable young man who appears to be somewhat "*unbalanced*," Sterling has recently been released from jail. He does not show any remorse for his crime, which was robbing a bank because he was tired of having no money, and he seems poised to go back to prison. This is not so much because Sterling is lazy, as Memphis claims, even though he seems unwilling to do hard manual labor. Instead, the play suggests that work is very difficult to find for poor black people, and Sterling continually looks in vain for a job.

Sterling's character description reads that he is wearing a prison-issue suit and an old-fashioned straw hat and that he uses "*unorthodox logic*" and has a "*straightforward manner.*" Sterling is certainly straightforward about what he wants, which is money and a girlfriend, and he flirts persistently with Risa until she begins to fall for him. He is susceptible to influence and becomes interested in the black power movement, Malcolm X, Prophet Samuel, and Aunt Ester, though it is unclear exactly where his political or spiritual convictions lie. Ultimately, Sterling expresses his sense of right and wrong with a belated and probably doomed gesture of affection for Hambone, when he steals a ham from Lutz. His attitude is generally that life is hopeless, but he also insists on enjoying each moment to the fullest, which makes him a likeable if somewhat confounding personality.

West

An undertaker who lives above his funeral home, West arouses the jealousy of his neighbors because he is comparatively wealthy. He is a widower in his early sixties and seems to continue to be saddened by the death of his wife, whom he loved deeply. He used to work in the gambling business, but he realized that he could make a lot of money by dealing instead with those who died from this kind of life, and he became an undertaker.

West's character description indicates that he "*has allowed his love of money to overshadow the other possibilities of life,*" and a symbol of this is the fact that he always asks for sugar with his coffee but never actually uses it. He is not entirely unsympathetic, however, since he is generally kind to everyone and even gives Risa and Memphis gifts (although he may intend these to encourage Memphis to sell the restaurant). He dresses immaculately in black and has a sense of pride and propriety; even though someone breaks the window of his funeral home, for example, he refuses to put a board in its place because that would not be classy enough for him.

Wolf

Wolf is a numbers runner who longs for female companionship but is unable to maintain or even begin a relationship. He earns a living recording bets and distributing winnings for an illegal lottery run by a white family organization probably tied to organized crime. He and Memphis have a strained relationship because Wolf continually receives phone calls related to his work at the restaurant, and Memphis is worried that he will get into trouble for allowing this. Wolf's confrontation with Sterling reveals that he has some mild discomfort with the nature of his work, not because it is illegal or even because it contributes to the impoverishment of the people who participate in it, but because those who run it do not always fairly distribute the winnings.

Wolf has feelings for Risa, which is why he is concerned about her relationship with Sterling and why he continually pays regard to her. He is completely ineffective in courting her, however, and deludes himself and others with stories of multiple lovers (possibly prostitutes) in Atlanta. Ultimately, he does not object to Risa's relationship with Sterling or even confront them about it, perhaps because he is insecure and unable to express his feelings.

THEMES

White Exploitation and Black Power

Two Trains Running is an explicitly political play that makes extended reference to the black power movement and its impact on poor urban communities like the Hill District of Pittsburgh. The issue of continued white oppression of African Americans and the response of the black community during the 1960s is at the foreground of the characters' experience. The community surrounding the restaurant is undergoing a major redevelopment, probably one which has been precipitated by the

TOPICS FOR FURTHER STUDY

- *Two Trains Running* was produced contemporaneously with a resurgence of interest in black power, marked perhaps most notably by Spike Lee's 1992 film *Malcolm X*. Watch Lee's film and research other treatments of the black power movement during the 1990s, and then deliver a class presentation analyzing why and how the movement was portrayed during the decade. How and why did such treatments tend to differ from historical reality? Why might they have been popular? What might they reflect about African American culture in the 1990s? How does Wilson's play compare to them?

- Wilson is known for his sensitivity to African American oral culture, including music. Listen to influential African American music of the 1960s, including bebop jazz musicians such as John Coltrane and black popular singers such as Aretha Franklin, and research the context and political associations of the music you have heard. Then, write a descriptive essay in which you speculate about how such music influenced the dialogue and rhythms of *Two Trains Running*. Which musical influences were most important to Wilson and why? Why might he have chosen Franklin's "Take a Look" as a backdrop to the love scene between Risa and Sterling?

How might live or recorded music be used to various effects in productions of the play?

- *Two Trains Running* seems divided in its articulation of theories of personal freedom and social determination. Memphis declares that he is and always has been free, and no one can take this freedom away from him, but Holloway meditates on the complex ways in which white oppression determines an individual African American's destiny. Write an essay in which you analyze Wilson's treatment of these themes. Describe the play's implied viewpoint on these matters, and determine the manner in which it impresses them upon the audience. Support your analysis with examples from the text.

- Write a short play in which Memphis travels to Jackson, Mississippi, in order to demand back his land. Carefully study Memphis's character as it develops through *Two Trains Running* in order to pursue his emotional development during this difficult quest. Study also his manner of speaking, and imagine how people might speak differently in the South. Consider what is at stake for Memphis in this journey, how it relates to the political atmosphere of its era, and what social themes and positions you will articulate in your drama.

---

social initiatives that came in the wake of the civil rights movement. However, the legal rights and privileges that the African American community won during the 1950s and 1960s do not seem necessarily to extend to impoverished city-dwellers. An underlying sense of tragedy and hopelessness pervades even short-term victories such as the city awarding Memphis thirty-five thousand dollars, since Memphis remains estranged from his wife and has the foreboding and dangerous plan of returning to Mississippi to claim back his land. Sterling seems doomed to return to prison, his relationship with Risa seems unlikely to have a future, and Wolf and

Holloway have as few prospects for the future as they did at the outset of the play.

Various religious and political organizations, which are tied loosely or explicitly to institutions such as the Nation of Islam or figures such as Malcolm X, provide a way of rallying and organizing as a community. Sterling repeats black power slogans, and other characters believe or participate in African American community initiatives to some degree. Even Memphis comes by the end of the play to feel affectionate towards Hambone, a symbol of unwavering resistance to white exploitation. All of the characters are skeptical about the effectiveness of individual organizations and movements, however, and none seems to find any direct benefits from them.

Gambling and Spiritualism in the Black Community

The characters in Wilson's play express their frustration and address their problems in a variety of ways, sometimes through political action. Frequently, however, they resort either to gambling in the numbers game or subscribing to supernatural beliefs or both, in order to find hope and comfort. Wilson characterizes these two pursuits in somewhat similar terms, stressing the ways in which they make poor blacks poorer. Memphis and Wolf believe that the numbers game helps its players rise from poverty once in a long while to enjoy a brief period of prosperity, but Risa points out that it is simply a way of throwing away money. Wilson also consistently associates religious and supernatural comforts with poor blacks' throwing away money, since Aunt Ester always advises her clients to throw money into the river and Prophet Samuel may have cheated people for donations. Spiritualism and gambling do help poor blacks to survive day to day, however, and Wilson's main goal in highlighting them may be to point out that the desperation among the black urban poor has no productive or effective outlet. They may be signs, rather than causes, of the desperate circumstances of African Americans living in Pittsburgh's Hill District.

Individual and Social Justice

Each of Wilson's characters feels some mix of resentment, anger, despair, and responsibility for his/her relationship to institutions of power, and Wilson is interested in comparing and evaluating these various attitudes. Memphis insists that he holds complete personal responsibility for his own freedom, for example, while Holloway is resigned to the idea that white people have always oppressed African Americans and will continue to do so for the foreseeable future. Other characters have a mix of personal and institutional allegiances, most of which have to do with race relations; while Wolf seems loosely comfortable with working for a white-run gambling association, Sterling feels that his situation is hopeless and turns to organizations such as the black power movement for support. Risa and Holloway find consolation and support mainly in religious beliefs that seem to distract attention from issues of justice altogether. Inescapably at issue in the play, however, is the question of how personal freedom relates to social forces, and Wilson is interested in expressing the limited possibilities available to individual black people within a system of continued inequality and turbulence.

STYLE

Unity of Place

Although *Two Trains Running* focuses on the changing circumstances of an entire community and describes large-scale events, such as rallies and funerals, the entire play takes place inside a small restaurant. Wilson thus follows a dramatic convention called the unity of place, a term invented to describe the tendency in ancient Greek drama for all of the action to occur in a single location.

One function of this formal choice is to achieve a sense of realism, since the audience does not have to imagine being transported for a change of scene. Wilson provides a full and sharp view of Memphis's restaurant, allowing the audience to experience a large range of emotion within a place that they begin to know well. The playwright establishes a kind of window on the world that he wishes to describe, one that can be both private and social. The restaurant provides a space in which the communal or external as well as the personal and intimate aspects of the characters' lives come into view.

Specific Character Descriptions

Wilson is known for his minutely detailed descriptions which state outright a character's fundamental motivations. Before the play begins, for example, the stage directions indicate that Memphis's *"greatest asset is his impeccable logic,"* a judgment that is not necessarily or entirely evident from the lines themselves, since Memphis's logic sometimes seems fuzzy or variable. Playwrights are often less aggressive in defining a character's role and purpose, since doing so leaves the work open to interpretation for individual productions or readers, although some may choose to view Wilson's character descriptions as suggestive but not definitive. Wilson's practice may be a method of assisting production companies and actors in fulfilling his intentions. Also, they may have the effect of bringing the characters to life for those reading the play.

HISTORICAL CONTEXT

African American Literary Culture before 1990

Mainstream drama in the United States changed significantly in the later part of the twentieth century, particularly during the 1980s and 1990s, to include more work by and about minorities. This was by no means a straightforward development, since

COMPARE
&
CONTRAST

- **1969:** The African American community has secured major legal victories as part of the civil rights movement, but blacks remain economically depressed in comparison to whites.

  1990: African Americans have made economic advances due in part to affirmative action and other social initiatives, and black-owned businesses are on the rise.

  Today: Despite major advances, African Americans continue to encounter discrimination and remain significantly more likely than whites to be poor.

- **1969:** President Richard Nixon leads the United States in the bloody and extended Vietnam War, which later ends in complete U.S. withdrawal.

  1990: President George H. W. Bush prepares to send U.S. forces into the Persian Gulf after Saddam Hussein invades Kuwait.

  Today: Years after President George W. Bush deploys U.S. forces to invade and conquer Iraq, the United States military remains engaged in the violent and unstable country.

---

there was continued opposition to theater, literature, and other arts that were seen as insufficiently American. Figures such as Wilson, however, widely increased the visibility and availability of theater that focused on the experience and traditions of cultural and racial groups that had long been sidelined or ignored.

When Wilson began writing drama in the 1970s, artists and intellectuals had been working for many years to focus less on a traditional canon of white drama and more on the unique history and culture of African Americans. Cultural figures, including W. E. B. Du Bois, Langston Hughes, Ralph Ellison, and James Baldwin, were part of black literary scene that flowered from the Harlem Renaissance of the 1920s and 1930s and continued through the civil rights movement of the 1950s and 1960s. Writers, including Maya Angelou, Toni Morrison, and Amiri Baraka, continued during the 1970s and 1980s to highlight African American cultural history and explore its relationship to white culture and structures of power. Angelou and Morrison have been important figures in relating African American cultural history as a whole to the experience of women, and they have helped to impress upon U.S. culture the ways in which minority categories overlapped and combined in patterns of oppression. Baraka, who was one of Wilson's greatest influences, was widely influential and controversial in emphasizing the relationship

between art and politics. Wilson himself was a pioneering figure, along with his mentor Lloyd Richards, in carving out a place for African American culture and history in the contemporary theater.

Late 1960s Political and Social Upheaval

Two Trains Running is set at a highly symbolic and significant point in African American political and social history, at the end of the U.S. civil rights movement and at the height of the influence of the black power movement. Martin Luther King Jr. (1929–1968) and other figures led a prominent and successful campaign to guarantee equal rights for all citizens under the law during the 1950s and 1960s. Nonviolent resistance tactics were perhaps chiefly responsible for achieving victories in the courts and in legislation that led to the dismantling of laws that discriminated against blacks and segregated U.S. society into racial groups. In 1968, shortly before the events of Wilson's play, President Lyndon Johnson signed the second Civil Rights Act, which outlawed discriminatory practices in housing.

By 1969, many African Americans continued to feel frustration and disappointment with their status in U.S. society. The civil rights era had marked major legal advances, but its victories did not translate into immediate or widespread improvements in economic circumstances, and great numbers of blacks remained extremely poor with very limited prospects. Many African Americans also continued to feel the loss of leaders, including Malcolm X (1925–1965) and Martin Luther King Jr.; major riots broke out in U.S. cities following the assassinations of King and Robert F. Kennedy (1925–1968). As a result of these and other factors, increasing numbers of blacks began to support institutions that did not confine themselves to peaceful resistance tactics, such as the Nation of Islam and the Black Panther Party.

So-called black power organizations did not necessarily share the same beliefs or goals; the Black Panther Party was explicitly revolutionary and violent in its philosophy, while Nation of Islam was a religious institution that preached black superiority over other races. However, such groups did tend to share a dedication to African American solidarity and self-assurance, which is why they have been identified as part of the black power movement. The phrase black power itself is a political slogan that was associated with black nationalism and self-determination. The black power movement had a wide following in the late 1960s and early 1970s, but its effects were limited at best, since it did not directly inspire clear economic or social gains for blacks. In part because of its violent associations and its tendency to identify blacks as superior to whites, it was widely viewed as dangerous and threatening to white U.S. society.

Black activists at a rally give the Black Power salute that would be familiar to the characters in Two Trains Running   © Flip Schulke/Corbis. Reproduced by permission

CRITICAL OVERVIEW

By the time *Two Trains Running* opened at the Yale Repertory Theater in 1990, Wilson had already achieved the status of a prestigious and eminent dramatist. The play itself was generally well-received, was nominated for a Tony Award for Best Play, and was the recipient of an American Theatre Critics' Association Award. Beginning with its 1992 Broadway opening, however, a critical debate raged about how *Two Trains Running* compared to Wilson's earlier work. As they had his previous play, *The Piano Lesson*, some critics in the mass media claimed that Wilson was becoming less poetic in his rendition of African American life. Mimi Kramer of the *New Yorker* suggested that *Two Trains Running* did not function as eloquently and subtly as Wilson's earlier efforts, and Clive Barnes of the *New York Post* criticized the play's lack of dramatic elegance.

Other periodicals praised Wilson's efforts; William A. Henry III writes in *Time* that *"Two Trains Running* is Wilson's most delicate and mature

work, if not necessarily his most explosive or dramatic." In *Massachusetts Review*, Robert L. King notes that the "civil rights movement rolls on past" Wilson's characters and highlights the political implications of the play: "Larger-than-life figures won't correct the injustices of their grocer and bookie, and saints don't connect to the Afro-American values that Wilson celebrates." Academic criticism also tends to discuss the work's upfront political agenda. In her influential book of criticism *The Dramatic Vision of August Wilson*, for example, Sandra Shannon notes Wilson's expression of loss over the "debris of an explosive era in black awareness" and his appeal to black youth "to look to the African continuum as inspiration for their cultural preservation and continued advancement."

CRITICISM

Scott Trudell

Trudell is a doctoral student of English literature at Rutgers University. In the following essay, he discusses Wilson's nuanced critique of African

American spiritual organizations and traditions, which in Two Trains Running *do not tend to act in the genuine interests of poor blacks.*

Two Trains Running is perhaps principally intended as an expression of the frustration and sense of tragedy on the part of lower-class, urban-dwelling African Americans who find themselves bypassed and sidelined by the civil rights victories of the 1950s and 1960s. Wilson creates a sense of doom surrounding even Memphis, who seems to have won a great victory in the amount of money that the city gives him for his restaurant. Taking instruction from Aunt Ester, the mysterious spiritualist who helps African Americans feel better about their problems, Memphis vows to go back and "pick up the ball," or regain his lost sense of pride and self-righteousness by winning his land from the white family that took it in Jackson, Mississippi. His glaring and ominous phrase, "if I get back from seeing Stoval," however, leaves a sense of gaping doubt and insecurity about the wisdom of this enterprise.

Even if Memphis were able to return and open a big new restaurant, it seems likely that he would leave his friends and neighbors behind. Holloway, Wolf, and Risa probably have even more difficult times ahead, since their neighborhood is about to be demolished, and Sterling is almost certainly bound for prison. Wilson thus alludes to the decline and desperation that would plague African Americans in inner city neighborhoods such as Pittsburgh's Hill District in the 1970s and 1980s. A complex variety of social and political forces and organizations are to blame for this grim reality, and Wilson highlights some of them individually or by implication in the course of the play. Continued white oppression is the greatest and most powerful threat, as Holloway stresses in his eloquent speech about the ways in which whites have always "stacked" African Americans. Wilson is sensitive to other problems as well, however, and in fact one of his most interesting critiques is of black spiritualism. The subtle, yet incisive, manner in which Wilson criticizes belief in the "*supernatural*," as he refers to religious or spiritual belief, is one of the most intriguing aspects of his politically charged drama.

Wilson is sympathetic to the idea that poor blacks must find some way of easing their minds and enjoying life despite their continued difficulties. When he brings up amusements and releases such as those offered by spiritualism and gambling, he carefully outlines the desperation that gives rise

> IN HIGHLIGHTING THE MISLEADING AND DANGEROUS ASPECTS OF SPIRITUAL LEADERSHIP, WILSON IS CALLING INTO QUESTION MANY HEROES AND TRADITIONS OF TWENTIETH-CENTURY AFRICAN AMERICAN HISTORY."

to them. Before she meets Sterling, Risa finds little comfort in life outside the counsel of Prophet Samuel, who seems to give her the empowerment and faith in herself that she needs to get through the day. Holloway, meanwhile, justifies the practice of throwing twenty dollars into the river at Aunt Ester's bidding based on the idea that it changes one's attitude and allows one to become comfortable with the inequities of the world. Aunt Ester is the only recourse he has in dealing with his infuriating grandfather, and Memphis comes to rely on her as well for advice on how to deal with his old demons. Similarly, Memphis explains that the numbers game may take money away from blacks, but it is also the only way that they are able to come by a large sum at once, with which they can buy something that they really want. He blames the "cheat[ing]" government for the fact that poor blacks are unable to save any money, while Wolf blames the rich white banker Mellon.

Understanding as he is of the conditions that lead poor African Americans to invest their time and money in gambling and supernatural belief, however, Wilson is sharply critical of the organizations that profit from them. Risa provides a blunt critique of the men for wasting their money in the numbers game, and the play seems to prove her point when the white Albert family cuts the winnings on Sterling. Sterling's encounter with Old Man Albert, in which he attempts a futile and somewhat pathetic gesture of pride by proclaiming that he has "something that belong to [Old Man Albert] for a change," leaves little doubt that poor blacks are accustomed to being cheated by the Alberts.

WHAT DO I READ NEXT?

- Wilson's *Fences* (1985) focuses on an ex-convict and baseball player who is locked in a desperate struggle with his son. Its sensitive depiction of themes which are widely supposed to be autobiographical has won it a place as one of the finest achievements in late-twentieth-century drama.

- *Dutchman* (1964), by Amiri Baraka, is a stark and shocking depiction of a white woman's efforts to take sexual advantage of a black man.

- In *Beloved* (1987), Toni Morrison's widely successful and influential novel about African American history and the supernatural, a black woman murders her own child to avoid her being returned to slavery.

- James Baldwin's *Tell Me How Long the Train's Been Gone* (1968) is not one of the prolific author's most well-known novels, but it provides a powerful meditation on social and political change and the impact of celebrity and art on a black man's development. Written at the very moment at which *Two Trains Running* is set, it is very much of its era.

- *New Day in Babylon: The Black Power Movement and American Culture, 1965–1975* (1993), by William L. Van Deburg, is a classic work of scholarship which analyzes what was at stake during the turbulent period in African American history that serves as the setting for Wilson's play.

Sterling's insignificant attempt at self-assertion, in which he gains a measly two dollars while the other half of his rightful winnings remain in Old Man Albert's pocket, reinforces the idea that gambling is little more than an extremely effective method by which white organizations are able to exploit the black poor.

Though perhaps more subtle in their process of cheating poor African Americans than groups tied to organized crime, spiritual organizations are little better at the end of the day in terms of the financial burden they impose on their followers. Evidence indicates, for example, that Prophet Samuel was adept and well-practiced at garnering large donations from the poor. Wilson is careful to emphasize that Risa's membership card to the First African Congregational Kingdom includes the phrase "having duly paid all tithing" and that Prophet Samuel's followers charged for admission to the visitation before West stopped them. There is no suggestion that Prophet Samuel managed to secure any real gains for the black community, however. On the contrary, Holloway indicates that the former income tax-evader has substantial and suspect connections to Mellon, the same white banker and speculator whom Wolf has blamed for keeping poor blacks poor.

Aunt Ester seems on the surface to be a more benign figure, and indeed she is effective at helping African Americans feel better about themselves. She makes it possible for Holloway to lead a peaceful life, contents Sterling for a brief period, and prompts some of Memphis's self-assurance at the end of the play. Beneath the surface, however, runs an indication that Aunt Ester is in fact a great threat to black prosperity. Her continual insistence that blacks throw significant amounts of cash into the river, her advice that Holloway ignore the dangerous and regressive behavior of his master-loving grandfather, and her ominous advice that Memphis "go back and pick up the ball," if indeed this means that he should return to Mississippi, seem counterproductive, if not dangerous. Supernatural beliefs may bring comfort to those who subscribe to them, but these pose a significant threat to their financial wellbeing and social advancement.

Wilson's implication against practicing supernatural belief is loaded with political significance, not least because the leadership of the African American community that was prominent before, during, and after the civil rights movement was so closely associated with religion and spirituality. Martin Luther King Jr. was a Baptist minister, Malcolm X was a leading figure in the Nation of Islam before he broke away from the organization, and black civil rights leaders continued to organize and develop community initiatives through religious bonds during the late-1960s and beyond. In highlighting the misleading and dangerous aspects of spiritual leadership, Wilson is calling into question many heroes and traditions of twentieth-century African American history.

Aunt Ester is a particularly rich symbolic figure in this regard, since she claims to have been alive for almost exactly the time period that Africans had lived in North America after they were abducted by European slave traders. As a figure of African American history and tradition, she represents many of the cultural ideas that Wilson is known to revere and identify as important. Furthermore, though his specific organizational association is left ambiguous, Prophet Samuel is strikingly reminiscent of leadership figures in the Nation of Islam. An institution known for preaching of signs from heaven, African superiority, and justice for black people, the Nation of Islam affirms many of Prophet Samuel's beliefs, as is clear from Risa's comments, such as "God sent him to help the colored people get justice" and, referring to the idea of the world coming to an end, "He said God was gonna send a sign." The Nation of Islam was known to be plagued by corruption and poor leadership decisions, and it might be an intended target of Holloway's criticism of Prophet Samuel's hypocrisy in his claim to be working towards the best interests of the black community.

Again, insofar as Wilson is critiquing or attacking the black spiritualist traditions, his is a mixed message. Prophet Samuel may not help Sterling and Risa to great fortunes, but they may be doomed in any case, unable to make any real advances until they feel comfortable and positive about themselves. Similarly, it is doubtful that ignoring Aunt Ester and refusing to play the numbers game in order to focus on moneymaking is a tenable solution to African American desperation. As Holloway points out, African American attempts to work within the white-dominated capitalist system is like toting a bucket of sand with a hole in it. West is a good example of this phenomenon, since he turns away from gambling in order to concentrate on money-making and refuses to follow Aunt Ester's advice but is deeply discontent and does not have a positive relationship with his neighbors. He may have lost all that was positive and meaningful in his life by capitalizing on the misfortunes of fast-living and fast-dying black people.

Nevertheless, Wilson's cynicism about black spiritualism during the late-1960s serves as a powerful reminder that it is dangerous to blindly idealize the spiritual heroes of the civil rights movement. *Two Trains Running* suggests that these leaders had a long way to go before finding effective solutions to African American segregation and exploitation. In fact, institutions and traditions posing as forthright contributors to black advancement may well have been corrupt, ineffective, misleading, and even dangerous to their followers. Aunt Ester and Prophet Samuel may have made Wilson's characters feel better about themselves in the short term, and they may have provided nuggets of wisdom about black pride and self-assurance with the potential to be very valuable. It may be that Memphis does, for example, have to confront the ghosts of his past before he can move on. The play provides a warning signal, however, that supernatural traditions and organizations are not necessarily to be trusted or emulated, since instructions of figures like Aunt Ester are as likely to worsen the situation of poor blacks as they are to provide any relief.

Source: Scott Trudell, Critical Essay on *Two Trains Running*, in *Drama for Students*, Thomson Gale, 2007.

Thomson Gale

In the following essay, the critic gives an overview of August Wilson's work.

Critics have hailed August Wilson as an important talent in the American theater since the mid-1980s. He spent his childhood in poverty in Pittsburgh, Pennsylvania, where he lived with his parents and five siblings. Though he grew up in a poor family, Wilson felt that his parents withheld knowledge of even greater hardships they had endured. "My generation of blacks knew very little about the past of our parents," he told the *New York Times* in 1984. "They shielded us from the indignities they suffered." Wilson's goal was to illuminate that shadowy past with plays that focus on black issues. *Ma Rainey's Black Bottom, Fences, Joe Turner's Come and Gone, The Piano Lesson, Two Trains Running*, and *Seven Guitars* are part of this ambitious project.

Wilson noted that his real education began when he was sixteen years old. Disgusted by the racist treatment he endured in the various schools he had attended until that time, he dropped out and began educating himself in the local library. Working at menial jobs, he also pursued a literary career and successfully submitted poems to black publications at the University of Pittsburgh. In 1968 he became active in the theater by founding—despite lacking prior experience—Black Horizons on the

TWO TRAINS RUNNING
CONTINUED WILSON'S PROJECTED
TEN-PLAY CYCLE ABOUT BLACK
AMERICAN HISTORY."

Hill, a theater company in Pittsburgh. Recalling his early theater involvement, Wilson described himself to the *New York Times* as "a cultural nationalist . . . trying to raise consciousness through theater."

According to several observers, however, Wilson found his artistic voice—and began to appreciate the black voices of Pittsburgh—after he moved to St. Paul, Minnesota, in 1978. In St. Paul Wilson wrote his first play, *Jitney!*, a realistic drama set in a Pittsburgh taxi station. *Jitney!*, noted for the fidelity with which it portrayed black urban speech and life, had a successful engagement at a small theater in Pittsburgh. Wilson followed *Jitney!* with another play, *Fullerton Street*, but this work failed to strengthen his reputation.

Wilson then resumed work on an earlier unfinished project, *Ma Rainey's Black Bottom*, a play about a black blues singer's exploitation of her fellow musicians. This work, whose title role is named after an actual blues singer from the 1920s, is set in a recording studio in 1927. In the studio, temperamental Ma Rainey verbally abuses the other musicians and presents herself—without justification—as an important musical figure. But much of the play is also set in a rehearsal room, where Ma Rainey's musicians discuss their abusive employer and the hardships of life in racist America.

Ma Rainey's Black Bottom earned Wilson a trip to the O'Neill Theatre Center's National Playwrights Conference. There Wilson's play impressed director Lloyd Richards from the Yale Repertory Theatre. Richards worked with Wilson to refine the play, and when it was presented at Yale in 1984 it was hailed as the work of an important new playwright. Frank Rich, who reviewed the Yale production in the *New York Times*, acclaimed Wilson as "a major find for the American theater" and cited Wilson's ability to write "with compassion, raucous humor and penetrating wisdom."

Wilson enjoyed further success with *Ma Rainey's Black Bottom* after the play came to Broadway later in 1984. *Chicago Tribune* contributor Richard Christiansen reviewed the Broadway production as "a work of intermittent but immense power" and commended the "striking beauty" of the play's "literary and theatrical poetry." Christiansen added that "Wilson's power of language is sensational" and that *Ma Rainey's Black Bottom* was "the work of an impressive writer." The London *Times*'s Holly Hill agreed, calling Wilson "a promising new playwright" and hailing his work as "a remarkable first play."

Wilson's subsequent plays include the Pulitzer Prize-winning *Fences*, which is about a former athlete who forbids his son to accept an athletic scholarship, and *Joe Turner's Come and Gone*, which concerns an ex-convict's efforts to find his wife. Like *Ma Rainey's Black Bottom*, these plays underwent extensive rewriting. Guiding Wilson in this process was Lloyd Richards, dean of Yale's drama school and director of the school's productions of Wilson's plays. "August is a wonderful poet," Richards told the *New York Times* in 1986. "A wonderful poet turning into a playwright." Richards added that his work with Wilson involved "clarifying" each work's main theme and "arranging the material in a dynamic way."

Both *Fences* and *Joe Turner's Come and Gone* were praised when they played on American stages. The *New York Times*'s Frank Rich, in his review of *Fences*, wrote that the play "leaves no doubt that Mr. Wilson is a major writer, combining a poet's ear for vernacular with a robust sense of humor (political and sexual), a sure instinct for cracking dramatic incident and passionate commitment to a great subject." And in his critique of *Joe Turner's Come and Gone*, Rich speculated that the play "will give a lasting voice to a generation of uprooted black Americans." Rich contended that the work was "potentially its author's finest achievement yet" and described it as "a teeming canvas of black America . . . and a spiritual allegory."

Wilson was intensely passionate about portraying the truth of the black experience, about being the voice of the ghetto. While he did not set out to create his plays in a series, it became clear to him that his plays in combination were creating a twentieth-century history of the black experience in America. "I'm taking each decade," Wilson said, "and looking at one of the most important questions that blacks confronted in that decade and writing a play about it. Put them all together, and you have a history."

In 1990 Wilson claimed his second Pulitzer Prize, this time for *The Piano Lesson*. Set during the Great Depression of the 1930s, this drama pits brother against sister in a contest to decide the future of a treasured heirloom—a piano, carved with African-style portraits by their grandfather, an enslaved plantation carpenter. The brother wants to sell it to buy land, while the sister adamantly insists that the instrument carries too much family history to part with. Acclaim for the play was widespread, although some commentators were put off by the supernatural elements that came to play in the climax of this otherwise realistic piece. "When ghosts begin resolving realistic plays, you can be sure the playwright has failed to master his material," wrote Robert Brustein in the *New Republic*. Brustein also found the play overlong and repetitious, and asserted that Wilson's focus on the effects of racism was limiting him artistically. Others praised the work unreservedly, however, including Clive Barnes of the *New York Post*. He declared, "This is a play in which to lose yourself—to give yourself up . . . to August Wilson's thoughts, humors and thrills, all caught in a microcosm largely remote for many of us from our own little worlds, yet always talking the same language of humanity." Frank Rich of the *New York Times* wrote that Wilson has given "miraculous voice" to the black experience, and William A. Henry III of *Time* dubbed the play's piano "the most potent symbol in American drama since Laura Wingfield's glass menagerie" in the Tennessee Williams classic. Barnes concluded, "This is a wonderful play that lights up man. See it, wonder at it, and recognize it." Wilson later adapted *The Piano Lesson* for a *Hallmark Hall of Fame* television production. It was judged a success by John J. O'Connor, who wrote in the *New York Times:* "If anything, *The Piano Lesson* is even more effective in this shortened version."

Two Trains Running continued Wilson's projected ten-play cycle about black American history. The play, which came to Broadway in 1992, is set in a run-down diner on the verge of being sold. Reactions by the diner's regular patrons to the pending sale make up the body of the drama. Some critics, such as the *New Yorker*'s Mimi Kramer, found the play less subtle and dramatic than its predecessors, but *Newsweek*'s David Ansen praised the "musical eloquence" of Wilson's language, which he felt enhanced a "thematically rich" work. And Henry wrote in *Time* that *Two Trains Running* is a "delicate and mature" play that shows Wilson "at his lyrical best."

Two Trains Running was followed by *Seven Guitars*. Set in the 1940s, it recounts the tragic story of blues guitarist Floyd Barton, whose funeral opens the play. Action then flashes back to recreate the events of Floyd's last week of life. *Seven Guitars* was the first major production of a Wilson play without the direction of Richards, who was forced to abandon the project due to illness. The task of directing fell to Walter Dallas, whose staging at the Goodman Theatre in Chicago William Tynan characterized as "skillful" in a *Time* review. Yet the critic's overall assessment was mixed. "Part bawdy comedy, part dark elegy, part mystery," he wrote, "August Wilson's rich new play, *Seven Guitars*, nicely eludes categorization. . . . But though full and strong in its buildup, the play loses its potency as it reaches its climax. . . . Though Floyd is as charming and sympathetic a protagonist as we could want, the surprising truth is that his death has little effect on us. We leave the theater entertained and admiring but not truly moved." Vincent Canby differed markedly in his judgment, writing in the *New York Times*, "Though the frame of *Seven Guitars* is limited and employs only seven characters, Mr. Wilson writes so vividly that the play seems to have the narrative scope and depth of a novel. When the curtain comes down, it's difficult to remember which characters you've actually seen and which you have come to know only through stories recollected on stage. . . . *Seven Guitars* plays with such speed that you begin the journey one minute, and the next thing you know, you're leaving the theater on a high."

Further praise came from *Newsweek* reviewer Jack Kroll, who called *Seven Guitars* "a kind of jazz cantata for actors," with "a gritty, lyrical polyphony of voices that evokes the character and destiny of these men and women who can't help singing the blues even when they're just talking." The play, he continued, "bristles with symbolism" and with "anguished eloquence." Kroll found the protagonist's death "shocking, unexpected, yet inevitable" and the characters overall "not victims, wallowing in voluptuous resentment," but "tragic figures, bursting with the balked music of life."

Not long after *Seven Guitars* opened, Wilson gave a keynote address to the Theatre Communications Group National Conference. The address, titled "The Ground on Which I Stand," was first published in *American Theatre* in 1996. Wilson's remarks created critical controversy and feud. According to Jonathan Little, writing for the *Dictionary of Literary Biography*, this address "can be read as the culminating manifesto of his personal politics, his aesthetics, and his vision for the future." A series of responses and counterattacks appeared in print both from Wilson and from critic Robert Brustein, leading to the culmination of a debate on January 27, 1997, at the New York City Town Hall. Little reported that critical reaction to the debate was mixed with both plaudits and criticisms given to the arguments made by both men.

In 2001, Wilson's ninth play in his cyclic history opened on Broadway for a surprisingly brief twelve-week run. *King Hedley II* is a dark retrospective, drawing upon the life of title character King Hedley, an ex-convict attempting to rebuild his life in 1990s Pittsburgh. Hedley, who first appeared as "a cracked old man who sees ghosts" in *Seven Guitars* (a technique the playwright uses often, according to Ashyia Henderson in *Contemporary Black Biography*), deals with his past while figuring out how to go "legit" in the midst of the brutality of a black ghetto. The play depicts the decline of the black family and the prevalence of violence and guns in contemporary inner-city neighborhoods.

Discussing Wilson's body of work, Lawrence Bommer stated in the *Chicago Tribune*, "August Wilson has created the most complete cultural chronicle since Balzac wrote his vast 'Human Comedy,' an artistic whole that has grown even greater than its prize-winning parts." As for the playwright, he repeatedly stressed that his first objective is simply getting his work produced. "All I want is for the most people to get to see this play," he told the *New York Times* while discussing *Joe Turner's Come and Gone*. Wilson added, however, that he was not opposed to having his works performed on Broadway. He told the *New York Times* that Broadway "still has the connotation of Mecca" and asked, "Who doesn't want to go to Mecca?"

In September of 2005, Wilson announced that he had been diagnosed with liver cancer. He died shortly after he made his illness known to the public.

Source: Thomson Gale, "August Wilson," in *Contemporary Authors Online*, Thomson Gale, 2006.

Jonathan Little

In the following essay, Little gives a critical analysis of August Wilson's work.

August Wilson is one of the leading American playwrights of the late twentieth century. He has been phenomenally successful, having won two Pulitzers, five New York Drama Critics Circle awards, and several Tonys in a long list of prestigious awards, grants, and fellowships. In a rare occurrence, in 1988 Wilson had two plays running simultaneously on Broadway—*Fences* (first performed in 1985) and *Joe Turner's Come and Gone* (1986). Dedicated to representing blacks from every decade of the century in a ten-play cycle, Wilson has completed seven of these plays. He has already expanded the range of American theater by documenting and celebrating black historical experience and by showing that embracing the African spiritual and cultural heritage can bring individual and collective healing for blacks.

In addition to his themes of the search for identity, racial exploitation and injustice, empowerment through the blues, and spiritual regeneration, his success results in part from how he has translated the specifics of black life into the conventions of realism and naturalism. While he adheres to traditional dramatic form, his plays imply no easy answers. Complex and mysterious, his plays show the poisonous effects of a bitter legacy on black individuals and their communities and include thrilling if infrequent moments of personal liberation.

Most of Wilson's plays take place in a tightly knit black neighborhood in Pittsburgh once known as the Hill, a sloping ten-block area that has now disappeared because of an "urban renewal" project. Wilson often laments the demise of the economically viable black community, an attitude informed by his experience growing up in such a community. Indeed, in a 1992 article written for *Life* magazine, "The Legacy of Malcolm X," Wilson, visiting from his home in Seattle, mourns the loss of the safe neighborhood he knew as a child when he was a newspaper carrier. Walking down streets blood-spattered by drug-related gang violence, he reminisces fondly about the former thriving community, where black-owned "stores and shops of every kind were wedged in among churches, bars and funeral homes" and where 55,000 people lived with a "zest and energy that belied their meager means."

August Wilson was born Frederick August Kittel in this Hill neighborhood on 27 April 1945, to an African American mother, Daisy Wilson Kittel, and a white German father, Frederick August Kittel, who all but abandoned them soon after August was born. August was one of six children and grew up in poverty in a two-room apartment above a grocery store. His mother supported her family with cleaning jobs and encouraged her children to read, teaching August to read at age four.

Wilson idolized his mother, who died in 1983, just a year before his first Broadway success. As an adult he changed his name to hers to reflect his allegiance to his mother and his African American heritage. Growing up in her household taught him the defining features of black culture and day-to-day life.

When Wilson was an adolescent, his mother remarried, to African American David Bedford, who moved them to Hazelwood, a mostly white suburb; there Wilson and his family were victims of racist vandalism and abuse. Wilson dropped out of high school at age fifteen after refusing to defend himself against false charges of plagiarism on a paper he had written about Napoleon Bonaparte, and after suffering from racist taunts.

After dropping out of school, Wilson spent much time in the library, preparing himself to be a writer and hoping for several months that his mother would not find out that he was not in school. He was largely self-taught, educating himself by reading all that he could by the writers in the black literature section of the library, including Richard Wright, Ralph Ellison, Langston Hughes, and Amiri Baraka, as well as books on black anthropology and sociology.

The year he was twenty, 1965, was a pivotal one for Wilson. He moved out of his mother's home into a rooming house and joined a group of young black intellectuals, poets, and playwrights. Then on 1 April 1965, Wilson bought his first typewriter and began his career as a poet. Although he recognizes his limitations as a poet, Wilson refers to his poetic work as a vocation that has deeply informed his playwrighting, especially in his expertise with metaphor. As a young poet, Wilson published in several small periodicals, including *Black World*, *Connections*, and *Black Lines*, and also read his work at local art houses. One of his poems, "For Malcolm X and Others," published in the *Negro Digest* in 1969, is a darkly cryptic homage to Black Power leaders he refers to as a "flock of saints."

Later in the fall of 1965, he heard Malcolm X's recorded voice for the first time. Although the media has tended to downplay this aspect of Wilson's career and life, the Black Power movement was, as he says in "The Ground on Which I Stand" (1996), "the kiln in which I was fired." He was drawn to the Black Power and Nation of Islam messages of self-sufficiency, self-defense, and self-determination, and appreciated the origin myths espoused by the controversial leader of the Nation of Islam, Elijah Muhammad. In 1969 Wilson married Brenda Burton, a Muslim, and briefly converted to Islam in an unsuccessful attempt to sustain

> " ... THE RACE RIOTS AND HEIGHTENED TENSIONS EXIST IN THE BACKGROUND. THEIR RELATIVE INSIGNIFICANCE HIGHLIGHTS WILSON'S BELIEF THAT POLITICS CHANGED LITTLE FOR BLACKS. INSTEAD OF CHANGE, THE PLAY FOCUSES ON THE FAMILIAR THEME OF OVERCOMING THE DESTRUCTIVE EFFECTS OF THE PERVASIVE ECONOMIC EXPLOITATION OF THE BLACK COMMUNITY BY MAINSTREAM WHITE SOCIETY AND OF THE TRAUMA OF THE PAST, INCLUDING SLAVERY."

the marriage. They had a daughter, Sakina Ansari-Wilson, and divorced in 1972.

Deeply moved by the messages of Malcolm X and the Nation of Islam, Wilson became a founder of the Black Horizon on the Hill Theater in Pittsburgh with writer and teacher Rob Penny. The theater operated from 1968 to 1978. It produced Wilson's first plays and allowed him and others to celebrate the Black Aesthetic, to participate in the Black Power movement, and to discuss the influences of Baraka and Malcolm X. In addition to Baraka, the black playwrights Wilson was most influenced by include Ron Milner, Ed Bullins, Philip Hayes Dean, Richard Wesley, Lonne Elder III, Sonia Sanchez, and Barbara Ann Teer.

However, in a 1984 interview with Hilary Davies, Wilson differentiated between black theater of the late 1960s and his own less didactic dramatic vision, calling his a more "internal examination" of African American life rather than the "pushing outward" of overt political propaganda. In "August Wilson and the Four B's: Influences," included in *August Wilson: A Casebook* (1994), critic Mark

William Rocha argues that while Wilson's plays, like Baraka's, center around confrontations with whites, there is the "signal difference that in Wilson's plays the confrontation occurs off-stage so that emphasis is placed not so much on the confrontation itself, but upon how the black community invests itself in that face-to-face encounter." Also, unlike the more exclusionary aesthetics held by Baraka and other Black Arts Movement proponents, Wilson often stresses the cross-cultural universals of drama and art. In his preface to *Three Plays* (1991) Wilson reflects on his first empowering experiences in writing drama: "When I sat down to write I realized I was sitting in the same chair as Eugene O'Neill, Tennessee Williams, Arthur Miller, Henrik Ibsen, Amiri Baraka, and Ed Bullins." He asserts that regardless of race, all playwrights face the same problems of crafting convincing drama and characters.

Besides a typewriter, the other important purchase that Wilson made in 1965 was a used Victrola and several 78 rpm jazz and blues records for five cents each from a nearby St. Vincent de Paul's store. He often speaks of the profound impact of listening to the blues, and specifically Bessie Smith, for the first time, including her hit song "Nobody in Town Can Bake a Sweet Jellyroll Like Mine." Hearing her voice validated the complexity, nobility, and spirituality of African American folk expression for him and increased his own self-esteem and sense of himself as a member of the black community. He has called the blues the wellspring of his art, and he frequently talks about the historical value of the blues as an emotionally charged and sacred vehicle for keeping an empowering African-based oral culture alive.

Besides the blues, the other chief influences on Wilson are black artist Romare Bearden, Baraka (mostly for his black nationalist ideas rather than his plays), and Argentinean fiction writer Jorge Luis Borges. Wilson admires how Borges tells a story in nontraditional ways to create suspense. He uses Borges's postmodern method of revealing the ending at the beginning and then working backward in *Seven Guitars* (1995), which begins and ends with a central character's funeral. Bearden's collages and paintings also provided direct inspiration for at least two of Wilson's plays. Wilson has called Bearden his artistic mentor; through drama Wilson seeks to reproduce Bearden's ability to capture the richness and diversity of black culture.

Wilson relocated to St. Paul, Minnesota, in 1978 after visiting his friend Claude Purdy, who was the director of the Penumbra Theatre, and after being introduced to Judy Oliver, a social worker in St. Paul who in 1982 became his second wife. At first Wilson worked for the Science Museum of Minnesota, writing plays to enhance their exhibits. He quit this job in 1981 but continued writing plays, and for three years he was also a part-time cook for a benevolent organization, Little Brothers of the Poor. While in St. Paul, he established ties with the Playwrights' Center in Minneapolis. Despite his close attachment to Pittsburgh, it was only after he moved far away from his Pittsburgh home that he was able to hear the black voices of his past and translate them effectively into drama. One factor that stimulated his growth was learning how to write plays by listening to his characters and asking them questions rather than by asserting his authorial control and forcing them into certain situations or political positions. Wilson lived in St. Paul until 1990, when he moved to Seattle and his marriage to Oliver ended.

Wilson's first taste of success came in 1981 when one of his first plays, *Jitney*, was accepted by the Playwrights' Center in Minneapolis, where it was staged in 1982 and met with critical acclaim. *Jitney* is set in Pittsburgh in the 1970s, in a gypsy (jitney) cab station scheduled for demolition. The plot bears some resemblance to Richard Wright's *Native Son* (1940), since one of the main characters—Booster—takes his revenge on a white girl who accused him of rape, by killing her and wounding her father. Academic critics highlight the importance of *Jitney* in Wilson's development as a dramatist. Sandra G. Shannon writes that the play "marks the beginning of both a private and professional journey for Wilson," since it takes place in Pittsburgh and anticipates many of the familiar themes of Wilson's later historical-cycle plays.

Wilson frequently talks about the liberation he felt as a writer in returning to and re-creating the voices and environment he knew growing up. His second play, "Fullerton Street," which was written in 1980, has remained unpublished and unproduced. Set in the 1940s on the night of the famous Joe Louis-Billy Khan fight, it concerns the loss of values attendant with the Great Migration to the urban North. In an interview with Shannon, Wilson reflects on the experience of writing "Fullerton Street," particularly his emotions when he killed off the central character's mother.

With the encouragement of a friend, in 1981 Wilson started submitting his plays to the National Playwrights Conference of the Eugene O'Neill

Theatre Center in Connecticut. After four of his early plays—including *Jitney*, "Black Bart and the Sacred Hills" (a satiric musical), and "Fullerton Street"—were rejected, *Ma Rainey's Black Bottom* was accepted. It opened at the Yale Repertory Theatre in New Haven on 6 April 1984 and ran through 21 April. The acceptance of the play marked the beginning of a long and fruitful relationship between Wilson and Lloyd Richards, Eugene O'Neill Center director and dean of the Yale School of Drama, who collaborated on most of Wilson's plays as they moved from first runs at the Yale Repertory Theatre to Broadway. Wilson frequently stresses the profound influence his collaborative work with Richards has had on his plays and on his revision process, and Richards frequently lauds Wilson's talent for creating authentic black voices for the theater.

Ma Rainey's Black Bottom opened at the Cort Theater on Broadway in October 1984 and ran for 275 performances. Wilson, relatively unprepared for the limelight and still struggling financially, was stunned by the enormous success of the play. It won the New York Drama Critics Circle Award and several Tony nominations; soon afterward, Wilson won several prestigious fellowships that allowed him to devote his attentions to full-time writing.

Unlike his other plays, *Ma Rainey's Black Bottom* is set in Chicago in 1927. The title of the play refers, on one level, to the historical Gertrude "Ma" Rainey (1886–1939), one of the first immensely popular African American blues singers. In "Speaking of Ma Rainey/Talking About the Blues," included in *May All Your Fences Have Gates: Essays on the Drama of August Wilson* (1994), Sandra Adell writes, "For the folk down home and down-home folk up North, Ma Rainey represented the epitome of black female wealth, power, and sensuality." The title of Wilson's play refers to Rainey's hit song "Ma Rainey's Black Bottom Blues" (also a black clog dance popular in the 1920s), while on another level it refers to her self-empowerment, effectively showing her white audience and record producers her "black bottom" in an act of defiance.

The play concerns a single afternoon in a studio in a disastrous recording effort. The play foregrounds the frustration and tension of racial exploitation and its explosive effects on blacks. It builds toward a stunning, and somewhat unexpected, climax in which one of the central characters, Levee, the trumpeter, stabs a fellow band-member, Toledo, for accidentally stepping on his shoe. Levee's motivation seems to stem not from Toledo's action but

more from the accumulated years of frustration and the bitterness of second-class citizenship. The first act ends, for instance, with Levee relating the horrific story of how his mother was raped and his father was murdered by white Southern racists. In interviews Wilson has repeatedly identified Levee as one of his characters possessing an admirable "warrior-spirit"—one who refuses to accept his oppression and lashes out against injustice in the manner of Nat Turner or Toussaint L'Ouverture. In this case Levee's revenge-inspired violence is misdirected, and perhaps stimulated by the white music producers' mistreatment of him; but the spirit is there nonetheless.

Despite the title of the play, the focus is not on Ma Rainey, but on the tensions and conflicts between the four male members of her backup band, who each represent different facets of the African American community and who chafe under the white producers' demeaning economic patronage, the artistic limitations of the outdated "jug"-band format, and Ma Rainey's control. They argue, for example, about which version of "Ma Rainey's Black Bottom" they are going to play—the traditional version or the updated one with a new introduction by Levee.

Despite her relative absence on stage, however, Ma Rainey plays a significant role in the play. She dramatizes one of Wilson's major influences—the blues. Once Ma Rainey finally arrives at the recording session late in the play, she speaks eloquently about the significance of the blues, despite the fact that the white recording industry and her white audience treat her like a "whore" or a "dog in the alley." As the Mother of the Blues, she summarizes their significance: they make it possible for African Americans to endure and to cope with and understand a difficult life. The bluesmen in the play alleviate their sense of frustration through soaring riffs and idiosyncratic renditions of classic songs, including her signature song. Despite all its intraracial and interracial conflict, the performance is a tribute to the sustaining power of the blues and their profound visceral impact.

Critics generally embraced the play for its seriousness during what a critic for *The Washington Post* (18 November 1984) called "a shockingly bankrupt season." Reviewers praised the superb acting, especially that of Charles S. Dutton as Levee, as well as the depiction of black vernacular speech in the play and the direction of Lloyd Richards. In his 12 October 1984 review for *The New York Times* Frank Rich argued that the significance of the play is that it "sends the entire history of black America crashing down upon our heads" through its "searing inside account of what white racism does to its victims." In his "spell-binding voice," Wilson crafts a play that is "funny, salty, carnal, and lyrical." In one of the few negative reviews of the play, Clive Barnes of *The New York Post* (12 October 1984) complained that, while he admired the fine acting and the sense of characterization, not enough happened in the play.

In a 1991 article for *Black American Literature Forum* Sandra G. Shannon answers Barnes's criticism of insufficient action by arguing that the play is a "disturbing look at the consequences of waiting, especially as it relates to the precarious lot of black musicians during the pre-Depression era." She posits that the play dramatizes this waiting motif through its constant use of stalling, delay, and deferment: "Forever practicing to become but never actually 'arriving' describes each of the musicians' predicament." In "August Wilson's Burden: The Function of Neoclassical Jazz," included in *May All Your Fences Have Gates*, Craig Werner makes the opposite point that the play affirms the call-and-response jazz or blues spirit, and seeks to identify the source of the historical Ma Rainey's popularity: "the people respond to Ma's response to the call of their own burdens, their lived blues."

Fences, Wilson's second major success as a playwright, was to a certain extent written in response to the more diffuse structure of *Ma Rainey's Black Bottom*. It was written quickly on the heels of the success of the latter play. In interviews Wilson admitted to being worried about being a one-time black playwright who achieved success and then sold out to an unsuccessful career in Hollywood—the fate suffered by several of his predecessors. After warm-up runs at the Eugene O'Neill Center, the Yale Repertory Theater, Chicago, Seattle, and San Francisco, *Fences* opened on Broadway in 1987 at the Forty-sixth Street Theater and ran for more than five hundred performances. It won four Tonys, the Pulitzer Prize, and the New York Drama Circle Critics Award and garnered almost unanimous praise from critics, especially for the acting of James Earl Jones, who played the lead character, Troy Maxson.

In an interview with Richard Pettengil, included in *August Wilson: A Casebook*, Wilson stated that in writing *Fences* he wanted to create a play that featured a single central character who is in nearly every scene. *Fences* is set in the late 1950s in Pittsburgh and focuses on fifty-three-year-old Troy, a former convict and baseball player, now a sanitation worker. Like the black characters in *Ma Rainey's Black Bottom*, Troy is still angry that he was denied the opportunity for economic and professional success. While he became a star in the Negro League after learning to play baseball in prison, he was unfairly denied the chance to play in the Major Leagues because of the color line; he is only angered by the success of Jackie Robinson and others in the now desegregated Majors. He possesses a "warrior-spirit" similar to Levee's, as he continues to battle the demons of injustice. He also repeatedly battles against Death, using his baseball bat. During the play Troy builds a fence around his backyard, at the urging of his wife. As critics have noted, the figurative meanings of the fences are many: the fences between the races, between past and present, between life and death, and between Troy and his family.

When his son Cory is offered an opportunity to play football in college on a scholarship, Troy forces the past to repeat itself by ruining his son's chances at the scholarship and, therefore, a professional career. Unlike Cory, who is part of a new generation more hopeful for social change, Troy sees manual labor as the black man's only reliable means of survival in a racist society. *Fences* includes strong scenes of father-son conflicts that are not even entirely resolved at the end of the play, set in 1965 at Troy's funeral.

Samuel G. Freedman, in a 1987 article on Wilson for *The New York Times Magazine*, points out that the plot of *Fences* and the character of Troy Maxson reflect an important experience in Wilson's own life, despite Wilson's often-quoted assertion that he does not write strictly autobiographical plays. After his stepfather, David Bedford, died in 1969, Wilson discovered that Bedford had been a high school sports star of the 1930s. Since no Pittsburgh college would give a black player a scholarship, Bedford turned to crime and decided to rob a store, killing a man during the robbery. He then spent twenty-three years in prison. Like Bedford, Troy turned to crime to support his family and was convicted of assault and armed robbery, spending fifteen years in prison. But whereas Troy encouraged his son to drop out of organized sports as a way of protecting him from disappointment, Bedford had been angry with Wilson for dropping out of football in his teens.

Unlike the critical response to *Ma Rainey's Black Bottom*, the reception of *Fences* was almost unanimously positive. Barnes, who had been somewhat critical of Wilson's first Broadway play, fully embraced *Fences*, calling it in the *New York Theatre Critics Reviews* (30 March 1987) "the strongest, most passionate American writing since Tennessee

Williams." A reviewer for the *Village Voice* (17 April 1987) called Wilson a mythmaker, a folk ethnologist, "collecting prototypical stories, testimonies, rituals of speech and behavior" while working with "basically naturalistic panorama plays" to create complex characters, none of whom are "unindicted or unforgiven." Another critic for the *New York Magazine* (6 April 1987) praised *Fences* for its universal qualities, calling it an "elegant play" not only because of its artful and fluid composition but also because in it "race is subsumed by humanity." The play "marks a long step forward for Wilson's dramaturgy."

Fences has not been made into a movie, perhaps in part because of controversy over a director. In "I Want a Black Director" (1990) Wilson reveals that Paramount Pictures, who purchased the movie rights in 1987, suggested white director Barry Levinson as their leading candidate. In his opinion piece Wilson gives his reasons for opposing a white director and attacks Paramount Pictures (and Hollywood in general) for not believing enough in black directors' abilities. Wilson argues that a white director does not share the same cultural specifics of black society that a black director would. He declined Levinson as a director, "not on the basis of race but on the basis of culture." Wilson ends the piece lamenting the fact that he is still waiting for Paramount Pictures to make the play into a movie. Yet, as Yvonne Shafer reports, *Fences* and *Joe Turner's Come and Gone* netted Wilson more than a million dollars in 1987-1988. The mayor of St. Paul named 27 May 1987 "August Wilson Day" to honor the fact that Wilson was the only Minnesota resident to win a Pulitzer for drama.

With his next play, *Joe Turner's Come and Gone*, Wilson achieved another notable success. Both *Joe Turner's Come and Gone* and *Fences* ran on Broadway at the same time; critics commented on how unusual this circumstance was for a black playwright. After a warm-up run at the Yale Repertory Production from 29 April to 24 May 1986, *Joe Turner's Come and Gone* ran on Broadway from 26 March 1988 at the Ethel Barrymore Theatre for 105 performances.

The play, which Wilson calls his favorite, is set in 1911 in a boardinghouse in Pittsburgh. As Wilson states in his preface to the play, the boardinghouse is a meeting place for those "sons and daughters of newly freed African slaves" who are trying to re-create their identity and to find "a song worth singing" that will make them self-sufficient. As his characters move to what is reputedly greater

opportunity in the North, they necessarily become more dependent on the empowering legacies of the past and on Southern black-vernacular culture.

As Wilson has stated in several interviews, the play was initially inspired by a Bearden painting called *Mill Hand's Lunch Bucket* (1978). The painting is an eerie and fragmentary collage depicting a boardinghouse with shadowy black figures. Fascinated especially by the mysterious man in the middle of the painting, who became a model for one of the central characters, Wilson first adopted the title of Bearden's collage as the title of his play. He changed the working title of the play after listening to the famous W. C. Handy blues song "Joe Turner's Come and Gone." Joe Turner was an historical figure who pressed Southern freedmen into servitude with impunity at the turn of the century because he was the brother of the Tennessee governor. Handy's song, thought to be one of the earliest blues songs ever recorded, is sung from the perspective of a woman who has lost her man to Joe Turner.

The most explosive character of the play, Herald Loomis, experiences firsthand the cruelty of the Reconstructed South and Joe Turner's reign of terror. He is falsely imprisoned for seven years of hard physical labor by the powerful Tennessee plantation owner. A former deacon, Loomis is a broken and angry man when he arrives at the boardinghouse after four years of searching for his wife with his daughter. He clashes with the other members of the boardinghouse, who are also looking for something that will bring them together and give them some peace. When the residents of the boardinghouse sing and dance a *juba*, an African call-and-response celebration of the spirit, Loomis cannot join in. Instead he is haunted by a horrifying vision of the Middle Passage: "I done seen bones rise up on the water."

Loomis's salvation comes only later in the play after he slashes his chest with a knife and finds the strength and the power to finally stand up on his own two feet and start afresh. He has found his own song, which Wilson calls the "song of self-sufficiency." This song helps him to attain the "warrior-spirit" and combat the racist environment in which he is forced to live. Bynum Walker, a mysterious African conjure man who "binds" people together and gives them their songs, plays an important role in Loomis's resurrection and healing. According to Bynum, Loomis becomes the spiritually charged shining man that Bynum has been looking for throughout his life.

Joe Turner's Come and Gone is a compilation of Wilson's most persistent themes. Through the play Wilson shows how embracing an African heritage—via the *juba* and Bynum's mysterious spiritual influence—can bring individual and collective healing to members of the African diaspora and the Great Migration north. Loomis's search for identity reaches a successful conclusion only when he confronts his painful past and the legacy of slavery within the framework of a communal response. Unlike previous heroes with the "warrior-spirit," such as Levee and Troy, Loomis achieves psychic unification and communal empowerment. That Loomis is able to attain his own redemption with Bynum's help is one of Wilson's strongest, most optimistic assertions of hope and possibility.

The critics were largely positive about Wilson's third Broadway showing. Writing for *The New York Times* (28 March 1988), Rich argued that *Joe Turner's Come and Gone* is Wilson's "most profound and theatrically adventurous telling of his story to date." The play "is a mixture of the well-made naturalistic boarding house drama and mystical, non-Western theater or ritual and metaphor." Writing for *Newsweek* (11 April 1988), Jack Kroll stated that *Joe Turner's Come and Gone* is Wilson's "best play to date and a profoundly American one."

Academic critics such as Trudier Harris stress Wilson's connections to such canonical African American folklorist writers as Zora Neale Hurston, Ralph Ellison, and Toni Morrison. In "August Wilson's Folk Traditions," included in *August Wilson: A Casebook*, she argues for the significance of Wilson's use of folklore and elevates Wilson's complex use of African American mythology in depicting Loomis's transformation to mystical "shining man": "When Wilson uses secular mythology as the source of religious conversion and overwrites Christianity with African American folkways, he merges the secular and the sacred in ways that few African American authors have attempted." Similarly, Shannon emphasizes the connections between *Joe Turner's Come and Gone* and Morrison's *Beloved* (1987): both Loomis and Beloved are mediums for "thousands of tormented slaves whose stories for centuries lay submerged beneath the currents of the Atlantic." Shannon also emphasizes Wilson's theme of reconnecting with African American heritage in the tradition of Black Nationalist writers Baraka and Larry Neal.

Another Bearden painting, *Piano Lesson* (1983), provided the inspiration for Wilson's next play. The silkscreen painting depicts a woman looking over the shoulder of her female student seated at a large piano. *The Piano Lesson* won Wilson his second Pulitzer Prize in 1990 before it opened at the Walter Kerr Theatre on Broadway in April that year and ran for 329 performances. Previous productions included a run at the Yale Repertory Theatre from 26 November through 19 December 1987. Charles S. Dutton, who had also acted in *Ma Rainey's Black Bottom*, was highly praised for his performance in the New York production. *The Piano Lesson* was adapted as a "Hallmark Hall of Fame" television production, also featuring Dutton as Boy Willie.

The Piano Lesson further develops the familiar theme of overcoming the bitter legacy of slavery through a revitalized connection with an African heritage. Set in 1936 Pittsburgh in the home of the main characters' uncle, the play centers on a conflict between Boy Willie and his sister Berniece over the fate of their most cherished possession from their enslaved past—their family's piano. Its legs had been carved with African-styled figures by their great-grandfather in an act of mourning the loss of his missing wife and nine-year-old son, who had been traded away for the piano as an anniversary present for the slaveowner's wife.

As if this symbolic weight were not enough, Boy Willie and Berniece's sharecropper father was killed in retribution for later stealing the piano from James Sutter, a descendent of the original slaveowners. Sutter suspiciously drowns in his well, perhaps pushed by Boy Willie, who celebrates his death. However, Boy Willie recounts the legend of the Ghosts of the Yellow Dog—the boxcar in which their father was burned along with three others—and blames them for Sutter's death. Sutter's ghost inhabits their uncle's home, giving the play supernatural overtones.

In contrast to Boy Willie, Berniece wants to keep the piano and emphasizes its priceless heirloom status. She recounts how their mother polished the piano every day for seventeen years, until her hands bled. It is a cumulative symbol of their family's tragedy—drenched in the blood of slavery, the hypocrisy of the Fugitive Slave Law, and the horrors of Reconstruction and Jim Crow. More practical-minded Boy Willie, who arrives in Pittsburgh ostensibly to sell watermelons, is interested in selling the valuable piano so that he can buy back the plantation on which his great-grandparents were enslaved.

Before either side can resolve their dispute, however, they must confront the ghosts of the past. Boy Willie must confront Sutter's ghost, which has followed the piano from the South, and Berniece must re-establish ties to her dead ancestors. Ever since the day her mother died, she has avoided playing the piano because she did not want to wake the spirits of her dead relatives. In the end, she plays a redemptive and empowering blues song on the piano that is "both a commandment and a plea"— it serves to exorcise the ghosts and to reconnect Berniece and her brother with her ancestors. Through music, in other words, the characters have accessed the power of the African heritage. Additionally the magic counterspell in the music has driven away the demons and ghosts of the white slaveowning past. Boy Willie departs for home in Mississippi, content to let Berniece keep the piano, after both characters learn a powerful individual and cultural "lesson."

A reviewer of the *Yale Repertory Theater* performance (Time, 30 January 1989) called *The Piano Lesson* "the richest yet of dramatist August Wilson" and the piano "the most potent symbol in American drama since Laura Wingfield's glass menagerie." Barnes, writing for the *New York Post* (17 April 1990), stressed the significance and power of the piano as a living symbol of the family's past and emphasized the effective confrontations in the play between the living and the dead, between the real and the supernatural. Writing for *The New York Times* (17 April 1990), Rich called attention to the effective use of music in the play. He concluded, "That haunting music belongs to the people who have lived it, and it has once again found miraculous voice in a play that August Wilson has given to the American stage."

A review for *New York Magazine* (7 May 1990), however, was largely critical of the Broadway production for having too many confusing subplots and contradictions and for the "uncompelling" use of the supernatural. The reviewer attributes the confusing and unconvincing aspects of the play mostly to its two-year period of testing in various venues before opening on Broadway. Critic Robert Brustein's scathing attack on Wilson in his review of *The Piano Lesson* for *The New Republic* (21 May 1990) marked the beginning of a bitter relationship between the playwright and Brustein, who called the play "an overwritten exercise in a conventional style" that does not have the poetry of Wilson's previous plays. Where other critics have celebrated Wilson's treatment of African American life, Brustein sees Wilson as having "limited himself to the black experience in a relatively literalistic style." He called Wilson's acclaim among white liberal audiences the result of "a cultural equivalent of affirmative

action." He also criticized the use of the supernatural as a "contrived intrusion," inappropriate in a realist drama, and concluded that "Wilson is reaching a dead end in his examination of American racism."

Some academic critics took a different, more positive view of Wilson's use of the supernatural or the mystical. In "Ghosts on the Piano: August Wilson and the Representation of Black History," included in *May All Your Fences Have Gates*, Michael Morales argues that the mystical and the historical are closely interrelated in Wilson's plays, especially *The Piano Lesson* and *Joe Turner's Come and Gone*: "In these two plays Wilson predicates the relationship of the past to the present for black Americans on an active lineage kinship bond between the living and their ancestors." In an answer to the critical controversy over the ending of *The Piano Lesson*, academic critics argue that the reliance of the play on the presence of the supernatural is a valid part of Wilson's overarching dramatic project of restoring a sense of historical-cultural connection with the past for contemporary blacks.

Two Trains Running, his next play, continues Wilson's ten-play historical cycle by examining urban black culture in the tumultuous 1960s. After a run at the Yale Repertory Theatre in New Haven from 27 March through 21 April 1990, and a year of fine tuning with the help of Richards, the play opened at the Walter Kerr Theatre on Broadway on 13 April 1992, with Laurence Fishburne playing Sterling, one of the central characters. The play won Wilson his sixth Drama Critics Circle Award. He also met his third wife, Constanza Romero, who was in charge of costume design, during the production. Together they have a daughter, Azula Carmen Wilson.

Two Trains Running is set in Pittsburgh in 1969, in a restaurant across the street from a funeral home and Lutz's, a white-owned meat market. As critics mention frequently, although the play is set in the 1960s, it does not foreground the political turmoil of that decade; instead, the race riots and heightened tensions exist in the background. Their relative insignificance highlights Wilson's belief that politics changed little for blacks. Instead of change, the play focuses on the familiar theme of overcoming the destructive effects of the pervasive economic exploitation of the black community by mainstream white society and of the trauma of the past, including slavery. As Shannon notes, Wilson's later plays, including *Two Trains Running*, feature characters who, "Instead of assailing white America's conscience . . . seem preoccupied with discovering, acknowledging, and grappling with both their collective and individual pasts in order to move their lives forward."

As in *Fences* especially, one of the central tensions exists between the older and the younger male generations. In *Two Trains Running*, Memphis Lee is the self-made man who owns the restaurant in which the play is set. Like Troy Maxson in *Fences*, Memphis rails against the younger generation. Perhaps because of the gap between himself and the younger generation, he scoffs at the Black Power rallies celebrating Malcolm X's legacy in his neighborhood, placing little hope in the power of the younger generation to change anything because of the loss of their work ethic. At the same time, however, he believes that the only way to make an impact on the white man is with a gun.

Wilson carefully balances Memphis's indignation against the younger generation with another older character, Holloway, who makes the connection between the lack of a work ethic in the younger generation and their lack of rewarding opportunity, a systemic problem that keeps the economic inequity of slavery intact. Holloway asserts a chilling logical equation: while times have changed since slavery, the basic economic policy of plenty of work for nothing and no work for pay is still in effect. Several of the other male characters in the play invest all their time and energy in playing the numbers as a seemingly viable alternative to working at a job or investing their money. Wilson's implication is that investment for the black community and the fixed, white-controlled numbers racket are essentially the same thing, since everything is set up to favor whites.

Despite their differences over how to cope with their economic disempowerment, the characters in the play seem obsessed by money and by redressing the economic exploitations of the past. For example, one of the characters, nicknamed Hambone, repeats a single line throughout the play until his death: "I want my ham." More than nine years before, the white grocery-store owner, Lutz, agreed to pay him a ham in exchange for doing a good job painting his fence. Instead of a ham, however, all Hambone gets is the offer of a chicken. Each day until his death Hambone confronts Lutz, receiving the same frustrating answer. In a symbolic act designed to redress the inequity of the past, one of the younger characters, Sterling, a former convict in his thirties, breaks the store window and steals a ham from Lutz's store to put in Hambone's coffin. Unlike Memphis, who seems paralyzed by contradictions and his own pessimism, Sterling,

as a disciple of Malcolm X, takes direct action. His act underscores Wilson's admiration for those who do something to counter pervasive racial injustice by enacting the "warrior-spirit."

Memphis dreams of returning to Jackson, Mississippi, to reclaim his farm, which he was forced to leave because of attacks by white racists in 1931. He hopes to sell his restaurant, which he bought with his numbers winnings and his disabled brother's insurance money, to the city for a good price. He plans to take one of the "two trains running" south every day from the Pittsburgh train station and buy back his farm. Memphis, like Troy Maxson, is pessimistic about the future of the black community and looks forward to leaving. Most of the stores and healthcare providers have already moved out in preparation for the city's "renovation" project. As Memphis grimly states, "Ain't nothing gonna be left but these niggers killing one another." By the end of the play, however, Memphis gets the money he wanted from the city, which is an unusually optimistic turn of events in Wilson's plays.

Two Trains Running features an offstage character—Aunt Esther—who, like Bynum in *Joe Turner's Come and Gone*, is the spiritual center of the play. She has the gift of prophecy, unlike the more suspect promises of the more popular, glitzy Prophet Samuel, minister of the First African Congregational Kingdom. Throughout the play different characters go to seek Aunt Esther's advice, including Memphis, who is told that he needs to take care of unfinished business—recovering his farm. Instead of boasting of the power to make people rich, as does the Prophet Samuel, the reputedly 123-year-old Aunt Esther has the "understanding" or wisdom of old age, which reinforces one of Wilson's consistent themes: that the older black generations offer empowering wisdom, experience, and spirituality. She represents the antimaterialism of true spiritual achievement, and tells several characters, including Memphis, to throw her twenty-dollar fee into the river. Aunt Esther's significance as a voice of wisdom and historical continuity cannot be overestimated; Holloway believes that she is actually 322 years old, roughly the same amount of time that Africans have lived in North America.

Critical reaction to *Two Trains Running* was less positive than to some of his earlier plays. Writing for the *New York Post* (14 April 1992), Barnes criticized the play, calling it the most diffuse play that Wilson has written. Some critics agreed with this assessment but found other aspects to praise. Chief among their criticisms was that the play lacked a strong plot and resolution, and that it was too long. Other critics, however, writing for *Time* (28 April 1992), and the *Christian Science Monitor* (27 April 1992), praised the sense of humor in the play and its lyric depiction of human suffering. Also prominent in the reviews of the play was a nearly unanimous appreciation for Wilson's use of language and for the acting, especially by Fishburne.

Academic criticism counters the criticisms in the mass media. Shannon, for example, writes that "the play's lax tempo and unconventional structure imitate the often unhurried, repetitive, and sometimes amorphous form of blues music." She compares the improvisational plotlessness of *Two Trains Running* to *Ma Rainey's Black Bottom*: both plays are "best viewed as a dramatic rendering of a blues song; form and structure are secondary to catharsis." Other critics affirm Shannon's central point: in an essay included in *Three Plays*, Paul C. Harrison emphasizes the oral-history quality of *Ma Rainey's Black Bottom* and the slow accretion of tension based on a pattern of "circuitous course of parenthetical anecdotes, asides and utterances."

Wilson's next play, *Seven Guitars*, returns to the blues as an explicit controlling metaphor. The play ran first in Chicago at the Goodman Theatre from 21 January to 25 February 1995 before it opened on Broadway on 28 March 1996 at the Walter Kerr Theatre. Wilson completed it after taking a three-year break from writing; the changes in his life during this period included his divorce from his second wife, his plans to marry Romero, and his success in giving up a heavy smoking habit.

Seven Guitars opens during a hot and humid summer in the familiar Pittsburgh Hill District in 1948. The dirt backyard set is a gathering place for the characters who occupy the apartments above and below the yard to play whist, sing the blues, dance, socialize, argue, and listen to the radio accounts of the latest Joe Louis victory over his white opponents. Despite the historical context of the country's economic boom after World War II, the Pittsburgh black community, made up largely of Southerners looking for greater economic opportunity in the North, seems completely isolated from the rest of the country and certainly does not share in its economic gains. Instead, as in many of Wilson's plays, the characters in *Seven Guitars* are fixated on money and on attaining some kind of financial retribution for past wrongs.

Seven Guitars begins and ends with musician Floyd "Schoolboy" Barton's funeral. The play creates some suspense by not answering the question of who murdered him until the final scene. The mystic and at times delusional character King Hedley dreams that someday King Buddy Bolden, a legendary blues player for whom Hedley is named, would appear and return to him his father's money. He plans to take this money, return south, and buy a plantation, like Memphis in *Two Trains Running*. When Hedley sees Floyd in the yard with $1,200 he had stolen during a robbery from the loan offices of Metro Finance, he feels his dream has come true and kills Floyd for refusing to hand over the money. Like Levee in *Ma Rainey's Black Bottom* and Herald Loomis in *Joe Turner's Come and Gone*, Hedley embodies the "warrior-spirit." He refuses to acquiesce to white economic disenfranchisement and wants to be famous someday. Near the end of the play he calls himself a "warrior" and a "hurricane," and warns that the "black man is not a dog!" Hedley sees himself cast in a biblical drama against the Satanic whites, and he hopes to father a son who will be the new black messiah born to conquer evil. Indicative of Wilson's complex sense of irony and realism, however, is the final act: instead of realizing his dreams, Hedley kills one of his friends, and the dollar bills that he had hoped would be his ticket to a new life instead "fall to the ground like ashes" from his hands in the closing scene, similar to the tragic denouement of *Ma Rainey's Black Bottom*.

One of Wilson's most pessimistic plays, *Seven Guitars* shows the black man caught in the inexorable web of white economic oppression that exploits the black artist and fails to see his music as anything more than a means to an economic end. As in *Ma Rainey's Black Bottom*, the musicians who occupy this play have been taken advantage of and cheated by the white-controlled music industry. Despite the fact that Floyd has a hit song, ironically called "That's All Right," he is still dependent on a white agent who eventually cheats him out of his advance money (and is convicted also of insurance fraud), thereby making it impossible for Floyd to get his guitar out of hock and return to Chicago. Like all the characters in the play, Floyd is tired of having nothing and decides to "take a chance" by robbing the loan offices. With the money he is finally able to provide a headstone for his beloved mother and, before he is killed, he performs in a night of singing and fun at the local nightclub, the "Blue Goose."

Several times in the play Floyd reminisces fondly about his mother, and his music reflects her love for gospel singing. In Wilson's "A Note from the Playwright," which precedes the play Wilson admits that this play is an homage to his mother's life, her cooking, her faith, and her superstitions. These aspects come alive as well in the female characters, who spend time preparing food and talking about men and the difficulties of love. The play begins and ends with one of the women, Vera, with whom Floyd was involved, claiming to have seen angels come to take Floyd to heaven.

Critical reaction to *Seven Guitars* was mixed. Writing for the *New York Post* (29 March 1996), Barnes praised the sad anger and the poetry of the play but criticized the lack of an effective climax. The reviewer for *The New York Times* (29 March 1996) also found fault with the ending but raved about the rest of the play and its spiritual power. Several other critics were impressed by the wisdom in the play, Wilson's use of language, the acting, and the homage to the blues spirit despite the less effective second act, which could have been improved.

Shortly after *Seven Guitars* opened, Wilson gave the keynote address to the Theatre Communications Group National Conference on 26 June 1996. This address, titled "The Ground on Which I Stand" and published in *American Theatre* in September 1996, can be read as the culminating manifesto of his personal politics, his aesthetics, and his vision for the future. In the address he differentiates between two traditions, the white and the black. While he recognizes his debt to great white dramatists, including William Shakespeare and Eugene O'Neill, the ground on which he stands as an artist is firmly in the black tradition, dating back to the spiritually empowering and functional art practiced not within the white slaveowner's home for white consumption, but within the slave quarters for an exclusively black audience. This art was designed to nurture the spirit, to celebrate black life, and to pass on strategies for survival in a hostile and antagonistic environment. Strategies for maintaining control over black cultural capital include rejecting colorblind casting (the practice of placing black actors in "white" plays or vice versa, such as an all-white cast of Lorraine Hansberry's 1959 play, *A Raisin in the Sun*) as cultural appropriation. Wilson also argues for increasing the number of black regional theaters. Out of the sixty-six theaters in the League of Resident Theaters (LORT), Wilson claims, only one is dedicated to black drama. Wilson challenges theater managers to increase the number of regional black theaters and to make theater more accessible to the masses.

Wilson goes on to reject the label of being a separatist, since he believes that whites and blacks can meet on a jointly constructed "common ground" of the theater in pursuing dramatic excellence, as long as that common ground allows blacks to explore and celebrate their cultural distinctiveness. He argues that in addition to the formalist commonalities of theater, which include plot and characterization, there are such human universals as love, honor, duty, and betrayal that all audiences can appreciate, regardless of race. Theater was developed by Aristotle and other Greek, European, and Euro-American playwrights; however, Wilson avers, "We embrace the values of that theatre but reserve the right to amend, to explore, to add our African consciousness and our African aesthetic to the art we produce." Wilson ends with an appeal to work together to create a common ground and to use the universal truth-telling power of the theater to improve all lives across the lines of culture and color.

Wilson's keynote address also includes attacks on the "cultural imperialist" critics who, like Brustein, are antagonistic to a diversified theater because they see a lowering of aesthetic standards. Wilson counters by arguing that the new voices in the theater represent a raising of the standards and levels of excellence in the theater.

Wilson's address was met with a veritable firestorm of print activity, including counterattacks by Brustein. In the next issue of *American Theatre* Brustein responded to Wilson's attacks with an article titled "Subsidized Separatism," to which Wilson also replied in the same issue. In the article, Brustein seeks to defend himself and to explore "troubling general issues" raised in Wilson's speech, which he calls a "rambling jeremiad." Brustein interprets Wilson's speech as a call for separatist theater and reads Wilson's comments about artistic universals and common ground as "boilerplate rhetoric," afterthought, and pretense. He repeats his objections to Wilson's plays, made clear especially in his review of *The Piano Lesson*, and adds a further complaint that "Wilson has fallen into a monotonous tone of victimization which happens to be the leitmotif of his TCG speech." Brustein asserts that Wilson is part of the "rabid identity politics and poisonous racial consciousness that have been infecting our country in recent years."

In his response following Brustein's article, Wilson defends himself against what he calls Brustein's misinterpretations of his speech and repeats his points about the cross-cultural commonalities inherent in great art. At the end of his response he turns around Brustein's scolding that he has left Dr. Martin Luther King Jr. out of his list of black American heroes by arguing that Brustein is the one who denies the possibility of a theater capable of absorbing or assimilating different traditions and cultural values.

The dramatic and well-publicized feud between Wilson and Brustein reached its peak during a 27 January 1997 debate at New York City Town Hall, moderated by Anna Deavere Smith and titled "On Cultural Power." In a review of the two-and-a-half-hour debate for *American Theatre*, Stephen Nunns emphasizes the evening as a flashy media spectacle. Accompanying photographs depict "a diverse and celebrity-studded audience." Nunns writes that both men began by repeating their earlier positions, with Brustein attacking multiculturalism as being without intellectual content and Wilson again emphasizing the need for more black regional theaters and his activist position that art has the power to transform society and individuals. While the two debaters were relatively civil, the 1,500-member audience had to be reprimanded several times by Smith for heckling the speakers.

Critical reaction to the debate was mixed. In *Newsweek* (10 February 1997) Kroll emphasized the significance of their debate and the need to explore issues of multiculturalism and cultural synthesis as the country becomes more diverse. An editorial in the *Boston Globe* (9 February 1997) praised the intelligence and depth of the evening. However, several critics noted that the event was not too enlightening because neither man seemed able to listen to the other or to come to any kind of reconciliation. Rich wrote in an article for *The New York Times* (1 February 1997) that both men ignored the larger crisis that serious theater is virtually dead: "Both men narcissistically fiddle (and bicker) while the world of serious culture they share burns." And a writer for the *Village Voice* (February 1997) found the evening disappointing because both men are stuck in "a monolithic modernism. Both hold faith in a capital-T Truth out there waiting to be uncovered."

In a 3 February 1997 article in *The New Yorker*, "The Chitlin Circuit," eminent literary and social critic Henry Louis Gates Jr. responded at length to Wilson's keynote address but mentioned the debate only in passing. While Gates calls Wilson the "dean of American dramatists" and "the most celebrated American playwright now writing and . . . certainly the most accomplished black playwright in this nation's history," Gates's article is largely critical of Wilson. Gates reviews the controversies around Wilson's "disturbing polemic," points out that many

black actors disagree with Wilson's condemnation of colorblind casting, and quotes Baraka's support for actors crossing color lines to get parts. Gates also attacks Wilson's "divided rhetoric" in calling for a self-determining black theater and government subsidies at the same time.

As if to answer the critiques of Gates and others, Wilson has become quite active in the cause of developing and nurturing serious black theater. He was featured at the opening of the foundation-subsidized new vehicle for black theater, The African Grove Institute for the Arts in partnership with the National Black Arts Festival. According to its brochure, the African Grove Institute, which is based at Dartmouth College, is "dedicated to the advancement and preservation of black Theater as an agent for social and economic change." Its initial event, which coincided with the National Black Theatre Summit II, was held in Atlanta in July 1998. The opening featured a performance of *Jitney* and included a closing conference session titled "A Vision for the New Millenium."

Not surprisingly, given Wilson's historically minded plays, Wilson's vision for the future concerns the past. He wants to see a new black community created in the South that emulates the closely knit, more economically self-sufficient black communities of the 1940s—such as the Hill—that Wilson knew and loved as a child and young adult. Wilson's play *King Hedley II* had its premiere in Pittsburgh in December 1999 and opened in Seattle on 13 March 2000. The main character in *King Hedley II*, the eighth play in Wilson's historical cycle, is an ex-con trying to rebuild his life in 1990s Pittsburgh. As part of his retrospective vision, the play depicts the decline of the black family and the prevalence of violence and guns in contemporary inner-city neighborhoods. While some critics may call this impulse to reject the present in favor of the past "sentimental separatism" or romantic illusion, Wilson sees nothing negative in revivifying a supportive separate black community or in attempting to reverse the mistake of leaving the South for a dream that did not come true. He also continues to support the idea of a diversified American theater, built on the common, cross-cultural ground of dramatic form.

Source: Jonathan Little, "August Wilson," in *Dictionary of Literary Biography*, Vol. 228, *Twentieth-Century American Dramatists, Second Series*, edited by Christopher J. Wheatley, The Gale Group, 2000, pp. 289–302.

Peter Wolfe

In the following essay, Wolfe declares that Two Trains Running *gives a faithful depiction of the decade-long progress, and its "effects," on black Americans. He also comments on Wilson's frequent use of the theme of "transience."*

Set in 1969, *Two Trains Running* provides a gritty, unflinching look at the effects of a decade of great progress for black America. The progress covered many areas. The year 1962 saw the election of the first black man, Jackie Robinson, to baseball's Hall of Fame and, thanks to the efforts of the Student Nonviolent Coordinating Committee, new highs in black voter registration in the deep South. Two years later, Dr. Martin Luther King won the Nobel Peace Prize and, a year after that, more than 3,000 people marched the 54 miles between Selma and Montgomery, Alabama. The list of breakthroughs continues. Justice Thurgood Marshall became the first black member of the U.S. Supreme Court in 1967, and 1968 brought the passage of the Civil Rights Act. But many would feel let down by this landmark bill. The benefits of hindsight explains why. The failure of the act to create more equality and justice for blacks could have been predicted from the ugliness that preceded it. The murders of Malcolm X in 1965 and of Dr. King in 1968 belong in the same continuum as the slaying of civil rights workers in Mississippi in 1964 and the deaths caused by riots in Watts in 1965 and Detroit in 1967.

This violence erupted for a reason. Despite the Black Power activism and the progress in civil rights legislation since 1962, blacks in America were still oppressed. Their future looked bleak. In the air were signs of the coming of cities that would be too fast, too crowded, and too smart to be easily endured by the black underclass, cities also marred by growing numbers of glue sniffers, heroin addicts, and hookers living in condemned buildings without electricity or running water. Unfolding in a transitional era, *Two Trains Running* (1992) describes urban blacks caught in the wash of social change. It depicts the clash of old and new energies— the relative ease of an old order faced by the anarchy of a new social agenda that includes the militant politics of the Nation of Islam. The ordeals of both the Middle Passage and the Great Migration have revived in the minds of Wilson's people. For another population displacement is at hand; city planners are razing Pittsburgh's Hill for an urban redevelopment plan without first providing for the residents' relocation. There are other forebodings. Besides flattening a friendly, vibrant community that has meant home to many people, the proposed renewal scheme will create new, uglier slums that

will aggravate Pittsburgh's present ghettoization— the division of the city's population by color and income. A larger public works program will replace neighborhood continuity with "projects," big low-income, high-risk public housing. Symbolizing both the doomed organic community and the warm socializing buzz of the street is Memphis Lee's homestyle restaurant, the setting for Wilson's 1992 play. Like the jitney station in Wilson's unpublished 1982 *Jitney*, Lee's has been targeted for demolition by the city. Across the street from it stand a funeral home and a meat market, suggesting rapacity and even cannibalism. This looming devastation rivets us because the restaurant, it soon becomes clear, is more than a place of business. It's also a makeshift community center and social club. People drop in at all hours for coffee and conversation. Neighborly and charitable, these denizens of Lee's take up a collection to bail a local man out of jail so he can attend his wife's funeral.

Yet Wilson is too ironic and socially aware to ride the flow of sentiment induced by the death of Bubba Boy's wife. Capable of being tender and tough minded at the same time, he deliberately sited *Trains* in a climate of "urban decay" (McDonough, 153). The local supermarket, the five-and-ten, two drugstores, and the local doctor and dentist, it comes out early, have all left the Hill or gone out of business. "Ain't nothing gonna be left but these niggers killing one another", says Memphis, forecasting the inevitable upshot of this erosion of amenities and services. Nor can he stop the slide. Once a thriving business, his diner now has a small clientele. At the time of the first act, its larder consists only of a little coffee, some beans, frozen hamburger, and a box of rice. Memphis goes shopping during the course of the action for limited quantities of chicken, meat loaf, and pie he'd have stocked— and sold—in abundance during the diner's earlier, palmier days.

On the subject of Memphis and his surviving clientele, Carla J. McDonough says, "a sense of detachment, decay, and dissolution pervades their talk. These men are separated from their families and are left very little in the way of companionship." Marginalized and wounded they have become. West the mortician is the only local whose business has been thriving. He can forget the days when it took two weeks to get a broken toilet fixed. So lucrative is his mortuary that he no longer replaces broken window panes with wooden boards; his livery includes seven Cadillacs; looking to add to his millions, he has been buying up much of the real estate on the Hill so he can sell it back to the city at a profit before it's razed. Memphis has also known prosperity, if not recently. Like West, he's a property-owning driver of a Cadillac. But the devastation that has enriched West—including that caused by black-on-black crime—is threatening *him*. This wise investor sees the forced sale of the building he has divided into a diner and rental apartments taking away from him both a steady source of cash and a means of self-validation.

He and his cronies lead half lives, a sad truth suggested by their mostly being known by one name. Holloway has no woman, and West is a widower (widowers outnumber widows in Wilson). Hambone, Wolf, and Bubba Boy (another widower) are known only by their nicknames. Memphis Lee, whose first name is probably also a nickname, has a wife he rarely sees. Loneliness also frets the two characters who develop the play's love interest. By default, the orphan-turned-bank-robber Sterling Johnson took the last name of an adoptive family he no longer sees. His putative mate, Clarissa Thomas, is always called Risa, denoting a loss of clarity or brightness in her life. The others share her plight. Gloom has gripped the doomed neighborhood with its shards of broken glass, thriving mortuary, and Bubba Boy's newly dead wife. Wilson told Mark William Rocha in a 1992 interview that his intention in *Two Trains Running* was to show "that by 1969 nothing . . . changed for the black man." In 1969, the efforts of the deceased Malcolm X and Dr. King, like the high-profile 1968 Civil Rights Act, did look futile. But futility hasn't swallowed all, thanks to the synergy created by the play's fusion of vision and voice. Supported by dialogue sinewy, charged, and sometimes hilarious, the ambiguity that permeates Wilson's beliefs about social progress for blacks provokes more debate than grief.

Life on the Edge

By all reasonable standards, the people in *Trains* qualify as losers—depressing to think about and painful to watch. That they fuse as a winning, engaging group whose doings fascinate us counts as a small miracle. This feat hinges in part on the deft and always entertaining techniques Wilson uses to drive a grim story. In part it hinges on Wilson's belief in the inadequacy of reason to explain life's mysteries. This belief, if unoriginal, is both hard won and moving. Wilson is the opposite of an ideologue. He hates ideologies and dogmas. To him, they're narrow and partisan, and they do great harm. They also make politicians look clumsy and stupid at times when they need flexibility and

" THE FREQUENCY IN THE CANON OF BOTH TRAINS AND THE BLUES, WILSON'S MAIN SOURCE OF ARTISTIC INSPIRATION, CALLS FORTH THE IDEA OF TRANSIENCE, SPECIFICALLY THE GREAT MIGRATION AND THE MANY FAMILY BREAKUPS IT CAUSED. **"**

breadth of outlook. This truth explains a great deal in *Trains*. A minute into the play a character says, "The NAACP got all kinds of lawyers. It don't do nobody no good." Wilson would probably approve this verdict. He's as hostile to collective solutions as was Ellison in *Invisible Man*. Pereira sees him directing that hostility toward recent attempts by black activists to improve their people's chances for justice and equality. The death of Wilson's Prophet Samuel, Pereira claims, coming soon after those of Malcolm X and Dr. King, signals the failure of the civil rights movement in the United States. The ballyhoo created by both Prophet Samuel's funeral and the monster rally for Malcolm X supports Pereira's claim.

Prophet Samuel confirms Wilson's genius for driving a plot with a character who never shows his face to the audience. That face *is* seen off-stage, though mostly by the undertaker West, since the prophet died just before opening curtain. But others have been thronging not only to see that face but also to touch it. Prophet Samuel had enjoyed roaring success preaching the doctrine of freedom and dignity through the acquisition of wealth. Though this dovetailing of material and spiritual blessings squares with mainstream Yankee Protestantism, Wilson rejects it with the same scorn he aims at the Black Power movement. Signs that Prophet Samuel represents a false direction include his sleazy background. Like Rinehart in *Invisible Man*, he's a huckster of religion with a criminal past who bleeds his own people. His death, which might have been caused by poison, suggests the same spiritual paralysis called forth by the dead priest in James Joyce's "The Sisters," from *Dubliners*. Sisters are what

Prophet Samuel's devotees might have called themselves, but the bonds he had with them were rumored to have been sexual. In fact, the poison that may have killed him would have been fed to him by a jealous female retainer.

Though based on hearsay, this possibility stays alive. For poison *could* have driven the disorder that follows his death: a fight caused by someone who tries to crash the line of mourners waiting to pay their last respects, an opportunist who would charge admission to see the corpse, and an attempted late-night burglary of the funeral parlor where the corpse was laid out all imply a poisoning of the social order Prophet Samuel had allegedly set out to redeem. He always walked with corruption and fraud. Shannon has discussed the carnival atmosphere he liked surrounding himself with both to amuse his followers and to distract them from his ignorance of the living God: "Even after his death, Prophet Samuel is able to attract hordes of people—the hopeless, the desperate, or simply the curious. While alive, he enjoyed a popular ministry based upon a mixture of showbiz antics, con artistry, and an immodest display of religiosity: he wore robes, went shoeless, and with much fanfare, baptized converts in a nearby river."

As is shown by the disruptions following Prophet Samuel's death, such extravaganza inhibits both social and spiritual uplift. Wilson, duly warned, resists imposing either an arbitrary aesthetic order or a political agenda on his materials. Reflecting the disarray he sees around him, his theater addresses the challenge of maintaining a belief that defies reason. Warrior spirits like Troy Maxson and Boy Willie Charles break so many rules making this provocative leap of faith that they foil themselves. The issue revives in *Trains*, a work that posits a new ontology with its fusions of logic and nonsense and of the outlandish and the factual. Defying huge odds, the number 621 hits for the second time within a week. Sterling's number will also win but with mixed results, since it's cut in half, paying only 300 to 1 rather than the customary 600 to 1. Reason and common sense come under question as early as midway through the first scene when, moments after claiming that she has been cleaning a chicken, Risa admits that the diner is out of chicken. Undeterred, her boss, Memphis, will soon tell her to fry the nonexistent chicken, to which she replies that she's already frying it.

Obviously, the world of Wilson's people regulates itself by a mystique far removed from Western pragmatism. Embodying this mystique is a 322-year-old woman named Aunt Ester, who lives at 1839 Wylie, just minutes away from Memphis's diner, the Wylie Avenue address of which is 1621. But the August Wilson of *Trains* varies his usual practice of siting salvation close to the miseenscène. Though suggesting sexual passion, the red door of Aunt Ester's apartment leads to inner peace and self-acceptance. But these blessings aren't open to all. She speaks in riddles, and, like that of Bynum in *Joe Turner*, her wisdom is more of a challenge than a quick fix. She makes Sterling come to her three times before admitting him. Her standards are high. She *will* rid people like Sterling of their bad energy, but anyone who approaches her with selfish motives will walk away empty-handed. In particular, she refuses to help those who want her to show them how to get rich. Indicative of the times they're living in, five characters in the play (four speaking parts and Prophet Samuel) ask her help. What she says to them reaches us only in rough outline, Wilson deliberately avoiding telling all. As he should; one of the privileges of being alive consists of moving forward in the dark. Were all life's riddles and mysteries disclosed to us, faith would be drained of meaning, and the afterlife would lack purpose. Thus Risa, a follower of the charlatan Prophet Samuel and a no-show at Aunt Ester's, gives Sterling his winning number, 781, but withholds its import from him. Defying reason, she also claims that the deranged Hambone has more sense than any of the other patrons of the diner.

Perhaps insight into the play's larger meaning lies in its title. Memphis says that every day two trains run back to his hometown of Jackson, Mississippi. He hopes that he'll soon board one to reclaim the farm that was stolen from him in 1931. He has judged his prospects well. Any train is a blind, amoral force, like money, a subject the characters argue about often. Memphis could hop on either of the two trains that leave daily from Pittsburgh. The sense of mission impelling him will endow the morally neutral train he takes with value; the moral drama must come from him if it's to come at all. Observing unity of place, Wilson ends the play before Memphis's long-awaited train ride to Jackson. But he does talk about the play's title in terms applicable to Memphis. His words appear both on the back cover of the 1993 Plume paperback reprint of the play and in the playbill (p. 34) of the 1992 Broadway production at the Walter Kerr Theater: "There are always and only two trains running. There is life and there is death. Each of us rides them both. To live life with dignity, to celebrate and accept responsibility for your presence in the world is all that can be asked of anyone."

Dignity and personal responsibility are virtues that members of an underclass, particularly a transient one, can rarely afford to cultivate. The frequency in the canon of both trains and the blues, Wilson's main source of artistic inspiration, calls forth the idea of transience, specifically the Great Migration and the many family breakups it caused. Romare Bearden, the black American painter and collagist whose work inspired both *Joe Turner* and *The Piano Lesson*, referred to trains more gently when he said in 1977, "Negroes lived near the tracks, worked on the railroads, and trains carried them North during the migration." Wilson prefers the darker tones. Doaker, who spent 27 years working on the railroad, says in *Piano Lesson* about train passengers, "They leaving cause they can't get satisfied." To him, trains symbolize failure to cope. Rather than staying home and trying to solve their problems, the fainthearted think that riding a train to a new town will make them go away.

They're wrong. Rather than staying behind in Mississippi, Sutter's ghost spent the three weeks before the opening curtain preparing for Boy Willie's arrival in Pittsburgh. Moreover, a train *will* sooner or later carry Boy Willie back to the Mississippi town where his journey began. Both the sound made by an approaching train at the end of the play and Boy Willie's last question "Hey, Doaker, what time the train leave?" reinstate the realities that rule most of Wilson's people—anxiety and the illusion of freedom.

A character whose financial and emotional distress converts to physical disquiet in *Trains* is Sterling. Recalling Wilson's other jobless young men just out of jail, such as Booster in *Jitney* and Lymon in *Piano Lesson*, Sterling is afraid that his new freedom offers no promise of a happy, productive life. So haunted is he by the fear of returning to jail that at times he seems to be inviting arrest. Self-preservation has never been his forte. Ten minutes after he robbed a bank, he was spending the stolen money. Yet, as Shannon says, he's no more of a monster than was the boyishly endearing Lymon: "Sterling is a strangely off-beat character. Far from presenting the hard-core image one might expect, he appears painfully naive—almost childlike." The good luck he claims to have been born with has deserted him. Unable to find work, he tries in vain to sell his watch. The job he held after his release from prison lasted only a week, at which time he was laid off. Or so he says; according to Memphis, Sterling quit. Holloway, the play's griot figure, agrees; if Sterling wanted to work, he'd have a job, Holloway believes. Holloway and Memphis could be

right. It's possible that Sterling's youthful charm stems from his immaturity. One of the most intriguing questions posed by *Trains* is whether Sterling (the Laurence Fishburne role in the 1992 Walter Kerr Theater production) can ever become a contented, peaceable member of society.

Alas, most of the evidence is negative. Lacking a sense of process, the boyish Sterling wants the rewards of labor without the toil: he steals some flowers from a memorial to give Risa because "it's silly to buy flowers" ; he also steals a five-gallon can full of gasoline. And it may also have been Sterling who broke West's window while trying to burglarize the mortuary after dark (he'll break a storefront window later in the play). Spending five years in prison didn't wipe out his criminal streak. Giving up his job search quickly, he buys a handgun, which he believes will help him access the material goods he wants but lacks the patience to work for. Holloway and Memphis both judge well when they envision him back in jail within weeks. Judging from his recklessness, they've skewed their timetables in his favor.

The person he'd sadden most by returning to prison is Risa. Like Lymon of *Piano Lesson*, he charms women rather than trying to over-power them. Risa is moved by his gentleness. He rejects her offer of beans in act 1, scene 1, explaining that he has been eating beans for the past five years. But a couple of days later, he gladly eats the beans she serves him, even asking for a second bowl. He has touched Risa. Within minutes, she twice uses the phrase "the right person" while discussing dancing partners, implying that she might welcome his attentions. But what kind of future would these attentions foster? Though uneducated, Risa is both sharp and caring. Other characters have misread this beguiling combination. Memphis miscues when he calls her "a mixed-up personality", and the numbers runner Wolf falls just as wide of the mark with his reductive summary, "all she need is a man." Risa defies definitions and formulas. Although constantly rebuked by Memphis, she's confident she won't be fired. She and Memphis both know that the diner is more than just a business establishment. To maintain its status as a surrogate home, it needs the female presence she gives it. Thus, without admitting it, Memphis prizes her kindness and warmth. What's more, the success he attains could well come from the wisdom he exercises by emulating her rarest quality—a fierce independence.

Like the others in the play, Risa is a lonely person awaiting redemption through love. But she wants love on her own strict terms, and it can only be shared with "the right person." Wilson fills in the background to the formation of these requirements. Some time before the play's present-tense action, perhaps as long as six years ago, she slashed her legs. Her scars depict her protest to being classified sexually or appraised as a possible bedmate. In the interest of building a long-term bond, she wants to turn the attention of any would-be male admirer to her inner self. She doesn't regret the 15 scars on her legs. To her, they still express a wish to be appreciated in her totality. There's much in her to appreciate. She speaks gently to Hambone, gives him a coat to wear, and feeds him whenever he comes into the diner. Though a follower of the Prophet Samuel, she'll attend neither his funeral nor the big rally for Malcolm X. She doesn't need the support of crowds to shore up her beliefs. Her values are personal, not collective, and she rates any leader's example over his mortal remains. (She will skip Hambone's funeral, too.)

Like everybody else, she knows, too, that love on one's own terms misses love. Thus she'll have to relax her agenda, fine as it is. Without protesting, she hears both Wolf and Sterling call her "baby." Protests wouldn't help her, anyway. She wants to share a special bond with a man she hopes might be Sterling. But she sees with a sinking heart that Sterling's sexual interest in her has put him on a par with all the other men who have courted her for the past six years; "You just want what everybody else want", she tells him. She wasn't expecting the reply she gets from him. By slashing her legs, he says, she violated nature. What's natural, he continues, is for a man to notice the charms of a pretty woman and then take steps to enjoy them. Instead of marring her legs, she should have simply used them to walk away from any man whose advances she found unwelcome.

Whether this argument convinces her is not clear. More obvious is her inability to fight the attraction she feels for him. Her reason tells her to resist him: "You ain't got no job. You going back to the penitentiary. I don't want to be tied up with nobody I got to be worrying is they gonna rob another bank or something." Her message is clear. She's doomed if she builds her life around an ex-con who doesn't know right from wrong. But within minutes of explaining to Sterling his unfitness as a mate, she's dancing with him and then kissing him. Her instincts have defeated her judgment. Wilson supplies the foreshadowing to show that Sterling has been wearing down her judgment longer than she suspects. Just as she violated her principles by accepting his bouquet of stolen flowers, so will she later accept him as a lover.

This cautious, self-protective woman's worst nightmare threatens to burst into reality. As has been seen, Sterling and the job that was waiting for him after he served his jail sentence parted company after a week. Nor has he learned from this setback. When told that he lacks the education to get "one of them white folks' jobs making eight or nine thousand dollars a year," he replies in terms redolent of Troy Maxson or Boy Willie: "I can do anything the white man can do. If the truth be told . . . most things I can do better." This arrogance can only land him back in jail. Within moments of voicing it, he starts shopping for a handgun. And not only is the handgun he buys illegal; it's also one he had already owned and gotten rid of because it malfunctioned. Spending five years in prison hasn't improved his judgment. Later, he takes the gun to the racketeer who halved the payout for the number that hit on the day Sterling bet on it. The four or five gorillas, or bodyguards, surrounding Mr. Albert show Sterling that his unannounced visit to the crime boss was a bad mistake. Wisely, he didn't start brandishing his gun in Albert's stronghold. He's probably as ready for an audience with Aunt Ester as he'll ever be.

Rocha says of this ancient conjuress whom death seems to have forgotten, "Aunt Ester is to be taken as the original African American, as old as the black experience in America" (Nadel, 128). Regardless of her exact age (three figures are mooted, ranging from 300 to 349), it approximates the length of time that Africans have been living in North America. The matriarch of the Charles family of Sunflower County, Mississippi, in *Piano Lesson* has the name Mama Ester. Perhaps the two like-named women embody the same ancestral wisdom. Holloway's claim regarding Aunt Ester, "She ain't gonna die, I can guarantee you that", besides reflecting a Borgesian acceptance of the bizarre, puts her beyond human processes. Her exemption from the categories that define the rest of us empowers her to boost Sterling's spirits. Before meeting her, Sterling believed that the world was about to end. Afterwards, he determines to marry Risa. Aunt Ester vitalizes him by advising him to be the best person he can, using the qualities given him. These qualities, she believes, will suffice him. If he stays within himself and cultivates what he finds there, he'll prosper. She closes their session with her usual mandate—that he throw $20 into the Monongahela River.

The session helps him, perhaps most of all because he obeys her mandate. Soon after returning to the diner, he sings. Then he and Risa dance and kiss to the accompaniment of an Aretha Franklin tune coming from the diner's recently repaired jukebox. Music has again promoted uplift and cheer in a Wilson playscript. But how long will its happy sway last? The next morning, Sterling robs a local store, reopening a path for himself to the jail where he just served time. He no longer regrets having been born. He'll even help further the continuance of the world he thought was about to end by having the children he had earlier forsworn. In fact, he may have fathered one in the hours that lapsed between the torrid kiss he shared with Risa at the end of act 2, scene 4, and the opening of the play's final scene the next morning.

But the criminal streak he discloses several times during the action implies that Risa will have to raise any offspring she has with Sterling alone. Having gone six years without sex, this paradigm of restraint and integrity finally lowers her guard for an amoral adolescent. His not being a Black Power activist has made him an anomaly among his peers. What brings this 30-year-old into the mainstream is his lawlessness. The numbers runner Wolf's comment, "every nigger you see done been to jail one time or another", applies more strictly to Sterling than to anyone else in the play. Unfortunately, the person who stands to suffer the most from its recoil action is Risa. In a truth borne out by Rose in *Fences* and Berniece in *Piano Lesson*, the women in Wilson's plays often suffer the most for the misdeeds of their men.

Source: Peter Wolfe, "Forever under Attack," in *August Wilson*, Twayne Publishers, 1999, pp. 110–20.

SOURCES

Henry, William A., III, "Luncheonette Tone Poem," in *Time*, Vol. 139, No. 17, April 27, 1992, p. 66.

King, Robert L., "Recent Drama," in *Massachusetts Review*, Vol. 32, No. 1, Spring 1991, http://web.ebscohost.com/ ehost/detail?vid=18&hid=d97a671 (accessed August 26, 2006).

Kramer, Mimi, "The Theatre: Unmanned," in *The New Yorker*, Vol. 68, No. 10, April 27, 1992, p. 84.

Shannon, Sandra G., *The Dramatic Vision of August Wilson*, Howard University Press, 1995, pp. 166, 167.

Wilson, August *Two Trains Running*, Plume, 1993.

FURTHER READING

Bogumil, Mary L., *Understanding August Wilson*, University of South Carolina Press, 1999.

Bogumil's useful and accessible overview of Wilson's career and dramatic output is directed towards students as well as nonacademic readers. It provides a biographical outline of Wilson and his place in African American drama and a discussion of each major play through *Seven Guitars*.

Elkins, Marilyn, *August Wilson: A Casebook*, Garland Publishing, 2000.

This collection of essays by leading scholars of twentieth-century African American theater includes a broad overview of Wilson's politics and their relation to his plays. It also contains two interviews, one with Wilson's longtime collaborator and mentor, Lloyd Richards, and one with Wilson himself.

Menson-Furr, Ladrica, "Booker T. Washington, August Wilson, and the Shadows in the Garden," in *Mosaic*, Vol. 38, No. 4, December 2005, pp. 175–91.

Menson-Furr's sophisticated article places Wilson against a broad historical backdrop, analyzing his place in twentieth-century African American history alongside major leaders who worked towards the advancement of black people.

Nadel, Alan, ed., *May All Your Fences Have Gates: Essays on the Drama of August Wilson*, University of Iowa Press, 1994.

The critical essays collected in this volume represent an important achievement, since they include the viewpoints of all of the prominent early scholars of Wilson's work. Each major play through *Two Trains Running* is considered in detail.

Women of Trachis: Trachiniae

SOPHOCLES

c. 440 B.C.E. to 430 B.C.E

One of the greatest tragedians of ancient Greece, Sophocles has remained the standard by which other playwrights are judged since his works were rediscovered during the western European Renaissance. He is the author of one of the most famous plays of all time, *Oedipus the King*, and a monumental figure from the so-called golden age of drama in classical Athens. Of the small fraction of his works that have survived the ages, however, not all are focused exclusively on male tragic heroes. In fact, Sophocles was able to probe sensitively and thoughtfully into the women's world that awaited these figures at home and was closely and complexly bound together with a hero's fate. *Women of Trachis* is one of these plays, focusing for the first two-thirds of its action not on the epic hero Heracles but on the suffering of his wife Deianira.

Also translated as *Trachiniae* or *Trachinian Women*, the play is commonly supposed to have been written and performed during Sophocles's early period, between approximately 440 and 430 B.C.E. The work has long startled audiences because of its unsympathetic portrayal of the mighty son of Zeus, Heracles, known as Hercules in ancient Rome and often called by that name in modern times. It has also puzzled critics who assume that Greek tragedy should have a single tragic hero because it places Deianira in this role only to kill her off with much of the play left to run. *Women of Trachis* has been widely published in various editions, but an able rendering of the drama in verse

is available in *Sophocles, 1*, translated by Brendan Galvin and published by the University of Pennsylvania Press in 1998.

AUTHOR BIOGRAPHY

Sophocles was probably born in either 497 or 496 B.C.E., in Colonus, a rural community just northwest of Athens. Because ancient biographies are often unreliable, there is little surety about the details of his life, but scholars believe that his father Sophillus was a businessman and a slave-holder. Sophocles was likely trained as a musician, since he led the paean, or choral ode, in celebration of a military victory over the Persians in 480 B.C.E. He was active in the Athenian political and social world throughout his life; he served as a treasurer in 443 or 442, and in 441, he was elected a general. While in the military, Sophocles may have helped to crush a revolt in Samos, and there is evidence that he was appointed a commissioner to impose order in Athens after the disastrous failure of the Sicilian expedition of 413. There is also some indication that he was a priest of a god of healing.

Highly acclaimed as a preeminent dramatist in his time, Sophocles wrote some one hundred and twenty-three plays. Sources suggest that he won the principal Athenian dramatic festival, called the Greater Dionysia, at least eighteen times, and never achieved less than second place. Of his prodigious output, only seven full plays and some fragments survive, and of those only two can be dated with accuracy. Nevertheless, scholars have surmised that *Women of Trachis* was an early play because its style does not seem mature. According to this supposition, Sophocles would have written the play between 440 and 430 B.C.E. This play is available in *Sophocles, 1: Ajax, Women of Trachis, Electra, Philoctetes*, which was published by University of Pennsylvania Press in 1998.

Some scholars believe that *Ajax* is also among Sophocles's early, less well-balanced plays, since as in *Women of Trachis*, the person who seems at first to be the tragic hero commits suicide well before the end. Ajax kills himself because he regrets having tried (and failed) to kill the Greek military leaders Menelaus and Agamemnon. In *Antigone* and *Electra*, Sophocles conjures deep sympathy for women caught in a murderous and tyrannical world. *Oedipus the King*, which focuses on the tragic hero who unknowingly kills his father and

Herm of Sophocles © Archivo Iconographico, S.A./Corbis.
Reproduced by permission

marries his mother, has been Sophocles's most influential play since Aristotle declared it the greatest tragedy in existence. *Oedipus at Colunus*, staged in 401 B.C.E. after Sophocles's death, follows Oedipus's fortunes after he blinds himself, while *Philoctetes* (409 B.C.E.) focuses on the recluse warrior whom Odysseus must convince to fight against Troy. The causes of Sophocles's death in 406 or 405 are unknown, although the comic poet Phrynichus claimed that he died without suffering, a happy man.

PLOT SUMMARY

Women of Trachis begins with Deianira's lament about her difficult life. She tells of Heracles rescuing her from the river god Achelous and marrying her, only to subject her to further suffering because Heracles is frequently away from home. Deianira's nurse advises her to send her son Hyllus to look for Heracles, and Hyllus tells her that he has heard that his father is at war with the city of Oechalia, which is on the island of Euboea. Deianira tells her son of a prophecy proclaiming that Heracles would either die on the island of

Euboea or enjoy happiness for the rest of his days, and Hyllus vows to find his father.

The Chorus intercedes to lament that Heracles is gone and advice Deianira to have hope for the future. Deianira tells the Chorus that Heracles left her a will, as though he had foreseen his death, and that this has left her deeply fearful. Immediately afterwards, the messenger arrives bringing word that Heracles is in fact alive and on his way home. Deianira disbelieves him at first, then she and the Chorus express their joy, and Lichas arrives to confirm the news. Lichas proclaims that Heracles is making sacrifices to Zeus as he vowed he would while conquering Oechalia. He says that Eurytus made Heracles angry, so Heracles killed Eurytus's son, and then in retribution, Heracles was caught and sold as a slave to Omphale. This made Heracles angry with Eurytus's city of Oechalia, so Heracles formed an army to destroy it and then abducted some of its surviving women as slaves.

Deianira says that she has reason to be joyful but feels pity for the female slaves and worries that her own fortunes will decline. She asks Iole who she is, but Iole refuses to speak, and Lichas suggests that they leave her alone. The messenger then approaches Deianira to tell her that Lichas is lying and that Heracles destroyed Oechalia and abducted Iole because he is in love with her. The Chorus advises Deianira to confront Lichas with the truth. Lichas dodges the messenger's questions about Iole, but Deianira implores him to tell the truth, stressing that she will not harm Iole or hold it against Heracles that he fell in love with her. Lichas confirms that Heracles destroyed Oechalia because he desired Iole, and Deianira tells Lichas to come inside.

The Chorus performs a meditation on the power of Aphrodite, the goddess of love, who inspired the brutal fight between Heracles and Achelous for Deianira's hand in marriage. Deianira then comes outside to tell the Chorus that she is jealous of Iole, who may usurp her place in Heracles's heart, but not angry at Heracles. Her plan to win her husband back is to follow the instructions of the centaur Nessus, whom Heracles killed with an arrow because he tried to rape Deianira. Nessus told Deianira to collect the clots of his blood that were poisoned by the Lernean Hydra and use them to charm Heracles into fidelity, and Deianira tells the Chorus that she has smeared the blood on Heracles's robe. Deianira gives the robe to Lichas, who agrees to follow her specific instructions about how to handle it.

The Chorus sings a prayer of longing for Heracles's return, and Deianira comes out to tell them that the ointment has dissolved the wool she used to apply it, and she worries that it is poison. She realizes that Nessus tricked her into murdering her husband and vows to die with him if it works. The Chorus implores her to retain hope, but Hyllus arrives and blames Deianira for killing Heracles. He says that Heracles wore the poisoned robe while he burned a sacrifice to the gods, and it began to devour his flesh. Heracles became furious at Lichas for delivering the robe and smashed his head to pieces on a rock. Heracles told his son to come to him and take him away from Euboea, and Hyllus helped transport him to a ship. Deianira goes into the house without defending herself while Hyllus curses and abuses her.

The Chorus declares that the prophecy of an end to Heracles's labors has come true, exonerates Deianira, and blames Aphrodite for the tragic events. The nurse then comes out to say that Deianira killed herself and that Hyllus grieved over driving his mother to this end. The Chorus laments Deianira's death and returns its attention to the dying Heracles, who is carried onstage, sleeping, by a group of grim and silent men. Hyllus tries to speak to his father, but an Old Man tells him to let Heracles sleep. Heracles wakes and bemoans his torment, blaming his wife for plotting against him. He tells Hyllus to bring Deianira to him, threatening to murder her and lamenting his former power to "punish evil," which is now eclipsed.

Hyllus tells his father that Deianira killed herself, and Heracles continues to curse his wife. Hyllus then tells his father of the centaur's trick, and Heracles explains that this fulfills the prophecies of his death. Heracles makes his son swear an oath to obey him and then commands Hyllus to burn him on a pyre. Hyllus refuses to do it himself but consents to have it done and then Heracles asks him to promise to marry Iole. Hyllus protests that this is impious but agrees to marry her. He then prepares to burn his father, blaming the gods for causing human suffering.

CHARACTERS

Achelous

Achelous is the river god who desires to marry Deianira. He appears as a bull, as a snake, and as a bull-faced man trying to court his would-be bride until Heracles conquers him in a violent fight.

Chorus

The play's Chorus consists of a group of women from the town of Trachis. These women are the commentators and advisors to whom the title of the play refers. According to the conventions of ancient Greek tragedy, they speak directly to the audience and help to explain the context of the plot, although they also become emotionally involved in the action and do not speak with complete objectivity. They are close to Deianira and attempt to advise her, and Deianira confides in them as friends even though she chides them for being young and "innocent," uninitiated into the tragedy of life. They criticize Deianira for losing hope in her husband and in the future, but they stress that she acted in good faith in preparing the supposed love charm.

The women continually praise Heracles and lament his suffering without blaming him for his bigamy or his violent behavior. They justify his actions as the results of the power of Aphrodite and stress their admiration for the famous Greek hero. Their failure to see anything wrong with Heracles's behavior may be an indication that they are not wise or discriminating. As Deianira points out, they come to see others suffer and are thus like a group of unreliable gossipers. Nevertheless, they display profound pity for the suffering family.

Deianira

Heracles's wife and debatably the tragic hero of the play, Deianira is a fearful woman with a trying life. She is the daughter of the Calydonian king Oenus, and when she was a beautiful young woman she was courted by the river god Achelous until Heracles came to destroy Achelous and take her as his bride. She loves Heracles and is devoted to him, but she has suffered as a consequence of his desertion of her in order to engage in various quests and pursue other lovers. Although he is the source of her fear and distress, Deianira never blames her husband for her problems.

Sophocles gives a subtle and compassionate portrayal of Deianira, and she is the central character for the majority of the play. Her fears seem excessive at first, but they are justified by the tragic course of her family's life and are not necessarily signs of a cowardly person. Deianira does not know where to direct her fear and unhappiness, but she proves the generosity of her character by indulging Heracles regarding his treatment of her and showing kindness to Iole. Even when she discovers that Heracles is in love with Iole, Deianira does not contemplate hurting or sabotaging the younger woman. She blames herself for inviting trouble under her roof, worrying that her womanly charms are "waning." Her failure to bring others (such as her husband) to account for her troubles might also be construed as a character weakness, and her failure to spot the centaur's trick soon enough might indicate a lack of intelligence or shrewdness. Because Deianira shares her doubts and insecurities in such an open and compelling manner, however, the audience is likely to forgive her frailties and sympathize with her plight.

Eurytus

Iole's father and Heracles's enemy, Eurytus is the king of Oechalia. Lichas and the Messenger relate conflicting stories about why he angers Heracles, but Lichas admits that Heracles destroys Eurytus and his city in order to capture Iole.

Heracles

Deianira's husband Heracles is a powerful and violent warrior who is half god and half man. The son of Zeus and the mortal woman Alcmene, Heracles possesses divine strength and is one of the most famous heroes of the classical world. He undertakes continual quests and labors, and according to most accounts this is due to the jealousy of Zeus's wife Hera, who wishes to subject her husband's illegitimate son to trials that are seemingly impossible. Although *Women of Trachis* stresses that Heracles suffers at the cruel whim of the gods, it does not mention Hera and dwells on Heracles's own initiatives as an angry conqueror. Heracles attacks Oechalia not because the gods require that he do so, but because he wishes to abduct the princess Iole. At this and other points, such as Heracles's brutal murder of his herald Lichas or his devious murder of Iole's brother Iphitus, the play implicitly criticizes Heracles's dangerous recklessness.

Heracles is fearless and boastful, citing the glory of his past adventures even as he cries out in his awful pain. He is quick to blame his wife for poisoning him, immediately threatens to murder her, and does not respond to Hyllus's defense of Deianira except to meditate on his own death and the truth of prophecies about him. He never approaches anything resembling penitence or sympathy towards Deianira or anyone else. Nevertheless, the Chorus and all of the characters are consistently uncritical of Heracles, praising him as a destroyer of evil and a magnificent warrior. Instead, the Chorus and characters, including Hyllus, blame the gods for causing human suffering and tragedy. They seem to expect that Heracles has the right to be brutal and impetuous, since he is such a monumental hero.

Heracles seems pious and dutiful toward his father Zeus, at least in the sense that he makes due tribute to the gods with great sacrifices. However, Hyllus gives voice to the potential impiety of Heracles's demand that his son marry Iole. Such contradictions about the famous warrior remain unresolved at the end of the play, when Hyllus stresses that the gods have worked out their struggles on the unfortunate Heracles and that the blame for the tragedy does not fall on Heracles's shoulders.

Hyllus

The son of Deianira and Heracles, Hyllus is a dutiful young man torn between his mother and his father. He admires his father greatly and his accomplishments, and he readily agrees to go to his father when he discovers that he may be in trouble. Hyllus is also devoted to his mother, although his loyalty is in doubt until after her death. When Hyllus blames Deianira for contriving his father's death and curses her viciously, he appears to have inherited Heracles's impatient tendency to break into a violent rage before hearing all relevant evidence. After his mother's suicide, however, Hyllus is overcome with grief and shame, blaming himself for driving her to this end.

The tragic events of the play test Hyllus's character further when he must decide whether to keep his promise and acquiesce to his father's dying wishes. In ancient Greek culture, it was not necessarily immoral to assist someone in killing him/herself, but it was doubtlessly traumatic, especially if the person was one's close relative. Hyllus proves his loyalty by agreeing to help Heracles to this end, but he has more difficulty accepting his father's request that he marry Iole. Not only is Iole his father's lover; Hyllus sees her as the cause of his mother's death. The question remains open at the end of the play whether Heracles has driven his son to act immorally and whether the gods will forgive him since he does so under a vow of obedience to his father.

Iole

Iole is the beautiful daughter of Eurytus and the princess of Oechalia. After he falls in love with her, Heracles destroys her town, enslaves its people, and abducts her. Iole refuses to speak, and Deianira notices that she has the bearing of someone with noble blood who has endured a tragic fall in fortune.

Iphitus

Eurytus's son and Iole's brother, Iphitus is the victim of Heracles's wrath. According to Lichas,

Heracles threw Iphitus over a cliff after he let down his guard because Heracles was angry with Eurytus.

Lichas

Lichas is Heracles's herald, or bearer of important news. He lies to Deianira about Heracles's motives for going to war with Oechalia and his plans for the captive Iole. When the messenger tips off Deianira to Lichas's deceit and Deianira confronts him about it, Lichas admits that he was lying and stresses that it was his own initiative. The Chorus damns him as a "scheming liar," and he certainly seems damned, since Heracles blames him for bringing the poisoned robe and smashes his head on a rock.

Messenger

Deianira describes the messenger who brings news that her husband is alive as an "Old man." He intercedes on Deianira's behalf to tell her the truth about Iole, seemingly because he wishes to be loyal to her and possibly because he expects a reward. He is a member of the town's male public and may represent public knowledge or rumor to some degree, since he discovers Heracles's plans for bigamy in the crowded Trachis marketplace.

Nurse

Deianira's nurse is a loyal servant who attempts to give her mistress prudent advice and mourns her when she dies.

Old Man

The old man who helps to conduct Heracles to Trachis pleads with Hyllus to let the hero sleep in peace. When the old man tries to help ease Heracles's suffering, Heracles tells him to stay away.

Omphale

Omphale is the "barbarian queen" who holds Heracles as a slave.

THEMES

Fidelity to the Family

A chief concern throughout *Women of Trachis* is in terms of loyalty and responsibility to one's family. Each of the main characters grapples with issues of duty and obedience, and none of them performs perfectly. Heracles displays what is perhaps the most extreme lack of family responsibility in the play, since he neglects his wife and abducts

TOPICS FOR FURTHER STUDY

- Ancient Athens was a prosperous environment for many intellectual activities in addition to drama, including the writing of history and philosophy. Choose an intellectual or cultural figure of the period, such as the philosopher Socrates or the politician Pericles, and prepare a class report about him. In your presentation, assess your subject's contributions to the era, place in Athenian culture and politics, and potential influence upon or relation to Sophocles and the tragic theater.

- With a group of classmates, perform a section of *Women of Trachis* that you feel expresses an important theme or a vital emotion in the drama. Make careful choices about issues such as whether the characters Deianira or Heracles should be painted as more or less sympathetic, and how to portray them as such with costuming, posturing, blocking (location and movement on the stage), and acting. Consider also whether to pronounce the lines rhythmically, render them closer to natural speech, or attempt some form of musical or dance accompaniment. Afterwards, discuss the performance with your classmates, answering their questions and explaining your choices and techniques.

- Critics have long debated the question of who is the tragic hero in Sophocles's play. Write an essay in which you argue that a particular character should be considered the tragic hero, justifying your contention by explaining what qualities and events make a character fit this role. Use examples of other tragic heroes to support your case. You may also choose to discuss whether the question over the tragic hero is important or useful in the first place, or you may wish to argue that there is no tragic hero at all.

- Write a short drama continuing the fortunes of Hyllus after the deaths of his parents. As you write, observe to the best of your ability Sophocles's rules of tragic drama, including the unities of place and time, the limit to the number of actors on stage at once, and the use of a Chorus. Consider how Hyllus copes with the loss of his parents, whether he marries Iole and under what circumstances, how Iole reacts to this situation, and how the gods view the morality of Hyllus's consent to obey his father's wishes.

---

another lover, in a sense instigating the tragic plot. Heracles has duties to the gods as well; his father Zeus seems responsible for his enslavement, while gods such as Aphrodite (and, implicitly, Hera) are perhaps to blame for his fall in fortune. Nevertheless, Heracles's own lack of respect for his wife is a prominent point of stress in the play, as is his demand that his son obey orders which may be impious or unjust.

Deianira's faith in her husband is under trial from the beginning, and the Chorus stresses that she must maintain hope for Heracles's safety and her family's well-being. This is no easy task, however, since Heracles is very rarely home to show her any affection, and Heracles's love for Iole and his plans to live with two wives deeply shakes Deianira's confidence. Deianira's plan to win back her husband's affections, although it is understandable and has no ill motives, may be interpreted as a failure to be entirely obedient to her husband.

Hyllus's character serves as another important example of the struggle that results from an obligation to be obedient to one's family. At first he finds it easy to obey his mother and go looking for his father, but his desire to act according to his parents' wishes rapidly becomes difficult. He laments his own failure to be just and respectful to his mother only when it is too late, and he fears that his improper and angry behavior led to her suicide. Then, when confronted with his father's imposing and perhaps immoral demands, Hyllus wonders to whom his highest allegiance is owed: to the gods or to his father. Indeed, he notes that "We call [the gods] our fathers" in his final monologue, emphasizing that familial demands have the potential to conflict and leave the correct moral choice difficult or impossible to determine. The play seems to seek to raise such questions rather than to resolve them definitively; fidelity to one's family remains a privileged ethical responsibility, but it is unclear whether it takes precedence over other moral responsibilities.

Women in Ancient Greek Society

Related to Sophocles's analysis of the family unit is his meditation on the role that women play in the male-dominated culture of ancient Greece. As Deianira stresses, women are often at the mercy of their husbands' whims and frequently have little power to shape their own destinies. Deianira's attempts to assert her authority and reestablish her position in Heracles's favor result in failure and tragedy. Perhaps the greater problem, however, is Heracles's refusal to allow his wife any influence and power and to neglect her. Heracles shows little regard for his wife and acts brutally towards women in general, and Sophocles may be criticizing such behavior.

Divine Control over Human Affairs

There is frequent mention is Sophocles's play of the influence that the classical gods have over mortal life. The notion of divine intervention takes a number of forms, however, beginning with the general trope of inevitable fate and cyclical fortune. As Deianira stresses, "he who rises / so high can also be brought low," and indeed this is a widespread formula in tragic drama. Plays such as *Women of Trachis* tend to contradict the notion that one is secure in one's prosperity or in control of one's destiny, stressing instead that humans rise and fall in fortune according to a divinely ordained cycle. The Fates, three goddesses traditionally associated with the variable nature of human prosperity, and other deities ensure that a prosperous family like that of Heracles endures their due allotment of suffering and heartache.

Sophocles also stresses the influence of the desires and loyalties of individual gods, however, as they impact human life. As the son of Zeus, Heracles is bound for strength and glory, but his father also is prone to punish him for misdeeds, such as killing Iphitus. The Chorus also draws attention to the cruel whims of the powerful goddess Aphrodite, who enjoys causing humans to fall in love even if she has nothing in particular against them. More often than not, gods enjoy torturing humans rather than aiding them, and it does not always seem that their punishments are deserved. Even when Hyllus stresses at the end of the play that the gods are unforgiving, however, it may be that they are justified in refusing to forgive humans for being impious or unfaithful. Whatever their motivations, the gods clearly seem to act harshly and cruelly towards their inferiors.

STYLE

Golden Age Dramatic Conventions

Sophocles wrote in a theatrical environment that had a specific and nuanced set of conventions which have inspired centuries of influence, admiration, and critical theory. Because commentary about ancient Greek drama survives only in often unreliable fragments, however, many of the rules which scholars associate with Sophoclean drama are based on supposition.

One formal convention common to all tragedians of the golden age is the use of poetic verse with strictly metered syllables. Sophocles achieves a sense of musical and rhythmical beauty with his poetry. Also, Aristotle and other sources have indicated that golden age dramatists such as Sophocles observed what are known as the unities. Using Sophocles's *Oedipus the King* as a model of perfection, Aristotle pointed out that tragedy should have unity of action and follow one main drama without complex subplots, and unity of time, which means that the events of the play should occur within approximately the same time that it takes to watch it. Later scholars added the third unity of place, which stressed that a dramatic plot should occur within a single physical space. *Women of Trachis* does follow these rules, a practice which arguably contributes to its aesthetic beauty and its ability to touch and affect its audience.

The Chorus

The Chorus, consisting of young women from Trachis, is a prominent example of a tradition that dates to the origins of ancient Greek drama. A group of commentators and onlookers that help to relate the plot and its context to the audience, the chorus developed from the ancient practice of singing lyrical odes to Dionysus, the god of wine, revelry, and fertility. Musical exchanges between a large group of singers and a leader developed into an entity with a storytelling function and a relationship with dramatic characters. Sophocles increased the size of Aeschylus's twelve-member chorus to fifteen and made the group more expressive and independent of the events of the drama. This tendency is particularly clear in the song-like interludes during which the Chorus of *Women of Trachis* meditates on deities or forces such as Aphrodite or the sun, relating detailed and exquisite imagery in brief, rhythmic lines. The Chorus also continues the tradition of giving advice to various characters and expressing their horror as tragic events unfold.

The Tragic Hero

Women of Trachis has long frustrated scholars because it does not seem to follow the rules that commentators since Aristotle have assigned to ancient Greek tragedy. These critics have claimed that tragic drama follows the rise and subsequent fall of a hero who has an important and characteristic fault or liability. The audience is meant to identify with this hero and feel catharsis, a sense of having been cleansed and refreshed, when he/she dies. The problem that *Women of Trachis* poses for this formula is that the play does not seem to have a single tragic hero, but two or even three characters that are tragic and heroic. Deianira is perhaps the main candidate for the tragic hero, but she dies with one third of the play left to run.

HISTORICAL CONTEXT

Ancient Athens and the Golden Age

The ancient civilizations that existed in what is approximately present-day Greece flourished during Sophocles's lifetime to become the most culturally and economically advanced societies in the world. In the sixth century B.C.E., power and influence were concentrated in the urban centers of Sparta, Corinth, Thebes, and Athens, whose powerful landowning aristocrats controlled the surrounding areas. As these cities grew wealthier, however, a mercantile class became increasingly influential and eventually contributed to the founding of the world's first major democracy (though only male citizens could vote), erected around 500 B.C.E. in Athens. At this time, Athens and the other Greek cities were united in war with Persia, and after the conflict abated Athens emerged unchallenged as the dominant power of the region.

Athenian dominance ushered in a period of cultural and economic prosperity marked by extraordinary advances in philosophy, literature, history, and the arts. Pericles, the leading politician of Athens, used taxes levied on Athenian allies to build the Parthenon, the famous temple to the goddess Athena, and other architectural marvels. It was this period, in the fifth century B.C.E., that became known as the golden age of drama. The three great tragedians, Aeschylus, Sophocles, and Euripides, and the comedic dramatist Aristophanes all lived and worked at this time, contributing to the famous and elaborate Dionysia festival each year. The philosophers Socrates and Plato, and the historians Herodotus and Thucydides, lived during this period. Though the epic poet Homer lived much earlier, possibly in the eighth century B.C.E., and the philosopher Aristotle lived in the fourth century, scholars consider Sophocles's life to have spanned the greatest single generation of cultural output in Athenian history.

Except for a brief war in 458 B.C.E., peace lasted between Athens, Sparta, and their allies, but growing resentment and Athenian disputes with Corinth led to the beginning of the Peloponnesian War in 431. Inconclusive fighting continued until 421, when the moderate Athenian politician Nicias signed a peace treaty, but war resumed three years later, and the Athenian war party led by Alcibiades was elected. After convincing the Athenians to attack the island colony of Syracuse, which was allied to Sparta, Alcibiades fled to Sparta and sabotaged the operation. The Spartan general Lysander defeated the Athenian navy after cutting off their supply of grain, and Athens lost the war. This defeat marked the end of the golden age and of Athenian supremacy in Greece.

Greek Mythology

The immortal gods of Greek mythology remained influential in Greek culture throughout the fifth century B.C.E. Accounts of the gods' lives and their role in human affairs frequently varied and conflicted, but Greeks generally believed that divine creatures who had human attributes controlled and created the world. The most powerful of deities was Zeus, god of the sky and of thunder, who overthrew his parents to become the king of the gods and ruler of Mount Olympus, home to the twelve principle gods. Zeus married his sister Hera, but frequently had affairs with other gods and mortals, often by disguising himself in other forms since gods were able to appear however they wished. When Zeus became infatuated with the mortal woman Alcmene, for example, he took the form of Alcmene's husband Amphitryon and fathered Heracles.

COMPARE
&
CONTRAST

- **430 B.C.E.:** Athens is a powerful and democratic city-state with a flourishing cultural and intellectual environment.

  Today: Athens is the capital of the Hellenic Republic, commonly known as Greece, a democratic, developed nation and a member of the European Union.

- **430 B.C.E.:** Greek city-states are primarily occupied with fighting amongst themselves, but tensions remain between Athens and Persia. Persia holds the island of Cyprus despite various Greek attempts to invade.

  Today: The island of Cyprus is a sore point in Greek and Turkish relations. Although the island is technically a European Union member state, this status is effectively limited to its Greek residents and excludes its Turkish population.

- **430 B.C.E.:** International multi-sport games are held every four years in Olympia, Greece. They are important for building diplomatic ties and for honoring the gods.

  Today: The Olympic Games are a worldwide tradition. In 2004, they are held in Athens, Greece, for the first time since the modern Olympic Games began in 1896.

Hera was angry and jealous when she discovered that Zeus had fathered Heracles, and she frequently tried to trouble and kill her husband's offspring. Zeus protected his son, however, who was a mighty demigod (or, half god, half man), and he helped him win fame and glory. Heracles's adventures included twelve seemingly impossible labors, numerous love affairs with women and men, and the conquest of Troy as an Argonaut. Variations on the tale that Sophocles relates in *Women of Trachis* include the idea that Heracles was a best friend and perhaps lover of Iphitus before he killed him and that Eurytus broke a promise to award Iole's hand to Heracles. Other gods of importance to Sophocles's play include Aphrodite, the goddess of love, who sprung from the foam when Cronus cut off Uranus's genitals and threw them into the sea.

Performance Practices in Ancient Greece

Sophoclean drama was a grand spectacle performed in a large outdoor theater. Evidence suggests that dancing and music were typically incorporated into the plays. Actors wore masks and costumes indicating their roles, and the same actor often played multiple parts. Aeschylus used only one or two actors on stage at once, and Sophocles increased the number to, at most, three or four. Productions occasionally made use of various stage equipment, including a wheeled platform and a tall crane that could raise, for example, an actor. A background was frequently designed on a revolving triangular piece at the back of the stage which could indicate a change in scene. The exact manner in which actors would recite their poetic lines is unknown, but the verse itself is carefully ordered, and actors may have recited their lines in a musical and rhythmic fashion.

CRITICAL OVERVIEW

Centuries of critical neglect have left scholars unsure of the original reception of *Women of Trachis*. Sophocles was the preeminent dramatist of the period in which the play was likely written, however, so the play may have been received well in the Dionysia festival. It is possible that the play was salvaged because it deals with the popular hero Heracles. After the decline of Athens, there is little or no extant critical commentary on the play until it was rediscovered and translated during the humanist movement of the Renaissance period in Western Europe (approximately 1400–1600). Criticism in English did not abound until the eighteenth century, when the play had been printed in English. At this time, literary figures, including John Dryden and Joseph Addison, appraised Sophocles and compared him to contemporary English dramatists in the so-called battle between the ancients and the moderns. *Women of Trachis* was infrequently singled out during this period, and it has generally not been among Sophocles's most admired plays.

August Wilhelm von Schlegel, a poet, translator, and critic of the German romantic movement, maintained that *Women of Trachis* was the least compelling of the surviving Sophoclean drama in his highly influential *Lectures*, published in 1815. The view that the play is an immature effort which fails to conform to the rules of tragedy largely continued throughout the nineteenth and twentieth centuries. The sensitive and important classicist Richard Jebb does not dwell on the play as a good example of Sophocles's genius for proportion and aesthetic subtlety, writing instead in *Essays and Addresses* (1907) that it "may be taken as [one of] those in which the dramatic irony is simplest." Cedric H. Whitman persists in the idea that play is simple or unsophisticated, contending in *Sophocles: A Study of Heroic Humanism* (1951) that it was "assuredly" composed earlier than *King Oedipus* because it "reads like the poem of a young man who has just realized the full cruelty of the world." Thus, critics like Whitman have concluded that *Women of Trachis* is one of Sophocles's earliest works on stylistic grounds.

Later critical approaches to the play have ranged from historical analyses of fifth-century Athens through the lens of *Women of Trachis* and other Sophoclean drama to formalist analysis of rhetorical structure. In *Vision and Stagecraft in Sophocles* (1982), David Seale analyzes the nature of virtual versus experiential knowledge in the play. Seale asserts:

> For the audience, in fact, there is, in the narrowest sense, no development of knowledge at all; the maxim is both the germ and the lesson of the drama. And yet the play is so designed that the audience too vacillates between this prepossession of the real situation and its engagement with the illusion and suspense of the moment.

Despite the cool praise, Sophocles's play has endured the millennia, and for that, it signifies an accomplishment and influence many writers could only dream about.

Engraving of The Death of Hercules. *Hercules, known to the Greeks as Heracles, is carried off to be burned alive as an end to his suffering in the final scene of this play* © Historical Picture Archive/Corbis. Reproduced by permission

CRITICISM

Scott Trudell

Trudell is a doctoral student of English literature at Rutgers University. In the following essay, he analyzes the role of the tragic Chorus in order to demonstrate a key method by which Sophocles develops frustration and dissatisfaction with the violent hero Heracles.

Women of Trachis is the only one of Sophocles's surviving plays whose title does not refer to a main character or tragic hero but instead to the group of onlookers who comment upon and explain the action. In much of Greek tragedy, the Chorus is generalized and even indistinct, circumscribed by a traditional role that does not leave much room for individuation or characterization. Often it resembles a collection of voices one might hear in the town square. It is frequently a reflection of the audience, liable to fade into the scenery except during its outbursts of tragic emotion intended to cultivate and intensify the feelings of the playgoers. In *Women of Trachis*, however, the title immediately directs the

> THE FACT THAT CHORUS
> NEVER COMES TO ANY
> BREAKTHROUGH IN WISDOM
> OR INSIGHTFULNESS AND FAILS
> TO RECOGNIZE HERACLES AS A
> BRUTE AND A TYRANT HAS THE
> INTERESTING EFFECT THAT IT
> MAY SOMETIMES INSPIRE THE
> OPPOSITE REACTION IN THE
> AUDIENCE."

audience's attention to the Chorus, which then remains an intriguing and distinctive group of women until it drops into near-silence with Heracles's arrival. Their major and important failing, however, is their blind and unjustified idolization of Heracles, an attitude which Sophocles subtly and implicitly criticizes through the course of the drama.

Sophocles begins his sharply drawn portrait of the Chorus by carefully emphasizing its allegiances and biases. From its opening song it is clear that the Chorus is close to Deianira; it begins by echoing her desperation and frustration, imploring the sun for news of Heracles and characterizing Deianira as a "fearful bird" who deserves to be pitied. In the same breath, however, the Chorus's language suggests that it is at great pains to exonerate Heracles from blame: "But her husband, of the line / of Cadmus, is pulled this way / and that, like waves moved / endlessly over the ocean." This passive construction, or grammatical format, in which Heracles is not the subject of the sentence, suggests that Heracles has no control over his situation. The Chorus stresses this point further when it says that "some god always rescues his descent/ to the house of Death," emphasizing that the gods and not Heracles control his destiny.

In fact, Sophocles's frequent enjambment, or division of a phrase across a line of verse, such as "this way / and that" or "moved / endlessly," creates the sense that it is not only Heracles who is floating on waves, but the Chorus itself. Indeed, the Chorus is given over to the idea that gods control one's fate so fully that they seem to deny any

human agency whatsoever. When, for example, Heracles sends Iole back to his house in chains, planning to use her as a concubine, the Chorus responds by blaming the goddess of love: "The power of Goddess Aphrodite / always wins." Again the Chorus blames Aphrodite when Deianira discovers that she has poisoned her husband: "But we know whose hand stirs / these events: it is the work / of Cyprian Aphrodite, the silent one." It would seem that the Chorus agrees with Hyllus's assessment at the end of the play that every tragic event in the drama is not due to human error or immorality, but results rather because Zeus and the other gods enjoy inflicting suffering on their mortal inferiors.

Even in Hyllus's speech, however, it is unclear that his family's suffering at the hands of Zeus is either random or unjustified. When he tells the Chorus, "You have seen / how little forgiveness the Gods show / in everything that's happened here," Hyllus implies that there was a reason for the punishment; otherwise there would be nothing for the gods to forgive. The gods certainly have the power to torture humans, but they do not necessarily do so without provocation. Zeus has always protected his son in the past, as the Chorus suggests (rather ominously) when it asks Deianira, "When has Zeus / ever neglected his children?" The riddle of *Women of Trachis* is over what parties are responsible and to what degree, for the gods' displeasure is at this point in the lives of Heracles and his family members.

The Chorus provides some clue to the answer to this riddle during its lapses from the conviction that fate is outside human control. In its first speech, while it is lamenting Heracles's submission to a divinely ordered destiny, the Chorus implies that, on the contrary, Deianira has some control over her situation. The language of this speech suggests not so much that the gods force her to cry and despair, but rather that she causes or creates her own suffering: "She nurses her fear with / the memory of Heracles's rovings / even as she lies in misery / on their bed empty of him, / expecting bad news." The Chorus then precedes to scold Deianira for this attitude and encourages her to hope for the best, as though this will make a difference.

Thereafter, the Chorus encourages Deianira along her path of tragedy. Its damnation of Lichas as a "scheming liar" and command that he tell the truth about Iole does not convey an attitude of stoic resignation to the will of the gods, but an incitement to act with personal agency. Their blessing of Deianira's attempt to charm Heracles with a centaur's trick is more subtle, but nevertheless a validation of the attempt to determine one's own

WHAT DO I READ NEXT?

- Sophocles's *Oedipus Rex* (c. 425 B.C.E.), also translated as *Oedipus the King*, follows the doomed Oedipus as he unknowingly kills his father and marries his mother, then realizes his fate and tears out his own eyes and banishes himself.

- Aristotle's brilliant work of aesthetic philosophy, *The Poetics*, was probably written between 335 and 322 B.C.E. Setting out to account for the poetic arts, it uses Sophoclean tragedy as a model, arguing that tragedy is the highest form of poetic representation. The rules and conventions by which Aristotle defined tragedy have remained extremely influential since they were rediscovered during the Renaissance.

- *Lysistrata* (411 B.C.E.) is Aristophanes's witty play that voices opposition to the Peloponnesian War. In an insightful attack on male politicians who neglect the advice of wiser women, its female characters refuse to have sex with their husbands in order to force them to end the war.

- Eugene O'Neill's masterpiece *Long Day's Journey into Night* (1941) is a deeply affecting work of American realism which uses many of the classical conventions of Sophoclean tragedy. Its intimate portrait of the severe troubles of a family from New London, Connecticut, in 1912 demonstrates the devastating failures in communication and support inside the home.

---

destiny. They begin with a careful and somewhat ambiguous avowal that Deianira is acting in a proper fashion: "If you believe in what you've done / we cannot say you have acted rashly." They then confirm, however, that she is justified in acting on her convictions: "What happens must be your proof. You have / no way of knowing, otherwise." The Chorus seems suspicious of the accuracy of Deianira's beliefs, but it fails to warn her of the obvious possibility that the centaur was lying, and it endorses her decision to intervene in affairs it previously claimed were completely under the control of Aphrodite.

This poor advice arouses suspicion about the Chorus's wisdom and reliability. Deianira has already claimed that they are "like the innocent girl who grows / in a safe place" until later in life, when "the young thing would feel / my burdens. She'd understand them from her own." This comment turns out to be prophetic if the Chorus is accurate when it says, "O Greece, if this man dies / your mourning will be endless." It suffers along with and on behalf of Heracles and his family and perhaps grows more mature in the process. Since the Chorus becomes silent when Heracles arrives, however, and fails to comment explicitly on how it has changed or matured, its newfound wisdom on human morality

and free will must be gathered from earlier and more subtle indications of where it is mistaken or naive.

It may have seemed less obvious to a fifth-century Athenian audience than it does to a contemporary reader that the Chorus's major error is its failure to attribute any blame to Heracles for the tragic events. Even those accustomed to revering the mythical hero, however, would have recognized that the group of young women holds Heracles to a different set of standards than it does any other character. While the Chorus scolds and blames Deianira explicitly for her weakness and despair, even as it encourages her down the path to doom, it criticizes Heracles only unintentionally. For example, its prayer that he come home swiftly and "wild with desire" is implicitly critical, since wildness and excessive desire is precisely Heracles's problem, the source for Deianira's suffering, and perhaps the true source of the tragic events. Yet this criticism is accidental (it is Sophocles's commentary expressed between the lines), and the Chorus blames everyone but Heracles for the tragedy. It even attacks Iole, the innocent victim of Heracles's rampage, for having "given birth / to a huge wrath in this house."

Sophocles is careful, therefore, that his notoriously unsympathetic portrait of Heracles is not apparent to the Chorus. Even Lichas proves that his is more attune to Heracles's failures than the young women of Trachis when he suggests that Zeus has punished his son for immoral behavior in the past. According to Lichas, who has no reason to lie on this point, Heracles's "act of murderous deceit" in killing Iphitus while his back is turned displeases Zeus and motivates him to enslave his son to a "barbarian queen." If Zeus is prone to punishing his son for such behavior, it seems plausible that he would allow him to be poisoned based on his betrayal and neglect of his wife and his destruction of a city to satisfy his personal desire. Insofar as any human action is to blame for the fall of his household, it is surely that of Heracles himself.

The fact that Chorus never comes to any breakthrough in wisdom or insightfulness and fails to recognize Heracles as a brute and a tyrant has the interesting effect that it may sometimes inspire the opposite reaction in the audience. A tragic Chorus often echoes and solidifies the sentiments of its audience, and it may be the case that many ancient Athenian theatergoers would have failed to see anything wrong with Heracles's behavior. The Chorus's unreliability, however, its innocent and naive nature, and its failure to judge Heracles according to the moral rules by which it judges other characters encourage the audience to move beyond its judgment. During the final section of the play, when the Chorus has only four lines, the audience is likely to find out of its shadow a wiser and more mature frustration with the wailing, raging Heracles.

Source: Scott Trudell, Critical Essay on *Women of Trachis*, in *Drama for Students*, Thomson Gale, 2007.

SOURCES

Jebb, Richard, "The Genius of Sophocles," in *Classical and Medieval Literature Criticism*, Vol. 2, Gale Research, 1988, originally published in *Essays and Addresses*, Cambridge University Press, 1907, pp. 1–40.

Schlegel, August Wilhelm von, *A Course of Lectures on Dramatic Art and Literature*, translated by John Black, Baldwin, Cradock and Joy, 1815.

Seale, David, "The *Women of Trachis*: The Verge of Knowledge," in *Vision and Stagecraft in Sophocles*, University of Chicago Press, 1982, p. 182.

Sophocles, *Women of Trachis*, translated by Brendan Galvin, in *Sophocles, 1*, edited by David R. Slavitt and Palmer Bovie, University of Pennsylvania Press, 1998, pp. 71–126.

Whitman, Cedric H., "Late Learning: *The Trachiniae*," in *Sophocles: A Study of Heroic Humanism*, Harvard University Press, 1951, p. 104.

FURTHER READING

Blundell, Sue, *Women in Ancient Greece*, Harvard University Press, 1995.
   This work provides an account of the female experience in male-dominated ancient Greek society. Carefully analyzing literary and historical sources, including golden age drama that seems to concentrate mainly on men, Blundell reconstructs the daily life, legal status, and social position of women of the era.

Bowman, Laurel, "Prophecy and Authority in *The Trachiniai*," in *American Journal of Philology*, Vol. 120, No. 3, Fall 1999, pp. 335–50.
   Bowman analyzes the powerful force of prophecy in *Women of Trachai*, arguing that it diminishes mortal free will, particularly on the part of women, and institutes social order.

Buxton, R. G. A., *Sophocles*, Oxford University Press, 1984.
   Buxton's broad overview of Sophocles and his works provides an introduction to twentieth-century scholarship on the poet, biographical information, explication of the performance conventions of the era, and interpretive analysis.

Easterling, P. E., ed., *Cambridge Companion to Greek Tragedy*, Cambridge University Press, 1997.
   This useful overview of tragic drama in ancient Greece includes twelve essays of explication regarding historical context, structural analysis, and twentieth-century critical reception of the genre.

Ehrenberg, Victor, *Sophocles and Pericles*, Blackwell, 1954.
   This discussion of Sophocles and his political era includes the playwright's reaction to fifth-century rationalism.

Glossary of Literary Terms

A

Abstract: Used as a noun, the term refers to a short summary or outline of a longer work. As an adjective applied to writing or literary works, abstract refers to words or phrases that name things not knowable through the five senses. Examples of abstracts include the *Cliffs Notes* summaries of major literary works. Examples of abstract terms or concepts include "idea," "guilt" "honesty," and "loyalty."

Absurd, Theater of the: See *Theater of the Absurd*

Absurdism: See *Theater of the Absurd*

Act: A major section of a play. Acts are divided into varying numbers of shorter scenes. From ancient times to the nineteenth century plays were generally constructed of five acts, but modern works typically consist of one, two, or three acts. Examples of five-act plays include the works of Sophocles and Shakespeare, while the plays of Arthur Miller commonly have a three-act structure.

Acto: A one-act Chicano theater piece developed out of collective improvisation. *Actos* were performed by members of Luis Valdez's Teatro Campesino in California during the mid-1960s.

Aestheticism: A literary and artistic movement of the nineteenth century. Followers of the movement believed that art should not be mixed with social, political, or moral teaching. The statement "art for art's sake" is a good summary of aestheticism. The movement had its roots in France, but it gained widespread importance in England in the last half of the nineteenth century, where it helped change the Victorian practice of including moral lessons in literature. Oscar Wilde is one of the best-known "aesthetes" of the late nineteenth century.

Age of Johnson: The period in English literature between 1750 and 1798, named after the most prominent literary figure of the age, Samuel Johnson. Works written during this time are noted for their emphasis on "sensibility," or emotional quality. These works formed a transition between the rational works of the Age of Reason, or Neoclassical period, and the emphasis on individual feelings and responses of the Romantic period. Significant writers during the Age of Johnson included the novelists Ann Radcliffe and Henry Mackenzie, dramatists Richard Sheridan and Oliver Goldsmith, and poets William Collins and Thomas Gray. Also known as Age of Sensibility

Age of Reason: See *Neoclassicism*

Age of Sensibility: See *Age of Johnson*

Alexandrine Meter: See *Meter*

Allegory: A narrative technique in which characters representing things or abstract ideas are used to convey a message or teach a lesson. Allegory is typically used to teach moral, ethical, or religious lessons but is sometimes used for satiric or political purposes. Examples of allegorical works include Edmund Spenser's *The Faerie Queene* and John Bunyan's *The Pilgrim's Progress*.

Allusion: A reference to a familiar literary or historical person or event, used to make an idea more easily understood. For example, describing someone as a "Romeo" makes an allusion to William Shakespeare's famous young lover in *Romeo and Juliet.*

Amerind Literature: The writing and oral traditions of Native Americans. Native American literature was originally passed on by word of mouth, so it consisted largely of stories and events that were easily memorized. Amerind prose is often rhythmic like poetry because it was recited to the beat of a ceremonial drum. Examples of Amerind literature include the autobiographical *Black Elk Speaks,* the works of N. Scott Momaday, James Welch, and Craig Lee Strete, and the poetry of Luci Tapahonso.

Analogy: A comparison of two things made to explain something unfamiliar through its similarities to something familiar, or to prove one point based on the acceptedness of another. Similes and metaphors are types of analogies. Analogies often take the form of an extended simile, as in William Blake's aphorism: "As the caterpillar chooses the fairest leaves to lay her eggs on, so the priest lays his curse on the fairest joys."

Angry Young Men: A group of British writers of the 1950s whose work expressed bitterness and disillusionment with society. Common to their work is an anti-hero who rebels against a corrupt social order and strives for personal integrity. The term has been used to describe Kingsley Amis, John Osborne, Colin Wilson, John Wain, and others.

Antagonist: The major character in a narrative or drama who works against the hero or protagonist. An example of an evil antagonist is Richard Lovelace in Samuel Richardson's *Clarissa,* while a virtuous antagonist is Macduff in William Shakespeare's *Macbeth.*

Anthropomorphism: The presentation of animals or objects in human shape or with human characteristics. The term is derived from the Greek word for "human form." The fables of Aesop, the animated films of Walt Disney, and Richard Adams's *Watership Down* feature anthropomorphic characters.

Anti-hero: A central character in a work of literature who lacks traditional heroic qualities such as courage, physical prowess, and fortitude. Anti-heros typically distrust conventional values and are unable to commit themselves to any ideals. They generally feel helpless in a world over which they have no control. Anti-heroes usually accept, and often celebrate, their positions as social outcasts. A well-known anti-hero is Yossarian in Joseph Heller's novel *Catch-22.*

Antimasque: See *Masque*

Antithesis: The antithesis of something is its direct opposite. In literature, the use of antithesis as a figure of speech results in two statements that show a contrast through the balancing of two opposite ideas. Technically, it is the second portion of the statement that is defined as the "antithesis"; the first portion is the "thesis." An example of antithesis is found in the following portion of Abraham Lincoln's "Gettysburg Address"; notice the opposition between the verbs "remember" and "forget" and the phrases "what we say" and "what they did": "The world will little note nor long remember what we say here, but it can never forget what they did here."

Apocrypha: Writings tentatively attributed to an author but not proven or universally accepted to be their works. The term was originally applied to certain books of the Bible that were not considered inspired and so were not included in the "sacred canon." Geoffrey Chaucer, William Shakespeare, Thomas Kyd, Thomas Middleton, and John Marston all have apocrypha. Apocryphal books of the Bible include the Old Testament's Book of Enoch and New Testament's Gospel of Peter.

Apollonian and Dionysian: The two impulses believed to guide authors of dramatic tragedy. The Apollonian impulse is named after Apollo, the Greek god of light and beauty and the symbol of intellectual order. The Dionysian impulse is named after Dionysus, the Greek god of wine and the symbol of the unrestrained forces of nature. The Apollonian impulse is to create a rational, harmonious world, while the Dionysian is to express the irrational forces of personality. Friedrich Nietzche uses these terms in *The Birth of Tragedy* to designate contrasting elements in Greek tragedy.

Apostrophe: A statement, question, or request addressed to an inanimate object or concept or to a nonexistent or absent person. Requests for inspiration from the muses in poetry are examples of apostrophe, as is Marc Antony's address to Caesar's corpse in William Shakespeare's *Julius Caesar:* "O, pardon me, thou bleeding piece of earth, That I am meek and gentle with these butchers! . . . Woe to the hand that shed this costly blood! . . ."

Archetype: The word archetype is commonly used to describe an original pattern or model from which all other things of the same kind are made. This term was introduced to literary criticism from the psychology of Carl Jung. It expresses Jung's theory that behind every person's "unconscious," or repressed memories of the past, lies the "collective unconscious" of the human race: memories of the countless typical experiences of our ancestors. These memories are said to prompt illogical associations that trigger powerful emotions in the reader. Often, the emotional process is primitive, even primordial. Archetypes are the literary images that grow out of the "collective unconscious." They appear in literature as incidents and plots that repeat basic patterns of life. They may also appear as stereotyped characters. Examples of literary archetypes include themes such as birth and death and characters such as the Earth Mother.

Argument: The argument of a work is the author's subject matter or principal idea. Examples of defined "argument" portions of works include John Milton's *Arguments* to each of the books of *Paradise Lost* and the "Argument" to Robert Herrick's *Hesperides.*

Aristotelian Criticism: Specifically, the method of evaluating and analyzing tragedy formulated by the Greek philosopher Aristotle in his *Poetics.* More generally, the term indicates any form of criticism that follows Aristotle's views. Aristotelian criticism focuses on the form and logical structure of a work, apart from its historical or social context, in contrast to "Platonic Criticism," which stresses the usefulness of art. Adherents of New Criticism including John Crowe Ransom and Cleanth Brooks utilize and value the basic ideas of Aristotelian criticism for textual analysis.

Art for Art's Sake: See *Aestheticism*

Aside: A comment made by a stage performer that is intended to be heard by the audience but supposedly not by other characters. Eugene O'Neill's *Strange Interlude* is an extended use of the aside in modern theater.

Audience: The people for whom a piece of literature is written. Authors usually write with a certain audience in mind, for example, children, members of a religious or ethnic group, or colleagues in a professional field. The term "audience" also applies to the people who gather to see or hear any performance, including plays, poetry readings, speeches, and concerts. Jane Austen's parody of the gothic novel, *Northanger Abbey,* was originally intended for (and also pokes fun at) an audience of young and avid female gothic novel readers.

Avant-garde: A French term meaning "vanguard." It is used in literary criticism to describe new writing that rejects traditional approaches to literature in favor of innovations in style or content. Twentieth-century examples of the literary *avant-garde* include the Black Mountain School of poets, the Bloomsbury Group, and the Beat Movement.

B

Ballad: A short poem that tells a simple story and has a repeated refrain. Ballads were originally intended to be sung. Early ballads, known as folk ballads, were passed down through generations, so their authors are often unknown. Later ballads composed by known authors are called literary ballads. An example of an anonymous folk ballad is "Edward," which dates from the Middle Ages. Samuel Taylor Coleridge's "The Rime of the Ancient Mariner" and John Keats's "La Belle Dame sans Merci" are examples of literary ballads.

Baroque: A term used in literary criticism to describe literature that is complex or ornate in style or diction. Baroque works typically express tension, anxiety, and violent emotion. The term "Baroque Age" designates a period in Western European literature beginning in the late sixteenth century and ending about one hundred years later. Works of this period often mirror the qualities of works more generally associated with the label "baroque" and sometimes feature elaborate conceits. Examples of Baroque works include John Lyly's *Euphues: The Anatomy of Wit,* Luis de Gongora's *Soledads,* and William Shakespeare's *As You Like It.*

Baroque Age: See *Baroque*

Baroque Period: See *Baroque*

Beat Generation: See *Beat Movement*

Beat Movement: A period featuring a group of American poets and novelists of the 1950s and 1960s—including Jack Kerouac, Allen Ginsberg, Gregory Corso, William S. Burroughs, and Lawrence Ferlinghetti—who rejected established social and literary values. Using such techniques as stream of consciousness writing and jazz-influenced free verse and focusing on unusual or abnormal states of mind—generated by religious ecstasy or the use of drugs—the Beat writers aimed to create works that were unconventional in both form and subject matter. Kerouac's *On the Road* is perhaps the best-known example of a Beat Generation novel, and Ginsberg's *Howl* is a famous collection of Beat poetry.

Black Aesthetic Movement: A period of artistic and literary development among African Americans in the 1960s and early 1970s. This was the first major African-American artistic movement since the Harlem Renaissance and was closely paralleled by the civil rights and black power movements. The black aesthetic writers attempted to produce works of art that would be meaningful to the black masses. Key figures in black aesthetics included one of its founders, poet and playwright

Amiri Baraka, formerly known as LeRoi Jones; poet and essayist Haki R. Madhubuti, formerly Don L. Lee; poet and playwright Sonia Sanchez; and dramatist Ed Bullins. Works representative of the Black Aesthetic Movement include Amiri Baraka's play *Dutchman,* a 1964 Obie award-winner; *Black Fire: An Anthology of Afro-American Writing,* edited by Baraka and playwright Larry Neal and published in 1968; and Sonia Sanchez's poetry collection *We a BaddDDD People,* published in 1970. Also known as Black Arts Movement.

Black Arts Movement: See *Black Aesthetic Movement*

Black Comedy: See *Black Humor*

Black Humor: Writing that places grotesque elements side by side with humorous ones in an attempt to shock the reader, forcing him or her to laugh at the horrifying reality of a disordered world. Joseph Heller's novel *Catch-22* is considered a superb example of the use of black humor. Other well-known authors who use black humor include Kurt Vonnegut, Edward Albee, Eugene Ionesco, and Harold Pinter. Also known as Black Comedy.

Blank Verse: Loosely, any unrhymed poetry, but more generally, unrhymed iambic pentameter verse (composed of lines of five two-syllable feet with the first syllable accented, the second unaccented). Blank verse has been used by poets since the Renaissance for its flexibility and its graceful, dignified tone. John Milton's *Paradise Lost* is in blank verse, as are most of William Shakespeare's plays.

Bloomsbury Group: A group of English writers, artists, and intellectuals who held informal artistic and philosophical discussions in Bloomsbury, a district of London, from around 1907 to the early 1930s. The Bloomsbury Group held no uniform philosophical beliefs but did commonly express an aversion to moral prudery and a desire for greater social tolerance. At various times the circle included Virginia Woolf, E. M. Forster, Clive Bell, Lytton Strachey, and John Maynard Keynes.

Bon Mot: A French term meaning "good word." A *bon mot* is a witty remark or clever observation. Charles Lamb and Oscar Wilde are celebrated for their witty *bon mots.* Two examples by Oscar Wilde stand out: (1) "All women become their mothers. That is their tragedy. No man does. That's his." (2) "A man cannot be too careful in the choice of his enemies."

Breath Verse: See *Projective Verse*

Burlesque: Any literary work that uses exaggeration to make its subject appear ridiculous, either by treating a trivial subject with profound seriousness or by treating a dignified subject frivolously. The word "burlesque" may also be used as an adjective, as in "burlesque show," to mean "striptease act." Examples of literary burlesque include the comedies of Aristophanes, Miguel de Cervantes's *Don Quixote,* Samuel Butler's poem "Hudibras," and John Gay's play *The Beggar's Opera.*

C

Cadence: The natural rhythm of language caused by the alternation of accented and unaccented syllables. Much modern poetry—notably free verse—deliberately manipulates cadence to create complex rhythmic effects. James Macpherson's "Ossian poems" are richly cadenced, as is the poetry of the Symbolists, Walt Whitman, and Amy Lowell.

Caesura: A pause in a line of poetry, usually occurring near the middle. It typically corresponds to a break in the natural rhythm or sense of the line but is sometimes shifted to create special meanings or rhythmic effects. The opening line of Edgar Allan Poe's "The Raven" contains a caesura following "dreary": "Once upon a midnight dreary, while I pondered weak and weary. . . ."

Canzone: A short Italian or Provencal lyric poem, commonly about love and often set to music. The *canzone* has no set form but typically contains five or six stanzas made up of seven to twenty lines of eleven syllables each. A shorter, five- to ten-line "envoy," or concluding stanza, completes the poem. Masters of the *canzone* form include Petrarch, Dante Alighieri, Torquato Tasso, and Guido Cavalcanti.

Carpe Diem: A Latin term meaning "seize the day." This is a traditional theme of poetry, especially lyrics. A *carpe diem* poem advises the reader or the person it addresses to live for today and enjoy the pleasures of the moment. Two celebrated *carpe diem* poems are Andrew Marvell's "To His Coy Mistress" and Robert Herrick's poem beginning "Gather ye rosebuds while ye may. . . ."

Catharsis: The release or purging of unwanted emotions—specifically fear and pity—brought about by exposure to art. The term was first used by the Greek philosopher Aristotle in his *Poetics* to refer to the desired effect of tragedy on spectators. A famous example of catharsis is realized in Sophocles' *Oedipus Rex,* when Oedipus discovers that his wife, Jacosta, is his own mother and that the stranger he killed on the road was his own father.

Celtic Renaissance: A period of Irish literary and cultural history at the end of the nineteenth century. Followers of the movement aimed to create a romantic vision of Celtic myth and legend. The most significant works of the Celtic Renaissance typically present a dreamy, unreal world, usually in reaction against the reality of contemporary problems. William Butler Yeats's *The Wanderings of Oisin* is among the most significant works of the Celtic Renaissance. Also known as Celtic Twilight.

Celtic Twilight: See *Celtic Renaissance*

Character: Broadly speaking, a person in a literary work. The actions of characters are what constitute the plot of a story, novel, or poem. There are numerous types of characters, ranging from simple, stereotypical figures to intricate, multifaceted ones. In the techniques of anthropomorphism and personification, animals—and even places or things—can assume aspects of character. "Characterization" is the process by which an author creates vivid, believable characters in a work of art. This may be done in a variety of ways, including (1) direct description of the character by the narrator; (2) the direct presentation of the speech, thoughts, or actions of the character; and (3) the responses of other characters to the character. The term "character" also refers to a form originated by the ancient Greek writer Theophrastus that later became popular in the seventeenth and eighteenth centuries. It is a short essay or sketch of a person who prominently displays a specific attribute or quality, such as miserliness or ambition. Notable characters in literature include Oedipus Rex, Don Quixote de la Mancha, Macbeth, Candide, Hester Prynne, Ebenezer Scrooge, Huckleberry Finn, Jay Gatsby, Scarlett O'Hara, James Bond, and Kunta Kinte.

Characterization: See *Character*

Chorus: In ancient Greek drama, a group of actors who commented on and interpreted the unfolding action on the stage. Initially the chorus was a major component of the presentation, but over time it became less significant, with its numbers reduced and its role eventually limited to commentary between acts. By the sixteenth century the chorus—if employed at all—was typically a single person who provided a prologue and an epilogue and occasionally appeared between acts to introduce or underscore an important event. The chorus in William Shakespeare's *Henry V* functions in this way. Modern dramas rarely feature a chorus, but T. S. Eliot's *Murder in the Cathedral* and Arthur Miller's *A View from the Bridge* are notable exceptions. The Stage Manager in Thornton Wilder's *Our Town* performs a role similar to that of the chorus.

Chronicle: A record of events presented in chronological order. Although the scope and level of detail provided varies greatly among the chronicles surviving from ancient times, some, such as the *Anglo-Saxon Chronicle,* feature vivid descriptions and a lively recounting of events. During the Elizabethan Age, many dramas—appropriately called "chronicle plays"—were based on material from chronicles. Many of William Shakespeare's dramas of English history as well as Christopher Marlowe's *Edward II* are based in part on Raphael Holinshead's *Chronicles of England, Scotland, and Ireland.*

Classical: In its strictest definition in literary criticism, classicism refers to works of ancient Greek or Roman literature. The term may also be used to describe a literary work of recognized importance (a "classic") from any time period or literature that exhibits the traits of classicism. Classical authors from ancient Greek and Roman times include Juvenal and Homer. Examples of later works and authors now described as classical include French literature of the seventeenth century, Western novels of the nineteenth century, and American fiction of the mid-nineteenth century such as that written by James Fenimore Cooper and Mark Twain.

Classicism: A term used in literary criticism to describe critical doctrines that have their roots in ancient Greek and Roman literature, philosophy, and art. Works associated with classicism typically exhibit restraint on the part of the author, unity of design and purpose, clarity, simplicity, logical organization, and respect for tradition. Examples of literary classicism include Cicero's prose, the dramas of Pierre Corneille and Jean Racine, the poetry of John Dryden and Alexander Pope, and the writings of J. W. von Goethe, G. E. Lessing, and T. S. Eliot.

Climax: The turning point in a narrative, the moment when the conflict is at its most intense. Typically, the structure of stories, novels, and plays is one of rising action, in which tension builds to the climax, followed by falling action, in which tension lessens as the story moves to its conclusion. The climax in James Fenimore Cooper's *The Last of the Mohicans* occurs when Magua and his captive Cora are pursued to the edge of a cliff by Uncas. Magua kills Uncas but is subsequently killed by Hawkeye.

Colloquialism: A word, phrase, or form of pronunciation that is acceptable in casual conversation but not in formal, written communication. It is considered more acceptable than slang. An example of colloquialism can be found in Rudyard Kipling's *Barrack-room Ballads:* "When 'Omer smote 'is bloomin' lyre He'd 'eard men sing by land and sea;

An' what he thought 'e might require 'E went an' took—the same as me!"

Comedy: One of two major types of drama, the other being tragedy. Its aim is to amuse, and it typically ends happily. Comedy assumes many forms, such as farce and burlesque, and uses a variety of techniques, from parody to satire. In a restricted sense the term comedy refers only to dramatic presentations, but in general usage it is commonly applied to nondramatic works as well. Examples of comedies range from the plays of Aristophanes, Terrence, and Plautus, Dante Alighieri's *The Divine Comedy,* Francois Rabelais's *Pantagruel* and *Gargantua,* and some of Geoffrey Chaucer's tales and William Shakespeare's plays to Noel Coward's play *Private Lives* and James Thurber's short story "The Secret Life of Walter Mitty."

Comedy of Manners: A play about the manners and conventions of an aristocratic, highly sophisticated society. The characters are usually types rather than individualized personalities, and plot is less important than atmosphere. Such plays were an important aspect of late seventeenth-century English comedy. The comedy of manners was revived in the eighteenth century by Oliver Goldsmith and Richard Brinsley Sheridan, enjoyed a second revival in the late nineteenth century, and has endured into the twentieth century. Examples of comedies of manners include William Congreve's *The Way of the World* in the late seventeenth century, Oliver Goldsmith's *She Stoops to Conquer* and Richard Brinsley Sheridan's *The School for Scandal* in the eighteenth century, Oscar Wilde's *The Importance of Being Earnest* in the nineteenth century, and W. Somerset Maugham's *The Circle* in the twentieth century.

Comic Relief: The use of humor to lighten the mood of a serious or tragic story, especially in plays. The technique is very common in Elizabethan works, and can be an integral part of the plot or simply a brief event designed to break the tension of the scene. The Gravediggers' scene in William Shakespeare's *Hamlet* is a frequently cited example of comic relief.

Commedia dell'arte: An Italian term meaning "the comedy of guilds" or "the comedy of professional actors." This form of dramatic comedy was popular in Italy during the sixteenth century. Actors were assigned stock roles (such as Pulcinella, the stupid servant, or Pantalone, the old merchant) and given a basic plot to follow, but all dialogue was improvised. The roles were rigidly typed and the plots were formulaic, usually revolving around young lovers who thwarted their elders and attained wealth and happiness. A rigid convention of the *commedia dell'arte* is the periodic intrusion of Harlequin, who interrupts the play with low buffoonery. Peppino de Filippo's *Metamorphoses of a Wandering Minstrel* gave modern audiences an idea of what *commedia dell'arte* may have been like. Various scenarios for *commedia dell'arte* were compiled in Petraccone's *La commedia dell'arte, storia, technica, scenari,* published in 1927.

Complaint: A lyric poem, popular in the Renaissance, in which the speaker expresses sorrow about his or her condition. Typically, the speaker's sadness is caused by an unresponsive lover, but some complaints cite other sources of unhappiness, such as poverty or fate. A commonly cited example is "A Complaint by Night of the Lover Not Beloved" by Henry Howard, Earl of Surrey. Thomas Sackville's "Complaint of Henry, Duke of Buckingham" traces the duke's unhappiness to his ruthless ambition.

Conceit: A clever and fanciful metaphor, usually expressed through elaborate and extended comparison, that presents a striking parallel between two seemingly dissimilar things—for example, elaborately comparing a beautiful woman to an object like a garden or the sun. The conceit was a popular device throughout the Elizabethan Age and Baroque Age and was the principal technique of the seventeenth-century English metaphysical poets. This usage of the word conceit is unrelated to the best-known definition of conceit as an arrogant attitude or behavior. The conceit figures prominently in the works of John Donne, Emily Dickinson, and T. S. Eliot.

Concrete: Concrete is the opposite of abstract, and refers to a thing that actually exists or a description that allows the reader to experience an object or concept with the senses. Henry David Thoreau's *Walden* contains much concrete description of nature and wildlife.

Concrete Poetry: Poetry in which visual elements play a large part in the poetic effect. Punctuation marks, letters, or words are arranged on a page to form a visual design: a cross, for example, or a bumblebee. Max Bill and Eugene Gomringer were among the early practitioners of concrete poetry; Haroldo de Campos and Augusto de Campos are among contemporary authors of concrete poetry.

Confessional Poetry: A form of poetry in which the poet reveals very personal, intimate, sometimes shocking information about himself or herself. Anne Sexton, Sylvia Plath, Robert Lowell, and John Berryman wrote poetry in the confessional vein.

Conflict: The conflict in a work of fiction is the issue to be resolved in the story. It usually occurs between two characters, the protagonist and the antagonist, or between the protagonist and society or the protagonist and himself or herself. Conflict in Theodore Dreiser's novel *Sister Carrie* comes as a result of urban society, while Jack London's short story "To Build a Fire" concerns the protagonist's battle against the cold and himself.

Connotation: The impression that a word gives beyond its defined meaning. Connotations may be universally understood or may be significant only to a certain group. Both "horse" and "steed" denote the same animal, but "steed" has a different connotation, deriving from the chivalrous or romantic narratives in which the word was once often used.

Consonance: Consonance occurs in poetry when words appearing at the ends of two or more verses have similar final consonant sounds but have final vowel sounds that differ, as with "stuff" and "off." Consonance is found in "The curfew tolls the knells of parting day" from Thomas Grey's "An Elegy Written in a Country Church Yard." Also known as Half Rhyme or Slant Rhyme.

Convention: Any widely accepted literary device, style, or form. A soliloquy, in which a character reveals to the audience his or her private thoughts, is an example of a dramatic convention.

Corrido: A Mexican ballad. Examples of *corridos* include "Muerte del afamado Bilito," "La voz de mi conciencia," "Lucio Perez," "La juida," and "Los presos."

Couplet: Two lines of poetry with the same rhyme and meter, often expressing a complete and self-contained thought. The following couplet is from Alexander Pope's "Elegy to the Memory of an Unfortunate Lady": 'Tis Use alone that sanctifies Expense, And Splendour borrows all her rays from Sense.

Criticism: The systematic study and evaluation of literary works, usually based on a specific method or set of principles. An important part of literary studies since ancient times, the practice of criticism has given rise to numerous theories, methods, and "schools," sometimes producing conflicting, even contradictory, interpretations of literature in general as well as of individual works. Even such basic issues as what constitutes a poem or a novel have been the subject of much criticism over the centuries. Seminal texts of literary criticism include Plato's *Republic,* Aristotle's *Poetics,* Sir Philip Sidney's *The Defence of Poesie,* John Dryden's *Of Dramatic Poesie,* and William Wordsworth's "Preface" to the second edition of his *Lyrical Ballads.* Contemporary schools of criticism include deconstruction, feminist,

psychoanalytic, poststructuralist, new historicist, postcolonialist, and reader-response.

D

Dactyl: See *Foot*

Dadaism: A protest movement in art and literature founded by Tristan Tzara in 1916. Followers of the movement expressed their outrage at the destruction brought about by World War I by revolting against numerous forms of social convention. The Dadaists presented works marked by calculated madness and flamboyant nonsense. They stressed total freedom of expression, commonly through primitive displays of emotion and illogical, often senseless, poetry. The movement ended shortly after the war, when it was replaced by surrealism. Proponents of Dadaism include Andre Breton, Louis Aragon, Philippe Soupault, and Paul Eluard.

Decadent: See *Decadents*

Decadents: The followers of a nineteenth-century literary movement that had its beginnings in French aestheticism. Decadent literature displays a fascination with perverse and morbid states; a search for novelty and sensation—the "new thrill"; a preoccupation with mysticism; and a belief in the senselessness of human existence. The movement is closely associated with the doctrine Art for Art's Sake. The term "decadence" is sometimes used to denote a decline in the quality of art or literature following a period of greatness. Major French decadents are Charles Baudelaire and Arthur Rimbaud. English decadents include Oscar Wilde, Ernest Dowson, and Frank Harris.

Deconstruction: A method of literary criticism developed by Jacques Derrida and characterized by multiple conflicting interpretations of a given work. Deconstructionists consider the impact of the language of a work and suggest that the true meaning of the work is not necessarily the meaning that the author intended. Jacques Derrida's *De la grammatologie* is the seminal text on deconstructive strategies; among American practitioners of this method of criticism are Paul de Man and J. Hillis Miller.

Deduction: The process of reaching a conclusion through reasoning from general premises to a specific premise. An example of deduction is present in the following syllogism: Premise: All mammals are animals. Premise: All whales are mammals. Conclusion: Therefore, all whales are animals.

Denotation: The definition of a word, apart from the impressions or feelings it creates in the reader. The word "apartheid" denotes a political and economic policy of segregation by race, but its connotations—oppression, slavery, inequality—are numerous.

Denouement: A French word meaning "the un-knotting." In literary criticism, it denotes the resolution of conflict in fiction or drama. The *denouement* follows the climax and provides an outcome to the primary plot situation as well as an explanation of secondary plot complications. The *denouement* often involves a character's recognition of his or her state of mind or moral condition. A well-known example of *denouement* is the last scene of the play *As You Like It* by William Shakespeare, in which couples are married, an evildoer repents, the identities of two disguised characters are revealed, and a ruler is restored to power. Also known as Falling Action.

Description: Descriptive writing is intended to allow a reader to picture the scene or setting in which the action of a story takes place. The form this description takes often evokes an intended emotional response—a dark, spooky graveyard will evoke fear, and a peaceful, sunny meadow will evoke calmness. An example of a descriptive story is Edgar Allan Poe's *Landor's Cottage,* which offers a detailed depiction of a New York country estate.

Detective Story: A narrative about the solution of a mystery or the identification of a criminal. The conventions of the detective story include the detective's scrupulous use of logic in solving the mystery; incompetent or ineffectual police; a suspect who appears guilty at first but is later proved innocent; and the detective's friend or confidant—often the narrator—whose slowness in interpreting clues emphasizes by contrast the detective's brilliance. Edgar Allan Poe's "Murders in the Rue Morgue" is commonly regarded as the earliest example of this type of story. With this work, Poe established many of the conventions of the detective story genre, which are still in practice. Other practitioners of this vast and extremely popular genre include Arthur Conan Doyle, Dashiell Hammett, and Agatha Christie.

Deus ex machina: A Latin term meaning "god out of a machine." In Greek drama, a god was often lowered onto the stage by a mechanism of some kind to rescue the hero or untangle the plot. By extension, the term refers to any artificial device or coincidence used to bring about a convenient and simple solution to a plot. This is a common device in melodramas and includes such fortunate circumstances as the sudden receipt of a legacy to save the family farm or a last-minute stay of execution. The *deus ex machina* invariably rewards the virtuous and punishes evildoers. Examples of *deus ex machina* include King Louis XIV in Jean-Baptiste Moliere's *Tartuffe* and Queen Victoria in *The Pirates of Penzance* by William Gilbert and Arthur Sullivan. Bertolt Brecht parodies the abuse of such devices in the conclusion of his *Threepenny Opera.*

Dialogue: In its widest sense, dialogue is simply conversation between people in a literary work; in its most restricted sense, it refers specifically to the speech of characters in a drama. As a specific literary genre, a "dialogue" is a composition in which characters debate an issue or idea. The Greek philosopher Plato frequently expounded his theories in the form of dialogues.

Diction: The selection and arrangement of words in a literary work. Either or both may vary depending on the desired effect. There are four general types of diction: "formal," used in scholarly or lofty writing; "informal," used in relaxed but educated conversation; "colloquial," used in everyday speech; and "slang," containing newly coined words and other terms not accepted in formal usage.

Didactic: A term used to describe works of literature that aim to teach some moral, religious, political, or practical lesson. Although didactic elements are often found in artistically pleasing works, the term "didactic" usually refers to literature in which the message is more important than the form. The term may also be used to criticize a work that the critic finds "overly didactic," that is, heavy-handed in its delivery of a lesson. Examples of didactic literature include John Bunyan's *Pilgrim's Progress,* Alexander Pope's *Essay on Criticism,* Jean-Jacques Rousseau's *Emile,* and Elizabeth Inchbald's *Simple Story.*

Dimeter: See *Meter*

Dionysian: See *Apollonian and Dionysian*

Discordia concours: A Latin phrase meaning "discord in harmony." The term was coined by the eighteenth-century English writer Samuel Johnson to describe "a combination of dissimilar images or discovery of occult resemblances in things apparently unlike." Johnson created the expression by reversing a phrase by the Latin poet Horace. The metaphysical poetry of John Donne, Richard Crashaw, Abraham Cowley, George Herbert, and Edward Taylor among others, contains many examples of *discordia concours.* In Donne's "A Valediction: Forbidding Mourning," the poet compares the union of himself with his lover to a draftsman's compass: "If they be two, they are two so, As stiff twin compasses are two: Thy soul, the fixed foot, makes no show To move, but doth, if the other do; And though it in the center sit, Yet when the other far doth roam, It leans, and hearkens after it, And grows erect, as that comes home."

Dissonance: A combination of harsh or jarring sounds, especially in poetry. Although such combinations may be accidental, poets sometimes intentionally make them to achieve particular effects. Dissonance is also sometimes used to refer to close but not identical rhymes. When this is the case, the word functions as a synonym for consonance. Robert Browning, Gerard Manley Hopkins, and many other poets have made deliberate use of dissonance.

Doppelganger: A literary technique by which a character is duplicated (usually in the form of an alter ego, though sometimes as a ghostly counterpart) or divided into two distinct, usually opposite personalities. The use of this character device is widespread in nineteenth- and twentieth-century literature, and indicates a growing awareness among authors that the "self" is really a composite of many "selves." A well-known story containing a *doppelganger* character is Robert Louis Stevenson's *Dr. Jekyll and Mr. Hyde,* which dramatizes an internal struggle between good and evil. Also known as The Double.

Double Entendre: A corruption of a French phrase meaning "double meaning." The term is used to indicate a word or phrase that is deliberately ambiguous, especially when one of the meanings is risque or improper. An example of a *double entendre* is the Elizabethan usage of the verb "die," which refers both to death and to orgasm.

Double, The: See *Doppelganger*

Draft: Any preliminary version of a written work. An author may write dozens of drafts which are revised to form the final work, or he or she may write only one, with few or no revisions. Dorothy Parker's observation that "I can't write five words but that I change seven" humorously indicates the purpose of the draft.

Drama: In its widest sense, a drama is any work designed to be presented by actors on a stage. Similarly, "drama" denotes a broad literary genre that includes a variety of forms, from pageant and spectacle to tragedy and comedy, as well as countless types and subtypes. More commonly in modern usage, however, a drama is a work that treats serious subjects and themes but does not aim at the grandeur of tragedy. This use of the term originated with the eighteenth-century French writer Denis Diderot, who used the word *drame* to designate his plays about middle-class life; thus "drama" typically features characters of a less exalted stature than those of tragedy. Examples of classical dramas include Menander's comedy *Dyscolus* and Sophocles' tragedy *Oedipus Rex*. Contemporary dramas include Eugene O'Neill's *The Iceman Cometh,* Lillian Hellman's *Little Foxes,* and August Wilson's *Ma Rainey's Black Bottom.*

Dramatic Irony: Occurs when the audience of a play or the reader of a work of literature knows something that a character in the work itself does not know. The irony is in the contrast between the intended meaning of the statements or actions of a character and the additional information understood by the audience. A celebrated example of dramatic irony is in Act V of William Shakespeare's *Romeo and Juliet,* where two young lovers meet their end as a result of a tragic misunderstanding. Here, the audience has full knowledge that Juliet's apparent "death" is merely temporary; she will regain her senses when the mysterious "sleeping potion" she has taken wears off. But Romeo, mistaking Juliet's drug-induced trance for true death, kills himself in grief. Upon awakening, Juliet discovers Romeo's corpse and, in despair, slays herself.

Dramatic Monologue: See *Monologue*

Dramatic Poetry: Any lyric work that employs elements of drama such as dialogue, conflict, or characterization, but excluding works that are intended for stage presentation. A monologue is a form of dramatic poetry.

Dramatis Personae: The characters in a work of literature, particularly a drama. The list of characters printed before the main text of a play or in the program is the *dramatis personae.*

Dream Allegory: See *Dream Vision*

Dream Vision: A literary convention, chiefly of the Middle Ages. In a dream vision a story is presented as a literal dream of the narrator. This device was commonly used to teach moral and religious lessons. Important works of this type are *The Divine Comedy* by Dante Alighieri, *Piers Plowman* by William Langland, and *The Pilgrim's Progress* by John Bunyan. Also known as Dream Allegory.

Dystopia: An imaginary place in a work of fiction where the characters lead dehumanized, fearful lives. Jack London's *The Iron Heel,* Yevgeny Zamyatin's *My,* Aldous Huxley's *Brave New World,* George Orwell's *Nineteen Eighty-four,* and Margaret Atwood's *Handmaid's Tale* portray versions of dystopia.

E

Eclogue: In classical literature, a poem featuring rural themes and structured as a dialogue among shepherds. Eclogues often took specific poetic forms, such as elegies or love poems. Some were written as the soliloquy of a shepherd. In later centuries, "eclogue" came to refer to any poem that was in the pastoral tradition or that had a dialogue or monologue structure. A classical example of an eclogue is Virgil's *Eclogues,* also known as *Bucolics.* Giovanni Boccaccio, Edmund Spenser, Andrew Marvell, Jonathan Swift, and Louis MacNeice also wrote eclogues.

Edwardian: Describes cultural conventions identified with the period of the reign of Edward VII of England (1901–1910). Writers of the Edwardian Age typically displayed a strong reaction against the propriety and conservatism of the Victorian Age. Their work often exhibits distrust of authority in religion, politics, and art and expresses strong doubts about the soundness of conventional values. Writers of this era include George Bernard Shaw, H. G. Wells, and Joseph Conrad.

Edwardian Age: See *Edwardian*

Electra Complex: A daughter's amorous obsession with her father. The term Electra complex comes from the plays of Euripides and Sophocles entitled *Electra,* in which the character Electra drives her brother Orestes to kill their mother and her lover in revenge for the murder of their father.

Elegy: A lyric poem that laments the death of a person or the eventual death of all people. In a conventional elegy, set in a classical world, the poet and subject are spoken of as shepherds. In modern criticism, the word elegy is often used to refer to a poem that is melancholy or mournfully contemplative. John Milton's "Lycidas" and Percy Bysshe Shelley's "Adonais" are two examples of this form.

Elizabethan Age: A period of great economic growth, religious controversy, and nationalism closely associated with the reign of Elizabeth I of England (1558–1603). The Elizabethan Age is considered a part of the general renaissance—that is, the flowering of arts and literature—that took place in Europe during the fourteenth through sixteenth centuries. The era is considered the golden age of English literature. The most important dramas in English and a great deal of lyric poetry were produced during this period, and modern English criticism began around this time. The notable authors of the period—Philip Sidney, Edmund Spenser, Christopher Marlowe, William Shakespeare, Ben Jonson, Francis Bacon, and John Donne—are among the best in all of English literature.

Elizabethan Drama: English comic and tragic plays produced during the Renaissance, or more narrowly, those plays written during the last years

of and few years after Queen Elizabeth's reign. William Shakespeare is considered an Elizabethan dramatist in the broader sense, although most of his work was produced during the reign of James I. Examples of Elizabethan comedies include John Lyly's *The Woman in the Moone,* Thomas Dekker's *The Roaring Girl, or, Moll Cut Purse,* and William Shakespeare's *Twelfth Night.* Examples of Elizabethan tragedies include William Shakespeare's *Antony and Cleopatra,* Thomas Kyd's *The Spanish Tragedy,* and John Webster's *The Tragedy of the Duchess of Malfi.*

Empathy: A sense of shared experience, including emotional and physical feelings, with someone or something other than oneself. Empathy is often used to describe the response of a reader to a literary character. An example of an empathic passage is William Shakespeare's description in his narrative poem *Venus and Adonis* of: the snail, whose tender horns being hit, Shrinks backward in his shelly cave with pain. Readers of Gerard Manley Hopkins's *The Windhover* may experience some of the physical sensations evoked in the description of the movement of the falcon.

English Sonnet: See *Sonnet*

Enjambment: The running over of the sense and structure of a line of verse or a couplet into the following verse or couplet. Andrew Marvell's "To His Coy Mistress" is structured as a series of enjambments, as in lines 11–12: "My vegetable love should grow/Vaster than empires and more slow."

Enlightenment, The: An eighteenth-century philosophical movement. It began in France but had a wide impact throughout Europe and America. Thinkers of the Enlightenment valued reason and believed that both the individual and society could achieve a state of perfection. Corresponding to this essentially humanist vision was a resistance to religious authority. Important figures of the Enlightenment were Denis Diderot and Voltaire in France, Edward Gibbon and David Hume in England, and Thomas Paine and Thomas Jefferson in the United States.

Epic: A long narrative poem about the adventures of a hero of great historic or legendary importance. The setting is vast and the action is often given cosmic significance through the intervention of supernatural forces such as gods, angels, or demons. Epics are typically written in a classical style of grand simplicity with elaborate metaphors and allusions that enhance the symbolic importance of a hero's adventures. Some well-known epics are Homer's *Iliad* and *Odyssey,* Virgil's *Aeneid,* and John Milton's *Paradise Lost.*

Epic Simile: See *Homeric Simile*

Epic Theater: A theory of theatrical presentation developed by twentieth-century German playwright Bertolt Brecht. Brecht created a type of drama that the audience could view with complete detachment. He used what he termed "alienation effects" to create an emotional distance between the audience and the action on stage. Among these effects are: short, self-contained scenes that keep the play from building to a cathartic climax; songs that comment on the action; and techniques of acting that prevent the actor from developing an emotional identity with his role. Besides the plays of Bertolt Brecht, other plays that utilize epic theater conventions include those of Georg Buchner, Frank Wedekind, Erwin Piscator, and Leopold Jessner.

Epigram: A saying that makes the speaker's point quickly and concisely. Samuel Taylor Coleridge wrote an epigram that neatly sums up the form: "What is an Epigram? A Dwarfish whole, Its body brevity, and wit its soul."

Epilogue: A concluding statement or section of a literary work. In dramas, particularly those of the seventeenth and eighteenth centuries, the epilogue is a closing speech, often in verse, delivered by an actor at the end of a play and spoken directly to the audience. A famous epilogue is Puck's speech at the end of William Shakespeare's *A Midsummer Night's Dream.*

Epiphany: A sudden revelation of truth inspired by a seemingly trivial incident. The term was widely used by James Joyce in his critical writings, and the stories in Joyce's *Dubliners* are commonly called "epiphanies."

Episode: An incident that forms part of a story and is significantly related to it. Episodes may be either self-contained narratives or events that depend on a larger context for their sense and importance. Examples of episodes include the founding of Wilmington, Delaware in Charles Reade's *The Disinherited Heir* and the individual events comprising the picaresque novels and medieval romances.

Episodic Plot: See *Plot*

Epitaph: An inscription on a tomb or tombstone, or a verse written on the occasion of a person's death. Epitaphs may be serious or humorous. Dorothy Parker's epitaph reads, "I told you I was sick."

Epithalamion: A song or poem written to honor and commemorate a marriage ceremony. Famous examples include Edmund Spenser's "Epithalamion" and e. e. cummings's "Epithalamion." Also spelled Epithalamium.

Epithalamium: See *Epithalamion*

Epithet: A word or phrase, often disparaging or abusive, that expresses a character trait of someone or something. "The Napoleon of crime" is an epithet applied to Professor Moriarty, arch-rival of Sherlock Holmes in Arthur Conan Doyle's series of detective stories.

Exempla: See *Exemplum*

Exemplum: A tale with a moral message. This form of literary sermonizing flourished during the Middle Ages, when *exempla* appeared in collections known as "example-books." The works of Geoffrey Chaucer are full of *exempla.*

Existentialism: A predominantly twentieth-century philosophy concerned with the nature and perception of human existence. There are two major strains of existentialist thought: atheistic and Christian. Followers of atheistic existentialism believe that the individual is alone in a godless universe and that the basic human condition is one of suffering and loneliness. Nevertheless, because there are no fixed values, individuals can create their own characters—indeed, they can shape themselves—through the exercise of free will. The atheistic strain culminates in and is popularly associated with the works of Jean-Paul Sartre. The Christian existentialists, on the other hand, believe that only in God may people find freedom from life's anguish. The two strains hold certain beliefs in common: that existence cannot be fully understood or described through empirical effort; that anguish is a universal element of life; that individuals must bear responsibility for their actions; and that there is no common standard of behavior or perception for religious and ethical matters. Existentialist thought figures prominently in the works of such authors as Eugene Ionesco, Franz Kafka, Fyodor Dostoyevsky, Simone de Beauvoir, Samuel Beckett, and Albert Camus.

Expatriates: See *Expatriatism*

Expatriatism: The practice of leaving one's country to live for an extended period in another country. Literary expatriates include English poets Percy Bysshe Shelley and John Keats in Italy, Polish novelist Joseph Conrad in England, American writers Richard Wright, James Baldwin, Gertrude Stein, and Ernest Hemingway in France, and Trinidadian author Neil Bissondath in Canada.

Exposition: Writing intended to explain the nature of an idea, thing, or theme. Expository writing is often combined with description, narration, or argument. In dramatic writing, the exposition is the introductory material which presents the characters, setting, and tone of the play. An example of dramatic exposition occurs in many nineteenth-century drawing-room comedies in which the butler and the maid open the play with relevant talk about their master and mistress; in composition, exposition relays factual information, as in encyclopedia entries.

Expressionism: An indistinct literary term, originally used to describe an early twentieth-century school of German painting. The term applies to almost any mode of unconventional, highly subjective writing that distorts reality in some way. Advocates of Expressionism include dramatists George Kaiser, Ernst Toller, Luigi Pirandello, Federico Garcia Lorca, Eugene O'Neill, and Elmer Rice; poets George Heym, Ernst Stadler, August Stramm, Gottfried Benn, and Georg Trakl; and novelists Franz Kafka and James Joyce.

Extended Monologue: See *Monologue*

F

Fable: A prose or verse narrative intended to convey a moral. Animals or inanimate objects with human characteristics often serve as characters in fables. A famous fable is Aesop's "The Tortoise and the Hare."

Fairy Tales: Short narratives featuring mythical beings such as fairies, elves, and sprites. These tales originally belonged to the folklore of a particular nation or region, such as those collected in Germany by Jacob and Wilhelm Grimm. Two other celebrated writers of fairy tales are Hans Christian Andersen and Rudyard Kipling.

Falling Action: See *Denouement*

Fantasy: A literary form related to mythology and folklore. Fantasy literature is typically set in nonexistent realms and features supernatural beings. Notable examples of fantasy literature are *The Lord of the Rings* by J. R. R. Tolkien and the Gormenghast trilogy by Mervyn Peake.

Farce: A type of comedy characterized by broad humor, outlandish incidents, and often vulgar subject matter. Much of the "comedy" in film and television could more accurately be described as farce.

Feet: See *Foot*

Feminine Rhyme: See *Rhyme*

Femme fatale: A French phrase with the literal translation "fatal woman." A *femme fatale* is a sensuous, alluring woman who often leads men into danger or trouble. A classic example of the *femme fatale* is the nameless character in Billy Wilder's

The Seven Year Itch, portrayed by Marilyn Monroe in the film adaptation.

Fiction: Any story that is the product of imagination rather than a documentation of fact. Characters and events in such narratives may be based in real life but their ultimate form and configuration is a creation of the author. Geoffrey Chaucer's *The Canterbury Tales,* Laurence Sterne's *Tristram Shandy,* and Margaret Mitchell's *Gone with the Wind* are examples of fiction.

Figurative Language: A technique in writing in which the author temporarily interrupts the order, construction, or meaning of the writing for a particular effect. This interruption takes the form of one or more figures of speech such as hyperbole, irony, or simile. Figurative language is the opposite of literal language, in which every word is truthful, accurate, and free of exaggeration or embellishment. Examples of figurative language are tropes such as metaphor and rhetorical figures such as apostrophe.

Figures of Speech: Writing that differs from customary conventions for construction, meaning, order, or significance for the purpose of a special meaning or effect. There are two major types of figures of speech: rhetorical figures, which do not make changes in the meaning of the words, and tropes, which do. Types of figures of speech include simile, hyperbole, alliteration, and pun, among many others.

Fin de siecle: A French term meaning "end of the century." The term is used to denote the last decade of the nineteenth century, a transition period when writers and other artists abandoned old conventions and looked for new techniques and objectives. Two writers commonly associated with the *fin de siecle* mindset are Oscar Wilde and George Bernard Shaw.

First Person: See *Point of View*

Flashback: A device used in literature to present action that occurred before the beginning of the story. Flashbacks are often introduced as the dreams or recollections of one or more characters. Flashback techniques are often used in films, where they are typically set off by a gradual changing of one picture to another.

Foil: A character in a work of literature whose physical or psychological qualities contrast strongly with, and therefore highlight, the corresponding qualities of another character. In his Sherlock Holmes stories, Arthur Conan Doyle portrayed Dr. Watson as a man of normal habits and intelligence, making him a foil for the eccentric and wonderfully perceptive Sherlock Holmes.

Folk Ballad: See *Ballad*

Folklore: Traditions and myths preserved in a culture or group of people. Typically, these are passed on by word of mouth in various forms—such as legends, songs, and proverbs—or preserved in customs and ceremonies. This term was first used by W. J. Thoms in 1846. Sir James Frazer's *The Golden Bough* is the record of English folklore; myths about the frontier and the Old South exemplify American folklore.

Folktale: A story originating in oral tradition. Folktales fall into a variety of categories, including legends, ghost stories, fairy tales, fables, and anecdotes based on historical figures and events. Examples of folktales include Giambattista Basile's *The Pentamerone,* which contains the tales of Puss in Boots, Rapunzel, Cinderella, and Beauty and the Beast, and Joel Chandler Harris's Uncle Remus stories, which represent transplanted African folktales and American tales about the characters Mike Fink, Johnny Appleseed, Paul Bunyan, and Pecos Bill.

Foot: The smallest unit of rhythm in a line of poetry. In English-language poetry, a foot is typically one accented syllable combined with one or two unaccented syllables. There are many different types of feet. When the accent is on the second syllable of a two syllable word (con-*tort*), the foot is an "iamb"; the reverse accentual pattern (*tor*-ture) is a "trochee." Other feet that commonly occur in poetry in English are "anapest", two unaccented syllables followed by an accented syllable as in inter-*cept*, and "dactyl", an accented syllable followed by two unaccented syllables as in *su*-i-cide.

Foreshadowing: A device used in literature to create expectation or to set up an explanation of later developments. In Charles Dickens's *Great Expectations,* the graveyard encounter at the beginning of the novel between Pip and the escaped convict Magwitch foreshadows the baleful atmosphere and events that comprise much of the narrative.

Form: The pattern or construction of a work which identifies its genre and distinguishes it from other genres. Examples of forms include the different genres, such as the lyric form or the short story form, and various patterns for poetry, such as the verse form or the stanza form.

Formalism: In literary criticism, the belief that literature should follow prescribed rules of construction, such as those that govern the sonnet form. Examples of formalism are found in the work of the New Critics and structuralists.

Fourteener Meter: See *Meter*

Free Verse: Poetry that lacks regular metrical and rhyme patterns but that tries to capture the cadences of everyday speech. The form allows a poet to exploit a variety of rhythmical effects within a single poem. Free-verse techniques have been widely used in the twentieth century by such writers as Ezra Pound, T. S. Eliot, Carl Sandburg, and William Carlos Williams. Also known as *Vers libre.*

Futurism: A flamboyant literary and artistic movement that developed in France, Italy, and Russia from 1908 through the 1920s. Futurist theater and poetry abandoned traditional literary forms. In their place, followers of the movement attempted to achieve total freedom of expression through bizarre imagery and deformed or newly invented words. The Futurists were self-consciously modern artists who attempted to incorporate the appearances and sounds of modern life into their work. Futurist writers include Filippo Tommaso Marinetti, Wyndham Lewis, Guillaume Apollinaire, Velimir Khlebnikov, and Vladimir Mayakovsky.

G

Genre: A category of literary work. In critical theory, genre may refer to both the content of a given work—tragedy, comedy, pastoral—and to its form, such as poetry, novel, or drama. This term also refers to types of popular literature, as in the genres of science fiction or the detective story.

Genteel Tradition: A term coined by critic George Santayana to describe the literary practice of certain late nineteenth-century American writers, especially New Englanders. Followers of the Genteel Tradition emphasized conventionality in social, religious, moral, and literary standards. Some of the best-known writers of the Genteel Tradition are R. H. Stoddard and Bayard Taylor.

Gilded Age: A period in American history during the 1870s characterized by political corruption and materialism. A number of important novels of social and political criticism were written during this time. Examples of Gilded Age literature include Henry Adams's *Democracy* and F. Marion Crawford's *An American Politician.*

Gothic: See *Gothicism*

Gothicism: In literary criticism, works characterized by a taste for the medieval or morbidly attractive. A gothic novel prominently features elements of horror, the supernatural, gloom, and violence: clanking chains, terror, charnel houses, ghosts, medieval castles, and mysteriously slamming doors.

The term "gothic novel" is also applied to novels that lack elements of the traditional Gothic setting but that create a similar atmosphere of terror or dread. Mary Shelley's *Frankenstein* is perhaps the best-known English work of this kind.

Gothic Novel: See *Gothicism*

Great Chain of Being: The belief that all things and creatures in nature are organized in a hierarchy from inanimate objects at the bottom to God at the top. This system of belief was popular in the seventeenth and eighteenth centuries. A summary of the concept of the great chain of being can be found in the first epistle of Alexander Pope's *An Essay on Man,* and more recently in Arthur O. Lovejoy's *The Great Chain of Being: A Study of the History of an Idea.*

Grotesque: In literary criticism, the subject matter of a work or a style of expression characterized by exaggeration, deformity, freakishness, and disorder. The grotesque often includes an element of comic absurdity. Early examples of literary grotesque include Francois Rabelais's *Pantagruel* and *Gargantua* and Thomas Nashe's *The Unfortunate Traveller,* while more recent examples can be found in the works of Edgar Allan Poe, Evelyn Waugh, Eudora Welty, Flannery O'Connor, Eugene Ionesco, Gunter Grass, Thomas Mann, Mervyn Peake, and Joseph Heller, among many others.

H

Haiku: The shortest form of Japanese poetry, constructed in three lines of five, seven, and five syllables respectively. The message of a *haiku* poem usually centers on some aspect of spirituality and provokes an emotional response in the reader. Early masters of *haiku* include Basho, Buson, Kobayashi Issa, and Masaoka Shiki. English writers of *haiku* include the Imagists, notably Ezra Pound, H. D., Amy Lowell, Carl Sandburg, and William Carlos Williams. Also known as *Hokku.*

Half Rhyme: See *Consonance*

Hamartia: In tragedy, the event or act that leads to the hero's or heroine's downfall. This term is often incorrectly used as a synonym for tragic flaw. In Richard Wright's *Native Son,* the act that seals Bigger Thomas's fate is his first impulsive murder.

Harlem Renaissance: The Harlem Renaissance of the 1920s is generally considered the first significant movement of black writers and artists in the United States. During this period, new and established black writers published more fiction and poetry than ever before, the first influential black literary journals were established, and black authors and artists received their first widespread recognition and serious critical appraisal. Among the major writers associated with this period are Claude McKay, Jean Toomer, Countee Cullen, Langston Hughes, Arna Bontemps, Nella Larsen, and Zora Neale Hurston. Works representative of the Harlem Renaissance include Arna Bontemps's poems "The Return" and "Golgotha Is a Mountain," Claude McKay's novel *Home to Harlem,* Nella Larsen's novel *Passing,* Langston Hughes's poem "The Negro Speaks of Rivers," and the journals *Crisis* and *Opportunity,* both founded during this period. Also known as Negro Renaissance and New Negro Movement.

Harlequin: A stock character of the *commedia dell'arte* who occasionally interrupted the action with silly antics. Harlequin first appeared on the English stage in John Day's *The Travailes of the Three English Brothers.* The San Francisco Mime Troupe is one of the few modern groups to adapt Harlequin to the needs of contemporary satire.

Hellenism: Imitation of ancient Greek thought or styles. Also, an approach to life that focuses on the growth and development of the intellect. "Hellenism" is sometimes used to refer to the belief that reason can be applied to examine all human experience. A cogent discussion of Hellenism can be found in Matthew Arnold's *Culture and Anarchy.*

Heptameter: See *Meter*

Hero/Heroine: The principal sympathetic character (male or female) in a literary work. Heroes and heroines typically exhibit admirable traits: idealism, courage, and integrity, for example. Famous heroes and heroines include Pip in Charles Dickens's *Great Expectations,* the anonymous narrator in Ralph Ellison's *Invisible Man,* and Sethe in Toni Morrison's *Beloved.*

Heroic Couplet: A rhyming couplet written in iambic pentameter (a verse with five iambic feet). The following lines by Alexander Pope are an example: "Truth guards the Poet, sanctifies the line,/ And makes Immortal, Verse as mean as mine."

Heroic Line: The meter and length of a line of verse in epic or heroic poetry. This varies by language and time period. For example, in English poetry, the heroic line is iambic pentameter (a verse with five iambic feet); in French, the alexandrine (a verse with six iambic feet); in classical literature, dactylic hexameter (a verse with six dactylic feet).

Heroine: See *Hero/Heroine*

Hexameter: See *Meter*

Historical Criticism: The study of a work based on its impact on the world of the time period in which it was written. Examples of postmodern historical criticism can be found in the work of Michel Foucault, Hayden White, Stephen Greenblatt, and Jonathan Goldberg.

Hokku: See *Haiku*

Holocaust: See *Holocaust Literature*

Holocaust Literature: Literature influenced by or written about the Holocaust of World War II. Such literature includes true stories of survival in concentration camps, escape, and life after the war, as well as fictional works and poetry. Representative works of Holocaust literature include Saul Bellow's *Mr. Sammler's Planet,* Anne Frank's *The Diary of a Young Girl,* Jerzy Kosinski's *The Painted Bird,* Arthur Miller's *Incident at Vichy,* Czeslaw Milosz's *Collected Poems,* William Styron's *Sophie's Choice,* and Art Spiegelman's *Maus.*

Homeric Simile: An elaborate, detailed comparison written as a simile many lines in length. An example of an epic simile from John Milton's *Paradise Lost* follows: "Angel Forms, who lay entranced Thick as autumnal leaves that strow the brooks In Vallombrosa, where the Etrurian shades High over-arched embower; or scattered sedge Afloat, when with fierce winds Orion armed Hath vexed the Red-Sea coast, whose waves o'erthrew Busiris and his Memphian chivalry, While with perfidious hatred they pursued The sojourners of Goshen, who beheld From the safe shore their floating carcasses And broken chariot-wheels." Also known as Epic Simile.

Horatian Satire: See *Satire*

Humanism: A philosophy that places faith in the dignity of humankind and rejects the medieval perception of the individual as a weak, fallen creature. "Humanists" typically believe in the perfectibility of human nature and view reason and education as the means to that end. Humanist thought is represented in the works of Marsilio Ficino, Ludovico Castelvetro, Edmund Spenser, John Milton, Dean John Colet, Desiderius Erasmus, John Dryden, Alexander Pope, Matthew Arnold, and Irving Babbitt.

Humors: Mentions of the humors refer to the ancient Greek theory that a person's health and personality were determined by the balance of four basic fluids in the body: blood, phlegm, yellow bile, and black bile. A dominance of any fluid would cause extremes in behavior. An excess of blood created a sanguine person who was joyful, aggressive, and passionate; a phlegmatic person was shy, fearful, and sluggish; too much yellow bile led to a choleric temperament characterized by impatience, anger, bitterness, and stubbornness; and excessive black bile created melancholy, a state of laziness, gluttony, and lack of motivation. Literary treatment of the humors is exemplified by several characters in Ben Jonson's plays *Every Man in His Humour* and *Every Man out of His Humour.* Also spelled Humours.

Humours: See *Humors*

Hyperbole: In literary criticism, deliberate exaggeration used to achieve an effect. In William Shakespeare's *Macbeth,* Lady Macbeth hyperbolizes when she says, "All the perfumes of Arabia could not sweeten this little hand."

I

Iamb: See *Foot*

Idiom: A word construction or verbal expression closely associated with a given language. For example, in colloquial English the construction "how come" can be used instead of "why" to introduce a question. Similarly, "a piece of cake" is sometimes used to describe a task that is easily done.

Image: A concrete representation of an object or sensory experience. Typically, such a representation helps evoke the feelings associated with the object or experience itself. Images are either "literal" or "figurative." Literal images are especially concrete and involve little or no extension of the obvious meaning of the words used to express them. Figurative images do not follow the literal meaning of the words exactly. Images in literature are usually visual, but the term "image" can also refer to the representation of any sensory experience. In his poem "The Shepherd's Hour," Paul Verlaine presents the following image: "The Moon is red through horizon's fog;/ In a dancing mist the hazy meadow sleeps." The first line is broadly literal, while the second line involves turns of meaning associated with dancing and sleeping.

Imagery: The array of images in a literary work. Also, figurative language. William Butler Yeats's "The Second Coming" offers a powerful image of encroaching anarchy: "Turning and turning in the widening gyre The falcon cannot hear the falconer; Things fall apart. . . ."

Imagism: An English and American poetry movement that flourished between 1908 and 1917. The Imagists used precise, clearly presented images in their works. They also used common, everyday speech and aimed for conciseness, concrete imagery, and the creation of new rhythms. Participants in the Imagist movement included Ezra Pound, H. D. (Hilda Doolittle), and Amy Lowell, among others.

In medias res: A Latin term meaning "in the middle of things." It refers to the technique of beginning a story at its midpoint and then using various flashback devices to reveal previous action. This technique originated in such epics as Virgil's *Aeneid.*

Induction: The process of reaching a conclusion by reasoning from specific premises to form a general premise. Also, an introductory portion of a work of literature, especially a play. Geoffrey Chaucer's "Prologue" to the *Canterbury Tales,* Thomas Sackville's "Induction" to *The Mirror of Magistrates,* and the opening scene in William Shakespeare's *The Taming of the Shrew* are examples of inductions to literary works.

Intentional Fallacy: The belief that judgments of a literary work based solely on an author's stated or implied intentions are false and misleading. Critics who believe in the concept of the intentional fallacy typically argue that the work itself is sufficient matter for interpretation, even though they may concede that an author's statement of purpose can be useful. Analysis of William Wordsworth's *Lyrical Ballads* based on the observations about poetry he makes in his "Preface" to the second edition of that work is an example of the intentional fallacy.

Interior Monologue: A narrative technique in which characters' thoughts are revealed in a way that appears to be uncontrolled by the author. The interior monologue typically aims to reveal the inner self of a character. It portrays emotional experiences as they occur at both a conscious and unconscious level. images are often used to represent sensations or emotions. One of the best-known interior monologues in English is the Molly Bloom section at the close of James Joyce's *Ulysses.* The interior monologue is also common in the works of Virginia Woolf.

Internal Rhyme: Rhyme that occurs within a single line of verse. An example is in the opening line of Edgar Allan Poe's "The Raven": "Once upon a midnight dreary, while I pondered weak and weary." Here, "dreary" and "weary" make an internal rhyme.

Irish Literary Renaissance: A late nineteenth- and early twentieth-century movement in Irish literature. Members of the movement aimed to reduce the influence of British culture in Ireland and create an Irish national literature. William Butler Yeats, George Moore, and Sean O'Casey are three of the best-known figures of the movement.

Irony: In literary criticism, the effect of language in which the intended meaning is the opposite of what is stated. The title of Jonathan Swift's "A Modest Proposal" is ironic because what Swift proposes in this essay is cannibalism—hardly "modest."

Italian Sonnet: See *Sonnet*

J

Jacobean Age: The period of the reign of James I of England (1603–1625). The early literature of this period reflected the worldview of the Elizabethan Age, but a darker, more cynical attitude steadily grew in the art and literature of the Jacobean Age. This was an important time for English drama and poetry. Milestones include William Shakespeare's tragedies, tragi-comedies, and sonnets; Ben Jonson's various dramas; and John Donne's metaphysical poetry.

Jargon: Language that is used or understood only by a select group of people. Jargon may refer to terminology used in a certain profession, such as computer jargon, or it may refer to any nonsensical language that is not understood by most people. Literary examples of jargon are Francois Villon's *Ballades en jargon,* which is composed in the secret language of the *coquillards,* and Anthony Burgess's *A Clockwork Orange,* narrated in the fictional characters' language of "Nadsat."

Juvenalian Satire: See *Satire*

K

Knickerbocker Group: A somewhat indistinct group of New York writers of the first half of the nineteenth century. Members of the group were linked only by location and a common theme: New York life. Two famous members of the Knickerbocker Group were Washington Irving and William Cullen Bryant. The group's name derives from Irving's *Knickerbocker's History of New York.*

L

Lais: See *Lay*

Lay: A song or simple narrative poem. The form originated in medieval France. Early French *lais* were often based on the Celtic legends and other tales sung by Breton minstrels—thus the name of the "Breton lay." In fourteenth-century England, the term "lay" was used to describe short narratives written in imitation of the Breton lays. The most notable of these is Geoffrey Chaucer's "The Minstrel's Tale."

Leitmotiv: See *Motif*

Literal Language: An author uses literal language when he or she writes without exaggerating or embellishing the subject matter and without any tools of figurative language. To say "He ran very quickly down the street" is to use literal language, whereas to say "He ran like a hare down the street" would be using figurative language.

Literary Ballad: See *Ballad*

Literature: Literature is broadly defined as any written or spoken material, but the term most often refers to creative works. Literature includes poetry, drama, fiction, and many kinds of nonfiction writing, as well as oral, dramatic, and broadcast compositions not necessarily preserved in a written format, such as films and television programs.

Lost Generation: A term first used by Gertrude Stein to describe the post-World War I generation of American writers: men and women haunted by a sense of betrayal and emptiness brought about by the destructiveness of the war. The term is commonly applied to Hart Crane, Ernest Hemingway, F. Scott Fitzgerald, and others.

Lyric Poetry: A poem expressing the subjective feelings and personal emotions of the poet. Such poetry is melodic, since it was originally accompanied by a lyre in recitals. Most Western poetry in the twentieth century may be classified as lyrical. Examples of lyric poetry include A. E. Housman's elegy "To an Athlete Dying Young," the odes of Pindar and Horace, Thomas Gray and William Collins, the sonnets of Sir Thomas Wyatt and Sir Philip Sidney, Elizabeth Barrett Browning and Rainer Maria Rilke, and a host of other forms in the poetry of William Blake and Christina Rossetti, among many others.

M

Mannerism: Exaggerated, artificial adherence to a literary manner or style. Also, a popular style of the visual arts of late sixteenth-century Europe that was marked by elongation of the human form and by intentional spatial distortion. Literary works that are self-consciously high-toned and artistic are often said to be "mannered." Authors of such works include Henry James and Gertrude Stein.

Masculine Rhyme: See *Rhyme*

Masque: A lavish and elaborate form of entertainment, often performed in royal courts, that emphasizes song, dance, and costumery. The Renaissance form of the masque grew out of the spectacles of masked figures common in medieval England and Europe. The masque reached its peak of popularity and development in seventeenth-century England, during the reigns of James I and, especially, of Charles I. Ben Jonson, the most significant masque writer, also created the "anti-masque," which incorporates elements of humor and the grotesque into the traditional masque and achieved greater dramatic quality. Masque-like interludes appear in Edmund Spenser's *The Faerie Queene* and in William Shakespeare's *The Tempest*. One of the best-known English masques is John Milton's *Comus*.

Measure: The foot, verse, or time sequence used in a literary work, especially a poem. Measure is often used somewhat incorrectly as a synonym for meter.

Melodrama: A play in which the typical plot is a conflict between characters who personify extreme good and evil. Melodramas usually end happily and emphasize sensationalism. Other literary forms that use the same techniques are often labeled "melodramatic." The term was formerly used to describe a combination of drama and music; as such, it was synonymous with "opera." Augustin Daly's *Under the Gaslight* and Dion Boucicault's *The Octoroon, The Colleen Bawn,* and *The Poor of New York* are examples of melodramas. The most popular media for twentieth-century melodramas are motion pictures and television.

Metaphor: A figure of speech that expresses an idea through the image of another object. Metaphors suggest the essence of the first object by identifying it with certain qualities of the second object. An example is "But soft, what light through yonder window breaks?/ It is the east, and Juliet is the sun" in William Shakespeare's *Romeo and Juliet*. Here, Juliet, the first object, is identified with qualities of the second object, the sun.

Metaphysical Conceit: See *Conceit*

Metaphysical Poetry: The body of poetry produced by a group of seventeenth-century English writers called the "Metaphysical Poets." The group includes John Donne and Andrew Marvell. The Metaphysical Poets made use of everyday speech, intellectual analysis, and unique imagery. They aimed to portray the ordinary conflicts and contradictions of life. Their poems often took the form of an argument, and many of them emphasize physical and religious love as well as the fleeting nature of life. Elaborate conceits are typical in metaphysical poetry. Marvell's "To His Coy Mistress" is a well-known example of a metaphysical poem.

Metaphysical Poets: See *Metaphysical Poetry*

Meter: In literary criticism, the repetition of sound patterns that creates a rhythm in poetry. The patterns are based on the number of syllables and the presence and absence of accents. The unit of rhythm in a line is called a foot. Types of meter are classified according to the number of feet in a line. These are the standard English lines: Monometer, one foot; Dimeter, two feet; Trimeter, three feet; Tetrameter, four feet; Pentameter, five feet; Hexameter, six feet (also called the Alexandrine); Heptameter, seven feet (also called the "Fourteener" when the feet are iambic). The most common English meter is the iambic pentameter, in which each line contains ten syllables, or five iambic feet, which individually are composed of an unstressed syllable followed by an accented syllable. Both of the following lines from Alfred, Lord Tennyson's "Ulysses" are written in iambic pentameter: Made weak by time and fate, but strong in will To strive, to seek, to find, and not to yield.

Mise en scene: The costumes, scenery, and other properties of a drama. Herbert Beerbohm Tree was renowned for the elaborate *mises en scene* of his lavish Shakespearean productions at His Majesty's Theatre between 1897 and 1915.

Modernism: Modern literary practices. Also, the principles of a literary school that lasted from roughly the beginning of the twentieth century until the end of World War II. Modernism is defined by its rejection of the literary conventions of the nineteenth century and by its opposition to conventional morality, taste, traditions, and economic values. Many writers are associated with the concepts of Modernism, including Albert Camus, Marcel Proust, D. H. Lawrence, W. H. Auden, Ernest Hemingway, William Faulkner, William Butler Yeats, Thomas Mann, Tennessee Williams, Eugene O'Neill, and James Joyce.

Monologue: A composition, written or oral, by a single individual. More specifically, a speech given by a single individual in a drama or other public entertainment. It has no set length, although it is usually several or more lines long. An example of an "extended monologue"—that is, a monologue of great length and seriousness—occurs in the one-act, one-character play *The Stronger* by August Strindberg.

Monometer: See *Meter*

Mood: The prevailing emotions of a work or of the author in his or her creation of the work. The mood of a work is not always what might be expected based on its subject matter. The poem "Dover Beach" by Matthew Arnold offers examples of two different moods originating from the same experience: watching the ocean at night. The mood of the first three lines—"The sea is calm tonight The tide is full, the moon lies fair Upon the straights. . . ." is in sharp contrast to the mood of the last three lines—"And we are here as on a darkling plain Swept with confused alarms of struggle and flight, Where ignorant armies clash by night."

Motif: A theme, character type, image, metaphor, or other verbal element that recurs throughout a single work of literature or occurs in a number of different works over a period of time. For example, the various manifestations of the color white in Herman Melville's *Moby Dick* is a "specific" *motif,* while the trials of star-crossed lovers is a "conventional" *motif* from the literature of all periods. Also known as *Motiv* or *Leitmotiv.*

Motiv: See *Motif*

Muckrakers: An early twentieth-century group of American writers. Typically, their works exposed the wrongdoings of big business and government in the United States. Upton Sinclair's *The Jungle* exemplifies the muckraking novel.

Muses: Nine Greek mythological goddesses, the daughters of Zeus and Mnemosyne (Memory). Each muse patronized a specific area of the liberal arts and sciences. Calliope presided over epic poetry, Clio over history, Erato over love poetry, Euterpe over music or lyric poetry, Melpomene over tragedy, Polyhymnia over hymns to the gods, Terpsichore over dance, Thalia over comedy, and Urania over astronomy. Poets and writers traditionally made appeals to the Muses for inspiration in their work. John Milton invokes the aid of a muse at the beginning of the first book of his *Paradise Lost:* "Of Man's First disobedience, and the Fruit of the Forbidden Tree, whose mortal taste Brought Death into the World, and all our woe, With loss of Eden, till one greater Man Restore us, and regain the blissful Seat, Sing Heav'nly Muse, that on the secret top of Oreb, or of Sinai, didst inspire That Shepherd, who first taught the chosen Seed, In the Beginning how the Heav'ns and Earth Rose out of Chaos. . . ."

Mystery: See *Suspense*

Myth: An anonymous tale emerging from the traditional beliefs of a culture or social unit. Myths use supernatural explanations for natural phenomena. They may also explain cosmic issues like creation and death. Collections of myths, known as mythologies, are common to all cultures and nations, but the best-known myths belong to the Norse, Roman, and Greek mythologies. A famous myth is the story of Arachne, an arrogant young girl who challenged a goddess, Athena, to a weaving contest; when the girl won, Athena was enraged and turned Arachne into a spider, thus explaining the existence of spiders.

N

Narration: The telling of a series of events, real or invented. A narration may be either a simple narrative, in which the events are recounted chronologically, or a narrative with a plot, in which the account is given in a style reflecting the author's artistic concept of the story. Narration is sometimes used as a synonym for "storyline." The recounting of scary stories around a campfire is a form of narration.

Narrative: A verse or prose accounting of an event or sequence of events, real or invented. The term is also used as an adjective in the sense "method of narration." For example, in literary criticism, the expression "narrative technique" usually refers to the way the author structures and presents his or her story. Narratives range from the shortest accounts of events, as in Julius Caesar's remark, "I came, I saw, I conquered," to the longest historical or biographical works, as in Edward Gibbon's *The Decline and Fall of the Roman Empire,* as well as diaries, travelogues, novels, ballads, epics, short stories, and other fictional forms.

Narrative Poetry: A nondramatic poem in which the author tells a story. Such poems may be of any length or level of complexity. Epics such as *Beowulf* and ballads are forms of narrative poetry.

Narrator: The teller of a story. The narrator may be the author or a character in the story through whom the author speaks. Huckleberry Finn is the narrator of Mark Twain's *The Adventures of Huckleberry Finn.*

Naturalism: A literary movement of the late nineteenth and early twentieth centuries. The movement's major theorist, French novelist Emile Zola, envisioned a type of fiction that would examine human life with the objectivity of scientific inquiry. The Naturalists typically viewed human beings as either the products of "biological determinism," ruled by hereditary instincts and engaged in an endless struggle for survival, or as the products of "socioeconomic determinism," ruled by social and economic forces beyond their control. In their works, the Naturalists generally ignored the highest levels of society and focused on degradation: poverty, alcoholism, prostitution, insanity, and disease. Naturalism influenced authors throughout the world, including Henrik Ibsen and Thomas Hardy. In the

United States, in particular, Naturalism had a profound impact. Among the authors who embraced its principles are Theodore Dreiser, Eugene O'Neill, Stephen Crane, Jack London, and Frank Norris.

Negritude: A literary movement based on the concept of a shared cultural bond on the part of black Africans, wherever they may be in the world. It traces its origins to the former French colonies of Africa and the Caribbean. Negritude poets, novelists, and essayists generally stress four points in their writings: One, black alienation from traditional African culture can lead to feelings of inferiority. Two, European colonialism and Western education should be resisted. Three, black Africans should seek to affirm and define their own identity. Four, African culture can and should be reclaimed. Many Negritude writers also claim that blacks can make unique contributions to the world, based on a heightened appreciation of nature, rhythm, and human emotions—aspects of life they say are not so highly valued in the materialistic and rationalistic West. Examples of Negritude literature include the poetry of both Senegalese Leopold Senghor in *Hosties noires* and Martiniquais Aime-Fernand Cesaire in *Return to My Native Land.*

Negro Renaissance: See *Harlem Renaissance*

Neoclassical Period: See *Neoclassicism*

Neoclassicism: In literary criticism, this term refers to the revival of the attitudes and styles of expression of classical literature. It is generally used to describe a period in European history beginning in the late seventeenth century and lasting until about 1800. In its purest form, Neoclassicism marked a return to order, proportion, restraint, logic, accuracy, and decorum. In England, where Neoclassicism perhaps was most popular, it reflected the influence of seventeenth-century French writers, especially dramatists. Neoclassical writers typically reacted against the intensity and enthusiasm of the Renaissance period. They wrote works that appealed to the intellect, using elevated language and classical literary forms such as satire and the ode. Neoclassical works were often governed by the classical goal of instruction. English neoclassicists included Alexander Pope, Jonathan Swift, Joseph Addison, Sir Richard Steele, John Gay, and Matthew Prior; French neoclassicists included Pierre Corneille and Jean-Baptiste Moliere. Also known as Age of Reason.

Neoclassicists: See *Neoclassicism*

New Criticism: A movement in literary criticism, dating from the late 1920s, that stressed close textual analysis in the interpretation of works of literature.

The New Critics saw little merit in historical and biographical analysis. Rather, they aimed to examine the text alone, free from the question of how external events—biographical or otherwise—may have helped shape it. This predominantly American school was named "New Criticism" by one of its practitioners, John Crowe Ransom. Other important New Critics included Allen Tate, R. P. Blackmur, Robert Penn Warren, and Cleanth Brooks.

New Negro Movement: See *Harlem Renaissance*

Noble Savage: The idea that primitive man is noble and good but becomes evil and corrupted as he becomes civilized. The concept of the noble savage originated in the Renaissance period but is more closely identified with such later writers as Jean-Jacques Rousseau and Aphra Behn. First described in John Dryden's play *The Conquest of Granada,* the noble savage is portrayed by the various Native Americans in James Fenimore Cooper's "Leatherstocking Tales," by Queequeg, Daggoo, and Tashtego in Herman Melville's *Moby Dick,* and by John the Savage in Aldous Huxley's *Brave New World.*

O

Objective Correlative: An outward set of objects, a situation, or a chain of events corresponding to an inward experience and evoking this experience in the reader. The term frequently appears in modern criticism in discussions of authors' intended effects on the emotional responses of readers. This term was originally used by T. S. Eliot in his 1919 essay "Hamlet."

Objectivity: A quality in writing characterized by the absence of the author's opinion or feeling about the subject matter. Objectivity is an important factor in criticism. The novels of Henry James and, to a certain extent, the poems of John Larkin demonstrate objectivity, and it is central to John Keats's concept of "negative capability." Critical and journalistic writing usually are or attempt to be objective.

Occasional Verse: Poetry written on the occasion of a significant historical or personal event. *Vers de societe* is sometimes called occasional verse although it is of a less serious nature. Famous examples of occasional verse include Andrew Marvell's "Horatian Ode upon Cromwell's Return from England," Walt Whitman's "When Lilacs Last in the Dooryard Bloom'd"—written upon the death of Abraham Lincoln—and Edmund Spenser's commemoration of his wedding, "Epithalamion."

Octave: A poem or stanza composed of eight lines. The term octave most often represents the first eight lines of a Petrarchan sonnet. An example of an octave is taken from a translation of a Petrarchan sonnet by Sir Thomas Wyatt: "The pillar perisht is whereto I leant, The strongest stay of mine unquiet mind; The like of it no man again can find, From East to West Still seeking though he went. To mind unhap! for hap away hath rent Of all my joy the very bark and rind; And I, alas, by chance am thus assigned Daily to mourn till death do it relent."

Ode: Name given to an extended lyric poem characterized by exalted emotion and dignified style. An ode usually concerns a single, serious theme. Most odes, but not all, are addressed to an object or individual. Odes are distinguished from other lyric poetic forms by their complex rhythmic and stanzaic patterns. An example of this form is John Keats's "Ode to a Nightingale."

Oedipus Complex: A son's amorous obsession with his mother. The phrase is derived from the story of the ancient Theban hero Oedipus, who unknowingly killed his father and married his mother. Literary occurrences of the Oedipus complex include Andre Gide's *Oedipe* and Jean Cocteau's *La Machine infernale,* as well as the most famous, Sophocles' *Oedipus Rex.*

Omniscience: See *Point of View*

Onomatopoeia: The use of words whose sounds express or suggest their meaning. In its simplest sense, onomatopoeia may be represented by words that mimic the sounds they denote such as "hiss" or "meow." At a more subtle level, the pattern and rhythm of sounds and rhymes of a line or poem may be onomatopoeic. A celebrated example of onomatopoeia is the repetition of the word "bells" in Edgar Allan Poe's poem "The Bells."

Opera: A type of stage performance, usually a drama, in which the dialogue is sung. Classic examples of opera include Giuseppi Verdi's *La traviata,* Giacomo Puccini's *La Boheme,* and Richard Wagner's *Tristan und Isolde.* Major twentieth-century contributors to the form include Richard Strauss and Alban Berg.

Operetta: A usually romantic comic opera. John Gay's *The Beggar's Opera,* Richard Sheridan's *The Duenna,* and numerous works by William Gilbert and Arthur Sullivan are examples of operettas.

Oral Tradition: See *Oral Transmission*

Oral Transmission: A process by which songs, ballads, folklore, and other material are transmitted by word of mouth. The tradition of oral transmission predates the written record systems of literate society. Oral transmission preserves material sometimes over generations, although often with variations. Memory plays a large part in the recitation and preservation of orally transmitted material. Breton lays, French *fabliaux,* national epics (including the Anglo-Saxon *Beowulf,* the Spanish *El Cid,* and the Finnish *Kalevala*), Native American myths and legends, and African folktales told by plantation slaves are examples of orally transmitted literature.

Oration: Formal speaking intended to motivate the listeners to some action or feeling. Such public speaking was much more common before the development of timely printed communication such as newspapers. Famous examples of oration include Abraham Lincoln's "Gettysburg Address" and Dr. Martin Luther King Jr.'s "I Have a Dream" speech.

Ottava Rima: An eight-line stanza of poetry composed in iambic pentameter (a five-foot line in which each foot consists of an unaccented syllable followed by an accented syllable), following the abababcc rhyme scheme. This form has been prominently used by such important English writers as Lord Byron, Henry Wadsworth Longfellow, and W. B. Yeats.

Oxymoron: A phrase combining two contradictory terms. Oxymorons may be intentional or unintentional. The following speech from William Shakespeare's *Romeo and Juliet* uses several oxymorons: "Why, then, O brawling love! O loving hate! O anything, of nothing first create! O heavy lightness! serious vanity! Mis-shapen chaos of well-seeming forms! Feather of lead, bright smoke, cold fire, sick health! This love feel I, that feel no love in this."

P

Pantheism: The idea that all things are both a manifestation or revelation of God and a part of God at the same time. Pantheism was a common attitude in the early societies of Egypt, India, and Greece—the term derives from the Greek *pan* meaning "all" and *theos* meaning "deity." It later became a significant part of the Christian faith. William Wordsworth and Ralph Waldo Emerson are among the many writers who have expressed the pantheistic attitude in their works.

Parable: A story intended to teach a moral lesson or answer an ethical question. In the West, the best examples of parables are those of Jesus Christ in the New Testament, notably "The Prodigal Son," but parables also are used in Sufism, rabbinic literature, Hasidism, and Zen Buddhism.

Paradox: A statement that appears illogical or contradictory at first, but may actually point to an underlying truth. "Less is more" is an example of a paradox. Literary examples include Francis Bacon's statement, "The most corrected copies are commonly the least correct," and "All animals are equal, but some animals are more equal than others" from George Orwell's *Animal Farm.*

Parallelism: A method of comparison of two ideas in which each is developed in the same grammatical structure. Ralph Waldo Emerson's "Civilization" contains this example of parallelism: "Raphael paints wisdom; Handel sings it, Phidias carves it, Shakespeare writes it, Wren builds it, Columbus sails it, Luther preaches it, Washington arms it, Watt mechanizes it."

Parnassianism: A mid nineteenth-century movement in French literature. Followers of the movement stressed adherence to well-defined artistic forms as a reaction against the often chaotic expression of the artist's ego that dominated the work of the Romantics. The Parnassians also rejected the moral, ethical, and social themes exhibited in the works of French Romantics such as Victor Hugo. The aesthetic doctrines of the Parnassians strongly influenced the later symbolist and decadent movements. Members of the Parnassian school include Leconte de Lisle, Sully Prudhomme, Albert Glatigny, Francois Coppee, and Theodore de Banville.

Parody: In literary criticism, this term refers to an imitation of a serious literary work or the signature style of a particular author in a ridiculous manner. A typical parody adopts the style of the original and applies it to an inappropriate subject for humorous effect. Parody is a form of satire and could be considered the literary equivalent of a caricature or cartoon. Henry Fielding's *Shamela* is a parody of Samuel Richardson's *Pamela.*

Pastoral: A term derived from the Latin word "pastor," meaning shepherd. A pastoral is a literary composition on a rural theme. The conventions of the pastoral were originated by the third-century Greek poet Theocritus, who wrote about the experiences, love affairs, and pastimes of Sicilian shepherds. In a pastoral, characters and language of a courtly nature are often placed in a simple setting. The term pastoral is also used to classify dramas, elegies, and lyrics that exhibit the use of country settings and shepherd characters. Percy Bysshe Shelley's "Adonais" and John Milton's "Lycidas" are two famous examples of pastorals.

Pastorela: The Spanish name for the shepherds play, a folk drama reenacted during the Christmas season. Examples of *pastorelas* include Gomez Manrique's *Representacion del nacimiento* and the dramas of Lucas Fernandez and Juan del Encina.

Pathetic Fallacy: A term coined by English critic John Ruskin to identify writing that falsely endows nonhuman things with human intentions and feelings, such as "angry clouds" and "sad trees." The pathetic fallacy is a required convention in the classical poetic form of the pastoral elegy, and it is used in the modern poetry of T. S. Eliot, Ezra Pound, and the Imagists. Also known as Poetic Fallacy.

Pelado: Literally the "skinned one" or shirtless one, he was the stock underdog, sharp-witted picaresque character of Mexican vaudeville and tent shows. The *pelado* is found in such works as Don Catarino's *Los effectos de la crisis* and *Regreso a mi tierra.*

Pen Name: See *Pseudonym*

Pentameter: See *Meter*

Persona: A Latin term meaning "mask." *Personae* are the characters in a fictional work of literature. The *persona* generally functions as a mask through which the author tells a story in a voice other than his or her own. A *persona* is usually either a character in a story who acts as a narrator or an "implied author," a voice created by the author to act as the narrator for himself or herself. *Personae* include the narrator of Geoffrey Chaucer's *Canterbury Tales* and Marlow in Joseph Conrad's *Heart of Darkness.*

Personae: See *Persona*

Personal Point of View: See *Point of View*

Personification: A figure of speech that gives human qualities to abstract ideas, animals, and inanimate objects. William Shakespeare used personification in *Romeo and Juliet* in the lines "Arise, fair sun,/ and kill the envious moon,/ Who is already sick and pale with grief." Here, the moon is portrayed as being envious, sick, and pale with grief—all markedly human qualities. Also known as *Prosopopoeia.*

Petrarchan Sonnet: See *Sonnet*

Phenomenology: A method of literary criticism based on the belief that things have no existence outside of human consciousness or awareness. Proponents of this theory believe that art is a process that takes place in the mind of the observer as he or she contemplates an object rather than a quality of the object itself. Among phenomenological critics are Edmund Husserl, George Poulet, Marcel Raymond, and Roman Ingarden.

Picaresque Novel: Episodic fiction depicting the adventures of a roguish central character ("picaro" is Spanish for "rogue"). The picaresque hero is com-

monly a low-born but clever individual who wanders into and out of various affairs of love, danger, and farcical intrigue. These involvements may take place at all social levels and typically present a humorous and wide-ranging satire of a given society. Prominent examples of the picaresque novel are *Don Quixote* by Miguel de Cervantes, *Tom Jones* by Henry Fielding, and *Moll Flanders* by Daniel Defoe.

Plagiarism: Claiming another person's written material as one's own. Plagiarism can take the form of direct, word-for-word copying or the theft of the substance or idea of the work. A student who copies an encyclopedia entry and turns it in as a report for school is guilty of plagiarism.

Platonic Criticism: A form of criticism that stresses an artistic work's usefulness as an agent of social engineering rather than any quality or value of the work itself. Platonic criticism takes as its starting point the ancient Greek philosopher Plato's comments on art in his *Republic.*

Platonism: The embracing of the doctrines of the philosopher Plato, popular among the poets of the Renaissance and the Romantic period. Platonism is more flexible than Aristotelian Criticism and places more emphasis on the supernatural and unknown aspects of life. Platonism is expressed in the love poetry of the Renaissance, the fourth book of Baldassare Castiglione's *The Book of the Courtier,* and the poetry of William Blake, William Wordsworth, Percy Bysshe Shelley, Friedrich Holderlin, William Butler Yeats, and Wallace Stevens.

Play: See *Drama*

Plot: In literary criticism, this term refers to the pattern of events in a narrative or drama. In its simplest sense, the plot guides the author in composing the work and helps the reader follow the work. Typically, plots exhibit causality and unity and have a beginning, a middle, and an end. Sometimes, however, a plot may consist of a series of disconnected events, in which case it is known as an "episodic plot." In his *Aspects of the Novel,* E. M. Forster distinguishes between a story, defined as a "narrative of events arranged in their time-sequence," and plot, which organizes the events to a "sense of causality." This definition closely mirrors Aristotle's discussion of plot in his *Poetics.*

Poem: In its broadest sense, a composition utilizing rhyme, meter, concrete detail, and expressive language to create a literary experience with emotional and aesthetic appeal. Typical poems include sonnets, odes, elegies, *haiku,* ballads, and free verse.

Poet: An author who writes poetry or verse. The term is also used to refer to an artist or writer who has an exceptional gift for expression, imagination, and energy in the making of art in any form. Well-known poets include Horace, Basho, Sir Philip Sidney, Sir Edmund Spenser, John Donne, Andrew Marvell, Alexander Pope, Jonathan Swift, George Gordon, Lord Byron, John Keats, Christina Rossetti, W. H. Auden, Stevie Smith, and Sylvia Plath.

Poetic Fallacy: See *Pathetic Fallacy*

Poetic Justice: An outcome in a literary work, not necessarily a poem, in which the good are rewarded and the evil are punished, especially in ways that particularly fit their virtues or crimes. For example, a murderer may himself be murdered, or a thief will find himself penniless.

Poetic License: Distortions of fact and literary convention made by a writer—not always a poet—for the sake of the effect gained. Poetic license is closely related to the concept of "artistic freedom." An author exercises poetic license by saying that a pile of money "reaches as high as a mountain" when the pile is actually only a foot or two high.

Poetics: This term has two closely related meanings. It denotes (1) an aesthetic theory in literary criticism about the essence of poetry or (2) rules prescribing the proper methods, content, style, or diction of poetry. The term poetics may also refer to theories about literature in general, not just poetry.

Poetry: In its broadest sense, writing that aims to present ideas and evoke an emotional experience in the reader through the use of meter, imagery, connotative and concrete words, and a carefully constructed structure based on rhythmic patterns. Poetry typically relies on words and expressions that have several layers of meaning. It also makes use of the effects of regular rhythm on the ear and may make a strong appeal to the senses through the use of imagery. Edgar Allan Poe's "Annabel Lee" and Walt Whitman's *Leaves of Grass* are famous examples of poetry.

Point of View: The narrative perspective from which a literary work is presented to the reader. There are four traditional points of view. The "third person omniscient" gives the reader a "godlike" perspective, unrestricted by time or place, from which to see actions and look into the minds of characters. This allows the author to comment openly on characters and events in the work. The "third person" point of view presents the events of the story from outside of any single character's perception, much like the omniscient point of view, but the reader must understand the action as it takes place and without any special insight into characters' minds or motivations. The "first person" or "personal" point of view relates events as they are perceived by a single character. The main character "tells" the story and may offer opinions about the action and characters which differ from those of the author. Much less common than omniscient, third person, and first person is the "second person" point of view, wherein the author tells the story as if it is happening to the reader. James Thurber employs the omniscient point of view in his short story "The Secret Life of Walter Mitty." Ernest Hemingway's "A Clean, Well-Lighted Place" is a short story told from the third person point of view. Mark Twain's novel *Huck Finn* is presented from the first person viewpoint. Jay McInerney's *Bright Lights, Big City* is an example of a novel which uses the second person point of view.

Polemic: A work in which the author takes a stand on a controversial subject, such as abortion or religion. Such works are often extremely argumentative or provocative. Classic examples of polemics include John Milton's *Aeropagitica* and Thomas Paine's *The American Crisis.*

Pornography: Writing intended to provoke feelings of lust in the reader. Such works are often condemned by critics and teachers, but those which can be shown to have literary value are viewed less harshly. Literary works that have been described as pornographic include Ovid's *The Art of Love,* Margaret of Angouleme's *Heptameron,* John Cleland's *Memoirs of a Woman of Pleasure; or, the Life of Fanny Hill,* the anonymous *My Secret Life,* D. H. Lawrence's *Lady Chatterley's Lover,* and Vladimir Nabokov's *Lolita.*

Post-Aesthetic Movement: An artistic response made by African Americans to the black aesthetic movement of the 1960s and early '70s. Writers since that time have adopted a somewhat different tone in their work, with less emphasis placed on the disparity between black and white in the United States. In the words of post-aesthetic authors such as Toni Morrison, John Edgar Wideman, and Kristin Hunter, African Americans are portrayed as looking inward for answers to their own questions, rather than always looking to the outside world. Two well-known examples of works produced as part of the post-aesthetic movement are the Pulitzer Prize-winning novels *The Color Purple* by Alice Walker and *Beloved* by Toni Morrison.

Postmodernism: Writing from the 1960s forward characterized by experimentation and continuing to apply some of the fundamentals of modernism, which included existentialism and alienation. Postmodernists have gone a step further in the rejection of tradition begun with the modernists by also rejecting traditional forms, preferring the anti-novel over the novel and the anti-hero over the hero. Postmodern writers include Alain Robbe-Grillet, Thomas Pynchon, Margaret Drabble, John Fowles, Adolfo Bioy-Casares, and Gabriel Garcia Marquez.

Pre-Raphaelites: A circle of writers and artists in mid nineteenth-century England. Valuing the pre-Renaissance artistic qualities of religious symbolism, lavish pictorialism, and natural sensuousness, the Pre-Raphaelites cultivated a sense of mystery and melancholy that influenced later writers associated with the Symbolist and Decadent movements. The major members of the group include Dante Gabriel Rossetti, Christina Rossetti, Algernon Swinburne, and Walter Pater.

Primitivism: The belief that primitive peoples were nobler and less flawed than civilized peoples because they had not been subjected to the tainting influence of society. Examples of literature espousing primitivism include Aphra Behn's *Oroonoko: Or, The History of the Royal Slave,* Jean-Jacques Rousseau's *Julie ou la Nouvelle Heloise,* Oliver Goldsmith's *The Deserted Village,* the poems of Robert Burns, Herman Melville's stories *Typee, Omoo,* and *Mardi,* many poems of William Butler Yeats and Robert Frost, and William Golding's novel *Lord of the Flies.*

Projective Verse: A form of free verse in which the poet's breathing pattern determines the lines of the poem. Poets who advocate projective verse are against all formal structures in writing, including meter and form. Besides its creators, Robert Creeley, Robert Duncan, and Charles Olson, two other well-known projective verse poets are Denise Levertov and LeRoi Jones (Amiri Baraka). Also known as Breath Verse.

Prologue: An introductory section of a literary work. It often contains information establishing the situation of the characters or presents information about the setting, time period, or action. In drama, the prologue is spoken by a chorus or by one of the principal characters. In the "General Prologue" of *The Canterbury Tales,* Geoffrey Chaucer describes the main characters and establishes the setting and purpose of the work.

Prose: A literary medium that attempts to mirror the language of everyday speech. It is distinguished from poetry by its use of unmetered, unrhymed language consisting of logically related sentences. Prose is usually grouped into paragraphs that form a cohesive whole such as an essay or a novel. Recognized masters of English prose writing include Sir

Thomas Malory, William Caxton, Raphael Holinshed, Joseph Addison, Mark Twain, and Ernest Hemingway.

Prosopopoeia: See *Personification*

Protagonist: The central character of a story who serves as a focus for its themes and incidents and as the principal rationale for its development. The protagonist is sometimes referred to in discussions of modern literature as the hero or anti-hero. Well-known protagonists are Hamlet in William Shakespeare's *Hamlet* and Jay Gatsby in F. Scott Fitzgerald's *The Great Gatsby.*

Protest Fiction: Protest fiction has as its primary purpose the protesting of some social injustice, such as racism or discrimination. One example of protest fiction is a series of five novels by Chester Himes, beginning in 1945 with *If He Hollers Let Him Go* and ending in 1955 with *The Primitive.* These works depict the destructive effects of race and gender stereotyping in the context of interracial relationships. Another African American author whose works often revolve around themes of social protest is John Oliver Killens. James Baldwin's essay "Everybody's Protest Novel" generated controversy by attacking the authors of protest fiction.

Proverb: A brief, sage saying that expresses a truth about life in a striking manner. "They are not all cooks who carry long knives" is an example of a proverb.

Pseudonym: A name assumed by a writer, most often intended to prevent his or her identification as the author of a work. Two or more authors may work together under one pseudonym, or an author may use a different name for each genre he or she publishes in. Some publishing companies maintain "house pseudonyms," under which any number of authors may write installations in a series. Some authors also choose a pseudonym over their real names the way an actor may use a stage name. Examples of pseudonyms (with the author's real name in parentheses) include Voltaire (Francois-Marie Arouet), Novalis (Friedrich von Hardenberg), Currer Bell (Charlotte Bronte), Ellis Bell (Emily Bronte), George Eliot (Maryann Evans), Honorio Bustos Donmecq (Adolfo Bioy-Casares and Jorge Luis Borges), and Richard Bachman (Stephen King).

Pun: A play on words that have similar sounds but different meanings. A serious example of the pun is from John Donne's "A Hymne to God the Father": "Sweare by thyself, that at my death thy sonne Shall shine as he shines now, and hereto fore; And, having done that, Thou haste done; I fear no more."

Pure Poetry: poetry written without instructional intent or moral purpose that aims only to please a reader by its imagery or musical flow. The term pure poetry is used as the antonym of the term "didacticism." The poetry of Edgar Allan Poe, Stephane Mallarme, Paul Verlaine, Paul Valery, Juan Ramoz Jimenez, and Jorge Guillen offer examples of pure poetry.

Q

Quatrain: A four-line stanza of a poem or an entire poem consisting of four lines. The following quatrain is from Robert Herrick's "To Live Merrily, and to Trust to Good Verses": "Round, round, the root do's run; And being ravisht thus, Come, I will drink a Tun To my *Propertius.*"

R

Raisonneur: A character in a drama who functions as a spokesperson for the dramatist's views. The *raisonneur* typically observes the play without becoming central to its action. *Raisonneurs* were very common in plays of the nineteenth century.

Realism: A nineteenth-century European literary movement that sought to portray familiar characters, situations, and settings in a realistic manner. This was done primarily by using an objective narrative point of view and through the buildup of accurate detail. The standard for success of any realistic work depends on how faithfully it transfers common experience into fictional forms. The realistic method may be altered or extended, as in stream of consciousness writing, to record highly subjective experience. Seminal authors in the tradition of Realism include Honore de Balzac, Gustave Flaubert, and Henry James.

Refrain: A phrase repeated at intervals throughout a poem. A refrain may appear at the end of each stanza or at less regular intervals. It may be altered slightly at each appearance. Some refrains are nonsense expressions—as with "Nevermore" in Edgar Allan Poe's "The Raven"—that seem to take on a different significance with each use.

Renaissance: The period in European history that marked the end of the Middle Ages. It began in Italy in the late fourteenth century. In broad terms, it is usually seen as spanning the fourteenth, fifteenth, and sixteenth centuries, although it did not reach Great Britain, for example, until the 1480s or so. The Renaissance saw an awakening in almost every sphere of human activity, especially science, philosophy, and the arts. The period is best defined by the emergence of a general philosophy that emphasized the importance of the intellect, the individual, and world affairs. It contrasts strongly with the medieval worldview, characterized by the dominant concerns of faith, the social collective, and spiritual salvation. Prominent writers during the Renaissance include Niccolo Machiavelli and Baldassare Castiglione in Italy, Miguel de Cervantes and Lope de Vega in Spain, Jean Froissart and Francois Rabelais in France, Sir Thomas More and Sir Philip Sidney in England, and Desiderius Erasmus in Holland.

Repartee: Conversation featuring snappy retorts and witticisms. Masters of *repartee* include Sydney Smith, Charles Lamb, and Oscar Wilde. An example is recorded in the meeting of "Beau" Nash and John Wesley: Nash said, "I never make way for a fool," to which Wesley responded, "Don't you? I always do," and stepped aside.

Resolution: The portion of a story following the climax, in which the conflict is resolved. The resolution of Jane Austen's *Northanger Abbey* is neatly summed up in the following sentence: "Henry and Catherine were married, the bells rang and every body smiled."

Restoration: See *Restoration Age*

Restoration Age: A period in English literature beginning with the crowning of Charles II in 1660 and running to about 1700. The era, which was characterized by a reaction against Puritanism, was the first great age of the comedy of manners. The finest literature of the era is typically witty and urbane, and often lewd. Prominent Restoration Age writers include William Congreve, Samuel Pepys, John Dryden, and John Milton.

Revenge Tragedy: A dramatic form popular during the Elizabethan Age, in which the protagonist, directed by the ghost of his murdered father or son, inflicts retaliation upon a powerful villain. Notable features of the revenge tragedy include violence, bizarre criminal acts, intrigue, insanity, a hesitant protagonist, and the use of soliloquy. Thomas Kyd's *Spanish Tragedy* is the first example of revenge tragedy in English, and William Shakespeare's *Hamlet* is perhaps the best. Extreme examples of revenge tragedy, such as John Webster's *The Duchess of Malfi,* are labeled "tragedies of blood." Also known as Tragedy of Blood.

Revista: The Spanish term for a vaudeville musical revue. Examples of *revistas* include Antonio Guzman Aguilera's *Mexico para los mexicanos,* Daniel Vanegas's *Maldito jazz,* and Don Catarino's *Whiskey, morfina y marihuana* and *El desterrado.*

Rhetoric: In literary criticism, this term denotes the art of ethical persuasion. In its strictest sense, rhetoric adheres to various principles developed since classical times for arranging facts and ideas in a clear, persuasive, appealing manner. The term is also used to refer to effective prose in general and theories of or methods for composing effective prose. Classical examples of rhetorics include *The Rhetoric of Aristotle,* Quintillian's *Institutio Oratoria,* and Cicero's *Ad Herennium.*

Rhetorical Question: A question intended to provoke thought, but not an expressed answer, in the reader. It is most commonly used in oratory and other persuasive genres. The following lines from Thomas Gray's "Elegy Written in a Country Churchyard" ask rhetorical questions: "Can storied urn or animated bust Back to its mansion call the fleeting breath? Can Honour's voice provoke the silent dust, Or Flattery soothe the dull cold ear of Death?"

Rhyme: When used as a noun in literary criticism, this term generally refers to a poem in which words sound identical or very similar and appear in parallel positions in two or more lines. Rhymes are classified into different types according to where they fall in a line or stanza or according to the degree of similarity they exhibit in their spellings and sounds. Some major types of rhyme are "masculine" rhyme, "feminine" rhyme, and "triple" rhyme. In a masculine rhyme, the rhyming sound falls in a single accented syllable, as with "heat" and "eat." Feminine rhyme is a rhyme of two syllables, one stressed and one unstressed, as with "merry" and "tarry." Triple rhyme matches the sound of the accented syllable and the two unaccented syllables that follow: "narrative" and "declarative." Robert Browning alternates feminine and masculine rhymes in his "Soliloquy of the Spanish Cloister": "Gr-r-r—there go, my heart's abhorrence! Water your damned flower-pots, do! If hate killed men, Brother Lawrence, God's blood, would not mine kill you! What? Your myrtle-bush wants trimming? Oh, that rose has prior claims—Needs its leaden vase filled brimming? Hell dry you up with flames!" Triple rhymes can be found in Thomas Hood's "Bridge of Sighs," George Gordon Byron's satirical verse, and Ogden Nash's comic poems.

Rhyme Royal: A stanza of seven lines composed in iambic pentameter and rhymed *ababbcc.* The name is said to be a tribute to King James I of Scotland, who made much use of the form in his poetry. Examples of rhyme royal include Geoffrey Chaucer's *The Parlement of Foules,* William Shakespeare's *The Rape of Lucrece,* William Morris's *The Early Paradise,* and John Masefield's *The Widow in the Bye Street.*

Rhyme Scheme: See *Rhyme*

Rhythm: A regular pattern of sound, time intervals, or events occurring in writing, most often and most discernably in poetry. Regular, reliable rhythm is known to be soothing to humans, while interrupted, unpredictable, or rapidly changing rhythm is disturbing. These effects are known to authors, who use them to produce a desired reaction in the reader. An example of a form of irregular rhythm is sprung rhythm poetry; quantitative verse, on the other hand, is very regular in its rhythm.

Rising Action: The part of a drama where the plot becomes increasingly complicated. Rising action leads up to the climax, or turning point, of a drama. The final "chase scene" of an action film is generally the rising action which culminates in the film's climax.

Rococo: A style of European architecture that flourished in the eighteenth century, especially in France. The most notable features of *rococo* are its extensive use of ornamentation and its themes of lightness, gaiety, and intimacy. In literary criticism, the term is often used disparagingly to refer to a decadent or over-ornamental style. Alexander Pope's "The Rape of the Lock" is an example of literary *rococo.*

Roman a clef: A French phrase meaning "novel with a key." It refers to a narrative in which real persons are portrayed under fictitious names. Jack Kerouac, for example, portrayed various real-life beat generation figures under fictitious names in his *On the Road.*

Romance: A broad term, usually denoting a narrative with exotic, exaggerated, often idealized characters, scenes, and themes. Nathaniel Hawthorne called his *The House of the Seven Gables* and *The Marble Faun* romances in order to distinguish them from clearly realistic works.

Romantic Age: See *Romanticism*

Romanticism: This term has two widely accepted meanings. In historical criticism, it refers to a European intellectual and artistic movement of the late eighteenth and early nineteenth centuries that sought greater freedom of personal expression than that allowed by the strict rules of literary form and logic of the eighteenth-century neoclassicists. The Romantics preferred emotional and imaginative expression to rational analysis. They considered the individual to be at the center of all experience and so placed him or her at the center of their art. The Romantics believed that the creative imagination reveals nobler truths—unique feelings and attitudes—than those that could be discovered by logic or by scientific examination.

Both the natural world and the state of childhood were important sources for revelations of "eternal truths." "Romanticism" is also used as a general term to refer to a type of sensibility found in all periods of literary history and usually considered to be in opposition to the principles of classicism. In this sense, Romanticism signifies any work or philosophy in which the exotic or dreamlike figure strongly, or that is devoted to individualistic expression, self-analysis, or a pursuit of a higher realm of knowledge than can be discovered by human reason. Prominent Romantics include Jean-Jacques Rousseau, William Wordsworth, John Keats, Lord Byron, and Johann Wolfgang von Goethe.

Romantics: See *Romanticism*

Russian Symbolism: A Russian poetic movement, derived from French symbolism, that flourished between 1894 and 1910. While some Russian Symbolists continued in the French tradition, stressing aestheticism and the importance of suggestion above didactic intent, others saw their craft as a form of mystical worship, and themselves as mediators between the supernatural and the mundane. Russian symbolists include Aleksandr Blok, Vyacheslav Ivanovich Ivanov, Fyodor Sologub, Andrey Bely, Nikolay Gumilyov, and Vladimir Sergeyevich Solovyov.

S

Satire: A work that uses ridicule, humor, and wit to criticize and provoke change in human nature and institutions. There are two major types of satire: "formal" or "direct" satire speaks directly to the reader or to a character in the work; "indirect" satire relies upon the ridiculous behavior of its characters to make its point. Formal satire is further divided into two manners: the "Horatian," which ridicules gently, and the "Juvenalian," which derides its subjects harshly and bitterly. Voltaire's novella *Candide* is an indirect satire. Jonathan Swift's essay "A Modest Proposal" is a Juvenalian satire.

Scansion: The analysis or "scanning" of a poem to determine its meter and often its rhyme scheme. The most common system of scansion uses accents (slanted lines drawn above syllables) to show stressed syllables, breves (curved lines drawn above syllables) to show unstressed syllables, and vertical lines to separate each foot. In the first line of John Keats's *Endymion,* "A thing of beauty is a joy forever:" the word "thing," the first syllable of "beauty," the word "joy," and the second syllable of "forever" are stressed, while the words "A" and "of," the second syllable of "beauty," the word "a,"

and the first and third syllables of "forever" are unstressed. In the second line: "Its loveliness increases; it will never" a pair of vertical lines separate the foot ending with "increases" and the one beginning with "it."

Scene: A subdivision of an act of a drama, consisting of continuous action taking place at a single time and in a single location. The beginnings and endings of scenes may be indicated by clearing the stage of actors and props or by the entrances and exits of important characters. The first act of William Shakespeare's *Winter's Tale* is comprised of two scenes.

Science Fiction: A type of narrative about or based upon real or imagined scientific theories and technology. Science fiction is often peopled with alien creatures and set on other planets or in different dimensions. Karel Capek's *R.U.R.* is a major work of science fiction.

Second Person: See *Point of View*

Semiotics: The study of how literary forms and conventions affect the meaning of language. Semioticians include Ferdinand de Saussure, Charles Sanders Pierce, Claude Levi-Strauss, Jacques Lacan, Michel Foucault, Jacques Derrida, Roland Barthes, and Julia Kristeva.

Sestet: Any six-line poem or stanza. Examples of the sestet include the last six lines of the Petrarchan sonnet form, the stanza form of Robert Burns's "A Poet's Welcome to his love-begotten Daughter," and the sestina form in W. H. Auden's "Paysage Moralise."

Setting: The time, place, and culture in which the action of a narrative takes place. The elements of setting may include geographic location, characters' physical and mental environments, prevailing cultural attitudes, or the historical time in which the action takes place. Examples of settings include the romanticized Scotland in Sir Walter Scott's "Waverley" novels, the French provincial setting in Gustave Flaubert's *Madame Bovary,* the fictional Wessex country of Thomas Hardy's novels, and the small towns of southern Ontario in Alice Munro's short stories.

Shakespearean Sonnet: See *Sonnet*

Signifying Monkey: A popular trickster figure in black folklore, with hundreds of tales about this character documented since the 19th century. Henry Louis Gates Jr. examines the history of the signifying monkey in *The Signifying Monkey: Towards a Theory of Afro-American Literary Criticism,* published in 1988.

Simile: A comparison, usually using "like" or "as", of two essentially dissimilar things, as in "coffee as cold as ice" or "He sounded like a broken record." The title of Ernest Hemingway's "Hills Like White Elephants" contains a simile.

Slang: A type of informal verbal communication that is generally unacceptable for formal writing. Slang words and phrases are often colorful exaggerations used to emphasize the speaker's point; they may also be shortened versions of an often-used word or phrase. Examples of American slang from the 1990s include "yuppie" (an acronym for Young Urban Professional), "awesome" (for "excellent"), wired (for "nervous" or "excited"), and "chill out" (for relax).

Slant Rhyme: See *Consonance*

Slave Narrative: Autobiographical accounts of American slave life as told by escaped slaves. These works first appeared during the abolition movement of the 1830s through the 1850s. Olaudah Equiano's *The Interesting Narrative of Olaudah Equiano, or Gustavus Vassa, The African* and Harriet Ann Jacobs's *Incidents in the Life of a Slave Girl* are examples of the slave narrative.

Social Realism: See *Socialist Realism*

Socialist Realism: The Socialist Realism school of literary theory was proposed by Maxim Gorky and established as a dogma by the first Soviet Congress of Writers. It demanded adherence to a communist worldview in works of literature. Its doctrines required an objective viewpoint comprehensible to the working classes and themes of social struggle featuring strong proletarian heroes. A successful work of socialist realism is Nikolay Ostrovsky's *Kak zakalyalas stal* (*How the Steel Was Tempered*). Also known as Social Realism.

Soliloquy: A monologue in a drama used to give the audience information and to develop the speaker's character. It is typically a projection of the speaker's innermost thoughts. Usually delivered while the speaker is alone on stage, a soliloquy is intended to present an illusion of unspoken reflection. A celebrated soliloquy is Hamlet's "To be or not to be" speech in William Shakespeare's *Hamlet*.

Sonnet: A fourteen-line poem, usually composed in iambic pentameter, employing one of several rhyme schemes. There are three major types of sonnets, upon which all other variations of the form are based: the "Petrarchan" or "Italian" sonnet, the "Shakespearean" or "English" sonnet, and the "Spenserian" sonnet. A Petrarchan sonnet consists of an octave rhymed *abbaabba* and a "sestet" rhymed either *cdecde, cdccdc,* or *cdedce*. The octave poses a question or problem, relates a narrative, or puts forth a proposition; the sestet presents a solution to the problem, comments upon the narrative, or applies the proposition put forth in the octave. The Shakespearean sonnet is divided into three quatrains and a couplet rhymed *abab cdcd efef gg*. The couplet provides an epigrammatic comment on the narrative or problem put forth in the quatrains. The Spenserian sonnet uses three quatrains and a couplet like the Shakespearean, but links their three rhyme schemes in this way: *abab bcbc cdcd ee*. The Spenserian sonnet develops its theme in two parts like the Petrarchan, its final six lines resolving a problem, analyzing a narrative, or applying a proposition put forth in its first eight lines. Examples of sonnets can be found in Petrarch's *Canzoniere,* Edmund Spenser's *Amoretti,* Elizabeth Barrett Browning's *Sonnets from the Portuguese,* Rainer Maria Rilke's *Sonnets to Orpheus,* and Adrienne Rich's poem "The Insusceptibles."

Spenserian Sonnet: See *Sonnet*

Spenserian Stanza: A nine-line stanza having eight verses in iambic pentameter, its ninth verse in iambic hexameter, and the rhyme scheme ababbcbcc. This stanza form was first used by Edmund Spenser in his allegorical poem *The Faerie Queene*.

Spondee: In poetry meter, a foot consisting of two long or stressed syllables occurring together. This form is quite rare in English verse, and is usually composed of two monosyllabic words. The first foot in the following line from Robert Burns's "Green Grow the Rashes" is an example of a spondee: "Green grow the rashes, O"

Sprung Rhythm: Versification using a specific number of accented syllables per line but disregarding the number of unaccented syllables that fall in each line, producing an irregular rhythm in the poem. Gerard Manley Hopkins, who coined the term "sprung rhythm," is the most notable practitioner of this technique.

Stanza: A subdivision of a poem consisting of lines grouped together, often in recurring patterns of rhyme, line length, and meter. Stanzas may also serve as units of thought in a poem much like paragraphs in prose. Examples of stanza forms include the quatrain, *terza rima, ottava rima,* Spenserian, and the so-called *In Memoriam* stanza from Alfred, Lord Tennyson's poem by that title. The following is an example of the latter form: "Love is and was my lord and king, And in his presence I attend To hear the tidings of my friend, Which every hour his couriers bring."

Stereotype: A stereotype was originally the name for a duplication made during the printing process; this led to its modern definition as a person or thing that is (or is assumed to be) the same as all others of its type. Common stereotypical characters include the absent-minded professor, the nagging wife, the troublemaking teenager, and the kind-hearted grandmother.

Stream of Consciousness: A narrative technique for rendering the inward experience of a character. This technique is designed to give the impression of an ever-changing series of thoughts, emotions, images, and memories in the spontaneous and seemingly illogical order that they occur in life. The textbook example of stream of consciousness is the last section of James Joyce's *Ulysses.*

Structuralism: A twentieth-century movement in literary criticism that examines how literary texts arrive at their meanings, rather than the meanings themselves. There are two major types of structuralist analysis: one examines the way patterns of linguistic structures unify a specific text and emphasize certain elements of that text, and the other interprets the way literary forms and conventions affect the meaning of language itself. Prominent structuralists include Michel Foucault, Roman Jakobson, and Roland Barthes.

Structure: The form taken by a piece of literature. The structure may be made obvious for ease of understanding, as in nonfiction works, or may obscured for artistic purposes, as in some poetry or seemingly "unstructured" prose. Examples of common literary structures include the plot of a narrative, the acts and scenes of a drama, and such poetic forms as the Shakespearean sonnet and the Pindaric ode.

Sturm und Drang: A German term meaning "storm and stress." It refers to a German literary movement of the 1770s and 1780s that reacted against the order and rationalism of the enlightenment, focusing instead on the intense experience of extraordinary individuals. Highly romantic, works of this movement, such as Johann Wolfgang von Goethe's *Gotz von Berlichingen,* are typified by realism, rebelliousness, and intense emotionalism.

Style: A writer's distinctive manner of arranging words to suit his or her ideas and purpose in writing. The unique imprint of the author's personality upon his or her writing, style is the product of an author's way of arranging ideas and his or her use of diction, different sentence structures, rhythm, figures of speech, rhetorical principles, and other elements of composition. Styles may be classified according to period (Metaphysical, Augustan, Geor-

gian), individual authors (Chaucerian, Miltonic, Jamesian), level (grand, middle, low, plain), or language (scientific, expository, poetic, journalistic).

Subject: The person, event, or theme at the center of a work of literature. A work may have one or more subjects of each type, with shorter works tending to have fewer and longer works tending to have more. The subjects of James Baldwin's novel *Go Tell It on the Mountain* include the themes of father-son relationships, religious conversion, black life, and sexuality. The subjects of Anne Frank's *Diary of a Young Girl* include Anne and her family members as well as World War II, the Holocaust, and the themes of war, isolation, injustice, and racism.

Subjectivity: Writing that expresses the author's personal feelings about his subject, and which may or may not include factual information about the subject. Subjectivity is demonstrated in James Joyce's *Portrait of the Artist as a Young Man,* Samuel Butler's *The Way of All Flesh,* and Thomas Wolfe's *Look Homeward, Angel.*

Subplot: A secondary story in a narrative. A subplot may serve as a motivating or complicating force for the main plot of the work, or it may provide emphasis for, or relief from, the main plot. The conflict between the Capulets and the Montagues in William Shakespeare's *Romeo and Juliet* is an example of a subplot.

Surrealism: A term introduced to criticism by Guillaume Apollinaire and later adopted by Andre Breton. It refers to a French literary and artistic movement founded in the 1920s. The Surrealists sought to express unconscious thoughts and feelings in their works. The best-known technique used for achieving this aim was automatic writing—transcriptions of spontaneous outpourings from the unconscious. The Surrealists proposed to unify the contrary levels of conscious and unconscious, dream and reality, objectivity and subjectivity into a new level of "super-realism." Surrealism can be found in the poetry of Paul Eluard, Pierre Reverdy, and Louis Aragon, among others.

Suspense: A literary device in which the author maintains the audience's attention through the buildup of events, the outcome of which will soon be revealed. Suspense in William Shakespeare's *Hamlet* is sustained throughout by the question of whether or not the Prince will achieve what he has been instructed to do and of what he intends to do.

Syllogism: A method of presenting a logical argument. In its most basic form, the syllogism consists of a major premise, a minor premise, and a conclusion. An example of a syllogism is: Major premise:

When it snows, the streets get wet. Minor premise: It is snowing. Conclusion: The streets are wet.

Symbol: Something that suggests or stands for something else without losing its original identity. In literature, symbols combine their literal meaning with the suggestion of an abstract concept. Literary symbols are of two types: those that carry complex associations of meaning no matter what their contexts, and those that derive their suggestive meaning from their functions in specific literary works. Examples of symbols are sunshine suggesting happiness, rain suggesting sorrow, and storm clouds suggesting despair.

Symbolism: This term has two widely accepted meanings. In historical criticism, it denotes an early modernist literary movement initiated in France during the nineteenth century that reacted against the prevailing standards of realism. Writers in this movement aimed to evoke, indirectly and symbolically, an order of being beyond the material world of the five senses. Poetic expression of personal emotion figured strongly in the movement, typically by means of a private set of symbols uniquely identifiable with the individual poet. The principal aim of the Symbolists was to express in words the highly complex feelings that grew out of everyday contact with the world. In a broader sense, the term "symbolism" refers to the use of one object to represent another. Early members of the Symbolist movement included the French authors Charles Baudelaire and Arthur Rimbaud; William Butler Yeats, James Joyce, and T. S. Eliot were influenced as the movement moved to Ireland, England, and the United States. Examples of the concept of symbolism include a flag that stands for a nation or movement, or an empty cupboard used to suggest hopelessness, poverty, and despair.

Symbolist: See *Symbolism*

Symbolist Movement: See *Symbolism*

Sympathetic Fallacy: See *Affective Fallacy*

T

Tale: A story told by a narrator with a simple plot and little character development. Tales are usually relatively short and often carry a simple message. Examples of tales can be found in the work of Rudyard Kipling, Somerset Maugham, Saki, Anton Chekhov, Guy de Maupassant, and Armistead Maupin.

Tall Tale: A humorous tale told in a straightforward, credible tone but relating absolutely impossible events or feats of the characters. Such tales were commonly told of frontier adventures during the settlement of the west in the United States. Tall tales have been spun around such legendary heroes as Mike Fink, Paul Bunyan, Davy Crockett, Johnny Appleseed, and Captain Stormalong as well as the real-life William F. Cody and Annie Oakley. Literary use of tall tales can be found in Washington Irving's *History of New York,* Mark Twain's *Life on the Mississippi,* and in the German R. F. Raspe's *Baron Munchausen's Narratives of His Marvellous Travels and Campaigns in Russia.*

Tanka: A form of Japanese poetry similar to *haiku.* A *tanka* is five lines long, with the lines containing five, seven, five, seven, and seven syllables respectively. Skilled *tanka* authors include Ishikawa Takuboku, Masaoka Shiki, Amy Lowell, and Adelaide Crapsey.

Teatro Grottesco: See *Theater of the Grotesque*

Terza Rima: A three-line stanza form in poetry in which the rhymes are made on the last word of each line in the following manner: the first and third lines of the first stanza, then the second line of the first stanza and the first and third lines of the second stanza, and so on with the middle line of any stanza rhyming with the first and third lines of the following stanza. An example of *terza rima* is Percy Bysshe Shelley's "The Triumph of Love": "As in that trance of wondrous thought I lay This was the tenour of my waking dream. Methought I sate beside a public way Thick strewn with summer dust, and a great stream Of people there was hurrying to and fro Numerous as gnats upon the evening gleam, . . ."

Tetrameter: See *Meter*

Textual Criticism: A branch of literary criticism that seeks to establish the authoritative text of a literary work. Textual critics typically compare all known manuscripts or printings of a single work in order to assess the meanings of differences and revisions. This procedure allows them to arrive at a definitive version that (supposedly) corresponds to the author's original intention. Textual criticism was applied during the Renaissance to salvage the classical texts of Greece and Rome, and modern works have been studied, for instance, to undo deliberate correction or censorship, as in the case of novels by Stephen Crane and Theodore Dreiser.

Theater of Cruelty: Term used to denote a group of theatrical techniques designed to eliminate the psychological and emotional distance between actors and audience. This concept, introduced in the 1930s in France, was intended to inspire a more intense theatrical experience than conventional theater allowed. The "cruelty" of this dramatic theory signified not sadism but heightened actor/audience involvement in the dramatic event. The theater of cruelty was theorized by Antonin Artaud in his *Le Theatre et son double* (*The Theatre and Its Double*), and also appears in the work of Jerzy Grotowski, Jean Genet, Jean Vilar, and Arthur Adamov, among others.

Theater of the Absurd: A post-World War II dramatic trend characterized by radical theatrical innovations. In works influenced by the Theater of the absurd, nontraditional, sometimes grotesque characterizations, plots, and stage sets reveal a meaningless universe in which human values are irrelevant. Existentialist themes of estrangement, absurdity, and futility link many of the works of this movement. The principal writers of the Theater of the Absurd are Samuel Beckett, Eugene Ionesco, Jean Genet, and Harold Pinter.

Theater of the Grotesque: An Italian theatrical movement characterized by plays written around the ironic and macabre aspects of daily life in the World War I era. Theater of the Grotesque was named after the play *The Mask and the Face* by Luigi Chiarelli, which was described as "a grotesque in three acts." The movement influenced the work of Italian dramatist Luigi Pirandello, author of *Right You Are, If You Think You Are.* Also known as *Teatro Grottesco.*

Theme: The main point of a work of literature. The term is used interchangeably with thesis. The theme of William Shakespeare's *Othello*—jealousy—is a common one.

Thesis: A thesis is both an essay and the point argued in the essay. Thesis novels and thesis plays share the quality of containing a thesis which is supported through the action of the story. A master's thesis and a doctoral dissertation are two theses required of graduate students.

Thesis Play: See *Thesis*

Three Unities: See *Unities*

Tone: The author's attitude toward his or her audience may be deduced from the tone of the work. A formal tone may create distance or convey politeness, while an informal tone may encourage a friendly, intimate, or intrusive feeling in the reader. The author's attitude toward his or her subject matter may also be deduced from the tone of the words he or she uses in discussing it. The tone of John F. Kennedy's speech which included the appeal to "ask not what your country can do for you" was intended to instill feelings of camaraderie and national pride in listeners.

Tragedy: A drama in prose or poetry about a noble, courageous hero of excellent character who, because of some tragic character flaw or *hamartia*, brings ruin upon him- or herself. Tragedy treats its subjects in a dignified and serious manner, using poetic language to help evoke pity and fear and bring about catharsis, a purging of these emotions. The tragic form was practiced extensively by the ancient Greeks. In the Middle Ages, when classical works were virtually unknown, tragedy came to denote any works about the fall of persons from exalted to low conditions due to any reason: fate, vice, weakness, etc. According to the classical definition of tragedy, such works present the "pathetic"—that which evokes pity—rather than the tragic. The classical form of tragedy was revived in the sixteenth century; it flourished especially on the Elizabethan stage. In modern times, dramatists have attempted to adapt the form to the needs of modern society by drawing their heroes from the ranks of ordinary men and women and defining the nobility of these heroes in terms of spirit rather than exalted social standing. The greatest classical example of tragedy is Sophocles' *Oedipus Rex.* The "pathetic" derivation is exemplified in "The Monk's Tale" in Geoffrey Chaucer's *Canterbury Tales.* Notable works produced during the sixteenth century revival include William Shakespeare's *Hamlet, Othello,* and *King Lear.* Modern dramatists working in the tragic tradition include Henrik Ibsen, Arthur Miller, and Eugene O'Neill.

Tragedy of Blood: See *Revenge Tragedy*

Tragic Flaw: In a tragedy, the quality within the hero or heroine which leads to his or her downfall. Examples of the tragic flaw include Othello's jealousy and Hamlet's indecisiveness, although most great tragedies defy such simple interpretation.

Transcendentalism: An American philosophical and religious movement, based in New England from around 1835 until the Civil War. Transcendentalism was a form of American romanticism that had its roots abroad in the works of Thomas Carlyle, Samuel Coleridge, and Johann Wolfgang von Goethe. The Transcendentalists stressed the importance of intuition and subjective experience in communication with God. They rejected religious dogma and texts in favor of mysticism and scientific naturalism. They pursued truths that lie beyond the "colorless" realms perceived by reason and the senses and were active social reformers in public education, women's rights, and the abolition of slavery. Prominent members of the group include Ralph Waldo Emerson and Henry David Thoreau.

Trickster: A character or figure common in Native American and African literature who uses his ingenuity to defeat enemies and escape difficult situations. Tricksters are most often animals, such as the spider, hare, or coyote, although they may take the form of humans as well. Examples of trickster tales include Thomas King's *A Coyote Columbus Story,* Ashley F. Bryan's *The Dancing Granny* and Ishmael Reed's *The Last Days of Louisiana Red.*

Trimeter: See *Meter*

Triple Rhyme: See *Rhyme*

Trochee: See *Foot*

U

Understatement: See *Irony*

Unities: Strict rules of dramatic structure, formulated by Italian and French critics of the Renaissance and based loosely on the principles of drama discussed by Aristotle in his *Poetics.* Foremost among these rules were the three unities of action, time, and place that compelled a dramatist to: (1) construct a single plot with a beginning, middle, and end that details the causal relationships of action and character; (2) restrict the action to the events of a single day; and (3) limit the scene to a single place or city. The unities were observed faithfully by continental European writers until the Romantic Age, but they were never regularly observed in English drama. Modern dramatists are typically more concerned with a unity of impression or emotional effect than with any of the classical unities. The unities are observed in Pierre Corneille's tragedy *Polyeuctes* and Jean-Baptiste Racine's *Phedre.* Also known as Three Unities.

Urban Realism: A branch of realist writing that attempts to accurately reflect the often harsh facts of modern urban existence. Some works by Stephen Crane, Theodore Dreiser, Charles Dickens, Fyodor Dostoyevsky, Emile Zola, Abraham Cahan, and Henry Fuller feature urban realism. Modern examples include Claude Brown's *Manchild in the Promised Land* and Ron Milner's *What the Wine Sellers Buy.*

Utopia: A fictional perfect place, such as "paradise" or "heaven." Early literary utopias were included in Plato's *Republic* and Sir Thomas More's *Utopia,* while more modern utopias can be found in Samuel Butler's *Erewhon,* Theodor Herzka's *A Visit to Freeland,* and H. G. Wells' *A Modern Utopia.*

Utopian: See *Utopia*

Utopianism: See *Utopia*

V

Verisimilitude: Literally, the appearance of truth. In literary criticism, the term refers to aspects of a work of literature that seem true to the reader. Verisimilitude is achieved in the work of Honore de Balzac, Gustave Flaubert, and Henry James, among other late nineteenth-century realist writers.

Vers de societe: See *Occasional Verse*

Vers libre: See *Free Verse*

Verse: A line of metered language, a line of a poem, or any work written in verse. The following line of verse is from the epic poem *Don Juan* by Lord Byron: "My way is to begin with the beginning."

Versification: The writing of verse. Versification may also refer to the meter, rhyme, and other mechanical components of a poem. Composition of a "Roses are red, violets are blue" poem to suit an occasion is a common form of versification practiced by students.

Victorian: Refers broadly to the reign of Queen Victoria of England (1837–1901) and to anything with qualities typical of that era. For example, the qualities of smug narrowmindedness, bourgeois materialism, faith in social progress, and priggish morality are often considered Victorian. This stereotype is contradicted by such dramatic intellectual developments as the theories of Charles Darwin, Karl Marx, and Sigmund Freud (which stirred strong debates in England) and the critical attitudes of serious Victorian writers like Charles Dickens and George Eliot. In literature, the Victorian Period was the great age of the English novel, and the latter part of the era saw the rise of movements such as decadence and symbolism. Works of Victorian literature include the poetry of Robert Browning and Alfred, Lord Tennyson, the criticism of Matthew Arnold and John Ruskin, and the novels of Emily Bronte, William Makepeace Thackeray, and Thomas Hardy. Also known as Victorian Age and Victorian Period.

Victorian Age: See *Victorian*

Victorian Period: See *Victorian*

W

Weltanschauung: A German term referring to a person's worldview or philosophy. Examples of *weltanschauung* include Thomas Hardy's view of the human being as the victim of fate, destiny, or impersonal forces and circumstances, and the disillusioned and laconic cynicism expressed by such poets of the 1930s as W. H. Auden, Sir Stephen Spender, and Sir William Empson.

Weltschmerz: A German term meaning "world pain." It describes a sense of anguish about the nature of existence, usually associated with a melancholy, pessimistic attitude. *Weltschmerz* was expressed in England by George Gordon, Lord Byron in his *Manfred* and *Childe Harold's Pilgrimage,* in France by Viscount de Chateaubriand, Alfred de Vigny, and Alfred de Musset, in Russia by Aleksandr Pushkin and Mikhail Lermontov, in Poland by Juliusz Slowacki, and in America by Nathaniel Hawthorne.

Z

Zarzuela: A type of Spanish operetta. Writers of *zarzuelas* include Lope de Vega and Pedro Calderon.

Zeitgeist: A German term meaning "spirit of the time." It refers to the moral and intellectual trends of a given era. Examples of *zeitgeist* include the preoccupation with the more morbid aspects of dying and death in some Jacobean literature, especially in the works of dramatists Cyril Tourneur and John Webster, and the decadence of the French Symbolists.

Cumulative Author/Title Index

Cumulative Nationality/Ethnicity Index

Shear, Claudia
Dirty Blonde: V24
Shepard, Sam
Buried Child: V6
Curse of the Starving Class: V14
Fool for Love: V7
True West: V3
Sherman, Martin
Bent: V20
Sherwood, Robert E.
Abe Lincoln in Illinois: V11
Idiot's Delight: V15
The Petrified Forest: V17
Shue, Larry
The Foreigner: V7
Simon, Neil
Biloxi Blues: V12
Brighton Beach Memoirs: V6
Lost in Yonkers: V18
The Odd Couple: V2
The Prisoner of Second Avenue:
V24
Smith, Anna Deavere
Fires in the Mirror: V22
Twilight: Los Angeles, 1992: V2
Stein, Joseph
Fiddler on the Roof: V7
Terry, Megan
Calm Down Mother: V18
Thompson, Ernest
On Golden Pond: V23
Treadwell, Sophie
Machinal: V22
Uhry, Alfred
Driving Miss Daisy: V11
The Last Night of Ballyhoo: V15
Valdez, Luis
Zoot Suit: V5
Vidal, Gore
Visit to a Small Planet: V2
Vogel, Paula
How I Learned to Drive: V14
Walker, Joseph A.
The River Niger: V12
Wasserstein, Wendy
The Heidi Chronicles: V5
The Sisters Rosensweig: V17
Wiechmann, Barbara
Feeding the Moonfish: V21
Wilder, Thornton
The Matchmaker: V16
Our Town: V1
The Skin of Our Teeth: V4
Williams, Tennessee
Cat on a Hot Tin Roof: V3
The Glass Menagerie: V1
The Night of the Iguana: V7
Orpheus Descending: V17
The Rose Tattoo: V18
A Streetcar Named Desire: V1
Sweet Bird of Youth: V12
Wilson, August
Fences: V3
Joe Turner's Come and Gone: V17

Ma Rainey's Black Bottom: V15
The Piano Lesson: V7
Two Trains Running: V24
Wilson, Lanford
Angels Fall: V20
Burn This: V4
Hot L Baltimore: V9
The Mound Builders: V16
Talley's Folly: V12
Wright, Doug
I Am My Own Wife: V23
Zindel, Paul
*The Effect of Gamma Rays on
Man-in-the-Moon Marigolds:*
V12

Argentinian
Dorfman, Ariel
Death and the Maiden: V4

Asian American
Hwang, David Henry
M. Butterfly: V11
The Sound of a Voice: V18

Austrian
von Hofmannsthal, Hugo
Electra: V17
The Tower: V12

Bohemian (Czechoslovakian)
Capek, Karel
The Insect Play: V11

Canadian
Highway, Tomson
The Rez Sisters: V2
MacDonald, Ann-Marie
*Goodnight Desdemona (Good
Morning Juliet):* V23
Pollock, Sharon
Blood Relations: V3
Thompson, Judith
Habitat: V22

Chilean
Dorfman, Ariel
Death and the Maiden: V4

Chinese
Xingjian, Gao
The Other Shore: V21

Cuban
Cruz, Nilo
Anna in the Tropics: V21
Prida, Dolores
Beautiful Señoritas: V23

Cuban American
Cruz, Nilo
Anna in the Tropics: V21

Czechoslovakian
Capek, Josef
The Insect Play: V11
Capek, Karel
The Insect Play: V11
R.U.R.: V7
Havel, Vaclav
The Memorandum: V10
Stoppard, Tom
Arcadia: V5
*Dogg's Hamlet, Cahoot's
Macbeth:* V16
Indian Ink: V11
The Real Thing: V8
*Rosencrantz and Guildenstern Are
Dead:* V2
Travesties: V13

Dutch
de Hartog, Jan
The Fourposter: V12

English
Anonymous
Arden of Faversham: V24
Arden, John
Serjeant Musgrave's Dance: V9
Ayckbourn, Alan
A Chorus of Disapproval: V7
Barnes, Peter
The Ruling Class: V6
Behn, Aphra
The Forc'd Marriage: V24
The Rover: V16
Bolt, Robert
A Man for All Seasons: V2
Bond, Edward
Lear: V3
Saved: V8
Christie, Agatha
The Mousetrap: V2
Churchill, Caryl
Cloud Nine: V16
Top Girls: V12
Congreve, William
Love for Love: V14
The Way of the World: V15

French

German

Greek

Hispanic

Indochinese

Irish

Subject/Theme Index

*Boldface denotes discussion in
Themes section.

Subject/Theme Index